■ A F T E R   T H E   L A W

A BOOK SERIES EDITED BY JOHN BRIGHAM AND CHRISTINE B. HARRINGTON

POLITICS BY OTHER MEANS

■ *AFTER THE LAW* A book series edited by John Brigham and Christine B. Harrington

Also published in the series:

Gigs: Jazz and the Cabaret Laws in New York City by Paul Chevigny

A Theory of Liberty: The Constitution and Minorities by H.N. Hirsch

Inside the State: The Bracero Program, Immigration, and the I.N.S. by Kitty Calavita

Explorations in Law and Society: Toward a Constitutive Theory of Law by Alan Hunt

Virtuous Citizens, Disruptive Subjects by Barbara Yngvesson

Contested States: Law, Hegemony and Resistance by Mindie Lazarus-Black and Susan F. Hirsch

Toward a New Common Sense: Law, Science and Politics in the Pragmatic Transition by Boaventura de Sousa Santos

POLITICS BY OTHER MEANS

LAW IN THE STRUGGLE AGAINST APARTHEID, 1980–1994

■ RICHARD L. ABEL

WITH A FOREWORD BY NELSON MANDELA

■ Routledge　　　　New York　　　London

Published in 1995 by

Routledge
29 West 35th Street
New York, NY 10001

Published in Great Britain by

Routledge
11 New Fetter Lane
London EC4P 4EE

Copyright © 1995 by Routledge, Inc.

Printed in the United States of America on acid-free paper.

Library of Congress Cataloging-in-Publication Data

Abel, Richard L.
    Politics by other means: law in the struggle against apartheid,
1980-94/Richard L. Abel.   p. cm. - (After the law)
    Includes bibliographical references and index.
    ISBN 0-415-90816-7 (hard) : - ISBN 0-415-90817-5 (pbk.)
    1. Race discrimination - Law and legislation - South Africa. 2.
Apartheid - South Africa. 3. Law and politics. I. Title. II. Series.
KTL2465.A93 1994
342.73'0873-dc20
[347.302873]   94-29579
                                                            CIP

Murals depicted on front and back covers by "Merrin Jr." and "Van."

CONTENTS

Foreword, Nelson Mandela   vii

Foreword, John Dugard   viii

Foreword, Geoffrey Budlender   x

Preface   xiii

Glossary of Acronyms and Foreign Words   xvii

Chapter 1   Speaking with the Ogre   1

Chapter 2   Politics by Other Means?   7

Chapter 3   Carving Loopholes in the Pass Laws   23

Chapter 4   White Resistance to the Military   67

Chapter 5   Seeking Recognition   125

Chapter 6   Mpophomeni and the War in Natal   173

Chapter 7   State Terrorism: The Response of Law and Medicine to Police Torture   211

Chapter 8   Censorship and the Closure of the *New Nation*   259

Chapter 9   The Alexandra Treason Trial   311

Chapter 10   Bakwena ba Magopa: The Last Forced Removal   385

Chapter 11   Moutse and KwaNdebele: Ethnicity and Gender in the Challenge to Grand Apartheid   435

Chapter 12   Disestablishing Oukasie   495

Chapter 13   The Roles of Law   523

Notes   551

References   597

Index   631

FOREWORD

BY NELSON MANDELA

This book documents the diverse struggles of the people of South Africa to resist and challenge the policies and practices of legalized racism, known as apartheid. In particular, the book reveals the significant part played by the law and the lawyers in these struggles. That some lawyers played a crucial role in these struggles is evident in this collection and indicates that these lawyers had more than a narrow professional concern for their clients. They employed their ingenuity in prying open the ever-widening cracks of apartheid's legal edifice.

This book, however, also documents the hardships endured and the courage displayed by many ordinary South Africans. Above all, it reveals that these South Africans had and have an enduring faith in justice. Our collective triumph in establishing a just and non-racial democracy, based on the rule of law, owes as much to these ordinary people as to their political and legal representatives, if not more. It is their consistent demand for justice, in the face of injustice, that now informs our constitutional vision.

Nelson Mandela is President of South Africa.

FOREWORD

BY JOHN DUGARD

South Africa now has a Constitution with a Bill of Rights protected by a Constitutional Court representative of all the people of the land. The Constitution is a response to apartheid, and memories of past injustices have guided those who drafted its provisions.

Apartheid was not merely a flawed and failed political policy, as some have suggested, but also an evil ideology. Fortunately, it was abandoned by its architects without war or bloody revolution, which has undoubtedly facilitated the process of healing. At the same time, the peaceful fall of apartheid has encouraged forgetfulness. For many, in the words of the novelist L. P. Hartley, "the past is a foreign country; they [did] things differently there." The foreign country that was the apartheid state is thus fast being forgotten.

Already, South African lawyers and scholars, excited by their new Constitution and the challenge of constitutional litigation, have started to address the future with little regard for the past. This makes the appearance of the present study both timely and necessary, for it reminds us of our recent history and of the legacy that we will have to overcome if we are to build a decent society.

Law played a pivotal role in the apartheid state. Racial discrimination and political repression were not practiced outside the law in an arbitrary and unregulated manner. On the contrary, racial injustice was perpetrated in accordance with legal rules, and political repression was administered according to carefully defined legal procedures. There was respect for rules of law, but not for the Rule of Law. These legal rules, abhorrent as they were, provided some opportunities for relief. Some good was to be found in the interstices of the laws of apartheid. This meant that while the law generally served as an instrument of oppression, on occasion it might present a salvation for the oppressed. It was both foe and friend.

Such was the anomaly of the apartheid state. And it is this anomaly that Abel portrays in ten case studies about the struggle of lawyers against the law in the last decade of apartheid. Abel's selection includes the pass laws, territorial apartheid, labor disputes, torture, censorship, conscription, and

John Dugard is Professor of Law at the University of the Witwatersrand and was the founding Director of the Centre for Applied Legal Studies.

treason. Each case is examined in careful detail so as to provide a complete picture of the law, its socio-political impact, the opportunities it provided for creative lawyering, and the strategies employed by lawyers and community to obstruct the consequences of the law. Together these studies provide a comprehensive overview of apartheid through the eyes of one of today's leading exponents of sociological jurisprudence.

This study is about the role of law in an unjust society. It is about the role that lawyers may play in an unjust society. It is about how lawyers may advance the cause of justice without a Bill of Rights or a "human-rights-friendly" Constitution. On the face of it, it is about that peculiar society that was Apartheid South Africa. But its lesson goes beyond South Africa, for many of the issues explored by Abel are not confined by place or time. They are universal jurisprudential issues that must be perpetually re-examined and re-assessed if law is to be brought closer to justice.

FOREWORD

BY GEOFFREY BUDLENDER

South Africa in the 1980s presented a paradox. On one hand, a repressive state systematically discriminated against the majority of its citizens, even to the extent of declaring that some of them were not citizens at all. On the other, there was an extensive and active human rights "industry," apparently thriving under these conditions.

The major source of the paradox is that the repression and discrimination were, for the most part, carried out through the mechanism of law. This book explains the nature of this paradox and demonstrates how it worked in practice. If the state is to use law to legitimize oppression then, in the words of E. P. Thompson:

> The essential precondition for the effectiveness of law, in its function as ideology, is that it shall display an independence from gross manipulation and shall seem to be just. It cannot seem to be so without upholding its own logic and criteria of equity; indeed, on occasion by actually *being* just.[1]

Lawyers in South Africa sought to exploit this internal tension in the use of law as a means of enforcing and legitimizing unjust power.

In reviewing those areas where there was success in this enterprise, it is necessary to analyze what distinguished the successes from the failures.

In the first instance, there was clearly no possibility of success if the legal attack threatened the very foundations of the system. A technically valid attack on the legality of racial discrimination per se, or on the constitutional foundations of the state, would have been either rejected by the courts or (if upheld) promptly reversed by legislation. The court's acquiescence to the government's abuses during the state of emergency shows once again that when courts perceive that "society" is under attack, they tend to close ranks with those in power. It is particularly striking that the reactionary position of the courts on "security" issues coincided with a more open-minded approach on racial issues, as shown by some of the cases described in this book.

Secondly, the legal work was most successful when its strategies were used in support of mass movements. At the obvious level, no number of suc-

Geoffrey Budlender is National Director of the Legal Resources Centre.

cessful court challenges could have stopped the removal of Oukasie (Chapter 12) if the authories had succeeded in bullying the residents into abandoning their homes. But more fundamentally, what breathed life into all of the successful legal work was a spirit of resistance and a rejection of unjust rule. It was the resistance and courage of the women of KwaNdebele that toppled the despots in that homeland (Chapter 11). Law was simply the mechanism that happened to be available because of the paradox of the South African legal system.

Thirdly, it was local and international opposition to apartheid that made it more difficult for government to reverse through law the gains that had been achieved through law. I have little doubt that if the successes in the "pass law" cases (Chapter 3) had been achieved in the early 1970s, they would promptly have been overturned through legislation. The reason this did not happen in the 1980s was due to the government's need and desire, at a time of growing local and international pressure, not to be seen to be acting in a reactionary or regressive manner.

This book vividly demonstrates the interplay between law and politics in a repressive society. We South Africans have reason to be grateful for the skill and care with which Rick Abel has analyzed the use of law in the struggle against apartheid. But I believe that this work has a significance that goes beyond South Africa. It speaks directly and in a telling manner to all who are concerned with the uses and limits of law and lawyers in fighting injustice.

PREFACE

During one of my field trips to South Africa it struck me for the first time that I had reached the furthest inhabited place on earth from my home in Los Angeles. Some explanation seemed in order for why I had embarked on this project.

Like many Americans reaching adulthood in the early 1960s, I saw the newly independent African nations as enormously hopeful and exciting. After law school I studied African law at the School of Oriental and African Studies in London and conducted research in Kenya on how the transformation of its judicial system had affected customary law. But when I returned to teach law in the United States I drifted out of African studies. American law students were uninterested. And I could neither uproot my family nor leave it for long periods.

At the end of the 1980s, when I finished a lengthy research project and my youngest daughter was about to go to college, I considered what to do next. I had long been interested in the relationship between law and fundamental social change. But most of the countries engaged in radical experiments did not speak English, and I had become resigned to incorrigible monolingualism. When I put a grid over the world with two variables—revolution and English—they crossed only in South Africa.

I had three reservations. If my concern was racism, there was plenty to study at home. I accept the criticism that my fascination with South Africa contains elements of escapism and exoticism. Yet the value of comparing the American and South African experiences is vividly illustrated by the work of historian George Frederickson and Judge Leon Higginbotham. The second objection was the cultural boycott. Talks with several ANC leaders—Kader Asmal, Aziz Pahad, and Albie Sachs—convinced me that the boycott was not intended to prevent research on the role of law in the struggle against apartheid. Finally, I worried about intellectual imperialism. Surely the South African human rights lawyers could tell their stories better than I. The brief answer is that they have done so, but the constant demands of their clients deny them the control over their time that is the greatest luxury of academia.

Even before I visited South Africa I was encouraged and aided by many people. Geoffrey Bindman, who chaired the 1987 International Commission of Jurists investigation, was endlessly helpful with documents, contacts, and advice. I was fortunate to teach Reagan Jacobus as a graduate student at xiv ■ POLITICS BY OTHER MEANS

UCLA and to meet John Dugard in London, Dennis Davis in Los Angeles, Arthur Chaskalson at Columbia, and Richard Goldstone at Harvard.

My first exposure to South Africa in February-March 1989 immediately followed P.W. Botha's stroke and coincided with the massive hunger strike by detainees, which forced their release and signified another breach in the apartheid state. Like so many other visitors I found the experience overwhelming and contradictory. On my first day in Johannesburg I made an unplanned (and probably unwise) trip by a third-class (i.e., black) train to Springs and then combi (mini-bus taxi) to its township, KwaThema, where I met with considerable suspicion from a very large comrade and spent the afternoon with a proto-capitalist, watching football on his wide-screen television and hearing him extol investment opportunities. Later that week I met Raymond Suttner, recently released from indefinite detention in solitary confinement for two years and still severely restricted, and Azhar Cachalia, the UDF treasurer, also just out of detention, as well as many human rights lawyers: Ismail Ayob, George Bizos, Priscilla Jana, Krish Naidoo, Kathleen Satchwell, and Raymond Tucker. I shared a compartment in the overnight train to Cape Town with three young white conscripts, who spoke mostly Afrikaans and seemed indifferent to my presence rather than hostile. At the University of Cape Town, Dennis Davis, Dirk van Zyl Smit, Hugh Corder, Sandra Burman, and Wilfried Schärf showed me the most beautiful city in the world, the verdant farmlands of Stellenbosch and the miserable townships of Crossroads and Khayelitsha. I met human rights lawyers at Bernardt, Vukic & Potash, Mallinicks, and the Legal Resources Centre. Himan and Jean Bernardt introduced me to their founding generation of opponents of apartheid.

Financial support from the National Science Foundation's Program in Law and Social Science (SES-9012250) and UCLA's International Studies and Overseas Programs, Academic Senate Research Committee, and Law School Dean's Fund allowed me to spend nine and a half weeks in Johannesburg in 1990 and 1991. Despite the regime's awesome security apparatus, I had no difficulty obtaining a tourist visa by declaring (truthfully) that I was not a journalist—a practice a Nationalist MP has denounced as an "execrable defrauding of the hospitality of a country" [Hansard col. 5869 (J.G. van Zyl, April 19, 1989)].

I am deeply indebted to many people and institutions within South Africa. The University of the Witwatersrand Law School provided me with an office, computer, photocopying, telephone, and fax and arranged accommodation and car rental. Dean Etienne Mureinik and his wife Amanda added their personal help and hospitality. At the Centre for Applied Legal Studies the successive directors, John Dugard and Dennis Davis, offered information and interpretation, and librarian Lydia Levin provided invaluable documentation. Cherie van Onselen translated the Afrikaans. CALS also is publishing more comprehensive versions of the ten case studies. I am grateful for the friendship of Denis Kuny, Cathi Albertyn, Janet Hirsch, Matthew Kentridge, Vicki

Bernstein, Heinz Klug, and Gaye Seidman. The human rights lawyers whose cases I studied gave me full access to their documents and spent hours answering my questions: Amanda Armstrong, Paul Benjamin, John Brand, Martin Brassey, Geoffrey Budlender, Edwin Cameron, Arthur Chaskalson, Halton Cheadle, Peter Harris, Nicholas Haysom, Carrie Kimble, Denis Kuny, Norman Manoim, Gilbert Marcus, Edwin Mohahlehi, Peter Mohtle, Clive Plaskett, Mpueleng Pooe, and James Sutherland. I also benefitted greatly from conversations with parties, witnesses, and activitsts: Obed Bapela, David Bruce, Aninka Claassens, Nan Cross, Lydia Kompé, Wendy Orr, Mandy Taylor, Gabu Tugwana, and Joanne Yawitch. Three academics who have written essential books about South African law during this period provided helpful guidance: David Dyzenhaus (University of Toronto), Stephen Ellmann (New York Law School), and Michael Lobban (University of Durham).

Two South African institutions made it possible to complete the research from thousands of miles away. The Institute for Contemporary History at the University of the Orange Free State provides a well-indexed clipping service, at reasonable cost, for the dozens of South African newspapers unavailable in the United States. The Government Printer heavily subsidizes the production and distribution of Parliamentary debates, perhaps in the belief that they will enhance the regime's image abroad. It shipped eight years of *Hansard*— 57 thick gold-tooled, leather-bound volumes containing upwards of 100,000 columns—to Los Angeles for about $200!

In the United States, I am grateful to the Ford Foundation for helping to distribute this book in South Africa, Cecelia Cancellaro at Routledge and the series editors Christine Harrington and John Brigham for accepting it on the basis of a brief prospectus, Adam Bohannon and Claudia Gorelick at Routledge for production and promotion, Austin Sarat for inviting me to present an early version of the conclusions at an Amherst conference (to be published by University of Michigan Press as "The Paradoxes of Rights" in 1995), UCLA law and graduate students Richard Marcus, John Muñoz, Farouk Abrahams, and Kathy Thomas for research assistance and tape transcription, and Emily Abel, William Forbath, Joel Handler, and Lucie White for comments on drafts.

My greatest debt, however, is to those who suffered in the struggle against apartheid. Like many, I was drawn to law by its aspiration toward justice. Most lawyers, law teachers and law students, however, lose sight of that ideal in the quotidian preoccupation with making a living. We become obsessed with craft at the expense of ends—what Charles Derber calls ideological proletarianization. The dedication of South African lawyers and litigants to the struggle against apartheid redeems law's promise by reminding us of its potential nobility.

Santa Monica, California
February 1994

GLOSSARY OF ACRONYMS
AND FOREIGN WORDS

AAC	Alexandra Action Committee (Mayekiso's group)
ACA	Alexandra Civic Association (Beea's group)
ACC	Alexandra Crisis Committee (organized funerals)
ACLA	Advisory Commission on Land Allocation
ACO	Alexandra Civic Organisation (successor to AAC)
AD	Appellate Division (of Supreme Court)
ALC	Alexandra Liaison Committee (became ATC)
amabutho	warriors (Zulu)
amaqabane	comrades (UDF/ANC supporters) (Xhosa)
ANC	African National Congress
AO	Adjutant Officer (subordinate police officer)
ARA	Alexandra Residents Association
askari	former MK member turned state agent (Swahili for soldier)
ASCO	Alexandra Student Congress
assegai	spear (traditional Zulu weapon)
ATC	Alexandra Town Council
AWB	Afrikaner Weerstandsbeweging (Afrikaner Resistance Movement, Eugene Terre'Blanche's organization)
AWO	Alexandra Women's Organisation
AYCO	Alexandra Youth Congress
AZAPO	Azanian People's Organisation (black power)
AZASO	Azanian Student Organisation (black power)
BAC	Brits Action Committee
balaclava	mask concealing all but eyes
Black Sash	white liberal women's group opposed to apartheid
boer	farmer (Afrikaans; pl. boere)
Bophuthatswana	one of four "independent" homelands, ruled by Lucas Mangope
Broederbund	elite Afrikaner secret society
buffel	armored car
CALS	Centre for Applied Legal Studies
casspir	armored car
charterist	movement associated with ANC Freedom Charter
combi	minibus or taxi
comrade	UDF/ANC supporter

comtsotsi	gangster (tsotsi) pretending to be comrade
CONTRALESA	Congress of Traditional African Leaders of South Africa (UDF/ANC supporters)
COSAS	Congress of South African Students (black student group)
COSATU	Congress of South African Trade Unions
COSG	Conscientious Objector Support Group
CP	Conservative Party
CTDB	Cape Town Development Board
CTrDB	Central Transvaal Development Board
dagga	hemp, hashish
DET	Deparment of Education and Training (Black)
dikgosana	heads of lineage groups (Tswana)
dompas	pass book (Afrikaans)
donga	gully
DP	Democratic Party (successor to PFP)
EAC	Ekangala Action Committee
ECC	End Conscription Campaign
ERAB	East Rand Administration Board
ERADEBO	East Rand Development Board
ETDB	Eastern Transvaal Development Board
FCI	Federated Chambers of Industry
FOSATU	Federation of South African Trade Unions (Cosatu predecessor)
FRELIMO	Mozambique liberation movement
Hansard	Official record of South African Parliament
hippo	armored truck
HNP	Herstigte Nasionale Partie (to the right of the National Party)
ICFTU	International Confederation of Free Trade Unions
IDASA	Institute for Democratic Alternatives in South Africa
IFP	Inkatha Freedom Party (Mangosuthu Gatsha Buthelezi's group)
impi	warrior phalanx (Zulu)
impimpi	informer (Xhosa)
interdict	injunction
ISA	Internal Security Act
kaffir	derogatory word for Black (Afrikaans)
kgoro	lineage group, clan (Tswana)
kgotla	council (Tswana; properly lekgotla, pl. makgotla)
kitskonstabel	instant policeman (Afrikaans)
KLA	KwaNdebele Legislative Assembly
knobkierrie	walking stick with knob on end (Zulu traditional weapon)
kombi	minibus or taxi
kraal	courtyard (often fenced)

KwaNdebele	one of six "national states" (Simon Skosana the original chief minister)
KWAYCO	KwaNdebele Youth Congress (UDF/ANC supporter)
KwaZulu	one of six "national states" (Buthelezi chief minister)
KZP	KwaZulu Police
Lebowa	one of six "national states" (Cedric Phatudi chief minister)
LLG	Louis le Grange Square Police Station (Port Elizabeth)
LP	Labour Party (in "Coloured" House of Representatives)
LRC	Legal Resources Centre
MACWUSA	Motor Assemblers and Component Workers Union of South Africa
MASA	Medical Association of South Africa (establishment professional group)
matric	examination at end of secondary school qualifying for university entrance
MAWU	Metal and Allied Workers Union (later NUMSA)
mbokotho	KwaNdebele vigilantes (alternative spellings: imbokhoto, mbokoto, mbhokoto, mbokodo)
MDM	Mass Democratic Movement (successor to banned UDF)
MI	Military Intelligence
MK	Umkhonto we Sizwe (Spear of the Nation in Xhosa; ANC armed wing)
mkhukhu	shack, hut (pl. mekhukhu)
MLA	Member of Legislative Assembly (homeland MP)
MLO	Municipal Labour Officer
Mogopa	Western Transvaal "black spot" whose people (Magopa) were moved next to Bophuthatswana
Moutse	North Sotho speaking area taken from Lebowa and given to South Sotho speaking KwaNdebele
MPLA	Mozambique People's Liberation Army
NAAWU	National Automobile and Allied Workers Union
NADEL	National Association of Democratic Lawyers (ANC supporters)
NAMDA	National Medical and Dental Association (ANC supporters)
NCAR	National Committee Against Removals
NECC	National Education Crisis Committee
NGK	Nederduitse Gereformeerde Kerk (Dutch Reformed Church) (white)
NICRO	National Institute for the Correction and Rehabilitation of Offenders
NP	National Party
NPU	National Press Union
NRP	New Republic Party
NTA	Ndzundza Tribal Authority
NUM	National Union of Mineworkers
NUMSA	National Union of Metalworkers of South Africa
NUSAS	National Union of South African Students (white)
OCA	Oukasie Civic Association
PAB	Publications Appeal Board

PAC	Pan African Congress
panga	machete (Swahili)
Pass Laws	Until 1986 adult Blacks were required to possess a pass and present it on demand
PE	Port Elizabeth
PEBCO	Port Elizabeth Boycott Committee
PEYCO	Port Elizabeth Youth Congress
PFP	Progressive Federal Party
Pondo	tribe related to Xhosa
Poqo	PAC armed wing
PPSA	People's Party of South Africa (Indian House of Delegates)
R	rand (worth thirty-five to forty cents during 1980s)
Reef	Witwatersrand gold mining area
Renamo	Mozambique guerrilla movement backed by South Africa
SAAWU	South African Allied Workers Union
SABC	South African Broadcasting Company (government owned)
SACBC	South African Catholic Bishops' Conference
SACC	South African Council of Churches
SACLA	South African Christian Leadership Assembly
SACP	South African Communist Party
SACTU	South African Congress of Trade Unions (banned ANC affiliate)
SADF	South African Defence Force
SAMDC	South African Medical and Dental Council (self-regulatory body)
SANSCO	South African National Student Congress (banned)
SAP	South African Police or Save Alexandra Party
SARMCOL	South African Rubber Manufacturing Company Ltd (British Tyre & Rubber subsidiary)
SASO	South African Student Organisation (banned)
SAWCO	Sarmcol Workers' Co-operative
SAYCO	South African Youth Congress
SC	Supreme Court or Senior Counsel
SEIFSA	Steel and Engineering Industrial Federation of South Africa
sjambok	leather whip
SRC	Student Representative Council
SWAPO	South West African People's Organisation (Namibian liberation party)
TFCC	Trust Feed Crisis Committee
toyi-toyi	dance with singing (associated with protest)
TPA	Transvaal Provincial Administration
TRAC	Transvaal Rural Action Committee
tsotsi	gangster
UAW	United Auto Workers (American union)

UCT	University of Cape Town
UDF	United Democratic Front
Umkhonto we Sizwe	Spear of the Nation (Xhosa); ANC armed wing
UNISA	University of South Africa
UNITA	Jonas Savimbi's rebel movement in Angola (South African supported)
UWUSA	United Workers Union of South Africa (Inkatha affiliate)
veld	rural land
verkrampte	strict believer in apartheid (Afrikaans)
verligte	enlightened reformer of apartheid (Afrikaans)
Voortrekkerhoogte	monument to Boer great trek; location of SADF training camp
WCAB	Western Cape Administration Board
witdoek	vigilantes (white headbands in Afrikaans; pl. witdoeke)
Wits	University of the Witwatersrand
WO	Warrant Officer (subordinate police official)
workerist	belief that workers are revolutionary vanguard
WRAB	West Rand Administration Board

CHAPTER 1

SPEAKING WITH THE OGRE

> The Ogre does what ogres can,
> Deeds quite impossible for man,
> But one prize is beyond his reach
> The Ogre cannot master speech.
>   W.H. Auden*

The struggle against apartheid is one of the great contemporary moral dramas. Together with proletarian revolutions, the defeat of fascism, wars of liberation, and the labor, civil rights, and feminist movements it defines our century. The April 1994 election, which launched democracy in South Africa, signified the end of the colonial era and official racism.

Law has played a central role in this struggle for several reasons. The white regime effectively excluded Blacks from the political arena. Africans could not vote for national offices.** Their local governments had little autonomy. No foreign country recognized the ten "homelands," whether "independent" or "self-governing." Elections were infrequent and often rigged, and military coups were common. The South African military kept homeland leaders in power (and restored them when overthrown), and the central treasury heavily subsidized their unviable economies. Although the regime purported to leaven totalitarian white control over urban Blacks with appointed and then elected black township councils, these were just as corrupt as their homeland counterparts and less legitimate, if anything, since

---

*O 26 (9.8.68). This was Auden's response to the Soviet tanks that crushed the Prague spring. I encountered it in Francis Wilson's foreword to the 1989 reissue of Charles Hooper's powerful account of women's resistance to the pass laws in the Western Transvaal in the 1950s.

**It is impossible to write about South Africa without employing the regime's racist terminology. I generally use Black as synonymous with African and as distinguished from "Coloured" and Indian. Beginning with the black power movement of the 1970s, however, the three groups sought to weld a united front in opposition to apartheid, so I use black to include all three.

local elections were frequently boycotted. Although the 1983 constitutional "reform" created Houses of Representatives and Delegates for "Coloureds" and Indians in the new tricameral Parliament, the United Democratic Front boycotted elections to those bodies (securing minimal turnouts), and the white-dominated President's Council could and did override their vetoes.

The principal opposition groupings—ANC, SACP, and PAC—had all been outlawed by 1960. Although they re-established themselves in exile, often with considerable diplomatic and media visibility, they could only operate underground within the country. Using detention without trial, torture, informers, and agents provocateurs, the security police managed to infiltrate and disrupt much of the underground movement. The ANC military wing, Umkhonto we Sizwe (Spear of the Nation), greatly strengthened by the exodus of youths after the crushing of the 1976 Soweto rebellion, smuggled arms and personnel back into the country. But though it demonstrated an increasing capacity during the 1980s to detonate bombs and land mines (hitting "soft" civilian targets more easily than "hard" military objectives), it never posed a threat to the regime or seriously impaired white morale. Staffed through the universal conscription of white men, who served two years and did reserve duty for another two, and endowed with the most advanced technology, the South African Defence Force exceeded the military capacity of all the rest of sub-Saharan Africa combined. Despite its name, the SADF actually defended white power by patrolling black townships, preserving colonial rule in South-West Africa (Namibia), assisting insurgents in Angola and Mozambique (Unita and Renamo), and freely attacking ANC targets (and innocent civilians) in the front-line states (Botswana, Zimbabwe, and Zambia).

Other forms of extraparliamentary politics were severely curtailed. Government either banned all outdoor meetings or refused to issue the requisite permits. It outlawed numerous organizations. It excluded and deported foreign correspondents and television crews. It regulated the entry of all foreign books, newspapers, magazines, and films. It controlled television and dominated radio. It severely limited what the domestic media could publish, seized offending issues, banned books, and punished publication and even ownership with fines and prison terms. It curtailed access to scenes of unrest or opposition. It prosecuted and jailed opponents for long terms—most notoriously Nelson Mandela and the other Rivonia accused for life on Robben Island. Using ever more restrictive security legislation it detained opponents indefinitely without trial or banned and restricted them (so they could not be quoted, meet with others, or even leave their homes). During the 1985–90 Emergency it jailed more than 35,000 people, some for years.

If the opposition had few avenues other than litigation through which to challenge the regime, there also were good reasons for choosing law as a means of struggle. South Africa repeatedly proclaimed its respect for the rule of law, to both foreign and domestic audiences. Courts occasionally invalidated racist actions by the executive or legislature, such as segregation of public accommodations, or disenfranchisement of Cape Coloured voters. If such decisions were exceptional, they also were repeatedly lauded as evidence of the independence of the judiciary. White politicians never tired of making comparisons with the one-party authoritarian regimes prevailing throughout black Africa. Because the regime used legal institutions to construct and administer apartheid, it was vulnerable to legal contestation. All this helps to explain why the opposition might choose law strategically. But it also embraced legality as a fundamental principle—most notably the ANC in its Freedom Charter.

Yet law was an unpromising ally. The South African Parliament was supreme. No bill of rights restrained it, nor was there any tradition resembling the unwritten constitution that inhibits its Westminster antecedent. The National Party ruled for nearly half a century—from 1948 to 1994—generally disregarding an opposition that dwindled to the lonely voice of Helen Suzman for thirteen years. Well before the 1980s the Nationalists had appointed every judge, increasingly guided by political loyalty. Legal challenges to the regime rarely succeeded and hence were rarely attempted. The legal profession, naturally conservative and timid, remained silent.

South Africa, therefore, presents the ideal setting in which to explore the central question of jurisprudence: the circumstances under which, extent to which, and ways in which legality constrains state power. Law claims authority by offering reasons for the exercise of power. It relies on human speech rather than brute action. Could the South African ogre speak? Would it heed opposing arguments? Reflecting on eighteenth-century England, E.P. Thompson declared that "the regulation and reconciliation of conflicts through the rule of law" is "a cultural achievement of universal significance."[1] Alan Paton (who testified for Mandela and the other accused in the 1964 Rivonia trial) unconsciously echoed this sentiment. The rule of law "is one of the noblest achievements of sinful man," "the greatest political achievement of humankind," "a miracle."[2] Would South Africa fulfill or disappoint these hopes in the 1980s?

This book seeks to understand the value and limits of legality in resisting authoritarian regimes—the art of speaking with the ogre—by examining ten pivotal legal campaigns during the last years of apartheid. In choosing them I sought to cover the three principal arenas of struggle—political authority, land, and labor—and the two strategic postures—law as shield and as sword. The victories and defeats, the resort to legality and its evasion, all illuminate law's potential for the oppressed. Here I preview the stories in chapters 3–12.

Chapter 3. The pass laws (which regulated the residence of Africans and required them to produce identity documents on demand) were one of the most pervasive and hated facets of apartheid, separating husband from wife, parent from child, banishing "surplus" labor and "unproductive" Blacks to impoverished "homelands" while exposing millions of urban residents to brutal bureaucrats, midnight raids, summary arrest, demands for bribes (of money or sex), and imprisonment or forced labor. Two challenges tested the utility of South Africa's first public interest law firm and the judiciary's capacity to control street-level bureaucrats.

Chapter 4. Resistance to conscription was one of the few contributions by whites to the struggle against apartheid (and one of the most visible). Those who failed to meet the narrow criteria for conscientious objection (or refused to apply) faced up to six years in prison. The handful willing to pay this heavy price to be absolved from complicity with apartheid became the focus of a highly effective campaign against conscription. The challenge to their sentences forced the Appellate Division to interpret unusually clear statutory language mandating fixed prison terms.

Chapter 5. Responding to big capital's insistence on greater productivity, government created a structure for collective bargaining by black trade unions, which allowed them to grow rapidly in membership and influence. For years the Metal and Allied Workers Union (the second largest black union and the most militant) engaged in frustrating contract negotiations with a recalcitrant SARMCOL (owned by the multinational British Tyre & Rubber). In 1985 the company retaliated against a wildcat strike provoked by growing worker anger, locking out and then dismissing the entire workforce and negotiating a sweetheart contract with the far more compliant United Workers Union of South Africa. MAWU's complaints about unfair labor practices led to the longest labor trial in South African history and an ambiguous judgment on the protection that law offered labor in disputes with management.

Chapter 6. After the Inkatha-linked (and government-financed) UWUSA ousted MAWU (which sympathized with UDF and the ANC), Inkatha launched a campaign to take over Mpophomeni, the SARMCOL company town. It sent a hundred armed youths to stage a deliberately provocative rally. During the preceeding night they kidnapped four MAWU activists (murdering three) and murdered a fourth Mpophomeni resident the next day. Summoned to the township, the police intervened to protect Inkatha from the angry populace, escorting them out of town with their weapons. The inquest tested the will of the legal system to name and punish the killers despite intimidation of witnesses by an armed Inkatha warlord, police delays, and prosecutorial indifference.

Chapter 7. The security forces routinely used torture to extract information, repress the masses, eliminate leaders, and take revenge. When government declared the Emergency in July 1985, Eastern Cape security police rounded up and systematically tortured hundreds of prisoners. Wendy Orr, working for the Prisons Department in her first job since qualifying as a doctor, was horrified by the wounds she treated and the stories she heard. Eight years earlier her superior had certified the tortured Steve Biko as fit for the 800-mile trip to Pretoria, which killed him. Fearing a new scandal, he instructed Orr to photocopy all the medical records to ensure that any blame fell on the security police rather than the Prisons Department. Her affidavit in support of an injunction, and those of the prisoners, illuminated the role of courts in restraining state abuses by exposing evil and mobilizing public opinion.

Chapter 8. Government also used the Emergency to strengthen its already elaborate censorship apparatus by empowering the Minister of Home Affairs to suspend a newspaper for three months—a sanction that could bankrupt it. The principal target was the "alternative press" and especially the *New Nation*, the largest black weekly, sponsored by the South African Catholic Bishops' Conference. The court had to decide whether the requirement that the Minister conclude that the paper fanned uprisings or unrest, stirred up feelings of hatred toward the security forces, or promoted the public image of any unlawful organization placed sufficient limits on his discretion to allow judicial review.

Chapter 9. In the mid-1980s the government launched three major treason trials, the first two targeting the UDF. A judge dismissed one when transcriptions of video- and audio-taped meetings proved hopelessly inaccurate. Heavy prison sentences in the second—the longest trial in South African history—were overturned on procedural grounds. Consequently, government had a great deal riding on the third, intended to discredit the trade unions and civic associations by accusing them of aspirations to "dual power" and implicating them in the excesses of people's courts. Justice van der Walt, educated during the trial by his first visit to a black township and lengthy colloquies with the accused about South African politics, had to decide whether the activities of the Alexandra Action Committee, documented in its fortuitously preserved minutes, demonstrated treason, sedition, or subversion.

Chapter 10. Grand apartheid was South Africa's ultimate obscenity, compared to the Holocaust, the destruction of aboriginal communities in the Americas and Australia, and contemporary "ethnic cleansing." In a vain effort to consign all Blacks to independent homelands so as to justify treating them like aliens, South Africa forcibly removed an estimated 3.5 million Blacks. The Magopa were the last victims. Three months after losing its nerve under the scrutiny of television cameras, security forces swooped down in the middle of the night to cart off residents. Although the Appellate Division later invalidated the removal, government had already nullified this victory by expropriating the land. After years of wandering in the wilderness, Magopa began to return, first to clean ancestral graves and then to resume farming and herding. Although the Supreme Court granted an eviction decree, the Appellate Division had to reconcile the government's legalistic entitlement with its commitment to reform after the unbanning of the ANC and release of Mandela.

Chapter 11. When the government no longer could remove Blacks physically, it tried to incorporate them into the homelands and persuade the six that had not done so to accept "independence." Only the corrupt rulers of KwaNdebele could be swayed, bribed by the offer of Moutse, an adjacent territory nearly as large and far better endowed. Justifiably terrified of KwaNdebele oppression, Moutse invoked the apartheid ideology of ethnic purity, asking the courts to nullify incorporation because of linguistic and cultural differences between the two groups. While this case was pending, many KwaNdebele residents continued to resist independence. One tactic was to attack the disenfranchisement of women by arguing, in the world's only country with a racially-exclusive franchise, that a sexually-exclusive franchise violated natural justice.

Chapter 12. Government's remaining tactic was to make life so unpleasant for black township residents that they would move "voluntarily." In Oukasie, the "old location" of Brits, a court ordered the white superintendent to reallocate vacant houses and plots to residents, moved in part by his vulgar rebuff of an applicant. Government responded by "disestablishing" the township and then declaring it an "Emergency Camp," which authorized government to promulgate intolerably restrictive regulations on movement and economic activity and to raise rents. This time residents asked one of the more conservative judges to invalidate the declaration on the ground that people living in their own houses, however miserable, were not homeless.

To lay a foundation for these narratives of resistance through law, the next chapter offers a framework for approaching the relationship between law and politics and an overview of the pertinent post-war South African history. After presenting the ten case studies I synthesize what we have learned about the roles of law in the struggle against apartheid and extrapolate this experience to post-apartheid South Africa and resistance to other oppressive regimes.

CHAPTER 2

POLITICS BY OTHER MEANS?

> The Rule of Law is the greatest political
> achievement of humankind. The Rule of
> Law is a miracle; it is nothing less than
> man protecting himself against his own
> cruelty and selfishness. (Alan Paton)[1]

Law and Politics

Rechtsstaat: the ideal of apolitical law

The relationship between law and politics is the central question of
jurisprudence. Is law, like war, merely politics by other means? Or can legal
institutions be relatively autonomous, reaching decisions that do not simply
reflect political forces and significantly constraining state power?

The controversy has been most intense with respect to adjudication. On
one side are those who believe in the possibility and desirability of apolitical law: German pandectists striving for Weberian formal rationality, English
positivists claiming that judges discover rather than make law, and Americans
championing the passive virtues, strict construction, and original intent. On
the other are those who maintain that law is inescapably political: German
"free decisionists," natural lawyers, American legal realists, jurimetricians
scrutinizing judicial background and personality, and critical legal theorists
proclaiming indeterminacy.[2]

The myth of the judge as a passive vehicle through whom the law
mechanically finds expression encounters a number of inconvenient facts. If
judicial identity is insignificant why did the U.S. Senate reject Nixon's
Supreme Court nominations of Carswell and Haynsworth? Why all the fuss
about Robert Bork and Clarence Thomas?[3] Indeed, why do scholars refer to
the "Warren" and "Rehnquist" Courts? Why did death penalty advocates and
other conservatives spend $11 million to recall Rose Bird, Joseph Grodin, and

Cruz Reynoso from the California Supreme Court?[4] Why the outrage that Nazis removed Jews from the German bench?[5] Or the debate about Roosevelt's plan to pack the Supreme Court when it kept invalidating New Deal legislation? Or the interminable controversy about the best method of judicial selection? Or the contemporary demand that women and minorities be proportionally represented in the judiciary? Why do litigators carefully strategize to appear before particular judges? Jurisdictions using juries confront these issues even more explicitly in the definition of the venire, voir dire and challenges, and government vetting of potential jurors. Judges may sequester juries during high-visibility trials, prohibit public discussion of matters that are sub judice, and even restrain media access to jurors after they deliver their verdict.

Jury nullification is notorious—e.g., white jurors acquitting whites of crimes against blacks in the American South or South Africa. Independent of personnel, sociologists have demonstrated class, race, and gender bias in judicial outcomes. The media highlight leniency to the well-born and powerful: aristocratic drunk drivers in England, Patty Hearst, John De Lorean, Ivan Boesky, and Michael Milken in the United States. Police who assault or kill civilians rarely are punished, while civilians who assault or kill police rarely are acquitted.[6] If adjudication were truly mechanical there would be no concurring and dissenting opinions—indeed, opinions would be superfluous since the inevitability of the outcome would be transparent; stare decisis would be absolute; and there would be little need for the elaborate structures of appeal, revision, and collateral attack. In fact, however, review by federal or supranational courts—the U.S. Supreme Court, the Privy Council for the Commonwealth, the European Court of Human Rights, the International Court of Justice—provokes vigorous political controversy.

Those who maintain or concede that adjudication cannot be apolitical remain concerned to understand the ways in which politics shapes law— what it means to say that law is relatively autonomous.[7] The question is both normative—when legal institutions may and must resist political influence— and positive—the circumstances under which they can do so. Some attacks on judicial independence are blatantly illegal, such as corruption (bribing judges, tampering with juries) and violence (e.g., the killing of judges by organized crime in Sicily, drug traffickers in Colombia, or Maoist guerrillas in Peru). Regimes circumvent obstreperous courts by curtailing their jurisdiction or shifting functions to specialized judges more amenable to influence and insulated from appellate review: military and labor tribunals, Diplock courts in Northern Ireland, the Volksgerichthof and Sonsgerichte in Nazi Germany, and administrative agencies generally.[8] The state may prohibit courts from evaluating its actions by invoking such doctrines as sovereign immunity, political question, and act of state. It may forbid review of executive discretion or curtail judicial discretion through strict sentencing guidelines (as the

U.S. Congress did recently). Finally, it may simply halt trials in progress or suspend an entire court, as Yeltsin closed the Constitutional Court when it blocked his reforms.[9]

Because the other two branches of government are explicitly political, tensions between law and politics assume different forms. Here the central question is the ways in which law restrains illegitimate political power. The legislature, like the judiciary, may suffer blatant interference: military coups and threats, executive suspension or arrogation of emergency powers. Its authority may be undermined more subtly by meddling with the selection process: violent or corrupt elections, the banning of parties or jailing of leaders. Even without such gross distortions, money, incumbency, districting, and choice of a voting algorithm will affect who achieves power. Absent external interference with the legislature, its edicts still may be challenged for insufficient generality, prospectivity, precision and notice, or because they discriminate, violate human rights (life, liberty, property, citizenship, information, privacy, speech, religion, association, movement), or inflict unacceptable punishments (torture, the death penalty). Some argue that the state also has an obligation to prevent private violations of fundamental rights.

When legislatures submit to or indulge in such abuses, we look to the judiciary to correct them. E.P. Thompson documented the opposition of common law judges to state absolutism in eighteenth-century England.[10] Robert Cover analyzed similar tensions in the enforcement of fugitive slave acts in ante-bellum America.[11] Because Nazism used legal forms for evil purposes, its judges faced the conflict between law and morality in particularly acute form—and totally failed to meet the challenge.[12]

Although procedures for selecting and dismissing the executive also affect its integrity, two other issues dominate the tension between law and politics in that branch. The first is respect for legislative supremacy—has the executive exceeded its delegated powers? Those subjected to economic regulation have made the claim of ultra vires central to administrative law. Recipients of welfare benefits also have challenged arbitrary or discriminatory treatment.[13] The second issue is respect for basic rights, whether enshrined in a constitution or derived from natural law. Police behavior receives particular scrutiny: unlawful arrest, coerced confessions, unreasonable search and seizure, excessive force, entrapment, use of informers and provocateurs, detention without trial, suppression of exculpatory evidence, coaching and coercing of witnesses. Police may kidnap suspects from foreign countries: Adolf Eichmann by Israel, Klaus Barbie by France, Ebrahim Ismail Ebrahim by South Africa, and the murderers of Klinghoffer by the United States. Or police may accept bribes to allow influential criminals to escape: Pablo Escobar in Colombia, the murderers of Chico Mendes in Brazil. Police excesses can be motivated by career incentives for apprehending and convicting criminals,[14] or by racial or political prejudice.[15] In extreme cases, police condone or participate in executions of revolutionaries, common criminals, or simply the poor, young or homeless. Custodial institutions like prisons, mental hospitals, and schools are empowered and tempted to abuse inmates. Alternatively, the executive may use clemency and pardon to frustrate the criminal process (Nixon by Ford, and Weinberger by Bush) or to appear omnipotent and merciful—as the South African executive did in commuting death sentences.[16]

The legal profession also plays a role in enhancing the autonomy of law. The Nazi regime sought to compel defense lawyers to place their obligations to the state above their loyalty to clients.[17] To discourage the emergence of an independent legal profession, Israel refused to allow Palestinian lawyers to engage in self-regulation.[18] Lawyers often are a central target of authoritarian regimes.[19] Professional associations have a spotty record of resisting threats to the rule of law: bar associations did not stand up to McCarthyism in the United States, the German occupation in France, or fascism in Italy or Brazil;[20] but professional bodies in Ghana and Malaysia have threatened to strike in support of the judiciary,[21] and the organized profession supported legal aid in many countries (if partly for selfish reasons).

Political Trials

The popular image of the clash between law and politics is the political trial—a prosecution motivated or distorted by animus.[22] In its most transparent manifestation the state mobilizes the criminal process to eliminate, silence, cow, discredit, or incapacitate opponents: Socrates and Jesus are the most notorious examples. Capital used criminal (and civil) law to frustrate workers' efforts to organize and bargain collectively in the nineteenth and early twentieth centuries and again during the neo-conservative 1980s.[23] Governments create and fuel moral panics over alcohol, drugs, mugging, gangs and pornography to distract attention from other issues, denigrate opponents as "soft on crime," and stigmatize entire populations as criminal.[24] The Cold War often abused the legal process under cover of anti-communism.[25] The state used criminal law to suppress the civil rights movement, as well as civil unrest provoked by institutional racism.[26] The state engaged in mass arrests of anti-war protesters and invested enormous resources in prosecuting their leaders.[27] Both fascist and communist regimes conducted show trials of opponents, recently General Ochoa Sanchez in Cuba and the Tiananmen Square demonstrators in China.[28] Governments use criminal law to discourage publication of embarrassing information.[29] States misuse police and prosecutions against terrorists and suspects.[30]

State opponents are not always passive victims of the criminal process. Sometimes they invite prosecution through civil disobedience or other forms of defiance in order to expose the regime's moral bankruptcy: suffragists in the US and UK, Gandhi's *satyagraha* (passive resistance) against British colonialism, conscientious objectors to war, the American civil rights, anti-nuclear and anti-war movements, sanctuary for Central American refugees, environmentalists and campaigners against blood sports, the anti-abortion movement, feminists against pornography, and AIDS activism.[31] In the ensuing trial defendants challenge the government's policies and very legitimacy, while prosecutors and judges try to treat the matter as an ordinary crime.

Politics also colors another kind of trial: when a new regime (often the product of war or revolution) seeks to redress the crimes of its predecessor: the Nuremberg trials of Nazi war criminals and German de-Nazification;[32] Israel's prosecution of Eichmann and Demjanjuk; France's continuing attempt to deal with Vichy collaborators;[33] the aftermath of dictatorship in Latin America;[34] internal colonization—aborigines in the United States, Canada, and Australia, blacks in the United States and South Africa; Chinese and Korean claims for reparations from Japan; and now the crimes of communism and the war crimes of Serbia.[35] Similar tensions are visible when the international community seeks to judge an entrenched regime: South Africa for its domination of Namibia, Rhodesia after UDI, the United States for mining Nicaraguan waters.

Law as a Sword

Although legislation and executive action are explicitly political, and prosecution can be turned to political ends, civil litigation usually manages to present itself as apolitical, routine, mechanical. Ever since the founding of the ACLU and NAACP, however, social movements have mobilized law proactively to challenge the state and, less often, private adversaries. The civil rights movement is the preeminent success story (despite recent revisionism).[36] During the last three decades law has played an increasingly pivotal role in movements for the rights those oppressed because of race, ethnicity or religion, the poor, women, consumers, the environment, gays and lesbians, the incarcerated, and the disabled.[37] Legal aid, domestic public interest, and international human rights lawyers have multiplied, although funding is always inadequate.[38] As a sword, however, law may be ornamental or two-edged. Many victories, legislative or judicial, are largely symbolic, difficult or impossible to implement in practice.[39] And vested interests may be better situated to invoke rights, derived from the constitution or natural law, in opposition to legislative or executive reforms: property rights against the New Deal, equal protection against affirmative action, the Fourth Amendment prohibition of unreasonable search and seizure against health and safety regulation, the Fifth Amendment on takings against environmental measures, the First Amendment on free speech against limitations on tobacco advertising, the Second Amendment against gun control.[40]

The Centrality of Law in South Africa

De Tocqueville's classic description of the newly-independent United States applied even more accurately to South Africa a century and a half later:

> Scarcely any political question arises... that is not resolved, sooner or later, into a judicial question. Hence all parties are obliged to borrow, in their daily controversies, the ideas, and even the language, peculiar to judicial proceedings.*

Law has played a central role in the struggle against apartheid for several reasons. First, few other weapons were available. Soon after it took power in 1948 the National Party completed the disenfranchisement of blacks. Although the 1983 constitutional "reform" created a tricameral Parliament, few Indians and "Coloureds" bothered to vote for chambers that could always be trumped by the white-dominated President's Council. Similarly, some nine out of ten Black voters boycotted elections for local councils, the only urban government in which they had any voice. The ten homeland regimes were notoriously corrupt, and few criticized South Africa, on which they were totally dependent. The state drastically restricted extraparliamentary opposition. The African National Congress, South African Communist Party, and Pan African Congress had been outlawed—driven into exile and underground. Thousands were detained under the Internal Security Act; many were placed under house arrest, banned (forbidden to meet with others), or listed (unable to be quoted).

Public gatherings required permission, which usually was denied. Domestic media were severely censored and foreign reporters excluded; books, periodicals, plays, and movies were banned; government owned all television and most radio stations. The Emergency, declared in July 1985 and renewed annually for five years, restricted actions and words even more severely. Finally, although the ANC military wing, Umkhonto we Sizwe ("spear of the nation" or MK), increased the number, magnitude, and audacity of its attacks in the 1980s, it never seriously threatened state stability. The South African military, whose firepower exceeded that of the rest of sub-Saharan Africa combined, contained guerrilla warfare in Namibia for decades, supported rebels in Angola and Mozambique, and freely raided the ANC in the front-line states of Botswana, Zimbabwe, and Zambia.

Not only were most other routes closed, but law also appeared promising. South Africa had a long liberal tradition, if greatly weakened by four decades of Nationalist rule.[41] Officials and other apologists constantly boasted about the government's respect for the rule of law and the exalted reputation of its judiciary, both within the country and outside.[42] In a 1985 Parliamentary debate, for instance, a Nationalist MP insisted:

---

*De Tocqueville (1958: vol.1, p.290). Consider the importance of law, trials, and repression in the fiction, plays, and autobiography of such internationally-known authors as Alan Paton (see Black, 1992), Athol Fugard, Nadine Gordimer, Richard Rive, Es'kia Mphahlele, André Brink, and Breyten Breytenbach, for instance, or others less well known: Boetie (1989); Malan (1990); Dangor (1990); Fugard (1984); Joubert (1980); Driver (1969); du Plessis (1983; 1989); Eprile (1989); Ramgobin (1986); Wicomb (1987).

the South African administration of justice and the judicature stand out as a symbol of hope and confidence. Even South Africa's severest critics readily concede that the standard of the administration of justice in South Africa is of the highest order. ... Mr. [Andrew] Young [former U.S. Ambassador to the U.N.] spontaneously and readily conceded that the South African administration of justice complied with the highest standards.[43]

Three years later a Nationalist MP declared: "The impartiality of judges of our Supreme Court has gained world-wide respect." Invidiously comparing the Russian legal system, he continued: "Every citizen of this country is assured that, whatever offence he commits against the laws of the country, he will have a fair trial...."[44] During that debate, however, a colleague revealed the superficiality of his party's commitment: "The rule of law operates politically, and there is a liberal insistence on maximum individual freedom regardless of how the exercise of these so-called freedoms encroach upon the rights of others and of the State. It is a kind of humanistic absolutising of individual rights."[45]

The state exploited the judiciary's reputational capital by appointing judges to conduct commissions of inquiry into highly sensitive issues.[46] Perhaps most important, the infrastructure of apartheid—an administrative nightmare more complex and bureaucratic than the combined tax code, criminal law, regulatory apparatus, and welfare system of most countries— was constructed out of law and thus susceptible to legal challenge.[47]

Opponents honored the regime's pretensions by judging it in terms of legality. The ANC's Freedom Charter, adopted by the Congress of the People in 1955, contains an enumeration of rights that have furnished critical criteria and a blueprint for the post-apartheid society for nearly half a century.[48] Although the government censored indiscriminately and banned the Charter's author, it never proscribed the document itself. Over three decades the International Commission of Jurists repeatedly condemned South African violations of the rule of law.[49] Foreign governments and media, international organizations, and officials were equally censorious.[50] In May 1990, 200 Dutch judges urged 133 South African colleagues to abolish apartheid, invoking the historical links between their countries and the fact that Verwoerd, the architect of grand apartheid, had been born in the Netherlands.[51] Dutch lawyers expressed outrage at the trial of Heleen Passtoors, a Dutch citizen.[52] American and British lawyers, judges, and legal scholars wrote critically for more than 30 years.[53] These attacks clearly stung. The regime refused to readmit Geoffrey Bindman after he chaired the 1987 ICJ inquiry.[54] Chief Justice Rabie, addressing a meeting of the South African legal profession, condemned *The Times* for calling the judicial system "little more than a charade...terror tailored to the purposes of the state" after the Appellate Division failed to review the death sentences of the Sharpeville Six.[55]

Many South African lawyers and legal scholars have been profoundly troubled by the role of law in constructing apartheid and repressing opposition. They, too, grounded their criticisms in the rule of law and respect for human rights.[56] Many condemned the death penalty, noting that the rate of executions was one of the highest in the world and almost all those hanged were black.[57] Lacking a bill of rights or tradition of judicial review based on an unwritten constitution or natural law, lawyers sought to develop administrative law principles to rein in the executive behemoth.[58] Although Nationalists had appointed the entire bench by the 1980s, observers focused on small differences in judicial personality, distinguishing the few liberal judges from the mass of "executive-minded" apparatchiki.[59] The inability of even liberal judges to find significant legal purchase to resist the apartheid state led to a vigorous debate over whether they should resign.[60]

Although South Africa purported to respect academic freedom, even mild criticism provoked prompt retaliation. Barend van Niekerk was cited for contempt for daring to document racial discrimination in sentencing (although he was strongly defended by academics).[61] Government embargoed a doctoral dissertation on prison conditions.[62] The Minister of Justice angrily reprimanded one critic.[63] As late as December 1993 the Appellate Division allowed a judge to sue a human rights lawyer for suggesting the judge had been guilty of racial bias in sentencing.[64] And academic activists suffered grievously: Raymond Suttner spent nearly a decade in jail, including years in solitary confinement, Albie Sachs lost an arm and an eye to a bomb attack in Maputo, and David Webster was assassinated in Johannesburg.

As de Klerk accelerated the reform process in 1989 and embraced majority rule, lawyers turned to drafting a post-apartheid bill of rights and devising structures for judicial review.[65] Yet this entire normative discourse has been strangely disembodied, uninformed by the role law actually played during this crucial decade. And those who narrated and analyzed concrete political struggles tended to disregard the role of law.[66]

The Politics of Law in South Africa

Law has been a terrain of political contestation throughout South African history.[67] Courts have oscillated between being compliant, even enthusiastic, instruments of white domination and erecting obstacles, if only temporary, to the apartheid project. Early in this century the Appellate Division allowed Cape schools to restrict enrollment to children of "European parentage."[68] A half century after the U.S. Supreme Court's notorious Dred Scott decision, it upheld the segregation of post offices absent evidence that facilities were unequal.[69] After its 1948 victory, the National Party lost no time in translating its racist ideology into law: the Mixed Marriages Act 1949, Population Registration Act 1950, Group Areas Act 1950, Suppression of Communism Act 1950, and Immorality Act 1951.[70] The Defiance Campaign of 1952, using non-violent tactics pioneered by Gandhi in Natal in 1907, was quickly crushed by overwhelming force.[71] At the same time, however, the Appellate Division invalidated regulations segregating transportation: the exclusion of blacks from white railroad coaches (because whites could travel in black coaches), the denial of taxicab licenses, and the conviction of a black for entering a white waiting room.[72] Demonstrating the limitations of judicial review in the face of parliamentary supremacy, the legislature nullified these decisions with the Separate Amenities Act 49 of 1953.

Starting in the 1950s, government tried to eliminate the last vestige of black political participation by disenfranchising the Cape Coloured. Twice rebuffed by the Appellate Division for failing to obtain the two-thirds vote necessary to amend an entrenched clause, government expanded the upper house (ensuring the requisite supermajority) and enlarged the Appellate Division from six to eleven, packing it with friendly judges, who promptly approved the disenfranchisement ten to one.[73] The reconstituted court also upheld the core of grand apartheid: segregation of residence and land ownership.[74] And it perpetrated its own petty apartheid, affirming a contempt citation issued against the law clerk of Mandela and Tambo for refusing to sit at a segregated table in the magistrate's court.[75]

In 1956 government prosecuted 156 members of the opposition for treason. After a five-year trial, which cost the defense £200,000, the court dismissed all charges.[76] But this victory coincided with the Sharpeville massacre and the declaration of the first Emergency.[77] Government banned the ANC and PAC under the Unlawful Organizations Act 24 of 1960. Convinced that peaceful change was impossible, both organizations formed military wings—Umkhonto we Sizwe and Poqo—in anticipation of armed struggle. Before any attacks, however, many ANC leaders were surprised at Rivonia (a farm outside Johannesburg) and, with Mandela (already imprisoned on other charges), were convicted under the "Sabotage Act" and sentenced to life imprisonment.[78] Government repression intensified, and courts offered little resistance. The Appellate Division rejected Albie Sachs's request for visitors and reading material during his indefinite detention—a decision that provoked the *first* article strongly critical of the judiciary.[79] Government responded by doubling the length of detention orders to 180 days, empowering the executive to make regulations governing prison conditions, and ousting courts of jurisdiction to pass on those regulations.[80] Government promptly authorized the officer in command to deny access to reading and writing material.[81] Courts upheld the admissibility of coerced confessions and the denial of legal advice to detainees.[82] Government passed the Terrorism Act 83 of 1967 to close any loopholes and again ousted courts of jurisdiction. Nevertheless, a few judges found ways to assert their authority.[83]

After nearly a decade of repression, political activity revived in the 1970s and with it prosecutions of anti-apartheid activists. Government convicted thirty-three Namibian resistance leaders, sentencing most to life or long prison terms. Yet twenty-one people (including Winnie Mandela) charged under the Terrorism Act were acquitted.[84] The growing black power movement led to many trials and convictions.[85] The state crushed the 1976 Soweto rebellion, driving thousands into exile (and into Umkhonto we Sizwe) and trying hundreds of others.[86] Most of the ninety-five accused in thirty political trials between 1976 and 1979 received lengthy sentences.[87] Breyten Breytenbach, who returned to South Africa in a transparent disguise, was convicted of sabotage and jailed for nine years.[88] Prominent clerics like Beyers Naudé and the Anglican Dean of Johannesburg were prosecuted.[89] The state constantly expanded the legal and institutional framework of its security apparatus.[90]

The struggle against apartheid changed qualitatitvely in the 1980s.[91] Under pressure from big capital seeking greater productivity, the Wiehahn Commission recommended and Parliament enacted the Labour Relations Act of 1981, stimulating the rapid growth of black trade unions, many of which joined to form the Congress of South African Trade Unions (Cosatu) in 1985.[92] The ANC demonstrated an increasing ability to attack targets throughout the country, although it never posed a military threat to the SADF.[93] The international community strengthened its economic boycott and disinvestment policies, whose effect was aggravated by the recession of the early 1980s.[94] Anger at the 1983 constitutional "reform," which gave Parliamentary chambers to Indians and "Coloureds" (subordinate to the white-dominated President's Council) but nothing to blacks, stimulated the creation of the United Democratic Front, a coalition of 600 residential, youth, women's, religious, sports, and other organizations, which claimed a membership of several million.[95] Discontent took the form of boycotts of rent and service charges, shops, and elections, stay-aways from school and work, and attacks on local councillors and police.[96] As the cycles of protest and repression grew more violent, P.W. Botha declared the second state of emergency in the country's history in July 1985, renewing it annually until 1990. Government used it to detain more than 35,000 people—including thousands of children—some for several years.[97] Nevertheless, Botha opened the 1986 Parliament with an extraordinary declaration:

> We believe in the sovereignty of the law as a basis of the protection of the fundamental rights of individuals as well as groups. We believe in the sanctity and indivisibility of law and the just application thereof. There can be no peace, freedom, and democracy without law. Any future system must conform with the requirements of a civilized legal order, and must ensure access to the courts and equality before the law. We believe that human dignity, life, liberty, and property of all must be protected, regardless of colour, race, creed or religion.[98]

Most legal challenges to detentions, Emergency regulations, and security force actions failed.[99] At first the Supreme Court asserted its authority to judge executive action: circumventing ouster clauses to review both the Attorney General's denial of bail[100] and an Emergency regulation,[101] finding a prohibition on "subversive" speech impermissibly vague,[102] rejecting a Minister's claim that his discretion to detain was purely subjective,[103] insisting that a prisoner be given reasons for detention and access to a lawyer,[104] and releasing a detainee because the state failed to make the requisite showing that detention would accelerate the lifting of the state of Emergency.[105] But in a notorious 1987 review of three consolidated cases, the Appellate Division upheld the central Emergency regulations and the legislature's exclusion of judicial review.[106] Only when Corbett replaced Rabie as Chief Justice in January 1989 (coincident with Botha's incapacitating stroke) did the Appellate Division begin to reassert judicial authority.[107]

The tide began to turn in 1989. Massive hunger strikes forced the release of a thousand detainees. A defiance campaign, imitating tactics that had failed nearly forty years earlier, successfully integrated beaches, public accommodations, and hospitals.[108] F.W. de Klerk became State President in August and began freeing prominent political prisoners, culminating in the release of Nelson Mandela and the legalization of the ANC and other opposition groups in February 1990. With the adoption of a transitional constitution in December 1993 the stage was set for the first democratic election in April 1994.[109]

The South African Legal System

The central feature of the South African legal system is Parliamentary supremacy. As mentioned above, the Nationalists were even able to abrogate the clause entrenching the voting rights of Cape Coloured by expanding both the Senate and the Appellate Division. Despite repeated boasts about the independence of judges and the respect they enjoyed, the judicial structure offered little more support for the rule of law than did the constitutional framework.[110] Most blacks encountered the legal system only when charged with petty offenses, especially pass law violations, appearing without legal representation before magistrates, some of whom were not qualified lawyers. Many were former prosecutors, most were Afrikaners, almost none was black, and all were members of the executive.* Their lack of independence was dramatically illustrated in August 1985, when the security police secretly

---

*In 1984 Minister of Justice H.J. Coetsee declared that "the administration of justice in the Supreme Court and the magistrates' courts has been and is independent of executive authority." *Hansard* col. 948 (5.17.84). A year later the PFP replied that the government's Hoexter Commission had said exactly the opposite: "the Commission's attention was drawn to the fact that magistrates in fact perform certain executive functions which are totally incompatible with the judicial nature of their office." Hoexter Commission (1983: 57), quoted in *Hansard* cols. 6778–80 (P.H.P. Gastrow) (6.4.85).

briefed Durban magistrates and prosecutors at the instance of Chief Magistrate J.J. Pienaar.[111] Judges, by contrast, enjoyed lifetime tenure. But selection exclusively from the ranks of senior counsel effectively excluded blacks, the first of whom, Ismail Mohamed, accepted an appointment only in August 1991.[112] The Nationalists increasingly disregarded the tradition of meritocratic selection.* Judicial deference to the state was particularly evident among chief justices (who assigned their brethren to Appellate Division cases.) L.C. Steyn was a government law adviser appointed to the Transvaal bench in 1951 (over the objection of the Bar, which attempted a boycott), promoted to the Appellate Division after just four years, and elevated to chief justice ahead of his seniors four years later.[113] Toward the end of his twelve-year tenure (the second longest) he declared it would "be an evil day for the administration of justice if our Courts should deviate from the well recognized tradition of giving politics as wide a berth as their work permits." It was "very improper" for a judge

> to rush into a political storm or into the wake of it, in a strongly contested matter in which Parliament has, by way of firm, deliberate policy, knowing what it was about and in the valid exercise of its legislative powers, laid down what is to be done. In such a matter, it is not our function to write an indignant codicil to the will of Parliament.[114]

At the beginning of his term in 1972, Ogilvie Thompson declared that "once a judge has determined what he conceives to be the intention of the legislature, he must perforce give effect to the intention so determined."[115] Rabie, his successor, commented toward the end of his term that "once Parliament says this is the law, it is the law." The Bill of Rights had produced a "bit of a shambles" in the United States, which suffered from "freedom run mad."[116] Although Rabie reached mandatory retirement in January 1987, the State President took the unprecedented step of making him Acting Chief Justice for another two years, allegedly because Botha considered the potential successors (Jansen and Corbett) insufficiently loyal to government. He also promoted Natal Judge President Milne to the Appellate Division, allegedly to stop him assigning political cases to judges hostile to government.[117]

Parliament, which cavalierly overturned judicial decisions and prohibited courts from reviewing executive action, suddenly displayed solicitude for judicial independence when the opposition criticized judges. The Appellate Division twice had reversed death sentences of blacks imposed by Justice J.J. Strydom, calling them "fundamentally fallacious" and a "serious misdirection." In 1988 he heard the case of a white farmer who tortured a black

---

*Cameron et al. (1980); SALJ (1980); S. Kentridge (1982). The opposition PFP declared in Parliament that a Nationalist Minister of Justice, F.C. Erasmus, had admitted that he took politics into consideration in appointments to the Supreme Court. *Hansard* col. 6746 (B.R. Bamford) (6.4.85).

employee to death over two days for accidentally running over two of the farmer's dogs eight weeks earlier. Strydom gave him a suspended jail sentence, R3,000 fine, and an order to pay restitution of R130/month for five years. The Speaker of the Assembly refused to allow Helen Suzman to petition for Strydom's removal on the ground that she had failed to state a prima facie case, and he overruled her points of order. When he finally allowed debate on a revised censure motion the Minister of Justice defended the sentence on the ground that the accused had been drinking, was nice to blacks, and employed forty of them. The restitution order was a form of "community service," he said, which would humiliate the accused worse than jail. Parliament defeated the motion 103–18, Suzman's last Parliamentary action after thirty-six years in the House, and overwhelmingly passed the Minister's substitute motion condemning her for ignoring the facts and events preceding the sentence.*

The legal profession also failed to champion the rule of law. Although eighty-five percent of the population was black, there were only thirteen African attorneys, twenty-six Indian, and five Coloured (out of 3,000) in 1962, and almost no black advocates (who had to demonstrate competence in Latin, a subject not offered by African secondary schools). Although all eleven white universities had law schools (Witwatersrand, Cape Town, Natal-Durban, Rhodes, Port Elizabeth, Pretoria, Rand Afrikaans, Stellenbosch, Potchefstroom, Free State, and Unisa), there was only one "Coloured" law school (Western Cape), one Indian (Durban-Westville), and five African (Bophuthatswana, North, Zululand, Transkei, and Fort Hare).[118] In the mid-1980s blacks constituted about ten percent of the 6,500 attorneys and about seven percent of the 650 advocates, but there were only two black senior counsel (who alone were eligible for the bench).[119] Attorneys were organized into provincial law societies, which formed the Association of Law Societies; advocates were organized by city and belonged to the General Council of the Bar. Professional organizations rarely took progressive political positions. The Transvaal Law Society moved to strike Mandela off the roll for his conviction for organizing the 1952 Defiance Campaign (although the Supreme Court refused). Unification of the bar was delayed by racial barriers in the Orange Free State and Transvaal. Apartheid prevented black attorneys and advocates from practicing in the Central Business Districts.[120]

The Association of Law Societies refused to seek the release of nine attorneys detained during the 1985–90 Emergency, disavowing any responsibility.

---

*Hansard cols. 2367–72, 2451–56, 2665–69, 2793–98, 10009–60 (3.8.89, 3.13–14.89, 5.23.89); Suzman (1993: 270-71). These events were reported in England (*The Times, Guardian, Daily Telegraph*) and Canada (*Toronto Globe and Mail*). The opposition Progressive Federal Party had earlier condemned magistrates for excessive leniency toward whites who attacked blacks. *Hansard* col. 6744 (D.J. Dalling) (6.4.85). Clearly stung, Justice Minister H.J. Coetsee replied by quoting Justice Coetzee's claim that he had never encountered racial sentencing disparities in 17 years on the bench and the liberal Justice Goldstone concurring based on six years experience. *Hansard* cols. 6796-98 (6.4.85).

The Transvaal Law Society vice president accepted the police assurance that no one was detained because he was a lawyer or had political clients. "I am absolutely satisfied with the bona fides of the Commissioner of Police." He urged lawyers not to make unreasonable demands for access to detained clients since "the police have tremendous logistical problems." "We must encourage things like human rights. But there are two sides to this story." Unidentified intruders broke into the office of human rights attorney Krish Naidoo three times, taking nothing of value. Police raided the office of human rights attorneys Cheadle Thompson and Haysom. They charged a King Williams Town lawyer with "publishing untrue matter" about the police by declaring they had taken "unnecessarily provocative action" in firing tear gas at a peaceful demonstration.[121] Toward the end of the decade, however, the organized profession became a little bolder, criticizing Justice Strydom's light sentence, the annual renewal of the Emergency, retroactive legislation, and laws denying courts the power to review their validity.[122]

Legal aid was badly funded and inadequately staffed, providing little more than routine representation in family matters.[123] The state contribution, only £5,304 in 1960, grew to £85,000 in 1970 and R12 million in 1988—still grossly insufficient. It handled only 6,000–7,000 criminal cases a year. To gain experience newly-qualified advocates accepted pro deo briefs in serious cases—including those carrying the death penalty.[124] A pilot public defender program was launched in the Johannesburg Magistrate's Court in 1992, but later that year the Appellate Division held that accused had no right to free representation.[125]

Although the vast majority of practitioners and the organized profession actively or passively supported the government, a handful of lawyers opposed it—Gandhi being a pioneer at the beginning of the century. Mandela and Tambo were law partners in Johannesburg in the 1950s, until they decided that only political activity could advance liberation. Few attorneys (if more advocates) accepted political cases in the first three decades of Nationalist rule.[126] In 1966 the government outlawed the South African Defence and Aid Fund, which had helped pay for representation in political trials. The Appellate Division upheld that decision the following year, refusing to review the Minister's discretion or require him to give the Fund an opportunity to be heard.[127]

The legal resources available to the anti-apartheid movement grew exponentially in the 1980s. The Centre for Applied Legal Studies was established at the University of the Witwatersrand Law School in 1978 to conduct research; soon afterwards it founded the human rights and labor law firm of Cheadle Thompson and Haysom and launched the *South African Journal on Human Rights*. The Legal Resources Centre was founded in 1979; in its second full year of operation the four attorneys, four advocates, and four law graduates were supported by a budget of R290,000 (most of it from American foundations but including a R1,000 contribution from Percy Yutar, the prosecutor in the 1956–60 treason trial). By 1990 it had thirty-three lawyers in six regional offices, supported by R8.5 million (mostly still from foreign donors).[128] Several organizations established or cooperated with legal advice centers, staffed primarily by laypeople and located outside the principal urban centers: Black Sash, the Transvaal Rural Action Committee, the University of Natal-Durban Street Law Project and Community Law Centres, and the University of Cape Town, Institute of Criminology, Legal Education Action Project.[129] The International Defence and Aid Fund, supported by North American and West European governments, churches, trade unions, and private philanthropy, paid £100 million to some 150 attorneys and eighty advocates over a quarter century; unbanned in 1990, it returned to South Africa the following year.[130] Three new professional bodies emerged: the Black Lawyers Association in 1977 (initially to defend the right of its members to practice in the Central Business Districts), the liberal Lawyers for Human Rights; and the ANC-oriented National Association of Democratic Lawyers (Nadel).

The next ten chapters illuminate the ways a handful of human rights lawyers were able to use law on behalf of opponents of apartheid.

CHAPTER 3

CARVING LOOPHOLES IN THE PASS LAWS

During an investigation into the living circumstances at 213 Makula Section, Katlehong, it was found that your client's wife and family are in fact living on the premises and have been so living for some time.

We regard this inexplicable conduct of your client as a total breach of any bona fides... and your client's conduct is unacceptable.... (Government lawyer to Legal Resources Centre lawyer, December 15, 1981)

[Y]our client's wife has completely ignored your self and our clients and simply proceeded to squat at the abode of your client.... The fact that your client's wife is at present residing where she is... you must concede, is highly irregular. (Government lawyer to LRC lawyer, February 5, 1982)

Mr Rikhoto does not CONSIDER it necessary to give any explanation to your client, nor does he consider his desire to live with his wife inexplicable. (LRC lawyer to government lawyer, February 5, 1982)

The Hated Dompas

Apartheid oppressed black South Africans in myriad ways: disenfranchising all, impoverishing most, relegating them to Bantu education and thus permanent economic inferiority, expelling millions from ancestral land, imprisoning hundreds of thousands, and killing many. The pass laws, how-ever, may have inflicted the greatest indignity. Every African who ever lived or visited outside the homelands—the vast majority—suffered personal harassment and humiliation.[1] Every adult had to carry a properly endorsed pass (dompas in Afrikaans) and display it on demand. Township residents were repeatedly awakened in the middle of the night by black Peri-Urban police. Those unable to hide, flee, or bribe their captors were arrested, con-victed in summary trials without legal representation, and fined or jailed: an estimated 17 million throughout the century, nearly 700,000 during the peak year of 1968, at least a quarter of a million annually from the 1950s through the 1970s, an average of a 200,000 in the 1980s.[2] Many convicts were forced to work for months as virtual slaves of white farmers.[3] The requirement in 1953 that women carry passes led to years of resistance.[4] The ANC engaged in passive disobedience against the pass laws in 1959, and the PAC followed in 1960, leading to the Sharpeville massacre.[5] The laws were tightened in 1964 and 1968, rendering Blacks even more vulnerable. Labor migrants could not acquire urban residence rights even after ten years with a single employer because each annual leave terminated the employment contract. The dependents of urban residents could not join them unless they entered the city "lawfully."[6] The crushing of the 1976 Soweto rebellion and the sub-sequent wave of repression precluded collective challenge. This chapter recounts two legal campaigns to win rights of urban residence for black workers and their dependents.

Komani

On June 11, 1975, Veli Willie Komani of Guguletu township, Cape Town, sued the Bantu Affairs Administration Board for the Peninsula Area for the right of his wife, Nonceba Mercy Meriba Komani, to live with him.[7] He had resi-dence rights under §10(1)(b) of the Bantu (Urban Areas) Consolidation Act by virtue of having worked for the same employer since July 1960 and never hav-ing been sentenced.[8] He claimed rights for her as a dependent under §10(1)(c) of the Act. When his wife entered Cape Town on May 13, 1974, the Board allowed her to remain until the end of the month, extending permission to July, October, and January 1975; but on April 1 it refused further renewals on the ground that Mr. Komani lacked suitable accommodation for her, having only a lodger's permit. It cited Regulation 10(1): "No person...shall reside in a Bantu residential area unless he has first obtained a [lodger's] permit." Without a permit, she could not "ordinarily reside" with him.

Three and a half years later Justice P. Schok dismissed the action with costs.[9] There was "no warrant whatsoever" for Komani's contention that the regulation applied only to men. Although it effectively nullified the law's extension of residence rights to dependents, "there is...nothing anomalous in requiring that...a Bantu wife...must comply with regulations ensuring proper housing conditions."

This outcome was less surprising than Komani's persistence. His attorney filed a notice of appeal but the Legal Aid Board was unwilling to continue paying for representation. Early in 1979 Noël Robb wrote from the Athlone Advice Office, operated jointly by the Black Sash and the South African Institute of Race Relations, to Geoffrey Budlender of the recently established Legal Resources Centre in Johannesburg.

> We are most anxious to know whether you could accept the Komani case since it is going to be very costly and Legal Aid are not prepared to finance the appeal to the A.D. [Appellate Division]. They did pay for the appeal [sic] to the Supreme Court. ... We will try to raise this money from our members but cannot afford to pay the likely legal fees. Mr Komani is not in a position to pay anything. ...
>
> Up to the present Fuller & More, Mr Fisher has handled this case but I'm sure he would be happy if you are prepared to take it over because he realises we can't afford to pay full fees....

In response to Budlender, Fisher sent the record on appeal, adding "we do not feel that there is much chance of success of the Appeal but in our opinion, as the matter in principle is of the utmost importance, the matter should run to its final determination." When Fisher complied with Budlender's request to "tactfully" ask his correspondent attorneys in Bloemfontein (the venue of the Appellate Division) "to attempt to keep down their [costs] as a result of the nature of this matter," McIntyre & van der Post agreed to act "pro amico."

An LRC memorandum (probably by Budlender) noted that the Appellate Division had denied a wife rights in 1963 and was unlikely to reconsider the issue.[10] Nevertheless, it concluded:

> If there is any reasonable prospect of success, a case of this nature should be undertaken, as it affects the rights of an enormous number of people. Failure will not adversely affect any person because of the way in which the law is presently being applied.

LRC Director Arthur Chaskalson commented that

> this is obviously the sort of case we should do. What concerns me is whether there is any substance in the appeal. ... Can it be argued that 10(1)(c) permits wife to reside at any place where husband lawfully resides? Mabasa's case and dicta in Mapheele's case are against this.

In the brief filed a year later Chaskalson and Felicia Kentridge acknowledged that §10(1)(c) did not grant rights to unlawful residents. However, a

section requiring dependents to obtain permission from the location superintendent, which had made Mrs. Mapheele's residence unlawful, was
subsequently repealed.[11] Furthermore, the regulation requiring a lodger's
permit for residence was ultra vires.

> The implementation of the regulation interferes radically with
> the right of persons...to enjoy a normal married life and to live
> together with their dependents as a family. This is destructive of
> the fabric of society and inimical to public policy.

The state responded with the legalistic claim that §10(1) did not "confer a
right to remain within a prescribed area" but merely granted "a qualified
immunity against prosecution" not amounting to residence. On the larger
issue it

> submitted that regulations restricting the right of residence at a
> particular place within a prescribed area cannot be construed as
> being unreasonable if it is accepted that the Minister is empow-
> ered to determine the precise extent of that residence.

Komani's reply brief invoked the classic liberal notion of limited government.

> [T]he question is not whether the Black (Urban Areas) Act con-
> fers a right on the Appellant to live with her husband in a black
> residential area. The question is rather whether the Black (Urban
> Areas) Act or any other statute has deprived the Appellant of that
> right, or has authorised the Local Authority or the Minister to
> deprive her of that right.

During oral argument in March 1980, Chief Justice Rumpff appeared sympathetic and took the unusual step of requesting additional briefs.[12]
Following his hints, the LRC argued that because the Act exempted from control "natives born and permanently residing" in the area, "a permit system
which detracts from the 'qualified rights' of such persons and makes them
dependent on the discretion of the location superintendent ... is inconsistent
with the Act and accordingly invalid." Reiterating its legal position, the state
also articulated the fundamental assumption of apartheid that "a Black can
only be 'satisfactorily' absorbed in an urban community when he is able to
be accommodated in that community"—a fact only white administrators
could ascertain. Budlender wrote to a friend:

> Initially some members of the Court seemed fairly hostile...but
> as the argument went on they began to see the difficulties and
> contradictions in the Regulation. ... At this stage we are still feel-
> ing fairly optimistic about what at one stage seemed a rather
> hopeless prospect in the light of the weight of authority.[13]

Writing for a unanimous court on August 19, the Chief Justice rejected the
argument that legislative changes had nullified *Mapheele*. "[E]ven before 1910

Blacks had no absolute freedom of entry to or freedom of residence within white urban areas." Oral argument, however, had raised an issue "of much more importance"—whether the regulation was ultra vires. The legislature had consistently recognized rights based on birth and continuous residence, extending them to fifteen-year residents in 1964. Consequently, the government had exceeded its legislative authority in promulgating regulations limiting residence to those with permits. The court acknowledged Mrs. Komani's right to remain in Guguletu.[14]

The English press applauded the victory. The *Rand Daily Mail* splashed a banner headline across the entire front page, "Reprieve for Thousands," and quoted Black Sash leader Sheena Duncan: "This is the most exciting news we've ever had.... The judgment actually makes nonsense of the whole house permit system. It means that no permits will be required except by persons who are not entitled to residence under the law."[15] A day later reality set in. The judgment was only "an improvement within an existing system of control," said the Sash, and would intensify the urban housing crisis. Duncan warned that if the government nullified the ruling "Minister Koornhof's claim that he has declared war on the dompas will finally lose all credibility."[16] The *Rand Daily Mail* noted caustically that the need for "a decision of our highest court to grant this most elementary of human rights is in itself a commentary on our society." To overrule it legislatively "would be unforgiveably cruel. ... For once can't we hope for practical expression of the fine words which Government leaders have been uttering since Mr P W Botha became Prime Minister nearly two years ago?"[17]

Noël Robb wrote to Budlender to exult but also to ponder the next step.

> Congratulations and *very* many thanks to all of you at Legal Resources.... The success is almost unbelievable and we are thrilled through. We don't read as much into it as Sheena does. For instance, it is impossible for a Black man who qualifies to move from bachelor quarters into lodgings. They will not cancel his rent. So even if he and his wife live together as lodgers they will be said not to be 'normally residing' because he is legally in the bachelor quarters. We must try a test case.... We have been inundated with phone calls of congratulations and requests for statements.

In reply, Budlender shared both her joy and reservations, concluding: "I am personally delighted to have been involved in the Komani case, as it was the Athlone Advice Office which first aroused my interest in the whole problem of pass laws and influx control."

The government's initial response was discouraging. Dr. Piet Koornhof, Minister of Co-operation and Development, insisted the ruling was based on a single case in one province. "It would be competely wrong to infer that a large-scale influx of wives and children...will now be possible, as each case will have to be judged on the facts concerned." Mrs. J. Nicholson, supervisor of Durban Black Sash, replied: "Although Dr Koornhof might think otherwise, any statement he may make regarding this regulation is not the law." "[H]e's a professed practising Christian and has promised a new deal for blacks...[but] once again this has been shown up as total hypocrisy."[18] Several newspapers condemned his response.[19] Urging Koornhof to embrace this "court-sent chance" to "serve the cause of better family life and improved race relations," the *Rand Daily Mail* quoted his statement to the National Press Club in Washington fourteen months earlier.[20]

> I detest the dompas. I declared war on the dompas. That thing must be ousted completely and totally out of my country and I have requested my officials to work on it. They have been doing it and the dompas will be ousted in my country sooner than later and I am working as far as this is concerned on a month time-span and not a year time-span.

The foreign press echoed the mix of elation and caution. The *Christian Science Monitor* exaggerated: "One of the legal linchpins of apartheid—South Africa's system of racial discrimination—has been sheared by a court decision."[21] The *Boston Globe* observed more realistically that "the basics of apartheid are not going to be altered."[22] *The Economist* welcomed the "notable victory for the Legal Resources Centre" but warned that its extension to others would be "a vital test of the sincerity of government statements about its desire to relieve the pressures which such control imposes on black family life."[23]

Less than two weeks after the decision the Director General of the Department of Co-operation and Development issued a circular further confusing the situation. Acknowledging that a lodger's permit was no longer required for legal residence, it nevertheless maintained that "the Urban Areas Act was not affected by the court ruling and consequently people who do not qualify to be in an urban area must still get permission to remain in such an area." Dependents could only join legal residents who obtained "approved accommodation" meeting "health regulations relating to overcrowding and slum conditions."[24] Responding to Noël Robb's request for guidance, Budlender maintained that a couple required the permission of a landlord but not a lodger's permit issued by the township superintendent. He feared, however, that

> much of this debate may become largely irrelevant next year, as it seems certain that new 'Riekert' legislation will completely replace the Urban Areas Act...[predicating residence rights] on employment and 'approved' accommodation.

Black families, the Black Sash, and the LRC now began the long, tedious, and frustrating process of enforcing *Komani*. The first success was deceptively easy. Beauty Senego joined her parents in Johannesburg, where they had §10 rights, but the West Rand Administration Board (WRAB) refused to add her name to their house permit. After the AD decision she took her parents' reference books, marriage certificate, and house permit to the Board's New Canada office but was told to prove that she had worked for one employer for ten years. Armed with an LRC letter threatening legal action, she obtained the endorsement from the Albert Street office three days later. Mr. Kruger, a spokesman, thought he remembered a circular about the AD decision but speculated the clerk had not seen it. More ominously, Labour Director Armand Steenhuizen commented: "I have nothing to do with the judgement's practical application, but all I can say is that there will be absolutely no change."[25]

Others encountered more obstacles. Pozisa Patricia Mpofu, whose husband had §10 rights, had been seeking an endorsement since the end of 1979. When phone calls and letters produced no response, Budlender filed an action at the end of November 1980.[26] The Department declared its intention to defend but sought extensions of time to reply, which Budlender granted. The WRAB Chief Commissioner denied a similar application by Evelyn Manana Mmapaletsebe more than a month after *Komani*, causing her employer to fire her. Budlender was referred by Mr. Bezuidenhout to Mr. Botha, who referred him to Mr. Oosthuizen, who said he had instructed Mr. Pretorius to issue the endorsement. But two weeks later Pretorius told Mr. Mmapaletsebe he had to buy a house. Why had he gone to the LRC? It could not help him because Pretorius was not afraid of a letter from "your friend." The couple was trying to take advantage of what had happened in Cape Town, but those things would not happen in Johannesburg. Pretorius said his superior, Mr. Ras, would telephone Budlender. Mr. Erasmus phoned instead, promising to investigate and get back. But when Budlender inquired two days later he was told Erasmus was meeting with Ras. Then Pretorius said Erasmus wanted to see the couple. When Budlender phoned Ras after that meeting he was told Ras had an appointment to see the Director the following day. Budlender spoke to Mr. Toerien, the WRAB legal adviser, that day and was told the Director had referred the matter to Pretoria, promising an answer by the end of the day. When there was no reply, Toerien suggested that Budlender sue but promised an answer in two days.

Budlender waited six days, only to be told that Evelyn did not qualify because she had entered Johannesburg without permission. The state declared its intention to defend this lawsuit as well and again sought an extension to reply. When Evelyn visited the Diepkloof Superintendent on January 14, 1981, to collect her husband's lodger's permit he said WRAB had ordered him to evict her, threatening her with six months' imprisonment if she did not return to her homeland voluntarily. Five days later van Wyk, de Vries, Malan & Steyn, the attorneys representing WRAB, agreed to settle the two cases and pay disbursements of R45.45. Even this did not end the matter. Six months later the New Canada office refused to add the couple's children to their lodger's permit. Only when Budlender threatened another lawsuit did it capitulate.

A pattern began to develop. While the government flouted *Komani* some applicants would find their way to the Black Sash, which referred them to the LRC for a "lawyer's letter" threatening legal action, usually producing prompt compliance. As government intransigence persisted, Budlender's letters became more peremptory: "your official was not entitled to make this endorsement or order," "we cannot understand why your officer has acted in this fashion," "there was no lawful basis on which this endorsement or order could have been made." He wrote Sheena Duncan at the end of November 1980 that "the rights of unmarried daughters are being recognised fairly readily, but the MLO is being very difficult about wives. I hope that when the SC applications land on his desk, he may revise his attitude." She replied that she was "entirely frustrated" and wished "we could think of some way of forcing...[the cases] through in bulk. There must be thousands of people sitting out there and how are we going to handle them one by one in this way?" He promised fortnightly reports to help both of them keep track of the myriad applications but shared her vexation.

> [I]t is utterly ridiculous that this procedure should be gone through in each case—and of course, there must be literally thousands of people who do not reach us and as a result receive no assistance and therefore do not have their rights recognised. ... we really need a 'class action' in the American style. All I can think of at the moment, is that when these matters reach court we should prepare a detailed analysis for the press and let them attempt to push the Administration Board.

Three days after the van Wyk firm agreed to settle the first two cases, Budlender wrote angrily that they were indistinguishable from other pending matters. "[W]e frankly find your client's attitude incomprehensible. When asked for an explanation, your clients consistently attempt to justify their attitude on the basis that our clients 'entered the area without permission' and therefore did not enter lawfully." But the Appellate Division had held in *Mabasa* as early as 1976 that WRAB exceeded its authority in requiring a §10 rights-holder to obtain its permission to bring his wife to live with him.[27] "In light of what has transpired in the Mpofu and Mmapaletsebe matters, would you now kindly advise whether your clients require us to launch further Supreme Court matters in the Mokgomane and Mhlongo matters, or whether they will now recognise our clients' rights." Although he received no written reply for half a year, LRC attorney Leizel Stals got a disconcerting phone call from Mr. Swart of the van Wyk firm on April 13, 1981. He was awaiting instructions from WRAB but volunteered "with respect" that he disagreed with *Komani*, which violated the spirit of the act and made it difficult to understand and interpret the legislation. He had prepared recommendations for WRAB to submit to the government. Stals's file note concluded: "I gained the impression that these recommendations were to undo the 'harm' done by the Komani decision. Sounded ominous!!" A week later she reported a

> long and interesting conversation with Mr Toerien, legal adviser, WRAB, who told me the following. Because of Mrs Mpofu and Mrs Mmapaletsebe they obtained legal opinion—the gist of which was that cases which substantially agree factually with the above should automatically be endorsed. This opinion was brought to the attention of both Commissioner's offices, Johannesburg and Pretoria. Mr Toerien is of the opinion that the Chief Commissioner for Witwatersrand (Mr van Heerden) falls directly under the Minister, thus not under jurisdiction of WRAB. The enforcement of WRAB opinion can therefore only come via Minister's office. He feels that the "buck" has been passed to and from without anybody giving a directive in terms of the opinion. He suggested (off the record) that should he not get a clear response to the queries in connection with...[pending cases] we should approach the "highest power that be" and request them to give a directive. He is prepared to come to us for a meeting and discussion and to put us into contact with the correct 'powers.' He feels in this way we shall be able to achieve our aim far better!!

Black Sash and the LRC compiled a memorandum on twenty-one women refused endorsements since the judgment.[28] Sheena Duncan was scathing:

> The Nationalists have always clung to Old Testament righteousness—it is right because it is the law.
> Now we have a radical departure from this....
> They have come to see themselves as omnipotent, uncontrolled either by law, judgments of the courts or decisions of Parliament.

WRAB chairman John Knoetze offered lame excuses: "This is a sensitive matter. We obviously cannot and will not ignore a court ruling...[but] every case is different. The Appeal Court didn't spell out what is to happen in every case."[29]

Each case *was* different but only in the arbitrariness of official action. Applicants were asked to provide irrelevant documentation (lengthy residence, school attendance, permission to enter), told to obtain employment, or rejected because they were too old or had inadequate housing. Some officials openly defied the Appellate Division. Five months after its decision Inspector J.M. Knudsen of the Western Cape Administration Board (WCAB) arrested Virginia Yapi in Constantia for violating the regulation invalidated in *Komani*. Although the defense offered uncontested evidence that she was married to §10 rights-holder, Magistrate L. van Wyk of the Langa Commissioner's Court held: "The law has not been repealed despite the Appeal Court decision and the requirements still apply as far as this court is concerned." At the end of 1981 the Supreme Court rejected the state's argument that Mr. Komani had had a lodger's permit, which Mr. Yapi could not get for twenty years. The court noted that the AD decision "will prevent the enforced separation of families so that they are not compelled to reside apart at great distances." It remarked, however, that they still could be evicted from any site they occupied unlawfully.[30]

Blacks were inured, if not resigned, to a hostile and incompetent bureaucracy. For the rare white who took up a black employee's cause, it was a revelation. Mrs. D.N. Bodley of Cleveland, Johannesburg, wrote to the *Rand Daily Mail*.[31]

> Why has it taken me nine months to get a South African maid registered to be employed in my home as a domestic? ...

> Why is it that a Wrab official can send you from Johannesburg to Pretoria, back to Johannesburg, and maybe even to Standerton and dozens of trips to Polly Street, Albert Street, Market Street, Diepkloof and back and forth several times? ...

> Eventually, after going to endless departments and finally being directed to "misplaced persons," the maid and I faced a man who was adamant that the maid was "a liar" and from then on he made it very difficult.

> He insisted she bring signed forms (supplied by him) stating where she previously worked, signed by the previous employers. This we did. ...

> Wrab somehow 'mislaid' the forms the maid and I so diligently searched for, found and got the previous employers to sign. So we started all over again.

> Before long the maid got 72 hours to leave the premises. It certainly was a shock. The Wrab official was determined to 'deport' her to Standerton and told us we both were liars. ...

> Together, the maid and I went to the Black Sash for help. Within five minutes I was told that Regulation [sic] 10(1)(c) applied to the maid and that I should not distress myself any further because the maid was entitled to a pass and to work in my area.

> They prepared the affidavits, giving the maid's history, the mother's history, etc and asked for a reversal of the decision and the application of Reg 10(1)(c). Another four months passed— and she was again advised that her appeal had failed and that she again had 72 hours in which to vacate my premises.

> Again the Black Sash had the solution. They sent the maid to an attorney and after several visits to Market Street, Diepkloof,

the attorneys etc. the maid made a final trip to Polly Street to see the very man we started with nine months ago. On being instructed by letter to grant her a pass, he showed his displeasure by saying to her: 'You are clever, eh?'

Even litigation did not always secure compliance. Although Ntema Johanna Moitse's husband had §10 rights and a lodger's permit, WRAB denied her application and appeal. Two weeks after taking an LRC letter to Market Street and being sent to Albert Street, her husband was summoned by the Orlando West (Soweto) Superintendent on June 16 (the anniversary of the 1976 uprising) and told his wife had to leave immediately or face arrest. Budlender phoned the Township Manager the next day that he had filed a Supreme Court application, which was granted by default.[32] The following day Mrs. Moitse took a letter from Budlender demanding compliance with the court order but was told Pretorius was sick. Budlender phoned and was told that Ras, the Chief Municipal Labour Officer, was on leave, the deputy was out of the office, and Pretorius was still sick; du Toit would say only that Pretorius "deals with these cases" and would not respond, even when threatened with contempt. At last Budlender spoke to Toerien, the WRAB legal adviser, who promised to get the endorsement. Du Toit issued it after his intervention. The next day, however, Budlender received a letter from N. Malan, Chief Executive Officer of Soweto.

> I refer to your communication of 17th ultimo and in particular to the application filed with the Supreme Court in this connection.
>
> If it is accepted that the Supreme Court is entitled to overrule a point of law of whatever nature and specifically where an inforcement [sic] of law is concerned, we should be glad to learn on what ground you base your submissions.
>
> Please see this enquiry as purely of an informative nature and for our guidance in future. ...
>
> My contention is inter alia that her appeal could have been settled with our labour department in collaboration with the Department of Co-operation and Development, once certain requirements have been met.
>
> However, what we are really interested in, are your grounds on which you base your appeal and we shall consider a formative [sic] precis a well meant gesture.

Budlender replied with a memorandum on *Komani* (decided a year earlier) and the court papers in *Moitse*.

In one instance its flagrant lawlessness hurt the government. Mafiri Maria Mashiane married William Silika Mhlongo in 1959 and came to live with him in Old Pimville, where he had §10 rights and a lodger's permit. When she sought an endorsement the New Canada office ordered her out of the city ten days after the *Komani* decision. Phoned by Budlender in January 1981, Pretorius justified the denial on the ground that she had entered Johannesburg without permission (twenty-two years earlier). The LRC sued, and the state defaulted on July 21 before Judge Richard Goldstone, who noted on the brief "Court's displeasure to be made known to Minister." Felicia Kentridge, who appeared for the LRC, wrote Budlender: "If there are any further applications of this nature we should remember to ask at the hearing that the judge order the official concerned to appear before him to explain his refusal of the endorsement." Mrs. Mhlongo obtained her stamp the next day. More important, the press widely reported Goldstone's displeasure: "Court raps Koornhof for trying to keep couple apart,"[33] "Urban boards accused of flouting law."[34] Goldstone issued a statement denying he had rebuked Koornhof personally but expressing

> the extreme displeasure of the court at the apparent disregard by Wrab of the recent judgment of the Appellate Division. ... [T]he failure of Wrab to oppose the relief sought by Mr Mhlongo in a similar matter which I was informed came before the court a week previously [*Moitse*], indicated that Wrab was aware of the decision of the Appellate Division. The consequence of this action is that affected persons are being compelled to approach the court for relief which according to the Appellate Division they are entitled to claim.

During the previous parliamentary session Helen Suzman, the opposition PFP's chief spokesperson on urban black affairs, had tabled a question asking if the government had informed officials of the *Komani* judgment. Dr. George de Villiers Morrison, Deputy Minister of Co-operation and Development, replied that it had in a circular dated a week after the judgment. Mrs Suzman now commented: "That circular is apparently being disregarded by certain officials."[35]

From the Black Sash, Sheena Duncan wrote Budlender thanking him for summaries of the cases she had referred and rejoicing over *Mhlongo*.

> We really did feel elated last week and just hope that the judgment will prove to be the end of this particular hassle. ...[T]hank you and Legal Resources a thousand times. It just shows how important the firm is proving to be. I look back on the 17 long years since the 1964 amendment to 10(1)(c) and could weep for the time we have wasted and the families for whom this has all come too late.

The press refused to drop the story. A *Rand Daily Mail* editorial asked "Why is the law being ignored?"[36] *The Star* concurred—"Put justice back into the Law"—and carried a front-page story about the Mhlongo family's hardships.[37] It editorialized the next day:

> Families within touching distance, able to communicate their love continuously and sharing the sublime experience of living in this blessed country. That, we should have thought, was the picture of contentment.... Yet, that is one of the problems in this country: we completely fail to see the obvious. Does anyone really believe that men prefer being crowded into huge monastic hostels to enjoying normal family life? Of course not.[38]

The *Rand Daily Mail* followed with a feature story entitled "This unique inhumanity."[39]

Clearly stung, WRAB chairman John Knoetze declared that his agency knew and was following the law; no one had to apply to the courts.[40] "We are aware of the Supreme Court decision; we realise the implications, and we are carrying them out.... I don't expect any repetition of what has occurred in this particular case." Although the AD had ruled a year earlier, he conceded: "As far as I know, we hadn't studied the full effects of the Komani judgment." A Department of Co-operation and Development spokesman, asked if officials had been instructed to follow *Komani*, said "I think so."[41] Knoetze elaborated in another interview.

> I realise the implications of the judgment and we will carry it out strictly according to the letter of the law and with understanding and empathy.
>
> We have made it perfectly plain that it's not necessary for any further blacks to go to the Black Sash or to lawyers or to court.
>
> They can come along now and get their endorsements...we will treat each case on its merits.
>
> What has gone before is water under the bridge. Sooner or later you must start collecting yourself and putting things right if they are wrong.[42]

Three days after Goldstone's public rebuke attorneys for WRAB and the Chief Commissioner telephoned Budlender, undertaking to recognize the rights of Mrs. Moitse and Mrs. Mhlongo and pay costs. They also assured Budlender that a memo had been sent instructing all MLOs to recognize such rights in the future. The same day those cases were settled, the state attorney's office agreed not to contest two others.[43] Budlender wrote H.B. Rhoode of the van Wyk firm that "We will try to resolve such matters administratively in the future through Mr Ras and Mr Toerien."

By this time Black Sash had interviewed 150 women who had been refused endorsements and sent the LRC forty-five, of whom thirty-four had been successful. On July 29 the Sash issued a pamphlet describing local

WRAB officials as "pressed between the tube and the tyre" by conflict between a Pretoria directive that women were not entitled and WRAB lawyers' insistence that they were. They sent their lawyers' written opinion to Pretoria for clarification but got no response despite repeated reminders.[44]

Yet the *Mhlongo* embarrassment did make a difference. Refused an endorsement two months after *Komani* because she lacked her children's birth certificates, Esther Kabinde returned to the New Canada office with a letter from Budlender on July 13, 1981:

> There is absolutely no basis on which you are entitled to require our client to produce the birth certificates of her children, as they are entirely irrelevant to her status.... The only conclusion which we can draw is that your officials are deliberately trying to frustrate the effect of the decision of the Appellate Division in Komani....

Noting the three other judgments, he gave the department forty-eight hours to comply before filing suit. Two weeks later he received a gratifying letter from Kabinde's husband.

> Dear Sir,
>
> how are you? I hope you are well.
>
> I am Victor Molepo. I am also well and with my family thank you. I am one of that case you have of sees of qualified about the pass book yes I went to arlbert Str in the pass office in the room 124 inside they geve my wife the next day she went the next day they geve her qualified 10 1 c at the same place. the following day we go to the sperdent they put my wife to the lodges pemit and they put us to the waiting list of the house. that you don a big think for us. now they waiting the children birth certiefket. We report that also we waiting for birth certiefket now. That you don a wonderfully think for us. that we wish yu the god he must help you must also help the poor people the god she will help you must grow up like oliphant.

Dozens of women whose applications and appeals had been denied received prompt endorsements after presenting a threatening letter from the LRC, although officials outside Johannesburg took longer to comply.[45] A private attorney in Cape Town telegraphed the LRC: "your recent successes on section 10(1)(c) of great interest to us shall appreciate a copy of the Goldstone judgment as soon as possible." Four months later he was able to report a similar triumph in his own appeal of Virginia Yapi's conviction.[46]

Increasingly frustrated at the failure of bureaucrats to grant endorsements without a lawyer's intercession, Budlender wrote H.B. Rhoode of the van Wyk firm on August 4.

Unfortunately, it seems that despite the six Supreme Court applications that have now been brought against your clients, and despite the contents of your letter, they are still not complying with the law. ... When we discussed these matters on 24.7.81 you advised that your clients had sent out a circular in regard to these matters, and you undertook to furnish us with a copy of same. In light of what has happened, there seem to be only three possibilities:

(1) No circular has in fact been sent out; or

(b) A circular has been sent out, but it is not correct; or

(c) A correct circular has been sent out, but it is being ignored by your clients' officials.

He asked Rhoode to keep his promise to provide the circular. After two reminders and a two-month delay, Rhoode reassured Budlender that a circular had been issued. Budlender reiterated that "particularly at the New Canada office, either the circular has not been received or is not being applied."

Just prior to the *Mhlongo* victory Budlender began providing Sheena Duncan with a running tally of their successes, summarized in the table.

Claims for Section 10(1)(c) Endorsements

Date of report	Granted by administrator	Granted by Supreme Court (cumulative)	Pending	Client did not return
July 17, 1981	25	3	3	
July 22, 1981	28	4	2	10
Oct. 7, 1981	57	6	3	3
Dec. 12, 1981	66	6	3	3
March 31, 1982	86		4	1
April 30, 1982	88		2	1
Sept. 6, 1982	108		4	1
Oct. 25, 1982	113		1	3

He accompanied his October 7, 1981, report with a letter.

It seems quite clear that the July flurry of Supreme Court applications and Mr Justice Goldstone's remarks in the Mhlongo matter at that time, have had an effect. ... The flow from Johannesburg seems to have slowed down again, but in the past month we have had three ERAB cases [East Rand Administration Board]. In all of these, it took some prodding before the wife's rights were recognised. In at least two (and probably the third), the officials telephoned Pretoria for instructions and then agreed that we were correct. While it is satisfying that Pretoria seems finally to have accepted our view, it is disturbing that no directive seems to have been sent out to this effect. The key, of course, is the circular which has apparently been sent out by the Department. I understand that Helen Suzman is trying to obtain that in Parliament.

The Chief Commissioner, Co-operation and Development, had issued a long circular on August 7; Budlender sought Helen Suzman's assistance in obtaining it but did not succeed for many months. In October, however, she sent him her recent parliamentary question and Koornhof's answer.

Question No. 100: What were the contents of the circular minute issued by his Department and sent to all Chief Commissioners and Administration Boards on 26.8.80 concerning the ruling of the Appellate Division in the Komani case?

Minister of Co-operation and Development: The Chief Commissioners of my Department were informed of the contents of my statement to the media on the matter on 22.8.80 and were advised the regulation…was declared ultra vires by the court ruling and that it would serve no purpose to promulgate any further fees payable in respect of lodger's permits. Furthermore the Chief Commissioners were requested to inform administration boards accordingly.

The pattern of official obstruction (demands for unnecessary affidavits and irrelevant children's birth certificates, as well as peremptory rejections) followed by capitulation under legal pressure continued in 1982. On March 31 Budlender gave Duncan his assessment of the situation.

I had finally been able to obtain a copy of the instruction sent to the Chief Commissioners (and through them to the administrative boards) by the Department of Co-operation and Development. …

You will see that the Department has rather reluctantly accepted that once it has been shown that a woman is married to a qualified man (and this includes a partner in a customary union), and usually lives with him in the area, then she is entitled to the qualification. There is no legal provision which requires that housing should be available. … [I]t is now clear that a dependent or unmarried son of a 'registered occupier'…does not require a lodger's permit.

> Would you please treat the enclosed circular with great discretion as my source would be embarrassed if it became known that we have obtained a copy.

Two days later Budlender sought confirmation of his understanding from the WRAB chairman. He began by reminding Knoetze of his public response to *Mhlongo* eight months earlier that further appeals to Black Sash, lawyers, and courts would be unnecessary.

> Unfortunately, this prediction has not been borne out in practice. Since the Mhlongo judgment we have taken up the cases of approximately 40 wives and children who qualified…but whose rights had not been recognised by your officials.

> In each case, we have sent the people concerned directly to Mr Ras who has dealt with them promptly and efficiently. However, we are extremely disturbed that it has continued to be necessary for qualified wives and children to come to us before their rights are recognised. We are also concerned that there may be very many more qualified wives and children whose rights are not recognised by your officials…because they do not know that they can readily obtain assistance through the Black Sash or lawyers.

> Most of the problems appear to arise in your New Canada office, where the officials concerned either do not know the law or choose to ignore it. …

> We have drawn the situation to the attention of Mr Ras, but nothing appears to have changed. …

> It is intolerable that people with clear legal rights, which have been defined by the Supreme Court, should be compelled to take a roundabout tour of various WRAB offices and finally consult an attorney before they can have their rights recognised.

Knoetze promptly assured him the Board was complying "and no problems are experienced in regard to any legal implications." Budlender had to "realise, however, that officials also have a responsibility to ensure that their decisions are based on substantiated facts…." These included the couple's marriage, the husband's §10 rights, the availability of "suitable accommodation for the wife and children," and evidence that the children were those of the married couple (proved by birth and school certificates and affidavits).

Budlender commented to Duncan that Boards could no longer require applicants to demonstrate accommodation.

> I think the most appropriate follow-up would be to write
> [Knoetze] again next time we have a specific case, giving details
> of the various demands which have been made of the person
> concerned. Perhaps if we tie them to a specific matter it may be
> more difficult for them to escape through generalisations.

He wrote Knoetze on April 20, 1982, protesting that officials continued to demand irrelevant documentation, such as children's birth certificates when wives were applying. He wrote again on May 11 as he had proposed to Duncan, complaining to Knoetze that New Canada had required a child's birth certificate from Setshego Maria Thupudi and "an affidavit of her life history" from Thayini Lettie Moswane. Two reminders elicited a somewhat disingenuous reply from WRAB Chief Director C.J. Bezuidenhout more than three months later. New Canada wanted the birth certificate to grant a simultaneous endorsement to Mrs. Thupudi's child. It wanted proof that Ms. Moswane was the daughter of a §10 rights-holder because her mother's surname, Mapule, was different. Budlender asked why Mrs. Thupudi's endorsement could not have been granted while her child's was being processed and corrected the bureaucratic error: Mapule was the *first* name of Ms. Moswane's mother. (It is striking that white officials whose job was ruling blacks would not know the difference between given names and surnames.) Budlender's tone, however, was placatory.

> We naturally appreciate that, in an organisation as large as
> WRAB, it is only to be expected that from time to time individual officials will make mistakes. What has concerned us has
> been the apparent systematic disregard in the past of the implications of the Komani judgment. It does seem that the position
> has improved to some extent, and if we have any further problems in this regard we shall be in touch with you again.

Little changed. Applicants were sent from office to office, asked for irrelevant documentation or rebuffed; those who found their way to the LRC generally got endorsements as soon as they returned with a lawyer's letter. New Canada told the unmarried daughter of a §10 rights-holder to marry. Budlender protested: "If our client were to follow your officials' advice, she would of course lose her right to remain in Johannesburg." Budlender denounced as "pure obstructiveness" New Canada's demand that Beauty Makutu produce school certificates and find a job. It required two other clients to furnish birth certificates and affidavits, prompting Budlender to reiterate that "officials at your New Canada offices either do not know the law, or are refusing to apply it."

On June 1, 1983, more than a year after his last exchange with Knoetze, Budlender made another effort to enlist a superior. For a long time he had treated the New Canada actions as individual errors, which Mr. Ras readily corrected.

> However, in the past two weeks there has been a startling increase in these problems, and evidence of clear obstructiveness on the part of officials at New Canada. Persons who have clear §10(1)(c) rights have been required:
>
> (a) to make several fruitless visits to your New Canada offices
>
> (b) to produce affidavits when there was clear documentary evidence of all relevant facts
>
> (c) to produce school certificates which are plainly irrelevant
>
> (d) to produce birth certificates which are plainly irrelevant.
>
> In many instances, officials at New Canada have simply refused to place §10(1)(c) endorsements in the reference books of clearly qualified people.

That the Albert Street office made no such demands showed that New Canada was either ignorant of the law or flouting it. "This has now been dragging on for nearly three years since the Appellate Division gave judgment in the Komani case." He did not want to appeal to higher authorities, but the situation was intolerable.

Knoetze replied promptly, expressing "regret for any inconvenience caused by my officials at the New Canada office." They asked for birth certificates only to give those born in Johannesburg a §10(1)(a) endorsement, which was more desirable. There was no record that the five clients Budlender named had ever applied at New Canada. "My office at New Canada qualify an average of 110 similar cases a month and it is not clear why your clients were turned away." Budlender challenged this account but acknowledged that "the position has again improved to some extent." Toward the end of the month, however, Sheena Duncan told a reporter that "some administration boards are still being obstructive about implementing the [Komani] decision."[47] And Budlender continued to intercede successfully for clients who were asked for irrelevant documents.

The situation was worse outside Johannesburg. In August 1983 the Roodepoort WRAB office told Mercy Seoposengwe Tswekae that she first had to be added to her husband's lodger's permit. When she did this she was told he had to obtain a house of his own and could not accept lodgers. Two months later Mr. de Lange demanded her marriage certificate, husband's name and identity number, lodger's permit, and a TB55 form from Dobsonville Council indicating that the house was large enough. According to the LRC file note

> Mr de Lange indicated that the problem that they have with such applications is the delay after the date of marriage. ... Their point is that while living in a house and without such approval a person is living illegally in the township for a substantial length

of time and is therefore not lawfully in the area and therefore not entitled to a 10(1)(c) recognition.

The Appellate Division had rejected precisely this argument three years earlier.

In 1984 the Eastern Transvaal Development Board (the latest euphemism) refused to endorse Celiwe Rita Nkosi because her husband Johan lacked his own house. After three letters from Budlender over three months they devised new reasons: by working in Johannesburg Mr. Nkosi had forfeited his §10(1)(a) rights in Amersfoort and would lose his lodger's permit there; and Mrs. Nkosi's presence was illegal since she had been ordered to leave Amersfoort when she first applied in February 1983.

> Although my Board at all times endeavour to treat cases such as the present with compassion, it should be borne in mind that its first and foremost responsibility rests with local residents and that overpopulation of the Amersfoort Black residential area (where an acute housing shortage is experienced) by other ethnic groups (non-Swazi) should be avoided as far as possible.

The following week the ETDB cancelled Mr. Nkosi's lodger's permit. The LRC responded in July that Mr. Nkosi worked in Johannesburg only when he could not find employment in Amersfoort; several cases held that this did not alter his residence. Whatever the legality of the Board's preference for Swazis, Mr. Nkosi *was* Swazi and should not be penalized because his wife was Zulu. After a reminder, the LRC wrote to protest the cancelled lodger's permit as a breach of natural justice. "We are very surprised that the response to our letter to you is not a reply, but a summary action by an official at a lower level." In August the ETDB wrote that it would allow Mrs. Nkosi to remain and thanked the LRC "for the comprehensive exposition furnished by you in connection with this matter."

On March 20, 1985, Budlender made a final effort to involve Knoetze in disciplining New Canada. Complaints continued; after the LRC intervened, Ras promptly remedied them. The only explanations were ignorance or recalcitrance. The problem continued nearly five years after the Appellate Division decision, "at a time when senior Government spokesmen are at pains to emphasise the need for good relations in our country. It is not difficult to imagine the impact of this sort of bureaucratic obstructionism on the feelings of people who are subjected to this treatment." A reminder was necessary before Knoetze replied after two months.

> I wish to advise that due to the high incidence of various malpractises, e.g. women professing to be married to permanent residents and producing forged marriage certificates; people claiming parenthood of the children of relations and the submission of fraudulent evidence in support of certain claims, each

application for recognition of rights in terms of Section 10(1)…must of necessity be thoroughly investigated.

Knoetze claimed that many applicants provided inadequate proof; they received prompt endorsements after LRC intervention because the Centre ensured full documentation. Some of Budlender's clients had never applied to New Canada, and others had never returned. "I can assure you that all cases are dealt with in a responsible manner and it is endeavoured to cause the minimum inconvenience." Budlender again rejected these explanations. Albert Street turned down many fewer applicants with similar cases. Anyhow, New Canada persisted in requiring irrelevant papers, such as school certificates. He credited Knoetze's solicitude; "the problem is that this does not appear to be the attitude of at least certain of the officials of your New Canada office."

The last word, typically bureaucratic, went to WRAB Chief Director Bezuidenhout on June 28, 1985.

> An investigation into the procedures currently in force and applied at the New Canada Offices was carried out by my Management Audit Team. No evidence pointing to wilful or intended obstruction to the processing of applications made in terms of above judgment was found. Officials interviewed expressed dismay at the allegations and they certainly have nothing to gain by adopting a negative stance.
>
> A Senior Official at the Centre will however personally interview applicants endeavouring to obtain 10(1)(c) rights in terms of the judgment and record each case referred to him. …
>
> We are confident that this arrangement would serve to expedite affairs and trust that this matter has now been settled to your satisfaction.

Rikhoto

Contemporaneous with the campaign to expand the rights of workers' dependents was a potentially even more important struggle on behalf of workers themselves. Section 10(1)(b) of the Act conferred residence rights on Blacks who had "worked continuously" for one employer for ten years. The government consistently ruled that the contracts of migrants terminated with each annual leave, preventing them from ever qualifying. Khazamola Samuel Chauke, who had gardened for a Johannesburg family for twelve years, was turned down on these grounds by the MLO. When the LRC appealed to the Chief Commissioner in October 1980 (two months after *Komani*), Mr P.A. van Heerden granted the endorsement. He told the press he could not remember why and denied any change in policy. "We must have been influenced by the facts in this specific case. We will continue to treat each case on its merits." Sheena Duncan objected: "The commissioner's personal decision in individual cases is not good enough. One wants either a firm ruling from the commissioner or, failing that, that the matter should be tested in court." She advised some 200 others to apply, while the LRC prepared similar appeals.[48]

In January 1981 D.G. Scott, a Cape Town advocate, gave an opinion on the legal status of two men who had worked for a single employer more than ten years. Courts had interpreted the alternative criterion of fifteen years continuous residence to mean without a break. Scott felt this would be absurd with respect to work, since everyone took off weekends and holidays. The Appellate Division had held that the purpose of the law was to exclude only those who could not "usefully or satisfactorily be absorbed into the economic life of the urban community in question."[49] In this respect there was no difference between a contract of employment for an indefinite time and a worker re-employed annually through a call-in card.

On April 27 Sheena Duncan described a potential plaintiff to Charles Nupen at the Johannesburg LRC.

> Mr Rikhoto came to see us first on 23rd April 1981 [about a week after he had obtained a lodger's permit for a room in Katlehong]. He signed an affidavit asking for 10(1)(b) in Germiston on that day on the grounds that he had been employed by Hargram Engineering from August 1970 to April 1981. When he took the application to the Labour Bureau they returned the employer's letter to him having written on it that he was first registered only on 2.1.73. The employer then produced their own record for him showing his date of engagement and "1 year contract from 25.8.70." They also gave him a photostat of his Administration Board Registration Certificate made on 29.1.1974 when his contract was renewed for that year which also shows his date of engagement as 1970. I believe this is sufficient proof because I don't think the date of engagement would have been filled in like that on an official document and stamped by them if they had not had it on the official records at that time.
>
> On 24th April Mr Rikhoto signed an appeal affidavit and on 27th April the Labour Bureau in Germiston wrote on the affidavit "Refused, must be registered before April 1968 [the effective date of Proclamation R74] for a sect 10(1)(b) qualification."

Mehlolo Tom Rikhoto had left school in Standard 4 because his father, Sixpence Rikhoto, a retired Kimberley diamond miner, had been too old to work. Sixpence had to raise Tom and his four siblings after Mrs. Rikhoto died when Tom was four. Like most black workers, Tom took annual leave each December. Shortly before the case he had planned to leave his job as machine operator or had been dismissed (which would have nullified any claim to §10 rights) but had changed his mind or been rehired when the "pass office" said he could not register for a new job. "I couldn't understand why I was refused because I have been working in the city for ten years and thought I was allowed to stay and work here. ... I just remember my boss telling me in 1970 when I started working for him that after ten years I would be able to get permanent residence rights." He had learned about the Black Sash advice office from a newspaper directed at Soweto readers.[50]

Nupen telegraphed Rikhoto in Katlehong on May 6 and interviewed him two days later. He also interviewed Hewitt (a Hargram supervisor) and René Charles Estcourt Barrois de Sarigny (company secretary). On June 10 the LRC filed a notice of motion in the Supreme Court in Johannesburg, seeking an order declaring that Rikhoto was entitled to §10(1)(b) status.[51] De Sarigny's supporting affidavit declared: "From time to time the applicant has had to return to the district of Ritavi, near Tzaneen [Gazankulu], for the purposes of renewing his contract of employment with the company. From our point of view this has been merely a formality."

The state answered, as expected, that homeland residents could not qualify under the section because annual leaves broke continuity of employment. The Germiston MLO insisted that the 1968 regulations were "specifically intended" to prevent people like Rikhoto from ever qualifying. On July 30 Nupen spoke by phone to attorney J.J. Scholtz, who acted for the state; they agreed that neither would raise technical matters. The LRC reply on August 3 denied that the regulation had this intent and argued that it would be ultra vires if it did. The same day Nupen told Scholtz the hearing was scheduled for Wednesday, September 2. Four days later Scholtz confirmed this was acceptable to counsel, reiterating that on August 17.

Late in the afternoon of Thursday, August 27, however, Scholtz asked Nupen for permission to file a supplemental affidavit. Because it would deal with the "call-in" card system, which Scholtz claimed was new matter, he sought a postponement. In a letter hand-delivered on Friday Nupen denied the matter was new, reminded Scholtz of his agreement about the hearing date, and complained that the suggestion "comes at a very late stage and may cause substantial prejudice to the Applicant." Scholtz promised the same day to deliver the supplemental affidavit on Saturday. Nupen gave Scholtz his home phone number and that of the LRC's junior counsel, Karel Tip. Scholtz telephoned Nupen at 11 a.m. Saturday but only to say he would ring back in an hour. At 3:30 p.m. he said he could not complete the affidavit and again sought a postponement. When Nupen refused, Scholtz threatened to ask the judge. They compromised that Scholtz would deliver the affidavit on Monday and seek no postponement. When it was still not ready, Nupen hand-delivered a letter to Scholtz reviewing this history and adding:

> We do not wish to be placed in a position in which an affidavit
> is tendered on the day of the hearing and we are required to take
> hasty decision without time for proper consideration. We cannot

understand why it has not been possible for you to let us have a draft affidavit or at least an indication of the facts which you hope to establish through it.

Scholtz replied on the eve of the proposed hearing.

[A]t all times the parties envisaged the present mattter as a test case and have approached it on that basis. In our view it is therefore essential that as complete a picture as possible be given to the Court.

The relationship between yourself and ourselves has been most amicable in the past.... It is clear that the matter is not one of urgency and that neither the Applicant nor the Respondent will suffer any prejudice by a further delay of even a month or more. [He claimed that the applicant's reply affidavit introduced new matter and circumstances beyond the respondent's control delayed its supplemental affidavit.]

In all the circumstances we are at a loss to understand your attitude.... In view of your attitude we will be constrained at the hearing of the matter to apply for leave to hand in whatever affidavit we are able to have prepared by then and obviously tender wasted costs.

On the day of the hearing the respondent submitted a supplemental affidavit noting that this test case affected thousands and requested a postponement to allow amplification. Arthur Chaskalson, the LRC's counsel, opposed this on the ground that Rikhoto wanted his wife and children to join him as soon as his status was legalized. The court rejected the state's request and heard the case the next day. Three papers noted its importance.[52]

Justice J.B. O'Donovan gave judgment on September 22. He rejected the state's argument that Rikhoto had failed to exhaust his administrative remedies by not appealing the MLO's decision to the Chief Commissioner. The MLO had to grant residential status to those who met the statutory requirement. If Rikhoto satisfied them, the MLO's " 'decision' was not reached as a result of valid proceedings, nor was it duly given in terms of any Act. ...[it] was in fact a 'decision' not to perform his functions...." O'Donovan summarily dismissed the contention that Rikhoto could not obtain §10 rights because he was a Gazankulu citizen, since he retained South African citizenship. Even citizens of the "independent" homelands could obtain §10 rights.

The Act did not require "a Black employee to interrupt his work at intervals so as to ensure that he does not qualify" under §10. Although his initial contract could not exceed a year, nothing prevented extensions. The Supreme Court had held that "a native who has...continuously worked for one employer in the area for ten years...may fairly be said to have given practical proof that he is at least prima facie not an undesirable."[53] Continuity was not broken by temporary absence due to illness or injury or other legitimate purpose unconnected with a change of work. As Justice Schreiner had said about the alternative criterion of fifteen years continuous residence: "no one could imagine that the useful or satisfactory absorption of a native in an urban community could in any way be affected by occasional departures from the area, not amounting to changes of residence."[54] If the call-in card system of annual renewals appeared to break continuity, this was the responsibility of a state motivated by the illegitimate purpose of preventing Blacks from qualifying. "This objective was not one which is authorised by the legislature." O'Donovan concluded:

> [A]lthough [Rikhoto's] services were rendered under a series of separate contracts, he and the company had a common and continuing intention that he should remain in employment; ...the arrangements for the renewal of his contract were made each year before he went on paid leave; ...he worked for no one other than the company; and...his absences from work for other causes have occurred on isolated occasions only. On these facts the Applicant has, in my view, satisfied the requirement of continuity in his work for a period of at least ten years. The question is one of substance, and not of form.

Having adopted virtually all the applicant's arguments, the judge declared Rikhoto entitled to remain and ordered the MLO to endorse his reference book accordingly.

Three papers gave the victory front-page headlines.[55] LRC lawyers jumped to their feet on hearing the outcome, "hardly believing that they would not have to be appealing [sic] the judgment." Rikhoto, by contrast, displayed little emotion, smiling only when Sheena Duncan asked if he understood what had happened. She declared that the judgment's implications were "immense" and would "give the authorities a headache by vastly increasing the privileged group entitled to a city life." In Cape Town, Helen Suzman called on the government to accept both this decision and *Komani* (now a year old): "The sooner the whole sorry business [of §10] is cleared up by the new bills we have to see emanating from the Grosskopf Committee's inquiry into Dr Koornhof's original bills, which were rejected by all who looked at them, the better." The South African Allied Workers Union immediately announced its intention to help members in Durban and elsewhere qualify. Few attended to an ERAB spokesman warning that the Board would probably appeal.[56]

The opposition press applauded the decision while criticizing the government. The *Sunday Times* unequivocally condemned influx control.[57]

> Apartheid worships many fictions. Not the least of them is its belief that people can be bureaucratised out of existence, that the men and women who keep South Africa's factories rolling, its

roads tarred, its cities lit, are—to coin a famous Verwoerdian phrase—not people, but units of labour. …

[T]he Government should resist its growing impulse to ignore laws it does not like, or remake them closer to its heart's desire.

Although the *Sowetan* applauded the "blow to influx control," it warned that "the jubilation…should be tempered with a certain amount of caution…people will continue being bulldozed out of their jobs, out of towns, and sometimes out of their minds. As is usual, this will be done by petty officials who simply disregard, or even worse, are ignorant of such breakthroughs or changes in the law."[58] The *Rand Daily Mail* also warned it was "too soon to celebrate." Although the court had ended the "trickery" of the Department of Co-operation and Development, the Chief Commissioners had shown their "scorn for the law" by refusing to follow *Komani*. They treated law "as the mere instrument of policy at best, or an obstacle at worst."[59] *The Natal Mercury* expressed the ambivalence of many white liberals. The "vital ruling" "should be a matter for rejoicing." At the same time, "there must be some barrier to uncontrolled movement to the cities," though regulations "should be logical and acceptable to those who are expected to abide by them. And above all else they should be human in concept."[60]

Feature stories depicted Rikhoto as a model citizen. During eleven years of marriage he had been able to visit his family in Ritavi only twice a year, at Christmas and Easter. He spent his evenings and weekends washing his car, gardening, reading the Bible, and attending the New Apostolic Church. He hoped to move from his rented room into a house when his family arrived.[61] The overseas press called the judgment a "breakthrough for South African blacks," which affected "thousands—perhaps hundreds of thousands."[62]

Large employers welcomed the decision. Reinald Hofmeyr, executive director of Barlow Rand, with responsibility for personnel and industrial relations, said "it will enable people who have come to regard themselves as urban workers to build homes in the townships and, most important, have their families with them." His company would help them obtain loans to buy houses. Industrial relations adviser Richard Sutton asserted that "responsible employers…have for some time made no differentiation between contract workers and those with permanent residence rights…[and] have regarded the whole contract system as a nuisance.…" Urban Foundation director Jan Steyn acknowledged that "in the past we have underestimated the way in which the courts can be used as an additional catalyst towards the combating of abuse of administrative authority."[63]

The critical question, of course, was how the government would respond. Koornhof temporized.

Seeing that standing court decisions must be acted upon, there will be no deviation from the rule in this case. The record of the case will be obtained and the judgment as well as the implications of it will be thoroughly studied and then action will be taken accordingly.[64]

He refused to say whether the government would appeal, disclaiming responsibility for that decision.[65] Helen Suzman got no further with a parliamentary question on October 2.

ERAB Chief Director Frans Marx was far less guarded: "I foresee that we will have to appeal because this has to be seen as a test case." (J.J. Scholtz, the ERAB attorney, had told Nupen two days after the judgment that he intended to appeal.) Marx's West Rand counterpart, John Knoetze, was studying the judgment. "This has far-reaching effects and we have two cases of a similar nature pending."[66] The ERAB deputy director said the judgment was "in abeyance" until that decision.[67] The Board resolved to appeal a week after the judgment.[68] Since the LRC had always seen this as a test case it consented to the appeal. Yet delegates from fourteen East Rand community councils met the ERAB executive committee two weeks later to urge reconsideration. Mr. Mpiyake Khumalo, East Rand Community Council Liaison Committee chairman, reported: "We contended that Mr Rikhoto had won a court case and that the board should not tamper with the law, in spite of being in a position to appeal. The Minister of Cooperation had indicated that he was not going to interfere with the course of justice." A.J. Niemand, acting chairman of the ERAB executive committee, promised to refer the decision to the full board.[69] But though the board met monthly, it postponed its decision in November and December 1981 and January, February, and March 1982. The board confirmed its original decision only on April 15.[70]

The government soon gave concrete proof it had not surrendered. Two days after the judgment Nupen asked Scholtz to allow Rikhoto's family to join him. The government refused to endorse Rikhoto's reference book but would consider a visit if told the number and ages of the children, where the family would live, and for how long. Nupen said that Rosina would bring Helen (five), Tony (three), and Terence (one), while Esther (eight) would stay in school in Ritavi. More than a week later Scholtz demanded this in writing. Nupen objected; Rikhoto was prepared to return to court unless his family was allowed to live with him for a year or until the appeal was decided. It took Scholtz two weeks to reply.

> As you know, our client is a statutory body and as such is bound by the statutory provisions relating to the admission of Blacks to urban areas. Consequently it is unable to summarily waive compliance with the regulations and it is our view that there was no unnecessary delay in dealing with the matter. ... What was intended by our client...was not to proceed against your client in any way prejudicing his stay in the area concerned, until finalisation of the appeal, and not to bestow on him a kind of section

> 10(1)(b) status.... hence the requirement that your client
> reduces to writing exactly what is required by him, because
> compliance with regulation 19 of GN1036/1968...is necessary.
>
> The main concern of our client at this stage is the nature of the
> available accommodation referred to in your letter. Our client's
> information is that the said accommodation is entirely inade-
> quate and illegal.

Nupen responded promptly that Rikhoto had a room and access to washing and cooking facilities; "due to the shortage of accomodation [sic] in black townships it is not uncommon for a family to be accomodated [sic] in this way."

Four days later Rikhoto and his family moved into a Zozo (corrugated iron hut) on the premises. Two weeks after that Scholtz objected.

> Your client's accomodation [sic] of the particular structure is ille-
> gal as for example the lodger's permit was granted to enable him
> to live with the occupants of the dwelling on the site in their
> house and not in an illegal structure.

Nupen immediately interviewed Rikhoto and his landlords, Philemon and Martha Nkosi. The property contained a legal hut, for which the Nkosis had been paying rent and in which Rikhoto lived. They had built a second illegal hut in 1980, which was discovered when the municipal police inspected the premises in October 1981 (presumably in response to the judgment). Nupen explained this to Scholtz on November 11. "We do not understand how in good faith your client can charge rent in respect of the structure and at the same time categorize it as illegal...." In any case, Rikhoto was now living in the house. The government also harassed Rikhoto by ordering him to remain in Katlehong over the Christmas holidays because of his involvement in a traffic accident. But the police declined to file charges, and he went home.

A month later Scholtz wrote Nupen that he felt personally betrayed by discovering that Rikhoto's family "are in fact living on the premises and have been so living for some time."

> We regard this inexplicable conduct of your client as a total
> breach of any bona fides on the part of your client against the
> spirit and essence of the negotiations.... [O]ur client demands an
> immediate explanation for this wrongful and illegal
> conduct...before replying to your aforesaid letter....

Scholtz sent a reminder after a month and again three weeks later.

> We fail to appreciate your attitude in this matter.... [Y]our client's
> wife has completely ignored your self and our clients and sim-
> ply proceeded to squat at the abode of your client. Yet you
> deem it fit not to give us any explanation of her conduct.

The fact that your client's wife is at present residing where she is, without any agreement thereanent between your client and our clients, you must concede, is highly irregular. We find your silence thereanent very strange indeed. ... [T]he fact that your client's wife has not yet been ejected and removed from the area, is done out of courtesy and with a view to arriving at some amicable solution to the problem, if at all possible, and is in no way to be construed as a waiver of any kind on the part of our clients.

He threatened to take "further action" if there was no reply within ten days and to bring the correspondence "to the notice of the forum concerned."

Nupen had seen Rikhoto the day of Scholtz's first reminder and learned that he had returned from Ritavi without his family. His answer, which crossed in the mail with Scholtz's testy second letter, attributed the delay to the holiday leaves of both his client and himself.

Mr Rikhoto does not consider it necessary to give any explanation to your client, nor does he consider his desire to live with his wife inexplicable. His attitude all along has been that he qualifies to be in the prescribed area of Germiston and is entitled...to have his wife and children live with him longer than the statutory 72 hours.... [W]e see no purpose in taking the matter further. ... If Mrs Rikhoto and her children should choose to reside with her husband and in consequence be prosecuted, the matter will be dealt with by way of a defence at the criminal trial.

Scholtz's rejoinder echoed the tone of moral outrage.

We are somewhat surprised...that [Mr Rikhoto] regards it as unnecessary to explain his conduct. We, on our part, do not in the least regard his desire to live with his wife as inexplicable and it was never contended by us.... Our clients sincerely appreciate the "desire" of your client to live with his wife and attempted to assist him within the framework of the Act to the best of their ability. Your attitude in the matter, now that your client has taken the law into his own hands, is not accepted.... The very fact that your client's wife has not been ejected from the premises she occupies is evidence of the bona fides and goodwill of our clients. ... You and your client have quite clearly expressed, in your letter under reply, that you are flaunting [sic] our client's authority in the matter, and because of the attitude expressed in said letter, you have left our clients no option for further negotiations....

Nupen immediately contacted Rikhoto, who reaffirmed that his family was in Ritavi and promised to inform Nupen if they returned. A year later Rikhoto sought the Centre's help in getting on the waiting list for houses because of a threat that those unhoused would be forced into hostels or deported to the homelands. "I am anxious to have my name placed on the waiting list before the threatened changes occur...[but] I fear that if I approach the authorities now to put my name on the list, I will have problems because of my case against ERAB re 10(1)(b) endorsement."

The appellate briefs filed in July and August 1982 reiterated those at trial. The state maintained that annual contracts broke the necessary continuity of employment since a mandatory seventy-two hours separated the termination of one from the commencement of the next. Furthermore, "the Black concerned is a willing and free contracting party who willingly accepts the aforesaid prescriptions and conditions and accordingly willingly enters into a written contract." Since the main purpose of §10 was segregation it conferred no rights on Blacks. The Appellate Division heard oral argument on May 20, 1983. Six days later the LRC told the press it feared that the Minister of Co-operation and Development planned legislation to nullify both *Komani* and *Rikhoto*.

On Monday, May 30, nearly two years after the Supreme Court decision, Justice van Heerden dismissed the appeal in a unanimous opinion of less than five pages.[71] It again was front-page news. Helen Suzman denounced the fact that "it required the courts to make this decision, which in a normal, democratic country is taken for granted," warning that severe housing shortages would frustrate implementation.[72] Nic Olivier, a nominated PFP MP, praised the judgment, which "places the final approval of the Courts on the sanctity of family life. It is very significant that our Courts in recent years have adopted an increasingly humane approach in the interpretation of the law which contrasts sharply with its application by the Government and the administration boards."[73]

With a day to reflect the press began to take positions. *The Citizen*, which supported the government, predicted it would "introduce legislation to normalise the influx control situation." That the government anticipated the decision suggested it had appealed only for delay.[74] *The Daily News*, by contrast, called the decision a "precious concession" and condemned "alarming...reports that the Government may act to plug the loophole."[75] *The Star* criticized "the deliberate creation of instability" among black workers and families and praised the willingness of the courts "to interpret unclear areas [of the pass laws] in terms of natural justice and human rights."[76] The *Rand Daily Mail* employed sarcasm.[77]

> It is embarrassing, in this last quarter of the 20th century, to have to plead for the right of people to a family existence. Elementary humanity together with the encouragement of a stable society...should place beyond any need for argument the right of husbands and wives to live together and the right of fathers and mothers to live with their children.

> To have to support the goodness and desirability of these rights
> is like having to defend the idea that the earth is round.

The *Sunday Tribune* praised the ruling as expressing "the highest traditions of an unfettered and independent judiciary" and deplored the
possibility of a legislative reversal. "For the Government to act so cynically
is a complete negation of any concept of justice. There can be no justice
in a society where the Government overrules the independent judiciary
whenever the findings displease."[78] The *Sowetan* welcomed this "blow at a
cornerstone of Government influx policies" but feared that legislation
would reverse it and bureaucrats obstruct its implementation. The paper
called upon civic organizations, Azapo, and Inkatha to help blacks claim
their rights. It urged the government to "prove its sincerity in the move
towards reform," redress "years of misery and pain," and erase the "polecat image" of South Africa abroad.[79] *The Natal Mercury* again reflected
white ambivalence.

> From the human aspect the ruling should be a matter for rejoic-
> ing, since it opens the way for tens of thousands of black
> migrant workers to live permanently in the cities with their fam-
> ilies. But it would be foolish not to temper one's gratification
> over the human benefits with some sober reflection on the prac-
> tical consequences.

Koornhof had warned that the backlog in black housing would double to
more than 500,000 units. The paper concluded lamely that "the emphasis
should be on studying fully its practical implications and trying to make it
acceptable."[80]

The foreign press seized on the decision to flog the government while
praising the courts. The *Guardian* called it "one of the most important judgments ever delivered by South Africa's highest court."[81] Three American papers
carried an article by a South African liberal describing the decision as "a three-
fold embarrassment for the government."[82] *The New York Times* warned that
the ruling applied to "only a small percentage of the nation's 22 million blacks"
and might be ignored or reversed.[83] Its editorial extolled the rule of law.

> Even as it dishonors humanity's basic codes, South Africa wor-
> ships forms of law. ...
>
> It is a paradox that can still serve conscience, and some coura-
> geous lawyers in Johannesburg are trying to make the most of
> their country's residual scruple. ...
>
> The judges hardly proclaimed a bill of rights for blacks, but they
> at least held the Government to the letter of its own law.
>
> While Parliament remains free to alter that letter, any true sense
> of justice will inspire respect for its common-sense meaning.[84]

Domestic voices mediated foreign responses. As the American disinvestment campaign gathered steam, Fred Ferreira of Ford (SA) warned the Afrikaanse Handelsinstituut (Afrikaner Chamber of Commerce) that Parliamentary reversal of *Rikhoto* could create "furore to the nth degree."

> The Americans are certain to view an attempt to circumvent the judgment as an attempt to muzzle the courts. They are particularly sensitive to this sort of issue as their own Supreme Court played a key role in the desegregation initiatives of the 50s and 60s. ... For this and many other reasons, I believe the Government would do well to implement the judgment.[85]

The Black Sash greeted victory in the case it had initiated by calling on migrant workers to apply to labor bureaus before the government could close the loophole, promising to help those who encountered obstacles. It had more than 800 applications pending before the Western Cape Administration Board, and local unions and employers had hundreds more.[86] It applauded the triumph of "rationality and compassion," declaring that the judgment

> underscores that even the ideology of apartheid must bow down to the law. The highest court in the land has spoken and its will must prevail. This is law and order at work and the Government, which professes to be a champion of law and order, must let its officials know that to frustrate the court order is a punishable contempt.[87]

In the first week after the judgment hundreds of applicants filled Black Sash offices, which had to turn many away.[88]

Within two days of the decision, however, Koornhof showed signs of resistance. The previous October he had told the Cape National Party congress in East London: "We will have to come with amending legislation to deal with the Komani case because it is causing problems."[89] Bills had been referred to committee in 1982 and again in 1983.[90] Now he said that *Rikhoto*'s "far-reaching implications" had to be "studied carefully." A spokesman for the Deputy Minister of Co-operation and Development affirmed that the department had to analyze the Appeal Court documents (an unambiguous opinion of fewer than five pages). By the end of the week an unnamed government source said: "Those rulings defeat the purpose of government policy. Contract workers were not meant to get Section 10 rights." It was rumored that the June 7 Cabinet meeting would consider a response, with an eye to the National Party caucus scheduled the next day.[91] An anonymous government source said "unofficial" legislation to overturn the decision had already been drafted.

The PFP stoutly defended the decision. An unidentified spokesman said Koornhof "is now universally distrusted. Even his own MP's watch him like a hawk."[92] Helen Suzman and Ken Andrew (party spokesperson on black affairs in the Western Cape) urged Koornhof to accept the decision before Parliament voted on his departmental budget the following week.[93] Nic Olivier deplored the government's "sad record of constantly overriding court decisions." Here was an opportunity for reform "without the need to amend the existing legislation." Government should show its commitment by implementing the decision "graciously and expeditiously."[94]

Although the Department of Co-operation and Development said it had taken notice of the judgment and people should apply to their local boards, these just stalled.[95] ERAB chairman Frans Marx conceded that "somehow or other" he would have to implement "part of the court judgment," but he was still awaiting instructions. When the Paper, Wood and Allied Workers Union brought 60 members, an ERAB office told them the computer was broken. Five applicants at the Edenvale office were told to return in a month. WRAB chairman John Knoetze said the judgment "has a number of implications and should be studied thoroughly to see how much of it could be carried out most effectively." When 300 employees of a Johannesburg company applied to a WRAB office, however, they were told the judgment was "simply an individual case." The office was waiting for guideliness from Pretoria, which could take two weeks.[96] Although nearly a thousand applications were pending before the WCAB, its Langa office told several applicants they had not heard of the case. Gert du Preez, the Board's chief liaison officer, said it had to study the judgment and was awaiting instructions from the Department.[97] Although he promised that the Board would begin processing applications on Monday, workers were turned away away then, and another twenty-two were rebuffed on Wednesday.[98] In response to a Parliamentary question by Helen Suzman two weeks after the judgment, Koornhof said ERAB had endorsed 143 men, and no other board had acted.[99]

Unions and employers pushed for implementation. The Council of Unions of South Africa threatened to litigate or take other action "if Minister Koornhof tries to ignore the decision and tries to push legislation through which attempts to regain control over urban black workers." Camay Piroshaw, its general secretary and representative of the National Mine Workers' Union, warned of a "tough line of action." The Federation of South African Trade Unions denounced all forms of influx control. South African Allied Workers Union secretary Sam Kikine spoke of a "terrible worker backlash" and was echoed by Building, Construction and Allied Workers' Union organizer Frank Mohlala. David Lewis, general secretary of the General Workers' Union, said: "It is interesting that the WCAB, which justified its excesses at KTC [squatter camp] by insisting that inhumane laws should be respected, should now be unwilling to implement a decision of the country's highest court." Rod Ironside, president of the Federated Chambers of Commerce, declared: "if the law and the courts mean anything, then obviously we would expect this judgment to be followed through." At least ten major Cape Town firms were helping employees apply.[100] Anglo American, Barlow Rand, the Premier Group, Federale Volksbeleggings, Ford, AECI, and the Association of Chambers of Commerce supported the decision. But the Urban Foundation sat on the fence: although "it is impossible to question the judgment of an SA Appeal Court," its implications were "a different kettle of fish." Afrikaanse Handelsinstituut president Hennie Klerck was even less enthusiastic.

> Although...there may be dozens of humane reasons to reunite contractual workers with their families, we believe the realities of a massive influx of blacks to the metropolitan areas is [sic] totally impractical and nowhere in the Western world would any country be able to cope with such a situation. ...it is in the best interests of blacks to avoid the chaos that would result from a loosening up of influx control.[101]

Rikhoto heard about the judgment on the radio on Monday night in Ritavi and read about it the next day when he returned to Germiston. On Thursday he visited the ERAB office with Charles Nupen. They were taken directly to office manager Scholtz Kruger, who personally filled out the forms and endorsed the reference book. Rikhoto said: "I feel great, not only for myself but for the thousands of other migrant workers who will be allowed to live in urban areas. The next time I go home I am going to slaughter an ox to say a big thank you to my gods." "I believe it was through prayer that I managed to acquire city rights. [Zion Christian] Church members and I prayed hard during the East Rand Board's appeal.... I am happy God answered our prayers." He was disappointed the South African Broadcasting Company had not interviewed him. "I expected that such an important matter that affects thousands of my black brothers would be televised." As he left, other applicants shook his hand and congratulated him. One said: "You have struck South Africa. This will be good for all of us." Hundreds returned to the office in response to publicity about the judgment, despite the "computer breakdown" the previous day, and obtained endorsements. But the office expelled a trade union leader who had brought eighty applicants. When Rikhoto visited the LRC two weeks later, however, he was told he had to apply to ERAB for his wife's §10(1)(c) endorsement and the Centre could not help him with accommodation.[102]

If Rikhoto credited his victory to prayer, the LRC naturally sought some recognition. Geoff Budlender declared:

> On his own, without lawyers, Mehlolo could not have had his rights recognised. Indeed, such an action...would have been beyond the means of any but the very richest of individuals. ... so many others will now benefit. ... this is a very worthwhile job if you believe the law can be used to build a fairer society.

The Centre, which raised forty percent of its support locally, used the occasion to solicit donations. The *Sunday Times*, whose National Charity

Fund contributed fifteen percent of its local support, said that one of the Centre's "obvious" strengths was its refusal to handle "political cases, particularly those that relate to the Terrorism Act."[103]

When Parliament debated the Department of Co-operation and Development budget on Monday, June 6, Koornhof decried the judgment as inconsistent with the accepted interpretation of the law. While the government had the highest respect for the courts, the ruling had serious social, economic and financial implications. The best influx control was development of the "National States," which had just created 2,150 jobs. "Show me a place in Africa or the world which can equal this." Government might recognize the §10 rights of those already qualified, depending on their numbers, but was considering closing the loophole prospectively. When Helen Suzman warned Koornhof this would destroy his "almost non-existent credibility," he retorted: "That sort of remark should not be made. It is stupid. If you want to go and joke, don't be so personal." When she condemned his "complete bungling" of the black portfolio and called for his dismissal from the Cabinet he protested that this cut him to the marrow. "It is a terribly serious accusation when a man's personal credibility is brought into doubt, especially when he is a Cabinet minister and one dealing with such sensitive issues. ... What has been happening here today has been most unfair. I don't deserve it."[104] Sources reported that next day's Cabinet meeting postponed a decision; although Ministers agreed that interim legislation was necessary, they could not decide whether to make it retroactive.

Government was under pressure from the right. In a front-page story the day before the Parliamentary debate, *Rapport* warned of "Die Swart Stroom" (The Black Flood) of 1.5 million new migrants.[105] Three days later the SABC predicted that the "destructive influence on community identity and stability" of uncontrolled urbanization "would be little less than a short-cut to social disintegration." During the Parliamentary debate Frank le Roux, Conservative Party MP for Brakpan, protested that failure to overturn the decision would constitute abandonment of the policy of apartheid.[106] Helen Suzman replied it would be "madness" to strengthen influx control. "Leave it alone. June 16 [the anniversary of Soweto] is coming up soon and we don't want to enrage people." Koornhof might contend that *Rikhoto* was bad law, "but eight judges disagree with him."[107] The *Sowetan* hinted it might have "similar views but the danger of raising them outside Parliament often leads to accusations of incitement."

> [T]here has been a heightening of tension. There has been a re-awakening of political activism even from your man in the street. ... There have been a series of serious political cases. There have been bombings. This was climaxed by the ANC hanging the other day. We who have been through similar times in the past have a way of sensing these things.[108]

In response to right-wing fulminations about the "swart gevaar" (black threat), supporters of the two decisions sought to minimize the number who might seek endorsements. University of Cape Town economist Charles Simkins had just published a book arguing that South Africa was under-urbanized compared to countries with similar populations and per capita incomes.[109] Making conservative assumptions about who might qualify under *Rikhoto* and bring dependents, one researcher concluded that 145,000 might do so immediately and 55,000 annually thereafter.[110] Sheena Duncan reassured whites that "The *Rikhoto* judgment won't swamp cities."[111]

> It does NOT overthrow the whole of the influx control mechanism. It does NOT presage an overnight growth in the size of the urban population. ...
>
> These tens of thousands of workers [who will qualify] are NOT a new influx into the cities. They have all been in town working legally and productively for a minimum of 10 years.

She criticized boards for delay and for demanding unnecessary information. "The employment records of every legal worker are in the keeping of the labour bureaus and are computerised." Governmental dilatoriness was "straightforward disobedience of the law."

Almost three weeks after the judgment *Nasionale Pers* newspapers reported that the government planned to introduce legislation to "give effect" to *Rikhoto* by the end of the Parliamentary session on June 30. Helen Suzman denounced this as "a typical Nat ploy. If you can't win, change the rules." Sheena Duncan called it "specious and dishonest."[112] At its third weekly meeting since the judgment, the Cabinet remained divided: those from the Cape took a hard line, while Koornhof wanted to avoid blatant rejection.[113] On June 22 the government finally announced that it accepted *Rikhoto* but planned to limit *Komani* by requiring dependents to demonstrate adequate housing. Koornhof sought to appease the right.

> [T]he government is obviously bound by the judgment...[but] it is my duty to avoid at all costs that unrealistic expectations of instant accommodation in urban areas are not created in the minds of migrant workers and their families.... [T]hey have not...acquired legal rights to demand a house in black urban residential areas. ...squatting will not be permitted under any circumstances.[114]

Apparently defying *Komani*, he declared that §10 right-holders would have to prove adequate housing before bringing their dependents. He adopted the conservative estimate of 144,000 eligible workers but believed many fewer would gain endorsements—perhaps only 5,000! Deputy Minister of Co-operation and Development George Morrison, who had opposed compliance, discouraged any hope of additional housing. "We have a backlog of 260,000 houses already; it would be most unfair to expect us to make provision for these people who now qualify."[115] On August 10 Koornhof assured his "colleagues in the CP" that the government was not "throwing in the towel as regards so-called influx control." (Unsatisfied, one replied: "From available statistics we know that before the end of the century 19 cities the size of Soweto will have to be built.") At the same time, he was "filled with pride that the courts in this country have built up a very good name worldwide," and "the Government has a high regard and respect for our courts." (Another CP representative rejoined: "it goes without saying that we respect the decisions of our courts. It has never been the task of the Appeal Court, however...to make the laws of this country. When Acts have to be amended, it is the task of this House of Assembly....")[116] Two weeks later the government passed legislation restricting *Komani*.[117]

The Urban Foundation offered a rare public criticism. "We are convinced the government does not wish to give recognition to the separation of husband, wife and family.... After all, workers affected by the Rikhoto judgment have shown by length of service that they are a stable and loyal component of the free market system."[118] Helen Suzman welcomed Koornhof's belated compliance but feared that the requirement of adequate housing would be a "Catch-22."[119] The PFP warned that "the tremendous administrative powers" of discretion granted to boards might be used to defeat the ruling.[120]

The day after the government announcement WCAB Chief Director J. Gunter fueled these fears by refusing to endorse those with lengthy absences during their ten-year employment. This openly defied a Supreme Court judgment two months earlier ordering his board to endorse a man with three absences totalling eighteen months. "A man cannot be expected to work day in and day out for 10 years without a break of any kind. If he left the area for a lengthy period and his employer agreed to his absence he could not be said to have abandoned his employment."[121] The board had not granted one of the more than 1,000 pending applications in the three weeks since the judgment.[122] Less than two weeks later WRAB chairman John Knoetze ruled that citizens of the four "independent" homelands would not qualify unless they had completed their ten years of employment or fifteen years of residence *before* independence—a view declared "absolutely wrong" by a lawyer specializing in influx control and "totally unlawful" by Sheena Duncan.[123]

A year later the Minister of Co-operation and Development revealed that 54,679 people had applied for §10(1)(b) rights and 38,907 had been endorsed by May 31, 1984.[124] The following year the Minister reported that the number of endorsements had reached 60,000.[125] But a study found that only twenty-one percent of the more than 10,000 Western Cape applicants in the first twenty months were successful.* In June 1985 Parliament passed the Laws on Co-operation and Development Amendment Act, granting §10(1)(b) rights to those who had lived or worked in an urban area for ten years (even

*69 percent were rejected and 10 percent pending. Although 65 percent of married men would bring wives and children if influx control permitted and accommodation were available, only 10 percent of hostel dwellers lived with their wives and only 19 perecent of fathers with their children. CP (6.9.85).

if for several employers). The government acknowledged that "the feelings in regard to influx control is [sic] one of the strongest causes of bitterness in Black communities that exists at present." But "it is definitely not the Government's objective to do away with the essential measures for ensuring orderly urbanization."[126] Although the PFP believed that "racial restrictions on the mobility of people in South Africa should be removed completely and immediately," it supported the bill.[127] The CP naturally opposed it because "Blacks are pouring illegally from Ciskei and Transkei to the Western Cape on a large scale."[128]

Aftermath

Although *Komani* and *Rikhoto* certainly were not the only causes, they did contribute to the gradual dismantling of explicitly racist laws regulating movement. Legislation in 1984 and 1986 (exactly a decade after the Soweto uprising) repealed the notorious §10 and that most Orwellian of titles, the Blacks (Abolition of Passes and Coordination of Documents) Act—which had *mandated* registration books.[129] Calling the Abolition of Influx Control bill "one of the most important" of the 1986 session, the Minister of Constitutional Development and Planning proclaimed that it "gives effect to the Government's philosophy about the elimination of racial discrimination and the extension of equal opportunities to all South Africans." It placed urbanization "in juridical perspective for the first time" by repealing laws that "gave the bureaucracy comprehensive and arbitrary powers" and "directly or indirectly constitute an infringement of the administration of justice." A Nationalist backbencher concurred that this was "the most important legislation with regard to Black affairs since the party came to power in 1948." "[N]o single statutory measure has harmed South Africa's image...as much as section 10...we are finally burying apartheid today. [Interjections]."[130] Helen Suzman observed that the PFP had been urging this step for decades and asked "the hon the Minister, when he has finished dishing out sweets, to tell us why it has taken the Government forty years to appreciate the mistake it has made."[131] Another Nationalist generously acknowledged that "she had better insight into the problems and could see further than many other people in South Africa." "[S]he, without any assistance, took up the cudgels in this House for many years.... I hardly think there will ever again be anyone in the history of this country who could do as much for human rights as she has done."[132] The Conservative Party called this a "fatal moment," warning of "chaos and untold misery on a large scale" and integration in "schools, residential areas, and community life." The Nationalist Party was "going to bring a curse upon itself because of what it is doing to its spiritual forefathers." "[W]as there nothing good in the policy of separate development and division? Did it contain no virtues and no idealism?" "Government has placed us inexorably on the way to a unitary state in South Africa."[133]

Perhaps anticipating a "post-apartheid" South Africa, the government relied increasingly on ostensibly non-racial laws: laying the foundation for a requirement that everyone carry identification documents,[134] using alienage to discriminate against "citizens" of the four "independent" homelands,* and limiting settlement in the name of public health and safety.[135] On the eve of majority rule, four years after de Klerk's accession to power, the Witwatersrand Regional Director of the Department of Home Affairs reported that in the first two months of 1993 his officers had apprehended nearly 5,000 people on suspicion of being aliens, deporting more than 3,500. He observed that under the Aliens Control Act "No court of law shall have any jurisdiction to review, quash, reverse, interdict, or otherwise interfere with any act, order or warrant" of an immigration officer.[136]

Analysis

Komani and *Rikhoto* were defining moments in the legal struggle against apartheid, revealing both its strengths and limitations. The choice of a legalistic strategy contrasts sharply with earlier challenges to the hated pass laws, from the 1952 Defiance Campaign through the women's resistance in the Western Transvaal to the 1960 Sharpeville massacre. Komani initiated his case the year before Soweto; only a legalistic challenge could have survived the repression that followed.

These actions were individual rather than collective as well as legal rather than political. Neither plaintiff was supported by any political group. Indeed, Rikhoto belonged to the Zion Christian Church, which not only was avowedly apolitical but even invited the State President to its annual gathering. A private lawyer acting under the legal aid scheme initiated Mr. Komani's action. Both plaintiffs were referred to the LRC by Black Sash, which acts on behalf of individuals seeking to secure rights under existing law, rather than groups struggling to change the regime. In both cases the plaintiffs remained ciphers, whose personalities and biographies emerged only in feature stories after their victories. It was fortunate that the government was equally uninterested in personal detail. The LRC had inherited the Komani case; although it chose Rikhoto, he was not the ideal plaintiff. Had he left his employer before the lawsuit, as planned, he would have lost his §10 rights. After it was filed the state might have used his illegal residence and traffic violation to deny the endorsement.

The case was ideal for the LRC, however, most of whose funding came from American foundations seeking to export the test case strategy pioneered

*G. Budlender (1986; 1989); Schoombee & Davis (1986). The misnamed Restoration of South African Citizenship Act, No. 73 of 1986, together with the Aliens Act, No. 1 of 1937. Before the repeal of §10, the government had categorically disqualified the children of "citizens" of the four "independent" homelands. G. Budlender (1984). Afterwards, it stalled in processing applications for South African citizenship, forcing the LRC to bring numerous test cases. When it finally capitulated, 250,000 applications were pending. LRT (1987-88: 15-16).

by the NAACP in civil rights and generalized by legal services and public interest lawyers. Individual claimants had sought and obtained §10 rights before, but those decisions by lower officials had not established any precedents. Only a public interest lawyer would pursue such chancy cases.

Why did these challenges succeed? The courts could have ruled for the government. There was nothing outrageous in the Supreme Court decision that Mrs. Komani did not "ordinarily reside" in Guguletu because she lacked legal accommodation. The Appellate Division could have held that the legislature, knowing about the "call-in" card system, intended to preclude migrant workers like Rikhoto from ever qualifying for urban residence. After all, those interpretations had prevailed for more than a decade. The courts could have avoided a substantive decision by finding a procedural impediment, such as the failure to exhaust administrative remedies through an appeal to the Chief Commissioner.

The plaintiffs, however, could mobilize a variety of resources. First, any complex regulatory structure inevitably contains inconsistencies that can be exploited by those seeking to frustrate it—tax avoiders, tenants opposing eviction, war resisters fighting conscription, and of course criminal defendants. This is a basic dilemma of the liberal state: it can coerce only through law, which simultaneously endows subjects with powers of resistance. Second, blacks enter the struggle against apartheid with an enormous moral advantage. Here they could not only assail racism but also invoke the sanctity of the family. The separation of husbands from wives and fathers from children is the contemporary equivalent of that ultimate outrage of American slavery—breaking up families by selling members down the river. It is publicly indefensible. Opposition figures like Sheena Duncan and Helen Suzman and the liberal English press took every opportunity to expose the ethical bankruptcy of Nationalist policies. The government's pretended concern that black families have adequate accommodation convinced no one, given its adamant refusal to build housing.

Third, the Nationalists were divided by the basic contradiction of apartheid. To retain electoral support among ordinary whites, the party had to ensure their racial superiority. But black labor drove the economy; to increase productivity, industry required a stable, contented, increasingly well-trained black work force. Large employers therefore favored continuity of employment [§10(1)(b) rights] and happy workers [§10(1)(c) rights for their dependents]. Furthermore, wealthier whites wanted male workers' wives available for domestic service. At the macrolevel, these pressures contributed to the Wiehahn and Riekert Commission reports, which recommended collective bargaining and liberalization of influx control.[137] Defending repeal of influx control in 1986 against Conservative Party criticism, the Minister of Constitutional Development and Planning declared that "economic realities are at odds with [the CP's] political philosophy."[138] At the microlevel, they were visible in Hargram's sponsorship of Rikhoto's application and the support many employers gave their workers after the Appellate Division decisions. For similar reasons, government sought to present a reformist image to South African blacks and white liberals and external critics. (White liberals were themselves divided, wishing to appear morally superior while continuing to enjoy the privileges of apartheid.) Nevertheless, the courts took no cognizance of moral, economic, or political factors, resting their decisions exclusively on the narrowly legalistic ground that the regulations were ultra vires or misinterpreted.

The government's response was even more mysterious than the decisions themselves. It had ample power to overturn them. Koornhof assured the Nationalist Party in 1982 that government was· contemplating such action, and bills were drafted toward that end. But the government backed off. Disagreements within the party had aborted passage of Koornhof's earlier "reforms." Government found it much harder to annul "rights" the courts had recognized than to deny them in the first place. Black leaders denounced the government's appeal from Rikhoto's Supreme Court victory as "tamper[ing] with the law" and "interfer[ing] with the course of justice" (although Komani had appealed the government's Supreme Court victory). Justice Goldstone sharply reprimanded government for relitigating matters that had been conclusively resolved by the Appellate Division. And the English press, which showed almost no interest in the routine enforcement of influx control, unanimously condemned reenactment of judicially discredited practices.

Most perplexing was the bureaucratic reaction. Geoff Budlender seems to have retained a stubborn faith that an authoritative declaration of legal rights would ultimately be respected. Like Pharaoh oppressing the Israelites, however, local Municipal Labour Officers repeatedly promised compliance only to renege. Was this behavior directed from the top? It is hard to imagine otherwise: when the Minister of Co-operation and Development wanted to *restrict* influx control, his orders were promptly executed. It seems likely that higher officials sought to preserve the facade of respect for law while secretly instructing subordinates to resist. This slowed the pace of change, winning them several years. Even the doomed appeal in *Rikhoto* delayed enforcement for two years. There are obvious parallels with nullification of federal decrees by southern American states before the Civil War and after 1954, although the South African adversaries were equal branches of a unitary government. Consistent with my suggestion that these cases exposed the major contradiction of apartheid, the government complied more readily with *Rikhoto* (which served industry's need for a stable workforce) than *Komani* (which threatened to intensify the housing shortage and increase wage demands by allowing dependents to leave rural areas, where they were supposed to be self-supporting).

There are other plausible interpretations, however. Any large bureaucracy is constructed of myriad loose couplings, some of which inevitably fail.

Inertia, incompetence, and indifference are powerful brakes on change. A command to comply by higher officials might have incited revolt by lower middle class Afrikaners resentful of English reformers. Clerks insecure about their fragile authority may have claimed unfettered discretion to tyrannize over black supplicants. Much enforcement of influx control appears to express whites' determination to dominate and humiliate blacks, granting favors as acts of grace rather than being compelled to recognize rights. Pass laws (like other comprehensive regulatory schemes) constantly criminalize everyone, subjecting them to autocratic whim and power. South African whites, like Southern whites in the United States, proclaimed paternalistic solicitude for victims. These attributions of motive have practical as well as academic implications: cooperation was an appropriate LRC strategy with officials who could be persuaded to comply; confrontation and denunciation were the only response to the incorrigibly intransigent. Motive often was opaque, however; New Canada clerks were clearly being obstructionist, but was Scholtz acting in good faith when he sought more time to file an additional affidavit or required a letter about Rikhoto's family?

A legalistic strategy offered the LRC some leverage but also imposed serious limitations. It seems to have made an ally of Mr. Toerien, the Department's legal adviser, who urged his superiors to comply with the judgments. Even Mr. Scholtz, the private attorney representing ERAB, sometimes heeded appeals to legality. But the government also hid behind legalism. Higher officials maintained that the decisions applied only to the particular parties. Lower officials demanded irrelevant documentation. Scholtz first claimed that the law prevented ERAB from allowing Rikhoto's wife to join him in Katlehong—although boards flouted the AD ruling in *Komani* for five years. Scholtz tried to regain the moral high ground by denouncing Rikhoto's alleged illegal residence and deceit. Rikhoto's wife "simply proceeded to squat" with him. Such behavior was "highly irregular." Lapsing into legalese in a vain effort to assert authority, Scholtz moralized: "We find your silence thereanent very strange indeed." Your "client has taken the law into his own hands." You are "flaunting [sic] our client's authority." But this strategy failed; Nupen dared Scholtz to prosecute Rikhoto, knowing it would be political suicide (and the issue was moot).

Test cases offer lawyers the lure of dramatic victories but also threaten to bog them down in the mire of endless enforcement. Another interpretation of the aftermath of *Komani* and *Rikhoto* is that the state made the LRC do its dirty work, disciplining applicants by conducting interviews and preparing the dossiers necessary to establish §10 rights. The LRC, however, did not want to become another legal aid office, handling routine, repetitive matters. Black Sash already performed that function; encouraged by its funders, the Centre saw itself as an agent of law reform. In any case, the number of applicants far exceeded its resources. These cases vividly illustrate the essential lesson that judicial victories are embedded in political struggles; they are neither self-realizing nor self-effectuating; appellate decisions are the beginning of the fight, not the end. A powerful adversary like the South African government does not surrender because of a single legal defeat.

The last question, and perhaps the most difficult, is the long-term effect of these campaigns. Although it is always dangerous to impute causality in large-scale events, judicial invalidation of two essential components certainly encouraged the government to abandon influx control (even though this was foreshadowed by the Riekert Commission report, which antedated *Komani*). Yet some have argued that the iron hand of brute force was simply replaced by the velvet glove of economic compulsion.[139] The decisions had no effect on segregation, poverty, wages, unemployment, education, housing, or infrastructure. The persistence of these inequalities does not depend on racist laws. Johannesburg, like Paris, equally forbids the rich and poor to erect shantytowns (although only Johannesburg prevents the construction of housing for blacks and then hypocritically uses that shortage as the basis for denying them residential rights). Although jubilant about its legal victories, the LRC ruefully had to tell Rikhoto it could not help him jump the endless queue and obtain housing for his family. These extra-legal obstacles help explain why only about a fifth of those entitled to §10 rights obtained them in the year following *Rikhoto*.

If the material gains were limited, what about the psychological consequences? Did legal victories empower blacks? They may well have alleviated the sense of defeat and paralysis following suppression of the 1976 Soweto rebellion. At least they demonstrated that the white minority government was not omnipotent. But if they lessened the tyranny of hostile white clerks they may have increased dependence on liberal white allies. Before going to the Municipal Labour Officer for an endorsement, black workers and dependents now appealed to Black Sash and the LRC, often expressing profound gratitude for their intervention. Reformers often worry that efforts to humanize government oppression will legitimate it. There is no evidence that blacks became more accepting of white minority rule as a result of these campaigns and victories. Even the plaintiffs do not seem to have seen law as their salvation. Rikhoto persisted in attributing his victory to God and the prayers of his fellow Zionists. The greatest effect appears to have been on the reformers themselves, whose faith in law was strengthened. The LRC took justifiable pride in its achievement, which validated its basic strategy.[140] Indeed, the lawyers sometimes seemed more excited than litigants about the victories. And liberal allies like the English press, the PFP, and the Urban Foundation extolled the courts, whose decisions demonstrated that non-violent, legalistic strategies could move the government. Yet there was nothing co-optative about the tactics used or the ends achieved. These campaigns helped lay the foundation for a decade of cumulative, and ultimately victorious, challenge to the apartheid regime.

CHAPTER 4

WHITE RESISTANCE TO THE MILITARY

I take this stand because I believe that in a sense it is the one time that I have a choice as a white South African. I can choose to go to prison... rather than to be part of the SADF. (Ivan Toms)

My understanding of what happened in Nazi Germany was that for me to be able to say that what happened there was wrong... I had to be able to say to myself that if I had been a German soldier at that time I would actually have taken the stand against what was going on there.... [L]eaving the country would be actually running away from racism once again. My mother is a refugee from racism. I am not prepared to be another refugee from racism. (David Bruce)

The struggle against apartheid has been waged almost entirely by blacks, who cannot avoid its pervasive oppression. The vast majority of whites silently enjoyed the benefits of racism. A few openly resisted: Black Sash, political parties (the Democratic Party and its precursors, the South African Communist Party until it was banned), the nonracial United Democratic Front from 1983, some churches, and small minorities within occupations: journalists on the opposition press, human rights lawyers, artists and writers, educators at nonracial or black schools, organizers in nonracial trade unions. Many emigrated; a handful became guerrillas.

Military service, however, posed a stark moral dilemma for whites who questioned apartheid. Despite its name, the South African Defence Force has consistently been the aggressor. Equipped with greater firepower than the rest of sub-Saharan Africa combined, it supported Renamo in Mozambique and Unita in Angola, fought Swapo in Namibia, and carried out raids in Zambia, Zimbabwe, Botswana, Swaziland, and Lesotho. It also repressed political activity in black townships during the 1985–90 Emergency.[1]

Collective Opposition: 1980–87

There is a long, if morally ambiguous, tradition of opposition to the military in South Africa. When the government invaded German South-West Africa during World War I the Afrikaner commander defected to the Germans, and other Afrikaner generals engaged in an insurrection, which the Afrikaner and English churches refused to condemn. World War II provoked much sympathy for the Nazis. B.J. Vorster (later Prime Minister) went to jail, and Magnus Malan (Defence Minister in the 1980s) also refused military service. The Dutch Reformed Church recognized a right to resist, and the Free State synod urged civil disobedience.[2]

South Africa adopted peacetime white male conscription in 1957. In the 1980s boys registered at sixteen and performed two years of National Service as soon as they left school unless granted deferment for further study. Over the next twelve years they completed two years of ninety-day Commando camps, graduating to five years of Active Citizen Force Reserve and then the Controlled National Reserve until fifty-five.[3] During the height of the Emergency the Standing Operational Force was 160,000, but half a million could be mobilized.

In 1961 the government allowed members of recognized "peace churches" to serve as noncombatants. Many refused, however, enduring up to four years in Detention Barracks.[4] In 1974 the South African Council of Churches, declaring that the SADF was "defending a fundamentally unjust and discriminatory society," challenged Christians to become conscientious objectors. Prime Minister Vorster responded by warning "those that are playing with fire in this way to rethink before they burn their fingers irrevocably." The government made it a crime punishable by six years imprisonment to encourage or assist another to refuse or fail to render military service. Even the opposition Progressive Party condemned the SACC for "spread[ing] a defeatist spirit towards peaceful change"; and the United Party accused it of "giving terrorism a cloak of sacrilegious respectability." When the Quakers urged that objectors be allowed to serve as ambulance drivers, community health educators, and black hospital workers, Deputy Defence Minister Kobie Coetsee said the proposal would "give each coward and rotter a sanctuary where he could evade his responsibilities to his country." Instead, the government made it a crime punishable by two years imprisonment for nonmembers of peace churches to refuse to serve; and they could be recharged repeatedly.[5] The SADF Chaplain General denounced conscientious objection in 1980 as "playing into the hands of the Marxist powers by way of indirect support."6 Opposition continued to grow, however. Because an average of 1,750 men (about ten percent) failed to report for each semi-annual call-up between 1975 and 1978, the National Union of South African Students appointed a committee to explore alternatives to military service. Conscientious Objector Support Groups (COSGs) were formed in 1980.7

In 1983 Parliament passed the Defence Act after a seven-day debate, one of the longest ever.8 It created a Board for Religious Objection chaired by a judge and composed of military officers and chaplains and church representatives (although the Roman Catholic, Presbyterian, Congregational, and Anglican churches refused to participate). The original bill offered successful applicants noncombatant service; if they refused to wear a uniform their military service increased fifty percent; if they refused all military duties they had to perform community service for two times their outstanding obligation; those who did not qualify but refused to serve were imprisoned for two times their outstanding obligation. The PFP urged recognition of conscientious objection on non-religious ethical grounds, provoking other MPs to condemn them as Marxists, ANC supporters, part of the onslaught against South Africa, "a bunch of hon pansy-pushers." A CP member opposed any broadening of the grounds of objection, pointing to the American experience during the Vietnam war, when the number of COs increased from 17,900 in 1964 to 40,000 in 1970.9 The Defence Minister maintained that the PFP amendments would "destroy the system of national service."10 After two full days of debate the House rejected the PFP proposal by defeating its motion to refer the bill to select committee, 89-22.

At the committee stage after the second reading, the Chairman refused to accept renewed PFP amendments to broaden the grounds for objection. W.V. Raw (New Republic Party) moved to amend the bill so that community service (and thus imprisonment) was only 1.5 times the outstanding military obligation or "six years' continuous community service."11 The PFP promptly moved to reduce the period to 1.25 times.12 The Defence Minister accepted Raw's motion that "community service will be just less than six years" while warning that if there were "a tremendous influx" of applicants he would have to consider an amendment extending the term.13 As amended, the clause passed 87-17.

The PFP then moved to amend the penalty for those refusing to serve to "community service for a period of service *not exceeding* one-and-a-half times" the outstanding obligation and imprisonment for those not qualifying as religious objectors "for a period *not exceeding* three years." The PFP believed "that good legal procedure provides that as a general rule it should be left to the court to apply in their discretion, taking the circumstances of each case into account, the penalty." This was particularly true here, since those liable for prison would range from "the ordinary draft-dodgers, the layabouts who just do not want to serve" to "people who have moral and ethical objections to participating in any form of warfare." "[T]he courts can very well take into account the person's background, his circumstances, his genuineness."[14] The NRP and Conservative Party rejected this as "simply a back door to achieve what the official Opposition failed to achieve by the front door."[15] A PFP member asked "why we should suddenly now tell a judge that we do not have confidence in him." The NRP member had said "he does not trust judges...it is necessary for Parliament to tell the judge what he should do."[16] Another NRP member retorted: "What discretion is left to the judiciary if a man gets up and pleads guilty.... That is black and white."[17] A PFP member responded that "the purpose of this kind of legislation...ought to be to prevent the S.A. Defence Force from coming into conflict in high profile trials...."[18] The Defence Minister commended W.V. Raw for having "definitely caught the official Opposition out when they wanted to slink in through the back door." The PFP wanted those with non-religious objections "to have a lesser offence than the religious objector." He rejected this. The penalty of "one-and-a-half times," he reterated, "amounts to more or less 6 years." The PFP motion was defeated 16-87.[19] The bill finally passed 110-20.[20]

Between February 1984 and September 1989 the Board granted over ninety percent of the nearly 2,000 applications (one percent of those called up). Almost all belonged to peace churches, however, and the harsh penalty apparently discouraged any nonreligious objector from refusing service between 1983 and 1986.[21] Yet there were other forms of resistance. As immigration declined and emigration increased, South Africa experienced a net outflow in 1986 (for the first time since 1978), which increased in 1987.* Polls found that more than half the male students at Rhodes University in 1987 and two-thirds of those at the University of Cape Town in 1988 were contemplating emigration; the number of degree-holders emigrating annually was a fourth of the degrees awarded.[22] Many others refused to serve. At the first call-up after troops were deployed in the townships following the 1985 Emergency only *half* the conscripts appeared (although the Defence Minister later withdrew this figure). In 1987 and 1988 more than a third of Commando and Citizen Force members sought deferments or failed to appear. Suicide attempts increased from 261 in 1985 to 404 in 1987.[23]

Black Sash's 1983 annual conference issued the first call to end compulsory military service. At the fourth national COSG conference a few months later a hundred delegates from numerous anti-apartheid organizations

---

*In response to the Vaal uprising, immigration declined from 10,775 to 7,959 in the first four months of 1985 compared to that period in 1984, while emigration increased from 2,459 to 2,948. WM 12 (8.23.85). White emigration outstripped immigration in 1986, 12,679 to 6,947, a dramatic inversion of the previous year's 10,709 to 17,195. *Hansard* q.930 (reply by Home Affairs Minister to N.J.J. Olivier, PFP) (9.17.87). The *Weekly Mail* began carrying advertisements like "Moving Overseas? Aran International Furniture Removals & Storage." WM 28 (5.16.86). The outflow was pronounced among professionals in 1987: doctors (93/52), attorneys (51/1), architects (28/10), scientists (133/86), health services (274/142), computer scientists (131/65), accountants (222/64), and educators (253/91). *Hansard* q. 95 (Home Affairs Minister to P.G. Soal, PFP) (2.24.88).

launched the End Conscription Campaign, which immediately established branches in Cape Town, Johannesburg, and Durban, expanding to most English-speaking university towns within three years. Although it sought to appear apolitical by declining to join UDF, it was supported by some fifty organizations, most of which belonged to UDF. In 1984 COSG established the Conscription Advice Service for men seeking alternatives to the military. Protests at English-speaking universities prevented the SADF from establishing Military Units (similar to ROTC). The Anglican Church resolved in 1985 to ban cadet programs from its secondary schools.[24] The ECC quickly attracted political hostility. During the debate on the Defence Appropriation bill in May 1985 a Conservative MP accused it of "sabotaging" military preparedness and "committing treason by doing so" and called for an investigation.[25]

When the ECC organized its first mass event in September 1985, a Stop the Call-Up Peace Festival at the University of the Witwatersrand, the government denied a visa to a Brazilian cardinal, searched the homes of twenty ECC members, and detained five leaders for two weeks. Nevertheless, several hundred people heard anti-apartheid notables and statements of support from 150 foreign organizations.[26] At the same time the ECC launched its "Troops Out of the Township" campaign with a three-week fast in support of the demand that conscripts be able to refuse township service. Harald Winkler and Ivan Toms (both refusing call-ups) fasted the entire time, as did Richard Steele (a detained ECC leader); more than a thousand joined for a day or two. Toms was visited by some sixty conscripts uneasy about National Service and received support from Jewish, Hindu, and Moslem groups in South Africa, as well as Christian groups abroad. The local press gave extensive, sympathetic coverage. Thousands attended rallies in Cape Town, Port Elizabeth, and Grahamstown to celebrate the end of the fast. Toms told supporters: "As a Christian I am obliged to say no, to say never again will I put on that SADF uniform." A week later he criticized cadet programs to secondary school students who had just formed the Pupil Awareness and Action Group.[27] Deputy Defence Minister Adriaan Vlok promptly accused the ANC of using the ECC to "achieve evil goals"; Defence Minister Malan added his condemnation two weeks later. An Afrikaans newspaper headlined "Onslaught on White Boys...To Cause the Government to Fall" and "The ECC's Politics Reveal Red" but was forced by the Media Council to concede distortions and give the ECC space to state its case. In November the police briefly detained Ivan Toms.[28]

At its second national conference in February 1986 the ECC launched an alternative service campaign "Working for Peace: Construction not Conscription," placing more than 600 volunteers in a wide variety of projects. In June the South African Catholic Bishops' Conference called for an end to conscription, and the Methodist Synod declared that members entering townships as soldiers violated church principles.[29]

Again there was a strong counterattack. In February Defence Minister Malan refused to reply to a Parliamentary question by the PFP about the number called up who had failed to report because the previous year's figures had been "misused by a certain organisation."[30] In March the House of Assembly debated a motion supporting conscription. The proponent condemned conscientious objection for political reasons, declaring that "anyone who supports the cause of the terrorist against South Africa and its people and whose sympathy lies with the ANC and with Swapo does not deserve to be a South African." Such people should be court-martialed. A Nationalist quoted a letter to the *Sunday Times* describing the ECC as part of a peace movement "in which innocent people are manipulated by activists who carry out the aims of the Soviet Union." The PFP replied by moving that conscription of whites be replaced by non-racial volunteers. This prompted the Conservatives to call for conscription into three racially separate forces and condemn Defence Minister Malan (whom they ridiculed as "Magtelose" or "powerless," a pun on his first name, Magnus) for allowing "any Black soldier" to "become the head of the SA Defence Force."[31]

Two months later a PFP member urged that "the whole question of objection on moral, ethical and religious grounds be reexamined" but hastened "to make it very clear" that he was "not a supporter of the End Conscription Campaign." His Conservative opponent inisisted that "the young Progs and the End Conscription Campaign, the ECC, are hand in glove." The ECC was "financed from countries abroad" and had "an ally in the United on Apartheid of the UNO." It was "actually concerned with support for an onslaught with the aim of overthrowing the Government of South Africa by means of violence." He rejected any expansion of conscientious objection beyond religious grounds because "in the case of religion... one can test it against a basic, consistent standpoint adopted by a specific denomination [but] in the case of conscientious objections one has no such objective test."[32]

In March police arrested Janet Cherry, Port Elizabeth ECC chair, for possessing illegal drugs (which she claimed they planted in an outside bathroom) but never charged her. Under the second Emergency declared on June 12 government promulgated regulations making it illegal to "incite the public or any person... to discredit or undermine the system of compulsory military service." Although the ECC challenged them, Justice John Didcott found them sufficiently precise to be enforced. The government detained at least seventy-five ECC activists, raided offices and homes, confiscated documents, restricted those released to their homes, and forced another thirty underground. The Cape Town Police Commissioner banned the ECC "Arts Festival '86: Towards a People's Culture" a few days before it was to begin. Activists suffered obscene telephone calls, death threats, assaults, and fire bombs; their cars' tires were slashed, wheel nuts loosened, and brake fluid drained. Defence Minister Malan denounced the ECC as "political agitators... [who] are possibly unconsciously being used by the ANC." The right-wing *Aida Parker Newsletter* published an enlarged special issue with three times the usual press-run, linking the ECC to a "vast Soviet active measures apparatus" and denouncing it as part of a "foreign subsidised tele-guided psychological warfare weapon aimed at gutting our defences and delivering us, bound, to our foe." Copies were sent to 1,300 white school principals and distributed to soldiers by the SADF.[33]

The SADF began 1987 by taking full-page advertisements in two Sunday newspapers reassuring conscripts about military service. Emergency regulations prevented the ECC from publishing a full reply. A Nationalist MP used the February budget debate to brand the ECC an ANC tool because Oliver Tambo had praised it in a speech celebrating the Congress's seventy-fifth anniversary and the two organizations received funds from the same international sources and had similar objectives. The ECC had "forged open personal links with the Helsinki-based War Resisters International... [which] has been identified as a component of the Moscow strategy of 'active measures.'" Ignoring the Chairman's ruling that he was out of order he demanded an investigation.[34] When the ECC sent call-up papers to Defence Minister Malan under the "Peace Act of 1987," he accused them of being "a direct enemy of the SADF" and subsequently told Parliament that South Africa could not allow the ECC to destroy the country's ability to fight communism. Nearly a hundred ECC activists remained in detention, although the state declined to prosecute nine charged with disseminating subversive statements. A new edition of the *Aida Parker Newsletter* contained documents the police had confiscated from the ECC (reinforcing charges that government supported the publication). Despite this onslaught, however, twenty-three men announced in a Cape Town church in August that they would refuse to serve, and many of them subsequently addressed student and religious meetings. Later that year politicians, corporations, clerics, academics, writers, and journalists endorsed the "Let ECC Speak" campaign.[35]

In 1987 Justice Stegmann sentenced Lotz, a religious objector, to community service for 1.5 times the period for which he *had been* called up. In response the government tabled the Defence Amendment Bill, 1987 retroactively reaffirming that the mandatory sentence was 1.5 times the period for which a serviceman *could be* called up (community service for religious objectors and prison for all others), while giving the Minister discretion to shorten it. A Nationalist MP denounced variation in sentences as an "untenable situation." The PFP condemned both the severity and rigidity of sentences. "The purpose of providing alternative service for conscientious objectors is not to 'straf' [punish] them." There had been no "rush" to qualify; aside from Jehovah's Witnesses, only about forty men a year were categorized as religious objectors. "[V]ery few servicemen ever serve the maximum term for which they can be called up." Furthermore, "six years' imprisonment is an extremely harsh sentence.... This is a sentence imposed on people who have been convicted of murder, rape, sedition.... In order to find some form of comparison we have to look to the Eastern Bloc countries, because in none of the Western countries will we find anything that comes close to this." The "administrative convenience of a Government department" was "not sufficient reason to make the legislation retrospective." A Nationalist insinuated that his PFP colleague "wants to create some leeway for members of Parliament or from his party who do not wish to do national service." If the bill failed "it will be the thin end of the wedge, and we shall be allowing the white-anting activities aimed at undermining our Defence Force to gain momentum and eventually succeed." "[E]veryone who refuses to perform national service for his fatherland is behaving like a parasite towards those loyal people who do their share for their country." A PFP MP replied that the children of some members—though certainly not his own— had fundamental objections to military service. "I do not then want to place that son of mine in the position of either having to go to jail for six years or having to do community service for six years of his life." A Nationalist responded by endorsing "punishment for those who want to do nothing at all." Otherwise "there would be a deluge of applicants, because then one is opening the gate to all the end conscription campaigners and similar people who, for all kinds of negative reasons, amongst them communistically inspired reasons, do not want to do national service." He quoted the Defence Minister in the 1983 debate—"community service will be just less than six years"—and added: "With all due respect...we cannot quite understand how the Supreme Court's decision could be the very opposite." A PFP MP sought to minimize the issue: the 755 categorized as religious objectors by June 1986 were 0.2 percent of those called up, "an absolutely insignificant number." In Europe, eight out of twenty-one countries had volunteer armies, and the others allowed objection on broader grounds, without punishment. "All of the objectors I have ever spoken with or met are absolutely sincere in their beliefs." A Nationalist retorted that any extension of the grounds for objection "will surely be giving the End Conscription Campaign a blank cheque." He quoted the *Aida Parker Newsletter* that the "heavily foreign-financed" ECC was "potentially the most dangerous political movement to emerge in the current national crisis." The Chairman had to cut off these attacks. The Deputy Defence Minister concluded the debate by reiterating that the bill was "necessary for the creation of uniformity and to remove the possibility of differing interpretations." "It is our interests, South Africa's interests, that are at stake and our freedom that is being threatened. This country's survival is at stake." He assured members that the Minister would show "great compassion" for religious objectors doing community service. But it was impossible to "make provision for the so-called political and conscientious objector," some of whom "lack the moral fibre to defend this country." The bill passed 122-18, with only the PFP and NDM objecting.[36]

At the year's end, just hours before completing their National Service, three soldiers were arrested for allegedly disclosing military secrets and held in solitary confinement for twenty-one days. Heinrich Mönnig, Peter Pluddemann, and Desmond Thompson, good friends, served at Western Province Command Headquarters in Cape Town. The court-martial president rejected their lawyers' objection that the military could not give them a fair trial. A fourth "friend" who had taped their conversations testified that Pluddemann was outraged by the SADF campaign against the ECC and wanted to warn it. Pluddemann agreed; Mönnig said he only wanted to expose lax military security and planned to denounce the others; and Thompson claimed he had never planned to act. Although the SADF conceded it had sought to discredit the ECC, the court martial denounced the accused's "despicable act of undermining the SADF in a time of crisis." Finding that their actions came close to "mutiny," it sentenced them to eighteen months in Detention Barracks, ordering their immediate incarceration. The Western Province Commanding Officer released them pending confirmation of sentence on condition that they speak to no one. When it was confirmed a month later they were told to report to military police that afternoon. Just before the deadline they obtained a stay of execution from the Supreme Court, which also gave them access to the court martial record for the first time. *The Cape Times* immediately broadcast the allegations of SADF dirty tricks on its front page, and the Sunday papers followed suit the next day.

Two weeks later, when the Defence Ministry obtained an order restricting the record to the court and lawyers, much of the damage had been done. The ECC had held a press conference to condemn the smear campaign. The record disclosed that, under cover of the fictitious Anti-Liberal Alliance, the SADF had plastered posters all over Cape Town: ECC Does It from Behind, ECC—Every Coward's Choice, ECC Members Are Yellow, ECC Believes in Fairy Tales, ECC's Rautenbach Exposed as Branch Informer, ECC Probes Gay Membership, ECC Talks with Irish Guerillas Refreshing. Pamphlets accused the ECC of being an "extension of Moscow's web" and helping Umkhonto we Sizwe. T-shirts declared "End Communism Campaign" and "I Love SADF." In May 1987 an army helicopter dropped pamphlets on an ECC fair.*

In June the SADF review council upheld the court martial convictions while reducing the sentences. But in August 1989 the Supreme Court held

*The Defence Minister had denied at the time that the helicopter belonged to the SAP or SADF. *Hansard* qs. 154–56 (P.G. Soal, PFP; J. van Eck, Independent) (6.16.87). After an "investigation," Law and Order Minister Vlok maintained that the helicopter in question had been at an aviation company for servicing but refused to identify the company. *Hansard* q. 1087 (P.G. Soal, PFP) (10.6.87), qs. 2-3 (Soal) (2.16.88). He would not disclose whether the pilot had filed a flight plan. *Hansard* q. 324 (P.G. Soal, D.J.N. Malcomess, PFP) (3.8.88). But the Minister of Transport Affairs later acknowledged that flight plans were required and there were only two helicopter service companies in Cape Town. *Hansard* q. 536 (Soal) (3.16.88). Malan ultimately claimed he had learned it was an SADF helicopter only in June 1988, when he informed Vlok and the Deputy Defence Minister. He had not corrected the earlier "error" in reply to an August 1988 Parliamentary question because the matter was sub judice! *Hansard* q. 2210 (S.S. van der Merwe, PFP) (8.30.88), q. 249 (S.S. van der Merwe) (3.7.89).

that the military tribunal was insufficiently impartial and nullified the convictions. The SADF claim that civil courts lacked jurisdiction because the country was in a state of war would have "a dramatic, if not devastating, impact on the rule of law in this country." The court found that the prosecution witness had entrapped the accused, offering them military documents provided by his superiors. The Appellate Division dismissed the state's appeal three years later.[37]

On the basis of the court martial's exposure of dirty tricks the ECC applied to the Supreme Court in March 1988 for an order restraining SADF harassment. Five hours after being served, the SADF asked the court to hold all hearings in camera. When the court granted the ECC interim relief four days later it prohibited the organization from publicizing the victory and extended the secrecy order. A ten-page annexure to the founding affidavit detailed seventy incidents: damage to property (including tampering with cars, which endangered lives), burglary and robbery, assault, defamatory and homophobic graffiti, harassing and obscene telephone calls, counterfeit posters and pamphlets, false advertisements offering ECC members' property for sale, and death and bomb threats. In April 1987 Ivan Toms had called the police, who apprehended four young white men with military haircuts putting up anti-ECC posters. After a secret conversation with the suspects, the police allowed them to "escape" and failed to investigate further, although Toms had reported the car registration number.

The state admitted putting up posters and dropping leaflets, but its campaign was "necessary for the efficient defence and protection of the Republic of South Africa." Because the ECC had "reduced the effectiveness of any overt counter-measures… it has accordingly become necessary for the SADF to resort to covert measures in order to meet the propaganda threat." The ECC had not shown that these "legitimate counter measures" caused harm. Again the SADF contested the court's jurisdiction and justified its actions on the ground that "a war in which the RSA is engaged actually prevails within the territory of South West Africa and elsewhere in Southern Africa." There was a "real danger" the ECC would demoralize and demotivate conscripts and "weaken the will to war… of the population as a whole." The ECC displayed "sympathy with, if not allegiance to, at least some of the forces with which the SADF is currently involved," as evidenced by the ANC's approbation. Appearing for the applicants, Sydney Kentridge SC called these arguments "the pretension of a junta of South American generals in a country in which the army acts as an independent force."

Justice Selikowitz ordered the application heard in open court (while prohibiting disclosure of some court martial documents). War did not actually prevail, nor had martial law been declared. The ECC was a "lawful organisation. It has a legal right to recruit members and to canvass for funds without unlawful interference." "The deliberate use of false statements of a type calculated to cause harm is an abuse of the right to criticise and is *prima facie* unlawful." He accepted Kentridge's contention that "it hardly lay in the mouths of the respondents to question the harm they avowedly set out to create." He made the interdict permanent in October 1988, awarding costs for the government's "vexatious" request to hear the case in camera and its "unrepentant attitude."[38]

In May 1988 a Nationalist MP resumed the attack, associating the PFP with the ECC, commending the University of Stellenbosch for prohibiting Ivan Toms from speaking on campus, and praising the Home Affairs Minister for issuing a warning to the ECC publication *Out of Step*. The Deputy Defence Minister thanked the backbencher for having "exposed that organisation as it has not been exposed for a long time." He reported that the SAP had just arrested "four suspected White terrorists" in possession of "the biggest consignment of arms the Police had ever seized…the kind used to commit acts of terror among innocent civilians." "[T]hey were clearly members of the ECC" and two were national service evaders.[39]

Individual Defiance: 1980–88

While collective opposition to conscription mounted, an increasing number of individuals refused to serve.[40] Between 1978 and 1983 a dozen non-members of peace churches suffered up to two years in Detention Barracks and prison, sometimes in solitary confinement and on dry rations. In 1982 the first black Namibian claimed conscientious objector status but was rebuffed by the courts.[41] The Board for Religious Objection rejected David Hartman's application on the ground that his Buddhism did not include belief in a Supreme Being; but the Free State Supreme Court overruled it, and a bill to add this requirement failed to pass.[42] Dr. Leslie London was the first Jew to be granted noncombatant status, with support from rabbis in Cape Town and Bloemfontein.[43] After Rashid Rooinasie refused to serve in the South-West Africa Territorial Force, Imam Rashid Omar, president of the Muslim Youth Movement, warned against conscripting Muslims: "Islam views apartheid and the present government as an embodiment of evil and immorality."[44] Philip Wilkinson, an unemployed butcher who had completed National Service and three Commando camps, refused further service in June 1985 after visiting Port Elizabeth townships with workmates. Denied exemption because his universal pacifism was not based on religious belief, he refused fourteen call-ups over fifteen months before being arrested during an ECC rally in May 1986 and sent to Detention Barracks. Although the charges were provisionally dropped, government detained him under the Second Emergency and refiled the charges. There were seven postponements in this first prosecution under the new law, partly because the state was unable to prove that call-up papers had been issued. Instead of contesting guilt, however, Wilkinson accused the SADF of military atrocities in Namibia and the townships and support for apartheid. He concluded: "I have in my heart an absolute conviction that what I am doing is right. I will not sacrifice my life or lend my body to the defence of apartheid." Declaring that he could not allow Wilkinson to "disrupt the SADF and the entire administration of the country," the magistrate fined him R200 immediately and four monthly installments of R100.[45] Shortly after his conviction, the two most widely publicized prosecutions began to take shape.

Ivan Toms

During a national tour against conscription Ivan Toms publicly declared his refusal to attend a July 1987 camp. "I feel there is a need to strengthen non-racialism in a small way by showing that whites can also make a costly commitment to the struggle for justice."[46] When his call-up was cancelled with five days' notice he reiterated his intention not to serve at the next camp on November 12. His mother offered unqualified support, but his father, a World War II veteran, had reservations: "I don't agree with what Ivan is doing but I admire how he stands out." At an ECC meeting in Port Elizabeth in early November he stated: "I have thought hard and prayed about my decision and it is not something I'm doing lightly... nor do I consider myself a martyr."

Two nights before the camp a meeting of 500 people gave him three standing ovations, while UDF Western Cape chairman Dullah Omar and independent MP Jan van Eck saluted him. He responded with typical modesty: "We are all struggling in our small ways for a new South Africa. I unfortunately just often get pushed to the front, but we are all part of that growing group."[47] He attended a prayer service at St. George's Cathedral the morning he was to report, thanking the 200 present for their "incredible support." "Members of the congregation were called to lay their hands on Dr Toms... and tears streamed down his cheeks as he was given a prolonged hug by Moulana Faried Essack of the Call of Islam." An hour later he was arrested at 3 Medical Battalion for refusing to serve. He wore an ECC tie but not his military uniform "because it's an identification with the apartheid system and I want to be rid of it."[48] While awaiting trial he addressed student meetings at the Universities of Natal and the Witwatersrand. Expressions of solidarity came from the South African Council of Churches, South African Catholic Bishops' Conference, Methodist Church of South Africa, European Parliament, and Australian Board of Missions. The day before his trial Moulana Essack and Archbishop Tutu addressed an open-air inter-church service for him.[49]

During the trial the Wynberg Magistrate's Court, Cape Town, was filled with supporters, who had to take turns, and Toms was interviewed by foreign reporters at every recess. The Attorney General took the unusual step of assigning the prosecution to P.J. Marais, who had an LL.B. degree. The first witness, Dr. Nikolaas Liebenberg, commanding officer of the 3 Medical Battalion, testified about the call-up. Toms's attorney had written in August protesting the last minute cancellation of the July call-up and noting a similar occurrence in May 1984.

[I]t should now be clear to you that our client is not prepared to perform any form of service in the SADF whatsoever.... [O]ur client cannot help but gain the impression that you will persist in your pattern of calling our client up and cancelling the call-ups shortly before they are due to commence. This is a source of considerable inconvenience to our client and, if it were to happen again, would be indicative of a campaign simply to harass our client.

He threatened to seek Supreme Court relief. Liebenberg replied in October, explaining the practice of calling up more men than needed (because of uncertainty about who would be available) and urging Toms to apply to the Board. Before this arrived, however, the attorney sent a registered letter reiterating Toms's refusal to serve and declaring that another cancellation would be viewed as harassment. The attorney wrote a third time three days before the camp, stating that Toms would refuse to serve. A lawyer later commented that the defense had deliberately "forced the issue."

Cross-examined by advocate Edwin Cameron, Liebenberg said Toms was the first person who ever expressed reluctance to serve in the townships and denied that service could endanger his excellent medical work in Crossroads: "in the north of Southwest [i.e., Namibia], where we work in our uniforms amongst the local population... there is no animosity whatsoever." He had never seen the Geneva Conventions and did not know where there were copies. (Col. J.T. Nel, commanding officer until May 1987, said the unit used to have a copy but it might have been misplaced. In a unit of 1,800 "it is obviously impossible to have every fine detail carried over to all members.")

Capt. Stanley Russell, personnel officer of the 3 Medical Battalion, related Toms's military record. Toward the end of his first year of National Service in 1978 Toms wrote the Surgeon General:

I have been a committed Christian trying to follow the teaching and leading of Jesus Christ for seven years. In the last year and a half I have been challenged as to what following him means especially in the case of loving one's enemy. ... Though I do not feel called to refuse all military service, I believe I can only fill a non-combatant role. ...on grounds of Christian conscience I will not be willing to carry a weapon in the operational area or elsewhere.

Both Liebenberg and Nel testified that doctors were urged to carry sidearms in Namibia. The Senior Medical Officer of the Eastern Province Command granted Toms's request, noting "your personal convictions are respected by this headquarters," but he reprimanded Toms for going over his head to the Surgeon General.

Toms was not called for a camp in 1980 (thereby receiving credit for sixty days) but sought deferment for a February 1982 call-up.

> I am presently the only doctor in charge of the Empilisweni
> SACLA Clinic. This is a private clinic recognized and subsidized
> by the Cape Provincial Administration Hospitals Department
> which provides primary medical care for Xhosa speaking blacks
> in the squatter camp of Crossroads near Cape Town. ... We see
> approximately 90 patients per day six days a week.

Granted that request, he refused a one-day shooting parade later that year
as a "recognized non-combatant." He obtained deferment from a February
1983 camp on the same ground as the previous year, noting that he accepted
a salary of R575/month: "I do not know of a doctor who would work for this
salary as a locum with all the other responsibilities as well." Closing the clinic
would deprive some 2,500 patients per month of medical care, "dental, nutri-
tion and relief work and Christian outreach." "As a Christian I seek to live by
the Bible and see this community as the place where God has called me to
serve at present." Col. Nel granted the request, testifying that Toms's "duties
were more needed [in Crossroads] and we did have enough doctors in other
places at that stage."

Even though he had not attended camps in nearly four years, Toms wrote
Nel in September 1983:

> After prolonged prayer and seeking God's guidance I regretfully
> find that my Christian conscience will not allow me to continue
> to serve in the SADF, even as a non-combatant Medical Officer.
>
> I have not come to this decision lightly or easily, but I am con-
> vinced that in the light of the Gospel of Jesus Christ this is the
> only option open to me.
>
> I have been doing "National Service" to the nation of South Africa
> by serving the squatter community of Crossroads as the only
> Medical Doctor at a salary of R661 per month for over three years.

After refusing another one-day shooting camp as a non-combatant, Toms
saw Nel in December and wrote him the following March, reiterating his conscientious scruples. Nel replied in April that he had to call Toms for a June
camp, adding that attendance would "be in the best interest of the community you are serving." In court he expressed "sympathy with [Toms's]
viewpoints because... it was really a religious thing with him" but urged the
sensible course of doing the one-month camp each year and continuing to
serve the clinic. "I had no doubt about his sincerity." The June 1984 call-up
was cancelled at the last minute because there were more physicians than
needed and Toms's excuse had "merit... in our Command Group's eyes."
Toms was not called in 1985 or 1986.

That ended the prosecution case. The magistrate was "quite surprised" by
the defense decision to offer no evidence but was equally brief. "It is as the
prosecutor has indicated that the record speaks for itself. The evidence

before the Court is undisputed evidence which clearly proves the commission of the offence charged. In the circumstances then you are found guilty as charged."[50] Although the prosecution offered no evidence on the sentence, the defense now put the SADF on trial.

Toms began with his biography. The son of a meter reader, he attended high school in Durban and then spent a year in the United States. On returning,

> I was very much challenged by a friend of mine who had been at school with me, who had... played rugby and "jolled" around.... [H]e was changed by a conversion experience and that was a real challenge to me and then personally I looked at the whole Bible afresh and was involved in a deep personal commitment in August '71....

At the University of Cape Town he served on the YMCA committee for three years and headed the Christian fellowship at his residence hall. Joining a hundred students demonstrating against Bantu education at St. George's Cathedral in 1972, he saw some dragged from behind the altar and beaten; his nose was broken and he had baton weals on his back. He interned at Kimberley Provincial Hospital.

> [F]or the first time I met blacks who were my equal or my superior.... [T]he best physician in the hospital by far was an Indian doctor.... [I also saw] the disparity between the white side of hospital where there were many empty beds and lots of nurses and the black side of the hospital which was overcrowded, understaffed and pressurised.

Through the Anglican Church's Nomad Programme he became close to Pakamile Majebe, who "fell" to his death from a sixth-floor window during security police interrogation.

Deeply troubled by his call-up for National Service, Toms considered emigrating to the United States, telephoning the family with whom he had been an exchange student. He consulted Archbishop Denis Hurley in Durban and attempted to contact the Quaker Church to become a conscientious objector. He even booked a flight to London, cancelling it the day before reporting.

> I went in confused and unhappy but feeling that I did not really have any voice. Most folk had advised me not to leave the country and rather to stay and use my skills in this country. I have gained them in this country and I really want to use them in service to this country.

After three months of basic training he was commissioned a full lieutenant and spent six months at Mount Coke Hospital and three at Cecilia Makawane Hospital (both in Ciskei).

I was briefed by a major in military intelligence who told me as he perceived it my role was to gather information from the patients that I saw. He went so far as to say that if teachers and doctors and development officers in the civic action programme had done their work properly they would have known about Soweto '76 before it happened. And that really disturbed me as it was in conflict with my medical ethics which called me to not divulge any information about my patients to others.

From April through September 1979 he served at 2 Military Hospital in Cape Town. Whereas there had been one physician for 10,000 people in Ciskei, this pediatric ward had more doctors than patients. He spent the first and last quarters of 1979 on the Namibia-Angola border.

[From] the black people in the hospitals and in the clinics [I felt] that there was this coldness, this sense of being rejected.... Perhaps even more or just as disturbing for me as a Christian was that the missionaries who worked in the Lutheran hospitals there, they are nursing sisters from Norway and Sweden, were also cold and rejecting towards me because I wore that uniform. ... [B]eing a noncombatant was a compromise and it was in conflict now with my conscience. I had felt that I was just part—a cog in that machine, the military machine....

His only further military service was two lectures, one on the threat of Soviet domination in Southern Africa and the other a graphic demonstration of the reasons for switching to the R4 rifle, whose high projectile bullet "tumbles and then loses all its power in the body and damages people and kills much more readily than the old R1."

After eighteen months in the military he obtained leave to attend a South African Christian Leadership Assembly (SACLA) meeting.

There were 3,000 Christians, both black and white, meeting in Pretoria for a week trying to discern the way forward for the church in South Africa, to be true to God.... We had many speakers, including people like Dr Koornhof and Chief Gatsha Buthelezi, and [I] felt very first of all depressed and confused and then felt challenged to actually, if I was going to be a white South African Christian doctor in this country then I needed to really do something positive to change things, rather than to just be at a hospital or working in private practice. ...[I] looked at the medical needs close at home, close to Cape Town, and Crossroads at that stage had 30,000 Xhosa-speaking blacks and no permanent medical facilities.... I spoke to the government to ask them if they planned to put up a day hospital there and their response was that Crossroads was a temporary phenomenon and it would go away.... So I talked to 25 people from Crossroads who had gone to the SACLA conference and with Rev David Russell about the needs there and the possibility of a Christian clinic that would really be expressing Christ's love to the poor and the oppressed and they were very excited about that and from those small beginnings the clinic opened in June 1980.

During the six years Toms directed Empilisweni Clinic (Xhosa for "the place where people are healed") he became deeply involved in Anglican activities, serving as associate member of the staff at St. John's Parish, sharing Holy Communion every Wednesday morning, chairing the social responsibility committee for five years, and serving on the Parish Council for four, the Missionary and Training Committee for five, and the Diocesan Council. As a delegate to the Cape Town Diocesan Synod in 1983 he seconded a motion to establish an alternative to National Service; as a delegate to the all-South Africa Provincial Synod two years later he seconded a motion to end conscription and proposed a motion on conscientious objection. He studied theology by correspondence at UNISA, expecting to complete a B.Th. degree at the end of 1988.

He also was active in ECC from its founding. During his three-week fast in September-October 1985 he spoke to nearly 3,000 people: "There were Muslims, Jews who came to join me and fast for a day or longer in the cathedral and just confirmed for me I think that you cannot separate one's faith from one's politics and one's action...." His opposition to SADF activities intensified.

> [S]ince October 1984 the SADF have been actively involved in the black townships of South Africa.... [W]hat was a border war in Namibia thousands of kilometres away has now become effectively a civil war in the black townships of our country.... It just suppresses people and oppresses people and actually has now become the ultimate pillar of apartheid rather than in any sense a shield behind which political change is taking place.

Three events at Empilisweni intensified his antipathy for the military. The severe drought of 1983 filled the squatter camps bordering Crossroads.

> [T]he South African government's approach was to class them as illegal immigrants and their structures as illegal structures, and day in and day out for three weeks the Administration Board officials and riot police would come into Crossroads, break down those shelters, burn the plastic and branches and stand around till half past four, leaving mainly women and young children in the rain and cold of the Cape winter, and we in the clinic were treating numerous cases of bronchitis and people who were sick from this result. That only ended on the one Friday

> when some of the women tried to hold onto those branches, they were tired of cutting more branches from the forest and to the riot police that constituted a riot and they used teargas, sneeze machines, rubber bullets and police dogs to quell the riot and we in the clinic treated the injuries, a woman with a fractured skull from a rubber bullet, another with a ragged dog bite of the calf muscle, children with an allergic response to the teargas.... [U]p till that point I had had an intellectual problem with going into the army, and now having seen the realities of apartheid and the viciousness of apartheid and seeing black people treated as if they were a non human people, as if they were animals, meant that I could not be part of that system. The court might think that that was the riot police, not the SADF, but to the people in Crossroads and to the children in Crossroads they were all seen as the "amajoni," the soldiers, to be feared and hated.... [To] the black communities that I work in at present... if I put on that uniform and especially to the youth in that community I would be identified with the enemy.

In February 1985 the government began destroying Crossroads and moving inhabitants to Khayelitsha, thirty-two kilometers from Cape Town, in furtherance of grand apartheid. In two days the police

> killed 18 people from Crossroads and we treated in the clinic alone 178 injuries. ... The majority were shot in the back when they were running away, with birdshot and buckshot. We had one man brought in shot in the groin with buckshot with a severed femoral artery and even though we put up two drips we could not save his life and he bled to death in front of us and the clinic was like a field hospital with bleeding people all around. We had five bodies in the clinic. Ambulances would not come into the community to pick up the injured...those that were sent into hospital were being arrested and charged with public violence and the proof of their public violence was their injuries.... [Later that year] the army and security police actually surrounded the clinic and asked us for information about shot patients....

In 1986 the witdoeke (vigilantes identified by white headbands) were used to destroy Crossroads squatter settlements.

> Our black staff were threatened because the clinic is in the centre of the Witdoeke area and [staff] live in New Crossroads, which was a more progressive area. The clinic was closed because of those threats to the black staff and within a week, very symbolically on June 16th, the tenth anniversary of the Soweto uprising, the very unit that I belonged to, the South

Africa Medical Service Corps, moved into our clinic, took it over, and army doctors in uniform and with pistols on their belts started treating patients there and medics with rifles in the corner of the dressing room [were] doing dressings, and a clinic that had been a community based clinic, controlled by the community, was now taken over and used by the SADF.

Toms redirected his energies, launching the SACLA Health Project to train community health workers in the townships and exposing UCT medical students to "the real primary health care needs in our country."

Toms concluded by explaining why he had not applied to the Board. To "separate religious objectors from political objectors or moral objectors... is an incredibly arrogant decision that implies that... non-religious people do not have a conscience." He criticized "punitive community service," which was "still compromised" by being "located within the government structure."

> I take this stand because I believe that in a sense it is the one time that I have a choice as a white South African. I can choose to go to prison... rather than to be part of the SADF. I also hope that... in some small way by the symbolic stand and as others who might follow me in this stand, that that might as in the past where the previous 12 COs brought about a change in the Defence Act allowing community service for religious objectors.

Marais, the prosecutor, began his lengthy cross-examination by characterizing Toms's objections as political rather than religious. Toms agreed that he opposed all apartheid institutions but turned around the question whether he would work in a segregated government hospital: "I have not fully thought it through because I have been actively involved in medical work for eight years now outside of the government structures...." Marais got Toms to admit he would be a noncombatant doctor in a just war. He had not been required to carry weapons or violate the Geneva Conventions and felt he performed a valuable service in the Ciskei. Marais tried to use Toms's National Service to throw doubt on the conscientiousness of his scruples.

> *Prosecutor:* The point I am trying to make [is] that living in South Africa it is very difficult to isolate one institution such as the Defence Force and say I am not going to comply with the needs of the Defence Force, but I am prepared to compromise myself regarding all other government institutions....

> *Toms:* I think one does live a life of compromise in South Africa. ... But... I felt this was one choice that I had....

Marais tried to blame the trial on Toms's stubbornness, since the Defence Force had always been "sympathetic" and "would probably" grant further deferments. Toms replied that he "wanted to deal with the issue rather than have it hanging over my head ad infinitum." Marais accused Toms of being "melodramatic" in characterizing the two cancelled camps as "harassment." Toms insisted it was "incredibly psychologically disturbing" and provoked nightmares. "[T]he fear of the unknown is often greater than what you actually deal with.... [O]nce I finished my potential time of imprisonment, I will no longer be liable for call-up...." Marais described the cancelled camps as a mere "inconvenience," insinuating that they primarily affected

> the campaign, the lecture tours, the support groups, the pamphlets that get distributed.... [O]ne of the aims of the ECC at that time was to publicise your stance...as extensively as possible...and a cancellation at the last minute is inclined to let the whole publicity fizzle out a little bit and it has to be built up with the next call-up.

But Toms observed that the repeated call-ups and cancellations actually generated more publicity.

Marais sought to embarrass Toms in several ways. He tried to show that the requested transfer from Ciskei was motivated by the desire to be near his friends and fiancée in Cape Town.

> *Prosecutor:* Is it possible that you did not want the Court to see you as any other person that would use—do things for his own selfish needs and not for some or other altruistic end?

> *Toms:* No, I would like the Court to see me as an ordinary person, a person like anybody else who tries to be true to what he believes.

Marais then tried to paint Toms not as a disinterested doctor but rather as a partisan of the comrades against the established Crossroads leadership. Toms responded that he had consulted the Crossroads mayor about his refusal to serve and that during the conflict between vigilantes and squatters the clinic was "very careful always to offer equal medical treatment to both sides." He had personally followed a witdoek to ensure "there was no prejudice [in] treatment against him by anyone on the staff." He admitted, however, that the witdoeke were happy to have the SADF running the clinic.

Marais's final strategy was to depict Toms as a dangerous radical. After the SADF took over the clinic he traveled for seven months, taking a State Department tour of the United States and visiting France, the Netherlands, England, and Nicaragua. Marais naturally was most interested in the last, but Toms parried that he wanted to see whether this "post-revolutionary society" was "going to be doctor orientated or were they going to be more orientated at a community level in terms of health care, and also to look at church/state relations...." Toms admitted attending the 1987 Harare conference on apartheid and violence against children; thirteen members of the ANC executive were present, and he had spoken to Ruth Mompati and Joe Slovo.

The prosecutor saved his lowest blow for last—a smear tactic reminiscent of Senator Joseph McCarthy.*

> *Prosecutor:* To what extent do you consider yourself to be a champion of gay and lesbian rights?
>
> *Toms:* I do not consider myself to be a champion, but it would be an issue that I am concerned about.
>
> *Prosecutor:* You have mentioned a large number of communities and organisations and committees in your evidence in chief of which you have been members or in which you have been involved, but you never dealt with any of your involvement in this particular issue, and you were also involved in...the Lesbians and Gays Against Oppression Committee, you were a founding member, were you not? ...
>
> *Toms:* [admitted being involved] [T]he aims of the organisation were to work towards a non racial, a non sexist, democratic non heterosexist...South Africa....
>
> *Prosecutor:* ...[D]id you also enjoy the full support of your church in this particular line of activities?
>
> *Toms:* I received the support of my parish priest and of the majority of the staff....
>
> *Prosecutor:* How would you anticipate...the Synod of the Province would have reacted?
>
> *Toms:* I know of many bishops who would be supportive of my involvement and many priests but I would not like to know what the vote would have been.

Marais had assured defense counsel Cameron before the trial that he had decided not to use a lot of damaging information. Cameron believed this was alleged ANC links or the fact that Toms was gay. The defense had deliberated about airing the issue, since Toms had identified himself as gay on several university campuses. But though some gay activists urged this strat-

---

*McCarthy attacked the character of a young assistant of the Army's counsel, Joseph Nye Welch, by publicly disclosing that he had once been a member of the National Lawyers' Guild, provoking Welch's famous rebuke: "Have you no shame, sir?" See De Antonio (1964). Winnie Mandela used the same tactic in defending against charges of complicity in the kidnapping and assault of four youths from the Soweto house of Rev. Paul Verryn, whom she accused of homosexuality and seduction. George Bizos SC, one of the most famous anti-apartheid advocates, continued the smear in what was his last trial in private practice. Gilbey (1993: 183–99, 205–06, 259).

egy, the defense decided to make it a "single issue case." The Organisation of Lesbian and Gay Activists supported the decision. Cameron felt Marais had played the homophobic card because Toms's testimony had gone so well and was "absolutely livid" Marais had reneged on an implied undertaking.[51]

Patrick Russell, diocese bishop of Grahamstown and the second defense witness, had written his doctoral dissertation on "A Theological Critique of the Christian Pacifist Perspective with reference to the Position of John." He met Toms in 1974 when they were praying in St. George's Cathedral for those arrested. After the 1979 SACLA conference they had a long conversation about Toms's plan to establish a Crossroads clinic, which Russell saw as "a most wonderful witness of missionary involvement in a great area of need." The 1982 Provincial synod resolution on religious objectors expressed "our serious doubts about the legitimacy of a military system whose role is increasingly seen as the protector of a profoundly immoral and unjust social order." Russell also helped draft the 1985 resolution calling for alternative service (which passed 147–1). It criticized the flawed distinction between ethical and religious convictions, narrow range of alternatives, and punitive length.[52] "[W]e must seek to love our enemies… one should not enter any army. And… no Christian should need to justify any decision in conscience not to fight."

Another resolution (passed 147–8) deplored the deepening SADF involvement in supporting apartheid, recognized conscripts' crises of conscience, and urged pastoral assistance to young men "as they seek God's will for them in this matter." Russell called this "a resolution in which we noted the stand that Dr Ivan Toms was taking and not only noted it but gave him full support…." Although Cameron sought Russell's endorsement of Toms's gay activism, the bishop evaded the issue by talking about the constantly changing nature of church doctrine and offering "general sympathy." The prosecutor contented himself with eliciting an admission that the church did not require members to refuse military service.

Rev. John Freeth, rector of St. John's Parish and Toms's friend since 1980, testified to his religious commitment while criticizing the Board for its false dichotomy between universal pacifism and concrete political objections. The Parish Council issued a statement of support for Toms just before the trial, affirming "that his Christian faith is the mainspring from which his action is taken." Just the previous Sunday Archbishop Tutu had said "he was privileged to belong to a church which produced people of the calibre of Dr Ivan Toms." Unlike Russell, Freeth was unequivocal that both he and the executive of the Parish Council supported Toms's involvement in gay and lesbian organizations.

As an expert on international law, Professor John Dugard testified that South Africa had failed to fulfill its obligation under the four Geneva Conventions to educate soldiers about their duties. Given South Africa's illegal occupation of Namibia and its aggressive acts in Angola, Mozambique, Lesotho, Botswana, Zimbabwe, and Zambia, soldiers constantly found themselves in a "conflict situation." It was arguable that individuals would be criminally responsible under the International Convention on the Suppression and Punishment of the Crime of Apartheid and subject to prosecution in any of the eighty-one signatory nations. Marais sought to undercut Dugard's evidence by showing that it reflected his position as "an opponent of the government in a number of fields." They conducted an inconclusive technical exchange over the domestic enforceability of international human rights.

Oswald Shifite, secretary of the Ovamboland Legislative Assembly, graphically described some of the 632 complaints of SADF atrocities he had investigated in the previous six years: a man's face burned by being pressed against an exhaust pipe while soldiers revved the motor, a thirteen-year-old boy burned with cigarette lighters and held over a fire, a woman nine months pregnant raped twice and stabbed when she refused to perform oral sex.[53] Cameron called his performance the best he had seen in seven years of practice: "The effect was electric on the audience, on the public, and on the magistrate...[who] listened with great consideration and attentiveness."

The magistrate passed sentence immediately. The Defence Amendment Act imposed "a mandatory or a compulsory sentence" to "a specific period of imprisonment," which the accused could avoid only by agreeing to serve. It was "a pity" that Toms refused. His unit was consistently "sympathetic" and "very lenient." He had been granted noncombatant status and allowed to serve "in a protected environemnt as opposed to the young soldier who is in the front line." It was "counterproductive" for "a professional man, a medical doctor" to go to jail. The reported atrocities showed that Toms was "more needed upon on the Border than down in Crossroads." But he was "not a criminal. Our jails are there for people who are a menace to society, you...are just the opposite, you have always been an asset to society in the services that you have rendered." Nevertheless, he was compelled to sentence Toms to 1.5 times his unserved obligation, or 630 days, while noting that "you yourself have the power to terminate your imprisonment at any time you wish" by agreeing to serve. Toms embraced and shook hands with many supporters and hugged his father before being led away.[54]

The extensive newspaper coverage was strongly sympathetic. *The Cape Times* front-page headline deplored "Maximum sentence for Toms." Several days later it ran a cartoon showing an armed prison guard looking into Toms's cell while a companion said: "Dangerous customer in there, Van der Merwe...stands for peace and justice and refuses to take up arms."[55] *The Star* declared "'Angel of Crossroads' chooses to follow his conscience."[56] The *Sunday Times* headlined "'Good Samaritan' is sent to jail," noting that Rev. Edward King, Dean of Cape Town, called it "preposterous," evidence that "our system of values has become perverted," while Amnesty International had adopted Toms as a prisoner of conscience.[57] *The Natal Witness* called the sentence "severe" and "excessive." "Surely the court could have exercised its powers of discretion in such a case? Justice has not been seen to be done."[58]

Several papers highlighted the plight of objectors who were not universal pacifists.[59] Two published letters from objectors doing alternative service expressing support for Toms and calling for reform of conscription.[60] Two focused on South Africa's violations of international law.[61] *The New York Times* featured Toms in a long article headlined "More Whites in South Africa Resisting the Draft," which documented increasing emigration and evasion and the anguish of young conscripts.[62] An ECC call for Toms's release was echoed by PFP MP Ken Andrew.[63] Students at the University of Natal-Pietermaritzburg held a silent vigil.[64] The Black Sash passed a resolution supporting all conscientious objectors, with particular reference to Toms.[65] Two UCT pediatricians wrote a letter to the *South African Journal of Medicine* supporting Toms and deploring the loss of physicians unwilling to serve in the military.[66]

Toms appealed to the Supreme Court on two grounds. First, he should be given credit for the two camps from which he was deferred, reducing his jail time to eighteen months. Alternatively, the magistrate had discretion to differentiate between "an accused who acts out of pure self-interest and an accused who acts on the basis of deeply-held beliefs." Penal law should be interpreted for the benefit of the accused. It was "inconceivable" that Parliament intended such a harsh sentence; it used more explicit language when it wanted to fetter courts. Toms's work in Crossroads was equivalent to community service; he should either be released or allowed to do alternative service.[67]

Justice J.G. Foxcroft decided the appeal on November 17.[68] He began by agreeing with Toms's counsel that the case had "some of the elements of a Greek tragedy. It does go to the core of the stresses and strains of the South African situation." Like the magistrate he lauded Toms but also held him responsible for his own punishment.

> It is of course a matter for regret when the provisions of a statute compel a Court to impose imprisonment upon a person whom it does not regard as a criminal. However, it is the onerous duty of the Court to apply the law. One may express the hope that the lawgiver will ameliorate the harshness of the compulsory provisions of this statute by allowing a discretion to the Court. It is a matter for regret that a person of the undoubted quality of the Appellant should have had to serve imprisonment at all.

> On the other hand he is an intelligent man and must have been aware of the consequences of his election not to serve in the SADF as required by the Act. The path which he has taken is not an easy one path but it is one which he has himself chosen.

Because a companion section used the words "not exceeding" to denote a maximum sentence, the legislature must have intended the sentence to be mandatory. Agreeing with the other defense argument, however, he reduced Toms's sentence to 540 days.

On November 29, making similar claims, Toms sought leave to appeal to the Appellate Division, which was granted the next day. Although the state did not oppose bail, the magistrate said Toms had the burden of demonstrating that he would complete his sentence if the appeal failed. The nine months Toms had served, however, was "a fairly severe sentence for a man of your standing and must have been traumatic for you." He released Toms on November 30 on R1,000 bail.[69] Archbishop Tutu welcomed him at the home of Rev. Freeth: "You don't know how proud you make us through the stand you have taken…each person can make a difference by taking a stand—it encouraged the more timid." Toms was "incredibly joyful," "so hyped up about being out that I don't think I will be able to sleep for a week." "But the important thing is that I went in on my own and now we have a real peace movement going." He expressed solidarity with David Bruce, in the fourth month of a six-year sentence, and Charles Bester, facing the same sentence.[70]

Toms related the horrors of prison.[71] For five months he was locked in a six by eight foot cell without any natural light for 22.5 hours a day. He received only one letter a month and no newspapers. "Late at night I felt incredibly lonely and alone. After 10:30 when they switched the lights off it was totally dark, quiet. … I would lie on my bed and the tears would just run down my face." He had been able to cope knowing "there were hundreds of people supporting me." Although Helen Suzman asked Justice Minister Coetzee to allow Toms to work as a prison doctor, that was forbidden. Authorities even deleted "Dr" from his return address. Once, however, Toms saved a prisoner who tried to hang himself.

> I got a taste of what happens to blacks in South Africa, how people are dehumanised by the system. Possibly it is the only time a white person feels what it is like to have the system dehumanise him and treat him as less than a person.

In his fourth month Toms shared a bathroom with Daniel Knipe, known to have severe personality problems manifested in violent behavior. Knipe once was removed from a psychiatric hospital for ripping all the doors off the hinges. The second time Knipe sexually assaulted Toms he responded with a punch—he had never before struck anyone. Knipe beat him severely, inflicting a wound under his eye that required stitches. After being pulled off by other prisoners Knipe was isolated in chains; but ten days later he returned to share the bathroom for twelve days before the incident was publicized. At Knipe's prosecution a psychiatrist testified that Knipe had been assessed several times at Valkenberg Hospital and hospitalized at Stickland and Weskoppies maximum security hospitals. "Reports of street fighting and sexual promiscuity are present with repetitive assaultive behaviour directed at his parents and family members. He is severely personality disordered with a low-normal intelligence." Because he had shown extreme strength he "should be considered highly dangerous." Knipe was convicted of assault, and the Department of Prisons later paid R10,000 to settle Toms's civil claim. Despite all this he was "twice as committed to working for a new South Africa."[72] A year later he called the "total lack of trust" the most disturbing aspect of prison life, especially to those "used to the trust and support that we often find in progressive organisations." Prison authorities treated him as a "Politico," "terrorist" and "communist," and prisoners (all white, of course) would not talk to him.

> [I]nterestingly, as time dragged on and some of the prisoners began to see me as "the doc", there developed an insight that ran something like this. I had stood up to the system that had unjustly (they thought) put them in prison. Therefore I was OK and later on some of the prisoners wanted to know how they could help fight the unjust system when they came out of prison.[73]

David Bruce

When David Bruce was fifteen in Standard 8 (the year schools registered boys for military service) he said to himself some nights: "I'll never serve in the SADF."[74] Of the four other politically conscious boys in his class of 150, one went straight into the army, one secured repeated deferments, one obtained an exemption but stopped doing community service after a year and joined the army, and the last dropped out of university, entered the army, and "came back a complete fascist... so brainwashed, hating SWAPO." Bruce went to university only to avoid the army and became involved with the left, where it was "virtually unacceptable to be in the army," but was so alienated by factionalism that he quit student politics in 1986. "I just find it difficult to cage myself in political organizations." He could not forget the threat of conscription, however. Sitting at his desk writing an essay he would find himself "going over this issue again and again... I don't know how many times." "I was basically in a continual state of uncertainty and indecisiveness and confusion about the whole thing... that's one of the most destructive states of mind that a human being can possibly be in." He rarely talked to people about his moral anguish, however, because when he said "I'm going to go to jail, people would say: 'Oh, you're ridiculous, you're an idiot, you're a fool, completely crazy.'"

At the end of 1986 he failed African Politics 2, his only remaining degree requirement, and was excluded from the university. This was "the time when the South African government was coming down on the democratic movement in the severest kind of way." Seeing a newspaper photograph of trade unionists besieged in COSATU House "I just had the sense of them coming and hauling us out of our houses and shooting us on the pavement outside." The government "was very definitely on a course which would have involved intensifying military conflict in Southern Africa... bloodshed and hatred and racism and madness." When he received a call-up in February 1987 "this was the first time in my life that I'd ever actually had to make a decision about what I was going to do about my call-up." "I prepared myself to confront this decision... making the effort to get physically fit... and to avoid drinking." If the university did not readmit him he decided to go to Zimbabwe, write that he was unavailable for military service, and return. When the university readmitted him at the last minute, Bruce felt "this incredible sense of relief at not having to confront this decision."

Because he had "absolutely no interest in being at university," however, he decided not to apply for another deferment in 1987. He felt temporary "euphoria... this burden of decision at least was off my shoulders." Although his father said he should leave the country, his parents always supported him. A friend who was articled to human rights attorney Kathleen Satchwell introduced Bruce to his employer, who misled him that he might be sentenced to less than six years. Nevertheless, "I didn't anticipate being out of jail prior to the time that I was say, thirty years of age." Satchwell agreed to extricate him from the army if they simply inducted him when he refused service. Bruce even worried they would suspect him of being ANC and torture him. But those fears proved groundless. When nothing happened for five or six months after his August 5 refusal, Bruce decided against joining the 143 men who publicly refused to serve under the aegis of the ECC because "that would have been pretty much putting myself on the line. I still had a hope that they would choose to steer clear of the issue."

Instead, Bruce was charged with refusing to serve and appeared in the Johannesburg Magistrate's Court for the first time four days before Ivan Toms's trial.[75] Although a support group was formed, Bruce refused to let it influence his decisions. He continued to go through "internal agonizing," "fear and anxiety," and "continual uncertainty." Still, he toured South Africa to publicize the case.[76]

The trial before Additional Mag. P.H. Bredenkamp began on July 19. After introducing affidavits showing Bruce's refusal to serve, prosecutor Louisa van der Walt called Staff Sgt. Johan Flattery, a Military Police investigator who had supervised intake on August 5.

> A youngster was brought to me, that was called up for his national service. [H]e stated to me that he is not prepared to do national service. I explained to him, your worship, that there were other avenues of doing national service without the combat units, such as the medical sections, alternatively the administration side of it, or as a chef where he will not be required to do actual fighting. He could not accept that, your worship. ... I then explained to him again that the military set-up in South Africa was not one where we go out and fight battles. We are for the safekeeping of the country.

When the audience of ECC supporters and Wits students erupted with laughter, van der Walt interjected:

Prosecutor: Your worship, with due respect....

Magistrate: [to Flattery] Just a moment please. [to audience] If anyone wish to attend this hearing, it will be appreciated if you remain silent and if any of the members of the public cannot behave themselves, they will be ordered to leave the court immediately. The court hope that this warning is quite clear to everybody. Thank you.

Edwin Cameron, again defense counsel, remembered that he "actually squirmed" when the audience jeered because the young, inexperienced, Afrikaans-speaking prosecutor used ungrammatical English.

Under cross-examination, Flattery testified that deferment was available for "medical disablement, study purposes," but he did not know whether Bruce could have invoked either. He had dealt with conscripts seeking non-combat alternatives.

I refer them to the Exemption Board, with advice from the military police side that we consider him not fit for combat. ... It does not happen very often, but we do find people that are scared of a rifle and they cannot handle it. Those people we do refer and where there is a physical disablement that prevents him from handling a fire-arm, we also refer him to the other side, where there is no combat situation for him.

This was the first time Flattery had encountered political objections, however, which the Board would not consider. Cameron also asked Flattery about the Board for Religious Objection.

Flattery: [T]hey get referred to a special court-martial where they go on trial and they get treated totally different as to the normal solider. They serve with the Department of Manpower after sentence had been passed on them. ...

Cameron: Did you discuss that with the accused?

Flattery: I did, your worship. He was still very serious about his situation as far as refusing to serve under the present government. [They had a long talk.] He said that he was not going to support the government in their effort to suppress the other side of our nation. He was not prepared to support apartheid was his distinct words, your worship.

Cameron: Did he say that the SADF was being used to uphold a racist system?

Flattery: Those were his words, your worship. ... My advice to him was to join the Defence department and that way stay out of prison.

Cameron: Did you respect him though for his moral and political decision in not doing that?

Flattery: Yes, your worship, I did.

After this perfunctory prosecution case, Bruce testified at length.

> From when I was in primary school I just say became aware of the kind of thing that happened in Germany during the period of the Holocaust and say became aware that my own family or my mother's family had suffered as a result of those things and as a result of racism. ... I sort of had a Jewish upbringing in the sense that I went to say a Jewish school... on Saturday mornings...up to the time that I had my Bahmitzvah [sic]...I would not call myself an observant Jew, for quite a long time I regarded myself as an agnostic, someone who believed in God [sic]. ... So in some ways I actually saw racism itself as something that actually personally threatened me... not just something that... threatens other people in this country.

Describing SADF intervention in Cape townships and "occupation" of Namibia, Bruce declared: "the basic function which the SADF plays in this country is one of upholding and defending a racist system." He objected to fighting, perhaps even dying, for a country that systematically deprived him of truthful history and accurate news.

Although Wits had admitted Bruce to its four-year LL.B. course, he decided not to apply for further deferments. When he declared his refusal to serve on August 5, an MP took him to an officer, who recorded his SADF number and said he could leave. Another MP intervened, taking Bruce to a senior officer, who said the boy was just being disobedient and should be sent to Phalaborwa to get him in line. Sgt. Flattery overheard this and offered to sort out the situation. When Bruce mentioned a knee problem in response to a question about physical disabilities, Flattery assured him "We can find you a job behind a desk." A noncombatant position was available if he was afraid. Bruce responded that "anyone who is not afraid of those kind of situations is quite stupid, but if I was prepared to fight for the particular political system, then I would." After five months of silence Bruce received a telephone call, which he ignored. He answered a second call, however, agreeing to meet Flattery at MP headquarters to make a statement. He and some national servicemen tried to dissuade Bruce. "They just sort of said to me why do you not go there and get it over and done with that that is not actually such a big deal to do that. And basically during the course of the day I was... offered any posting which I would have chosen in SADF." He did not seek religious objector status because

"I am not a pacifist… my objection is based on my understanding of the situation in this country rather than on particular religious beliefs that I have."

When the prosecutor tried to categorize Bruce as a political objector, however, he resisted. "I feel personally threatened by racism and so I feel it is in my own personal interests to… oppose racism." She then tried to convince him of the error of his ways, in what Cameron called a "very fiery and rather passionate cross-examination." Punishment was inevitable since he had broken the law.

> *Bruce:* I do not regard it as an offence.

> *Prosecutor:* But by law it is an offence? … What I cannot understand is if you, because of your beliefs, are prepared to go to jail…. I mean what is the purpose of that?

> *Bruce:* [T]he purpose of the decision for me is to resolve this quite major dilemma in my own life….

Since racial conditions had improved, she argued, he should be as willing to seek deferment now as he had been before.

> *Prosecutor:* And would you agree that… racism is not as intensified as it was ten years ago?

> *Bruce:* No, it is much more complicated than that. … [T]here are people who are now talking about fighting a war for a white future for this country. …

> *Prosecutor:* Ten years ago there would not have been a black or coloured employee in the state….

Her attempt to persuade Bruce that the SADF performed important functions reignited audience laughter.

> *Prosecutor:* Your worship, I would request the court to warn the people who apparently has no respect for the court to behave properly. …

> *Magistrate:* Thank you, Mrs Prosecutor. The court furnished a warning yesterday to the members of the public inside court. The court will issue this final warning today. If anyone wish to be present inside the court, he is welcome to do so, but then it is expected from such person to behave properly, due to the fact that this is a court of order. It is definitely not a circus.

Undaunted, the prosecutor asked Bruce if he also objected to the SAP.

> *Bruce:* My understanding is that the SAP in say the area where I live they actually might play a quite useful role…. But say in the townships their role is basically one of suppressing what are

protests against the present system of government. I mean I am aware for instance that 19 people were shot by the SAP at Uitenhage....

Prosecutor: And you base these allegations on what you have heard and what you have read in the newspapers?

Bruce: I am fully convinced that 19 people were shot by the SAP at Uitenhage. ...

Prosecutor: [Y]ou have never been in a black township where you saw exactly what happened....

Bruce: I have been say to some of the townships say during some elections that were taking place. I saw the kind of things that the police were involved in during that.

Prosecutor: And the useful things that the police officers do and the SADF do also include the blacks, not so?

Bruce: Well, no. What I have heard is that say in the black townships that the police do not actually play such a useful function.

To the prosecutor's conventional criticique of pacifism—"I am sure you would like to have your mother protected against bombs, terrorism"—Bruce responded "I do not think that I would be protecting my mother by serving in defence of a racist political system."

She again expressed bewilderment: why the trial if Bruce admitted guilt?

Prosecutor: Do you want to be regarded as some sort of a martyr for certain beliefs, or what is your problem?

Bruce: I do not regard myself as being guilty of any kind of offence. ...

Prosecutor: [Y]ou said a person who is not [afraid to be in a combat situation] is stupid. ... Now I want to know what do you think a person is that knows he is most probably going to jail and irrespective he puts him in a position where he has no option than to go to jail?

Bruce: I did not choose the options.

Prosecutor: Did you not have the opportunity to serve in any section you wished at the SADF that were not directly linked to any combatant situation or to the promotion of racism or oppressment of blacks or whatever?

Bruce: I would be part of an institution which is involved very basically in perpetrating the violence of a racist political system. I am not prepared to do that.

Prosecutor: You had the opportunity to leave this country and go to Germany or wherever…if you are so unhappy about the situation.

Bruce: My understanding of what happened in Nazi Germany was that for me to be able to say that what happened there was wrong…I had to be able to say to myself that if I had been a German soldier at that time I would actually have taken the stand against what was going on there…leaving the country would be actually running away from racism once again. My mother is a refugee from racism. I am not prepared to be another refugee from racism.

When she remained perplexed about Bruce's conduct, his explanation resembled that of Toms: "I realised I have a decision about what I am going to do about my service in the SADF, [which has been] hanging over me from when I was in Standard 8."

Van der Walt concluded by trying to place responsibility for punishment on Bruce rather than the law (and by implication herself).

Prosecutor: Now lastly I just put it to you that, although you do not agree that you are guilty in terms of your personal beliefs, you are guilty in terms of the section of the act. …

Bruce: That is for the court to decide.

Prosecutor: You have already admitted all the elements. What is then left over?

Bruce: I pleaded not guilty to the charges.

Prosecutor: The court has no option. You have already admitted each and every element. The court has no option.

Bruce: That is for the court to decide, that is for the court to decide.

Prosecutor: To convict you.

Bruce: That is for the court to decide.

The magistrate's judgment was brief: "Accordingly, none of the elements of this offence as set out in the Act had been in dispute and accordingly the court is satisfied that allegements to this offence had been proved and the Accused is accordingly convicted to the main count as charged."[77] Asked for her reaction, van der Walt said: "I had no option. He is guilty in terms of the law. Yes, he is not like the criminals I see in this court. His mother is a very intelligent woman. I too know people who died in the Holocaust."[78]

Bruce's mother was the first defense witness in mitigation of sentence. She shunned publicity, and David worried about seeming dominated by his parents, but Kathleen Satchwell persuaded both of them. Mrs. Bruce had fled Germany at the age of ten, in the face of the Holocaust.

> *Mrs. Bruce:* I became increasingly aware of a growing sense of fear among the adults, a growing furtiveness, people were afraid of speaking to one another and people in the community at large were avoiding us. We were increasingly being excluded from activities and normal civil contact and access to normal places. ... I had been expelled under an act... which precluded Jewish children from attending school where they were in contact with Aryan children. ... One of the children at school, largely prompted by her mother, used to come to us secretly and let me copy the work from her exercise books.

> *Cameron:* Was this child pressured to stop visiting you?

> *Mrs. Bruce:* Very much so by the leader of the female counterpart of the Hitler Youth. She was threatened repeatedly. ... [S]he was on one occasion called out of our garden and ordered to go home at once. Towards the end of our stay, we had access to practically nothing. My uncle was not even able to visit the barber shop, because it was said that a brush and razor used on a filthy Jew could not be used on Aryan customers. ... [After Kristallnacht] the SS presented themselves at our door and commanded that we report to the police station. My mother took me out into the fields to hide... until they were informed that the people who had come to arrest us and burn the house were in a pub some distance away and had become too drunk to carry out whatever they had in mind. ... [O]n the following morning the headmaster of the local school took the children down and instructed them to break up the synagogue, which they did very effectively.

> *Magistrate:* [with great hostility] Sorry Mr Cameron, just before you continue, can you just indicate to the court the relevance of this evidence in regard to this matter please?

> *Cameron:* ... [T]he accused's beliefs are being formed in a close family, most of them who were wiped out in the Holocaust, made an impression on his early mind....

Mrs. Bruce lost two aunts in Auschwitz, a grandfather in Theresienstadt, twelve other members of her immediate family, and many remote relatives; three of the five Jewish families in her village were exterminated. She drew parallels between Nazism and apartheid.

> [T]he concept that any group of human beings is different from another group, that generically it is inferior or less reliable or less

intelligent, anything of that nature, I think dehumanises and degrades the people who are being perceived in that way, but I think ultimately it also dehumanises the perceivers. ... The other point of similarity which troubles me very much is the instance of forced removals... to take people forcibly from their environment and dump them somewhere in the veld where there are no adequate facilities of food, housing or other basic amenities is not gas ovens, but it is not dissimilar from the kind of environment to which people were conveyed in a place [like] Theresienstadt where they were just left to die from lack of food and sanitation. ... [T]hose perceptions and the general value judgments within the family have helped to form [David's] attitudes and opinions. ... [W]e are proud of him, although we are terribly appalled at the severity of the sentence and also at the lack there seems to be for anybody with strong moral convictions to have an alternative choice.

The prosecutor wisely did not cross-examine her.

The other witness in mitigation of sentence was Dr. Nthatho Motlana, who practiced in Soweto and was a member of its Committee of Ten and president of the Soweto Civic Association. He described experiencing racism at high school, university, and Baragwanath Hospital, the structures of apartheid, and the black community's attitude toward the SADF.

I can never forget my visit to New Brighton, your worship, where I found an army unit sitting atop an old abandoned beer hall with machine gun nests and a nest of searchlights which, I was told, they turn onto the township at night. ... I can recall, your worship, sitting in my rooms and being rung up by one woman who says to me—come and see what is happening in Mafolo, where the army has cordoned off a section of Mafolo village. The army units are going from house to house, evicting people and seizing their property.

His community saw David Bruce as "a hero" for being "a young man who could take such a stand over such a principle."

Noting that "legal matters would not really be your cup of tea," the prosecutor tried to get Motlana to agree that "starting from 1957 up to now, the lives of the black people in South Africa are less affected by racism." But while conceding improvements in "peripheral areas," he insisted that "the racism we are talking about is entrenched in our constitution." Then she advanced the common white complaint that blacks were treated better than whites, as shown by government tolerance of the refusal to pay rent, electricity, or water charges. (She seemed unaware that Motlana's SCA had organized those boycotts.) He responded that white citizens controlled housing charges through democratically elected governments, whereas unelected white officials fixed charges for blacks. This provoked an inconclusive power struggle over who defined the question. Van der Walt posed it narrowly: why should blacks get away without paying when whites must pay? Motlana kept enlarging the issue: "I was going to show you that it is because of lack of representation, lack of legitimacy...." Then the prosecutor made the mistake of challenging Motlana's factual assertions, allowing him to demonstrate detailed historical knowledge about Soweto housing.

Van der Walt was no more successful in examining Motlana about the military.

> *Prosecutor:* Now you said that the attitude of the army can be described as to protect white South Africa against black South Africa for the maintenance... of white supremacy. Have you ever served in the SADF?
>
> *Motlana:* Oh no, they would not let me.
>
> *Prosecutor:* How can you then say exactly what the attitude of the SADF is?
>
> *Motlana:* When the South African Government puts their major bases opposite the entrance of black townships throughout the country... there is only one conclusion that can be drawn from that....
>
> *Prosecutor:* Are those the only places—your worship, at this point in time the state again requests your worship to warn the crowd, who apparently cannot behave themselves and apparently have contempt for the court, that if they do not behave with their making remarks and laughing whilst the state is busy, the state is not prepared to proceed. ...
>
> *Magistrate:* Thank you, Miss Prosecutor. The court did not overhear any certain remarks at this stage, but the court [would] just like to appeal to the public again in order to maintain proper order in this court and to show respect for the court proceedings as such....
>
> *Prosecutor:* Why do you not mention some of the good deeds of the SADF? For instance, the flood disaster or even in Lesotho? ...
>
> *Motlana:* But your worship, we are talking about the maintenance of racism. ...
>
> *Motlana:* I meet a lot of blacks who serve in the SAP, not many in the SADF, and over the 30 years that I have been in practice,

your worship, some of those people have been my patients and their attitude generally is one of incredible unhappiness with their role in the police.

Prosecutor: How did you assess that?

Motlana: Most of them, your worship, join the police because at the time when they could not move from Pampoenstroomfontein into urban areas and required influx control regulations amended, they joined the police in order to get into Johannesburg. [The second reason was unemployment.] ... The third reason that they are so unhappy is that up to about 2, 3 years ago a black major... could not give orders to a constable who was white and entered the police force three days before. ... [T]he constable could send the black colonel to go and buy him cigarettes and this is the kind of thing, you know, overt and open discrimination that takes place in the police force everywhere in this sick society, that makes the policemen so unhappy.

The prosecutor concluded by reattempting the strategy that had failed with Bruce: Motlana also expected and benefitted from SADF protection against "terrorists coming over the border."

Motlana: Oh yes, but particularly coming over the border. I do not expect an army based opposite my township. ...

Prosecutor: But surely you are aware that lots of the terrorists coming over the border have bases in some of the townships. ...

Motlana: No, I have not read about bases in the townships, your worship.

Prosecutor: Not really bases, but homes where they stay. ...

Motlana: When they do that kind of work, your worship, presumably they will be welcomed in that kind of role, but not as people who maintain our racist structure.

Prosecutor: So would you in the end then agree that the SADF is not as bad as you want it to look from the outset?

Motlana: On balance, your worship, I am afraid that the SADF is regarded in the most adverse light, as an unfriendly force, as a force intended purely for the maintenance of the structure of this country, which is racism.

The defense case was extensively reported in the press under headlines like: "SADF upholds racist system, says objector," "Objector's mother was a refugee from Nazis," "Blind mom tells court of Nazi terror," and "Objector Bruce says no to 'racist' army, risks jail."[79]

In passing sentence the magistrate offered his theory of political authority and moral obligation.

> [N]o state exists where the final authority is not vested in an organised defence force. The competence to apply an armed force in order to combat any armed resistance, and thereby securing the maintenance, securing and maintaining state security, law and order results typically from the historical foundation of any state. In South Africa too, the state has the duty to protect all individuals by securing law and order. In that regard the state is competent to compel and prescribe to its subjects in order to compile an effective defence force.
>
> On the other hand it is also the duty of the subject in return to respect the aforementioned claim by the state. That is the basis of the obligation to render service in the Defence Force.

The Supreme Court had upheld the statutory framework in seven cases.

He claimed that "the attitude by the accused and his motivation for refusing to do national service was carefully considered" (though he never mentioned it). "However, such motivation leads to the compromise of the said legal objects of the State. General indulgence of such motivation can only lead to absurd results."

Impressed by the severity of the sentence, the magistrate interpreted the statute by looking at its "ordinary meaning."

> It is clear that due to the seriousness of the offence, the legislator intended to prescribe the longest possible sentence as an obligation. A lesser sentence or a suspended sentence will counterfeit the purpose of the act.

He criticized Bruce for refusing a noncombatant role, which would give him "full opportunity to get his personal knowledge of what the real purpose of the defence force is in perspective" and to "do much better service to the community of South Africa." He concluded by reminding the accused that §126A(7) allowed him to leave prison by entering the military.

> The consequences of serving imprisonment are in your own hands, Mr Bruce. You have the options as set out by the court to avoid it and still be a useful member of the public. The court has given consideration to your personal circumstances as set out in this court. However, as already pointed out, the court is bound to the Penalty Jurisdiction as set out in the act. ...
>
> *ACCORDINGLY THE ACCUSED IS SENTENCED TO IMPRISONMENT FOR A PERIOD OF SIX YEARS.*

Supporters wearing yellow buttons and flowers wept and sang Nkosi Sikelel' iAfrika with fists raised.[80] The English press gave extensive critical coverage.[81] Wits students picketed, although Rand Afrikaans University students said he "got what he deserved."[82] Many papers reported Helen Suzman's prompt condemnation of the outcome as a "tragedy."[83] Dr. Allan Boesak wrote Bruce: "Your courage is a shining example for millions. At a time when many are doubting the viability of non-racialism in our struggle you have given me faith."[84] Khulu Sibiya's column drew parallels between Bruce and Jackie Selebi, just appointed to the ANC National Executive Committee: "One has chosen to go to jail instead of joining what he describes as a racist institution, and the other has decided to join an organisation perceived by the majority of the people in this country to be fighting racism."[85] Editorials in six papers urged that non-religious objectors be allowed to do alternative service.[86]

The right attacked this celebration. Conservative Party justice spokesman Chris de Jager said Bruce's assertion that the SADF upheld a "racist system" was "revolution against the Government."[87] Bruce was "no hero" to *The Citizen*.

> One can have little sympathy for David Bruce. ... He chosen [sic] not to serve at all.... [His convictions] are not shared by the great majority of young South Africans, who accept national service as a patriotic duty or as a necessary obligation. ... The true heroes ... are the young men who fight on the Border or help to bring peace to the townships. ... The SADF does not play a political role ... [or] defend a racist system, as Bruce claims, but defends the people of this country.

It called for "severe action against those who are involved" in weakening military morale but acknowledged that the sentence seemed long.[88]

Bruce's appeal to the Supreme Court, modelled on that of Toms, was rejected by Justice H. Coetzee on March 3, 1989. He was "not a 'criminal' in the ordinary sense of the word. His evidence showed him to be a firm believer in his principles but that is not in issue in this case." Coetzee accepted the defense argument that the correct sentence was 2,176 days instead of 2,191, adding "the deprivation of an individual's liberty for each day beyond that which is allowed by statute cannot be countenanced." The statute was "clear and unambiguous," however.

> Much as one would like to come to the assistance of the appellant ... this section shows how the legislature has taken away the court's discretion completely. The basic jurisprudential principles of the ends of criminal justice which are cherished by our common law and which have been eloquently expounded by the highest court in the land are with one stroke of the pen, in a case like the present, removed from the ambit of the presiding

judicial officer... [who] requires a calculator and cannot use his innate sense of justice inculcated through the centuries. The sentence may just as well be passed and imposed by an administrative official with a rubber stamp because no legal skill is required.[89]

Bruce remembered prison as an obsessive effort to qualify for less punitive conditions. When he finally reached Category Four after a year, "your whole life changes." He became entitled to thirty contact visits annually (forty minutes each) with up to two people at a time, who could buy food. Family and friends visited often, as did someone from War Resisters International, a conscientious objector from the Netherlands and one from the United States. Although warders treated him like any other white male, "prisoners in general treat each other very badly." They assumed he was a Jehovah's Witness. When he explained that he refused "to serve in defense of a racist political system... that would just kill the conversation... the next question [would be] 'So, you think the kaffir should be equal to the white man?'" When he said "Yah, I think so," one man replied, "Well, yeah, I agree with you." He received the Reebok Human Rights Award in December 1988, and several papers noted the end of his first year in prison.[90]

Collective Opposition: 1988–89

While the government was prosecuting Toms and Bruce, the ECC took the offensive. Although Defence Minister Malan still refused to release the number refusing to report, he did acknowledge that thirty percent of those called for the Citizen Force and Commando camps applied for deferments.[91] In August 1988, at simultaneous news conferences in Johannesburg, Cape Town, Grahamstown, and Durban, 143 men publicly refused to serve. They included a grandson of a former cabinet minister and a Rhodes scholar; the Johannesburg contingent contained seven doctors, five clerics, nine university lecturers, six teachers, four engineers, two architects, two physicists, and four lawyers. More than a hundred faced six-year sentences. Those who had served (some rising to the rank of captain) described SADF atrocities. Etienne Marais saw soldiers murder a thirteen-year-old Namibian girl and torture a sixteen-year-old Angolan girl for eight hours. "Collecting ears and fingers as souvenirs happens quite often on the border." He had seen a soldier "use the corpse of a Swapo guerrilla as a pillow." Steven Louw had been stationed in the townships of the Eastern Cape and the Vaal triangle. As a Buffel driver he had been instructed to plow "into a crowd of people to provoke them to offer resistance." He often saw soldiers sjambok small boys.[92]

Defence Minister Malan announced that he had "broken off relations with the ECC," accusing it of threatening state security. "No citizen can decide of his or her own free will which laws to respect." *The Citizen* proclaimed: "The government will have to act firmly to prevent the rot spreading and it will have the support of most South Africans."[93] Later that month the government banned the ECC—the first white organization to be suppressed since the Congress of Democrats in the early 1960s. Law and Order Minister Adriaan Vlok explained:

> The ECC attempts to create an impression of political neutrality, but it is not difficult to see the organisation's role in the revolutionary onslaught against South Africa. ... As a result of the ECC's campaigns, many liable for national service are influenced to refuse to do military service.

Many prominent figures denounced the ban, and six UCT students added their names to the list of resisters in front of an audience of a thousand. Labour Party leader Allan Hendrickse declared "the ECC is entitled to oppose conscription while the army is seen as undergirding and supporting the unjust policies of the National Party government." Malan denounced this as "reckless and irresponsible," "an emotional outburst," "condoning those who break the country's laws." Hendrickse "plays right into the hands of terrorists, who maim and kill our people."[94]

Two weeks later Charles Bester, eighteen, refused military service. His father had stood as a PFP candidate in 1981, and he had attended a multiracial school. A committed Christian from the age of fourteen, he resisted conscription on the ground that South Africa was engaged in an unjust war: "I cannot go into the townships on the back of a Casspir and say as a Christian, I have got good news." In December, the Potchefstroom Magistrate's Court sentenced him to six years. When Kathleen Satchwell argued that the term was not mandatory, Mag. J. van der Merwe snapped: "I did not ask for your comment." Journalists wept, and the audience, including Ivan Toms and some of the 143 who had publicly refused military service in August, rose to sing Nkosi Sikelel' iAfrika and shout Amandla and Viva. The magistrate, who had forbidden them to wear yellow flowers, locked the courtroom and threatened them with contempt. In February 1990 a petition by 70,000 calling for Bester's release was submitted to the British Parliament.[95]

Saul Batzofin, who had done National Service in Namibia in 1980–81 and six subsequent camps, was one of the 143 objectors. He pleaded guilty to refusing another camp in March 1989, describing SADF atrocities in his evidence in mitigation. Sentencing him to eighteen months in May, Mag. P.H. Bredenkamp (who had tried David Bruce) declared:

> It was not the purpose or duty of the court to judge the political structure in this country but to consider and impose a sentence in accordance with the limits of the relevant Act. ... Said words in respect of sentence are clear and unambiguous and makes [sic] it absolutely clear that in respect of sentence no discretion whatsoever remains with the presiding officer (as confirmed in the unreported decision of S v Bruce....). ... Consideration of a sen-

tence involving community service would have absurd consequences, in that a great number of potential trainees would try to
use it in order to avoid rendering the required service.[96]

Other organizations took up the struggle. A Black Sash meeting in
September 1988 called for alternative forms of national service. Groups representing 800 mothers held simultaneous services in three cities on the February
1989 call-up under the demand "Give Our Sons a Choice." Mothers Against
War was launched in Durban that month; one of its leaders was Millicent Toms,
Ivan's mother.[97] In May COSG launched the National Campaign on South
African Conscientious Objectors to Military Service, which organized meetings
in eight cities on International Conscientious Objectors' Day (May 15), focusing on the three in prison. South Africans in England burned their call-up
papers, demonstrations were held at South African embassies in twelve countries, and the European Parliament sent messages of support.[98]

Following de Klerk's election as State President in August 1989 the ECC
asked to be unbanned, with support from church leaders, Black Sash, and
Lawyers for Human Rights. As part of the Mass Democratic Movement's defiance campaign, several ECC chapters unilaterally unbanned themselves,
prompting the arrest of their leaders for "furthering the aims of a banned
organisation." At the Voortrekkerhoogte on August 14 Defence Minister Malan
attacked the ECC and other groups for supporting the "ANC-SACP alliance"
and committing internal acts of terror. Threatened with court action, he undertook not to repeat such comments but promptly linked the ECC and ANC at
a National Party meeting. The next month 771 men publicly signed a National
Register for Conscientious Objectors, soon complemented by an International
Register of South African War Resisters containing the signatures of 162 exiles.
The Citizen responded by condemning "conchies" (conscientious objectors)
as dupes of the ANC and SACP.[99] But though the government detained a few
organizers, its attitude toward conscription was changing. In March, Malan
denied any intent to shorten military service; but the following month he
reduced liability for camps from twelve years to ten, and in December he
halved National Service from two years to one. The COSG and ECC asked de
Klerk to make these changes retroactive and release jailed objectors. In
January 1990 the government halved community service for recognized objectors (from six years to three) and allowed those jailed remission of sentence
for good behavior.[100] In response to a petition by his attorney, Defence
Minister Malan released Saul Batzofin after nearly ten months in prison.[101]

The Appellate Division Surprises

The Appellate Division consolidated Toms's and Bruce's appeals and
heard argument on February 27, 1990—three weeks after the government
released Mandela and unbanned the ANC, SACP, and ECC (among other

organizations). The ECC demonstrated in Johannesburg the same day to launch its "Release Objectors Campaign."[102] The March 30 judgment included four separate opinions.[103]

Smalberger wrote the majority opinion (in which Nicholas concurred). "[T]he infliction of punishment is pre-eminently a matter for the discretion of the trial court," partly because "the individualisation of punishment … requires proper consideration of the individual circumstances of each accused person." A mandatory sentence "reduces the court's normal sentencing function to the level of a rubber stamp." The legislature "must express itself in clear and unmistakable terms" in order to eliminate discretion. The court followed the "ordinary, literal, grammatical meaning" of statutes unless this would lead to absurdity. Ambiguous penal provisions should be construed to favor the accused. The accused acted on "principles they hold no less sincerely, tenaciously and resolutely" than the religious beliefs the statute recognized.[104]

The words "whichever is longer" simply directed the choice between the alternative sentences of eighteen months or 1.5 times the remaining service obligation. The presumption in favor of judicial discretion survived in the absence of words unambiguously mandating a penalty, such as "shall be sentenced to." Although Parliament often imposed minimum sentences, it had never imposed a *fixed* sentence. According to the dictionary, the phrase "liable to" "would normally denote a susceptibility to a burden of punishment and not that the burden in question is mandatory or compulsory." The Criminal Procedure Act specifically provided that those "liable to" a specified period of imprisonment might be sentenced to a lesser term. Use of the words "not exceeding" in the next subsection did not mean that its penalty was a maximum whereas the present penalty was mandatory. The act did not systematically distinguish between mandatory penalties for refusal to serve and discretionary penalties for failure to serve.[105]

The act's deterrent purpose did not require that every offender serve the maximum, only that potential offenders know the threat. "Rigorous and harsh sentences do not necessarily effect their purpose and they are out of tune with a just society." The Criminal Procedure Act allowed suspended sentences; since the accused had refused military service, the appropriate condition would be community service.[106]

Chief Justice Corbett concurred separately "not without some hesitation." After "anxious deliberation," Botha dissented. The legislature used the words "not exceeding" when it wished to indicate a maximum. Since it had created an "elaborate machinery for alternative kinds of service" for religious objectors, courts should not suspend the sentences of those who did not qualify. However, he had "reached the conclusions stated in this judgment with profound regret." The statute was "a draconian provision which is not necessary or desirable for achieving the purpose of the Act"; it violated the "principle that the discretion of the courts in the matter of sentence should not be encroached upon, and that the individualisation of punishment should not be rendered nugatory"; and it "must inevitably lead to harsh and inequitable results." Kumleben felt that the sentence was mandatory but the court could suspend it.[107]

Allowing both appeals, the court passed sentence on Toms at his request. He was "a highly principled man of impressive qualities, not least of which is his sensitivity to the suffering of his fellow man, in whose service he so resolutely and compassionately stands." It reduced his sentence to the nine months served.[108] The ECC welcomed the court's "enlightened decision." Toms himself declared: "All that objectors and the ECC stood for has been vindicated."[109] Bruce was released on his own recognizance, having served twenty months. At his retrial three months later the defense called two witnesses: an SADF commandant and a Prisons Department social worker, who testified that he had matured in prison and would be harmed by further incarceration. With the prosecutor's agreement, the magistrate sentenced Bruce to time served. Since he was not "fundamentally opposed to conscription" he did not immediately join the ECC but instead worked in community health. Eventually, however, he became full-time National Office coordinator for the ECC.[110]

Individual Defiance: 1989–92

Douglas Torr had the only full trial after the AD decision. Although an Anglican priest, he (like Toms) declined to apply to the Board because it would not recognize moral or political objectors. One of the 143 who refused service in August 1988, he defied the July 1989 call-up but heard nothing for five months. Torr pleaded guilty in January 1990 and offered evidence in mitigation in May, including his own observation of SADF actions in Eastern Cape townships. When he quoted scripture in response to the prosecutor's usual argument about the essential functions the SADF performed, Mag. Hein Verhoef engaged the accused in a religious debate.

> *Magistrate:* I am also a Christian, by the way, that is why I can talk to you. I am not ashamed about it. I am very serious about that. That is why I am discussing the matter with you. We live in a broken world, never mind, society.
>
> *Torr:* Right.
>
> *Magistrate:* Right. We all believe that Christ, not all of us, but me and you believe that Christ is Our Saviour.
>
> *Torr:* Correct.
>
> *Magistrate:* Now, there are millions of people who do not believe that. ... The devil is present in our midst.

Torr: OK.

Magistrate: Shouldn't the Christian in order to uphold Christianity take a defensive action against the evil forces...?

Torr: My Christ is the Christ that takes the suffering of the world into himself.

Asked whether South Africa no longer had enemies, Torr answered that it was "very interesting that the enemies we considered we have are now the people we sit at the negotiation table with." The magistrate responded: "[U]ltimately I with my conscience have to sentence you."

Torr supported his request for community service with evidence from NICRO (National Institute for the Correction and Rehabilitation of Offenders), the Anglican Bishop of Johannesburg, the director of the St. Joseph's Home for "coloured" children (where Torr worked), the Community Service Office, and the Director General of the Department of National Health and Population Development (who supported Torr's request to do AIDS counselling). The presentence report by C. Vorster of the Department of Health Services and Welfare opposed this, however.

> [B]eside religious objections, the accused's actions are also inspired by political factors. ... [He] has brought forward a number of conditions [for performing community service, but] a community service sentence is under no circumstances to be a sentence of convenience. ... [I]f the Court is prepared to accommodate the accused regarding community service of choice, an inevitable precedent will be created regarding the punitive measures imposed on future conscientious objectors. ... The elements of punishment must still be there as well as the accused experiencing a degree of discomfort in rendering that service.

At the end of July Mag. Verhoef sentenced Torr to a year's imprisonment, criticizing him for a "rather arrogant" attitude toward the Board and for condemning the SADF on the basis of two instances. "I want to make it clear I am not referring to the contents of his perception, whether that is right or wrong... I will not partake first of all in expressing political opinions. That is not my job first of all." But he talked about the SADF building schools and teaching people to farm in Namibia and saving flood victims in Natal and the Orange Free State. "I am not taking judicial notice of such aspects and I am not praising it and I am not promoting anything. I am merely trying to explain that there is another side. ... Whoever wants to criticise me for mentioning this should say first of all that I am a liar."

Although the Bishop had expressed the Anglican Church's condemnation of apartheid, the magistrate refused "to promote or criticise apartheid." He did not know whether Torr would qualify as a religious objector, but "it is again not for me to say whether that is right or wrong…the court should interpret the law and not make the law." Because of Torr's evasions about whether he was a universal pacifist, the magistrate found that he was not a religious objector and therefore did not qualify for community service. Since Torr and the 142 others had defied conscription such refusals had increased twenty percent. Hence "the problem of people refusing to do military service is quite bigger than the one case before the court." He ignored the Defence Minister's halving of the length of military service in February "because a court is bound by the law, and this act has not been changed." He rejected a suspended sentence because Torr was committing a continuing offense and could be reprosecuted.

> I find no pleasure in finding that the only sentence I can impose is imprisonment…[which was] plainly stupid and a waste of his talents. This is the first time in my career…that I have before me exactly the kind of person who does not belong in prison. But there is an Act passed by Parliament and the court has to obey that Act…. [I]f a person with the qualities of Mr Torr and his background…elects to go to prison for six years because of a conviction that he based in a way on perceptions which are really not scientifically, I do not think even generally spoken accurate, then I think he is really wasting his talents.

He welcomed the AD judgment "because there is no more dissatisfying part of a criminal court magistrate's work, and is to be a rubber stamp when it comes to sentence." "[T]his sentence is one of a symbolic nature…to impress on others that they should do military service unless they want to face the music—bad music."

When Torr appeared in court the next day to seek bail pending appeal, he was handcuffed and shackled. Verhoef was livid: "I find it totally unacceptable that a man like Mr Torr should be in chains." Leading lawyers and politicians denounced the incident; Justice Minister Coetsee expressed regret and ordered an investigation. Nine months later the state conceded that the sentence violated the AD decision and urged the Supreme Court to sentence Torr itself. The court suspended imprisonment on condition that he perform 800 hours of community service at the Johannesburg AIDS Advice Centre.[111]

In August 1990 the Supreme Court released Charles Bester after twenty months, finding that he had "no less worthy a character" than Toms and Bruce. Declaring that he would do it again, Bester said he had been "unbelievably encouraged by the other objectors, especially David Bruce. Knowing David was with me was incredibly important, even though we were never actually together. And when the 771 objectors made their stand, I was just so happy I was in a daze." The *Daily Mail* called his imprisonment "an indictment of all of us" and welcomed the AD decision for "the discretion it now allows magistrates in passing sentence." *The Star* denounced his "wasted months" as a reminder that "society has need to evaluate its own code of conduct." *The Argus* agreed that it was "comforting to know that in punishment the final word rests with the judges."[112]

Gary Rathbone did not fit the mold of Toms, Bruce, Bester, or Torr. After four years in the Permanent Force (1979–82) he had had enough and managed to avoid camps for seven years, fleeing abroad for three months, enrolling in Wits, playing lead guitar in "The Spectres," and living underground. He refused a December 1989 camp and was arrested the next week. Two months after the AD decision Mag. Verhoef (who tried Torr) rejected Sgt. Flattery's testimony that Rathbone still owed 420 days of camps as unreliable, nonexpert, incomplete, and hearsay and dismissed the charge at the end of the prosecution case.[113] The government avoided confrontation in other ways. Andre Croucamp refused a December 1989 camp and was tried in March 1990, but the case was postponed to allow him to apply to the Board for Religious Objection.

> I do not belong to any formalised religion and I do not believe in a Supreme Being in a conventional sense. … I have assimilated and tried to integrate the insights of mystics, psychologists, historians and scientists alike. … I also experienced premonitions, dreams, visions, and insights. [Through meditation he had experienced death and resurrection.] After such an experience I can never take sides in any objective sense.

The Board granted an exemption.[114]

Michael Graff had performed National Service in 1980–81, the last half in Namibia. Having avoided camps for nine years he refused to serve in December 1989. "My main motive is a wish not to compromise myself. For me, maintaining a lifestyle of evasion has become a compromise…. [I also] wish to stand witness to a range of experiences which are normally hidden from public view…." In November 1990 the Pietermaritzburg Magistrate's Court sentenced him to a year's imprisonment, suspended on condition that he perform 2,400 hours community service—the first non-custodial sentence for an objector. He applied for indemnity as a political offender but missed the deadline by a week. In June 1991 the Natal Supreme Court ordered resentencing. But in August the State President granted indemnity—the first time to an objector.[115]

Jehovah's Witnesses, the first conscientious objectors and always the vast majority, posed a unique problem. Although the exemption had been created for them they would not apply to the Board for alternative community service. Instead, they refused conscription and were convicted, sentenced to prison, and then paroled to community service. More than a thousand went through this procedure between 1985 and 1990. To ensure uniformity, all cases were sent to the Bloemfontein Magistrate's Court. The AD decision reopened the 403 uncompleted sentences and unsettled all future cases by giving magistrates discretion. Mag. Landman convicted Colin Sangster less than three weeks later and sentenced him to what the magistrate still believed was the mandatory 2,175 days. The Bloemfontein Chief Magistrate referred the matter to the Orange Free State Supreme Court, where a full bench set aside the sentence in September. Mag. Landman reheard the case two weeks later. Sangster, who was unrepresented, described his religious beliefs and activites. The prosecutor called Maj. Fourie, secretary of the Board for Religious Objection, who urged that sentences remain uniform but noted that the Defence Minister had halved National Service the previous February.

After a postponement, Edwin Cameron appeared for the accused and called an elder of the Bloemfontein Jehovah's Witnesses. The magistrate said "this is one of the most difficult sentences I have ever been called upon to pass." Although cognizant of the AD decision and moved by "the element of mercy," he did not believe he had discretion. "[T]he sentence should be such that it does not provide for the accused to make a farce of the intention of a legislator." Because "the principle of uniformity must receive preference" it was "not really possible to individualise." Since the offense was "not regarded as particularly reprehensible [sic]," however, he halved the sentence. Sangster's attorney sought the intervention of Justice Edeling (who chaired the Board for Religious Objection), but he refused to get involved. On appeal the state conceded that the magistrate had erred. In March 1991 the OFS Supreme Court rejected the state's contention that three years should be the sentence unless the accused presented evidence in mitigation. Noting the "undesirability of a practice of standard sentences becoming established" and invoking the AD holding that "the court is not a rubber stamp," it sentenced Sangster to 850 days.[116]

Collective Opposition: 1990–92

When the ECC was unbanned in February 1990 it immediately reestablished branches in seven cities. There were further revelations of dirty tricks: the Harms Commission documented that the SADF Civil Cooperation Bureau had targeted ECC leader Gavin Evans for assassination; the Hiemstra Commission disclosed that the Johannesburg City Council had spied on ECC activists. The ECC called for Defence Minister Malan's resignation and prosecution.[117] He responded by establishing the Van Loggerenberg Committee to restructure military service and consider extending conscription to all races.[118] But this did nothing to staunch the hemorrhage: 1,300 men proclaimed their intent not to serve in the first seven months of 1990; thirty-eight percent of Citizen Force and Commando members requested deferments, and nine percent failed to report. At the end of the year ten exiles returned and invited prosecution. Matthew Temple declared: "We're an advance party for other resisters. This is a sort of upping of the tempo...."[119] The SADF floundered. Louis Bredenkamp obtained an exemption as a member of the

ANC! When he publicized this, however, the army conscripted him. The Defence Minister first declared that ANC and SACP members could serve and then reversed himself.*

In April 1991 a man was exempted because he worked for a rural relief organization and another had his call-up cancelled because he belonged to the ANC. In May Mag. Verhoef (who had thrown out Gary Rathbone's charges) acquitted Inkatha spokesman Peter auf der Heyde of failing to register on the ground that the offense was failure to produce proof of registration. "If the legislature intended to make it criminally liable, they should have said so in plain words so there could be no mistake." In June the state dropped charges against Rev. Alan Storey, twenty-two, who refused National Service, and Wally Rontsch, a forty-year-old businessman who refused further service in the Commandos.[120]

Having obtained a legal opinion in June that repeal of the Population Registration Act rendered whites-only conscription invalid, the ECC declared that "any person refusing to render service in the SADF on the basis of such a call-up will have a valid defence...." It cheered the demotion of its bitter adversary Malan to the Department of Water and Forestry and hoped for "constructive dialogue" with Roelf Meyer, his replacement. The Conscription Advice Service claimed that as few as ten percent had reported for National Service, camps, and Commando units in August and October 1991. The SADF seemed to concede defeat. Spokesman Maj. Charl de Klerk conceded that many were not reporting and added: "The Defence Act is still applicable to every white male. But we are looking into each case individually regarding the granting of possible deferment and if the person has a valid excuse then the Exemption Board will look into that. For a person to threaten not to go is not an offence." At the end of the year the far-right Boerestaat Party, Conservative Party Youth Wing, and Aksie Volkseie Weermag encouraged members to resist. Nevertheless, Defence Minister Meyer reasserted his commitment to whites-only conscription.[121]

The ECC began 1992 with an open letter to Meyer repeating that only thirty percent had reported the previous year, predicting only fifty percent would do so in January, and denouncing the SADF. "We believe that your government will try everything in its power, every devious manoeuvre, and every dirty trick, to delay relinquishing power to a democratic government. Who better to ensure by fair means or foul, continued white minority domination of the 'new' South Africa?" A Ministry spokesman rejected the ECC's "impatient and hysterical reaction." ECC leader Chris de Villiers characterized this response as "pathetic and an apparent attempt to draw attention away from the real issues"—"the legal invalidity of the call-up." When the SADF

*Hansard q. 813 (P.G.Soal, PFP) (4.17.90), q. 1007 (S.C. Jacobs, CP) (4.24.90). Malan explained that "an applicant's bona fides are naturally investigated, and because the SA Defence Force is an instrument of the government of the day, such persons' political feelings....[Interjections] I don't really mean political feelings. They must support the underlying principles of policy and the Constitution of the Government of this country...."

maintained that ninety percent of the January call-up reported, the ECC denigrated this as a "face-saving exercise." The Boerestaat Party reiterated support for any "Boerseun" who refused to serve. Leader Robert van Tonder said "the watershed was the events at Ventersdorp where army units were deployed to act against Boere and when Government forces shot at Boere" (see chapter ten). Whites should refuse to serve because blacks were not conscripted. The press recoiled from ECC (and right-wing) calls for massive civil disobedience but generally supported a volunteer force.[122]

Two weeks after the call-up Deputy Defence Minister Wynand Breytenbach announced a Cabinet decision not to prosecute those who failed to report. The ECC promptly claimed this meant "any further call-ups are effectively unenforceable." The next day, however, Breytenbach said he had been misinterpreted; he only meant it would be unfair to prosecute objectors before the Gleeson Committee reported. And Meyer added that anyone failing to report "without legitimate reason" would be prosecuted. Chris de Villiers called the conflicting statements "hot air," noting that no prosecutions had been brought since the previous June. The ECC advocated non-registration, which Mag. Verhoef had declared not to be an offense.[123]

Because the SADF would not expose itself to judicial review by prosecuting those who failed to report, the ECC and a conscript applied in March for a declaratory judgment that conscription was illegal. Denouncing the "outright lies, distorted facts and rumours spread by anti-Defence Force organisations and people," Meyer reintroduced sixty-day camps to control escalating unrest. The SADF circumvented the civil courts by court martialling fifty Citizen Force members for failing to report, fining twenty-three of them R400 while dropping charges against those with legal representation. But the Supreme Court affirmed the magistrate's decision that failing to register was no offense. The ECC called this "another nail in the coffin of whites-only conscription," but Meyer said it could be overturned by a "minor" amendment.[124]

At the beginning of May the ECC repeated its prediction that many would not report for camps, and the 8 SA Division acknowledged that nearly half sought deferments. Later that month the government tabled a Defence Amendment Bill, retaining white conscription, allowing those with sincere ethical beliefs to perform three years' alternative service, but mandating eighteen months imprisonment for those refusing to serve. Under pressure the government dropped mandatory sentencing and unilateral conscription into the police, and the act passed. As the mid-year call-up approached, thousands sought exemptions, and some lawyers engaged in price gouging. Chris de Villiers reassured the reluctant that only eight percent of those refusing National Service and six percent of those refusing camps were pursued. The ANC urged whites to defy the call-up. Gene Louw (the third Defence Minister in less than a year) condemned criticism of the SADF as revealing "a desire to seize power." Government continued selective court-martials of men who failed to report for camps and prosecutions of conscripts who refused National Service; but it gave the latter an extra month to apply to the new Board for Conscientious Objection, and often dropped charges against those who offered any defense. The ECC responded by forming a panel of thirty-five lawyers willing to defend conscripts without charge.[125]

In September the Supreme Court found the call-up legal and denied leave to appeal. The ECC responded with a Non-Co-Operation Campaign, publicized by a pamphlet showing black and white hands tearing a call-up paper. It advised hundreds that the maximum fine was R600, suggested ways of evading service, and opened a "Register of Non-Co-Operation." The SADF threatened to prosecute both individuals and the ECC, which had come "close to breaking the law." Defence Minister Louw issued a stern warning:

> South Africa cannot afford the disappearance of national service. Next year the same system as this year will still be in force.
>
> Furthermore, stricter measures will be taken against draft dodgers.
>
> This will apply to those who refused to do service in 1992 as well.

The ECC aimed at "destroying the country's preparedness." He admitted the need for change, however, because it was "unreasonable to discriminate against whites."[126]

Chris de Villiers dismissed these threats as "cynical bluster." "To even talk of prosecutions while the Government is scrabbling like ants on a hot-plate to get an indemnity for their own thugs and murderers is outrageous." In December the Appellate Division denied the ECC leave to appeal dismissal of its challenge to conscription. The ECC, ANC, Democratic Party, and Conservative Party criticized the SADF plan to recruit 6,000 two-to-six-year volunteers of all races to replace a similar number of white Citizen Force and Commando members. David Bruce, speaking for the ECC, noted that fewer than 700 of 3,000 called up reported to a 1 SA Infantry Battalion in July, and only six of 150 Citizen Force members reported for a camp in Germiston in December. A week later twenty-one men wrote the State President refusing to serve. The SADF reiterated its threat to prosecute but finally conceded that 1993 would be the last all-white call-up.[127] In July 1993 the ECC held a National Peace Festival, at which Mandela thanked it for a decade of white activism. The ECC then dissolved.[128] In August Defence Minister Kobie Coetsee announced that Parliament would consider a bill to create a nonracial volunteer army.*

---

*"January Call-up Cancelled!" Obj 1 (9.93); LAT A4 (8.26.93). In one of the many ironies of the transition from apartheid, the *Weekly Mail* urged continuing conscription to make the SADF "a stabilising influence in a multi-ethnic, multi-party South Africa." WM 28 (8.29.93).

Analysis

Conscientious objection is an unusual form of political protest because it is simultaneously intensely individualistic and a powerful magnet for collective action. When the state prosecuted individuals, the ECC produced hundreds of other resisters. Isolated in the hostile prison environment, objectors were sustained by feelings of solidarity with other protesters. Yet there were more differences than similarities among the dozen political objectors (and a fortiori among the thousand who publicly refused to serve). Most were English-speaking, but not all. Some were intensely Christian, but others showed little interest in religion, and Bruce was an agnostic Jew. Resistance fostered a rare ecumenical cooperation among Christians, Jews, and Moslems. Most had higher education, but not Wilkinson or Rathbone. They ranged in age from Charles Bester, who refused conscription at eighteen, through Ivan Toms, who was thirty-five at his trial, to Wally Rontsch, who was forty when he refused a camp. Some had never served, while Gary Rathbone had been a full-time soldier for four years. Some received moral support from their families, while others were disowned. Their occupations ran the gamut from physician to butcher, rock musician to priest, insurance clerk to rural development worker. The two whose trials received the greatest publicity could not have been more different (although the ordeal made them friends). Toms, more mature, had developed a coherent moral argument against conscription and carefully planned his arrest, prosecution, and trial for maximum political impact. Bruce had equally strong anti-racist convictions but expressed himself like Herman Melville's Bartleby—he just preferred not to serve and would have been happy had the SADF overlooked him. Toms was deeply involved in the ECC from its founding and planned his refusal with the advice of many. Bruce was a loner who went to his call-up without even a lawyer, did not join the 143 who publicly refused to serve, and kept his distance from the COSG created for him. By 1991 the left-wing EEC was joined by far-right groups, who no longer supported a regime fatally compromised by negotiations with the ANC.

The state response was no more coherent. When Bruce refused to serve for political reasons, the SADF was nonplused: some officers wanted to punish him, others to dissuade him, and one hoped he would just go away. The SADF displayed almost as much incompetence as malice: calling up Toms twice for shooting camps after granting him noncombatant status; and calling up both Toms and Bruce after they had been convicted for refusing to serve. Sgt. Flattery, although specializing in reluctant inductees, had a vague and partly erroneous knowledge of the Board for Religious Objection.

The state vacillated between systematic repression and ad hoc lenience. The Defence Act, which originally contained no exceptions, was amended to exempt members of peace churches, then universal pacifists, and finally those with sincere ethical beliefs. The restriction of alternative service to government employment was eventually relaxed. At the same time, those who did not qualify spent one and a half times longer in prison—initially in Detention Barracks. This severity seems to have had the desired effect: Fewer than one out of 10,000 conscripts refused service.

If government increasingly tolerated individual deviance, it responded swiftly and harshly to collective opposition. The state (and its private supporters and possible surrogates) illegally harassed ECC activists through verbal and physical attacks and groundless criminal charges; police refused to investigate "vigilante" violence; the CCB planned to assassinate Gavin Evans. The SADF brazenly claimed that "wartime" conditions justified its illegality and even immunized it from review by civilian courts. The state detained dozens of activists and eventually banned the ECC. It denigrated international law as mere politics.

The state equated the anti-conscription campaign with treason, just as it identified the UDF with the ANC and saw the *New Nation* as the mouthpiece of revolution (see chapters eight and nine). Although it could accommodate religious objectors, especially those belonging to marginal peace churches, it could not permit political objection without acknowledging the illegitimacy of apartheid. It felt so insecure that it feared the total collapse of authority if it did not punish each act of defiance. If the state exaggerated the threat to justify its overt suppression and covert attacks on the ECC, it was not simply paranoid. Many white middle-class young men, especially at English-speaking universities, were susceptible to moral suasion and often supported and protected by parents wielding political and economic clout.

As the ECC boasted and government warned, highly publicized individual resistance did encourage others. Banning organizations, detaining leaders, and jailing objectors further inflamed collective opposition through the "high profile trials" of which the PFP had warned in opposing the 1983 Defence Act. Just as draft resistance helped turn the tide of American public opinion against the Vietnam War, so South African opposition to conscription, together with the body bags shipped back from Angola and the hemorrhage of emigration, fostered an atmosphere in which de Klerk could initiate reforms. These, however, only emboldened the ECC openly to encourage refusals to serve.

The state consistently avoided confronting individuals who refused to serve. Toms's superiors readily granted him noncombatant status well before the Defence Act recognized conscientious objectors outside the peace churches. Both a court and the Board for Religious Objection extended exemptions to nontheistic religious believers (and the bill to overturn this died). Sgt. Flattery—a bluff, open fellow reminiscent of Ancient Pistol, Falstaff's companion in "Henry IV"—promised Bruce exemption from combat duty and encouraged him to seek a desk job because of his knee injury. At virtually every opportunity the SADF offered concessions and urged objectors to accept them. When confrontation was unavoidable, the state procrastinated. This, as much as harassment, seems to explain the repeated cancellation of call-ups; the state sought to regain control over timing. Although Toms refused to serve in 1983, the SADF did not insist until 1987. Bruce was not prosecuted for nearly a year after refusing induction. The state detained Philip Wilkinson under the Emergency regulations and eventually charged him with the lesser offense of failing to serve, whose penalty was only a fine.

Almost encouraging dissidents to emigrate, the prosecution repeatedly asked Toms and Bruce why they did not flee, insinuating unsubtly that they should "love it or leave it." After evading detection for four years, Gary Rathbone was deferred for several more. Following its Appellate Division defeat, the state appeared to lose direction. Resorting to court martials (exempt from judicial review), it abandoned prosecution when the accused showed any fight. It would not replace white conscription by a nonracial volunteer force (which would be mostly black); but it did not pursue the growing number of defaulters. It even exempted ANC members—until they flaunted their defiance. When all else failed, the State President extended the indemnity for political offenders. As its power disintegrated, the emptiness of state threats of prosecution mirrored the ECC's bravado a decade earlier.

State vacillation reflected uncertainty about the magnitude of the challenge posed by objectors. Although numerically insignificant, they symbolized treachery by fellow-whites. They intended to inspire others, with some success. They exposed the racism of whites-only conscription and SADF atrocities in Namibia and the black townships. They became heroes to many blacks, forging one of the few interracial alliances in the anti-apartheid movement. They radically repudiated state authority, elevating religion, personal ethics, and even politics above positive law. The magistrate who convicted Bruce stated this clearly: however well intentioned his objection, "general indulgence of such motivation can only lead to absurd results." Bruce's courtroom audience magnified this disrespect by openly laughing at the prosecutor. The state's reaction was unfocussed because it was mystified by the objectors. How could someone choose jail when the SADF made every effort to meet his special needs? Because these were not ordinary criminals jail was a waste, for society as well as the accused. The state's case was too easy: defendants did not deny their guilt, and the sentence was mandatory. Military police, prosecutors, and judges concurred that the defendants' behavior was "stupid."

The state adopted four trial strategies. First, it accepted the defense challenge to justify conscription into the SADF. This was a surprising choice, since the prosecution usually narrows issues in political trials, while the accused seeks to broaden them. The guilty pleas and mandatory sentence would have justified a refusal to hear any evidence in mitigation. Instead, the state countered with sweeping claims that race relations were improving, whites suffered from racism as much as blacks, the SADF protected all citizens, and it enjoyed the respect of blacks in Namibia and in South African townships. Prosecutors shamelessly advanced the clichéd refutation of pacifism: what would you do if the Hun raped your sister (ignoring the fact that the Hun was more likely to be the SADF and raping black "sisters"). In 1848 Thoreau spent a night in jail for refusing to pay taxes in protest against the Mexican-American War. When Emerson visited him and asked "Henry, what are you doing in there?" Thoreau is alleged to have replied, "Waldo, what are you doing out there?" South African officials seem to have felt obligated to answer that question.

The state may have felt compelled to engage the defendants' substantive arguments because they were religious. Afrikaners were deeply attached to their version of Christianity, which they invoked to justify apartheid. Piet Koornhof, a leading Nationalist cabinet minister, addressed the SACLA conference at which Ivan Toms had resolved to open a township clinic. Mag. Verhoef protested to Rev. Torr: "I am also a Christian, by the way, that is why I can talk with you. I am not ashamed about it. I am very serious about that." In passing sentence he maintained that Torr's beliefs were political rather than religious. The ECC decided not to join UDF in order to present an apolitical image.

Having agreed to play on the defendants' turf, however, prosecutors and magistrates made a poor showing. I can only attribute this strategic error to their unquestioning conviction in the moral rightness of the South African state. The young Afrikaner woman who prosecuted Bruce hoped moral fervor would strengthen her dubious authority. If once again the state denounced the "total onslaught" by blacks and reds, surely the white accused would acknowledge the military imperative. There was no other potential audience for this rhetoric. Courtroom spectators vociferously supported the accused. Most of the media were impressed by the objectors' moral courage and dismayed by the harsh penalties.

The second strategy sought to expose flaws in the defendants' characters in order to undermine their claim to moral superiority. Prosecutors portrayed the accused as deceitful, expedient, selfish, compromised, and confrontational. Far from being helpless victims, they actively sought martyrdom and publicity. What prosecutors could not prove they insinuated—political radicalism, communism, ANC sympathies, and homosexuality—particularly damning charges in South Africa. The SADF broadcast homophobic slurs against Ivan Toms; the prosecutor reiterated them at trial; Charles Bester, David Bruce, and the entire ECC were taunted as gay; homosexual attacks on Toms and Bester in prison may have been orchestrated. (It is ironic that "liberal" America continued to exclude homosexuals from the military a decade after "conservative" South Africa sought to conscript them.) By publicizing Toms's gay activism the prosecutor sought to convince the court (and newspaper readers) that he was not an exemplary Christian. Like most prosecution strategies, this backfired. Two distinguished clerics affirmed his

Christian character. And both the military and all the judges conceded the bona fides of Toms and Bruce.

The third strategy was conventional cross-examination of accused and defense witnesses to reveal inconsistencies. The prosecutor was most successful in showing that Toms repeatedly changed the reasons he gave the SADF for requesting transfer to Cape Town. Mag. Verhoef condemned Torr's beliefs as unscientific because based on insufficient evidence. Most of the time, however, witnesses outwitted prosecutors. Dr. Motlana, for instance, demonstrated greatly superior knowledge of township life. In any case, this strategy had no apparent relevance to either guilt or disposition.

Finally, state officials disavowed responsibility for the harsh sentences. They only administered the laws, they did not make them. The accused knew what would happen when they broke the law and had only themselves to blame. They could free themselves from prison by accepting military service; or they could apply to the Board for Religious Objection. Magistrates and judges seemed to feel that expressing sympathy absolved them of any guilt for sending the accused to prison.

The motives and goals of the accused were as diverse as their backgrounds.* Most wanted to reclaim autonomy, become active subjects rather than pawns of state power. Toms expressed this in clearly existentialist terms: "[I]t is the one time I have a choice as a white South African. I can choose to go to prison." By attacking the SADF for repeatedly cancelling his call-ups, Toms invited prosecution. For many, notably Bruce, the cathartic decision ended years of painful, ultimately unbearable uncertainty. Objectors also cleansed themselves of shameful compromises, bearing witness to whites still complicit in apartheid while expressing solidarity with black suffering. Michael Graff said "my main wish is not to compromise myself." In response to the prosecutor, Toms agreed "one does live a life of compromise in South Africa" but added "this was one choice that I had." Bruce sought moral consistency: If he condemned ordinary Germans who failed to oppose Nazism, he, as an ordinary South African, had to oppose apartheid. Toms and Torr refused to apply to the Board for Religious Objection; so did Jehovah's Witnesses (for different reasons). Similarly, the accused eschewed technical arguments (unlike those who resisted removal or censorship, see chapters eight, ten, and eleven). Prison was costly, to both themselves and others, but it offered moral purification. In claiming the moral high ground, the accused could invoke support from all the major English-speaking churches in South Africa—and, of course, the rest of the world. The moral repercussions of jailing conscientious objectors resembled those of Northern states returning fugitive slaves to the ante-bellum South.[129]

---

*On the motivations of Americans who resisted the draft during the Vietnam War, see Gaylin (1970).

By exercising choice, furthermore, objectors forced the state to take responsibility for inflicting punishment. Every time the prosecutor sought an admission of guilt, Bruce replied: "[T]hat is for the court to decide." When the prosecutor said to Torr "[W]hat sentence would you ask from the court today?" he responded: "[I]t is up to this court to make up its own mind." Both retorts resembled Jesus' answer to those who accused him of impersonating God: "Thou sayest."

Defendants often approach political trials as opportunities to educate, particularly in a country obsessed with controlling information. Defense witnesses in these trials testified about black life in the townships and Namibia, inadequate medical care, racism, SADF brutalities, disregard of the Geneva Conventions and other violations of international law, parallels between apartheid and Nazism, and religious objections to warfare and military service. Accused wrote from prison to denounce mistreatment and inhumanity (in apparent defiance of the Prisons Act). The state's attempts to maintain secrecy in the dirty tricks court martial and interdict application suggest fear of publicity. Such an interpretation, however, must deal with the question of audience. Prosecutors and judges were impervious to argument. Spectators were already ardent supporters. Condemnations by foreign observers (governments, churches, organizations) appeared to leave the regime unmoved. The only meaningful audience was the wider public (especially South African) who learned about the trial through the media. The defense enjoyed extensive and sympathetic coverage, but there is no evidence of public response.

If the defense staged the trials, judges had the last word. Two things happened during the arguments made to and by them. First, the scope of the controversy narrowed dramatically. From my perspective as an American lawyer, South African conceptions of relevance seem extraordinarily broad. One reason is legal: the absence of a lay jury to be protected from prejudicial evidence. But the more important reason is political: These trials offered a rare outlet for public debate of the issues tearing apart South African society. Defense, prosecution, and judge all wanted them aired, if for different reasons. The Toms trial gave eloquent voice to the attitude of the Anglican church toward military service. Although the magistrate asked Edwin Cameron why he was exploring Mrs. Bruce's childhood experience in Nazi Germany, he did not halt the inquiry (although he pointedly stopped taking notes). And it was the prosecutor herself who introduced the issue of housing and rent boycotts in Soweto.

If these substantive issues dominated the trial, however, they disappeared from the outcome. Magistrates ignored them in passing judgment and sentencing. Advocates and justices in the Supreme Court and Appellate Division focused exclusively on statutory construction. By joining the two cases, the AD eliminated all biographical detail. Every judge who ruled against the accused took refuge in a pedantic legalism. They became preoccupied with the arithmetic of sentencing. One justice paraded his solicitude by reducing Bruce's sentence less than one percent. Judges claimed to be unwilling instruments of the legislature, expressing personal regret in order to associate themselves with the conspicuous virtue of the accused. Judges joined the SADF and prosecutors in blaming defendants for their plight, reiterating that they could leave prison at will by accepting military service.

Law always narrows conflict; the extraordinary thing about these cases was the outcome. For seven years virtually all observers had read the statute as imposing a mandatory sentence of 1.5 times the outstanding period of military service. Four magistrates and four Supreme Court justices concurred in four cases. Suddenly the Appellate Division found, instead, that it established a maximum, within which magistrates had total discretion. The court disregarded Parliament's explicit rejection of the PFP proposal for discretionary sentencing in the 1983 debate, the Defence Minister's constant reiteration that alternative service (and thus imprisonment) would be six years, the refusal in both 1983 and 1987 to extend community service to those with ethical objections, and the statutory overturning in 1987 of a judge's departure from the mandatory sentence. The outcome clearly reflected the dramatic changes in the political climate between the 1989 convictions and first appeals and the ultimate review in 1991. The bench was selected by Chief Justice Corbett; his predecessor, Rabie, might have chosen, and voted, differently. Even Corbett joined the majority reluctantly, writing a separate opinion. The vote was only three–two. The dissenters' statutory interpretation was at least as compelling as the majority's. This demonstrates the indeterminacy of legal language once again (if further proof were needed).

The one theme uniting the eight opinions was the judges' deep resentment at legislative invasion of their domain. These judges were angry—but not about apartheid, not about SADF atrocities in the townships or Namibia, not even so much about the harsh punishment of objectors. They were angry that the legislature had violated judicial prerogatives, reducing them to "rubber stamps." Judicial concern for the rule of law may be evoked less by state oppression of citizens than legislative disrespect for judicial authority.* Ironically, however, it was the administrative reduction in the length of military service that first allowed courts to cut objectors' sentences. When

---

*Simpson (1988) interprets Lord Atkin's famous dissent in Liversidge v Anderson [1942] AC 206 as resentment at judicial inability to review a Minister's "subjective" discretion. South African Chief Justice Centlivres complained in 1956 about mandatory sentences of whipping for receiving stolen property and saw judicial discretion restored in 1965. Sachs (1973: 254). Both the trial judge who sentenced ANC member Oscar Mpetha and the Appellate Division criticized the mandatory five-year prison term. S v Mpetha 1985 (3) SA 702 (A); *Hansard* cols. 6740-42 (D.J. Dalling, PFP) (6.4.85). United States District Judges have expressed anger at mandatory minimum sentences, see, e.g., NYT §1 p.13 (8.29.93); Weinstein (1992).

discretion was restored, magistrates vacillated between abusing it and refusing it, seeking instructions in the name of preserving uniformity. It was the executive decision to stop prosecuting objectors that began the transformation from conscription to a volunteer force.

The media's fulsome praise for the AD decision should not distract from the courts' equally significant failures: the decision by Justice Didcott (the country's most liberal judge) upholding Emergency regulations constraining the ECC; the Supreme Court's refusal to invalidate whites-only conscription (and the AD's refusal to hear the appeal); and the continuation of SADF dirty tricks in defiance of the interdict. If courts were surprisingly effective shields against criminal prosecution, they were rubber swords against other forms of state power.

CHAPTER 5

SEEKING RECOGNITION

[M]anpower is simply one of the resources that is used in this process of an industry.... [I]f you were to allow the manpower body itself to dictate to the whole as to what size it should be and where it should be deployed—in which departments and on what activities—then I suggest to you, sir, that, other than in possibly a communist or maybe a socialist enterprise, that might be acceptable but, in a free enterprise competitive environment, there is no way that a management could hope to survive. (Reginald John Sampson, Administration Director, BTR SARMCOL)[1]

The Dispute

In 1919 the South African Rubber Manufacturing Company Ltd (SARMCOL) built a factory in Howick, eventually becoming the largest employer in the Natal Midlands. By the late 1960s most workers had been forcibly removed to Mpophomeni, a company town of some 15,000 with unfenced houses, untarred roads, no street drainage, one tap for every four houses, buckets for toilets, and few shops or schools. In the 1950s SACTU (the ANC trade union federation) helped launch the Howick Rubber Workers Union, which had enrolled 750 members by 1956; but SARMCOL refused to deal with it, and the arrest of Harry Gwala and other organizers destroyed the union.[2] The company created a works liaison committee of four nominated workers in the 1950s, allowing them to be elected in the 1970s.

In 1973 the newly-formed Metal and Allied Workers Union (MAWU) renewed efforts to organize SARMCOL (as well as Huletts Aluminium and Scottish Cables, two other Pietermaritzburg factories).[3] It charged that

SARMCOL called the South African Police to stop it recruiting members outside the factory gates. Reginald John Sampson (who joined SARMCOL in
March 1950, becoming director of administration and finance in 1968 and personnel director in 1975) conceded that "the police of Howick were concerned
when there were gatherings outside of the factory... [because] in 1973 there
was very widespread labour unrest in Natal...." When Sampson added it was
"quite possible" that security personnel at the gate called the police whenever
they saw the union canvassing members, he was pressed by P.E. Roux
(Deputy President of the Industrial Court and presiding officer in the trial).
Sampson was unabashed: "a good security man doing his job, if he saw a
major gathering outside of a factory, could well feel that it is his duty to
inform the police." Until MAWU interfered, according to Sampson, labor relations "were very healthy indeed. They were not a cause for anxiety at
management level at all." As late as the 1986–87 hearing, Sampson still
believed it had been illegal for blacks to join trade unions until 1979 (although
Smith and Nephew recognized the black National Union of Textile Workers
in 1975). "[T]he trade unions were certainly not welcome—they were seen as
an irritant in those days.... There was inevitably a relationship between the
SAP and our own Security Department which had its origin from the Security
Legislation in the country which imposed on the local police certain obligations insofar as our operation was concerned." In 1974 the police Central
Intelligence Division gave SARMCOL significant information about the union.

Lawrence Zondi, the MAWU organizer, wrote SARMCOL on July 17, 1974:

> As we hope that you are quite aware of the existence of Mawu
> through a number of phonic communications we have Made
> with you, we would like to extend our relationship to Sarmcol
> management. Our continues [sic] of 56% membership of black
> workers at Sarmcol. We also believe that recognition of our
> union will be made with peace dialogue between the manage-
> ment and its representatives union.

Rejected by management, MAWU called a meeting of African employees on
August 15, which declared that the workers had "no confidence in the present
works committee," called on its members to resign, and authorized union officials to represent them. Because "the pressure from workers in this regard can
no longer be sustained," Zondi sought a meeting with management to air
grievances. SARMCOL summarily refused. "[T]he works liaison committee system at Sarmcol has been in existence for more than 20 years as an established
and effective channel of communication...." Therefore management could not
recognize anyone else. In October, A.R. Hesp (later divisional managing director) told Zondi (and subsequently the works liaison committee):

> Sarmcol is an organisation which is self-contained. The company
> started the factory, have created the business and the company
> runs it on a day to day basis. The company pays the wages; the

company sets the bonus; the company has all the problems—
provides the canteen facilities, tries to help with public transport,
pension fund, all these things; the company spends a great deal
of money and a great deal of time in the running and the operation and that includes the welfare of the workers. No union
spends a cent or any time in assisting in the operations of
Sarmcol. ... We are prepared to do everything possible to solve
problems and difficulties but cannot agree to an outside organisation which knows nothing about running a rubber factory to
become involved.

Industrial relations officer C.S. "Steve" van Zyl reported the names of all those
attending an October union meeting to management and the company policeman. Management's adamant opposition and the five-year banning of MAWU
organizer Moses Ndlovu in 1976 effectively terminated this campaign.[4]

In 1979, having organized twenty-nine other Natal companies in an average of six months each, MAWU returned to SARMCOL. William Geoffrey
Schreiner, a recent graduate of the University of the Witwatersrand, joined
the union as an organizer at its Pietermaritzburg office, serving as branch secretary in 1983-85 and then national education secretary. He and John
Makhatini (branch secretary in 1979) urged workers to sign membership
cards as they entered or left the factory. Soon after they arrived each day the
police appeared, tried to seize their pamphlets, prevented them from talking
to workers, and threatened to arrest them for unlawful assembly. Schreiner
testified that because they were invisible from the main road "it seemed fairly
clear that the police were being phoned by somebody inside the company."
They detained Makhatini for questioning on June 12. The following month
SARMCOL rejected MAWU's request to discuss police harassment, access to
the factory, and shop stewards meetings. "We have no knowledge of the matters concerning the SAP to which you refer. As the Metal and Allied Workers
Union is unregistered, we are unable to enter into discussion or correspondence concerning the other matters related in your letter." MAWU replied:

[L]egally there is nothing whatsoever preventing you from communicating or entering into agreements with unregistered
multi-racial trade unions. Therefore we are only able to interpret
your response to our letter as reflecting that it is simply the policy
of Sarmcol not to communicate with unregistered trade unions.

Sampson wrote "yes" in the margin.

MAWU also wrote the managing director of SARMCOL's English parent
(British Tyre & Rubber—BTR), complaining about non-compliance with the
1977 EEC Code, which required companies to allow employees "to choose
freely and without any hindrance the type of organisation to represent them."
Although SARMCOL did not reply to this or other letters and phone calls, the
minutes of its October 1 management meeting disclosed concern.

> The chairman questioned whether it would not be wise to take the initiative in forming an in-house trade union.... Mr Hesp indicated that the workforce was aware that trade union involvement was not favoured or encouraged but he would be discussing this subject with the rubber industry shortly. In the meantime Mr Sampson would consider a suitable form of trade union constitution for use in case of developments in the direction of an industry union.

Sampson testified that he supported the idea of a sweetheart union as "a way of maintaining a union situation which was more easily accommodated within the company framework." As late as 1983 SARMCOL maintained that "Mawu is not an industry based union and we are not convinced they can effectively represent our workers in an honest and fair way." On December 12 Sampson initiated a fateful connection with the industrial relations consulting firm of Andrew Levy and Associates, who advised:

> Management should do nothing to drive people into unions. Incidents critical should be avoided. Supervisor who cannot handle blacks—no good. Issue statements of intent. Document for handling grievances. Some training for supervisors what the law says and company procedures. Must be important to MD [Managing Director] or won't be important in the works. They have pre-empted largely the union. Our attitude should be Mawu is not in the rubber industry, don't make management mistakes and incidents.

Soon after passage of the Industrial Conciliation Amendment Act 1979 MAWU and three other unions formed the Federation of South African Trade Unions (FOSATU) and applied to register non-racially. When MAWU was registered as a black union it appealed unsuccessfully to the Minister and then successfully to the Supreme Court, which held that the Registrar lacked evidence that the interests of black employees differed from those of others.[5] The following October MAWU again requested recognition, noting it was registered and claiming that a "sound relationship had been built between the union and the employees." But Sampson later testified that the union had "a very minor involvement."

> We had an industrial relations officer [van Zyl] who was a Zulu linguist one of whose functions was to keep his finger on the pulse of the organisation; to know what people were doing and what people were saying and we would have estimated at that time that if there were 200 or 300 members of the union that would have been about the length of it.

Sampson recorded the advice of managers from Hullets Aluminium, Scottish Cables, and NCI:

The union always makes a practice of suggesting the week in which a meeting should be held. This is considered an impertinence and management should never agree to a meeting in the week they suggest. They will do everything possible to make you talk as if you were in the dock by requesting you to outline your policy and questioning you about that policy. It is important to turn the tables on them by aggressive questions to them as to their credibility, who they are, who recognizes them, how many members they have and how many employees of yours they claim to represent. ... Ask them for a copy of their Constitution. ... Never agree to anything. ... They may try to create some sort of incident at the meeting so be on your guard. Agree beforehand that the meeting is to be conducted in English. Try and arrange a venue where tea can be served. Evidently this creates an interesting reaction as some union representatives will suspect it to be poisoned. ... One of the employer representatives must assume the role of chairman of the meeting. If necessary in a slightly aggressive manner. He should take a low key approach as welcoming the opportunity for consultation but that this should not be in any way confused with negotiation or recognition.

Sampson took three months to reply that MAWU "had to represent the interests of the workers, have the confidence of workers and management...." This meant more than numerical representativeness because "we had had unsatisfactory experiences with Mawu up to this time." Later in 1981 the managing director of the British parent declared:

Growth is the object, profit is the measure. ... Those educated post-war...have been taught, almost brainwashed, that it is socially undesirable to make much money. So they combine other objectives that it is important to have good personnel policy, decent factories, to play a significant social role. They blur the issues. The key is the bottom line.[6]

In March 1982 SARMCOL refused MAWU's request to issue stop orders for membership dues. Seven months later MAWU reiterated that it had been registered and believed it represented a majority of hourly employees. Apparently following the advice of other managers, Sampson requested "a copy of the registration certificate of your union showing that you are able to represent all sectors of our multi-racial work-force." He knew, of course, that the Registrar had disregarded MAWU's request to be classified nonracial. At trial he acknowledged that this demand "was certainly used to delay recognition." Schreiner observed that this demand was "odd coming from a company...[which had] separate sports days for separate so-called racial groups and separate facilities...." The minutes of a November meeting of the board of the South African parent noted "no objection to recognizing unions who were properly formulated and whose demands were reasonable"— which Sampson later construed to mean not "outside of, shall we say, the norm of the time."

The same month MAWU wrote the FOSATU representative in the UK: "Union members is plus minus 657 ie plus minus 52% of the total hourly paid work-force." Sampson testified at trial that when MAWU said this to SARMCOL: "[W]e were amazed at that claim. We even went so far as to wonder whether they had got hold of the wrong company." The two sides met in February 1983 (after five months of union pleas) but disagreed sharply about how to determine representativeness. SARMCOL demanded either access to union records or private interviews with each member. MAWU refused the former, insisted on being present during the latter, and sought a secret ballot. Management refused to process stop orders and accused the union of misleading workers into signing them but ultimately agreed to verify the union forms. It took two more months for SARMCOL to send its auditors, who concluded that MAWU had valid stop orders for only thirty-six percent of the workforce—more than SARMCOL expected. Sampson later reflected:

> [W]e were used to battling our way through all sorts of circumstances that may have been adverse so that we were not unskilled in the area of negotiation. We believed that we could reach an accommodation with this union but we proceeded with caution. ... in the Chamber of Industries in Pietermaritzburg there had been at least one very unhappy experience with this particular union.

While representativeness was being contested SARMCOL laid off many employees, denying that this was directed at union members. MAWU strongly condemned the company and threatened to declare a dispute if it did not agree to meet in five days. SARMCOL answered on the deadline, criticizing the union's attitude and declining to meet within the time period. MAWU's attorney replied that the union intended to apply for a Conciliation Board, but the dispute was settled before a hearing.

The parties met to negotiate a preliminary agreement in June. When the directors read the union proposal, Sampson later remembered, they remarked: " '[W]hat happened to the company?' Because the company is simply not mentioned in this agreement at all as having any rights. ... Everything is an expression of the rights of the union." Still, SARMCOL agreed to initiate stop orders on advice from the union, accept them as the criterion of representativeness, and allow union officials to spend an hour a week in the canteen. It was harder to agree on retrenchment procedures, and SARMCOL refused to specify a rule (like Lifo—last in, first out) or grant severance pay.[7] Sampson later explained this as "not an attitude only held by my company but by every company operating in the free enterprise, capitalist system… manning levels must be determined by management." SARMCOL previously had given *no* severance pay to employees with fewer than fifteen years' service and only R50 (plus R10 for each additional year) to those with more. Even this, Sampson testified, "was not really in the sense a severance pay policy as such." SARMCOL resisted greater generosity to long-term employees because it estimated the *average* length of service as twenty-five years. The union sought two weeks severance pay for each year of service; SARMCOL responded by offering two *days* and only to those with at least five years service. SARMCOL prevailed. The parties also promised to seek a procedural agreement within three months after MAWU became representative and then negotiate a substantive agreement.

In August SARMCOL notified MAWU of further retrenchments and its decision to contract out firm security but promised to try to find other jobs for the thirty employees affected. At trial Roux (the presiding officer) commented to MAWU's advocate: "there is some change… in tone or attitude in regard to the company. I am not saying that it has now put on a spotless garb and discarded a completely tarnished garb… but there does appear to be a change in attitude." MAWU promptly challenged the layoffs as a breach of the June agreement, which it was determined to enforce, adding: "this action is certainly not conducive to building mutual respect between our parties." SARMCOL responded with further layoffs later that month.

MAWU also submitted a draft recognition agreement that month. Because SARMCOL now maintained the stop orders it did not challenge representativeness, which had reached an astonishing ninety-five to ninety-eight percent, from just thirty-six percent four months earlier. Sampson rejected the two dates MAWU proposed for a meeting (following the advice he had noted three years earlier) and suggested others, claiming to need time to study the proposals. Schreiner reminded Sampson of his promise to offer counter-proposals promptly. Instead Sampson objected that the union negotiating team was too large. At the first meeting on September 15 SARMCOL agreed to negotiate severance pay, and the parties made some progress on a recognition agreement. But the next day MAWU complained about SARMCOL's attitude toward the union negotiating team. A month later SARMCOL replied that it still used the works liaison committee, although a union representative might appear at the "request of the individual." Schreiner testified to his consternation that the company continued to rely on a committee that "did not represent anybody or if anybody a very small number of people" and his skepticism that the company intended to reach an agreement soon.

SARMCOL broke its promise to comment on MAWU's proposals by September 22. At the first real negotiation on September 27 it just asked MAWU to read its proposals out loud. Sampson's contemporaneous notes reveal his flat refusal to allow the union any say about manning levels. The impasse was repeated the next month. Because the company had retrenched a thousand employees in the previous eighteen months, Sampson noted, the union's insistence on Lifo would create "a company of old men." SARMCOL needed "to maintain a balanced work force. To qualify only on skills and abilities is not sufficient." He was "amazed" at MAWU's insistence on a right to strike and "astounded" that union representatives refused to drink tea with management (apparently forgetting that three years earlier he was advised to offer tea to provoke such an incident).

A month later SARMCOL finally stated that Lifo would have to be qualified by consideration of special skills, the balance of age and experience, the standard of education, mental and physical capacities, and general attitude. Schreiner later testified that this made "nonsense" of the principle. He remembered Sampson reading from a book that "severance pay was a non-negotiable issue, it was an ex gratia payment which would be determined from time to time by the company." His own notes of that discussion agreed with Sampson's: "I mentioned to the board that the union is even questioning the company's right to manage the company and the company's right to control admission." He wrote in his journal: "Retrenchment a management matter. Not one for the recognition agreement." Both sides considered declaring another dispute.

SARMCOL's attitude emerged more clearly at trial. Martin Brassey, MAWU's advocate, had Sampson read out the union proposal: "the company agrees that it shall hold itself available to meet with the negotiation committee of the union on any proposed retrenchment for the purpose of reaching agreement...."

Brassey: Would you look for the clause in the agreement that deprives you of the right to dismiss unless the union agrees? ...

Sampson: We have just read it out, sir.

...

Brassey: Where does it say that?

Sampson: Sir, it requires the parties to reach agreement....

Brassey: Is that honestly the impression that you had over 21 months of negotiation?

Sampson: Yes, sir.

...

Brassey: If the demand had simply been, meet with us to negotiate over manning levels, you would have been happy with that?

Sampson: Sir, the word "negotiate" I think would have been a major problem. "Negotiate" implies that both parties have to have an input and that if one party does not agree then they can block or take steps to block the action that is being negotiated about.

When MAWU declared a dispute, SARMCOL proposed a one-year recognition agreement, after which it would consider adding a clause about retrenchment. In view of MAWU's "current inflexibility," however, "a period of time will be necessary for us to be satisfied that reasonable and proper working practices can be established with your union." Schreiner resented that SARMCOL was "basically treating the union as a child."

At the next meeting, Sampson testified,

> we had been amazed to find that the company was not mentioned as having any rights in this agreement and so we raised the issue of the management's right to manage the company. Their response to that was to say that, "if that is what you want put in the agreement then you must also have a clause specifying the union's right to strike".... We could not understand where a natural right—the management's right to manage— should have to be traded off against the union's right to strike.

In accord with the managing director's instruction to break off negotiations Sampson wrote Schreiner the same day:

> It is clear from the attitude adopted at meetings with our management that you are not interested in negotiating in good faith...but are merely stating your demands in an inflexible manner. We should add that the behaviour of your delegates at the [last] meeting... and the use of obscene language was disgraceful.

He later testified that Mr. Mbanjwa said "every time we meet with this so-and-so company to talk about so-and-so issues all we get is a so-and-so fight and we are simply not prepared to agree to the so-and-so retrenchments that have been proposed."

When MAWU reminded SARMCOL in November of its promise to seek an agreement within three months of accepting representativeness the company was condescending: "When we are again satisfied that you are willing and able to negotiate in good faith we will have further meetings with you." SARMCOL made its own application for a conciliation board on the ground that severance pay was a matter of substance and thus inappropriate for a recognition agreement. This second dispute was also settled just before the hearing.

Negotiations resumed in February 1984 between C.J. Albertyn and G.S. Giles, attorneys for MAWU and SARMCOL, because Schreiner felt he was getting nowhere with Sampson. A purely symbolic issue revealed the parties' radically divergent perspectives. SARMCOL proposed a clause declaring the "common objective" of benefitting "the shareholders, employees and customers." MAWU wanted that changed to "shareholders and/or employees."

Schreiner testified that "it is in the interests of shareholders to have their dividends maximised and it is in the interests of employees to have their wages maximised." Sampson, by contrast, believed that "the term 'company' was large enough to encompass its workforce."

The next month MAWU attended the BTR annual meeting to inform shareholders that management had resisted the union's request for recognition for ten years and document the "pitifully low" wages.[8] In May—after the parties had managed to meet only six times in nine months of negotiation—MAWU proposed embodying the existing consensus in an expanded preliminary agreement, but SARMCOL insisted on including a disputes procedure. Its suspicion and hostility toward MAWU emerged at the trial.

> *Sampson:* If [disputes procedures] were going to be left out of the whole agreement…then we were simply not interested because we had to say to ourselves, "what is there in this relationship at all if there is not going to be security and protection for the company and a logical way of resolving disputes". …

> *Wallis* [SARMCOL's counsel]: … [T]he only substantial stumbling block was the union demand for compulsory appointment of conciliation boards and compulsory access to the industrial court on an allegation of unfair labour practice?

> *Sampson:* Yes. This was no way to run a complicated company like ourselves, it was no way to deal with a representative trade union—rushing in and out of Conciliation Boards or in and out of the Industrial Court, which seemed to be the way in which Mr Schreiner wanted affairs to be run.

> *Roux:* Would it be a correct summary of the stance of the parties with regard to the one issue that where the company was opting for a domestic resolution of disputes the union was opting for…a more formal resolution of disputes within the framework of the act?

> *Sampson:* This would have served, I believe, Mr Schreiner's style of operating admirably because he could then do these things….

> *Roux:* That might have been your perception. It might very well have been Mr Schreiner's perception on the other hand that he did not have any confidence in the manner in which…the domestic resolution of disputes would be carried out by the company.

> *Sampson:* That was an entirely new notion, that there should be introduced a provision which would not allow the employer to make comment on an application for a Conciliation Board or an application to the court, comment which might influence the

Minister in deciding whether this was a proper matter to be dealt with....

Contemporaneously with this stalemate on a procedural agreement, the parties were at similar loggerheads on substantive issues. MAWU sought a seventy percent wage increase, while SARMCOL offered 8.5 percent. MAWU wanted the greatest increase at the lowest levels, but Sampson thought "this was completely upside-down so far as management thinking was concerned." Sampson testified that on May 17 "the union indicated it was not prepared to negotiate further; that those were the minimum demands that they were prepared to accept and they then said they were going to declare a dispute." The company proposed a mediator, whom MAWU accepted, but on July 30 SARMCOL wrote MAWU: "The offer is final and is open for acceptance" within twenty-four hours. MAWU immediately applied for a conciliation board, but the differences were settled before it met (apparently on the company's terms).

Sampson made what he thought was a major concession about May Day.

> [T]his country's productivity is extremely low in relation to most western nations. We have more public holidays I believe than most nations in the west and that to give a gratuitous additional paid holiday which would mean the loss of production and an added cost... was something we were not happy with. ... [Instead he offered unpaid leave.] This was certainly understood to be the first time in South Africa that a company had actually reached an accommodation with a trade union on May Day. ... I had a very rough time at the next meeting of the Chamber of Industries.

(In fact, the Chemical Workers' Industrial Union won a paid May Day holiday at the end of 1984.)[9] Sampson strongly resisted union efforts to negotiate working conditions, such as the definition of shifts or the work week. "You could not possibly have an open clause which would require you to negotiate virtually every message or every change that you made...." He refused a request by the secretary and the chairman of the shop stewards to attend a training seminar because "in the absence of an agreement between the company and the union there are no shop stewards as such."

SARMCOL cancelled an October 2 meeting on the recognition agreement, claiming insufficient time to review the union proposals; three weeks later it found "such wide differences" that it required more time to reply. The same day it refused to discuss pensions because "there is no such body as the SARMCOL pension fund.... [W]e are not in a position to discuss [the BTR of South Africa Ltd group pension fund] with the union.... [G]eneral subjects will in any case not be considered until the recognition agreement has been finalised." The next day MAWU telexed its intent to declare a dispute. Schreiner had found the company's rebuff "very very irritating"; it was "just inviting conflict and tension between the parties." Sampson, in turn, remembered his "exasperation" at MAWU for even raising the issue. He agreed to discuss it only after MAWU had applied for a conciliation board.

On November 14 SARMCOL notified MAWU of further retrenchments and agreed to meet two weeks later—the first meeting in three months. Sampson's contemporaneous notes reveal the fundamental conflict.

> I said management functioned to determine employment levels. ... Schreiner says union has a say in manning levels... it is a function of management, not an exclusive management prerogative. ... I indicated that survival is a management function but Schreiner believes it is a joint function. ... Unanimous decision on company negotiating committee and Mr Blackstock [Managing Director] that union's bottom line proposals are not acceptable.

At about this time Sampson telephoned his attorney, Giles, "with a sense of desperation, acquainting him with the latest developments...[and] asking for his advice. And he said to me, John, the only thing you can do is to go and get yourselves industrial relations experts... and we then telephoned Mr Andrew Levy... and appointed his firm as our consultants." This unremarkable action would have enormous implications two and a half years later.

On December 3 MAWU asked SARMCOL to respond to its proposed recognition agreement within two days, as promised. The company replied on the deadline, objecting that "the parties have gone way beyond the limits of the intended agreement" and urging elimination of "any reference to matters of substance." MAWU's anger suffused its December 7 reply. "It is abundantly clear to us that your company has no serious intention of entering an equitable and reasonable recognition agreement with Mawu." More than a year of discussion had borne no fruit. SARMCOL's refusal "will undoubtedly aggravate relations between employees and management." MAWU announced its intention to declare a dispute.

The union's interpretation of management strategy was closer to the truth than it knew. On December 6 SARMCOL's industrial relations officer submitted a confidential report:

> Although trade union support has reached 90 percent of the workforce, there are signs that the pendulum has reached its zenith and is beginning to swing the other way. A small nucleus of workers are reacting against what the Union is doing and the shop stewards and this reaction may actually be greater than is evident upon the surface. ...

> [He made thirty-four observations, including the following.]

> No. 11. Why do we not fire the shop stewards?

No. 20. Nkatha [sic] and Chief Gatsha Buthelezi are opposed to the union.

No. 27. When did workers just walk into the managing director's office? Why did he not shoot one of them? Even a white man cannot just walk into his office.

No. 31. It is not too late for management to show its teeth and retaliate. Workers want management to do that so that they can challenge the shop stewards.

The night of MAWU's reply the workers staged a go-slow. Sampson spent 10 p.m. to 2 a.m. at the factory trying unsuccessfully to restore normal production. His notes recorded that he told workers: "failure to work we will regard as breaking your contract... [T]he company pays your wages and your side is to give the company good work." He testified, however, that "I do not think we adopted a threatening attitude." Four days later the entire day-shift staged a sit-down strike in the canteen, demanding to know what had happened to the recognition agreement and who was going to be retrenched. At 11:10 the works director warned that the action was very serious, a breach of their employment contract, putting their jobs at risk. Three hours later he read a longer notice expressly warning about job loss. SARM-COL appealed to MAWU; in Schreiner's absence Ian Weir replied that the union did not support the work stoppage and had sent an organizer to the factory but added that the action "was occasioned by your unreasonable refusal to concede a procedural agreement" and urgently sought another meeting. Sampson credited Mr. D. Mbanjwa (whose vulgarity he had earlier condemned) with getting the night shift back to work. Sampson talked to Mr. Allen of Andrew Levy the next day and noted his advice.

> They have declared the dispute. They said it is final. This is how we win our case, by quoting telexes. ... We have all the cards. Schreiner is most unlikely to proceed with a conciliation board in the circumstances. Mr Weir from Pinetown—stubborn and very tough. A great big act. Keep very calm. Worse than Schreiner and younger.

At a negotiation session on December 12 SARMCOL marginally increased its severance pay offer and agreed with the union on thirty retrenchments. But when the factory closed for Christmas, 111 workers in the engineering division refused to stay and maintain the machines. SARMCOL responded by hiring fifty white high school pupils. MAWU declared a dispute and applied for a conciliation board over the lack of progress toward agreements on recognition and severance pay.

When the factory reopened in January 1985 MAWU banned overtime and weekend work in order to reduce retrenchments. Sampson characterized this as "industrial action of various types and threats." Believing that its conciliation board application satisfied the statutory requirements, MAWU asked SARMCOL for access and time to conduct a strike ballot. SARMCOL refused to set aside working time but allowed access to the canteen during lunch. At the same time it expressed renewed interest in negotiations, promising an amended recognition agreement in two weeks.

On February 5 MAWU informed SARMCOL that workers had endorsed the strike 964-3 (with one invalid ballot), adding that "the result of this ballot demonstrates the great degree of frustration caused by your refusal to conclude the agreement" and offering the company a day to reconsider. SARMCOL, however, saw the ballot very differently. Van Zyl told Sampson that each worker was "asked out loud whether he supported strike or not." Sampson did not think this improbable and was "astonished that a so-called secret ballot could be conducted in this manner." Van Zyl also reported that the strike's goal was "to smash the company." Workers, he said, believed that SARMCOL would have to give each striker a month's pay and their accumulated pension. Sampson believed van Zyl's report because he "had a very intimate knowledge of the African, he had been brought up with them and therefore we had to take account of his knowledge and his expertise in matters like this where we could not hope to have any concept as to what might be in the worker's mind."

When MAWU's strike threat persuaded SARMCOL to resume negotiations during the one-day grace period it was the union's turn to snub management by insisting on a conciliation board. SARMCOL rejected MAWU's three suggestions for a chair (two of whom were management oriented). Persisting in its strategy of always rejecting dates proposed by the union, SARMCOL postponed the board for a month, despite MAWU's fears that it could not hold off the strike. On February 15 MAWU reserved the right to strike, telexing that SARMCOL was "not actually interested in mediation." SARMCOL reiterated its "firm desire to settle these disputes as quickly as possible" and promised a revised draft the same day. MAWU replied the next day that it "fails totally to address seriously any of the major issues discussed last year." It reiterated its strike threat if SARMCOL did not respond within hours. The following week they finally agreed that the conciliation board would meet on the date SARMCOL originally suggested. During this period management was very unhappy with what Sampson called the "breakdown of discipline." Workers were taking long tea breaks, and shop stewards were circulating throughout the factory. It disciplined two shop stewards and demanded that they obtain permission from both their department and the department they wished to visit.

The March 7–8 informal conciliation board began with a discussion of disputes of right, which the parties eventually agreed to treat as disciplinary matters. MAWU offered to redraft its proposal within four days, but the board's chair said SARMCOL would not reply that quickly. Sampson's note that day reveals that he continued to negotiate with an eye to creating a record for litigation: "Andrew Levy believes, sooner or later, we are going to have a strike. We are going a long way to meet [Schreiner's] requests. Helpful to paint the view that we have done." When SARMCOL telexed on March 12—the union's deadline—that it was working on further documentation, MAWU called a strike, complaining that "the company had utilised two days of an expensive mediation process to discuss matters of principle amongst themselves which should have been discussed a long time previously." SARMCOL protested the next day that it thought it had until March 14, winning MAWU's promise to return to work if the company proposals arrived by then. They did (with management's condemnation of the "illegal" stoppage), and work resumed on March 15.

Sampson remembered these events differently. The workers started a go-slow during the conciliation board and resumed it on March 11, after the weekend. When he protested on March 12, MAWU denied it was happening, which Sampson found "astonishing," "immature and unacceptable." At 11 a.m., he wrote in his diary, he told the shop stewards: "We want you to warn your members at lunch-time today disciplinary action will be taken against them if the go-slow continues because it is an illegal strike in the middle of negotiations." (His diary entry the next day, however, revealed doubts: "Graham [Giles], is it a legal strike?") SARMCOL telexed MAWU at 1:40 p.m. on March 12 to protest the go-slow and an hour later met again with the shop stewards, who refused to terminate the job action until there was an agreement. This, Sampson testified, "was an extraordinary position from the union because we were losing production, day shift and night shift, on a continuing basis." The company was close to "desperation." There had been "nothing but disruption in the plant since the factory re-opened." They had lost R1 million during a period when they expected R1.5 million profit. "[W]e actually had a graph which showed the... loss, and it was quite a simple matter to extrapolate that line and to realise that unless we got to grips with the problem and got the factory back to normal operation the ultimate result would have been bankruptcy...."

Yet Sampson's diary note that day suggests he was not unhappy with industrial action.

> We have to show a concerted go-slow; three—we need a demand; four—get stewards in as a group, minute the meeting, production records to be shown to them that production has halved and why; five: why—will indicate the demand. If failed by tomorrow morning, find worst offenders in worst departments, give him final written warning; give him a couple of hours then fire him. If Giles unhappy, do it on a whole dept basis and warn summarily dismissed if, within plus/minus two hours, back up with telex to dept.

Sampson's diary continued on March 13:

Great joy—Schreiner backing off. Do not now meet shop stewards. Remember Schreiner gave us deadlines and he is now moving. He is worried he won't maintain strike. He says we are not panicking. They go back and we cannot belt them. Disadvantage. If they come back union will find it difficult to get them out again.

SARMCOL's actions seemed to follow this script. On March 14 it telexed MAWU that continued stoppage was a material breach of the contract. SARMCOL telexed its contract proposals the next morning, and MAWU acknowledged receipt, but at 11 a.m. SARMCOL threatened mass dismissal. Work resumed after lunch, at 1 p.m., but MAWU took "great exception to the issuing of this pamphlet, in particular the threats contained therein." At 2:30, however, SARMCOL reiterated that threat. Sampson's diary note recorded his strategy.

Lunch time pamphlet for lads.

1. Call shop stewards in. We have done our part. Three days are up and we are now warning. Can lead to termination, that failure to return will be loss of your jobs. Tell workers. Steve [van Zyl] to leave pamphlets in canteen. Likely to cause return to work.

2. Another pamphlet, close of plant, unless return Monday [March 18] and work normally you will be fired.

3. Fire Monday.

4. Start re-hiring x old faces, y new faces each. Union lads will be last back, that is no jobs. Schreiner will shout to talk to us. If return to work Monday will either work normally then meet Schreiner on Wednesday and either agree or break. If break, equals fire. If do not work normally, show section results or individual results, brief supervisors to watch shop stewards work performance. Exciting, etcetera, to bounce them out.

Because this was almost an exact script for the mass dismissals six weeks later, the union's advocate carefully dissected it.

Brassey: [T]he plan was, if the workers did not return, to fire them all…[and] because the union lads would be the last back, there would be no jobs for them…anyway, if there is a return to work your supervisors have to watch the shop stewards carefully so that if anything is detected they can be dismissed. Would you agree that that is a fair summary?

Sampson: That is the substance of the advice being given to us. …

Brassey: [Y]ou would certainly have been prepared to use this strategy?

Sampson: Sir, it would have been on our record as a strategy to use, yes, most certainly.

Brassey then turned to Sampson's March 15 diary note: "Schreiner might get them back—bad luck—before lunch."

Brassey: [I]f he got them back at too early a stage you would not be able to take punitive action against them?

Sampson: That is what that says, yes.

Brassey: And if that happens then you would not be able to fire the workforce and clean out the shop stewards? That is the bad luck part?

Sampson: That is the substance of Mr Levy's advice.

Sampson conceded that he generally followed Levy's advice.

After returning to work the employees learned the content of SARMCOL's proposals and expressed their anger through the shop stewards. On March 15 MAWU objected to SARMCOL's reference to "unlawful" industrial action and its threatened retaliation. The union questioned management's bona fides and urged it to be properly prepared to reach an agreement on March 20. Sampson's satisfaction with his strategy, by contrast, emerged in his March 18 note of a talk with Andrew Levy:

State of factory working best in two years. Grapevine message— initial upshot they had a lucky escape and next time they will be unemployed. Tell chaps they came close. Settle. Schreiner will shout and scream on [March 20]. We just say, "that is it, Mr Schreiner"—he has to make the moves. He is a very worried man.

The conciliation board, formally appointed by the Minister of Manpower on March 11 to resolve the dispute "concerning the failure of [SARMCOL] to accept the proposals of [MAWU] regarding a written recognition agreement," met at 2 p.m. on Wednesday, March 20. MAWU had already answered SARMCOL's latest proposals, suggesting three ways of protecting strikers engaged in lawful industrial action: no dismissals within fourteen days of the strike, no selective hiring and firing, and no victimization. In exchange it recognized the company's right not to reemploy those guilty of intimidation and violence. Late that night the parties exchanged final package offers with a deadline of 2:30 p.m. Thursday. Sampson's note of a subsequent midnight meeting with managing director Blackstock, attorney Giles and Andrew Levy employee Allen reveals the company strategy:

Strike two weeks. Would not fire or rehire for two weeks. This will erode Schreiner's power base. More acceptable to the UK. A clean surgical issue. Nothing we have done or proposed is unreasonable. If not broken by two weeks we could have a trickle

back and lose shop stewards by closing gates. Then perhaps fire
after due warnings, obtain new workforce. Aerial pamphlets.

SARMCOL responded to the union offer at noon Thursday, demanding a
reply by 2:30 p.m. MAWU said that was too little time to answer in full but
added: "this offer may provide a realistic basis for settlement...." SARMCOL
granted an extension to noon on Monday, giving Giles authority to deal with
"matters which do not involve principle or substance." At the same time,
Sampson's diary recorded Andrew Levy's advice: "Do not meet with
Schreiner." Schreiner telephoned Sampson at 3 p.m. Friday. Sampson noted
in his diary that Schreiner said "we are closer and [MAWU] might come up
with a proposal that the company can accept." He asked to meet the next
Monday, Tuesday, or Wednesday. Blackstock told Sampson to answer:
"There cannot be anything major bar your own statements. (c) Why do you
not just accept the good with the bad?" After talking to Andrew Levy at 3:20,
Sampson called Schreiner at 4 p.m.:

> [T]he package offered you is a final one open for acceptance by
> noon on Monday, after which it will be withdrawn.
>
> 3. The question of meeting with you therefore does not arise.

On Monday MAWU reiterated that "while we were not able to accept
these proposals without any single change, we nevertheless saw them as
constructive and conducive to a prompt settlement." It found SARMCOL's
refusal to negotiate further "unreasonable and not at all conducive to har-
monious industrial relations," especially since some elements in its final
proposal had never been discussed. Giles responded on Tuesday that SARM-
COL remained willing to negotiate matters "which did not involve principle
nor [sic] substance" if MAWU dropped any clause about severance pay.

After further controversy, MAWU submitted a new proposal on
Wednesday, and the conciliation board reconvened on April 10. SARMCOL
delivered its proposal at 7:30 that morning, which Schreiner testified was
"highly undesirable" and showed that the company lacked "the intention of
actually concluding an agreement." At 11:45 MAWU gave Giles three to four
pages of proposals. Ninety minutes later, Sampson noted, "Giles asked
Schreiner whether that document was in the nature of a demand or what the
union would expect to see included in the proceedings. Schreiner said that
he could tell the company that it was virtually a bottom line position."
Sampson also recorded that Brian Allen of Andrew Levy told him it would
be "a pity to break at this stage. Somebody has got to say that is it. Orderly
close-down pushing a bit and a few [time] periods. The agreement or the
[company] proposals would be perfectly signable." Sampson himself noted:
"Our view, far too much, just too much. Not willing to move on a number
of principles. Keep on giving. We keep on giving and we are not getting
much back. Or give him half an hour."

At about 3 p.m. Giles told Schreiner the company needed another half hour. Giles noted:

> Schreiner was agitated and quite angry and said that he was not prepared to wait as long as that and would only agree to wait until 15h15, so that gave the company about 10 minutes to make up its mind. ... Giles then went off quickly to speak to Schreiner at 15h15 and told him that the company had seriously considered all the points raised by the union but was not prepared to amend its offer.

Schreiner later testified: "The company said they were rejecting all the suggestions that we had put forward" without giving reasons. Sampson agreed:

> We just threw up our hands in dismay and said if that is the attitude of the union, if we simply cannot be given another 15 minutes then we had better get up from the meeting and go to the Conciliation Board and report our inability to reach agreement. ... I cannot speculate as to what our final decision might have been if we had had the additional 15 minutes, but it is unlikely that our position on some of the significant differences would have changed.

The conciliation board formally noted its failure because SARMCOL had rejected the union proposal and withdrawn its own.

Two days later SARMCOL gave workers a pamphlet blaming the failure of conciliation on the union. Four days after that Phineas Sibiya and Philip Dladla (secretary and chairman of the shop stewards committee) wrote SARMCOL accepting its last draft but incorporating union proposals the company had ignored and making minor amendments. They proposed meeting the next morning to sign the agreement. Sampson consulted Brian Allen three days after receiving this proposal and noted his advice: "Do not get upset with the final tone of their letter, it means we can still concede, not be obstinate. We have bust a gut over this agreement, it would be a pity to blow it now." Sampson telephoned Schreiner six days later, suggesting they meet alone. Schreiner replied:

> [I]t was against the policy of the union. ... [I]t puts an organizer in a very very invidious and vulnerable position if he, for whatever reason, gets into problems and management claimed that certain things have been agreed which in fact have not been agreed. It is also contrary to our principle of building and developing worker leadership.

Sampson refused to reconvene the negotiating committees or send the company proposals by telex. He testified that such a tête-à-tête was "common practice in the United States." In the end their telephone conversation identified retrenchment procedures and discipline following industrial action as the two main problems, and they agreed to speak again in four days (on April 29).

On April 26 MAWU sought confirmation that the factory would close on May Day from 11:45 a.m. to 10 p.m. SARMCOL responded that the night shift would have to be back by 6 p.m. Schreiner and Sampson spoke by phone on April 29, as planned, but only to replay the dispute about May Day. Schreiner quoted the July 1984 wage agreement: "[T]he company undertakes not to prevent any of your members concerned from clocking out early on 1 May provided that it is not before the commencement of the normal lunch break on that day and provided further that such persons will only be paid for the hours worked on that day." He then offered to get the men back by 8 p.m., but Sampson remained adamant. At the trial, Roux asked Sampson "were you not in retrospect rather formalistic... could you not have accommodated these night workers at that stage?" Sampson replied that "our markets had been crumbling" and "there was still an overtime ban" (although the latter should have alleviated the problems caused by the former). "Every hour sir, when you have a labour force as large as ours—a thousand men working—you cannot afford to be accommodating in an issue like this."

Sampson was at work at 7:30 a.m. on April 30, some forty-five minutes after the day shift began. Twenty minutes later he "saw a very large number of workers pouring out of those factory departments which can be seen from my office window."

> I immediately thought about my telephone conversation with Mr Schreiner the day before. At the end of that call he had said to me there is going to be trouble... and I wondered if what I was now seeing in front of me was the trouble.

Van Zyl reported that the shop stewards said "quite emphatically that the strike had been caused through the company's failure to sign the agreement." Gavin Brown at Andrew Levy told Sampson: "Be careful of threats at this sensitive stage. Do this [i.e., issue threats] post May Day situation." Sampson himself noted:

> Very tense[,] staff dragged out. Consider that they may not come in tomorrow which we regard as due to May Day. We could prove that re buses [taking workers to the rally] etcetera. A wage strike is less likely but cleaner. [Brown] thinks it is a legal strike (bad publicity, too emotional). We could consider lock-out and only allow people in on basis that there will be no work stoppage on the question of recognition agreement.

SARMCOL immediately telexed MAWU that the strike was "an illegal industrial action and a breach of the individual contracts of employment of your members." MAWU replied that the strike was legal in light of the company refusal to conclude a recognition agreement, the failed conciliation board, and the February strike ballot. It urged SARMCOL to sign the union proposal, offering to meet first to consider "minor semantic changes." "[O]ur members wish this negotiating document to be signed by your company prior to their returning to work." A newspaper quoted Schreiner as saying that day: "Management have been procrastinating for too long now and the workers are not prepared to back down this time."[10] The next day it quoted Dladla telling the May Day rally that the workers "were tired of waiting for the company to sign the recognition agreement and they would not go back to work until the company signed."[11]

On May Day Sampson recorded a conversation with Andrew Levy:

> He goes along with no lock-out, no barred gates. He agrees dismiss but it is the worst timing for us due to international implications on BTR in U.K. This is total war mode. Andrew believes this is the route but very bad for us.... Make a list of those you are not taking back including those who have misbehaved.

The same day Sampson drafted a telex to Alan Bird (Managing Director of the South African parent):

> Options on strike agreement.
>
> 1. Sign the agreement as presented by the union.
>
> 2. Meet with the union and try to settle the five fundamental differences.
>
> 3. Meet as in (2) above under a mediator.
>
> 4. Stand fast on our ground, that is the agreement as presented by us to the union last month.
>
> The only option we see is (4) above. The fundamentals are such that there is no prospect of reaching agreement on them nor can we accept the union position on these fundamentals.

On May 2 SARMCOL protested about the intimidation of staff, concluding: "[P]lease immediately advise whether you condone this situation and we call on you to take immediate steps to have our staff released." MAWU asked for details so it could investigate. SARMCOL identified the victims as all non-white monthly paid staff and non-union weekly paid staff. "This is not the time to conduct an investigation." MAWU responded that the allegations were "extremely vague and highly improbable." It could do nothing without more information. Sampson's subsequent testimony provided it.

> [A] large gang of factory workers armed with sticks and with pipes...burst into the estimating department...demanding that the Asiatics...go with them to join a strike.... [A]nother gang of

> workers broke into the main office similarly armed and they said
> they had come to take the staff from the computer department
> to the strike. ... [T]hroughout those three days quite frequently
> I saw gangs of four or five or six blacks, sometimes with one or
> two Asiatics, with sticks and pipes going into the departments
> which were within my view at that time, each day looking to see
> if any of the staff that they had taken out had escaped from the
> canteen and gone back to their place of employment.

He later called it "the most devastating experiences, sir, during the three day
strike.... I cannot tell you the emotional impact that that had on management. These were men that most of us knew personally." He called them
"hostages" because they were "held" in the canteen but admitted that they
went home each night and voluntarily returned the next day.

On May 2 SARMCOL reiterated to MAWU that the strike was illegal and
the refusal to return to work "a material breach of the employment contracts" and criticized the union for rejecting management's offer. The same
day SARMCOL told the workers sitting in the canteen to resume work by 4
p.m. or face dismissal without further notice and said the same to the night
shift, which should have begun at 5 p.m. Sampson testified: "[T]herefore we
had complied we felt with the warning adequately for both the day and the
night shift people." At 8:43 p.m. it telexed MAWU: "Reluctantly the company
has now taken a decision to terminate the contracts of employment as indicated in this notice and this fact will be communicated shortly to those
concerned." Sampson testified that the decision had "enormous implications
for the company," which had "enjoyed an exceptionally good relationship
with our workers of all races." He attributed the loss of another R1 million
to "a crumbling customer base, our product performance had been very
poor during this period, our delivery promises we had not met." Because a
strike of even two weeks would destroy the customer base and threaten
bankruptcy, the only alternative was "to dismiss the workers and see if we
could not man this factory again by people who were prepared to work for
the company."

MAWU telexed the next day that the termination was "unlawful," although
Schreiner later admitted to Roux that he was "blurring the distinction"
between "fairness and lawfulness." MAWU warned that the company's
"provocative" action would "increase the possibility of intimidation" and
"encourage police involvement," which could "only exacerbate hostility and
bitterness towards management." The use of "scab labour" would "seriously
undermine the possibilities of settlement of this dispute."

On Friday, May 3, SARMCOL locked out the entire workforce (which had
sat in the canteen the previous day). When they milled about the gates, it
called the police to disperse them. The next day it advertised for new
employees on Radio Zulu, offering a preference to early applicants. At least
500 applied for work on Monday. The same day SARMCOL ordered strikers

to vacate their houses in the compound. Management also interrogated each one of its ninety monthly staff "to confirm that he was not a striker, that he had not gone to the strike of his own volition, that his absence was due to intimidation, and on his making that declaration sir he was reinstated." On Tuesday MAWU's attorney phoned SARMCOL's attorney offering to negotiate at any time or place, directly or indirectly, without precondition. On Wednesday Sampson recorded the advice of Andrew Levy's Gavin Brown about how to respond:

> The sooner you re-man the better and before any request from the union in the form of a demand. [Schreiner's] strategy is a long-term one. ... [D]on't talk unconditionally at this stage. It must be on the clear basis that they are prepared to make major changes. ... Giles should say as long as you come prepared to make significant concessions otherwise you are wasting your time; you must bring offers and proposals with you. ... We are not reinstating so that talks can continue. Hold him off.

When the strikers came that day to collect their weekly pay packets, they found that SARMCOL had inserted applications for re-employment. Sampson described their response.

> I was actually at the pay point... when the payout took place, and to our astonishment sir we found that there were a couple of shop stewards in the foyer and as each man received his pay the shop steward took the envelope from him, opened it, took out the application for employment form, then closed the envelope, handed it back to the man sir.... This was so serious an action in our view that I called the company photographer and he actually took one or two photographs of this activity taking place.

Because of intimidation, Sampson testified, the company escorted workers in and out of the factory. One or two houses were burned, and a worker was hospitalized after a beating. Of the 370 workers living in Mpophomeni, 240 returned to work but were coerced into resigning or fleeing the township.

MAWU's advocate tried to get Sampson to admit he was following Andrew Levy's strategy to destroy the union.

> *Brassey:* I am going to suggest to you that it was the hope of management that those compliant workers would return, but the union lads would be left out.

> *Sampson:* People who did not want to work for BTR SARMCOL were free to work anywhere they liked. ... [He rejected the word "compliant."] [W]e wanted a return of people who prized their jobs and were prepared to get back into the factory and get on with the job in the same loyal way they had done before.

Brassey: Was it your hope that the union lads would be left out in the course of the process?

Sampson: Sir, we would not have lost any tears if they had been.

Brassey: Was a union lad merely a person who happened to be a member of the union, or was it a person who felt very strongly, was he a leader amongst the union movement?

Sampson: ... [T]hat would have been the trouble-maker or the more militant or the more outspoken, more aggressive of the people in the union camp who probably would not have come back.

...

Brassey: I just put it to you Mr Sampson that the purpose of the dismissal was essentially to smash the union as an influence amongst your workers?

Sampson: It was not the aim... it was certainly one of the effects of the dismissal.

Brassey: It was one of the purposes too.

Sampson: Sir, to some extent that is true because the final strike was an absolute disaster for the company and we began to realise that the only hope of dealing with this union is if they are prepared to give up the impossible belligerance and disruption that we have been exposed to by them.

On Friday, May 10, MAWU warned SARMCOL that hiring scabs would create "immense friction between the Howick residents" with "very serious consequences." If the company ignored this advice the union refused to "accept any responsibility." Schreiner testified that the union called daily meetings in the Mpophomeni community hall starting Sunday, May 5, at which "the shop stewards emphasised to the strikers that it was essential to be disciplined, to be organised, and to act in a responsible manner." SARMCOL replied on May 11 that it was following its normal practice of giving preference to former employees. It denounced the "blatant and unlawful coercion and interference with the freedom of our dismissed workers to make decisions for themselves." Two days later MAWU declared that its members had "unanimously decided that since their dismissals were unlawful they wish all to be reinstated once the recognition agreement dispute has been resolved" and urged resumption of negotiations. Schreiner testified that workers had given the shop stewards the employment applications they found in their pay packets in accord with a collective decision taken several days before. Roux's comment reveals striking impartiality:

I do not see the problem as being a problem which places the onus squarely on the union in this situation. It is also a situation in regard to the company. ... A company faced with strike action might also equally say, well we have realised that you have gone on strike. We are prepared to take you back. We know you can go on strike again. Come back and we will now talk again, realising that you have shown your solidarity in your strike action.

SARMCOL would have none of this, however. The day after MAWU's telex it told the union to send any new proposals to Giles. Brand complied immediately: "Your client has advised we should direct matters for an agenda of a meeting re BTR Sarmcol to yourself which we do as follows: 1. Conclusion of recognition agreement; 2. Reinstatement of employees." The next day Sampson recorded the advice of Andrew Levy's Gavin Brown.

The most important message is there is no relationship any more. ...no open-ended debate or discussions but only specifics. ... Every day that goes by you [Sampson] are remanning the factory and his position [Schreiner's] is getting weaker. He must come with surrender terms. ... Graham [Giles] must just be a listener. He can say he has no instructions but if there is a settlement, it must be a final one. Gavin believes Brand sees the risk in the legal route, therefore they will try to get back and fight us another day on better grounds.

Giles followed the advice in telexing Brand that day.

[O]ur client was inviting your client to submit proposals to enable our client to decide whether or not there was any point in meeting with your client. Our client was not inviting matters for an agenda at any meeting. ... [O]ur client maintains that it lawfully terminated the contracts of employment of all the employees who, according to a telex from your client, were refusing to return to work until the recognition and procedural agreement... had been signed.

Replying two days later, Brand maintained that "[O]ur client is willing to negotiate at any place and time either directly or through ourselves." This elicited the same response from Giles: "[O]ur client was not seeking to initiate negotiations." On May 25 Schreiner wrote Sampson that "all our members wish to be employed notwithstanding their legal strike action" and sought a "clear response" about whether Sampson was prepared to attend a "settlement meeting." Giles replied that job vacancies remained and there was no point "in meeting to cover ground already canvassed." The next day Schreiner reiterated MAWU's desire for "bona fide discussions aimed at the resolution of such dispute," only to be coldly spurned by Giles: "[O]ur client denies that any dispute exists such as is alleged therein." When MAWU asked about salaries owed to monthly paid staff SARMCOL refused to concede its "right to represent these ex-employees... [who] are no longer employed by this company."

On June 10 MAWU switched from pleas to threats of legal remedies. "[I]t is going to be very time-consuming and expensive for both of us to get relief for your breaches of the UN, ILO and EEC codes... [and in] actions before the South African Courts." It urged SARMCOL to submit to binding arbitration. Sampson's diary note was unambiguous: "arbitration obviously not." Two days later he recorded Andrew Levy's advice.

> International field is where he is going now. Nothing to hang us on in SA. ... Will (a) get British trade union movement and British MPs in Parliament; (b) pressure via the EEC Code; (c) institutional investors in U.K.; (d) Church groups in U.K.; (e) Feature at BTR AGM in U.K.; (f) Will raise at ILO in Geneva; (g) Hold an enquiry at ILO as to whether took place dismissals under Section 158—I think that is (to prove flouted conventions); that does not matter to us; (h) UN General Assembly but no impact for us at all.

Two days after that SARMCOL replied brusquely that "we do not recognise that there is a dispute over which we could arbitrate," adding perfunctorily that it was "always willing to listen to any practical proposals you may care to address to our attorney." MAWU took up this "offer" on June 17: "Our practical proposals as follows: 1. suggest meeting 24.6 at 1:30pm at the factory. 2. Mawu to be represented by its negotiating committee. 3. Meeting to be unconditional with agenda as previously telexed to your lawyers." Only on the day suggested did SARMCOL bother to reply that "your proposals are simply a repetition of your previous position which remains unacceptable to the company." Sampson testified: "There was no way in which we could see ourselves meeting in an open-ended negotiation with the union with a pistol held to our heads... that we sign the union document otherwise the intimidation, violence, whatever it may be would continue."

On June 21 the strikers hand-delivered a letter asking Sampson to sign the union proposal and reemploy all the workers. "If you cannot meet our demands then you must go back to Britain where you came from." The next day some sixty workers travelled to Johannesburg. Police stopped them from picketing BTR headquarters, but they did hold a press conference decrying the wages (below poverty level), documenting the severe malnutrition of Mpophomeni children, and noting that BTR's national pretax profits had averaged more than R16 million in 1980–84, while productivity had increased an average of eighteen percent annually.[12] On their return early Sunday morning they marched through Mpophomeni calling people to a meeting; the 2,500 who attended condemned scabs and vowed to continue boycotting

Howick merchants. Police teargassed the crowd and attempted to arrest a youth, provoking a struggle in which four police were injured. The homes of several scabs were burned. The next evening a crowd stoned a bus carrying scabs and stabbed to death Dumisane and Khehla Ntombela, one of whom worked at SARMCOL. Vulindlela Magistrate T.E. Strachan imposed a twenty-one-day ban on meetings in the township. When Father Larry Kaufmann offered a Roman Catholic church hall in Howick for meetings, Town Clerk Ron Robbins prohibited them there, too.[13]

On June 26 (two days after both SARMCOL's latest rebuff and the killings) MAWU denied that it had adopted any "position." "[W]e are prepared to meet yourselves on an unconditional basis.... If you are unhappy about the items suggested for your agenda we are quite happy for you to suggest other and/or additional matters." It feared that the recent violence, which it opposed, was "only the beginning." But it was "unable to make much progress in calming the situation for as long as your company is unwilling to meet and try and settle matters." SARMCOL replied on June 28 in a tone intended to end the dialogue. "[W]e see no purpose in meeting to discuss that agenda.... We have no other or additional matters to discuss with you. We see no purpose in continuing the present exchange of telexes...." Nevertheless, MAWU issued a press release in July offering to "drop some or all of its demands or agree to amend some of its demands" and "meet unconditionally to try and resolve the dispute."

The strikers sought to increase pressure locally as well as abroad. On June 29 a convoy of eleven buses paralyzed traffic in downtown Durban until police escorted them to Edendale Lay Ecumenical Centre for a meeting with community and student organizations.[14] MAWU visited neighboring communities to condemn scabs, distributing leaflets explaining the reasons for the strike and singing "Uthinta MAWU undakwe yini" [You must be drunk to play with MAWU].[15] At about the same time Inkatha organized counter-demonstrations in Mpophomeni, shouting "Down with the strikers," "Get out of Mpophomeni if you don't obey the KwaZulu government," and "Join Inkatha or go and live elsewhere."[16] Violence spread to Pietermaritzburg, where many workers lived and meetings were held after being banned in Howick. On June 30 MAWU organized a street demonstration under the slogan "Rats out of SARMCOL."[17] A week later 2,000 people attended a rally calling for a general stayaway. On July 16 strikers coming from court, where several had been charged with intimidation and assault, fought scabs coming from the factory, leading to the arrest of fifty and charges of obstruction against thirty-eight MAWU members.[18] Escalating school boycotts intensified the tension.

MAWU was able to enlist the support of the local Chamber of Commerce but not the Chamber of Industry or the Afrikaanse Sakekamer (the Afrikaans Chamber of Commerce). With the backing of FOSATU it called a general stayaway on July 18. Although all three business groups denounced it as concerning "a matter which has no direct influence on [workers'] lives and which could be resolved by way of court procedures," almost nobody worked in Pietermartizburg that day because the transport workers halted all movement. Shops were looted and administration board offices and beerhalls burned. Several thousand workers held brief stoppages in Durban. Scabs' houses in Mpophomeni were burned, and the fire could not be extinguished because water had been cut off two days earlier. Barricades of old cars and excrement from bucket toilets stopped police from entering the township. The consumer boycott, begun in Howick and extended to Pietermaritzburg, lasted more than forty days. Despite scab purchases, the Pietermaritzburg Chamber of Commerce estimated that black shopping was down sixty to seventy percent.[19] More than a dozen organizations supported the strikers.[20] The *Daily News* commented over-optimistically: "Those few employers who had still believed that the old order continued—that workers making unreasonable demands could simply be dismissed and replaced by others off the street—will now be revising their ideas."[21]

The British TUC and the trade unions of Dunlop (which BTR had bought in 1984) pressured the multinational without effect. The BTR personnel director called it "invidious for unions in Britain to raise this matter. BTR South Africa was completely independent and acting within its rights." When the chairman of BTR South Africa endorsed the state of emergency and opposed rapid change, MAWU declared there was "no place for [BTR] in South Africa.[22] MAWU received support from two international unions, as well as ICFTU. Later in the dispute workers at South African Dunlop factories engaged in work stoppages and strike ballots but were deterred by the threat of legal action.[23] The EEC eventually held hearings on SARMCOL, but the ILO refused to get involved because of its total boycott of South Africa.

Learning from an intermediary that he might get a more favorable response from Managing Director Blackstock, Schreiner phoned him on July 22, abandoning any prerequisite that SARMCOL sign the recognition agreement and stressing the workers' desire for phased reinstatement. He conceded that those charged with serious crimes might be excluded. Blackstock insisted that the union first sign management's proposed agreement. At his suggestion Schreiner phoned a week later and was asked for written proposals about phased reinstatement. But on August 2 SARMCOL irrevocably closed this door by offering permanent jobs to its hitherto temporary workforce. Apparently unaware of this, MAWU made two further conciliatory approaches on August 6 and 8, which Sampson characterized at trial as "totally unacceptable because we could simply foresee a picking up of where we had been before, back to the untidy, difficult situations that we had just come through."

MAWU's August 12 meeting with Sampson and Blackstock was a fiasco. When the union sought reemployment of a "significant" number of strikers, SARMCOL said only fifty vacancies remained. (In the end, only sixty-six of the nearly 1,000 original workers were rehired.) Schreiner felt humiliated.

Schreiner: One of the questions that Mr Blackstock kept repeating in that meeting, which we found very strange, was he kept asking us to motivate [explain] why the company should settle the dispute. ...

Roux: In other words, was his attitude that there was no obligation upon the company to settle?

Schreiner: Very much so, yes.

Roux: If he did settle, it was an ex gratia settlement?

Schreiner: Absolutely.... I got the impression that what Mr Blackstock was looking for was almost for the union to sort of come crawling to the company and begging now to be given some left-overs.

Sampson's own notes of the meeting recorded that "Schreiner said that the recognition agreement as an issue has dimmed into insignificance. If this meant compromising on the agreement they would even be prepared to do that."

Once it was obvious the company would not rehire the strikers MAWU, which was providing food worth R20,000 a month, created the SARMCOL Workers Cooperative (SAWCO), chaired by Phineas Sibiya (former chair of the shop stewards committee). SAWCO bought goods in bulk, made t-shirts, ran a health project, engaged in dairy and vegetable farming, and produced three plays about the struggle, which toured the country and visited England in 1987.[24] But all this effort provided a bare subsistence for just 100 of the 1,000 workers fired.[25] An August 1986 survey found that three-fourths of the households of former workers lived on less than R500 per month and more than half on less than R300 (compared to thirty percent and five percent in neighboring communities). Only a quarter were looking for work; forty percent were over forty-five and unlikely to find any, and many still considered themselves employees of SARMCOL, whose management they called "our fathers." Former workers displayed significant psychological distress at their inability to support their families, often turning to alcohol, violence, and crime. Many lost furniture bought on the installment plan, took their children out of school, could not afford medical care, and had insufficient food.[26]

Abandoning faith in negotiation, MAWU considered a §43 proceeding but rejected it because the case was too complicated. To obviate a pointless conciliation board, MAWU asked SARMCOL to refer the matter directly to the Industrial Court, but the company refused and on November 29 opposed MAWU's application for a conciliation board. The reasons for such obstructionism emerged in Sampson's notes of his December 13 conversation with Andrew Levy.

Fosatu has virtually given this one up and [MAWU] are now doing a one-man war. [The proposal to go directly to the Industrial Court] is Brand's work. … We do not mind fighting a lawyer, but not one who also behaves like a trade unionist. Group should take work away from Bowman's Gilfillan [sic]. Brand is a senior partner. We have every right to expect him to act ethically. The position is intolerable. Feeding the hand that bites me. We should respond strongly to the press by telex today. I should write and telex it through Andrew [Levy]. It is bluster; they will never do it. What they are trying to [do is] to manoeuvre us into a situation where they are saying: you said you acted lawfully, let the court decide. Therefore let us go to the court to arbitrate. This is not the point at all. We are not preapred to go to arbitration with anyone or anywhere. You think your members were wrongfully dismissed, go and talk to the court. But understand whatever you do, we are going to oppose. You must raise the action and we will defend it on the basis that there is no dispute firstly. Our second line of attack will be that it was an illegal strike. Our third line of attack will be that we were justified in dismissing and will take all the technical points we can on the way. It is typical of the type of advice that comes from that quarter [Brand] where the law is seen as a means to an end. … They will never lodge papers.

Despite SARMCOL's objection, a conciliation board was established in January 1986. After meeting for three hours the next month it found, not surprisingly, that agreement was impossible. SARMCOL simply rejected MAWU's proposals and offered none of its own. The Minister of Manpower referred the dispute to the Industrial Court in May. Two months later MAWU formally claimed reinstatement of all workers who sought it (retroactive six months) and an order that SARMCOL resume negotiations for recognition.[27]

The Industrial Court

In September, the Industrial Court President (Ehlers) and Deputy President (P.E. Roux) met lawyers for both sides to discuss venue and the composition of the panel. MAWU proposed the Mpophomeni community hall, but the court chose the Ecumenical Lay Centre outside Pietermaritzburg, which could hold all thousand strikers. Roux, who was to chair the hearing, wanted two other members because of the complexity of the case and asked the parties to comment on his nominees—C.C. de Witt and M.J. Oosthuizen. MAWU welcomed the invitation, but SARMCOL objected, obtaining rulings from the Johannesburg and Durban Bar Councils that it would be "undesirable" for advocates to comment. Nevertheless, MAWU placed on record that de Witt currently held a grant from Anglo-American Corporation, consulted for management, and had written in favor of returning to the common law in industrial disputes. This would be ground for seeking his recusal, although MAWU declined to move it. Roux rejected the objection, noting that de Witt was prepared to advise labor as well (even if he had never been asked). On October 14, Brand tried another tactic, urging Giles to accept arbitration and proposing the director of the Independent Mediation Service of South Africa, a professor at the University of the Orange Free State (whose thesis concerned the right to strike), and an Asian or African advocate. Brand added: "A panel of this sort...would...represent a cross-section of South African society." SARMCOL naturally rejected the proposal.

The Industrial Court hearing consumed thirty-nine days between November 4, 1986, and July 10, 1987, making this labor case the longest in South African history.[28] Opening arguments alone took a week. Roux ordered frequent Zulu summaries of the proceedings for the hundreds of workers and their supporters, who attended daily and began and ended each session with freedom songs. During a recess a month after the hearing began Inkatha murdered Phineas Sibiya, chair of the shop stewards committee, and three other Mpophomeni residents (see chapter six).

The trial created a record of 4,250 pages, supplemented by some 3,000 pages of exhibits. Schreiner and Sampson related and documented the narrative presented above. The central issues were the differences between the parties, the reasonableness of their positions, and responsibility for the failure of negotiations. MAWU called four other witnesses. A University of Natal psychologist presented his survey of the effect of mass dismissal on the workers and their families. A shop steward described the May Day strike. An organizer testified about both police harassment in the 1970s and the February 1985 strike ballot. And the secretary of the shop stewards committee spoke about worker attitudes and the ballot. SARMCOL called two white supervisors to describe the intimidation of monthly salaried workers.

MAWU portrayed SARMCOL as conservative, inexperienced, and inept. Brassey got Sampson to admit that he knew little about the 1979 Wiehahn Commission (which transformed labor relations), confused two very different professional journals, and was ignorant of the ILO code. But when Schreiner alleged that management came to meetings unprepared and without authority to negotiate, Sampson responded that it drafted eighty percent of the proposals discussed.

Sampson testified before the hundreds of workers he had fired: "We were a company that was concerned for the workers that we had. I do not believe anyone present in this hall today would gainsay that, sir, that this was a company that was a good employer." But SARMCOL's advocate, McCall, virtually conceded MAWU's characterization of his client in the course of cross-examining Schreiner.

[W]hen you went into Sarmcol to negotiate surely you had to take them as you found them...as they had grown up in Howick in a rural community compared to Metal Box which had branches all over the country and was in cities and so on... [T]hey had no obligation to you to have sophisticated procedures. ... [Y]ou could not expect Sarmcol if it was going along quite happily as it appears to have done, making large profits and having very contented workers who had been there for 25 years, to actually go out of its way to equip itself to start negotiating with Mawu?

MAWU should have "set its sights lower." "You knew it was going to be a hard uphill struggle." Sampson admitted that the company had "ratcheted" up its position as negotiations continued.

As evidence of SARMCOL's incomprehension or misrepresentation of the union position, MAWU offered the account by the managing director of the South African parent to his board of directors on July 25, 1985:

1. The Trade Union wanted to decide how many people were to work in specific departments, thus seeking to take away management's right to manage.

2. In the event of a strike, whether legal or illegal, the company was not to take any action, thus blocking management's legal rights.

3. The Trade Union wanted retrenchments to be on a last in first out basis regardless of skills involved.

Although Sampson admitted that he had terminated negotiations with MAWU after the May 1985 strike, less than two years later he signed a recognition agreement with UWUSA—the trade union sponsored by Inkatha. The moment was highly significant: half-way through the hearing and just a few months after Inkatha had murdered four Mpophomeni residents in an attempt to intimidate and take over the township. Although UWUSA was unregistered, Sampson explained that "a lot has happened since 1982/83 when that was our policy" (his refusal to talk to MAWU because it was unregistered). He recognized UWUSA because it had achieved "something in excess of 65% support" (although MAWU had enrolled ninety-five to ninety-eight percent).[29] He insisted that UWUSA represented SARMCOL's multiracial workforce (although its constitution limited membership to Zulus).

SARMCOL's version of these events was a mirror image of MAWU's. The union was militant, intransigent, unreasonable. In cross-examination, McCall asserted: "[T]he union expected that there would be many more struggles in the future." Schreiner "viewed everything the company did...with suspicion." Why was there so much industrial action? "Was the union whipping up this anger?" "Was this something that only started when the union was recognised?"

McCall found it "strange that the chaos was introduced into BTR from the time that the union was recognised and the negotiations regarding this agreement commenced." SARMCOL felt it was being targetted. BTR South Africa Chairman Peter Fatharly wrote the English parent after the mass dismissal: "It is mainly multinational companies... that have been selected as MAWU's targets for disruption." To Sampson "it was almost as if BTR Sarmcol was being set up as a guinea pig in which the union was going to attempt to move into new knowledge, into new ground, into new concessions."

McCall insisted that "almost from the outset there was a note of hostility from the union," citing the refusal to drink tea with management in October 1983 and the overtime ban and canteen boycott. The union was impatient; two and a half years was not an excessively long time to negotiate recognition. MAWU's demand for severance pay revealed "a very aggressive approach and quickness to... suggest the declaration of a dispute as soon as one ran into some sort of a deadlock."

Controversy naturally was most intense about the final strike. McCall repeatedly attacked the adequacy of the February 1985 vote and MAWU's failure to retain the ballot papers for the requisite three years. When he persisted, Brassey objected (perhaps embarrassed by the union's negligent or intentional misconduct), producing one of the rare angry exchanges between counsel. McCall blamed MAWU for prolonging the strike by refusing to sign the company's proposed recognition agreement. He condemned MAWU's failure to investigate and discipline members for intimidating strike breakers.

McCall constantly baited Schreiner, impugning his veracity in an unsuccessful attempt to provoke an outburst:

> You made that statement either deliberately or recklessly and you have persisted along the same lines until, towards the end, you shifted your ground.

> I suppose you know what is coming, so now you are trying to shift from that position.

> I have asked you before, do words have no meaning for you?

> You are never very clear, Mr Schreiner, when you are in a corner.

> I presume you weighed your words carefully for once, before making a statement to the press, is that right?

He accused Schreiner of failing to acquire "any knowledge about economics and managing a company before you started negotiating with the company." He taunted Schreiner for having "lost your first workforce at Hewlett's and... your next one at BTR."

As chairman of the hearing, Roux was the pivotal figure (the other judges were entirely passive). Many of his interventions sought to curtail the lengthy and tedious trial. Although he sometimes tried to understand the union perspective, his sympathies clearly were with management, as revealed in his questions to Schreiner:

> [What McCall] is suggesting is that possibly as a result of earlier dealings you had adopted a preconceived attitude toward the company and because of that you were not prepared to recognise concessions that were being made.

> [W]hilst you were still insisting on the recognition agreement how could the company take the persons back if...you could immediately threaten to go on strike again?

> If in fact you wish to draw the company's attention to the problem [failure to reach a recognition agreement] why is the process not adopted of possibly sending a telex or a letter... some preliminary procedure prior to actually adopting industrial action?

He accused Schreiner of making "misleading" statements to the press and disbelieved his disclaimer of responsibility for the May Day strike.

During a recess two months before the trial ended MAWU raised a procedural issue with momentous consequences.

> *Brand to Roux* (May 19): Our client has seen a brochure advertising a seminar "for management and senior legal practitioners" on labour law... "presented by" Andrew Levy and Associates. This firm, we need hardly say, was retained to give industrial relations advice on the dispute that is the subject of the litigation... and the nature and propriety of its advice is pertinently in issue in the proceedings. Other speakers at the seminar include...the complete legal team of the company. Finally, it seems that the seminar will have a partisan quality, since only "management perspectives" are being given. Our client has instructed us to record its formal objection to your participation in this conference. The objection extends to your acceptance of the invitation to speak.

> *Roux to Brand* (May 20): I entertain not the slightest doubt that the legal representatives of the Metal and Allied Workers Union would entertain ["no" is crossed out] any doubt that by acceptance of the invitation, nor of my addressing the conference would or could in any way effect [sic] either my objectivity nor impartiality in respect of the application for the determination to which you refer.

> If however you find that neither yourself nor your counsel whose advice I would request you to obtain, would be able to convince your clients of this fact, then I am prepared to reconsider whether in the interest of justice being seen to be done, I should refuse to attend or address such conference.

Is the implication of your objection that I in future also consult you before I and other members of the court address any other conferences arranged at the instigation of management....

I might add that neither Mr Levy nor his associates are known to me. That both the president of the court and I have been requested to attend, and wish to attend the conference for the instructive value which we hope it may provide us in the field.

Should you in light of this telex see your way clear to withdrawing your objection, I undertake (not that I consider that it might have been necessary) that no reference will be made directly nor indirectly at the conference in my presence to the case in which your clients are involved.

Brand to Roux (May 20): We regret to inform you that our client does not withdraw its objection.

Roux to Brand (May 22): In the rapidly evolving new labour dispensation, both the president and I...welcome every opportunity presented to us to attend conferences on labour relations.... In fact, we consider it as part of our duty to do so. ... I am...not being compensated for my contribution.... I am consequently in no way beholden to the firm who arranged the conference, nor will I be in a position of informal association with Sarmcol's representatives either before or after such conference. That the present conference happens to have been arranged by a firm of labour consultants, who at one stage were engaged by Sarmcol in respect of the present dispute, or that it eventually emerges that respondent's complete legal team are also to be speakers at such conference, is entirely incidental to and insufficient reason to justify the perception that my objectivity and impartiality may be affected thereby. My withdrawal from participation in such conference as a result of your client's objection, may however give rise to unwarranted inferences, or undesirable assumptions which I consider should be avoided.

Brand to Roux (May 25): Our client notes your attitude and the reasons that underlie it. Our client's objection still stands, however, and it will be placing this correspondence on record at the renewed hearing of this matter.

Roux delivered the keynote address the next day, after which the SARMCOL legal team gave four of the seven talks: Wallis on "Inter-Union Competition in Your Plant," McCall on "Legitimate Activities in the Course of Industrial Action," Trollip on "Protection of Strikers in Recognition Agreements in Law," and Giles on "Legal Remedies and Relief against Unions and Strikers"—all central issues in the ongoing trial. The audience of more than 300 executives from some 170 companies included five from BTR SARMCOL; there were no labor representatives. When Wallis completed his re-direct examination of Sampson four days after the seminar, Brassey placed the telexes in the record but hesitated to move for recusal. Roux insisted that he do so or withdraw them. The next day McCall agreed, demanding to know "whether the objection is also intended to be an attack on either the integrity or the independence of the members of our legal team?"

After a day to allow Brassey to take instructions from the shop stewards, who had consulted with those ex-workers attending the trial, he formally moved for recusal "based on the fact that, by attending the conference in question and addressing it, [Roux] gave a reasonable apprehension of bias to a reasonably [sic] lay person." He hastened to add that "neither I nor Mr Brand would in any sense be expressing any personal opinion, nor in any sense seeking personally to impute [impugn] your integrity or bona fide[s], nor in any sense to indicate to you any alternation [alteration] in the personal respect and affection that you enjoy from us."

Roux predictably rejected the application. He often attended conferences and constantly dealt with the same parties. Recusal would taint the other members of the court, with whom he had been discussing the case. "I am entirely convinced in my own mind that I have in no way been influenced by attending the conference or that I acted improperly in doing so and I find it unacceptable that any of the gentlemen sitting in this court, who have been sitting here for weeks on end, could entertain any real thought in their hearts that I might be biased...."

On September 9, two months after the hearing ended, Roux gave judgment in writing (although he had promised twice to read it in open court).[30] He commented on the duration of the case and size of the record, "the orderly and disciplined behaviour of the union members" during the hearing, and the court's visit to the factory and Mpophomeni. He thanked the lawyers for their effective preparation of the evidence and documentation, "especially Mr Giles on whom the main burden" fell.

He began by noting that the work force had shrunk from a peak of 2,160 in 1974 to fewer than 900 by 1985. Since the average length of employment was seventeen years, "the dissatisfaction amongst the weekly-paid work-force must have been pronounced." "Although BTR initially endeavoured to promote works committees in line with general labour policy at that time they adopted a more realistic approach to unionism in the late 1970s." Their "initial reluctance" to enter a recognition agreement may have reflected resentment that the union treated SARMCOL as "a soft target." The nineteen months of negotiations after MAWU demonstrated representativity exhibited "increased industrial unrest attended by industrial action." "Notwithstanding what could properly be described as undisciplined action by union members," BTR took the "progressive step" of allowing a half shift of unpaid leave on May Day.

The court found that the union had directed the final strike, believing it was legal, in order to force recognition. "Possibly as a result of union solidarity and intimidation" the strikers rejected SARMCOL's generous offer of re-employment, with preference for ex-employees. Strikers wrongly viewed the new workforce as "scabs," some of whom were killed or injured or lost their homes.

The court found both principal witnesses partial but "honest"; Sampson, however, was more reliable. The court believed his representation that "had the dismissed workers returned, negotiations with the union with regard to the recognition agreement would have continued." It disbelieved Schreiner's testimony that he thought the strike was legal and the mass dismissal illegal. Of MAWU's three African witnesses, the court discredited one for "inexplicable memory lapses during cross-examination" and found that the others were "not impressive" and "lacked candour."

On the central issue, the court found that neither party failed to negotiate in good faith. Despite "signs of intransigence," both shared an "overall commitment" to reach agreement, as shown by the length of the negotiations and their reliance on "independent expert advice." SARMCOL could not be compared to other companies because of different circumstances and requirements and MAWU's "continued and sustained industrial action." The mass dismissal was substantively and procedurally fair and not intended to "smash" the union. SARMCOL had no obligation to reemploy the entire workforce, nor was there evidence that it discriminated against "union lads" in rehiring individuals. Strikes were "an extremely serious matter," and criminal and other "unreasonable" acts were unacceptable. The court explicitly criticized:

(a) The complete insensitivity of the union to the economic losses which were being occasioned to BTR....

(b) The nonchalant manner in which the union treated the request by BTR to discipline its members and to restrain them from acts of intimidation and violence and the union's and shop stewards' total lack of leadership during the earlier days of the strike.

(c) [The loss of life, injuries, damage to 30 homes, and stoning of six more.]

(d) The removal of the application forms for re-employment...depriving members of the opportunity of the independent exercise of individual discretion.

(e) The lack of any approach by the union suggesting temporarily to call off the strike on the reciprocal undertaking by BTR to continue the negotiations.

(f) The manner in which the principal strike was conducted without prior warning and with machines simply left running and also accompanied by intimidation of some of the monthly-paid staff.

In contrast... the responsible manner in which BTR, under intense provocation, was prepared to keep the union members' jobs open to them for a period of three months stands in stark contrast.

The court found "disturbing" the "form of collective democracy practised by this union," which deprived it of "responsible and strong as well as sustained leadership." Roux had "reservations whether this philosophy, if correctly understood, can properly be entertained or even tolerated by present-day society in this country."

Although it did not have to determine the strike's legality, the court noted that the workers' demand had not been presented to the conciliation board (creating technical illegality), criticized the "haphazard way in which the ballot was taken," and denounced "conduct which falls to be categorized if not unlawful as certainly unfair." It disregarded the EEC Code and ILO Tripartite Agreement. It did not take seriously the requested relief of reinstatement retroactive six months. There was a "total lack of evidence" of the cost of such an order, which might further aggravate the dispute. "Without even giving consideration to union rivalry, how could any order which may have the effect of ousting these persons, who are innocent to the present dispute, ever be countenanced as being fair and equitable." It dismissed the application with no order for costs.

The few newspapers reporting the judgment took predictable positions. *The Citizen*, a pro-government paper, observed that the union proposal "contained clauses that would have severely hampered the company's operation."[31] *Finance Week* called it a "severe defeat for radical trade unionists," who "essentially espouse Marxist rather than western government philosophies." The judgment affirmed the right of employers to replace all strikers within a short time period, which militant unionists were unlikely to meet.[32]

In the absence of any procedure for substantive review, MAWU asked the Supreme Court in February 1988 to set aside the judgment on the ground of Roux's participation in the Andrew Levy seminar at a time when there was a reasonable possibility SARMCOL might call Levy employees to testify. "Probably the best known and certainly the biggest firm of industrial relations consultants in the country," Levy had published *I.R. Data* since 1980. Without revealing its crucial role in advising SARMCOL, the journal presented highly partisan accounts:

[S]omeone in the union slipped badly. ... [O]nce the firestorm broke MAWU seemed to have little option but to climb in with every weapon available. ... [T]here seems little chance of a settlement without MAWU having to make major and perhaps unacceptable concessions. [August 1985]

The impression conveyed by witness Schreiner is far from the obdurate and unyielding negotiator which many Natal employers have come to know. ...

Nevertheless, some of his evidence... has hinted at many inconsistencies in his approach to the SARMCOL dispute. ... Zondi suffered a complete lapse of memory.... [December 1986][33]

[A] number of opportunities to end the war that no one could win were missed because of the all-or-nothing approach adopted by the union leadership and their advisers. Conciliation and pragmatism were repeatedly rejected in favour of a collective and often highly personalised belligerence which continues even after the judgment. [October 1987]

MAWU offered other evidence of Roux's bias: fifty-five adverse and twenty-two sympathetic interventions during Schreiner's testimony, nine adverse and eighty-two sympathetic interventions during Sampson's. The union concluded by challenging Roux's factual findings and substantive judgment.

SARMCOL raised numerous procedural objections, most of them frivolous. It defended Roux's participation in the seminar as customary and valuable and the topics discussed as innocuous. SARMCOL had never intended to call Levy employees since "it was no part of the case of [MAWU] that Andrew Levy and Associates had given bad advice which the [company] had unwisely followed."

Roux also opposed the motion as "no more than a transparent and impermissible attempt to take the judgment in question on appeal." The seminar did not have a management perspective (despite its subtitle) because McCall spoke on "legitimate activities in the course of industrial actions." Visibly angered by the applicants' insinuations, Roux protested too much, allowing his true feelings toward Schreiner to emerge:

I deny emphatically that there was any likelihood that I would consciously or unconsciously be influenced in my approach to the proceedings before the court by what had transpired at the seminar.... This is but a figment of Schreiner's imagination....

Schreiner's statement as to the avowed objective of the conference is clearly recklessly made. ...

[Schreiner] has been guilty of ignoring findings on the probabilities and of distortion by quoting certain passages in the transcript either out of context or truncating certain events and giving selective and incomplete extracts of evidence from the transcript. He has also been guilty of certain incorrect factual assumptions and other errors of fact....

At the time of the seminar, Roux knew that Andrew Levy was "a well-known firm of industrial relations consultants" but not that it advised only management; he had not read its publication *I.R. Data*. He was also defensive about his choice of the other two hearing officers and his failure to deliver the judgment in open court, as promised. Ehlers, the president of the Industrial Court, offered a supporting affidavit.

Andrew Levy's affidavit was a masterpiece of false naievete.

> I invited [Roux] for no other reason than that the Industrial Court has and still does play a major role in industrial relations developments. ... The fact that four of the invited speakers were [SARMCOL's] legal representatives in a matter against Mawu and would also be at the seminar was never a consideration. ... [T]here is only a small group of legal practitioners with expertise in the field of labour relations and the pool from which speakers with the requisite expertise can be drawn is limited.

(It was just accident that they were all management lawyers, although there are roughly equal numbers of union lawyers.)

More than 150 former SARMCOL employees attended the seven-day Supreme Court hearing in Durban in February 1989.[34] The union was lucky to appear before John Didcott, the most adamant opponent of apartheid on the bench, who gave judgment on March 4.[35] He saw his task as merely ceremonial, without any power to judge the credibility of witnesses, exercise discretion, or grant interim relief.

> Three days have been spent in argument and enormous costs have been incurred, to no end which I can see but to confer jurisdiction on the Appellate Division to...consider the entire case from the beginning, its task unlightened and unenlightened by anything I may say. ... [T]he best I can possibly do in all the circumstances will be ill considered, hastily conceived and superficial. I hope it will influence nobody....

He was characteristically forthright on the issue of bias, however.

> Andrew Levy & Associates were seen by the workers and the trade union to be in the employer's camp, and therefore partisan with regard to the litigation, indeed to some considerable extent to be the éminence grise behind the employer.

Although Roux was unpaid and had good motives and the papers were innocuous, this "misses the point entirely." The objection was not to Industrial Court members attending seminars in general but rather to Roux's participation "in the middle of litigation" in a seminar organized by "somebody who was involved to a very substantial degree in that litigation, and involved in a most partisan way," especially since there was "no compelling or even cogent reason" for his presence.

The standard for recusal (and thus for declining the seminar invitation) was not actual bias but whether a reasonable lay litigant would fear the likelihood of bias. Didcott rebuked Roux's counsel for insisting on the former test on the basis of "passages in judgments [taken] out of context." Although SARMCOL's counsel sought to distinguish the "semi-public" seminar from a private dinner party, Didcott pointed out that even the seminar created "all sorts of opportunities for private hob-nobbing."

> Labour disputes aroused particularly intense emotions. ... The advice given by the Levy firm was very much in the firing line. ... [I]t was unquestionably perceived as a strategy to undermine the union and to victimise workers. ... [T]o a trade unionist such things are mortal sins. ... [Y]our average lay litigant in the position of those concerned in this case... would have been disturbed that it was more important to [Roux] to go hobnobbing with these people over a weekend in the northern suburbs of Johannesburg than to take account of the understandable sensitivities of the workers involved.

Didcott set aside the Industrial Court decision and ordered a de novo hearing by different judges. He awarded partial costs against SARMCOL and Roux for the four days of argument devoted to the bias issue and granted leave to appeal both his reversal and the order about costs.

When the audience of workers heard the outcome they shouted "Amandla," congratulating each other as "my learned friend." Raphael Nzimande said he was as happy as if a child had been born. "All my children were born during my 21 years of service with Sarmcol, but this one we have all waited for a long time, and it has come at last." Philip Dladla (shop steward chair, plaintiff, and witness) declared: "After four years of hardship we have seen justice to be done." NUMSA (MAWU's successor) again called on SARMCOL and its British owners to negotiate. Although union lawyers were "jubilant," they warned that SARMCOL might appeal.[36] Both sides promptly did so, although the litigation was estimated to have cost R2 million already.

In July 1991, while the appeal was pending, the *Weekly Mail* exposed government funding of UWUSA, the Inkatha-linked union, which had organized SARMCOL's new work force and gained recognition four years earlier. At least five Inkatha leaders were implicated: Buthelezi, his personal assistant M.Z. Khumalo, two KwaZulu cabinet members (Interior Minister Stephen Sithebe and Justice Minister C.J. Mtetwa), and Inkatha Institute director Gavin Woods. An October 1989 police memo referred to UWUSA as "a project under the control of the SAP." Two days later the Natal deputy security police commissioner wrote his superior: "Chief Buthelezi was very emotional when a copy of the receipt (for R100,000 for Inkatha rally 19.10.89) was handed to him." UWUSA used some of the money to prevent the Mass Democratic Movement from renting King's Park Stadium in February 1990 to welcome the ANC leaders released from prison. In the wake of these revelations, NUMSA publicly demanded that SARMCOL disclose "details of all dealings with Uwusa, the SAP, the security police, the SADF and Inkatha."[37]

The Appellate Division heard oral argument in March 1992 (three years after the Supreme Court's reversal) and gave judgment on May 25.[38] Although the court had instructed the parties to limit themselves to the recusal issue, it began by describing the "prolonged and bitter struggle" and massive retrenchments, which led to "much dissatisfaction and uneasiness on the part of the workers" and twenty-one months of "protracted power play" over recognition. Like Roux, it noted the "sustained industrial action… in the form of mass meetings, a ban on overtime work, go-slow techniques on night shifts, a sit-in at the canteen and a refusal to work on the part of the solid woven belting department." After the May Day strike and mass dismissal, the company's offer of "re-employment to all workers…was rejected. Thereafter BTR maintained its offer of re-employment to all dismissed workers…." MAWU failed to submit an unconditional written agreement to return to work until after SARMCOL had made its temporary work force permanent.

Sampson had testified that he sought the advice of Andrew Levy and Associates (ALA) "at every juncture" and relied on it "very heavily" during the negotiations. The court commented:

> It is clear from the evidence that in advising its client ALA espoused the cause of BTR very zealously. On the one hand ALA viewed BTR's labour problems with sympathetic understanding. Towards MAWU's trade union aspirations and the strategies employed by it, on the other hand, the attitude of ALA was one of undisguised hostility mingled, on occasion, with disgust.

ALA's advice "was often couched in acerbic language." It expressed the hope that the strikers would not return so that BTR could "belt" them and advised management to watch the shop stewards in order to be able to "bounce out" troublemakers. The court added, however, "it is well known that struggles between management and labour are often fiercely waged…[and] the pugnacity which often characterised the advice given by ALA to BTR was well matched by the obduracy sometimes shown by MAWU's negotiating team…."

Ten days before this judgment the AD had reaffirmed the standard of a "reasonable suspicion" of bias in preference to that of a "real likelihood."[39] "In the end the only guarantee of impartiality on the part of the courts is conspicuous impartiality. … If suspicion is reasonably apprehended then that is an end to the matter." "[I]t would be difficult to imagine a case in which a suspicion of bias harboured by an applicant was ever more clearly manifested." The court reprimanded Didcott for exaggerating the length of the seminar (a day rather than a weekend), using overly colorful language ("untoward hobnobbing"), and describing Andrew Levy as "involved to a very substantial degree in that litigation" when it was involved only in the negotiations. But because "in the eyes of MAWU's members and officials, ALA was in the camp of the enemy," the Supreme Court had correctly applied the test for recusal. The court dismissed the appeal with costs.

Almost twenty years since MAWU had started organizing SARMCOL workers, nearly a decade since it had enrolled ninety-five percent of the workforce and requested recognition, and seven years since the mass dismissal MAWU was back to where it had been in 1986. Nevertheless, NUMSA's lawyers welcomed the decision. "I would rather be fighting the case in 1992 than in 1984," said John Brand, because of the creation of the Labour Appeal Court, decisions favoring reinstatement, and legislation protecting strikers. SARMCOL denounced the judgment for not "ruling on the merits of the case" and warned that it exposed any judge who attended a seminar to accusations of bias.[40]

Analysis

The struggle between MAWU and SARMCOL revealed their diametrically opposed images of the employment relationship. The adversaries started from a common acceptance of paternalism: management saw itself as caring; workers reciprocated by calling managers "our fathers." This reflected real dependence: most workers had spent their entire adult lives at SARMCOL and were too old to obtain new jobs, whose numbers drastically declined during the recession. The mass dismissal was a total betrayal—equivalent to the evictions of tenant farmers and forced removals (of which many Mpophomeni residents had been victims). Workers persisted in believing that the company would relent. At first, MAWU seems to have shared the workers' faith, accepting management's last draft as the basis for negotiations after the mass dismissal.

SARMCOL demanded unquestioning obedience and passivity from its employees. Only management could realize the common interest of labor and capital in maximizing production. When the workers began to assert themselves management saw red. South African whites had demanded absolute submission from blacks for more than three centuries. SARMCOL was even less willing to tolerate threats to its authority than government or other employers. To Sampson the union was an "outside organisation which knows nothing about running a rubber factory." It refused to acknowledge "a natural right—the management's right to manage," which included unilateral decisions about retrenchment. Severance pay could only be ex gratia. Even negotiation was an intolerable surrender of control; union proposals had to be "reasonable" according to criteria determined by management. The entire capitalist system would collapse if it made any concessions to unions.

This ideological fundamentalism guided SARMCOL's actions. Whatever it disliked must be illegal: all black trade unions, any converse with unregistered unions. The police were there to do its bidding: obstruct MAWU's organizing campaigns in 1973 and 1979, control MAWU after the May 1985 strike. Even after MAWU demonstrated representativeness, management refused to recognize shop stewards, continuing to deal with the works liaison committee (the workplace equivalent of homeland governments or township councils). Although other companies had accepted Lifo, SARMCOL refused to negotiate retrenchments.

SARMCOL was convinced its employees would be perfectly content absent MAWU's agitation (paralleling the government's feelings about blacks and the ANC). Because apartheid succeeded in rendering whites almost totally ignorant of blacks, SARMCOL relied on its Zulu-speaking industrial relations officer to interpret the feelings of its workforce. Van Zyl told his bosses what he thought they wanted to hear: The union was alienating its members; managers should shoot workers who invaded their offices; Buthelezi and Inkatha would deliver more compliant workers. He was remarkably prescient: UWUSA made no "unreasonable" demands.

SARMCOL shared the ideology of individualism pervasive among whites; only coercion could explain collective action. Were they free to choose, workers would reject the union, vote against the strike, and accept re-employment (just as blacks would repudiate the ANC and defy work stay-aways and election, consumer, bus, rent, and utilities boycotts). Paradoxically, SARMCOL treated black workers as a collectivity only when it sought to smash their unity by the mass dismissal, forcing them to reapply as individuals and allowing management to separate the loyal from the rebellious, a divide-and-conquer strategy similar to the government's construction of tribalism to dominate the black majority. SARMCOL could not see its unilateral retrenchments or the mass dismissal as coercive; such acts merely reflected natural authority. Sampson said the fired workers were "free to work anywhere they liked." Roux agreed that it was each striker's "independent exercise of individual discretion" not to accept re-employment at SARMCOL. MAWU's overtime ban and strike, by contrast, were an illegitimate "resort to power." Insisting that MAWU must have coerced the monthly workers into striking, SARMCOL made them sign statements to this effect before reemploying them, unable to perceive the coercion in this demand.

If management held black workers to an ethos of individualism, it simultaneously embraced a fundamental collective principle—racism. As a minority, whites were naturally solidary. Government and police would help employers crush black unions. Whites who sided with blacks were traitors—hence the detestation of Schreiner shared by SARMCOL, Andrew Levy, and even Roux. Brand betrayed his race by vigorously championing MAWU, Brassey by moving for recusal. "Asiatic" monthly employees would naturally ally themselves with their white superiors. Whites like Schreiner must be running black unions like MAWU (which explains Sampson's April 1985 invitation to a tête-à-tête). Union democracy and grassroots control were inconceivable—even morally wrong—to both SARMCOL and Roux.

Negotiations were troubled from the start by the personal clash between Sampson and Schreiner, which often seemed oedipal. (Their names were ironically inappropriate. The union leader should have been Samson, blindly pulling the temple down on his head to destroy the high priest. The manager should have been Schreiner, a famous South African family.) Relations became so bad they delegated negotiation to their attorneys, who preserved civility but made no progress.

SARMCOL saw the union as disruptive and confrontational, pointing to its five applications for conciliation boards, wildcat strikes, go-slows, work-to-rule, refusal to maintain the machines over Christmas 1984, threat of worsened labor relations, and of course the May 1985 strike. Because its British parent seemed vulnerable to international pressure, Schreiner had targeted SARMCOL for ratcheting and leapfrogging.

MAWU reciprocated by accusing SARMCOL of conservatism. Not only did management accept the charge, but its counsel actually argued that MAWU should have moderated its demands accordingly. Schreiner supported his accusation that SARMCOL was unsophisticated in labor relations by documenting its persistence in maintaining incorrectly that negotiations with black trade unions were illegal. It came to meetings unprepared, sent officials without authority to negotiate, submitted complex proposals at the last moment, and harped on technical details. Its strategy of deliberate delay alternated long periods of inaccessibility with frenzied demands and impossible deadlines. Management intransigence forced MAWU to apply for conciliation boards, which SARMCOL aborted at the last moment by conceding (just as the government repeatedly defied the AD decision in *Komani* until the day before the Supreme Court was to hear an urgent application for an interdict). Each time they approached consensus Sampson added unacceptable conditions. When Schreiner persuaded the workers to return following the March 1985 strike by promising them an agreement Sampson reneged, undermining Schreiner's credibility with his members.

Sampson's scrupulous note taking thoroughly documented SARMCOL's bad faith (just as the prison doctors recorded torture by the Port Elizabeth security police in 1985 and Richard Mdakane's detailed minutes of the Alexandra Action Committee showed its respect for legality, see chapters seven and nine). Sampson seems to have followed Andrew Levy's advice religiously: demanding MAWU's registration certificate in 1982 (though it was irrelevant), building a record in anticipation of litigation during the December 1984 dispute, provoking the workers to strike illegally over May Day so he could dismiss the entire work force. There were plenty of smoking guns: van Zyl's advice to fire the shop stewards and enlist Buthelezi's help in replacing MAWU members with Inkatha; Sampson's diary entry of a plan for mass dismissal followed by selective rehiring in order to get rid of the "union lads," who would not apply until all jobs were filled; his instruction to supervisors to scrutinize the work records of shop stewards during the go-slow to find grounds for dismissal; the March mass dismissal; and Andrew Levy's May Day phone call urging just what SARMCOL did—mass dismissal and selective re-employment to eliminate troublemakers. Knowing

Schreiner's reputation for impatience, Sampson sought to goad him into rash action. This succeeded brilliantly in March 1985, when SARMCOL's demand for another half hour made Schreiner snap and refuse to concede more than fifteen minutes—an impetuous act that temporarily eclipsed the company's recalcitrance during the preceding eighteen months. SARMCOL's counsel continued this strategy during the trial in the vain hope Schreiner would blow up.

Throughout the struggle each side sought moral superiority by appealing to emerging (but still amorphous) labor law: how to phrase offers and responses, the timing of negotiations, what and when to threaten. MAWU blamed the final rupture on SARMCOL's refusal to negotiate in good faith, about which it had applied for a conciliation board and taken a strike vote; SARMCOL maintained that MAWU had struck in support of wage demands or May Day, either of which would have been illegal. Just as apartheid's apologists sought to distract attention from their crimes by focusing on black violence (people's courts in the Alexandra Five treason trial, the Port Elizabeth boycott in the exposure of security police torture, ANC terrorism in the prosecution of conscientious objectors, intimidation of those who "chose" to leave in the destruction of Oukasie, see chapters four, seven, nine, and twelve), so SARMCOL kept returning to the threats against monthly employees, shop stewards' "seizure" of re-employment applications from the pay packets of fired workers, and attacks on its new workforce. MAWU responded lamely by attributing all the violence to SARMCOL's mass dismissal and resort to scabs.

The struggle was over respect as well as money and power. Every interaction implicated honor, amplifying the significance of trivial details. Sampson followed Andrew Levy's advice never to accept a proposed meeting date. It sent lower officials to demean its adversary. It demanded that MAWU cut its negotiating team. Schreiner felt that SARMCOL treated union members like children. Blacks compensated for their powerlessness by refusing to drink tea, using profanity, and walking into the managing director's office without invitation. MAWU appealed over the heads of local managers to their British superiors, shareholders, and world opinion. Given South Africa's rigid racial hierarchy, these actions succeeded in shocking. Management responded by demanding that shop stewards obtain permission from two departments before leaving their machines—an unsubtle reminder of the hated pass laws.

Power ultimately determined the struggle. Declining demand and rising unemployment associated with the 1980s worldwide recession (accentuated by the international boycott) sharply reduced MAWU's leverage. If that was the excuse for SARMCOL's retrenchments, they also served to punish the rank and file for organizing and to oust their leaders. MAWU's appeal to outside authority (five applications for conciliation boards, two proposals for arbitration, the request for access to the boards and the Industrial Court without ministerial approval) reflected its weakness at the bargaining table. The lengthy and pointless prerequisites for a legal strike drove workers to prefer go-slows, work-to-rule, and wildcat strikes. Because SARMCOL correctly viewed most threats of industrial action and recourse to law as empty, they did little more than anger management. The company was less eager for third-party intervention because it could just work its will. Furthermore, the law gave it a trump card—the right to fire and replace strikers. This disabled the union in much the same way that the disenfranchisement of blacks, the denial of free speech, assembly, and the press, and the use of detention without trial crippled the political opposition.

From 1984 both parties engaged in an accelerating game of chicken, threatening a final rupture and then pulling back. SARMCOL's failure to retaliate for the December 1984 and March 1985 strikes misled MAWU into the fatal miscalculation that it would never do so. The May 1985 strike was an act of desperation, with no visible plan of action and little chance of success. The mass dismissal fundamentally altered power relations. Inside the factory workers control production; outside they can only protest. SARMCOL had achieved its ultimate goal of destroying the union. Although MAWU pretended to be on strike, its weakness was evident in its progressive concessions. Even had Inkatha permitted, MAWU could not have tried to organize the new workforce without betraying the old. SARMCOL's strategy reflected its enhanced power: escalate demands to forestall agreement while hiring replacements. Once that was complete SARMCOL announced with a straight face that there was no labor dispute because MAWU no longer represented any workers. It had succeeded in turning the clock back to the early 1980s.

Unable to restart negotiations, MAWU had only two alternatives. It mobilized pressure both inside South Africa (stay-aways and boycotts) and outside (foreign trade unions, governments, and international organizations). SARMCOL's response was the typical South African laager—circling the wagons. MAWU went to the Industrial Court reluctantly: Litigation was long and expensive; given the inchoate state of South African labor law and the court's management bias it was a long shot. But it was all that remained.

The hearing began promisingly. Roux appeared openminded, even criticizing the company's conservatism. The immaturity of South African labor jurisprudence allowed the union to mine the decade-long struggle to illustrate the unreasonableness of SARMCOL's behavior. Whereas parliamentary supremacy and a weak tradition of judicial review of executive action usually compelled or excused the judges' passivity, the Industrial Court had a virtual tabula rasa on which to write a new law of labor relations. As the trial dragged on, however, Roux's sympathy for Sampson became obvious, as did his impatience with Brassey's relentless cross-examination.

The court's judgment was incredibly one-sided. It believed Sampson and distrusted Schreiner and the black workers. It condemned the aggressiveness of MAWU's efforts to win recognition and bargain over substance and found its frequent resort to industrial action intolerable. Roux shared management's view that the union constantly disrupted production and intimidated workers. Indifferent to the plight of a thousand workers fired after a lifetime of service to SARMCOL, he exuded solicitude for the scabs who replaced them. Despite the numerous memos in which Sampson, Levy, and van Zyl described the plan to fire the entire workforce and rehire selectively in order to break the union he found no unfair labor practice. Even the Supreme Court and the Appellate Division expressed skepticism about the union's case, although they had no need to address the merits.

Lawyers always prefer procedure to substance in order to shift debate from a terrain where lay opinions are equally valid and politics inescapable to one where lawyers enjoy a monopoly of esoteric technique that conceals moral choices. From the outset the parties jockeyed for procedural advantage: MAWU made suggestions for the Industrial Court bench, objected to de Witt, and urged arbitration; SARMCOL countered with opinions from the Johannesburg and Durban bars that it was improper for advocates to engage in such discussions. Procedural fetishism resurfaced when SARMCOL criticized MAWU for failing to preserve the February 1985 ballot papers for the mandatory two years, although the vast majority of workers clearly supported the strike.

As union lawyers realized they were losing, the discovery that Roux was the keynote speaker at Andrew Levy's seminar must have seemed a deus ex machina. They cleverly put him on the defensive by criticizing his acceptance of the invitation. This had the desired effect: Rather than withdraw, Roux justified his decision and secured the approval of the Industrial Court president (who also attended the seminar). Having participated in the seminar, it was inevitable he would refuse to recuse himself, especially after more than three weeks of trial. This strategy was risky, however. Even more than others, judges hate having their judgment questioned. Roux's resentment was visible in the exchange of telexes, courtroom colloquy, and his arguments on appeal. The motion clearly destroyed any residual sympathy he felt for the union; fortunately, he fell into the trap and dug himself even deeper in denying his mistake.

In many ways the victory was pyrrhic. The cost in time, emotion, and money was immense. If the workers felt morally vindicated they were no closer to their real goal: a return to work and apology by SARMCOL. The fait accompli of a new work force is almost impossible to reverse.

Should MAWU have followed a different strategy? Given SARMCOL's documented intransigence it is unlikely that a more conciliatory approach would have secured an acceptable agreement. Further concessions might have lost the loyalty of workers justifiably impatient at two years of fruitless bargaining. The Industrial Court application may have been doomed from the outset, but the only alternative was ignominious defeat. Like earlier reversals—the 1952 Defiance Campaign, the 1960 Sharpeville massacre, the 1976 Soweto uprising—MAWU's loss to SARMCOL may have been unavoidable but transitory, just one battle in a war whose motto appropriately was: Victory is inevitable, defeat impossible.

CHAPTER 6

MPOPHOMENI AND THE WAR IN NATAL

We say
  very well
always

We shall remember
your smiling and simple faces
…
Your smiling and simple faces
meant sleepless nights
to bosses, rulers and their puppets

Your smiling and simple faces
gave hope to SARMCOL workers' struggle
to our liberation struggle

Your death now
comrades
proclaims our earthly triumph.[1]

I am now coming closer to believing that the only reconciliation there will ever be in this country is the reconciliation of the most powerful with those who pay homage to the powerful. We are talking about a life and death struggle. We are talking about all-or-nothing victories. We are talking about the final triumph of good over evil. (Chief Mangosuthu Gatsha Buthelezi to the Inkatha Central Committee, December 1987)[2]

Background

In the struggle against apartheid, law must protect blacks not only from an oppressive state but also from each other. Although the media have sensationalized "black-on-black violence," attributing it to tribalism and savagery, the reality is more complex. The state is deeply implicated in promoting it: constructing and fueling "tribalism," training and arming vigilante groups, conducting attacks in blackface, and infiltrating resistance movements with spies and provocateurs. Much of the violence occurs within tribes. Many of the targets are state surrogates: black councillors, police, and informers. And the combatants are not equally culpable.

Violence increased throughout South Africa during the 1980s and 1990s.[3] Because it is impossible to do justice to the myriad incidents in which thousands have been killed and tens of thousands injured or displaced, I have focused on a particular event occurring at the beginning of the deadliest struggle—between the UDF and COSATU on one hand and Inkatha on the other—before the mounting toll deadened the sense of outrage. Inkatha is a Zulu nationalist movement revived by Chief Mangosuthu Gatsha Buthelezi in 1975.[4] To "encourage" KwaZulu residents to join, officials have required membership cards before issuing and endorsing passes, paying pensions, providing housing, allocating land, and hiring civil servants and teachers. In 1980 Inkatha "impis" (a warrior phalanx) attacked school children who joined the national boycott and University of Zululand students who criticized the organization and its leader. The next year the university banned the national black student organization (AZASO); another attack in 1983 left four students dead and more than a hundred injured.[5]

In the violence following the murder of Durban attorney Victoria Mxenge in August 1985, "amabutho" (Zulu warriors) attacked UDF supporters throughout Natal, killing dozens.[6] Another ten were killed after the King Shaka Day rally in Umlazi Stadium in September.[7] Zulu attacks on Pondo shack settlements in November 1985 and January 1986 killed some thirty.[8] In January 1986 residents of Chesterville sent the Attorney General a thirty-eight-page account of murders and beatings by Inkatha supporters calling themselves the A-team.[9] Because the police took no action, lawyers filed eight urgent applications for interdicts, but the perpetrators ignored them with impunity. Police disregarded complaints, sometimes arresting complainants, one of whom died in police custody.[10]

Murder in Mpophomeni

Mpophomeni, the BTR/SARMCOL company town, is located in the Natal Midlands, fifteen kilometers from the factory. Although the area supports Inkatha, Mpophomeni is one of the pockets of equally strong UDF/COSATU loyalty. Even the Inkatha-aligned council had resisted a 1983 increase in rents and bus fares.[11] In May 1985 SARMCOL fired all 1,000 employees, nearly a third of whom lived in the township (see chapter five). Violent clashes between the replacements and the strikers caused property damage, personal injury, and two deaths. The KwaZulu Police occupied the township in June. When MAWU organized a school boycott, one-day work stay-away, and forty-day consumer boycott, Inkatha opposed it and condemned the intimidation of those who resisted.[12] After a year of fruitless efforts to restart negotiations, MAWU initiated an unfair labor practice action in the Industrial Court in July 1986. The same year, however, Inkatha launched the rival United Workers Union of South Africa (UWUSA) and sought to organize the new BTR work force, gaining recognition early in 1987. South Africa spent nearly R3 million (more than $1 million) upgrading the township in 1986.[13]

The Industrial Court hearing began on November 4, 1986. About the same time Inkatha decided to lay claim to the township, where it had only three members: M.M. Mchunu (local Inkatha "chairman" and councillor), Romanus Mzolo (vice-chairman), and M. Zuma. Mxegeni Joseph Mabaso, Assistant National Youth Organizer for Inkatha, and at least five older men accompanied a busload of 100 youths to the community hall on Friday, December 5. Shortly after midnight youth "security guards" encountered four township residents. Phineas Sibiya had been chairman of the BTR shop stewards committee; after the mass dismissal he chaired the SARMCOL Workers' Co-operative. He was driving a car borrowed from Phillip Dladla, the principal MAWU organizer at BTR and a named plaintiff in its lawsuit. Simon Ngubane was head of the Co-operative's cultural project. Phineas's brother Micca Mnikwa Sibiya, thirty-seven, was a MAWU member. And Nomuza Flomena Mnikathi, twenty-three, Phineas's girlfriend, was the daughter of a former SARMCOL worker. The security guards took the four to the community hall, where they were interrogated by Mabaso and others and badly beaten. Two residents were summoned to identify them: the hall's caretaker (Thusi) and the local Inkatha chairman (Mchunu). About 2 a.m. the captives were driven to a deserted area in two cars and shot. Micca escaped, but the others were killed and their bodies burned in one car. Micca made his way to the MAWU office, told his attorney, and then made a statement to the police, who had already found the bodies. The same weekend two other MAWU members were killed in Chesterville.[14]

Later that morning Inkatha youths marched through the township, pulling people out of houses and forcing them to join the demonstration. Several fights occurred, and a resident was murdered. The police separated the two groups and dispersed the residents. They searched the Inkatha youths, confiscated many weapons (including two guns), and videotaped the entire contingent. About 3 p.m. they returned the weapons and escorted Inkatha out of town.

The police immediately initiated an investigation, photographing the car, summoning relatives to identify the deceased, and taking numerous statements.[15] Micca Sibiya, the survivor, named one of his assailants, whom MAWU organizer Pauline Sanford said was well known in the township. The police claimed to be "doing their utmost to locate the chap."[16] Calling the incident "horrifying," *The Natal Witness* said the police should not find it "beyond their powers to establish who perpetrated this outrage." "Talk about a civil war in South Africa is easy—and dangerous. One way to counteract such talk is for the authorities to demonstrate, clearly, that they are unaligned in such conflicts."[17] Indeed, the government's Bureau of Information offered an account similar to that of MAWU, calling the murderers "allegedly Inkatha members."

This prompted rationalizations and rebuttals. V.V. Mvelase (KwaZulu Urban Representative for Vulindlela) and V. Ndlovu (Imbali MP in the KwaZulu Legislative Assembly) said the Inkatha Youth Brigade had been sent to "protect" the community hall. "The KwaZulu Minister of Health and Welfare was scheduled to address an Inkatha meeting in the township on Saturday and we had to make sure there were no bombs in the hall."[18] Claiming he had conducted his own investigation, Oscar Dhlomo (Inkatha Secretary General and KwaZulu Minister of Education and Culture) issued a press statement three days after the killings denying responsibility.

> For reasons unknown to Inkatha, members of the COSATU-affiliated MAWU were against the holding of the Inkatha Rally at Mpophomeni. MAWU therefore began to mobilise themselves with the aim of disrupting the Inkatha Rally and attacking those who attended the Rally. A letter written to the Manager of a Merry-Go-Round show in Mpophomeni by the Mpophomeni Youth Organisation and dated 30 November 1986 clearly states that this Youth Organisation was preparing to attack Inkatha on the day of the Inkatha Rally. The other signatories to the letter were Mpophomeni Students Committee, Mpophomeni Civic Association and the Workers' Interim Committee....

> When Inkatha Youth learned of these plans on Friday evening the 5th December, they decided to send an advance party to the hall where the meeting was to be held, to ensure that MAWU members did not plant bombs as they had allegedly planned to do and as clearly stated in their letter of warning to the Manager of a Merry-Go-Round Show.

> When this party of Inkatha Youth arrived at Mpophomeni Township all the lights in the township had been switched off— allegedly by MAWU members who wanted to attack Inkatha in the dark to avoid being identified.

Dhlomo continued: "This was violence between two warring factions and not a one-sided Inkatha attack." He threatened legal action against newspapers linking the murders to Inkatha and condemned "the irresponsible attitude of the Bureau for Information." "Newspapers have suddenly forgotten their complaints about the bureau's reliability. People should make their statements to the police instead of making newspaper headlines."[19]

MAWU naturally disagreed. "The cold-blooded murder of three people in itself shows the weakness in Inkatha's version" since none of its members was killed or injured. In retaliation, local "comrades" allegedly drove out two former councillors and a school principal allied with Inkatha.[20]

The funeral for the three victims followed a memorial service in the township church. The Natal Divisional Commissioner of Police forbade a joint burial, outdoor services, procession, and speeches, pamphlets, and banners. Buses carrying hundreds of workers from as far away as Durban were turned back. A large security force abused and assaulted the mourners. Police also warned residents that Inkatha was determined to drive UDF/COSATU out of the township. South Africa delivered the township to KwaZulu on January 1, 1987.[21]

Detective Warrant Officer Mattheus Henning reported on April 5, 1987, that "the deceased were murdered and set alight by person or persons unknown at this stage. Extensive investigation and enquiries were made but to date we have been unsuccessful in locating any suspects." Three weeks later MAWU attorney John Brand filed a notice of claim for the assaults and murders with the KwaZulu Police; receiving no reply, he sued Mabaso, Thusi, Inkatha, and the KwaZulu Minister of Police for compensation.[22] Because he practiced in Johannesburg, Brand asked Richard Lyster of the Durban Legal Resources Centre to sign and file the papers. Lyster had reservations, however; he and his colleagues had received death threats for suing Inkatha. He convinced Brand to sign the papers because he would be less at risk in Johannesburg. A week later Inkatha's attorneys, Friedman & Friedman, objected that Brand's signature violated a local rule of court, since he was not admitted in Natal, and moved to dismiss the case against the KwaZulu Minister of Police (the principal solvent defendant) because the statute of limitations had run.

In order to encourage the criminal prosecution Brand wrote the senior public prosecutor, Ms. K.N. Wentzel, noting that he and his counsel, Wim Trengove, had urged a formal inquest. She replied that the docket had been returned to the South African Police (SAP) for further investigation and suggested he check in about a month. He did so promptly and was told by prosecutor N.J. Strydom that the matter was still under investigation. Brand sent further reminders in each of the next two months, eliciting perfunctory replies. In the beginning of November, five months after his initial inquiry P. Coetzee, a third prosecutor, wrote Brand that "no inquest is to be held regarding the deaths of the above mentioned persons. Criminal proceedings are being instituted in connection with the above deaths. This office will keep you informed." Understandably distrustful, Brand asked for details about who was being prosecuted, on what charges, in which court, and when. Coetzee answered that there were outstanding warrants for six of the Inkatha youth "security guards."

The Inquests

In fact, two inquests were held.[23] The first, into the death of Alpheus Mziwakhe Nkabinde, was conducted by Magistrate J.J. Scholts (who, in his executive capacity, had issued the permit for the Inkatha rally that led to the killings). Goodenough Bhekinkosi Chonco told the police that he and the other Inkatha youths were awakened about 5 a.m. on Saturday, December 6. When they started to sing, the township residents gathered outside the fence. Joseph Mabaso told the youths to drive away the "opposition." About 100 youths chased the residents up the hill, where a fight broke out. Mabaso followed in his car, telling the youths to stop fighting and return to the hall. N.M. Mvelase, a former BTR employee, was awakened at 6 a.m. Going outdoors, he saw a car driving slowly, followed by about ten armed youths. Half an hour later he saw a man with a gun and minutes later heard a gunshot. He ran into the bush to escape Inkatha. David Zuma, another resident, also heard the shot and saw a boy fifty paces away crying and holding his leg. Armed youths attacked the gunshot victim and then ran away. Recognizing Nkabinde, Zuma sought help from a police van and ambulance. The police took Zuma to the community hall, but he was unable to identify the assailants. SAP Lt. Gerrit Botha was called at home at 6 a.m. and reached the community hall at 6:20. Botha's statement recorded that Mabaso told him, "[T]hey had marched through the streets of Mpophomeni informing the residents of an intended meeeting that was to have taken place the following morning, when they were attacked by the local residents." Botha saw youths armed with sticks, assegais, pangas, axes, and shields. The autopsy found deep wounds from sharp weapons in Nkabinde's left chest and abrasions and fractures caused by sjamboks or reinforcing rods. Det. Sgt. Mzakelwa Alpheus Nkomo was responsible for the investigation but got nowhere.

> I have tried all my best to trace the culprits in this matter but with negative results. None of the witnesses can point out the culprits. More than 10 people were attacked on the day in question. The culprits attacked people on the roads and even in houses. The culprits are believed to be members of Inkatha. Since these people were not local it made it difficult for the victims to be able to identify them or point them out.

The inquest watched the police video of Inkatha members and then adjourned sine die, unable to reach a finding.

If the police could not identify the culprits, they made quick work of the victims. On Saturday evening a rumor spread through Mpophomeni that Inkatha was returning. N.M. Mvelase gathered with others at the junior school only to be arrested by three policemen. One kicked him several times with his boot while another, Bhengu, hit him in the face with a fist, breaking Mvelase's tooth. At the police station Bhengu said Mvelase had stabbed him with an assegai. He was charged with assault and public violence and only released on bail after a week.

Inquest 13 of 1988 into the other three deaths began on February 22, 1988. Magistrate Mrs. S.M. Nieuwoudt presided; the prosecutor was P. Coetzee; MAWU retained Wim Trengove to represent the families. After the first three witnesses had testified, advocate W.S. von Willich arrived, instructed by Friedman & Friedman. He referred to the civil action but was vague about whom he represented. Later the instructing solicitor explained that von Willich appeared only for Inkatha and the KwaZulu Minister of Police.

The prosecutor introduced three statements by Micca Sibiya, the survivor, but did not examine him further (and posed only perfunctory questions to the other witnesses). Before Trengove asked anything he raised the issue of intimidation, which pervaded the entire investigation.

> This witness has been in hiding since the incident to which he is just testifying [i.e., more than 15 months]. He is in fear of his life for very obvious reasons. He believes that there are people who are hostile to him and may want to kill him. There is in this court a man by the name of Ntombela. Mr Ntombela is a senior official of Inkatha. He may well be sympathetic to the cause of the people hostile to this witness. Mr Ntombela has been recently a respondent in two applications in the Supreme Court in which allegations have been made about him, amongst other things that he has incited people to murder and that he has participated in murder himself. [During the Natal Supreme Court hearing of one application, ten days earlier, Ntombela had threatened to shoot a man who had assisted Cosatu to serve legal papers on him.[24]] I don't object to his presence in court because I presume because it is a public hearing he has every right to be here. I am instructed, however, that Mr Ntombela is armed. He is carrying a firearm at this very moment.

The magistrate responded sternly: "Mr Ntombela please rise. Sergeant and the Orderly please accompany Mr Ntombela outside, search him and remove whatever weapon he may have on him. The weapon will be held until the court's further order." After the first two witnesses testified, Trengove told the court that others in the audience were armed. The magistrate was visibly angry.

> I was just going to make an announcement about it Mr Trengove. I understand that there are some of you people sitting there in the gallery with weapons on. You will all now give those weapons over to the police before leaving this room. If anyone comes into this courtroom again with a weapon of whatever kind, I shall deem it contempt of court. I shall not give a fine, I warn you now. That person will be locked up for three months, my maximum that I can impose. Is that clearly understood? It also goes for uttering any threat of any kind to any person here. Is that clearly understood?

The press reported this dramatic opening, although nothing further.[25]

Planning for the Inkatha rally had begun in November, when Joseph Mabaso visited the Amandleni Camp of the Inkatha Youth Movement and told Goodenough Bhekinkosi Chonco about it. KwaZulu Urban Representative V.V. Mvelase had told Moses Majola, who had told Andreas Mncube (both Inkatha officials in Ashdown). They attended a meeting at Mabaso's house on December 2, together with Shiyaboni Zuma and Mgagashe (both from Slangspruit). (Zuma's house had been burned the previous June, and he had received death threats.)[26] Those four were selected to be security guards for the rally under the direction of Mabaso, who confirmed the arrangements with Majola the next day. On December 4 Chonco and some thirty youths met at "Ma Snacky's," an Inkatha hangout near Edendale Hospital, where Mabaso chose Thulani Mchunu, Bhekukwenza Mtshali, Bhekisisa Majozi, Mzikayifani Cele, Nhlanhla Shabalala, and Vela Mchunu as youth security guards "to guard the Mpophomeni Community Hall during our stay at the hall and to see to it that no unknown people entered the hall or the grounds surrounding the hall." Zuma explained that the adult security guards were "to see to it that the youth were kept in an orderly manner and to see to it that the opposition 'UDF' did not disrupt the rally." Asked about the relevance of this line of questioning, Trengove said he sought to show that Inkatha planned the meeting knowing and intending that it lead to conflict. "With due respect to you," said the magistrate, "it is a little bit far removed from our present enquiry where we already have the conflict and we already have the deaths." But she allowed Trengove a few more minutes to show who was responsible.

On Thursday, December 4, Mag. Scholts issued a permit for a meeting at the community hall at 10 a.m. on Sunday "to inform the community of Mpophomeni regarding the need to pay rent, the need to see to the further education of children and to address the problem of intimidation." The chair was to be V.B. Ndlovu (KwaZulu MLA for Pietermaritzburg); the speakers were to be E.S.C. Sithebe (KwaZulu Minister for Pensions and Welfare), V.B. Ndlovu, and V.V. Mvelase. In fact, the event was to begin on Friday and continue with a march through the township on Saturday. Mabaso told Majola "that the reason for us going to Mpophomeni Township was to strengthen the Inkatha Movement there as there was only three members of Inkatha left." Mabaso told the police that Sithebe was to address the residents about "what the future holds for Mpophomeni"—a veiled threat to join Inkatha.

V.V. Mvelase and Joseph Mabaso drove their cars, and a KwaZulu government car and hired bus transported 100–200 youths. The township must have expected them. The previous Wednesday two Inkatha supporters had discussed the event, and so had the weekly meeting of BTR strikers. Even Inkatha Secretary General Oscar Dhlomo claimed that the Mpophomeni Youth Organisation had written on November 30 opposing the rally.

Mabaso arrived at the Community Hall about 10 p.m. and told its caretaker, Morris Sipho Thusi, to take him to M.M. Mchunu (local Inkatha "chairman"). Thusi led the way in his car and then back to the hall, where Mchunu noticed that the electricity was out (a common occurrence during thunderstorms). When Mabaso asked whether the youths should march from the township entrance to the hall or continue by bus, Mchunu urged the latter. The other vehicles arrived before midnight and left after depositing their passengers. Thusi and Mchunu lit candles they had bought, placing them on the verandah and in the conference room. The youths were in the yard, singing and shouting slogans. They were armed with knives, spears, knobkierries, and shields, and one youth security guard had a pistol. At the command "attention" they fell into groups. Mchunu welcomed Inkatha and thanked them for coming "as the inhabitants of Mpophomeni have opposed Inkatha and have forced most of Inkatha people out." He hoped "this show of force could show the people of Mpophomeni how strong Inkatha was." Shiyaboni Zuma introduced himself to Thusi as one of the adult security guards and asked how many gates there were. While he was being driven home by Thusi, Mchunu saw two Inkatha youth security guards questioning Zakwe, a local resident. Mchunu told them Zakwe was mentally ill and escorted him twenty meters up the road to ensure that he was not harmed.

Micca Sibiya was at home in the township with his mother and wife. About 9 p.m. his brother Phineas arrived with Phineas's girlfriend Nomuza Mnikathi, and Simon Ngubane. Phineas wanted a place to sleep with his girlfriend, but Micca said the house was full so the four drove around in Phillip Dladla's well-known car looking for a trysting place. Armed Inkatha youth security guards followed them back to Micca's house. They were led by Mzikayifani Cele, a former township resident who knew the four. When the youths ordered the four to go with them Micca refused to leave his home. After a youth stabbed him in the back, the guards took all four to the community hall and put them in the kitchen.

Mabaso summoned Zuma, Majola, and Mncube to the kitchen, where Cele identified the four as "staunch UDF supporters." Mabaso asked "why they were roaming around in the streets of Mpophomeni after dark?" Majola testified:

> I then asked the male captives: "you have [been] assaulted now. What were you doing here? What do you want here?" One captive said: "We were looking for the place to sleep with the female." I asked: "There is one female and three males, how will you sleep with one female and you are three males?" They said they were going to fetch other females if they found a place in the hall. I asked: "What made you to come to the hall because you knew that the hall on that day is occupied by us? Now look you are being assaulted." They said: "We knew that you were coming but we came into the hall not to fight or to be against you, just to look for the place to sleep."

Having learned they were MAWU supporters, Mabaso asked "whether they were aware that people from COSATU are going around killing people?"

Mabaso told the police that a youth security guard had found a bag of bullets in the car trunk (not offered in evidence) and that Nomuza said Phineas had a gun (never found).

Majola and Mncube claimed they left the kitchen. The youth security guards beat the captives badly. When Zuma saw that "blood was all over" he intervened because, "as we did not know them, we should get someone that knows [them] and could positively say that they [are] from the opposition, namely UDF." Trengove challenged this incredible explanation.

> *Trengove:* Mr Zuma, why was Mr Mchunu [local Inkatha chairman] called to tell you whether or not these people were members of the opposition? ...
>
> *Zuma:* It's because the others had assaulted them.
>
> *Trengove:* That answer doesn't make sense. They had been assaulted, they could have been taken to the hospital or the police, why was it important to know whether they were members of the opposition?
>
> ...
>
> *Zuma:* The other members were not supposed to beat these four people without consulting Mr Mchunu. When Mr Mchunu arrived he looked at them and then he said "these are the people who caused the violence." ... I then instructed that they should be taken to the police station.

Thusi had returned to his room in the hall. Although he claimed he had gone to sleep, the noise of youths singing and dancing and captives screaming made this unlikely. The first time the youths asked him to identify the captives he claimed to have refused. When they returned "he was curious to see who the people were" and "peeped through the window" of the kitchen (so that he would not be seen). He identified them to Mabaso, who told him to summon Mchunu. Again Trengove wanted to know why.

> *Trengove:* It's gone midnight, why take the trouble of going out, waking up a township supervisor and bringing him in?
>
> *Thusi:* As he was the person that arrived with the letter mentioned that they were going to use the hall and he knew about the meeting, I thought it was a good idea to call him so that he can see what's happening.
>
> *Trengove:* Mr Thusi, it was an absurd idea, wasn't it?
>
> *Thusi:* Yes, it was an absurd idea on my own seeing. ...
>
> *Trengove:* Mr Mchunu came in and his verdict, in your own words, was "They are bad people. You can do with them what you want."

[Thusi confirmed this.]

Mchunu first told the police he had spent the whole night at home after greeting the Inkatha delegation. (Majola corroborated this alibi, apparently unaware that Mchunu had disavowed it.) Four hours later Mchunu thought better and returned to the police. "I have made a sworn statement before Col. Marx...but I now wish to state the truth and nothing but the truth as I have left certain very important facts out of the statement." He now claimed to have been awakened at 1 a.m. by Thusi (who said there was a problem with the candles!) and two youth security guards (who said they had captured unknown people patrolling around the hall). Mchunu immediately recognized the impounded car as Dladla's. He observed the captives, taking care not to be seen by them, and named them to Mabaso, calling them "definitely the opposition." He claimed, however, that he told Mabaso this was a matter for the police and Mabaso agreed. Thusi said Mchunu told him he was "scared to see these people about the bad situation of the township." Mchunu walked home and went back to sleep.

Everyone tried to distance himself from what happened next. Mncube told the police he had returned to guard duty. "I never saw these people leave the hall as I was too busy guarding the hall." He fell asleep either standing up or just before daylight. But both Mabaso and Majola maintained that Mncube continued to participate in the questioning. Inkatha advocate von Willich made one of his rare interventions, protesting that Mabaso's statement did not mention Mncube's first name and many Zulu shared the same surname. Trengove parried by calling the witness "the Mncube, Inkatha member from Ashdown." When von Willich persisted, Mncube himself undermined the stratagem.

> *Von Willich:* Can you exclude the possibility that there was another Mncube at the community hall on the evening in question who also came from Ashdown?

> *Mncube:* If there was... I would have known about it because all the people were together now.

Majola told the police that Mncube joined Zuma and him in urging Mabaso to send the captives to the doctor before taking them to the police. Trengove added that Mabaso had said the same thing. Again Mncube would not take the hint, although this story tended to exculpate him and he could offer no reason why Mabaso would falsely implicate him.

In testimony Majola recanted his police statement that Mncube participated in the interrogation. Trengove pressed him.

> *Trengove:* So the statement is false?

> *Majola:* It is false because of Mr Mncube.

> *Trengove:* When you read this statement on Monday, swore under oath and swore that it was true, that oath of yours is false?

Majola: It wasn't false.

Trengove: You were here on Monday in the company of Mr Mncube, is that correct?

Majola: Yes.

Trengove: And you and him travelled to Mpophomeni together at lunchtime during his cross-examination.

Majola: Yes.

Trengove: He is a friend and colleague of yours?

Majola: We were only colleagues in Inkatha movement, he is not my friend.

Trengove: And I would like to suggest to you that he told you that in your evidence today you should leave him out of your story.

Majola: He didn't tell me.

Mncube also denied that the captives were injured or crying; but on cross-examination he offered one of the great understatements of the inquest: "seeing the appearance of their faces I would say they were not happy at that time."

Although he claimed to have spent the night on guard ten meters from the kitchen door, Mncube denied seeing the youth security guards leave with the captives. Von Willich intervened again, to clarify the layout of the Community Hall. The magistrate seemed impatient, asking whether he represented the witness, which he denied. After further exchanges about the layout, which seemed to upset Mncube, the court adjourned for lunch. During the break Trengove went to see the hall himself, where he encountered Mncube, Majola, Mchunu, and David Ntombela (the gun-packing Inkatha warlord). After lunch Mncube testified he had made the visit at the behest of Ntombela.

Zuma's initial strategy was to emphasize his solicitude for the captives, telling the police that he and the others wanted to send them to the doctor, even though their injuries were "slight," whereas Mabaso insisted they go to the police. In testimony, however, he inexplicably reversed himself. Trengove expressed mystification about why beating victims should be sent to the police. He kept asking why they were not just released, but Zuma remained evasive.

Trengove: Your worship, I must appeal to you because this witness....

Magistrate: Do you understand the question?

Zuma: I do understand the question, your worship.

Magistrate: You have no problems about the Zulu that's being spoken to you?

Zuma: No trouble with the Zulu, your worship.

Magistrate: Thank you, now it's a very simple and easy question and the court wants you to answer it with a yes or no. When you got to where these four people were with your youth brigade and Mabaso, why did you not order their release? No, Mr Zuma, you are not answering the question. The court can hear you. Please answer the question.

Zuma: The only reason is that they had assaulted them and injured them.

Magistrate: Even though they were assaulted and even though they were injured, why did you not order the youth to let those four people go? That is the question. That's all you have to answer.

Zuma: Your worship, I told Mr Mabaso that what the youth has done it is something which is unlawful, it is something....

Magistrate: No, Mr Zuma, is there any objection that you have to answering the question?

Zuma: No objection, your worship.

Magistrate: Would you like to answer the question or must the court take it that you refuse to answer the question?

Interpreter: Your worship, the witness says, when he arrived on the scene these four people had been already injured and he thought that their actions, the youth actions were unlawful and he thought the best solution was to hand over the matter to the police officers.

Majola also contradicted himself about whether the captives were to be sent to a doctor or the police. Trengove returned to the incomprehensibility of the latter course.

Trengove: Why were they to be taken to the police? What had they done wrong?

Majola: I saw the way they were injured. I don't know anything wrong which they had done.

Trengove: You mean you wanted to give them an opportunity to complain to the police about the assault?

Majola: Yes.

Majola offered inconsistent stories about his role in the interrogation, blaming the police for reading back his statements in English and the translator for skipping some parts. He concluded: "I cannot place every events on my mind because I have got so many things to think about."

Micca Sibiya (the surviving victim) confirmed that the four were taken out of the hall and told they would see a doctor. When Simon Ngubane tried to escape someone shot at him and others recaptured him. Micca heard him cry: "Oh, you are killing me." The security guards put Simon in the trunk of Dladla's car, pushed Nomuza Mnikathi into the front seat and bundled Micca and his brother Sibiya in the back. One of the youth security guards (Dumusani Mkhize) drove, and another (Bhekukwenza Mtshali) rode in front. Thusi drove his car with Zuma and seven other youths. He claimed they were taking the captives to the hospital. At trial, for the first time, he said the youths were armed with pangas and knives and threatened him. Trengove got him to admit this was "an afterthought created this morning." Furthermore, Majola testified that he would have seen such weapons. Thusi had told the police he could recognize the eight occupants of his car and might be able to identify the two youths in the other car. At trial, however, he was unable to recognize anyone. He could only identify the youths if they were wearing the clothes they had on that night: "[T]here's a word which I cannot understand very well, 'identify'. I don't know whether to identify a person is to see his face or either to see him by his clothing...." Von Willich again objected that Zuma was a common last name (although Majola had testified that only one Zuma was a security guard). Thusi admitted Zuma had been introduced to him by name but insisted he could not remember him because he had not known him previously. When Zuma stood in the audience, Thusi claimed not to know him. Majola inadvertently referred to "an elder person" in the car before recanting.

Thusi refused to acknowledge the implausibility of his story that youth security guards, having severely beaten members of "the opposition," would take them to the hospital. If that was their destination, Trengove asked, why were they armed? Thusi answered: "As I am wearing my jacket now, I cannot leave it. ... [W]hen they came to the hall they were armed with their own weapons. When they were in the vehicle with their weapons I thought maybe they don't know where to leave them, but I didn't think what they were going to do with them." Pressed further, he admitted: "I don't know the need [for the weapons] because I didn't ask them. ... Even on that day it didn't make sense to me."

Trengove also asked Majola why a second car full of security guards had to accompany the captives to the hospital.

> *Majola:* [T]hey must go with two vehicles because if they are going to Edendale Hospital they must leave the captives at Edendale Hospital and then leave the captives' vehicle at Sutherlands Police Station and then they must come back with Thusi's vehicle to the meeting.

Trengove: Why were these people not simply given their car and their car key so that they could go on their own?

Majola: They were afraid they would run away.

Trengove: Run away from whom?

Majola: Those assaulting them.

Trengove: So why shouldn't they run away?

Majola: I don't know.

Trengove: What right did you have to keep them?

Majola: We didn't keep them.

Trengove: Of course not. You were taking them to the hospital [he means the police] so that they could lay a complaint and you were taking them to hospital so that they can be treated. You weren't holding them. Is that right?

Majola: No, that's not right.

Trengove: What's wrong with it?

Majola: It's lawful that if I caught you doing something which is wrongful I must escort you to the police station.

Trengove: You didn't know of anything that they had done wrong?

Majola: Yes. ... I didn't know the reason why they were kept or detained. That's why I gave instructions that they must be sent to the police station so that everything could be found out why they were detained. ...

Trengove: Why is it necessary to send more than two people, a driver for each car?

Majola: I don't know because I'm not one of the leaders in the Inkatha organization. The person who was the leader there, it was Joseph Mabaso alone.

Trengove: Mr Majola, as far as you know it was quite senseless to send all those guards along.

Majola: It's senseless. ... Thusi was only told to go and show them the police station.

Trengove: That explanation can't be true, can it? The captives were Mpophomeni inhabitants. They knew very well where the police station was, correct?

Majola: Yes, correct. ... I only told him that because he was an adult person and he was also the caretaker of the hall.

Trengove: There is one service that Thusi could render, though. He could show the murder party a desolate spot where they could commit murder without interference. ...

Majola: I have no knowledge about that. ... I wanted them to send the captives to the police station.

Trengove: So that the captives could lay a complaint against the security guards who brought them to the police station?

Majola: Yes.

Trengove: And then they would say to the policemen on duty, "Good evening, sir, I have come to lay a charge of assault. Here are all the people who have beaten me up"?

Majola: Yes.

Trengove: And then they would go through the formalities of taking a statement, laying a charge?

Majola: Yes.

Trengove: And then all of them would get into the two cars again?

Majola: Yes.

Trengove: And they would ride to hospital?

Majola: Yes.

Trengove: And they would say to the doctor, "Good evening doctor, as you can see I have been injured badly." And the doctor will say, "What happened to you?" And they would say, "I was beaten up by these people with me." And then the security guards would say, "Would you excuse us, we have to go now."

When they left the hall, Zuma told Thusi to turn away from the hospital toward Nottingham Road. At Lion's River Thusi made a u-turn and halted; his headlights illuminated the second car stopped on the other side until his passengers told Thusi to douse them. All but Thusi and another rushed to the other car. Micca testified that on the drive the guards had demanded money. Phineas offered a R10 note but was told to hand over all he had—R200, which he claimed was MAWU's money. When the guard in the rear seat got out at Lion's River, Micca jumped out after him. The guard shot at his head, but Micca blocked it with his right hand. He rolled down the embankment and ducked underwater, successfully evading the guards. He heard five more shots. He hid until dawn and then fled; smoke still was rising from the burnt out car.

Thusi also heard the five shots and saw the other car overturned and set on fire. All nine security guards jammed into his car, making it difficult to drive property. Although two had flashlights, the courtesy lights went on each time the doors opened, and he was thirty centimeters from the nearest passenger, he could not identify anyone. No one spoke during the drive back.

When they reached the hall about 3 a.m. Thusi saw the security guards approach those in charge. Mabaso admitted seeing them return but claimed he did not talk to them until 7 a.m., when they said they had handed the captives over to the police. Majola also witnessed the return but "I did not take much notice of them as I was also lying down." Although he saw them again later "I didn't get any chance of speaking to anybody in the morning. No one was speaking to each other." Furthermore, "I don't like to ask. You are not supposed to ask questions if you are not a leader." Mncube saw Mabaso after the car returned but did not inquire what had happened because Mabaso was always busy. The prosecutor made one of his rare interventions.

> *Prosecutor:* If it is suggested to you by myself that you didn't ask any questions because you knew what happened to those people, what would your reply be?

> *Mncube:* I cannot say anything if you say so.

> *Prosecutor:* Don't you want to comment on my suggestions which is based on the evidence totally before the court?

> *Mncube:* What I can suggest is only that there was a person who was in charge of everything.

Thusi claimed he told Mabaso he was leaving for Durban. He took a bath, packed his things, and departed at 5 a.m. Zuma told police he had encountered Thusi, who reported "everything went off very well and [the captives] had been handed over to the police." Both denied this encounter in testimony. Majola claimed to have seen Thusi leave Saturday morning with two women. Thusi said he was alone; the trip to Durban had been planned earlier (even though Inkatha would occupy the hall for two more days); and the person he had planned to pick up at the bus stop was not there. In his first statement, Thusi said he had not reported the murders to the police out of fear. His second statement declared he had stopped at the Mpophomeni Police Station and said "there is trouble that happened at the hall" without specifying its nature. In testimony, however, he admitted that he had not reported the murders until Tuesday. "I thought that the people who were in the hall and the people of the community would have killed me." He admitted, however, that he only feared Inkatha. He denied that a guilty conscience prompted his precipitate departure from the township but admitted he was still afraid of Inkatha "because I don't know what they think the way I told the police officers." Thusi had been a KwaZulu employee since July 1983 and supported Inkatha. In April 1987 he was transferred to Ulundi, the homeland capital.

As soon as it got light on Saturday Micca made his way to a nearby farmer, who took him to the MAWU office in Howick, where he waited for his colleagues before calling the police. He made a statement to them and then to Chris Albertyn, a MAWU lawyer. Sgt. Perumal Reddy heard at 6:20 a.m. that a car was burning on the old main road toward Lidgton. When he arrived about ten minutes later he found it still smoking. The gas cap had been removed. A woman was in the front seat, a man in the back, and another man in the trunk. Dr. Dhanraj Maney, the assistant district surgeon, performed the autopsies. Nomuza died from a stab wound to her left lung, Simon Ngubane from two bullet wounds to his chest, and Phineas from a bullet or stab wound to his heart. The first two probably were still alive when the car was set on fire, although Phineas probably was dead.

M.M. Mchunu and Romanus Mzolo (two of the three Inkatha members in Mpophomeni) woke up at 5:30 a.m. and drove in Mzolo's car to buy milk for the youths and a goat for the KwaZulu cabinet minister scheduled to speak on Sunday. When they saw Inkatha and the "amaqabane" (comrades—UDF supporters) fighting and found the police at the community hall they went home. Shortly after 8 a.m. Mzolo found about 150 people in front of his house, singing and throwing stones. He chased them away by shooting three times, but they threatened to return at night and burn his house. When Mchunu walked to the hall about 9 a.m. a group accused him of bringing Inkatha to the township to kill residents. They chased him home and threatened to kill him and his family. At 2:45 p.m. a stone-throwing crowd returned to Mzolo's house; this time it took eight shots to scare them off. Both men fled the township that night.

On Saturday afternoon the bus deposited the Inkatha youths at Edendale Hospital. Chonco saw the five security guards say goodby to each other (Vela Mchunu was missing). Nhlanhla Shabalala shook hands with the others, saying "Comrades, you have done good work." When Chonco got something to eat at "Ma Snacky's," Thulani Mchunu said that he and the others had killed some people and burned them in a car. Chonco claimed he never saw the security guards again, although he knew where they lived.

Mabaso claimed to have heard about the deaths for the first time on the 6 p.m. radio news on Saturday. He confronted Vela Mchunu and Thulani Mchunu (two of the youth security guards) with this at a restaurant near his office Monday morning, but "they denied all knowledge." He made a statement to the police that afternoon and gave them his pistol.

The magistrate ruled that the last witness, M.M. Mchunu (Mpophomeni Inkatha chairman), was superfluous. Trengove argued that Mchunu could help affix responsibility. By identifying the four captives as "the opposition," Mchunu "virtually passed the death sentence." The magistrate called this an exaggeration. It was

common cause that these people were killed and they were
killed by certain members of a certain organisation, namely
Inkatha. ... Where we can name people we will name
them...but the court would say that if we are going to name
names we might as well name every single person who gave evidence here because as I understand the evidence, which we had
over and over again, it was quite clear that nobody was going to
divulge the most important features of this mess and they will
protect each other and the court feels that all of them, on that
score, could possibly have been charged but obviously that
would not be the right thing to do either. [Trengove persisted,
but the magistrate cut him off.] I think if I was in your position
I would also argue exactly like you did. ... I am sure that this
will not be the end of this matter. I have the belief in justice and
I am sure that arising from what has happened here there will
be a thorough investigation and whoever is responsible apart
from those that the court may or may not name, they will be
brought to book.

Trengove urged the court to admit the affidavits of Mabaso, who had died in
a car accident. However, he lacked standing to submit them, and the magistrate held she could not act on her own. Von Willich objected to their
admission on various inconsistent, legalistic, and probably incorrect grounds.
The magistrate finally accepted them at the prosecutor's behest. Trengove
and von Willich addressed the court, but the prosecutor declined.

At the end of three days of testimony, the magistrate began her judgment
by addressing the audience.

The court is not going to give a summary of all the evidence
which is heard here. Most of you were here, you have heard the
evidence yourself. What you must understand is that the proceedings were not a trial. It was an enquiry into the death of
these three persons.... [A]part from the evidence of the doctor
who conducted the post mortem report and the police witnesses, the only two witnesses of those present at the hall whose
evidence was not seriously challenged or shown to be patently
false were Micca Sibiya and Goodenough Chonco. It was quite
clear to the court that the question involved here were that of
two opposing factions. That was common cause. It was also evident to the court [that] all the other witnesses who were there at
the Mpophomeni Hall on the tragic evening of 6.12.86 were
lying witnesses. It was also clear to the court that they knew a
lot more than they were prepared to divulge. It's also clear that
they all tried to exculpate themselves. ... [W]here the court has

a doubt it will not name those people even though there is a strong suspicion that they may very well have participated in some degree or other. Unless the suspicion is of such a nature that it amounts to certainty, the court thinks it is wrong to name them. What is happening here today is not the end of the matter. The Attorney General will receive a full report with the record of these proceedings. Ultimately it is his decision of who should be charged and if so what the charges shall be. [She enumerated the causes of death.] The court further finds prima facie it appears that the death of all three deceased was brought about by the act or omission amounting to an offence on the part of one or more members of the Inkatha organisation, including the Inkatha Youth Brigade, who are, inter alia, Joseph Mabaso, Nhlanhla Shabalala, Tulani Mchunu, Bekisiswa Majozi, Bhekekwensa Mtjalie, Usikayifani Cele, Vele Mchunu, Dumisani Mkhize and Morris Thusi.[27]

No one was ever charged with the murders. Indeed, only one charge ever was brought. As Phillip Mnikathi, father of the murdered Nomuza, left court at the end of the first day of the inquest he commented out loud on the guns Ntombela and other Inkatha supporters were carrying: "Did you see those Inkatha bastards came to kill us!" Someone reported this to the police, who immediately arrested him and charged him with crimen injuria. MAWU attorney John Brand testified in his defense, but Mnikathi was convicted.[28]

At the end of 1991, nearly four years after the inquest, Vela Mchunu was still wanted for the three murders in Mpophomeni and another in Mpumalanga.[29] He also was accused with KwaZulu MLAs Khawula (Umzinto) and Ndlovu (Hammarsdale) of killing Zazi Khuzwayo, Clermont businessman and member of the advisory board, on the orders of KwaZulu cabinet minister Samuel Jamile (who was convicted in 1990). He also was thought to be the Vela who accompanied Jamile in killing Joseph Khumalo on April 5, 1987.[30] In March 1992 Vela Mchunu and Sibongeseni Nzama were arrested in Mpumalanga as supects in the murder of Hammarsdale taxi drivers Sipho Mkhize and Richard Duma. Mchunu showed a KwaZulu Police (KZP) identity card with the name Alfred Masongo. He was one of 200 Inkatha men trained by the SADF at its Hippo camp in the Caprivi strip and later absorbed into the KZP. Another member named Mchunu as part of the "offensive" unit hit-squad; his name also appeared on the list of trainees, which M.Z. Khumalo gave the Goldstone Commission.[31] In April 1992 Mchunu confirmed this account. Joseph Mabaso had recruited him in Hammarsdale in 1986. After six months in Caprivi he and twelve others were issued guns by Inkatha leader M.Z. Khumalo. Following the Mpophomeni murders he and others hid in the back room of Khumalo's shop in Ulundi. He served as Khumalo's security guard in Hammarsdale but in 1987 murdered Robert Dlamini, the brother of his fellow-trainee Bheki. He was charged with murder and possession of an unlicensed gun at Camperdown Magistrate's Court in 1987, but the charges were dropped. Although he was dismissed from the KZP, Khumalo got him a false KZP kitskonstabel (instant policeman) card in the name of Alfred Masongo and hid him and four kits-konstabels implicated in the Trust Feeds murders in the secret KZP Mkuze camp. In 1991 he was given a new police card and a machine gun and became a security guard for headman Ndlovu in Ixopo district.[32]

The Goldstone Commission's final report refused to draw these connections: "Although certain Caprivi trainees may be involved in some current acts of violence there is no evidence to suggest that such involvement was a direct result of the training they received in the Caprivi.... Vela Mchunu one of the trainees testified that he was involved in certain acts of violence. [The Commission] can however not find that he committed those acts as a direct consequence of his training at the Caprivi." In September Justice McCall acquitted Mchunu of the murders of Duma and Mkhize; although he did not believe the accused, the state had not proved its case.[33]

Spiraling Violence

Uncontrolled, indeed encouraged, by the state, violence continued to escalate.[34] A month after the Mpophomeni murders Inkatha raided the home of UDF activist and KwaMakhutha Youth Organisation member Victor Ntuli, killing four of his relatives and nine others (including seven children). Fifteen months later he was ambushed and shot in the neck. He saw two KZP running toward him, one of whom fired and missed.[35] Two weeks after the first attack on Ntuli, killers looking for Hammarsdale Youth Congress (HYC) president Vusi Maduna (an Inkatha defector) murdered Sthembiso Mngadi by mistake because he had playfully snatched Maduna's characteristic brown hat half an hour earlier. Witnesses identified two of the killers, but no arrests were made. Three more HYC members were killed in the next ten days. Maduna accused the local councillor and named three killers, but the police took no action. Maduna then offered to surrender to the killers to end the bloodshed. Instead he was attacked by forty people, stabbed, doused with gasoline, and burned to death. More than fifty were killed in Durban townships in the first three months of 1987. In response, police prohibited all outdoor funerals, limited the number of mourners, and banned public address systems, banners, and posters.

UDF president Archie Gumede and Inkatha general secretary Oscar Dhlomo negotiated peace in September and signed a truce in October. But the previous weekend a youth was killed in Mpumalanga.[36] Addressing the Inkatha Women's Brigade several weeks later, Buthelezi accused Gumede of "toadying" to divisive elements within UDF and resorting to "provocative political polemic in responding to my speech at the weekend."[37] The government foreclosed further negotiations by banning the UDF in February

1988 and forbidding COSATU to engage in political activity. KwaZulu MLA V.V. Mvelase (who had helped plan the Mpophomeni rally) accused UDF of bribing black police to win support.[38] The next week KwaZulu MLA Velaphi Ndlovu (accused with Vela Mchunu of killing a Clermont businessman) endorsed Inkatha revenge attacks. At least 138 people had been killed in the Pietermaritzburg area in the first ten months of the year.[39]

In October 1987 David Ntombela (the gun-toting Inkatha warlord at the Mpophomeni inquest) led five men to the Mkhize house, where they murdered Angelica Mkhize and her daughter Petronella; two younger children escaped into the bush. Later that night the gang killed Sithembiso Khumalo, apparently mistaking him for a relative. When Mangethe Mkhize (another son) started to cry at the police station a white policeman offered him a gun to shoot Ntombela. "When I moved towards the gun, he took it out of my reach. A number of policemen who were present thought this was funny." After the interview a policeman told him to wash his car, which Mangethe did "because we did not wish to antagonise the police." When Mandla Mkhize, another son, visited the police three days after the killing he was told the investigation was complete. The SAP charged Ntombela but released him on R100 bail. The surviving family members sought an interdict against further violence, provoking threats against the youngest children if they testified. The entire family went into hiding just before their home was raided again. The interdict was granted in November. At the March 1989 inquest into the deaths the magistrate found Ntombela and others responsible and referred the matter to the Attorney General. No one was prosecuted.[40]

In August 1987 Inkatha murdered the four daughters of Johannes Mthembu. In defending themselves, the family injured the attackers, including Dumisani Awetha, the son of Imbali town councilor Abdul Awetha. At a November memorial service Mthembu and his four sons—Elphas, Smalridge, Simon, and Ernest—were arrested for assaulting Dumisani and severely beaten. In January 1988 KZP officer Thulani Ngcobo shot Elphas in the foot and just missed Smalridge. Later that day Ngcobo and Harewood Inkatha Youth Brigade chairman C.S. Zuma threatened Johannes and Simon. When Johannes took Elphas to make a statement, he saw the police chatting with Ngcobo. A week later the Mthembu family applied for an interdict against attacks by Zuma, Ngcobo, and Imbali town councilor Jerome Mncwabe (already under interdict in two other cases). Furious at being served, Zuma went to the Mthembu house the day before the hearing and shot Smalridge in the shoulder and then shot Simon twice, paralyzing and eventually killing him. At the hearing the applicants urged the court to hold Zuma in contempt. The police responded by arresting Ernest for public violence for attacking Zuma's car. Ernest, who was to have testified at the August 1988 hearing on the permanent interdict, was shot the previous month. Before dying in hospital he identified Ngcobo as the killer. Now the applicants asked that Ngcobo be held in contempt as well.[41]

At least thirteen Inkatha members were the object of interdicts (some of several). Shiyaboni Zuma (the adult security guard at the Mpophomeni rally, who allegedly accompanied Thusi on the death ride) was accused in one of kidnapping a couple in June 1987.[42] Halton Cheadle, whose firm filed eleven applications, explained the strategy.

> [O]nce the Supreme Court spotlight was on [the warlords] they'd be curbed. ... [I]f we brought many applications the effect would be overwhelming. ... [They] would force the top Inkatha leadership either to take responsibility for its members, and in particular for those warlords who held leadership positions in Inkatha, or to distance themselves completely from their actions. ... [Because] Inkatha defended them all the way...we ended up citing Inkatha as a respondent.... There's no doubt that Inkatha suffered propaganda setbacks here and overseas because of the interdicts.... Another part of our approach was not to cite the police directly, but still present horrendous allegations against them in the papers.

Buthelezi, however, ridiculed the strategy in his answer to one application.

> The relief [sought] inevitably is an order seeking to restrain the members of Inkatha cited in those applications from murdering the members of the UDF or COSATU. As such illegal acts may carry capital punishment, no meaningful advantage can be obtained through a court order.... Accordingly, such applications I submit have been brought as political strategy.

> When the initial cases were brought before court certain leaders of the UDF and COSATU became deponents including Jay Naidoo, the leader of COSATU. Immediately after interim interdicts were obtained, a "Press Conference" was held by COSATU and UDF leaders to ensure that their organisations obtained maximum publicity from such facts.[43]

Inkatha Youth Brigade official Ntwe Mafole (convicted of attempted murder and public violence) declared in November 1987: "If somebody takes my eye out, I will take somebody's eye out; if they take my tooth out I will take somebody's tooth out; if they stab me I will stab. That is defence." KwaZulu MLA Velaphi Ndlovu (accused of murder) agreed: "As far as Inkatha (who is being attacked) is concerned, there is no difference between self-defence and retaliation." IFP (Inkatha Freedom Party) head Musa Zondi added that Inkatha was entitled to its "inalienable right" of self-defense: "When you are attacked someone will retaliate in some or other way depending on what you did." Buthelezi capped these threats in December. UDF and COSATU were "not worthy" of reconciliation, he told the Inkatha Central Committee. "I am now coming closer to believing that the only reconciliation there will ever be in this country is the reconciliation of the most powerful with those who pay homage to the powerful." A month later he warned Archie Gumede and the UDF that in Zulu tradition "the use of vitriol is a declaration of war."

In February 1988 the Natal Supreme Court conducted the first full hearing of an interdict application. Witnesses overheard David Ntombela threaten to shoot a man who had served legal papers on him.[44] Ntombela, V.V. Mvelase, and another defendant agreed not to assault anyone until the hearing. COSATU representative Alec Erwin explained that the interdicts were "attempts to break down the wall of prejudice against our organisations...." A witness testified that at a meeting in Mpumuza on January 31 Philip Zondi, brother of the local chief, said the UDF and COSATU were "Indian" organizations. "Any 'Indian' who did not move or repent and apologise, would be killed." Parents should kill children who had joined the "other camp." KwaZulu MLA Velaphi Ndlovu told parents whose children had not joined Inkatha to bring them to the chief to apologize. Otherwise they would be expelled or killed. The Ladysmith chief incited the crowd:

> "What should we do about them? Abajojwe! [stab them] Let's stop them! Abajojwe! Finish them off! Abajojwe!... Kill them." At each stabbing of the spear, the women would ululate and the men would stab into the air with their spears or sticks. As the pace increased the crowd became more frenzied.

The last speaker, David Ntombela, said anyone who did not want to belong to Inkatha should be killed. He asked the chiefs to end the meeting so he could lead an attack. Two men were killed and many injured by those leaving the rally. V.V. Mvelase's reply affidavit acknowledged that the demonstrators had attacked Ashdown residents, but Inkatha would not condemn such self-defense. "The police and defence force did not disarm the attackers because they had been provoked beyond all endurance by having their houses set alight, and then attacked by radicals." Ntombela said his sister had been attacked by a "well-known UDF supporter" and his house bombed in 1979 but he still opposed violence.

Later that month two Supreme Court judges summoned the Natal Deputy Attorney General to explain why the crimes alleged in the interdict application had not been prosecuted.[45] In April 1987 Samuel Jamile (KwaZulu MLA for KwaMashu and Inkatha Central Committee member), together with Vela Mchunu (one of the youth security guards in Mpophomeni) and three others, abducted Joseph Khumalo and his fiancée, Thokozile Shabalala. They killed Khumalo and gouged out his eyes; they beat Shabalala and left her for dead with a panga cut across the throat, broken jaw, fractured arm, and severe blood loss. Jamile was a wealthy businessman and national president of the Traditional Healers' Association. He commanded the hit-squad trained by the SADF in Caprivi. SAP security police Col. James Louwrens told the investigating officer to release Jamile before the investigation was complete. In

March 1988 Shabalala won a R15,000 default judgment against Jamile, but the Attorney General withdrew the murder and attempted murder charges without explanation, prosecuting only when Jamile's driver wrote the State President that his boss was bragging about the murders. After the civil judgment he was appointed KwaZulu Deputy Minister of Interior. In June 1991 he was sentenced to life imprisonment and finally dismissed from the cabinet.[46] Less than two years later, however, the Indemnity Board decided to release him.[47]

In May 1988 six Inkatha members pleaded guilty in the Pietermaritzburg Supreme Court to beating and stabbing an elderly woman to death in the belief that she supported UDF. Because the accused had acted in a state of "mass psychosis" induced by the loss of family and friends, the judge sentenced them to three to seven-and-a-half years imprisonment, half suspended.[48] In April the Natal University Centre for Adult Education estimated that more than 600 had died in two years of violence; Inkatha attacked three times as often as UDF and suffered half the losses.[49]

In September a lawsuit by COSATU against Inkatha was settled by creating a Complaints Adjudication Board chaired by a retired Natal Supreme Court judge, with one assessor from each side. COSATU dropped all its interdict applications, even though hearings had begun, having concluded that Inkatha planned to drag them out indefinitely.[50] A week later, however, violence in Sweetwaters took six lives and forced at least 100 families to flee.[51] In November COSATU filed complaints against two senior Inkatha members, who promptly refused to participate because criminal charges were pending. Retired Judge John Trengove gave Inkatha a month to reply and then another, without any effect. A witness before the Board was murdered in April 1989, after which it dissolved, having heard only two complaints.[52]

In February, seven of the eleven men charged with murdering seven KwaMashu school children three years before were convicted on the testimony of the survivor. Defense counsel argued in mitigation that the accused were following the orders of Inkatha Central Committee member Thomas Mandla Shabalala, who had heard a false report that KwaMashu people had kidnapped his son. Calling the event "an efficient, well organised, well executed slaughter," Justice Broome sentenced five to eight to sixteen years and two to death. The death sentences were subsequently commuted to twenty-five years. As a result of the Pretoria Minute (granting amnesty for political crimes), three men were released after twenty-two months and another after thirty-six.[53]

That month David Ntombela (the intimidating warlord at the Mpophomeni inquest) was elected unopposed to the KwaZulu Legislative Assembly. A week later a Pietermaritzburg inquest found him and six others responsible for killing Angelica Mkhize and her daughter Petronella in October 1987. Interviewed about that time, Ntombela proudly displayed the gun he always carried fully loaded. Brig. Jacques Büchner, Pietermaritzburg security police chief, said Ntombela had a firearm license and could carry the gun anywhere, even in court. "Look, David Ntombela is a legally appointed representative of the KwaZulu government; he has to rule with an iron hand or he loses respect and authority." He dismissed all the allegations against Ntombela as unproved.[54]

Towards the end of March COSATU released its "Report on Imbali Stage One," alleging police complicity with Inkatha in detaining, interrogating, harassing, and shooting UDF supporters. Police Commissioner Hennie van Wet's only response was to investigate whether COSATU had violated the Emergency regulations by holding a press conference. Inkatha secretary general Oscar Dhlomo replied that COSATU and the UDF were allied with the police. COSATU declared its loss of faith in the police when they detained and tortured Mandla Mthembu, whose testimony the Report had quoted.[55]

On March 19, Inkatha members left a rally at kwaNxamalala, killed several people in kwaHaza, and advanced on Mpophomeni. Residents summoned Democratic Party MP Pierre Cronjé and called the police, who were slow to arrive and then ignored the Inkatha invaders, attacking residents instead. They also arrested and roughed up Cronjé. The next day they imposed a curfew, whipping people on the streets. Vincent Sokhela did not run home fast enough.

> When I got to the kitchen door a policeman fired a shot. The bullet struck me in the back of my left thigh…. I fell down. The policeman came up to me. He turned me over and placed his foot on my leg just above the wound. He pointed a gun at my head… and [another] policeman began to cut at my leg with a small blade, and picked at the flesh of my leg. As a result of my injury, my left leg was amputated.

A month later a large force from kwaShifu attacked Mpophomeni, killing five, injuring four, and torching many houses. At the end of April Mpophomeni residents, ministers, and NUMSA applied to the Durban Supreme Court for an interdict against harassment, to which the police consented. In May it was made permanent and extended to the Minister of Law and Order. In September, however, more than a hundred Mpophomeni women complained that the Howick police were favoring Inkatha. Ten days later a clash between hundreds of Mpophomeni and kwaShifu residents left one dead and at least seventeen injured. A few days later Mpophomeni residents burned five homes in kwaShifu as their owners attended Shaka Day celebrations, threatening (in the words of David Ntombela) "that people should not attend the celebration to see Inkosi (King Goodwill Zwelithini) and noMntwana (Chief Buthelezi)."[56]

The government constantly frustrated peace efforts. In November 1987 it detained UDF leaders reporting back on proposals to meet with Inkatha in Pietermaritzburg. The following February it detained UDF and COSATU leaders during peace talks and restricted UDF soon thereafter. When DP MP Peter

Gastrow tried to persuade Law and Order Minister Vlok to ease restrictions he insisted that UDF was composed of "revolutionaries." The Complaints Adjudication Board failed in April 1989 partly because UDF could not participate. When church leaders sought to mediate that month, Vlok said they were "being inspanned by the ANC/SA Communist Party to do their devilish work" and promised an "iron fist" policy of massive police intervention, blaming UDF and COSATU for all the violence. When the parties were about to meet in June, Vlok placed UDF leaders Archie Gumede and Azhar Cachalia under house arrest.[57]

In June four high school pupils obtained an interdict against Thomas Mandla Shabalala and his son, alleging that they had been kidnapped and tortured at his headquarters. Two months later Shabalala was tried for murdering high school pupil Bheki Gcabashe and attempting to murder others. He had been free on R500 bail. After his acquittal Justice Combrink remarked that he had never known a trial in which there were so many overt lies. Shabalala's supporters carried him out on their shoulders.[58]

Despite Vlok's opposition, Inkatha met UDF and COSATU twice in June, although killing increased. At the Inkatha annual general meeting in July, however, Buthelezi condemned UDF and COSATU for allowing comrades to sing insulting songs. As he spoke, youths sang: "The amabutho support us/Hit the comrades/O Buthelezi; Attack/Kill/The Comrades; the amabutho are with us/O Buthelezi." Inkatha withdrew from talks in September, angered by ANC leader Thabo Mbeki's derogatory remarks about Buthelezi, violence, and UDF and COSATU demonstrations.[59]

A few whites who had gone to stay with black families in Imbali to discourage violence were ordered to leave in November, accused of bias toward UDF and failing to introduce themselves to local councillors. David Ntombela said if such "squatters" did not leave as soon as possible "we will be forced to take the law into our own hands." The effective amaqabane leader, Bogart Ndlovu, responded: "These are our whites; they eat our food and sleep in our homes and not in the opposition's. We are supposed to be fighting discrimination and apartheid with its Group Areas Act." A week later both retracted. Ntombela could not have issued threats: "I am an old man and I don't believe in violence." Ndlovu insisted "these whites are here for everyone—they do not belong to any political organisation and will stay with anyone who requests them through the established channels."[60] In March 1990, the day after his granddaughter was badly burned in a fire-bombing, Ntombela participated in an attack by a 1,500-man impi on settlements in lower Vulindlela Valley, where buses had been stoned while carrying Inkatha supporters to a Durban rally. More than 115 homes were burned and many people killed.[61]

At the end of March groups from kwaHaza and kwaShifu attacked Mpophomeni, which retaliated the next day. A month later Mpophomeni residents sought permission to march through Howick and present their grievances to the police. The magistrate allowed only twenty to do so. Some

5,000 marched in the township instead, calling on the police to end "harassment, shootings and killings." The Mpophomeni Youth Organisation, Women's Organisation, Residents Association, and Council of Churches and the Howick Student Congress demanded an end to Inkatha attacks and removal of the riot squad, invoking the Supreme Court interdict of the previous year. In July KwaZulu Interior Minister Sithebe led an armed group to the township, guarded by security forces, and berated the Mpophomeni Residents Association for resisting homeland control.62

In August Justices Didcott and Wilson, in separate cases, deplored the intimidation that discouraged witnesses from testifying about violence. Justice Wilson criticized the police for lax investigation verging on protection of the accused.63

When the Durban LRC urged the SAP to stop Inkatha from carrying weapons, it replied that "cultural" weapons like assegais, axes, and knobkierries had been exempted from the Natal Code of Zulu Law by de Klerk in August and eliminated from the KwaZulu Code of Zulu Law and Notice 8 under the Dangerous Weapons Act in November (although the SAP enforced that Act in Transvaal). In January 1991 the KwaZulu Minister of Justice gazetted government notices eliminating the minimum sentences for dangerous weapons offenses. The next month journalist Lechesa Tsenoli asked the Durban Supreme Court to invalidate de Klerk's order on the ground that it discriminated against him as a Mosotho. When armed Inkatha members prevented the southern Natal ANC from conducting a mock trial of Buthelezi in July 1992, 10,000 ANC members marched through Inanda the following month carrying spears, sticks, shields, axes, and pangas and singing traditional fighting-songs.64

Stories began to emerge in September 1990 that four years earlier at its Hippo base in the Caprivi Strip the SADF trained 200 Inkatha warriors, who then joined the KwaZulu Police. De Klerk admitted this a year later.65 SADF Military Intelligence channeled more than R7 million through front organizations to maintain the KZP secret Mkuze camp for three years. Evidence accumulated of police complicity with Inkatha attacks. MI trained Transvaal Inkatha leaders before violence broke out on the Reef in 1990. A KZP officer trained in guerrilla warfare led the attack on an ANC funeral in Wesselton; he was released after being arrested and his group's AK47s were returned to the KZP.66 The government paid the expenses of a trip to Norway by Musa Myeni, IFP executive member and head of international relations, who declared at a press conference: "Apartheid is dead. Today we are suffering under an emerging African National Congress dictatorship backed by communists all over the world." The government also contributed at least R250,000 to an Inkatha rally at King's Park, Durban in March 1990, which sparked the "Pietermaritzburg War." Maj. Louis Botha, head of Durban security police, declared it was of "cardinal importance" that the rally "show to everyone that [Buthelezi] has a strong base." In January 1991, nearly a year after de Klerk publicly terminated government funding for Inkatha, there was evidence that Maj. Botha paid for another rally. The government also supported UWUSA, the Inkatha union, which police described in 1989 as "a project under the control of the SAP." At least five people knew of these payments: Buthelezi, Interior Minister Stephen Sithebe (who was to have spoken at the 1986 Mpophomeni rally), Justice Minister Mtetwa, Gavin Woods, and Buthelezi's personal secretary M.Z. Khumalo (who led the Caprivi-trained hit-squad and hid Vela Mchunu, who had participated in the Mpophomeni murders).[67]

In an October 1990 interview David Ntombela blamed all the violence on UDF/ANC/COSATU.

> Whenever we have a meeting, they distribute pamphlets and say any person will be killed or have his house burned if he goes to that meeting. ... [They engage in] attacks and insults on Inkatha leaders. Most of the Inkatha leaders have been attacked, myself even.

His son, a special constable, recently had been shot in ambush. He defended the March 1990 attack on the ground that the stoning of buses had kept people from working. "[T]here's not one time I will allow anybody to tell people not to go to work." He supported Inkatha because of its "commitment to non-violence." UDF had to "stop calling the Honourable Chief Minister a dog; they must also stop swearing Inkatha, calling us 'theleveni' and warlords and so on." He repudiated the title (though he had clearly been flattered when another interviewer recently had called him "Inkatha warlord number one"). "I'm 65, never convicted. I'm clean, my hands are clean—if I had money I would sue because they can't prove it that I'm a warlord." KwaZulu Police Commissioner Jacques Büchner called him "a rural somebody" who held "the Elandskop area together" by loyalty rather than intimidation.[68] A month later Ntombela told a rally of a thousand: "There is no nation without the young men or the army—they must protect the Zulus. They must not keep quiet when the minister is insulted and people are trying to divide us. Bring back the dignity of the Zulu nation."[69] Immediately after he addressed a National Party meeting the following week an ANC member was killed.[70] When KwaZulu transport buses came under fire in January 1991, injuring a driver, Ntombela warned "bloodthirsty ANC supporters" there would be "revenge missions" if the shooting continued.[71]

In March 1991 Chief Maphumulo, president of Contralesa (the pro-ANC Congress of Traditional Leaders of South Africa) was assassinated. Hours earlier another Contralesa chief was killed in his car with two companions. In response there was an attempt on the life of David Ntombela. A month later Maphumulo's brother-in-law survived an attack, but Maphumulo's close friend was murdered before the inquest. At the inquest an SAP constable testified that he and other police had attacked Maphumulo's home before the assassination. Sipho Madlala, a security police agent, told reporters he had been recruited for the assassination. At the inquest he named four policemen as his handlers, picking two out in an identity parade.[72]

When the state charged two KwaZulu MLAs with separate murders in June 1991, Buthelezi explained that they were not suspended from the Legislative Assembly because they were

> victims who have not been able to carry the burden of peace that the rest of black South Africa carries. They are wrong and their apprehension by the law and being brought to trial is right. ... The ANC has waged an ugly war against kwaZulu.... It might be they feel more burdened and are subject to greater strain than other members of the republic.[73]

In July 1991 attacks on Mpophomeni left at least twelve houses burned, several injuries, and unconfirmed deaths. The ANC responded by suspending its branch treasurer and pleading for an end to fighting.[74]

In February 1992 KwaZulu MLA and Inkatha Central Committee member Winnington Sabelo was assassinated. The most senior Inkatha victim to date, he had led the 1985 attack on the memorial service for Victoria Mxenge, in which nineteen died, as well as the attack on the victims' funeral. His wife had died and his three children had been injured in a retaliatory raid the following year. Attempts on the lives of Imbali deputy mayor Abdul Awetha and Richmond IFP leader Paulus Vezi killed three children. Inkatha retaliated by murdering ANC Imbali chairman S'kumbuso Ngwenya the same month. At the end of October Reggie Hadebe, close associate of ANC Midlands leader Harry Gwala, was murdered as he and two other ANC officials returned from meeting the IFP and SAP. A few days later there was an unsuccessful ambush of David Ntombela as he came back from a National Dispute Resolution Committee meeting.[75] Imbali mayor Phikelela Ndlovu, deputy mayor Abdul Awetha, and Awetha's sixteen-year-old son were prosecuted for the Ngwenya murder. Ballistics tests pointed to Awetha's gun, one of twenty-four purchased by Pietermaritzburg security police for Imbali town council officials, four of which were connected to seventeen murders. Awetha had damaged the barrel and firing pin, exchanged barrels and slides with Ndlovu, and then asked the town council to replace the defective weapons to prevent identification. It took detectives twelve days to obtain a warrant to search Awetha's home. The trial was held in camera since one accused was a minor. Justice Combrink acquitted all the defendants because expert testimony conflicted. The gun parts could have been switched inadvertently while their owners were cleaning them. After judgment the deputy Attorney General ordered the guns be returned to the accused.[76]

Analysis

The legal system's response to the Mpophomeni murders was emblematic of its inability to end the war in Natal and, indeed, its complicity in the violence. A threshhold lesson is humility about the possibility of ascertaining the "truth" about what happened (a variant of the fact skepticism of legal realists like Jerome Frank). Why were the four MAWU supporters driving around the armed Inkatha encampment the night before the rally? Certainly not seeking a quiet place for Phineas and Flomena to make love. Were the youth security guards intending to capture "opposition" figures—especially someone as prominent as the head of the shop stewards? Who was implicated in the decision to murder? Another lesson is the inescapable role of chance. Had Micca Sibiya not escaped there would have been no one to challenge Inkatha's lies. Mabaso's accidental death made him a convenient scapegoat for his underlings.

In the face of state indifference to Inkatha violence (and later revelations of complicity), MAWU lawyers had to push hard for a formal inquest, through which they hoped to avoid a cover-up and compel a prosecution. This hearing allowed them to publicize the atrocity unconstrained by the Emergency Regulations (which limited unrest reports) and Inkatha's readiness to sue for defamation. The mere exposure in a public forum, and even more an official imprimatur on the narrative, would empower MAWU (and COSATU/UDF) supporters in Mpophomeni and throughout Natal. Trengove sought to destroy the web of lies in order to implicate Inkatha, and especially its leaders, in the assaults and murders. COSATU/UDF hoped this would curb violence and intimidation. As was tragically demonstrated, however, the legal system was impotent to halt the war. Inkatha, by contrast, was engaged in damage control. Officials denied all knowledge and responsibility. Von Willich ineffectively objected to witness identifications of Inkatha leaders and sought to exclude Mabaso's statements to the police. Intimidation—Inkatha's principal tactic—not only failed but backfired.

The state's objectives were more ambiguous. Although liberal theory requires it to enforce the law while remaining neutral between private parties, it betrayed both ideals. Magistrate Scholts allowed Inkatha to demonstrate in a township he knew supported MAWU; Inkatha was so confident of getting permission that they applied only a day before an event that had been planned for weeks. By contrast, the Natal Police Commissioner severely restricted the funeral for the murder victims.

The police displayed bias in other ways. Knowing that Inkatha youths had just committed four murders, they not only failed to interrogate them or even take their names but actually returned their weapons and escorted them home! Knowing the identity of the adults and the youth security guards, they made no arrests. They concealed the video from MAWU attorneys and did not offer to screen it at the inquests. The strongest evidence of a police cover-up is the statements they took from potential witnesses. Although the

SAP routinely tortured anti-apartheid activists to extract confessions and statements implicating others (see chapter seven), they uncritically accepted patent lies and inexplicable memory lapses. They failed to pursue inconsistencies within or between statements. They may even have encouraged perjury. Col. Marx took Mchunu's first statement; three hours later he took Mabaso's first statement. The next day his colleague Lt. Delport took Zuma's statement. Eight sentences (containing more than 230 words) in the statements of Zuma and Mabaso are *identical*; four of these sentences also appear in Mchunu's statement. Since Mabaso and Mchunu were speaking English, while Zuma was speaking Zulu, only the police could have been responsible. No other statement displays language even vaguely similar.

The Attorney General and his prosecutors were equally indifferent. No inquest might have been held but for constant pressure by John Brand. The prosecutor remained passive, leaving questioning to Trengove. He refused to call Mchunu as a witness. He declined to give a closing address. Yet even he sometimes rose to the occasion, rejecting von Willich's insinuation that there were other Zumas or Mncubes at the hall that night and offering Mabaso's affidavits over von Willich's objections.

Because the state abdicated responsibility to enforce the law, what should have been a public prosecution for murder became a private dispute between MAWU and Inkatha. MAWU lawyers represented the survivors seeking damages from Inkatha. MAWU lawyers insisted on a formal inquest and dominated the hearing. Even von Willich appeared on behalf of a private party. Elsewhere private parties and their lawyers sought interdicts against violence, shouldering the burden shed by the police.

The magistrate's role best reveals the complex relationship between law and politics. Magistrates need not be qualified lawyers, and most have never practiced privately (though many have been prosecutors). As civil servants they identify closely with the government, performing administrative as well as adjudicative functions. Magistrate Scholts issued the permit for the Inkatha rally, then conducted the inquest into one of the Inkatha murders, and terminated the hearing by accepting the police claim they could not identify the assailants.

Mrs. Nieuwoudt was less compliant. She was unused to dealing with either the media or an advocate of Trengove's calibre, who enjoyed greater professional and social status. She sought to establish authority at the outset, taking over Trengove's objection to Inkatha intimidation, questioning the relevance of his first extended cross-examination, and rebuffing his final request to have Mchunu testify. She openly displayed impatience with von Willich, demanding to know whom he represented, rejecting his proffered diagram of the community hall, and admitting Mabaso's statements over his objections. Like the judges who resented mandatory sentences or statutory presumptions, she jealously asserted her considerable discretion.

She certainly did not favor Inkatha, strongly reprimanding those carrying weapons, pressing evasive witnesses, and making Zuma stand to allow identification. Yet she also did not give Trengove everything he requested, such as a chance to question Mchunu (whom she may have known as a former Mpophomeni councilor). Her judgment offered further evidence of the tension between law and politics. Emphasizing the irreconcilable conflict between Inkatha and UDF/COSATU, she bluntly called most of the witnesses liars and did not hesitate to blame Inkatha. But she refused to accuse anyone whose guilt was not "certain," a reticence without legal foundation. Consequently, though she named the seven youth security guards (who could not be found) and Mabaso (conveniently dead), she did not name Majola, Zuma, Mncube, or Mchunu (who could readily be charged). Furthermore, she repeatedly affirmed her faith in the legal system, deferring to her superior, the Attorney General. And he filed no charges, even against Thusi, whom she named and whose whereabouts were known.

The inquest violated the basic criteria of a legal proceeding in three crucial respects. First, it was hopelessly politicized from the outset. Police inefficiency and obstruction allowed suspects to disappear, witnesses to forget, and physical evidence to be "lost." Intimidation was pervasive: everybody but the white magistrate and lawyers knew that David Ntombela and his followers were armed. Micca Sibiya had to remain hidden for fifteen months before the hearing, since Inkatha routinely murdered those with the temerity to testify against it. Trengove elicited admissions of fear from Thusi and Chonco. Although the magistrate repeatedly warned witnesses not to discuss their testimony, David Ntombela used the lunch recess to compel Mncube to join him, Majola and Mchunu in a visit to the community hall in order to coordinate their lies. Inkatha's threats even dissuaded a Durban attorney from suing Inkatha.

These threats within the courtroom merely reflected the fear dominating Natal. As several members admitted, Inkatha held the rally in order to force the township to change sides. Zuma testified that the appropriate response to identifying the captives as members of "the opposition" was to beat them. The armed "parade" early Saturday morning served only to cow Mpophomeni residents. Inkatha sought to justify its terror by similar allegations against UDF/COSATU.

The larger struggle contaminated the inquest. Almost everyone lied outrageously. They lied to the police (who may have orchestrated their inventions). Unlike witnesses in criminal cases, they could listen to each other. They felt no compunction about abandoning one lie for another. Sometimes the pressure was obvious, as when Majola exculpated Mncube after Ntombela took both of them to the community hall during lunch. Some stories were inherently implausible: Mchunu awakened in the middle of the night to identify captives whose names and loyalties were known; nine security guards escorting captives to the hospital and then to the police to complain about being beaten. Prosecution for perjury was an empty threat in this politically charged atmosphere.

Even with ample opportunity and police assistance, however, they were bad liars. Inkatha supporters constantly contradicted each other. Majola denied Mncube had interrogated the captives, although Mncube admitted it. Thusi told police Zuma was in his car, which Zuma naturally denied. Zuma said Thusi told him he had taken the captives to the police station, but Thusi denied speaking to Zuma. The adults could not agree whether they intended to take the captives to the police or the hospital. Self-interest always colors testimony, but witnesses rarely show such total contempt for truth and apparent indifference about their credibility.

Sometimes instead of lying they took refuge in silence and forgetfulness. Thusi could not identify Zuma, any of those he drove back from the murder site, or even Micca Sibiya, who lived in his township. Mncube and Zuma could not identify any of the youth security guards they commanded. When shown the police video of the Inkatha rally Zuma could not identify anyone. The participants were surprisingly incurious about the dramatic events in which they participated. When he saw Mabaso Saturday morning, Mncube did not ask what had happened to the captives. When Majola saw the driver of the death car that morning, he also did not inquire. When a security guard said he and the others had killed the captives and burned them in their car, Chonco did not ask why. The ethic of *omerta* is not restricted to Sicily.

Divisions of race, culture, language, and politics in South Africa obstruct attainment of the second prerequisite of legal proceedings—mutual comprehension. Most witnesses spoke through an interpreter, whose pivotal role emerged when he intervened to explain what the speaker really meant. Trengove deployed all the advocate's tricks to expose lies, but witness incomprehension of his (s)wordplay denied him an unambiguous victory. In any case, cross-examination is more effective as a shield, to generate doubt, than as a sword, to compel belief. Like the Alexandra treason trialists (see chapter nine), some witnesses took refuge in linguistic incomprehension. Thusi claimed confusion about what it meant to "identify" someone, although he had no difficulty making police statements in fluent English. Confronted with the contradiction between his stories to the police and to the inquest concerning his role in interrogating the captives, Majola claimed ignorance of English, poor translation, and "so many things to think about." Playing dumb is a common linguistic defense among oppressed people.[77]

Even had the court penetrated the smokescreen of lies, silence, and mutual incomprehension, it could not have affixed responsibility for the murders because of the difficulty of establishing a chain of authority between perpetrators and leaders. This problem arises whenever law seeks to control the behavior of large organizations, public or private. Most illegal acts are committed by dispensable foot soldiers. Indeed, some Inkatha hit-men were charged, convicted, and sentenced to long terms. An organization can be changed or destroyed only by attacking its commanders. Yet leaders often evade responsibility for compromising behavior (although this undermines the authority structure essential to any large organization).

Inkatha tried to have it both ways. Because it was a quasi-military organization, everyone at the rally acknowledged Mabaso's authority. Mchunu told the police that "he was the Senior Member of Inkatha present, at the Community Hall, and members of Inkatha were taking instructions from him." Majola testified that "when I made a comment that they mustn't do like that [beat the captives] I was instructed to leave the kitchen and go back to the hall," which he obediently did. He did not question Thusi about the captives' fate because "you are not supposed to ask questions if you are not a leader." Mncube disobeyed the magistrate's instructions not to discuss his testimony because Ntombela told him "to get inside the vehicle and then we must go." Mncube also asked no questions because "there was a person [Mabaso] who was in charge of everything."

At the same time, the adults sought to distance themselves from the murder by insisting they had challenged Mabaso's authority. Both Majola and Zuma claimed to have argued with Mabaso, trying to stop the beating and urging that the captives go to the hospital before the police. Alternatively, they blamed the violence on rogue youths who defied their authority. In other instances Inkatha leaders as high as Buthelezi protested their inability to contain their followers, especially given the justifiable anger at opposition atrocities. This strategy was remarkably successful (despite its fundamental contradiction). The youths had gone underground. The adults had either bent to Mabaso's will or courageously defied him. The only one left holding the bag was Mabaso—who conveniently had died.

The inquest could not transcend these political intrusions. Although Trengove demonstrated and the magistrate affirmed that Inkatha witnesses were lying, the court never determined what actually happened. Trengove had relatively free rein to question witnesses, but only after the police had botched the investigation so badly that essential evidence and suspects were lost irretrievably. The magistrate strongly condemned the intimidation of witnesses but could not stop it. Just as the police returned weapons to Inkatha youths when they left Mpophomeni, so the magistrate returned Ntombela's gun as he left the court. High visibility behavior in the courtroom exhibited the trappings of legality; low visibility behavior in the community and the police station was blatantly political. One magistrate (if not the other) showed signs of judicial independence; the police and prosecutors did not. State indifference to the murders (and possible police and prosecutorial complicity in the cover-up) transformed a public prosecution into a private dispute, but MAWU alone could not convict. Culpability was displaced onto missing youths and a dead leader. Secure in its support by the state, Inkatha was unabashed about its notorious criminal behavior; leaders did not even seek to concoct a convincing story. Skilled advocacy caught witnesses in lies and evasions; but these had no consequences, either legal (perjury, loss of credibility) or informal (public embarrassment). The magistrate found foul play, named the perpetrators, and declared her faith in the criminal justice system—but nothing further happened.

Although I cannot detail the myriad other stories of private violence in South Africa during the 1980s, Mpophomeni was not an isolated incident. Politics repeatedly trumped law, whose impotence was proclaimed by the failure of the criminal justice system to deter thousands of murders. As Buthelezi asked rhetorically, what was the point of interdicting a crime already punishable by death? Publicity discourages wrongdoing only when perpetrators are shamed by public opinion. In the Natal civil war, however, reactions were uncompromisingly partisan. Inkatha leaders openly flouted interdicts with impunity, just as they evaded investigation, prosecution, conviction, and punishment. The police condoned Inkatha's criminality while protecting members from retaliation.[78] Prosecutors did not charge or vigorously prosecute Inkatha leaders. Of the few convicted, most received light sentences. David Ntombela kept committing assault, arson, and murder and intimidating witnesses with impunity for over six years. Like other warlords, he was rewarded with election to the KwaZulu Legislative Assembly. Even those imprisoned were released through general amnesties or the commutation of individual sentences.

Covert state partisanship eventually was exposed. The government rewrote laws to allow Inkatha to carry "cultural weapons." It propagandized on behalf of Inkatha at home and abroad. It funded Inkatha demonstrations and obstructed those of the ANC. It was the largest financial backer of the Inkatha trade union, UWUSA, which could not have survived independently. Most shocking of all, it trained Inkatha's hit squad, supported it financially, armed it, and condoned its incorporation into the KwaZulu Police. It frustrated every effort to negotiate peace. While publicly sensationalizing the horrors of "black-on-black" violence, it secretly fueled such conflict. Neutrality was impossible or ineffective: the few whites who sought to interpose their bodies between the ANC and Inkatha were seen as partisans by both; peace negotiations went nowhere.

Thus, the Mpophomeni murders epitomized and foreshadowed the civil war that has raged for almost a decade. The attack was planned by KwaZulu MLA V.V. Mvelase. Shiyaboni Zuma, an Inkatha warlord implicated in other murders, directed the youth security guards and rode with them to the murder site. Vela Mchunu committed the murder after being trained by the SADF. Afterwards he was protected by Buthelezi's personal assistant, M.Z. Khumalo, and hidden for almost six years within the KwaZulu Police—first openly and then, after murdering a colleague's brother, covertly. He continued to murder on the orders of Inkatha leaders like Samuel Jamile. While a warrant was outstanding against him for the Mpophomeni murders, he was arrested and charged with another murder and then released. The courage of Micca Sibiya in testifying, the energy of Wim Trengove in representing him, and the integrity of Mrs. Nieuwoudt in naming the murderers came to naught. As Chief Buthelezi bombastically declaimed: "We are talking about a life and death struggle. We are talking about all-or-nothing victories. We are talking about the final triumph of good over evil." In such conflicts, law is impotent.

CHAPTER 7

STATE TERRORISM: THE RESPONSE OF MEDICINE AND LAW TO POLICE TORTURE

> We were also informed...that we could
> only use fair violence. (Affidavit of Lt. Eric
> Alexander Taylor in reply to the interdict
> application by Dr. Wendy Orr)

The South African Police have a well-deserved reputation for brutality.[1] In the eight years following their 1977 murder of Steven Biko, twelve political detainees died in police custody; another eight political prisoners died in 1984 and early 1985.[2] The Eastern Cape, with a long history of political activism, was particularly dangerous.* During the thirtieth annual Black Sash conference beginning March 14, 1985, in Port Elizabeth, Molly Blackburn and other participants investigated and exposed police torture of detainees, including children, charges that were repeated four days later when Parliament debated the SAP Special Account Bill.** On March 21—exactly a quarter century after the police murdered sixty-nine people in Sharpeville—a group of mourners waited at the Langa bus terminal to attend a funeral in KwaNobuhle (both townships of Uitenhage). The police opened fire with shotguns and rifes, killing twenty and wounding twenty-three. The same day the Minister of Law and Order informed Parliament of that "most unfortunate

---

*Port Elizabeth had organized a four-month bus boycott in 1949. The Eastern Cape accounted for seventy-one percent of arrests nationwide during the 1952 Defiance Campaign. Lodge (1983: 47, 51). Police at the Algoa Park station were particularly brutal in the wake of the 1976 Soweto uprising. J. Jackson (1980: chap. 18 et passim).

**Spink (1991: 171–73); *Hansard* cols. 2455–57 (K.M. Andrew, PFP) (3.19.85); col. 946 (reply by Minister of Law and Order to H. Suzman, PFP) (4.9.85). A Conservative MP denounced Blackburn for having "entered the property of the SA Police uninvited and unlawfully" and having "kicked up a big fuss." "[E]very officer worth his salt deserves the protection of the Minister of Law and Order." *Hansard* cols. 2810–12 (J.H. Hoon) (3.26.85).

incident," explaining that the police "had no alternative but to order fire in self–defence" and "later found traces of exploded petrol bombs."[3] When a PFP member complained that police had refused to cooperate with his party's investigation, the Minister sought to block Parliamentary debate on the ground that the State President had appointed a commission of inquiry, making the matter sub judice; but he was rebuffed by the Speaker.[4] Even the South African ambassador to England, Dr. Dennis Worrall, declared there was no justification for the shootings.[5]

Helen Suzman used the vote on the police during the April 29 Appropriation Bill debate to condemn the Minister for accepting "without question everything the Police do or tell him" and moved that his salary be reduced to that of a police constable. Opponents condemned her as "a favourite in the eyes of revolutionaries" and a "granny for criminals." The CP declared that "the SA Police acted within its rights and has to be protected at all costs. We should not create a psychosis of suspicion around it." The Minister complained that his predecessors had not been subjected to "such a sustained, venemous, derogatory and personally insulting campaign" since the early 1960s. Despite PFP attacks he would "not come down like a ton of bricks on a policeman who oversteps the mark" and refused "to hammer policemen left and right." Of the more than two dozen complaints about police behavior, the Attorney General had prosecuted six (of which two were acquitted and four pending.) But the Minister reiterated that "neither the Commissioner of Police nor I am prepared to permit any member of the Police Force to break the law or Standing Orders deliberately." Concerning "the so-called unnecessary shooting of rioters" he reminded members of "the atrocities carried out in those areas, how portions of bodies were swung around at funerals…and eaten as well. [Interjections.] Only yesterday a member of the SA Police was murdered horrendously in Uitenhage. He was burnt and we came upon his half-charred body lying under burning tyres in the street. The houses of councillors and police are attacked, their families are also attacked and murdered…." "I regard myself as a friend of every member of the Police Force and I am sure that every member for the Police Force regards me as a friend as well."[6]

Three weeks later a PFP MP who was also a medical doctor sought to use the budget debate on the Department of Health and Welfare to raise questions about the role of district surgeons in "the inspection of health facilities in prisons and the examination of detainees," noting that two men had recently died of brain damage while in custody. He had not seen "any report by a district surgeon on an injury sustained in prison as a result of police action" or any instance where a policeman had been brought before an inquiry as a result. When the Chairman of Committees ruled that this could only be taken up under the Prisons vote, the member warned "that the practice of allowing a private practitioner only to attend the post–mortem of a prisoner is destroying the good name of South African medicine not only here but overseas. ... [T]he South African Medical Association has already been banned from the World Medical Association following the Biko affair."[7]

The commission of inquiry by Justice Kannemeyer criticized the police for the Langa shootings but assigned no individual responsibility.[8] During the June 13 debate on the report, Helen Suzman again condemned "the blind loyalty which is so often displayed by the hon the Minister of Law and Order" and demanded his resignation. "Let us not have another Biko dogging us throughout the following years." The CP objected that it was not the function of Parliament "unnecessarily to pillory before the whole world those men whose duty it is to maintain and promote peace and security while most of us are sleeping." An NRP member urged that "charges of perjury should be laid against those who made willfully false allegations" to the commission. The PFP, however, regarded the Kannemeyer report as a "totally devastating...indictment of senior officers in the Police and of the whole administration of law and order." A month before the massacre, government had rejected the party's call for a commission of inquiry into police behavior in the Eastern Cape. The PFP member urged both the Minister and the State President to think of any eleven-year-old girl they knew, remember the killing of such a girl at Uitenhage, and ask "Had I acted sooner...would this tragic event have happened? ... Do I share the blame?" The Minister should not be allowed to resign—he should be fired. The NP retorted that it was "unheard-of that a political party should involve itself in this way in an investigation by a commission of inquiry...[an] unbalanced and prejudiced action." PFP members "took down uncontested sworn statements and presented them as gospel." Peter Gastrow replied with "the assurance that we in the PFP will go on monitoring and critically examining police action throughout the country" and denounced "poor discipline among the Police in the Eastern Cape" and its command structure, which required a "visible shake-up." The Minister ended the debate by dismissing "the frivolous demands, by a small leftist group in the PFP, for my resignation" and the denunciations of the "equally leftist newspaper friend *The Cape Times*."[9]

Following allegations about mistreatment of juvenile detainees, the Port Elizabeth Chief Magistrate visited North End Prison on March 15 and 17 and found inmates "had no complaints." In response to Helen Suzman's renewed charges about the prison on June 5, the Minister of Justice directed an inspection by Justice J.W. Smalburger, who rejected the allegations as unfounded or misleading. Suzman's refusal to name her informants "seriously hampered our investigation." The Minister declared that "every complaint will be dealt with on its own merit," but he and others had "come to the conclusion that some representations and complaints in the Eastern Cape are aimed at disrupting public institutions and to irritate it to such an extent as to make it impossible to perform their normal task. Effective government is thus sabotaged."[10]

On May 8 Qoqawuli Godolozi, Sipho Hashe, and Champion Galela (president, general secretary, and organizing secretary of the Port Elizabeth Black

Consumers Boycott Committee [PEBCO]) disappeared on their way to collect a British visitor at the local airport, never to be seen again.[11] On June 27 UDF activists Sparrow Mkhonto and Fidelo Mhlawuli and Craddock Residents Association executive committee members Matthew Goniwe and Fort Calata disappeared after leaving a meeting in Port Elizabeth. Their mutilated burned bodies were discovered a few days later. Tens of thousands attended the July funeral.[12] Attorney Victoria Mxenge, who spoke at the funeral (and whose attorney husband Griffiths had been murdered in 1981), was murdered ten days later.

Consumer boycotts, one of the few weapons available to black protesters, were particularly effective in the Eastern Cape. UDF and PEBCO organized boycotts against the Master Bakers' Association, Eastern Cape Development Board liquor stores, businesses operated by black township councils, and Port Elizabeth Tramways.[13] In response to growing unrest, State President P.W. Botha declared a state of emergency (except for the Western Cape) effective Sunday, July 21. By the end of the year police had detained 7,000 people, nearly three times as many as after the 1976 Soweto uprising.[14] During the first three months the crackdown was most severe in the Eastern Cape, which accounted for sixty percent of all detentions. Two-thirds of all Eastern Cape detentions came from Port Elizabeth (PE) and Uitenhage.[15] The next section recounts the experiences of some of the 2,000 PE detainees and the police rebuttal.[16]

Port Elizabeth in the 1985–86 Emergency

As general secretary of the Motor Assemblers and Components Workers Union (MACWUSA), Dennis Neer was an important figure in both the trade union movement and UDF. On the night the Emergency began police stormed his house in Zwide township (PE). "[A] black policeman...hit me with a [knob]kierrie while I was still in bed. I jumped out of bed and the policeman tried to hit me again but my wife intervened.... Lt. Strydom witnessed the assault but did nothing to stop it...." Indeed, Strydom slapped Neer for refusing to disclose the whereabouts of MACWUSA chairman Thobile Mhlahlo. The police threw Neer in the back of a Land Rover and drove through several townships looking for trade unionists. The driver deliberately started, stopped, and swerved abruptly to throw the prisoners around; a black policeman sprayed teargas on them. Security Branch policeman Neil Coetzee declared: "Should there have been any discomfort to the people in the Landrover this was not done on purpose." Strydom beat Neer again when police could not locate Mhlahlo and Themba Duze, another MACWUSA official. Strydom insisted that Neer "was in the vehicle and it would have been impossible for me to have assaulted him through the wire." Sgt. M.A. Tungata added: "None of these persons resisted arrest and there was no need to use any force in performing any of the said arrests."

The team arrested and beat James Michael Tamboer, an organizer for National Automobile and Allied Workers Union (NAAWU), accusing him of instigating strikes at Ford and GM. They found Themba Duze and MACWUSA treasurer Eric Mapuma. In Motherwell township (PE) they arrested another MACWUSA official, Vusumzi George. They beat him and his very pregnant wife and ransacked the house, confiscating a list of people who had attended the Goniwe funeral. During booking at Algoa Park Police Station police smashed detainees' unshod toes with rifle butts. Strydom and Coetzee took Neer aside and questioned him about missing union officials. "Frustrated by my answer, [Strydom] began to punch me. The first blow caught me off guard and connected with some force." Strydom demurred: "[T]here were senior officers in the charge office and... it is highly unlikely that such assaults would have taken place in their presence." When the detainees stripped for admission to St. Alban's Prison Tamboer saw Neer's wounds. He also saw Henry Fazzie (UDF vice president for Eastern Cape and PEBCO vice president) bleeding from the mouth. Neer and Tamboer saw red weals on Themba Duze's back.

Leslie Mangcotywa was a fieldworker for the PE Advice Centre, which provided bail, traced missing people, and helped assaulted detainees lay charges against the police. He was detained at the beginning of the Emergency by Sgt. Phumzile Jam, who hit him on the back with a three-foot stick because he took too long to dress. When he could not state the whereabouts of the secretary of the PE Youth Congress (PEYCO), Lt. G.J. Niewoudt sprayed teargas in his face. Four days later the police interrogated him at Louis Le Grange Square (LLG).

> [Freddie] van Wyk wanted to know where Mkhuseli Jack [PEYCO president] was. I told him I did not know. He pulled out a red quirt and began to hit me with it. I tried to protect myself by moving around the room. Van Wyk was apparently enjoying himself. [Rodwell] Ndiyane then took the quirt and followed suit. All laughed at my rather desperate efforts to avoid being hit.

Neil Coetzee told Ndiyane to get handcuffs. Mangcotywa was made to crouch, a long piece of wood was placed beneath his knees, his arms passed below the stick, and his wrists handcuffed in front of his shins. He was suspended upside down between two tables in this notorious "helicopter."

> This position is a very awkward one. Firstly, one is suspended upside down with one's head hanging down, causing blood to rush to the head. Secondly, one is constantly trying to keep one's head up causing a great deal of strain in the neck. Thirdly, one's whole weight is suspended on one's wrists, held by the handcuffs and the back of the knees. The handcuffs are tight, making the hands numb. The back of the knees ache. Fourthly, one would pull with one's arms on occasions to relieve the pres-

sure of the knees—with the resulting strain on that part of the body. Fifthly, one would sweat, which would run into one's eyes and one was unable to clear them. Sixthly, in lifting the head a pain developed in one's spine. I was then prodded on the buttocks and this caused me to swing, causing a great deal of pain to the inside of my knees and forearms.

If the police did not like his answers they hit him on his bare buttocks.

I pleaded with them to release me. They said that I must answer all the questions. I screamed when I was hit, and as the pain became quite excruciating I began to cry. It was a terrible indignity for me to break down like this. When my screams were becoming too loud, they tied a cloth over my mouth, which they would only release for my answers… Finally, they released me. … I just lay on the floor. They asked me further questions. I could not move. Any movement caused me terrible pain.

He could not sit because of the pain in his buttocks, nor could he sleep that night. Freddie van Wyk claimed to have been sleeping that day because he had been busy the previous night making arrests.

Mangcotywa was taken back to LLG the next morning before he could speak to the medical orderly and again tortured by the "helicopter." "Faku, I remember, grabbed me around my Adam's apple causing me to start suffocating. He would intermittently release and tighten his grip. I was hysterical and I think at this time I fainted." When he returned to St. Alban's in great pain other detainees saw his injuries. He complained to the medical orderly but did not see a doctor until six days after the torture began. The physician prescribed some pills; when he saw Mangcotywa again in five days he treated the bruises and abrasions on Mangcotywa's buttocks, thighs, back, and forearms. When his mother finally saw him after a month in detention he "looked well."

Alex Rala, who worked at the Eastern Cape Adult Learning Project, was detained the first night of the Emergency and interrogated the same day as Mangcotywa, hearing his screams and seeing him afterwards. Coetzee, Ndiyane, and M.A. Tungata tortured Rala with the "helicopter." Tungata hit him in the buttocks with a sharp instrument; Ndiyane hit him with a sjambok; someone perforated his eardrum.

They generally assaulted me when they were dissatisfied with my answers, though sometimes I was hit quite arbitrarily. … Ndiyane kept claiming that I was responsible for burning policemen's houses and where were they going to live. When I did not reply to this, he would strike me. This was no longer an interrogation. It was simple revenge on me for his own unfortunate experiences in the township.

Tungata denied involvement, sounding hurt. "Alex Rala is well known to me since the time of his boyhood. He went to the same school as my sisters and on many occasions visited our home to visit my sisters." Ndiyane admitted interpreting for Coetzee but denied everything else.

> The first time that I heard of [the "helicopter"] was when I was told of the allegations in the various affidavits. I may add that during the unrest, black policemen, including myself, have been subject to various acts of abuse, violence and damage to our properties in the black townships. These actions against us are instigated by people with political motives and they attempt to do anything to discredit us in the townships. I can only assume that the allegations made in this regard against me are part of this campaign.... I am also aware of the so-called "Comrades" who have attempted to establish their own system of justice in the townships. They do not give people a proper opportunity of defending themselves and the "sentences" are harsh and unfair. As an example I may mention a relative of mine who was assaulted by "Comrades"....

Michael Xhego had seen Rala leave St. Alban's in good physical condition. On his return

> he scared all of us. He walked slowly and in great pain. His face was swollen. His pores were visible. He took off his clothes and showed us his injuries. There were fresh bruises on his forearms and bruising and abrasions just below the inside of the elbow. ... There were many sjambok marks on his back. There was a very big bruise and abrasion above the right buttock.

The next morning Rala saw a doctor, who gave him an injection and treated his bruises. Three days later Lt. Karl Edwards interrogated him about Janet Cherry, his employer.[17] When they heard the screams of other torture victims, Edwards said that could happen again. Rala saw Sgt. Butler Tungata beating Vusumzi George.

Edwards said Rala had declined his invitation to sit down. "We had a chat which was done on a friendly footing. He was very co-operative and forthcoming with information. ... [T]he door was closed and it seems unlikely that he would have been able to hear any screaming during our conversation." A week later Neil Coetzee interrogated him for the last time, asking him to sign a statement about the work he and Janet Cherry did in the townships. When he asked to see a lawyer Coetzee said: "It seems as if that I am not satisfied with what I have recieved" and went to get a sjambok. Fearing more torture he signed. Rala saw no visitors for two-and-a-half months, until Molly Blackburn intervened.

The police detained two elderly clergymen, Rev. de Villiers Soga (minister of the Reformed Presbyterian Church in New Brighton and president of the Interdenominational African Ministers' Association of South Africa) and Rev. Hamilton Dandala (superintendent of the Methodist PE North Circuit). At Algoa Park a security policeman interrogated Soga about the Goniwe funeral. When he denied having danced and sung freedom songs the policeman slapped him for lying, and others hit him to make him dance and sing. They did the same to Rev. Dandala. During admission to St. Alban's Prison he was stripped and made to stand in the cold for twenty minutes. It was humiliating for an elderly minister to be seen naked by much younger men, some of them members of his congregation. In their nine days of detention, Soga stated, "the daily appearance of the warder with the list of people who were to undergo interrogation became one of the focal points of fear."

Ihron Rensburg, a pharmacist and UDF activist detained at the start of the emergency, saw Michael Coetzee return to St. Alban's Prison after being interrogated on Sunday. "I examined him since I was the only detainee with any medical training. His jaw was tender and his hearing appeared to be impaired in one ear." The next morning he saw Percy Smith, whose face was swollen and tender. Both asked to see a doctor. Three days later security police interrogated Rensburg. Sgt. Faku told him to sing Xhosa freedom songs and toyi-toyi, returning with two other detainees. "There was no purpose to this exercise other than to humiliate us," but they complied out of fear. After the other detainees were removed Faku questioned Rensburg about his speeches at township meetings, hitting him in the face with his fist and kneeing him in the stomach. Faku ordered him to clean the blood off the floor, threatening to suffocate him with a bag and subject him to the "helicopter." Rev. Soga and James Tamboer saw his injuries that night. Faku said he could not have interrogated Rensburg because "I have been informed that he is a Coloured man. … I am involved with the interrogation of black people…."

Assistant District Surgeon Dr. Louw examined Rensburg the next day, sending him to hospital to see if his nose had been broken. At the hospital Dr. Daniels noted that his neck movement had been restricted by the assault. Rensburg complained about the torture to both Dr. Louw and the nurse in charge of the prison hospital. "[T]he next day I was asked to sign a form indemnifying the prison department. … [N]o one approached me in prison for the purposes of investigating my charge of assault." Lt. Beeton questioned Rensburg after his release on August 3:

> I think it is fair of me to say that Rensburg and I had built up a good rapport after he became known to me. … [H]is family also thanked me for the manner in which he was treated during his detention, and I find it inexplicable under these circumstances that he would not have complained to me should he have been assaulted during his detention.

Three doctors in the District Surgeon's office were responsible for the health of prisoners: van der Walt at St. Alban's, van Staden at the North End women's prison (Louw until she took maternity leave on July 31), and Wendy Orr at North End on Monday and Tuesday and St. Alban's Wednesday through Friday. Dr. Orr, 25, was the daughter of a Presbyterian minister who recently had been transferred to Port Elizabeth. She studied medicine on a government scholarship at the University of Cape Town and had just completed her internship in Port Elizabeth (which she chose to be near her parents). Although she had been brought up to dislike apartheid she had never been involved in politics. She did, however, have a vivid memory of her first lecture on medical ethics by Dr. Stuart Saunders, UCT Vice-Chancellor. He "spoke about doctors who treated prisoners during World War 2, and about how aware they had to be of the ethics involved. This was related to a South African context and for me it was very relevant." (About that time Saunders had publicly resigned from the Medical Association of South Africa to protest its failure to discipline Drs. Lang and Tucker, who had been responsible for Steve Biko's death and were now Orr's superiors.)[18] Having joined the District Surgeon's office to repay the government scholarship, she had participated in the post mortems of the twenty people killed by police in Langa in March.[19] She was troubled from the outset that prisoners regarded her as "a government employee," "on the other side," "not as a doctor dealing with her patients."

Prison regulations required doctors to examine each prisoner at admission, transfer, and release and made them responsible for prisoner health.[20] On admission a prison warder recorded identifying information, including injuries, and a prison hospital orderly entered medical complaints in the hospital register. Prisoners with subsequent complaints attended sick parade, where the district surgeon recorded them on the medical history card, distinguishing between old and new injuries. When they complained of assault, the medical officer filled out a Medical Report on Prisoner and entered progress reports on a Prisoner's Injury Form. Only one of these latter reports was completed before September 25, however. If the prisoner accused the police, the medical officer was to fill out a J88 form to initiate an SAP investigation, but such forms were rarely available or completed. "[T]he only thing that was happening," Orr remembered, "was that the prison would make the detainee sign an indemnity form saying it wasn't the prison warder who has assaulted me, it was during my arrest." Between July 22 and September 25 272 such affidavits were completed. Orr began examining the approximately twenty daily new emergency detainees in August. "[A]n inordinately large proportion of them complained to me that they had been assaulted by the police. They presented with symptoms consistent with their complaints, mostly severe multiple weals, bruising, and swelling." A morning visit by a single doctor was barely enough for the usual workload and entirely inadequate during the Emergency; she had to examine 160 detainees one morning and 360 another.

On Friday, July 26, Dennis Neer was taken to LLG by the security police, who "called us their customers." When he refused to disclose the where-abouts of Thombile Mhlalhlo, Lt. Strydom threatened (in Afrikaans): "Dennis, you're going to shit now."[21] Strydom and Coetzee were joined by Sgt. M.A. Tungata, who accused Neer of burning down the homes of black police. When he denied this Tungata

> hit me with his open hand on my back. They weren't hard blows. They were more designed to humiliate me than to hurt me. When I tried to avoid the blows he said to me: "No, Dennis, you are grown up—are you afraid of being hit?" Strydom and Coetzee were present and did nothing to stop him. In fact they just stood there and laughed.

Coetzee insisted that "Dennis Neer's interrogation was conducted in a rea-sonably good spirit." It was continued by Sgt. Faku, who handcuffed Neer's hands in back and tied his hooded tracksuit to his chest so that he could see only a small part of the floor. When his answers were unsatisfactory he was hit with a quirt or punched.

> One can hear the sound of the quirt before being hit, and I would tense at the sound, expecting a blow. Sometimes there wasn't a blow. I did not know the direction it was coming from or if it would hit me at all. There is no sound prior to a punch. Suddenly without warning I would be punched. It was excruci-ating. Although the blows themselves were painful, it was the helplessness, the disorientation, the constant tension and expec-tation of being hit and the sudden unexpected blows that was the worst.... At one stage someone grabbed me from behind by my trousers and lifted me off the ground while at the same time pushing me forward with his other arm. I lost my balance and fell to the floor. It was then, I think, that I hurt my left cheek-bone.... I skidded across the floor and hit the wall with my head. While I lay there, someone pinioned me with his knee in the small of my back while another twisted my neck. ... While I lay on the floor I remember something being put between my handcuffed hands. I think it was a piece of wood. Someone then twisted it.... It was exceptionally painful. Someone twisted slowly telling me to admit possessing the gun. When I denied it, he would twist further. I could stand the pain no longer. I admit-ted everything, pleading only that they should stop. ... I struggled to stand up and had to use the wall to snake my way up. I suddenly felt an excrutiating pain. Someone had stamped on my toes. ... [Faku] held me by the shoulders from the front and tried to butt me with his knee in the groin. I bent back to protect my genitals. Whilst in that position I was hit with a hard

object from behind. As I responded to that kick by moving involuntarily forward, Faku would try and kick me from the front. ... At one stage Faku threatened to kick me so hard in the genitals that I would become impotent if I did not cooperate.

The handcuffs had to be pulled off because Neer's wrists began to swell. Faku denied participating in the interrogation because he did not investigate trade union activities.

Because they were particularly interested in a gun they claimed he had, Faku handcuffed him again and drove to his home with "Loots" (G.J. Lutz) and Maj. R.F. Berg. They broke drawers, pulled up loose floorboards, ripped posters off walls, and broke a sofa. Lutz took Neer's passport, ID book, and coins he had been collecting since childhood, saying, "From today they are mine." Freddie van Wyk admitted taking the coins, some of which were from Lesotho, as evidence that Neer had undergone ANC training there. Back at LLG, Lutz led Neer up and down the corridor by the string of his tracksuit. "Passing policemen and policemen in offices would laugh as we went past. It was humiliating." Michael Xhego saw Neer.

> He was in terrible shape. His head was bent down, he was cradling his own arm with the other. He walked and moved in great pain. He was walking very slowly. He was being accompanied by Faku. His face was badly bruised. His hands and wrists were swollen.

Faku again had to pull off the handcuffs. Strydom said: "Dennis, I am coming for you again on Monday." When Neer said his head ached and he was nauseous, Strydom replied: "I hope you don't make a mess in my office."

Neer could not eat or sleep that night. He complained to the medical orderly the next morning, only to be told there was no doctor until Monday. The medical history card noted at 11:30 a.m. on Saturday: "Injured left forearm—blue purple bruises on the arm; arm is swollen; half-healed mark on the wrist; movement is limited, red cuts on the pulse." When Neer told Dr. van der Walt on Monday how he had been tortured the physician seemed shocked and prescribed medication. Because Neer's arm was worse the next day, van der Walt injected a powerful anti-inflammatory drug and sent him to Livingstone Hospital for x-rays. After four vain attempts the intervention of Black Sash secured Ethel Neer a three-minute visit with her husband five weeks after he was detained. More than a month after the assaults his face was still badly bruised. Dr. Orr saw Neer on September 11 for headaches, nausea, and a stiff neck. When he prepared an affidavit in prison on November 11 he still had visible marks on his thighs, knee, calf, leg, wrists, cheek, and shoulders.

PEYCO member Michael Xhego was detained on July 24. A policeman slapped him across the face, said the police could do what they liked, and hit his shaved head with a piece of wood; the wound was still sensitive three and a half months later. Police questioned him about working with Janet Cherry. When Ndiyane and Coetzee interrogated him two days later, Xhego heard Mangcotywa's desperate screams and "panicked." Because the only set of handcuffs was being used on Neer, Ndiyane started hitting Xhego with a piece of wood and shouting "What are you doing in the township?" Interrogation resumed on July 29. A white policeman and Ndiyane subjected him to the "helicopter" while Ndiyane laughed.

> I begged for mercy. Coetzee brought his chair next to me and interrogated me. ... Nieuwoudt came in and asked "Is he talking?" Coetzee said "No." He went out and came back with a blackish sjambok. He hit me all over my body. My arms and legs were extremely painful just from the strain of being suspended. He hit my head and my thighs. I could do nothing to protect myself but scream. ... Macici [Templeton Luthi] hit me with his open hand and then with his fist. I cried for mercy. ... Macici told me to swing. I said that it was too painful. He then came and swung me. I started crying. I have never experienced such pain before. I pleaded to be released. I was sweating and hot and my head throbbed.
>
> The interrogation continued. I then claimed that I was a heart patient and that my heart was painful. This seemed to frighten them and I was then quickly released. I just lay on the floor. I was weak. There was no strength left in my feet. My forearms were numb. They are still slightly numb [almost four months later].

When the handcuffs were removed Xhego asked for painkillers. The interrogation resumed, but he found it too difficult to speak. He was returned to the fifth floor and made to sit on the ground with Alex Rala. Lt. Dawid Flemmert stood on Xhego's ankles. Begged to get off, Flemmert knocked the ash of his cigarette in Xhego's face and stood on Rala's ankles. Siyolo Mashiqana saw the marks of the "helicopter" on Xhego when he returned to prison that night. The next morning Xhego complained to a medical orderly, who refused to put him on sick parade. He persisted for more than a week before being taken to a white doctor, who did nothing.

Luthi denied knowing Xhego, interrogating him, ever working with Coetzee, or ever seeing someone subjected to the helicopter. Like Tungata he was well known in the townships and blamed without justification.

Strydom and Niewoudt interrogated Vusumzi George on Monday, July 29. They made him sit on the floor with his hands handcuffed behind, forced his legs open by beating the inside of his thighs with sjamboks, and tried to kick him in the genitals. He would end up like Dennis Neer, they warned, if he did not tell the truth. They beat him on the back and chest with a sjambok and on the toes and head with a stick. James Tamboer, interrogated the same day, heard George scream and cry and saw him return from torture with his face puffy and red. Four black police made George crouch in an uncomfortable position while holding a chair above the head of other detainees. Butler Tungata beat him in the kidneys and shoulders, slapped his ears, and kicked him. When George told Tungata he belonged to MACWUSA, Tungata asked why he burned people. George denied this, and Tungata slapped his face and told him to stop talking shit. He bent George's arm behind him, making him scream. He and two other police beat George until he screamed again. A white policeman used a wet towel to suffocate him and then to choke him. Coetzee admitted interrogating George but asserted that "it is unlikely that a person on the fifth floor [where Tamboer was being interrogated] would be able to hear if there was any screaming and crying" on the seventh floor where Coetzee worked. When George told the medical orderly in prison on Tuesday that his ears were infected, he was told to wait until Wednesday, and then until Thursday, when he saw Dr. Orr (on her first day at the prison). She asked if he had hurt himself, and he replied he had been assaulted. The orderly filled her prescription on Friday. In the subsequent lawsuit Mbulelo Edgar Magamela, awaiting trial for murder, gave an affidavit for the state that he and George were punished by a people's court on August 11, which might have explained George's injuries; but Orr had seen them ten days earlier.

When James Tamboer was taken to LLG on July 29 he saw someone being tortured by the "helicopter." Strydom told him to write a statement about his union activities. A white policeman held his hands behind his back while "Billy Flemmer," a "coloured" policeman, walked on his ankles, inflicting intense pain. "Flemmer" also banged his head against the wall twice, causing headaches that continued for two months. Tamboer heard Butler Tungata interrogate a black student about burning Tungata's relative to death and saw him torture the student. Strydom denied any knowledge of the "helicopter." Coetzee, who participated in the interrogation, said "I had to leave the office for a few minutes and on my return Tamboer was busy smoking a cigarette and drinking tea with Lt Strydom." Tungata insisted he was "not at all involved in the questioning of persons detained in terms of the emergency regulations." Maj. du Plessis had ordered him and WO Mene "not to have anything to do with the investigation of matters concerning the state of emergency" because of the "many rumours and certain allegations" about them and prior threats and attacks. When Tungata lived with his parents from 1976 to 1980, stones and firebombs were thrown at his house eleven times. When he lived alone from 1980 to 1982 his house was attacked seven times. After he moved, his new house was attacked six times and finally burned down on March 13, 1985.

Lt. Dawid Flemmert, a "coloured" security policeman at LLG, said he was never called Billy, denied being present during the interrogation, claimed to have gone to Cape Town on August 2 (three days after the interrogation), said he was concerned exclusively with "coloured" students, and denied ever leaving his fifth-floor office to visit the seventh floor (where trade unionists were interrogated). Strydom expressed amazement "at the accusations made against the persons who interrogated the trade union members. Throughout the examinations they were treated well, supplied with cigarettes on request and also drank coffee with us."

Edward Mentoor was detained on July 22 by Adj. Officer Louis Wentzel among others and interrogated at LLG on August 6 by Wentzel and AO Tembile Gcani. Mentoor claimed they forced him to eat his hair. Gcani denied this.

> [I]t would be very difficult to pull one's own hair out. … [H]e showed no signs of visible injuries and as far as I can remember there were no signs on his head that his hair had been pulled out. I would like to mention that Mentoor is very well known to me. He is a very difficult man and I was aware that I would have to be very careful with regard to my conduct towards him, as any such conduct which he may have deemed to be unfair would have been followed up.

Wentzel added that Mentoor "has short hair." Brig. E.S. Schnetler, SAP Divisional Commander of Eastern Province, affirmed that it would have been impossible to pull out enough of Mentoor's hair and noted he had not complained.

Dr. Orr examined Mentoor the next day; he complained of being forced to eat his hair and had "an irritation in his throat and nausea." She prescribed a gargle and tablets, but he did not respond to this treatment. A month later he had lost five kilograms, his abdomen was slightly distended, and there were decreased bowel sounds. "Those symptoms are consistent with sub-acute intestinal obstruction." She referred him to Livingstone Hospital, which prescribed similar treatment.

Ernest Malgas (who had succeeded the murdered Champion Galela as PEBCO organizing secretary) was detained on August 9. The prison register described his physical and mental condition as "geskik" (no complaints). When he was interrogated five days later Michael Xhego heard him scream for a long time. Later that day Xhego saw that Malgas could hardly walk; his hands were puffy and his face swollen. Back at prison, according to Xhego,

> Malgas asked to see a doctor. This was still in the presence of the two escorts, Ndiyane and Faku. The prison officials were reluctant to take him and they wanted to know why he needed to see a doctor. He told them that he had been assaulted by the security police at Louis Le Grange. He took off his trousers. His buttocks and his legs were covered with purple bruises. He pointed out his swollen hand. Faku warned Malgas that they were coming for him tomorrow.

When Dr. Orr saw him the next day his injuries were so serious she remembered them vividly five weeks later. He showed "severe and deep bruising on the lower back and buttocks... not merely sub-epidermal but intra-muscular. The bruises were prominently purple, red and consistent with a particularly violent assault with a blunt instrument. His condition was such that I was unable to take a history from him." Lt. Patricia Prince (a prison hospital nurse) told her that Malgas had been interrogated and complained of police assaults. A number of prison officials came to look at his injuries. One commented "he probably needed it," and the others agreed. Lt. Prince noted on his medical record card "right arm and hand swollen, swollen cuts on the thighs, right ankle is swollen, bruises on left hip, complaining of pains in right side of chest." Lt. Pieter Steyn, assistant head in charge of the safety watch, admitted seeing Orr examine Malgas. He denied hearing the comment and reprimanded Orr for allowing others to observe an examination. He noted that Malgas had served time on Robben Island.

Ivy Gcina, a forty-nine-year-old mother of five children and activist in the PE Women's Organisation, was arrested the second day of the Emergency. When she tried to protect four of her children from police assault she was beaten. Luthi took her from prison for interrogation a week later and noticed she walked with a limp, but she said nothing was wrong. Coetzee, van Wyk, and Smith began the questioning. "Whenever they were unhappy with my answers, Smith and Coetzee swore at me, calling me a liar, a 'bitch,' 'rubbish,' and other abusive terms." Ndiyane joined them, and a white policeman told her to keep her knees together.

> Quite suddenly, I was hit behind the knees, causing me to fall. As I got up, Ndiyane hit me very hard with an open hand on the side of the face. I took off my spectacles to see if they were broken, when Ndiyane hit me again with his open hand. The white policeman standing behind me would hit me on the back of the neck. I tried to remain dignified and not call out or cry, but this only seemed to provoke them further. Van Wyk suggested that they should use teargas. One of the white policemen... grabbed me and pushed me into a nearby toilet. He sprayed me with teargas. I suffocated but I managed to prevent him from locking me in the toilet. I stood in the passage and coughed until the effect of the gas wore off.

> I was then taken by a white policewoman to her office. I sensed that she had taken me there to protect me from further assaults. When she heard voices in the passage she pretended to hit me. The white policeman who had sprayed teargas in my face came in and chided her for not hitting me. He took the baton from her and started to hit me on my arms and my shoulders. The police-woman left immediately.

> The tall policeman again sprayed me with teargas. This was done directly into my face. I immediately began to suffocate and

cough. I could hardly breathe. I rushed into the passage for air. I noticed that the gas had affected some of the policemen as well. A black policeman came down the stairway and told Coetzee not to use teargas since some of it had gone up to the upper floors. Coetzee told me that I would be assaulted every-day unless I "told the truth."

At North End Prison she complained about the assault and was given painkillers and an ointment for her bruises. Prison officials promised she would see a doctor the next day, but she was taken back for interrogation by Coetzee and Ndiyane. "Although they did not assault me that day...they went so far as to threaten to shoot my children if I did not tell them what they wanted to know." She saw a woman doctor the next day and a male doctor the day after. Her medical history card recorded bruises on her right upper arm and elbow, left upper arm and forearm, right buttock, left eye, left ear, and jaw. After several futile attempts, her sister Miriam saw her through the intervention of Molly Blackburn. Ivy was in solitary confinement and told Miriam she had been beaten.

Ndiyane admitted questioning her but naturally denied the assaults.

> I know Mrs Gcina well and while she was detained in North End Prison she requested me to take clothes to and fro from the prison to her house whenever she needed them. I did this and spoke to her husband on a number of occasions when doing so. He enquired after her health and I informed him that she was in good health as far as I could see. I have no reason to assault Mrs Gcina, more particularly, because her husband is a very good friend of my brother and they had worked together for a long time.

Mkhuseli Jack, twenty-eight, PEYCO president and PEBCO convenor, evaded detention until August 2. During booking at Kempton Road Police Station, Sgt. Jam beat him with a sjambok, holding his mouth closed so others would not hear his cries. A white policeman named George told Jack to give the raised fist salute until Mandela was released. He also told Jack to shout "Mayibuye iAfrika" (Africa must be free). He abused PEYCO and other community organizations and Molly Blackburn, stating "ominously that she would die one of these days if she kept stirring up trouble in the townships." (She died within four months in a car accident; investigation found no foul play.) The next day Nieuwoudt and Coetzee interrogated him. Coetzee told Jack: "We've got you and today we shall beat all the politics out of your head because you don't want to listen." They subjected him to the helicopter until Jack cried and pleaded to be released. Coetzee said "wait and see—you are going to talk the truth. This is the room of truth." Ndiyane, Strydom, and Bezuidenhout participated.

> Ndiyane rocked me so as to expose my buttocks about the level of the two tables. Bezuidenhout struck me with a sjambok,

accusing me of calling the Port Elizabeth police "Gestapo" at a meeting that I had addressed in Cape Town. ... Strydom picked up [the sjambok] and took a turn at hitting me on the buttocks. At some stage Niewoudt hit me with an object that looked like a hosepipe. ... [T]he overall effect of the blows to the head and to the buttocks, together with the rocking motion, was so painful and disorienting that I still have nightmares about the incident.

Released from the helicopter but temporarily paralyzed and lying on the floor, Jack was hit with a sjambok by Bezuidenhout, who joked to Ndiyane: "Give him a microphone to address the people." Ndiyane took him to the toilet, made him strip, and poured a bucket of dirty water over him. "It included an irritant of some kind, making me itch terribly." They resumed the interrogation, denouncing Molly Blackburn. "When I replied that Mrs Blackburn understands the hardships that blacks suffered, Niewoudt stopped writing and took up the sjambok, hitting me several times and shouting 'You lie, all Mrs Blackburn wants is a violent overthrow of the State and one man, one vote!'" Niewoudt warned Jack not to complain or he would disappear, as the PEBCO leaders had done three months earlier. Complaints would be futile, since the Emergency gave the police broad powers. Niewoudt told Jack about the torture of Neer, Rala, and Mangcotywa, who had been "thoroughly beaten" but never laid charges. Jack's experiences had merely been a "warm up," and he should expect more.

Nevertheless he protested the beating to Sgt. Kumm, the readmitting officer at St. Alban's. When he was stripped so that the warders could check his clothes, other detainees exclaimed about his wounds. Kumm invited the warders to come and look, remarking "he has been thoroughly beaten." The next day (Sunday) he complained to the medical orderly about headache and pain throughout his body. He saw Dr. van der Walt on Monday, who noted on his medical history card: "blue marks and marks left after a beating—left thigh, beating marks—right shoulder; head severely beaten." He prescribed drugs for bruises.

Coetzee, Strydom, and Ndiyane denied interrogating Jack. Niewoudt admitted taking him to Capt. J.C. Scheepers, who said, "It was not an interrogation in the true sense of the word, more an interview with him concerning the consumer boycott, among other things."

On August 7 Jack was interrogated by Maj. du Plessis, who told him to telephone the newspapers and call off the consumer boycott. Jack said the people would continue it. Du Plessis warned him not to be stubborn, again recalling the missing PEBCO leaders. Du Plessis admitted a "conversation" with Jack but denied telling him to call off the boycott or threatening him.

Jack's employer, Edward Chalmers, learned about the torture from Molly Blackburn on August 17. He telephoned John Malcomess, MP for PE Central, who got permission for a visit by a magistrate or physician. During the third week of detention Col. Paulsen interviewed Jack, who reiterated that he had been tortured, knew the perpetrators, and intended to lay charges but did not want to make a statement then for fear of retaliation. Paulsen reassured Jack, who wanted more time to think about it. Paulsen described this visit to Lt. Prinsloo, who told Chalmers that Jack was in good health. Chalmers got permission for Jack's mother and sister to see him. Soon thereafter two plain-clothesmen asked Jack for a statement. When he sought to consult a lawyer first they insisted that he put this in writing. A few days later Jack was taken back to LLG.

> Niewoudt took me to a certain office. He closed the door and pushed me backwards, jabbing his finger in my face. He said: "What did I say to you? Didn't I tell you not to lay charges against the police?" He said that he was going to deal with me and kill me on the spot. He was very angry and I was very scared.

Jack calmed Niewoudt by promising he had not laid a charge and had written a statement to that effect. Niewoudt took Jack to Coetzee, who said Jack had done the right thing but wanted to know how the torture leaked out. Jack suggested that released detainees might have spread the word. WO Nani took Jack to and from LLG on this occasion. "I have known [Jack] for about five years. He has long hair in an afro style and if he had sustained any head injuries on these occasions, I would have noticed it. I recall that he is a friendly person who smiles easily and that on these occasions... he acted in the same friendly manner as I have known previously." Lt. Taylor interrogated Jack on August 23, sending Luthi to buy food, which Jack ate in Taylor's office. "[T]he interview with Jack took place in a congenial and relaxed atmosphere." Luthi agreed that "he was still in good spirits."

In early September Gerrit Niewoudt, a uniformed policeman, interviewed Alex Rala, Michael Xhego, Dennis Neer, and Leslie Mangcotywa in response to their charges of assault by the security police.[22] They described their torture but were afraid to name their assailants or press charges while in detention. At Niewoudt's insistence Neer signed a statement declining to do so. Niewoudt remembered the occasion differently.

> Not one of the named persons was prepared to carry on with the charges of assault and made statements to this effect. Insofar as any one of these people alleged that they were put under pressure to make such a statement, I deny this emphatically. They did not describe how they had been assaulted. In the light of the said persons' attitudes it was not possible to further the investigations of assault.

On September 16 Maj. D.L.E. Laubscher asked the men if they still refused to lay charges, offering an identification parade where they could pick out the torturers. Rala said he "deliberately feigned ignorance. I personally believed that should I point a finger at Coetzee or Ndiyane, the two would take revenge." Laubscher rewrote what Niewoudt had drafted, added some clauses, and got them to sign again. In his reply affidavit to Wendy Orr's interdict application Brig. E.S. Schnetler, SAP Divisional Commander for Eastern Province, emphasized this reticence.

> [T]he police endeavored to thoroughly investigate the charges of assault laid. The investigations had to be stopped as a result of certain people refusing to make statements with regard to the alleged assaults. I really do not understand how the South African Police and the Prisons Department can now be blamed for not investigating the case when the persons on behalf of whom the grievances are made are not prepared to help with the investigation.

The day after the interdict was granted the four were given a last opportunity to complain when they were interviewed by Professor J.A. Olivier, an "independent" physician from the University of the Orange Free State. Xhego told him about the torture and his continuing pain and numbness. Rala described the assaults, but Olivier was interested only in complaints he had "at that particular moment." Rala said he had recovered, but Olivier persisted in taking his blood pressure, listening with a stethoscope, and looking at his ears and mouth.

After the police had caught the leading activists they cast their net more widely. They detained and beat five pupils at Ndzondelelo Secondary School in a vain search for "China," a student leader. Sgt. Mphokeli was personally outraged because his daughter, who attended the school, had been threatened. In the second week of August the police conducted a night sweep of Red Location, New Brighton township, detaining and torturing five to ten more pupils with the helicopter, suffocation, and threats of the necklace. On the night of August 15–16 they repeated the raid, bringing every adult male in front of headlights while hidden informers fingered 169. Taken to Berry's Corner (Kempton Road Police Station) for booking, they were beaten until their palms blistered, allegedly for refusing to accept corporal punishment at school. Each time they entered or left the interrogation room they had to run a gauntlet of police, who beat them with sjamboks. Those waiting were assaulted at random with pickhandles, a soft drink bottle, and a brick. Peter Ngcina, seventeen, whose tooth was knocked out, related that "a white policeman…fetched a dead branch from outside. This he used to strike us on our heads, while singing the notes of the musical scale on each blow." The police pelted the detainees with raw potatoes, which they were made to eat, together with splinters from the pickhandles with which they were beaten and pieces of paper. Paul Fani remembered Capt. Smith saying he was showing them they were fit enough to endure brutal punishment. The police would continue to harass them until they reported everything they saw in the township. They sinned against the police by attending funerals of unrest victims.

Mbulelo Sogoni was made to stand with arms outstretched; whenever they sagged he was hit with a sjambok, pickhandle, baton, or knobkierrie and kicked and punched. The assaults continued after he fell down. The police ordered him to lead freedom songs while they beat him. He was put in the helicopter, suffocated, and doused with gasoline. On admission to St. Alban's Prison he was too weak to stand. Friends spread mats so that he could lie on the floor. A warder took him in a wheelchair to be examined by Dr. Orr. Because he could not talk, friends described the assaults. He spent the night in the prison hospital.

The prison admissions register on August 16 recorded that more than 100 (i.e., substantially more than half) had fresh injuries consistent with assault, two-thirds of whom formally blamed the SAP. Dr. Orr examined all of them, finding fresh weals, bruising, and blisters over their backs, arms, and palms, lacerated lips, split cheeks, and perforated eardrums. She remembered Fezile Ngcezula, an old man on whose bare feet a brick had been dropped. "The top of his toes and the bridge of one of his feet were very badly bruised and swollen." She also had a vivid recollection of Sogoni.

> He had weals from his shoulders to his buttocks. There were so many weals that I could not count them. They were superimposed upon each other. ... I specified that I required to see him again to review his case a few days later. He was, however, never brought to me again. I recently searched for his yellow [medical history] card but found it was missing.

The police offered the routine denials. Capt. I.P. du Plessis, who led the raid on Red Location, insisted that "should people have been assaulted and they had screamed, I would have heard it; should detainees have been chased through rows of policemen who hit them, I would have been aware of this; if freedom songs had been sung, I would have heard them." Sgt. W.W.G. Bradley added: "All the policemen who were involved in this operation worked long hours, without a break, and in any case there was very little time available for the continual assaults on detainees." Const. V.M. Nesi noticed that the detainees had some injuries but did not know "whether these injuries were sustained before the arrests or during the arrests themselves. As far as I can remember they were not of a particularly serious nature. ... there was no bleeding. They looked to me more like sjambok marks." He denied making them eat raw potatoes: "[I]t is highly unlikely that food would have been wasted in this manner."

> The only reason that I can think of why my name has been mentioned in regard to the assaults is that I am well known in this area. I am the only black person in this area who plays rugby for the S.A.R.A. team. It is fairly well-known that this side plays under the auspices of the South African Rugby Board and that it is violently opposed by elements in the black and Coloured communities because it is allegedly a racist body. I have also

worked in the shebeens in the townships and am therefore generally well-known in the black townships.

Mbulelo Magamela, awaiting trial for murder, who had attributed Vusumzi George's injuries to a people's court, said the same about Sogoni's. He placed the alleged court six days earlier, however, and Dr. Orr recorded that the wounds were probably less than twenty-four hours old and certainly not more than thirty-six.

As Dr. Orr was examining the 170 new prisoners on August 16 her immediate superior arrived. Dr. Ivor Lang, assistant district surgeon for PE, was acting for District Surgeon Benjamin Tucker, who was on "extended sick leave." Lang noticed the large number of assault complaints Orr had recorded on the detainees' "yellow [medical history] cards" and expressed concern that they would require completion of many J88s to initiate police investigation of the allegations. Lt. Prince (head nurse of the prison hospital) said this would be unnecessary since all complaints were being handled by a single investigator—a prison official rather than a policeman. No investigation appears to have been conducted, however, since Dr. Orr was never questioned about the assaults. Lang told Orr she was taking too long with each detainee and should speed up the examinations.

Orr's superiors had good reason to fear investigations. Over five days in September 1977 Lang had examined Steve Biko three times and Tucker had done so twice. They disregarded signs of beating and serious injury and medical tests showing blood in the cerebrospinal fluid. Lang certified that he "found no evidence of any abnormality or pathology on the patient." After a five-minute examination of Biko, who was collapsed, glassy-eyed, hyperventilating, and frothing at the mouth, Tucker authorized the police to transport him 750 miles in the back of a Land Rover. He died shortly after arriving at Pretoria Central Prison. In December the inquest magistrate raised questions about the conduct of both doctors, sending the record to the South African Medical and Dental Council. Two years later, however, the SAMDC Medical Committee of Preliminary Inquiry found no prima facie evidence of improper or disgraceful conduct. In June 1980 the full Council upheld this decision eighteen–nine, reaffirming it in October over protests by the medical faculties of the Universities of Cape Town and the Witwatersrand. The Cape Midlands Branch of the Medical Association of South Africa (to which Tucker belonged) dismissed a complaint and was upheld by the Federal Council in August 1980. The British Medical Association and other national organizations resigned from the World Medical Association in 1981 to protest MASA's continuing membership. Under pressure MASA appointed an ad hoc committee, which criticized both doctors and the SAMDC. Two groups of doctors renewed formal complaints to the SAMDC, which again exonerated the accused in March 1983.

Some of the complainants then applied to the Supreme Court; in January 1984 it ordered the SAMDC to reopen its inquiry.[23] A Council committee held four days of hearings in July 1985. It found Dr. Tucker guilty of three counts of improper and disgraceful conduct and suspended him for three months (but then suspended the penalty for two years, knowing he was about to retire). It issued a caution and reprimand to Dr. Lang. The penalties were stayed pending review by the full Council. In response to public outcry, the Council struck Dr. Tucker from the roll on October 16.* Although Lang continued to function as acting district surgeon, Orr remembered that his attitude throughout was: "let's just do our job, and that was keep our noses clean, and cover our backsides. So that if anyone ever does bring a civil claim the Department of Health can say we did our job." When Orr took her concerns to Maj. Cecil Sandenbergh, Commander of St. Alban's Prison, he expressed no interest because the violence was being committed by the police, not his subordinates.**

In the later interdict application the state countered Orr's affidavit with one by Col. F.J. Fourie, who had twenty-nine years experience in the SAP Disputed Documentation Division. He alleged that Orr added notations on the medical history cards under the same date, insinuating that she had done so in anticipation of the lawsuit. She admitted doing so on two occasions but noted that she had used a different pen, showing she had not sought concealment. The first was the August 16 mass detention. She had not been asking if the police were responsible and often failed to record this when informed by the detainee. "It did not occur to me that, from a medical point of view, the identity of the culprit was material." After Lang expressed concern about the large number of assault complaints, however, he instructed her to note that the victim blamed the police, in order to protect the Prisons Department. Because the prison required her to complete the sick parade before lunch (the largest she had ever held) she simply recorded the medical findings and treatment and set aside the cards of those who complained of police assault, adding that fact after the parade. Almost none of the forty-three prisoners whose yellow cards Fourie examined submitted affidavits in the case, and none figured importantly.

The police continued to detain youths, often torturing them *before* admission to prison, perhaps to evade its medical records. Once a white captain

---

*In 1991 Tucker successfully petitioned the Council to restore his name to the register. Suzman (1993: 224–25). See generally Baxter (1985c); McQuoid-Mason (1986a); Rayner (1987; 1990); Berat (1989); WM 2 (10.18.85); NYT 7 (10.17.85); 1985 *Lancet* 136. Biko's murder a year after the Soweto uprising intensified international condemnation of South Africa. See U.S. Congress (1977); Hilda Bernstein (1978); Essa & Pillai (1987). Donald Woods, an expatriate South African journalist, virtually made a living out of publicizing it, see Woods (1978). The Royal Shakespeare Company dramatized the inquest, see Blair (1978). Richard Attenborough's attempt to make his film in South Africa in 1984 provoked outrage. *Hansard* cols. 1407–09 (T.G. Alant, NP) (2.20.84). The government declared that no permit would be issued to a foreigner to make the film. *Hansard* col. 2550 (reply by D.J.L. Nel, Deputy Minister of Information, to P.G. Soal, PFP) (9.5.86). The movie's appearance revived the issue for a much larger audience, see Attenborough (1987); Woods (1987).

**This and other quotations and comments by Wendy Orr come from my interview in July 1990.

warned Lt. Deon Els and Const. V.M. Nesi not to beat Mlungisi Ncane, eighteen, in the face since he had not yet been photographed. Later a white man in a suit saw blood on Ncane's face and warned both police that this could lead to problems. The dragnet extended to young and old, activists and the apolitical, leaders and followers, men and women, even those disabled. At 2 a.m. on September 5 the police—shouting "where's the cripple"—came for Welile Peter, who used crutches and foot braces. They put him in the trunk of the police car and drove him and others around Zwide township in search of "Stanley." AO Juan Lombard, who participated in the incident, admitted breaking down the door of Peter's house "because we could not stand around too long." "Although I cannot remember, it is possible that I asked after the cripple." He denied hitting anyone with a sjambok, but "I might well have told the people in the house that they should hurry." He put Peter behind the back seat of the station wagon because it was "more comfortable for him."

On September 4 Dr. Orr examined 360 new admissions, half of whom complained of assaults and presented consistent injuries, though not as severe as those on August 16. The next day she heard Dr. Lang telephone his superior, Dr. Japie Krynauw, Eastern Cape regional director of the Department of National Health and Population Development. Worried that many detainees complained of police assaults, Lang asked what to do. After the conversation he told Orr that Krynauw had instructed them to copy the medical history cards of every complainant, in case they sued the Department of Health. Although Orr was distressed that Krynauw seemed interested in protecting only the Department, not the prisoners, she asked the senior staff officer at St. Alban's Prison hospital, who passed the request to Brig. Johannes Hills, PE commander of prisons, who said he needed higher approval. On September 7 Hills instructed Orr through Lt. Georgina Toubkin, supervisor of physical care at St. Alban's Prison, to stop noting on medical history cards detainee requests for investigation of their assaults because this had nothing to do with the Prisons Department. Toubkin admitted saying "that [Orr] should essentially not write on the yellow cards that a statement should be made by the concerned person." Although Orr continued to urge investigation she saw that the necessary J88 forms were no longer being completed. Hills agreed that they were not routinely filed, since they were only for the convenience of the district surgeon, but he denied issuing any order not to investigate.

On September 11 the Azanian People's Organisation commemorated the eighth anniversary of Steve Biko's death, an event about which the PE police, prisons, and district surgeons had reason to be particularly sensitive. Ashraf Karodia, twenty-two, a systems analyst at Volkswagen, told the story. The police surrounded St. Gabriel's Church in Uitenhage, searched those inside, confiscated political literature, pins, and banners, and took about forty to a nearby rugby field. As they left the van for interrogation and returned to it they had to run a police gauntlet of blows from sjamboks, fists, and boots. Ashraf Mohamed, fifteen, had already been detained three times that year and tortured twice; he had been suffocated, beaten into unconsciousness, and subjected to electric shock just a few weeks earlier. On his return to the van he was knocked out again. His fellow prisoners shouted for help, but the police just laughed. Dr. Orr examined about forty male detainees at St. Alban's the next day and three female detainees at North End on September 16. All had been at St. Gabriel's, complained of police assaults, and displayed consistent injuries. Ashraf Mohamed had weals on his right elbow and behind both ears and right temple; bruises on the front of his neck supported his claim that a policeman had choked him. Five days after the beatings Helen and Moira Sauls, nineteen and seventeen, had clearly visible abrasions on their hands, shoulders, arms, buttocks, and thighs. A union official incarcerated a week later with thirty-four of the male detainees heard them tell the same story. After being questioned, they sought refuge in the van from police blows, but each time they opened the upper latch the police closed the lower one and vice versa.

Parents understandably anxious about their children encountered bureaucratic obstruction or outright refusal. NAAWU General Secretary Frederick Sauls (detained with other union members on August 12) was particularly concerned about Moira, who needed constant medication for chronic bronchial asthma. Prison officials initially denied having his daughters. Two days later he visited North End Prison with Halton Cheadle, a Johannesburg labor lawyer he knew through the union. Capt. H.D. Treurnicht, assistant head of safety watch services, refused to tell them anything. When Cheadle produced a copy of an interdict application he called his superior, who told him to answer the question. Believing the Emergency regulations prohibited this he asked the superior to tell Sauls himself.

Cheadle's chance involvement was momentous. In August Wendy Orr had confided her growing distress to her older sister, Kathleen, who lived in Johannesburg and who sought advice from her friend, Gilbert Marcus, an advocate and colleague of Cheadle at the Centre for Applied Legal Studies at the University of the Witwatersrand. Orr met Cheadle on September 3, when he visited Port Elizabeth on other business.

> Halton saw me that evening, and we discussed my experiences and what channels of action were available to me. I asked for time to think about it, consulted Gilbert Marcus and Dr Jonathan Gluckman [the foremost pathologist on police torture and a complainant against Lang and Tucker in the Biko case], and phoned Halton on Tuesday, September 10, to say that I was willing to prepare an affidavit. ...
>
> It was and it wasn't [a difficult decision]. You know I was terribly young and naive at the time, and I don't think I entirely knew what I was letting myself in for. It was somewhat of a

> relief to be given a way out almost...something effective to do,
> a way of helping these people.*

Cheadle told her "if you make an affidavit, give us information, your life is going to change dramatically. ... You're going to be thrown out. You're going to be subject to death threats. ... This is true betrayal." If she only complained to superiors, however, nothing would happen. She could provide information and remain "deep throat," "or she could come out, which is what I wanted of course.... She took about nine or ten days to actually make her mind up and I was just ants in my pants, I just could not handle it."[24]

After Cheadle returned from North End Prison the evening of September 13 they began her affidavit and worked all next day. On Sunday morning Orr called Cheadle and said: "You won't believe this. I don't know what the hell's happened. I've been phoned. I've been told to go to prison." Cheadle was fearful they had been discovered. Instead, Dr. Lang had summoned her because the Department of Prisons had finally approved his request to copy the medical history cards, and he wanted it done immediately. When she began on Monday, Brig. Hills summoned her and demanded to see everything she copied so he could note complainants' names. She explained she was making copies to protect the Department against civil and criminal claims, but he assured her they had legal defenses. When he saw her notation that the complaints should be investigated and asked what had been done, she said no action had been taken. He asserted that the Department of Prisons had no duty to investigate. Orr replied she was only asking for a referral to the SAP, but Hills said the police were invoking Emergency Regulation 11, which immunized them for any action taken in good faith to protect the safety of the public. Hills phoned Maj. Sandenbergh, commander of St. Alban's Prison, who visited him that afternoon, reaffirming that complaints were referred to the SAP only if the victim formally laid charges.

It took Orr three days to make two copies of 286 cards, one for Lang and another for her attorney. The records confirmed everything she had told Cheadle. "She has absolutely total recall...and she got to see hundreds of patients." She was disturbed that many were incomplete or missing, however, including those of Malgas and Sogoni. When an assault was clear from the detainee's affidavit or referral to Livingstone Hospital, she added the missing information to the card, always in a different pen, indicating no intent to deceive.

She noted that one out of four female detainees complained of assaults and presented consistent injuries, compared to only one out of 200 ordinary

---

*This 1990 recollection strongly resembles her statement two weeks after filing the lawsuit. "[W]hat finally decided me was that I knew I had to do something to help people in no position to help themselves." Asked if she had belonged to NUSAS, she laughed: "I have never been involved in politics. I took the action I did because I was not prepared to compromise my medical ethics." FM 85 (10.4.85).

female arrestees. Lt. Winnifred Nel, Commander of North End Prison, confirmed these numbers but noted that no one filed charges or was hospitalized. Lt. Prince added that Orr referred only three detainees to the St. Alban's Prison hospital and transferred none to outside hospitals. Orr replied that "only with great difficulty... was [it] possible to place an emergency detainee in the hospital at St. Alban's... [because] no contact was allowed between emergency detainees and other prisoners." Furthermore, Prince deliberately overlooked at least eleven detainees referred to Livingstone Hospital, including Dennis Neer, Ihron Rensburg, Edward Mentoor, and Vusumzi George.

Cheadle and his staff completed the application in ten frantic days, operating from a PE hotel to which they brought PCs and photocopiers from Johannesburg. The police entered their rooms but failed to identify the project. Unions provided invaluable assistance, raising funds, contacting community organizations, tracing detainees and their relatives, and allaying the inevitable suspicions of black victims. Because South Africa does not allow class actions, the applicants were chosen from various constituencies. Dr. Orr told the basic story in a forty-one-page affidavit. Two church leaders (Anglican and Methodist) represented their congregations, as NAAWU did its members. The elderly ministers were the only two immediate victims (because many were still detained), but thirty-five relatives and two employers also made affidavits.

The case was filed on September 24.[25] In addition to the Minister of Law and Order and local police commanders, the applicants gave incomplete names for five of the most notorious torturers and obtained permission to add others. They sought an order protecting all detainees, declaring that the police lacked immunity for willful assaults or threats, prohibiting interrogation at Louis Le Grange Square without an order by the Minister, and costs. The matter was heard the next day by Justice J.P.G. Eksteen and reported in a front-page headline: "Stop beating up detainees."[26] When the applicants' counsel introduced himself in chambers before the hearing, the judge said he was strongly inclined to grant the relief. The police did not resist, although it took a long time to negotiate the language. The following day the Registrar issued a rule nisi ordering the respondents to show cause on November 26 why it should not be made permanent.

The front page of *The New York Times* declared "Pretoria Ordered to Stop Beatings."[27] The *Cape Herald* headlined its congratulations: "Well Done, Wendy."[28] Noting a report that month by University of Cape Town researchers that eighty-three percent of Cape detainees were tortured, *The Argus* said "the volume and nature of complaints" had reached "alarming proportions" and called for "an urgent, full and credible public inquiry."* *The*

---

*Foster & Sandler (1985); Foster et al. (1987); A 28 (9.26.85); CT (9.12.85). Brig. Gert Odendaal, who had just resigned as Western Province divisional police commissioner, complained that the study was not "impeccably scientific" because it was based on reports by former detainees rather than "reliable sources" like the police. FM 61 (9.27.95). Six months later an MP denounced the authors as "enemies who act in an irresponsible way here in South Africa in order to present our country...in an unfavorable light abroad..." The report was "nothing but

Daily News condemned "the sort of random violence…that merely brings authority into disrepute" and praised "the Supreme Court which stands as a bulwark against a kind of technically legitimised law of the jungle."[29] *The Natal Mercury* used stronger language.

> We all know that the record of political detentions—at least 50 people have died in police custody in the past 20 years—is a national disgrace in a country that still professes adherence to the Rule of Law.
>
> After the infamous Biko and Aggett cases it seemed things might be getting better. Then came the State of Emergency, a wave of arrests, disturbing allegations of ill-treatment, and evidence of unprovoked brutality in the streets, much of it on television for all the world to see.
>
> Inured as we are to such things, anyone reading the catalogue of horrors that a Port Elizabeth district surgeon submitted to the Supreme Court this week cannot but fear that the country is edging closer to the dark shadows of a totalitarian police state.

It praised judges who "powerfully assert the Courts' role as protector of individual rights" and called for "an immediate and unequivocal statement from the minister…putting the restraints on the police beyond any doubt." It acknowledged, however, that the "undermanned and over-extended force…for the most part, is doing a tough job well and is aware of the need to win and keep public trust in these difficult times."[30]

The local *Eastern Province Herald* published the longest editorial. The application created "a hugely disturbing picture of police captives being thrashed, injured, and otherwise abused…." The "scale of the allegations" made the case "far more troubling." It was "astonish[ed]" that "the State Department of Prisons and Health appeared to turn a blind eye to what was going on." The Minister of Law and Order, who had to answer for the recent Langa massacre, "has to be able to check his own men, or resign if he cannot." It urged "a judicial commission of inquiry into the police handling of the unrest" and deplored "the harm being inflicted on South Africa's reputation abroad" and "the damage being done to racial attitudes."[31] Three weeks later the *Sowetan* condemned the "dark and sinister world" Dr. Orr had exposed, recollecting six other famous deaths in custody.[32] At the end of November *The Star* gave her its Woman of the Year Award; she was readers' overwhelming choice among the twenty-four nominated by the paper's senior editorial staff.[33] Calling 1985 "the unhappiest year of our lives," eighty-

a political attack on the South African Government and more specifically the SAP." It was funded by the notorious Ford Foundation. As long as the 176 torture victims "remain secret, the report is not worth the paper it is written on." The principal author was thinking of making a movie: "Does the proposed Foster film have any connection with the Biko propaganda film?" The report "should be tested in a court of law." *Hansard* cols. 2877–83 (G.C. Ballot, NP) (4.9.86).

two-year-old Alan Paton listed among the few good events Wendy Orr's bravery and Justice Eksteen's courage, speculating that "the rule of law [is] creeping back."[34]

Several doctors added their voices. Professor Trefor Jenkins of the Wits Medical School, a complainant against Lang and Tucker, praised Dr. Orr for adhering to the Declaration of Tokyo. Her allegations, if true, "would be a dreadful indictment of the Department of Health." Dr. Yusuf Veriava, another complainant, asserted that "this type of thing happens frequently" and commended Dr. Orr for taking a stand.[35] The (South African) National Council of Women and the British Medical Association joined the chorus of praise.[36]

The state was quick to respond. The day after the interdict the police brought a pathologist to St. Alban's, where he observed an assembly of detainees and examined a "random sample" of eighteen in the presence of prison officers, later declaring that none complained of assaults or showed any signs of injury.[37] The same day the District Surgeon's receptionist told Dr. Orr she could not leave the office, receive or make telephone calls, or talk to the press. Dr. Lang, who had flown back from vacation in Cape Town, told her he was "loyal to his department" and had "nothing to say...about the matter."[38] He instructed her to tell the receptionist where she was going when she left the office and when she would be back. The next day he told her by phone that she could no longer visit prisons, attend sick parades there, see prisoners held in police cells or detainees, or do any postmortems involving "unrest victims." She saw Dr. G.S. Watermeyer, Deputy Director-General of the Department of Health, in the office that day but did not talk to him. Reporters who called the District Surgeon were told that the "head office" would not let her speak.[39] Dr. Watermeyer denied forbidding her to see detainees but conceded she might have been subject to a "normal" rotation. Dr. Krynauw told her she had not been banned from the prisons but because her relations with them were strained it was wiser that she no longer visit them. When she asked to resume her duties he refused on October 24. Able to work no more than five hours a day, she was "nearly dying of boredom." She did not want to do "daily sick parades of people [in old age homes] without real ills."[40] She began to receive death threats. When anonymous donors paid off her bursary, she resigned on December 30.[41] Editorials and letters to the editor condemned her forced departure.[42]

The night after the interdict application was filed the police detained a number of men and beat them at Kempton Park Police Station. Two weeks later they arrested four high school pupils suspected of holding a people's court. Lulamile Matoto, seventeen, was crippled with polio.

> I was not given a chance to collect my crutches from my room. When Sgt Faku told me to go to the combi, I attempted to walk without my crutches, but Faku pushed me and I fell onto the ground. After that I crawled on my hands and knees to the combi. As I crawled, Sgt Jam kicked me. Sgt Faku pulled me

onto my feet and told me to walk. I told them that I was unable
to walk without crutches, but they just laughed, and Sgt Faku
threw me onto the ground again.

At LLG Faku announced to them: "Kwanja zivuthumlilo" (You have
arrived in hell). When they were ordered out of the combi, Matoto asked for
his crutches. Faku threatened to beat him until he shit. As Matoto tried to get
into the building Faku laughed and insisted he walk faster. In the elevator
Faku told Matoto to pray because he might not come out alive. He held
Matoto by the shirt and shouted "Do you hear me, cripple?" When Matoto
did not answer, Faku warned that he would follow Bubele Maneli, who had
died in custody. During interrogation Faku made Matoto do exercises, which
were very painful because of his crippled leg. He was made to lie on his
back while Sgt. Jam stamped on his stomach until he screamed. Then
Mpokeli stood on his stomach while Jam stood on his neck, pressing his
shoes into Matoto's throat. When Jam choked him with his hands, Matoto
rolled his eyes back to appear to be dying.

Very early the next morning Jam and Mpokeli drove him around New
Brighton township looking for "Michael." Mpokeli took out his gun and said
that now Matoto would talk or be jailed or killed. If he were not a cripple
he would go to Robben Island. When they returned to LLG at daybreak, Jam
told Matoto to make arrangements for his funeral because he was going to
die. The four were finally booked at Algoa Park (two days after being
detained) and sent to St. Alban's. Matoto got a new pair of crutches two days
later. None of the four was told about the interdict issued seventeen days
before their detention. The police denied everything, Sgts. Mpokeli and Jam
adding that they did not know Matoto was crippled or used crutches.

On October 11 the police detained and beat another thirty youths at Algoa
Park before imprisoning them. At North End Prison a wardress read the
female detainees the interdict but gave them no chance to complain of the
torture. The police detained and tortured three more on October 15.

The publicity generated by the application elicited affidavits from other
victims, including many caught in the raids on Red Location and the Biko
commemoration. The order also gave lawyers access to detainees. They
began operating a complaints office, helping relatives find and visit
detainees. By the November 11 deadline they had completed more than a
hundred additional affidavits, whose gruesome details were again reported
by the press.[43]

On December 28 Molly Blackburn was killed in a car accident in which
two others died. Some 20,000 blacks attended her funeral in Port Elizabeth
during the first week of January.[44]

The respondents filed their answering affidavit on December 24 and fifty-
nine affidavits by police and prison officials by January 23, 1986. Although
they denied that the police viewed the Emergency regulations as carte
blanche to torture detainees, inconsistent memories raised doubts.

> We were warned that we were protected by the emergency regulations against assaults on people and violence to property … [but] could only use fair violence that was necessitated when there was a resistance to arrest or to obtain access to a property when this was refused or to disperse crowds when such orders had been given. (Lt. E.A. Taylor)

> [A]t no stage where I was present was there any warning given to police officials with regard to the use of violence when arrests were undertaken. … [W]e were informed that we are not subject to any actions which may arise out of the arrests of people...[but] are not given any protection should [we] illegally assault people. (AO Freddie van Wyk)

The repertoire of denials, justifications and excuses lacked both credibility and consistency.

(1) Blanket denials: None of the events ever happened.

(2) Procedural objections: The allegations were hearsay or insufficiently specific; the applicants lacked standing.

(3) Mootness: The assaults had ended, and the detainees been released. (The affiants were unembarrassed by the negative pregnant.)

(4) Bureaucratic impossibility: The affiant interrogated another category of detainee (students rather than trade unionists, "Coloureds" rather than Blacks). Superiors repudiated responsibility for subordinates: Brig. Schnetler denied knowing Sgt. Butler Tungata, although Tungata said he was employed by Schnetler.

(5) Alibi: The affiant was posted elsewhere (even if only a few days out of the two-month period).

(6) Workload: The police were too busy to spend time assaulting prisoners.

(7) Physical impossibility of the assault: The victim was in the back seat while the accused was driving; the victim's hair could not be pulled out.

(8) Physical impossibility of the evidence: The witness was too far away to see or hear the alleged assault, or the door was closed. That is, the location was too private.

(9) Imprudence: The respondent would have seen or heard the alleged assault and did not; others (particularly superiors) would have done so, making it imprudent. That is, the location was too public.

(10) Pre-existing injury: The victim was hurt before interrogation.

> It often happens that members of the public are injured when crowds are dispersed. They fall on top of one another, run through fences and doors, fall over stones, clash with poles, motor cars and houses, sometimes fall in holes and often hang onto high enclosures made of corrugated iron. … [Because] such persons are then unwilling to report such injuries… hundreds of people within the confines of various residential areas

are walking around with injuries such as sjambok strikes, bruises, open sores, shotgun wounds to the body, as well as fractures. ... [T]here is often stone throwing and... bumps and bruises may occur as a result.... (Maj. Blignaut)

(11) Lack of necessity: Because detainees were not common criminals they offered no resistance, making force superfluous. (This contradicted the previous defense.)

(12) People's courts: The injuries were inflicted by the "comrades" of those complaining. M.E. Magamela, awaiting trial for murder committed by a people's court, declared:

Everywhere in the black residential areas people are sentenced on a daily basis by the People's Court and there are hundreds of people walking around with sjambok lash marks which have been inflicted... by the People's Court officials.

(13) Friendship: The accused was friendly to the accuser or his family, as demonstrated by favors given (cigarettes, coffee, information to relatives) and thanks received. You do not torture friends.

(14) Enmity: The accused was widely detested. Enemies falsely accuse you of torture.

(15) Police notoriety: Superiors ordered the accused not to arrest or interrogate because he was so widely detested that he would be accused without reason.

(16) Prisoner fame: The alleged victim was too well-known to be tortured.

(17) A policeman's lot is not a happy one. They, not the detainees, were the real victims. Their houses were burned and they and their families attacked. The townships were

very tense and anything but normal. Instances of public violence, arson, murder and assault often take place. There is large scale intimidation against the black members of the SAP. The situation had become so grave that I was forced to remove all the black policemen and their families. (Lt. Col. F.A. Pretorius)

The police seemed unaware that the last two defenses might offer motives to assault detainees.

(18) Enjoyment: The victim appeared to enjoy interrogation.

(19) Detainees did not complain; investigations by the Prisons Department and SAP found no misconduct. This is the most common response to charges of state terror.

(20) Some accused showed their contempt for the inquiry by not deigning to respond.

On January 29 the applicants filed a notice ordering the respondents to produce the medical history cards, prison registers, reports of departmental investigating officers, and other documents referred to in their affidavits.

Cheadle spent a week in prison photocopying 7,000 documents. On the applicants' motion Justice Jones added numerous applicants and respondents and ordered an oral hearing, extending the rule nisi until June 17 and the interim interdict until a decision on the merits.

Dr. Orr filed a sixty-eight-page reply affidavit on March 27. Police and prison records disclosed that 434 detainees had complained of assault, 406 named the SAP, and 296 laid formal charges and presented consistent injuries, at least 217 of which could only have been produced by torture. Dr. Orr was responsible for only 120 complaints, the others having been recorded by prison warders, prison hospital staff, and district surgeons. Although the Prisons Department Investigating Officers took 272 affidavits, they investigated only four.

Because the State President had lifted the Emergency, however, ending all emergency detentions, the applicants withdrew the interim interdict. In September, Law and Order Minister Louis le Grange (eponym of the torture site) agreed to pay costs, eventually calculated at R262,000, without admitting any allegations.[45] When the state actually made the payment a year later, the *Cape Times* called it "yet another indication of the need for police reform." Although "the truth of Dr Orr's individual allegations was not tested by the court," "the impression left in the public mind is hardly reassuring." The payment of R1.2 million to victims of police violence in 1986 was further evidence.[46] Reporting the payout, the *Sunday Tribune* remembered payments to other victims, as well as uncompensated victims.[47]

No police officer, prison official, or doctor was ever punished. On the second day of the Emergency WO Stanford Mene and Sgt. Butler Tungata (one of the most sadistic torturers) went to Phakamisa Junior Secondary School, where Mene murdered two pupils and Tungata shot two teachers, later seeking to cover up their conduct by filing public violence charges. In May 1986 Justice Solomon convicted both of defeating the ends of justice, Mene of two counts of murder with extenuating circumstances (necessary to avoid sentencing him to death), and Tungata of assault with intent to do grievous bodily harm. Calling Mene a blatant liar, he sentenced each to twenty-nine years but immediately granted leave to appeal and bail.[48] At midnight on December 14, 1989, a police car was destroyed by a limpet mine, killing Sgt. A.T. Faku (another torturer), two other policemen, and Charles Jack (a former ANC member turned police informer). The police were implicated in the June 1985 murder of Matthew Goniwe (whose inquest was in progress), and there were rumors that Jack remained a double agent for the ANC. In June 1993 the SADF accused the SAP of the killings, noting that its explosives expert, Maj. Gideon Niewoudt, was the first person on the scene and had lied to the first inquest.*

*WM 2 (6.11.93), 8 (6.18.93). Niewoudt originally testified that the explosion had been caused by a limpet mine, which he attributed to the ANC. He now admitted it had been 6 kilograms of explosives armed with a detonator. He could give no reason for his deception, for which he apologized.

In July 1990—five years after the torture—the state (still admitting no wrongdoing) settled the claims of eighty-two victims for R120,500, ranging from R400 for those with the least serious injuries to R8,000 for Dennis Neer, R5,000 for Leslie Mangcotywa and Mkhuseli Jack, R4,000 for Ivy Gcina, and R3,500 for Vusumzi George.[49] The *Daily News* called this a "small but significant vindication for an act of courage and conscience."[50] Wendy Orr, Mike Xhego (now ANC regional spokesman), Mkhuseli Jack (UDF publicity secretary), Dennis Neer (COSATU regional secretary), Ihron Rensburg (NECC national secretary), Ivy Gcina (ANC Women's League National Executive Committee member), Leslie Mangcotywa (SAYCO vice-president), and Rev. de Villiers Soga celebrated the payment at COSATU's Port Elizabeth office. Dr. Orr commented:

> I am pleased that the ex-detainees have received some form of compensation for all they went through. However, I feel it would have been better had the case gone to court.
>
> None of the police involved has been disciplined. ... I feel angry that there are still doctors, such as Ivor Lang, who have not been disciplined and are still party to the whole system.[51]

The *Natal Witness* commended her "rare courage" and "relentless pursuit and exposure of the truth."[52] Since leaving Port Elizabeth she had worked in the Alexandra Health Centre in Johannesburg and volunteered for the National Medical and Dental Association detainees' support service. Later that month she addressed a conference on Medicine and the Media at UCT Medical School, reiterating her 1985 disclosures and urging doctors and health-care workers to "shed their traditionally apathetic image." The police conceded that torture "does occur from time to time by individual members of the police who step out of line, but where it occurs the police have always taken the necessary steps to prevent a recurrence."[53] Accepting the Human Rights Award from the Civil Rights League in September, she noted that no district surgeon before or since had exposed police torture. Justice was unattainable under apartheid. "The struggle continues," she concluded.[54]

Legal Responses to State Violence

Even the limited success of Wendy Orr's interdict was rare.* Less than a week after it was filed the Durban Supreme Court heard seven similar applications, entering a consent decree restraining the police from assaulting Billy Nair of the Natal Indian Congress executive.[55] When the police were tried seven months later the defense lawyer declared "It is not far-fetched to

---

*See, e.g., Lawyers Committee for Human Rights (1986c) (seven deaths in April–May 1986); Hansson (1989) (Cape Town deaths 1984–86). When human rights lawyers sought an inquest following the death in custody of Amos Raditsela, police raided their office and seized the files. D. Unterhalter (1986).

accept that a person with his dedication could stoop to the depths of injuring himself to bring the police and the authorities into disrepute." Although they were convicted for injuring his eye and ear they were fined only R175 and R50.[56] In April 1986 the Minister of Law and Order complained that the PFP was demanding that he "always go around arresting and charging policemen and bringing them to trial." The Attorney General had reviewed two-thirds of the 310 complaints about police torture and decided to bring only two prosecutions. Although the UCT study of torture the previous year reported that eighty-three percent of detainees complained, "the official statistics... indicate that such complaints were received only in 13.78% of the cases."[57] With the renewal of the Emergency in June 1986 the police resumed mass arrests and torture in Port Elizabeth, although now they preferred to suffocate victims with a wet bag, which left no marks.[58]

On December 12, 1985, while Dr. Orr's application was pending in Port Elizabeth, seven victims applied in nearby East London for an "Anton Piller" order allowing them to search two police stations for torture instruments. Writing for a full bench, Justice Kannemeyer (who had investigated the Langa shootings) rejected the request a week later. Although the applicants had made a strong prima facie cause of assault and the instruments "would no doubt be strongly corroborative... and could be a conclusive factor," they were not essential nor would their absence "lead to a denial of justice" since the victims could testify about their torture. PFP MPs later read some of the torture affidavits to Parliament, one of them warning that "hon members of this House should be aware of what is going on in this country because when the Nuremburg trials are held in this country—and it will happen—I do not want any members in this House to say: 'I did not know.'" A Nationalist called this "definitely the most disgraceful of all the speeches" David Dalling had ever made.*

In May 1986 "homeguards" arrested 121 Zolani residents in the middle of the night, dragged them out of their houses, undressed and beat them. Arraigned before Mag. M.P.H. Stander two days later, they still had dried blood, black eyes, and bandages; two had plaster casts; some women wore only a torn half-slip. The Directorate of Justice explained the magistrate's failure to comment on their condition.

> When the magistrate entered the court, the accused were already present and due to the large number of persons present and the brevity of the proceedings—a mere formal reprimand—the magistrate could not and did not notice the particular apparel of

*Ex parte Matshini and others 1986 (3) SA 605 (E). Six months later the Cape Supreme Court issued such an order. WM 3 (6.6.86). *Hansard* cols. 8058–63 (P.G. Soal, PFP) (6.12.85), 7957–73 (D.J. Dalling, PFP; A.P. Wright, NP) (6.11.86). The Ciskei Supreme Court also issued an order in 1989. Ex parte Dyantyi and another 1989 (4) SA 826 (Ciskei). But in 1991 the Appellate Division upheld the Witwatersrand Supreme Court's refusal to grant an order ex parte, effectively eviscerating the remedy. Jafta v Minister of Law and Order and others 1991 (2) SA 286 (A); see Plasket (1986b; 1992).

each individual. The magistrate's attention was furthermore not directed to any injuries by any of the accused persons appearing before him.[59]

In the June 1986 debate on the Public Safety Amendment Bill the PFP moved a clause prohibiting government from indemnifying "the State or any official from civil or criminal liability for any unlawful act or omission." The Minister's only response was to protest references to "agents of the hon the Minister" or "agents of the Police," which are "the way the agents of the Gestapo or the KGB are referred to." "[A] member of the Security Forces who commits wrongful and unlawful actions is not protected." In preparing for the debate, he had remembered two police who had been punished. The proposal was defeated 106-15.[60]

Simon Marule, COSAS Deputy Chairman, died on December 23, 1986, hours after being transferred from detention in Modderbee Prison. The inquest nearly two years later revealed that the prison medical orderly had ignored repeated requests from other prisoners that Marule be examined. The District Surgeon who saw him on December 22 diagnosed an early stage of heart failure but did not stress urgency.[61]

On July 7, 1987, police surprised ANC guerrilla Ashley Kriel, handcuffed him, and killed him with a point-blank shot in the back. WO Jeff Benzien, who had fired the shot, found a poster with Kriel's photograph and the legend "Victory or Death. Freedom Is Certain." He scrawled "not for you" underneath. Although Benzien testified at the inquest two years later that he had not shot in self-defense, or to prevent Kriel from escaping, or to effect an arrest but was holding Kriel down on the ground with the help of another officer, Mag. G. Hoffmann found that the shot was fired by accident during a tussle, although he criticized the graffiti on the poster as "tasteless, disgusting and disturbing."[62]

A month after Cape Town police killed Kriel, Daveyton police killed Caiphus Nyoka, former executive member of the Transvaal Students Congress and SRC president at Mabuya High School. Three youths sleeping in the room with him were taken outside and heard the shots. At the police station they saw a white policeman write on the blackboard "999 Lemba Street—Caiphus Nyoka executed 6 shots—Hands of Death." He laughed and made them read it. The police claimed to have seen "something glittering in [Nyoka's] left hand." Inquest Mag. J.P. Myburgh accepted their evidence that they found a knife in the hand of Nyoka, whom he constantly called "the accused." "If they wanted to plant something surely they would not have planted a knife. They have access to hand grenades, hand-guns and all sorts of weapons." He disbelieved Caiphus's brother because he had a motive to lie.[63]

In the notorious "Trojan Horse" incident in October 1985 a flat-bed South African Transport Services truck slowly cruised Thornton Road in Athlone, where burning tires had been reported. When youths threw stones at it, police hiding in crates jumped up and fired almost forty rounds of buckshot and bird shot, killing three and wounding many. Three-and-a-half years later Mag. D. Hoffman found that the police were negligent, their lives had not been in danger, there was no evidence the deceased had thrown stones, and the police had falsely doubled the size of the crowd. The parents of two dead children brought a private prosecution after the Attorney General refused to prosecute (a decision criticized in Parliament). The Supreme Court rejected the defense demand of R1 million security since the state would pay the defendants' costs. It rejected a defense motion to dismiss on the ground that the parents had not been injured but separated the two parents' prosecutions. Four years after the event Justice Williamson acquitted all the accused in the first prosecution. Although the police "overreacted to a manifestly dangerous situation," they lacked the requisite intent.[64] Six months after that Free State police hired a truck and hid under a tarpaulin as it trolled the "war zone" called Vietnam. Youths surrounded the truck but could see the police and did nothing. Nevertheless, the eight white police jumped up and started shooting, killing two and wounding others.[65]

The December 1988 Trust Feeds massacre illustrated the brazen efforts of police to cover up their crimes. In February Law and Order Minister Adriaan Vlok had declared in Pietermaritzburg: "Radicals... will not be tolerated. We will fight them. We have put our foot in that direction, and we will eventually win in the Pietermaritzburg area." Residents at Trust Feeds near Hanover had formed a Crisis Committee (TFCC) to resist forced removal. Local Inkatha leader Jerome Gabela organized a Landowners' Committee to oppose them and launched a recruitment drive. TFCC chair Phillip Shango survived an assassination attempt, but his stores were burned. Police sent a special force to Trust Feeds in November to assist Gabela. On December 2 they declared a curfew, barred journalists, detained TFCC members, confiscated the weapons of UDF members, and razed their homes. That night Capt. Brian Mitchell picked up four kitskonstabels (instant police) armed with pump action shotguns and surrounded a funeral vigil for an old man who had died of natural causes. At 3 a.m., after the mourners had gone to sleep, police fired through doors and windows and then entered the building with flashlights and finished the job, killing eleven. When Gabela and the TFCC vice-chairman asked why Inkatha people had been killed, Mitchell said "a mistake occurred so you shouldn't talk about what happened. If you do, I will kill you." They blamed the attack on TFCC, forcing supporters to flee the township and allowing Inkatha to take control. Mitchell was promoted to captain and the kitskonstabels appointed to the KwaZulu Police.

The initial investigation by Capt. Wattruss recorded no evidence, not even the discovery of spent shotgun cartridges, specially made for the police, at the murder scene and in Mitchell's vehicle. Two other white police had seen Mitchell with the kitskonstabels that night and saw him throw spent cartridges out of the vehicle. Although a ballistic report connected the killings to guns issued to two kitskonstabels, warrants for their arrest were never executed. When Wattruss completed his report, Natal CID head Brig. Christo Marx took the investigation away from him. Three months after the crime Marx terminated the inquiry, accepting Mitchell's version and rejecting that of his two white subordinates. Several years later the police reopened it and assigned it to Lt. Gen. Ronnie van der Westhuizen, who was later replaced (on the objection of the Natal Attorney General). Seven police were put on trial three years after the killings. Although the indictment alleged that Pietermaritzburg Riot Unit head Capt. Deon Terblanche knew of the planned massacre, he was conveniently assassinated by Const. Roy Ngcobo, a subordinate, who confessed to doing so out of a personal grudge and coincidentally was killed the next day allegedly trying to escape.

Although the accused pleaded not guilty, four kitskonstabels admitted participating in the attack on Mitchell's orders. When the prosecutor put it to Mitchell: "You set up an organisation which supports the government of the day and you oust[ed] the one which would not follow the same principles," Mitchell agreed "that is what happened." He had decided to "jack up [Gabela] and get him to be more forceful." "Can we take it you mean a little more violent?" the prosecutor asked. Mitchell replied: "That's what eventually happened." Judge Andrew Wilson found Mitchell and four kitskonstabels guilty of eleven murders and two attempts. He rejected evidence in mitigation that Mitchell was drunk, had acted on the spur of the moment, and had shown great remorse.[66]

Despite its totalitarian aspirations, South Africa was underpoliced compared to western liberal regimes (two rather than seven or eight police for every 1,000 people). In response to growing unrest in the mid-1980s the government started deploying kitskonstabels after just three months of training, putting the first thousand on the street by September 1986.[67] Nine months later the Cape Supreme Court granted an interdict restraining the police from interfering with a Cape Youth Congress commemoration of the Soweto uprising, after kitskonstabels had disrupted a meeting and tortured members.[68] Nine months after that the Natal Midlands Council of Churches obtained an interdict against kitskonstabels who got drunk every weekend and abused residents. A beating victim who complained about a violation of the interdict was followed home and beaten further.[69]

Early in 1988 the Southern Cape Council of Churches sought an interdict against kitskonstabels in Bhongolethu, near Oudtshoorn, when they killed three and injured at least ten others six days after one of the most brutal kitskonstabels had been murdered. The police characterized the application as a campaign by "radical elements" to undermine the authority of the kitskonstabels, "the last line of law and order in the township." The commander of the local unrest unit said there had been no reports of bad behavior, although the Bhongolethu police station incident book contained twenty entries of kitskonstabels reporting for duty drunk, firing shotguns without cause, accidentally setting off teargas grenades, and assaulting each other.[70] The following month an independent MP criticized kitskonstabels during debate on the Police Amendment Bill. The Minister of Law and Order responded that, although "the SA Police are not perfect," "it is a fraction of a percentage of the Police Force that are guilty of contraventions." The attack was politically motivated. "[T]he radicals in South Africa fear the special constables. [Interjections.] The radicals have taken a beating from the special constables. The radicals tried to control the Black residential areas in South Africa. What did we do? We stationed the special constables there." The critic "is an advocate for the radicals in South Africa." A few months later the Deputy Minister of Law and Order added that special constables "maintain a vital presence in unrest situations. ... not a single request had been made by a Black area for the withdrawal of [the 4,389] Black special constables...they march through parts of Black townships, where they are received with great enthusiasm and delight. People even sweep the ground over which they are going to march."[71]

In a terrorism prosecution in Windhoek in February 1987 South West Africa Police frankly admitting torturing prisoners. WO Nikodemus Nampala declared: "You thrash [a prisoner] until he cracks—points out what has to be pointed out. ... It was right to beat men and go crazy." He saw an intravenous drip ripped out of the arm of one accused before questioning and a wounded man flogged with a hosepipe. Asked if there was a procedure to complain about such conduct, he responded: "For what purpose, your honour?" Capt. Frantz Ballack beat Andreas Heita because "he told lies...but after being assaulted he was completely willing to tell the truth." When Heita stripped in court, Justice Harold Levy called his injuries "inhuman." WO Hermanus van der Hoven testified: "I tried to explain to [Heita] why it was necessary to use violence.... We then had a discussion about how a person as a Christian repents and how you are sometimes subject to punishment, like a child would [be] had he done wrong."[72] When the SWA Attorney General prosecuted six soldiers for murdering SWAPO member Immanuel Shifidi at a November 1986 rally, the State President stopped the trial and was upheld by the Appellate Division.[73]

Although fame offered the living no protection from police violence and might even increase the risk, it complicated posthumous attempts to cover up, as Biko's death illustrated. On January 30, 1990, Clayton Sizwe Sithole, twenty, died in John Vorster Square (Johannesburg police headquarters), allegedly "hanging from a shower pipe." He had been arrested four days earlier for suspected membership in an ANC cell accused of ten murders. Although at least seventy blacks had died in police custody since 1963, Sithole was the father of Zinzi Mandela's son (the grandson of Nelson Mandela, released from prison the next month). Within hours of Sithole's death the State President promised to appoint the first judicial commission of inquiry ever held. Law and Order Minister Vlok declared uncharacteristically: "I wish to give the assurance that the law will take its course. I also wish to express my condolences to his next of kin." The state invited the family to choose a private pathologist to observe the postmortem.[74]

A month after Mandela's release police fired on Sebokeng residents protesting rent increases, killing twelve and wounding eighty-five. The ANC suspended negotiations, and de Klerk appointed Judge Richard Goldstone to conduct a commission of inquiry. Although he found no legal justification for the shootings there or in Boipatong, Lekoa, Sharpeville, and Evaton, there were no criminal prosecutions. In May police killed another eleven and wounded ninety-one in Thabong, near Welkom.[75]

When Cape Flats police fired on a demonstration against the September 1989 elections, killing at least twenty-three and injuring more than a hundred, the first policeman broke ranks. Lt. Gregory Rockman, a "coloured" policeman with twelve years experience, had tried to stop the riot police from attacking school children. When Col. John Manuel, the highest ranking "coloured" policeman, backed Rockman's accusations of brutality, the Cape Attorney General charged two riot police with assault. The SAP responded by investigating Rockman for unauthorized contact with the press. Although Mag. A.S. McCarthy found the assaults unlawful and police conduct "utterly despicable," he acquitted them under the indemnity clause because there was no evidence of bad faith. When Rockman launched the Police and Prisons Civil Rights Union to fight discrimination against black employees the SAP fired him and thirty-nine others for violating a standing order against unions.[76]

The next month, however, another insider blabbed. Former security policeman Butana Almond Nofemela obtained a stay of execution the day before he was to be hanged (for an apolitical murder of a white farmer) by revealing that he and three other police killed Durban attorney Griffiths Mxenge in 1981 at the direction of Capt. Dirk Coetzee. Nofemela also claimed a role in eight other assassinations. They had poisoned Mxenge's watchdogs and then slashed his throat, cut off his ears, crushed his skull, and stabbed him forty-five times to make it look like a robbery. Nofemela and Coetzee drove Mxenge's car to Piet Retief, stripped it, and burned it near the Swazi border. The four black policemen each earned R1,000. The 1983 inquest found the cause of death unknown.

Three weeks later Coetzee, who had taken disability retirement in 1985 and later fled South Africa, corroborated the story. He had led the hit squad from Vlakplaas, a secret base near Pretoria, using former ANC guerrillas called "askaris." After a mission to kill Marius Schoon in Botswana was aborted a letter bomb killed Schoon's wife and daughter in Angola. Coetzee also took responsibility for murdering Ruth First, bombing the ANC office in London, attempting to assassinate Chris Hani in Lesotho, murdering Patrick Makau and his child in Swaziland in 1980, bombing Bufana Duma in Swaziland, and attempting to poison ANC members in Maputo. In June 1981 he saw Sizwe Kondile at Jeffrey's Bay Police Station and was told by a doctor that this was "another Steve Biko case coming up" because Kondile had suffered brain damage. Coetzee saw Kondile given knockout drops provided by Gen. Lothar Neethling and then shot dead.[77]

SAP Maj. Gen. Herman Stadler first called the accusations "unfounded, untested and wild" and then suggested that rogue squads could have acted without authority. Another hit squad member, David "Spyker" Tshikalange, confirmed Nofemela's account before fleeing the country. Nofemela then described a 1983 raid led by Maj. Eugene de Kock (who replaced Coetzee), which killed three ANC members in Swaziland. Nofemela had accidentally shot fellow policeman Jeff Bosego, whose admission to Ermelo hospital was recorded. Coetzee was the target of a sophisticated package bomb, ostensibly containing a tape about the hit squads, mailed to him in Lusaka in May 1990; he narrowly escaped death when he refused to pay the postal charges.[78]

De Kock testified in the inquest into the killing of four Chesterville youths in 1986. Three "askaris" had offered them an AK-47 and then shot ninety rounds into their hut. Brig. W.F.S. Schoon (the immediate superior of Coetzee and de Kock) testified that he authorized the Vlakplaas unit to draw an AK-47 from police stores to establish credibility with ANC units they sought to infiltrate. Mag. B.J. Olivier exonerated the police of the killing, finding that they had intended only to arrest the youths.[79]

In February 1991 Coetzee (now an ANC member in Harare) named ninety-two people with knowledge about the hit squad, including Police Minister Louis le Grange, SAP Commissioner Gen. Johan P. Coetzee, Maj. Craig Williamson, Defense Minister Magnus Malan, and both State Presidents. In December Nofemela pleaded guilty to the murder of Griffiths Mxenge, claiming he acted under the instructions of Brig. Schoon. The family sued the Minister of Law and Order despite the six-month statute of limitations; the action was postponed while Dirk Coetzee sought indemnity to testify in South Africa (which was never granted). The Natal Attorney General refused to bring a murder prosecution. Four days before Coetzee was to testify in the civil case two South African agents flew to London (where he had taken refuge) to arrange for his assassination by IRA guerrillas; they were foiled by British intelligence. Leon William Floris, one of those arrested, was a former SAP officer at Vlakplaas, who had accompanied Maj. de Kock in killing four suspected ANC members in Piet Retief in June 1988.[80]

In 1989 two prominent opponents of the regime were murdered: David Webster, a University of the Witwatersrand anthropologist who had uncovered Renamo activity in Kosi Bay (in Johannesburg in March) and Namibian human rights lawyer Anton Lubowski (in Windhoek in September). In November the police arrested two former policemen, Sgt. Ferdinand Bernard and Det. Sgt. Calla Botha, for the murders, but Justice Kriegler released Botha on grounds of insufficient evidence. Successfully opposing a motion for Bernard's release in January 1990, SAP Brig. Floris Mostert asserted: "a secret organisation exists in this country, with members from all levels of society, which strives to terrorise left-wing radicals with the aid of violence and intimidation." He named retired Lt. Col. "Staal" Burger as a superior. Claiming he had only learned about it in November, President de Klerk appointed Judge

Louis Harms to hold a commission of inquiry. His backbenchers were not enthusiastic. One deplored the "one-sided witch-hunt, specifically on the security forces... whereas not a word is said about suspected malpractices on the other side." Another declared, "[I]f I should discover that my Government, in the circumstances in which South Africa finds itself has not got a special unit such as the CCB, I would have blamed the Government bitterly."[81] While Defense Minister Malan did not deny *The Star*'s charge that he had known about the "Civil Cooperation Bureau," he declared he was suspending it but deplored the "remorseless campaign against our security forces."[82] A year later, however, the Auditor General reported that the SADF subsequently approved a further R4 million for the CCB.

At the first day of the Harms inquiry in March 1990 the SADF admitted planting a bomb at an Athlone early learning center, blowing up a store owned by a Pretoria anti-apartheid activist, planning to tamper with the luggage of Rev. Frank Chikane (who later showed signs of poisoning), and plotting to send a baboon fetus to Archbishop Tutu. Abraham van Zyl described a botched attempt to poison human rights attorney Dullah Omar. Disbelieving most former CCB witnesses, Harms recommended further investigation of only two murders. The inquest into Webster's death was inconclusive.[83]

The 1985 murders of Victoria Mxenge (Griffiths's widow) and Matthew Goniwe and his three companions, just before the first Emergency unleashed police torture in Port Elizabeth, were ignored for three years. Mag. F.M. Vorster refused to hold a formal hearing about Victoria Mxenge (killed ten days after speaking at Goniwe's funeral), even when asked by the Attorney General. He ignored evidence proffered by by Bheka Shezi (former law partner of Griffiths and Victoria). At the hearing Vorster asked the family's advocate whether it was "the function of the open inquest to check the police. Why must we do this in open court with everyone here, hearing how the poor old investigating officer is being questioned about what he did and did not do?" He refused to allow the advocate to ask the investigator "what he did about certain information given to him." It was "not the course of the investigation that must be made known; but only the result." After a two-minute hearing he ruled that Mxenge had died of head injuries by persons unknown.

In the Goniwe inquest, Mag. E.L. de Cock failed to notify two families and notified the other two families late, forcing further delay. It began in February 1989, almost four years after the murders. Although two witnesses had stated that police showed the four victims to AZAPO enemies for identification and that two AZAPO men saw them killed and burned, they withdrew the statements. When the inquest reconvened Mag. E. de Beer denounced suspicions of the security police and declared the cause of death unknown.[84]

In May 1992, however, the *New Nation* published a June 7, 1985, message from Gen. Christoffel van der Westhuizen, now SADF Chief of Staff of Intelligence, to the State Security Council urging that Matthew Goniwe and two others be "permanently removed from society as a matter of urgency.

Widespread reaction can be expected, locally as well as nationally, because of the importance of these persons." Three cabinet ministers were on the Council when the message arrived. Lt. Lourens du Plessis, who signed the order to kill Goniwe, was then staff officer for intelligence at Eastern Province Command. Judge Zietsman, chairing the reopened inquest, heard evidence that the four had passed through a roadblock that night near where their bodies were found. Col. Eric Winter, a Cradock security policeman, testified that he had bugged Goniwe's telephone and transcribed the calls, including one the morning of his murder arranging a meeting in Port Elizabeth that day, on the return from which he was killed. Transkei ruler Bantu Holomisa threatened to release additional files implicating security forces.[85]

Notwithstanding the "reforms" initiated by de Klerk's release of Mandela and legalization of the ANC and SACP in February 1990, the police continued to abduct, torture, and execute. A letter bomb nearly killed an Anglican priest and ANC member in Harare in April.[86] Security forces still tried to recruit returning ANC members.[87] Those suspected of ordinary crime were tortured and died in custody.[88] In the Vaal triangle nineteen ANC members were killed or shot in the first four months of 1992.[89] At the end of July 1992 Dr. Jonathan Gluckman (whose advice Wendy Orr had sought before deciding to expose police torture) published a report on more than 200 deaths in custody. He was driven to do so after performing a postmortem on Simon Mthimkulu, nineteen, beaten to death in detention. The District Surgeon had found no suspicious circumstances. Two months later he performed an autopsy on Clement Hlengwa, who had died in police custody while in the last week of a four-year degree program at the University of Zululand. Although police said he was killed in a gun battle, the body was covered with bruises. Within a day of Hlengwa's death two other blacks were killed in police custody in the same area. Gluckman was asked to investigate fifteen cases of suspicious death the month after his report, up from an average of three to four a month.[90]

The indemnity for crimes committed before October 8, 1990, applied to police as well as civilians. In August 1992 the government proposed a general amnesty for all security forces in exchange for releasing the remaining 420 prisoners whom the ANC claimed as political. The President's Council overrode Parliament's defeat of the Further Indemnities Bill—the first time de Klerk had done this—apparently fearing evidence about to emerge in political trials. Former CCB head Joe Verster was believed to have documents withheld from the Harms Commission, which he threatened to use if forced to take the rap for actions ordered by superiors.[91] The same month de Klerk purged nineteen of fifty-five SAP generals in response to a highly critical report by a British police expert but retained three who were deeply implicated in illegal activities.[92] In December he forced twenty-three SADF officers to retire.[93] The interim constitution adopted in December 1993 repealed most legislation authorizing detention without trial, while retaining government authority to declare an emergency, which would permit such detentions.

Analysis

A comparison between Port Elizabeth during the first Emergency and the succeeding eight years of repression and "reform" offers valuable insights into state terror. The torturers are a mass of contradictions, illustrating the "banality" of evil.[94] Sadists enjoyed tormenting their victims. Some sought to revenge mistreatment by anti-apartheid activists. Many felt that the means were justified to defeat the ANC and SACP—just as police routinely feel about ordinary crime.[95] Some wanted their victims' respect—reenacting (almost to the year) George Orwell's classic portrayal of the use of torture to compel love for Big Brother.[96] Like the father with the strap telling a child "this hurts me more than it does you," police portrayed themselves as victims.[97] All expressed the violence that pervades South African society.[98]

The security police also were structurally contradictory. Although committed to preserving apartheid, they have had to integrate in order to repress effectively. Black police may surpass their white superiors in brutality to overcome lingering doubts about racial loyalty and enjoy the rare pleasures of dominance. This moral division of labor allowed whites to delegate the dirty work to blacks.

Even in totalitarian states the instruments of repression are inescapably flawed. Like any large, complex organization the parts are loosely integrated and often at odds. Although each component—security police, uniformed police, prison warders, and medical staff—was internally solidary, the groups differed in interest, composition, and function. It was the doctors' determination to cover their asses (highly vulnerable because the Biko inquiry had just reopened) that allowed some truth to emerge. Later conflicts between the SAP and SADF, black and white police, and South Africa and the homelands it had created exposed other secrets.[99] Even disavowals by individual police could only implicate others, given the undeniable physical evidence of torture. As a bureaucracy, the security apparatus kept detailed records. Like Nixon's White House tapes, however, these unimpeachable sources could be turned against their authors. Because torture requires invisibility it occurs at night, at remote locations, or inside buildings. But torturers seek to amplify fear by making one victim's suffering an example to others, through screams, sights, wounds, or stories, which simultaneously increases the number of witnesses. And systematic repression destroys anonymity as interrogators become intimate with their victims. Police are no better than criminals at committing the perfect crime. Indeed, their extraordinary power induces carelessness. Police testimony offered motives for otherwise gratuitous torture. By relieving Wendy Orr of her duties, the Prisons Department conceded complicity. Had the government, as usual, accepted the interdict without admitting the allegations, the story would have died more quickly.

Power corrupts. Although the state promulgated elaborate regulations restricting the use of force, police knew they were immune from discipline.

Abuses were rewarded, not punished. Even if superiors warned against "illegal violence," the declaration of the Emergency was an invitation to break heads. The respondents' "defenses" displayed contempt for law: No one was tortured, I wasn't there, I didn't do anything. The violence seemed inefficient: Among the two thousand detained in Port Elizabeth during the first two months of the Emergency, few were important leaders. And the torture often seemed unrelated to extracting information. But this was exactly the point. Random, arbitrary, unpredictable terror was the state's only hope of crushing the opposition.

The victims of state torture were unlikely heroes. Ordinary people who had known nothing but oppression displayed extraordinary courage. They defied tormentors knowing this would increase their suffering. They filed complaints knowing this would provoke retaliation rather than investigation. The experience of detention and torture strengthened resistence rather than producing the intended despair. State repression designed to destroy individuals paradoxically forged collectivity. The prison is to state repression what the factory was to capitalist exploitation—it aggregates, homogenizes, and fosters communication. Prisoners exchange tales of torture and care for each other. Prisons educate the politically naive and enhance the moral stature of inmates. Like their predecessors in the Bastille and the Soviet Gulag and the "graduates" of Robben Island, political detainees were ennobled by exemplary suffering. Virtually every black South African had a friend or relative who endured imprisonment. Their stories of police abuse were told and retold, creating a mythical charter of resistance.

If the discourse of torture is phrased in the language of pain, its subtext is humiliation. Pain can make anyone do anything, but only humiliation can change people. The state's declared goal was winning hearts and minds (WHAM). Torturers made detainees sing freedom songs, dance the toyi-toyi, shout their slogans, disavow their leaders, and publicly soil themselves. Police inflicted degradation to compensate their insecurities about authority and self-respect. The victims also identified humiliation as their worst torment. Helplessness was the greatest indignity, what they recounted most vividly—not knowing when the next blow would strike.[100] This partly explains why they defied their tormentors and complained—not to stop the torture (for which such actions were futile or counterproductive) but to reclaim their dignity, sense of agency, transforming themselves from objects to subjects.[101]

Powerlessness, ironically, can be a form of power. The state can abuse bodies only so far without killing. Deaths in detention are hard to conceal or explain. Two detainees bought a brief respite from torture by threatening to die.* Even Dr. Lang referred seriously injured prisoners to hospital, creating

---

*This, too, can produce incredulity. Both Lang and Tucker claimed to have believed that Biko was shamming brain damage. Rayner (1987: 30–31).

an independent record of their torture. And the threat of multiple deaths during the 1989 hunger strikes forced the government to release nearly a thousand detainees.

The strategy of terror always fails in the long run. States need authority to govern, not just brute force. The very abuses of power undermine authority. But the strategy was doomed in the short run as well. State terror was directed at two targets. Anti-apartheid leaders were few and notorious. While suffering the worst torture, however, they remained steadfast, their stature enhanced by martyrdom. And they were sufficiently prominent that death or torture could backfire on the state. If the state detained them indefinitely they became teachers in prison, demands for their release fueled further protests (most notably about Mandela), and others took their places. Torture might have discouraged some rank-and-file, whose desire for ordinary lives competed with their commitment. But there were too many. And random state terror was as likely to politicize as to frighten. Interrogating Mkhuseli Jack, Maj. du Plessis revealed his determination to end the consumer boycott. Instead it expanded to East London and became almost total. Suspended for four months when detainees were released, its April 1986 resumption forced a hundred firms into bankruptcy, and new detentions prompted a third boycott in November.[102]

With the exception of Wendy Orr, medical "professionals" displayed callous indifference to their patients. Dr Lang, rightly afraid that Biko's skeleton was about to re-emerge from the closet, was obsessed with creating a paper record to save himself and his department. No doctor or nurse took any action to protect the hundreds of tortured prisoners. They did not remonstrate with the police or publicize their crimes and barely treated the victims. Entrusted with the well-being of the elderly, orphans, the mentally ill, and school children, they failed utterly to defend the equally powerless and even more vulnerable population of prisoners. More perplexing than the routine cowardice of doctors, however, was the singular courage of Wendy Orr.* Like David Bruce (see chapter four), she was a reluctant hero, who acted alone and initially rebuffed the embrace of anti-apartheid organizations. Because massive repression always depends on broad complicity, individual acts of defiance can temporarily destabilize—as illustrated by the defections of

---

*There was much critical commentary on the ethical obligations of medical professionals to protect citizens from state violence. Levin (1986); Selvan (1986); McQuoid-Mason (1986a; 1988).

But professional integrity carries a high cost in South Africa. In 1987 a hundred doctors at Soweto's Baragwanath Hospital wrote to the *South African Medical Journal* condemning the appalling inadequacy of care. When the Department of Hospital Services threatened to fire those who did not formally apologize, forty-nine promptly complied. The *Journal* published their retraction, admitting inaccuracies, blaming senior staff for abusing their trust, withdrawing derogatory remarks, and acknowledging improvement. The thirty-one unrepentant doctors (some had retired or changed jobs) got official letters of reprimand, with a warning that any repetition would be punished more severely. *Hansard* col. 5771 (Dr. M.S. Barnard, PFP) (9.11.87),

Rockman, Nofemela, and Coetzee. Such bravery is effective, however, only when supported collectively: conscientious objectors by the ECC, PE detainees by the unions. And both individualists later became politically active, partly as a result of involuntary celebrity. But the basic question remains unanswered: Why did Orr and the few conscientious objectors feel morally compelled when all other doctors and conscripts disregarded the ethical issues?

In most respects the legal system failed to protect Port Elizabeth Emergency detainees from torture.[103] Police ignored legal restrictions on their power. Procedures for internal review by the Prisons Department and SAP did not discourage torture, uncover it, or punish the perpetrators. Prisons Department officials admitted a policy of doing nothing about complaints. Either the police chain of command was disregarded by inferiors or it implicated superiors. The police continued to torture detainees after the application was granted, simply doing so before they were admitted to prison. Police responses to the interdict revealed contempt for the legal system. The law itself shielded police from meaningful scrutiny by indemnifying security forces from punishment for actions taken in "good faith." After being charged with two attempted murders, Butler Tungata was allowed to continue torturing detainees. Sgt. Faku allegedly was executed by colleagues fearful he would implicate them in the Goniwe murder.

Such behavior was unexceptional. Police killings, torture, arson, and burglary almost never were punished. Hit squads operated in secrecy, and kitskonstabels ran riot. The Appellate Division eviscerated judicial power to expose torture chambers.* Magistrates held "informal" inquests, denying families the right to testify or examine police witnesses; formal inquests exonerated the police. Even when inquests named the killers, Attorneys General refused to prosecute. Private prosecutions failed. Courts that had applied the "common purpose" doctrine in sentencing dozens to death for spontaneous mob action in Sharpeville and Upington would not apply it to the police conspiracy in the "Trojan Horse" killings. The State President aborted prosecutions of South West African police. Commissions of inquiry performed the whitewash for which they were designed. Even a responsible

---

903 (reply by R.P. Meyer, Deputy Minister of Constitutional Development, to M.S. Barnard, PFP) (4.12.88); WM 1 (1.15.88), 1 (3.4.88), 7 (4.15.88), 5 (4.22.88), 7 (5.13.88).

MASA initially responded to Wendy Orr's disclosure by refusing to get involved since she was not a member and the matter was sub judice. Rayner (1987: 77–78; 1990).

The medical professional association that opposed apartheid, NAMDA, was condemned by the Australian president of the World Medical Association as "a frankly political body allied to the ANC which is stated to be largely under communist control." Its PE office was burgled in 1988, despite a sophisticated alarm system, and raided by the police twice the next year. WM 9, 14 (4.15.88), 11 (9.9.88), 4 (5.12.89).

*Victims silenced by torture can "speak" only through their wounds (with the aid of an interpreter like Wendy Orr) or the instruments of their torture. Scarry (1985: 15).

investigation, like Goldstone's into the Sebokeng massacre, led nowhere. The few police convicted generally received light sentences, on the basis of evidence in mitigation that judges would have rejected summarily if offered on behalf of a black citizen. The rare policeman given significant jail time benefitted from the blanket indemnity or was released on "parole."

Yet legal procedures were not empty forms. Wendy Orr's application pierced the veil of secrecy surrounding police torture. The hierarchical structure of the security forces fostered compliance with the order, which was more effective than interdicts against Inkatha violence (see chapter six). Restraint was temporary and local, however, doing nothing to reduce the numerous deaths and innumerable injuries inflicted on demonstrators and arrestees.

The application revealed the enormous disparity in the power of South African voices. Black victims (sometimes surrogates for whites protected by their skin) have loudly denounced police violence for decades. They have little access to media or courts, however, and less credibility with white audiences.* Torture doubly silenced them: police turned them into ventriloquist's dummies, and whites disregarded their complaints—the archetypical nightmare of the unheard scream.[104] This application succeeded because it was brought to a white judge by white lawyers based on the affidavit of a white doctor and publicized in the white press. Judiciary and media reinforced each other: litigation created an uncensored space within which the press could criticize security forces; newspapers returned the favor by extolling the court as the last bastion against tyranny. The English press and its liberal white readers were starved for white heroes with whom they could identify—hence the idolization of Wendy Orr and the conscientious objectors. Complicity in apartheid made whites yearn desperately for one just white who could alleviate their racial guilt.[105] These heroes were easier to celebrate because they were individual rather than collective, ethical rather than political, universal rather than partisan. The logic of apartheid diverted attention from the anonymous black victims of torture to their white champion, just as the aggregate compensation paid the eighty-two plaintiffs was less than half the fees awarded their few white lawyers.

Chance played a significant role here as elsewhere: Wendy Orr did not want a career within the Department of Health; her sister knew a leading human rights advocate; re-opening the Biko case scared Dr. Lang into ordering Dr. Orr to copy the prisoners' medical records.

Although the police resisted the application, mere publication of the torture significantly curtailed their power. Hearing the interdict read out in prison helped detainees resist further torture. Police throughout the country knew the conspiracy of silence could fail. Sunlight was the real deterrent: not

---

*The judge disregarded overwhelming evidence by the Sharpeville Six that confessions had been coerced. See Diar (1990).

the threat of internal discipline or criminal prosecution (which either never began or ended in acquittal), not the fact of civil liability (which the state was prepared to pay as a trivial part of the cost of repression).* Although unable to neutralize power, law can expose brute force as illegitimate. And power without authority is ultimately impotent.

---

*A year after his death Biko's family accepted R65,000. Lawyers' Committee for Civil Rights (1985: 67–68); H. Suzman (1993: 223). Two years after the Langa massacre the 51 surviving victims and families of the deceased accepted R1.3 million. WM 1 (7.31.87). Government paid R1,209,780 for police assaults on 124 victims in 1986. *Hansard* col. 176 (reply by A.J. Vlok, Minister of Law and Order, to S.S. van der Merwe, PFP) (2.20.87). On civil actions against the police, see Dendy (1987; 1989); Gauntlett (1989).

CHAPTER 8

CENSORSHIP AND THE CLOSURE OF THE NEW NATION

> It is not our function to pass an opinion, favourable or unfavourable, on what the State President appeared to think necessary or upon the Minister's opinion. ... [C]ensorship is very like a guillotine, and there is very little use in growing honeysuckle over a guillotine. (Justice Curlewis)

South African censorship is more comprehensive and oppressive than that of any self-styled "democracy."[1] Government previews all movies, many of which it bans, and can exclude any foreign publication. The South African Broadcasting Corporation monopolizes television and, until recently, radio. The South African Press Association news service has been cautious in criticizing government. Outdoor meetings were banned after the 1976 Soweto uprising; all meetings required prior permission, which often was withheld. "Listed" people could not be quoted; "banned" people could not attend gatherings. Government even regulated t-shirt slogans and funeral orations.

Although the Afrikaans press supported government and most English papers restrained their criticism, the small alternative press has been bravely independent.[2] Government counterattacked in many ways, directing its most virulent hatred at the *New Nation* and black journalists generally.[3] This chapter explores the government's practice of and justifications for censorship, the journalistic and legal strategies of its targets, and the failure of courts to protect press freedom.

Repression Under the Emergency, 1985–87

Government used the declaration of the Emergency in July 1985 to clamp down even more tightly. The Supreme Court upheld a subpoena compelling a *Star* reporter to reveal his sources about a meeting of the Vaal Civic Association, which had initiated the rent strikes.[4] After the SADF raided Gaberone, government detained a Dutch reporter and seized his notes. It arrested CBS and BBC television crews. Police sjambokked reporters for Agence France Presse and London World Television News in a Cape township. The SADF detained three foreign correspondents filming Winnie Mandela in Soweto in September, confiscating their film and tape. Police searched a *Cape Times* reporter covering a rally later that month.[5] Foreign Affairs Minister Pik Botha condemned foreign television reporters for presenting a distorted picture of the violence; his Department urged local journalists working for foreign media to register as foreign correspondents, thereby submitting to regulation. The next week his Deputy Minister said "it is time the government reconsiders whether its hospitality should be extended to people who share in the organized lying." Government deported a *Newsweek* reporter and denied visas to foreign correspondents seeking to cover the visit of the EEC Foreign Ministers. It arrested eight journalists reporting unrest at the University of the Western Cape, promptly deporting one. In November it prohibited all pictures of unrest.[6] When *The Cape Times* published a lengthy interview with ANC President Oliver Tambo, government prosecuted editor Anthony Heard for quoting a listed person (although it eventually accepted a R300 fine from his publisher).[7] Government arrested London World Television News cameramen for filming the Moutse removal (see chapter eleven) and detained two *Sowetan* journalists following Chris Heunis's tour of East Rand townships.[8]

In the April 1986 Parliamentary debate over the budget of the Bureau for Information, Deputy Minister D.J.L. Nel declared that "South Africa is an open community." Government was "prepared to co-operate with the Press on the condition that it is a free and responsible Press." Foreign journalists, however, had no right to enter the country; "they are here as a result of the grace of the Government… on the condition that they report fairly." They must not "be part of propaganda vendettas." He condemned *Newsweek* for referring to the "White regime." "There is of course not a 'White regime' in this country." *Newsweek* was "inaccurate" in saying that "funerals are the Blacks 'only real forum for political expression'" because "the State President has invited Blacks to come and discuss the future of the country with him."[9] In the budget debate on Home Affairs three days later, the PFP observed that nearly half the visa applications by foreign journalists had been rejected. The Minister warned: "I will not hesitate for one moment to withdraw the residence or work permits of foreign journalists who misbehave. I mean it in the strong sense." Although a "large section" of the press was observing the

Media Council code by exercising "due care and responsibility" in reporting "subjects that may cause [racial] enmity" and in "the presentation of brutality, violence, and atrocities," he criticized "the continually negative reporting in certain newspapers." The government expected "balanced presentation; which shies away from polarisation."[10]

That month a magistrate fined *Eastern Province Herald* reporter Juliette Saunders R100 for violating the Police Act because he found errors in two paragraphs of a 1,300-word eyewitness account of security forces using sjamboks, teargas, and rubber bullets on mourners. The following month Justice van Dijkhorst, presiding in the Delmas treason trial (see chapter nine), held a *Weekly Mail* editor and a reporter in contempt for three articles erroneously describing certain notes as "judge's notes" (for which they had apologized). Nearly two years later the Appellate Division upheld their fines.[11] In June the government banned a *Newsweek* edition and expelled its South African bureau chief. At least nine journalists were in detention.[12] Law and Order Minister Louis le Grange initiated the second Emergency by confiscating the *Weekly Mail*, although the Grahamstown Supreme Court later awarded it damages.[13] Bureau of Information director David Stewart told a news conference, "[W]e are not kidding, we will not hesitate to take action" and advised reporters to consult lawyers about the new law. Journalists should not call the government a "white minority regime" because the Cabinet included two non-whites (without portfolio). "Journalists who use this factually incorrect approach will place their position in South Africa in jeopardy."[14] The Deputy Information Minister Louis Nel condemned as "subversive" and thus illegal Lord Acton's famous dictum that "power tends to corrupt and absolute power corrupts absolutely."[15]

The State President summoned the heads of the four large media companies to meet him on November 28. Two months later he informed Parliament he had told them: "Listen, we cannot carry on this way. Wittingly or unwittingly the hand of a diabolical enemy is being strengthened." He had "brought peace" to black townships by banning foreign television cameras. Although he offered to exempt the established papers from the Emergency regulations if the National Press Union would "discipline itself," they declined.[16] In the subsequent debate over the PFP no-confidence motion the party deplored the fact that the South African press was no longer "relatively free" compared to that of other African countries. Government was now manipulating the news.[17]

In January 1986 the South African Catholic Bishops' Conference had launched the biweekly *New Nation*. Its editor, Zwelakhe Sisulu, son of Rivonia trialist and Robben Island life-prisoner Walter and UDF patron Albertina, had been the first president of the Writers' Association of South Africa and a Harvard Niemann fellow. Less than six months later he was detained after giving the keynote address to the National Education Crisis Committee. The paper increased its circulation from a target of 20,000 to 50,000 by December and started weekly publication in 1987. Acting editor

Gabu Tugwana remembered State President P.W. Botha's fury when he met with the SACBC.

> He said that if they want to play any positive role in this country they should do something about the *New Nation* newspaper. Charity begins at home. That newspaper is not worthy of any church belief. It is nothing but communism. ... The examples [he offered] were the carrying out of women's rights... the claim of labor rights and the struggle for recognition, as well as having comments about the communist leadership organizations.[18]

Government boldly confronted threats to public order. After the Johannesburg cabaret show "Famous Dead Man" had run for eight weeks, Home Affairs Minister Stoffel Botha urgently ordered a Publications Committee review, which found it "undesirable" (without seeing it) because "Dr Verwoerd [had been] chosen as a symbol of a large section of the Republic in an attempt to insult and degrade them." Three plainclothes police threatened the proprietor and actors with arrest and dispersed the audience. After they stopped performing the actors received telephone threats and were fired from their daytime jobs selling mock-tile roofs to southern suburbanites.[19] A Committee also banned the children's picture book "Two Dogs and Freedom" on the testimony of John Horack, formerly morning group manager of South African Associated Newspapers and now a major in the security police (for whom he had worked while employed by the *Sunday Times*). He noted that the book had been produced at The Open School, "a system of alternate education which endeavoured to break down society's existing structures and values and bring in a new order." It portrayed township children as a "suppressed group" and fostered hostility toward the security forces, seeking to radicalize the situation by promoting a White/Black confrontation. The title expressed township residents' feelings that they were treated like dogs. (In fact, it was a young boy's caption for his picture: "When I am old I would like to have a wife and two children, a boy and a girl, and a big house and two dogs and freedom. My friends and I would like to meet together and talk.") Horack acknowledged that he had no training in psychology or communciations and had urged the Directorate of Publications to ban some eighty publications that year. The Publications Appeal Board concluded that Horack's "frankness" did not constitute "sufficient evidence of expertise in the field of media-influence on emotions" and questioned his objectivity. Whereas the Committee viewed the likely readership as black school children, the PAB thought it was adults, some of whom would find it moving and optimistic, while others would see it as exaggerated and one-sided. It overturned the ban.[20]

At the end of 1986 the government consolidated its censorship laws, broadly proscribing "subversive statements" and descriptions of detentions, security actions, deployment, and technology.[21] Even the establishment

National Press Union was critical, although it realized "that South Africa is being subjected to a many-pronged but well co-ordinated revolutionary onslaught... [and accepted] the need to do everything in our power to avoid giving support and encouragement to those seeking revolutionary change by overt as well as covert means."[22] It opened negotiations with the Cabinet about forms of self-discipline that would exempt its members from censorship, but the State President cancelled the February 1987 meeting. Nasionale Pers managing director Ton Vosloo criticized the English press's failure to police itself and its employment of "journalists who have been punished in court for deeds of subversion and terrorism" (presumably a reference to Zwelakhe Sisulu).

On January 7 eleven newspapers carried full-page advertisements asking government to unban the ANC. Within a day Police Commissioner P.J. Coetzee prohibited publications from explaining the policies of banned organizations. The Argus and Saan newspapers immediately filed an urgent application for an interdict. Three weeks later Justice H. Daniels of the Rand Supreme Court, disregarding legislation ousting courts from reviewing Emergency regulations, found that the Police Commissioner lacked the power to make orders for the entire country. By midnight Law and Order Minister Adriaan Vlok issued regulations defining a new category of illegal subversive statement—encouraging support for unlawful organizations—and the State President had empowered the Police Commissioner to prohibit any publication in the interest of public safety. The next day the *Weekly Mail* carried the ad on its front page, but the Police Commissioner soon outlawed any advertisement "defending, praising, or endeavouring to justify any of these organisations' campaigns, projects, or actions." The UDF and the Release Mandela Campaign, which had dropped their earlier challenge in favor of the *Saan/Argus* lawsuit, sought an interdict against the new regulations. The State President directed Cape Judge President Munnik to investigate who had paid for the offending advertisement. He reported in April, criticizing First National Bank president Chris Ball for allowing an overdraft by attorney Krish Naidoo; the R100,000 cost was paid by businessman Yusuf Surtee. In September the Pietermaritzburg Supreme Court invalidated some of the regulations (notably the Police Commissioner's power to gazette new definitions of subversive statement) but upheld others (including the definitions of unrest and security action).[23]

Courts sometimes offered greater protection to the accused. A magistrate acquitted *Cape Times* deputy news editor Tony Weaver of violating the Police Act by giving a BBC interview, in which he described a police killing of seven alleged ANC guerrillas. It was the first time a local journalist had been charged for material published abroad. Weaver had reasonable grounds to believe what he had written—a story that the magistrate himself found more credible than the state's version.[24] When the *Eastern Province Herald* editor-in-chief and a reporter were charged under the Police Act for describing a

1985 confrontation in Lingelihle township, Cradock, they invoked a "gentle-man's agreement" allowing an NPU member to publish critical accounts if it gave the police "ample and fair opportunity" to comment. Although the SAP press liaison officer denied any agreement, the defense offered two sets of NPU minutes detailing its content. The magistrate convicted them anyhow, finding some statements untrue and reading the agreement to require simul-taneous publication of the police version.[25] Courts would not release journalists detained under the Emergency regulations.[26]

The alternative press continued to suffer disproportionately. Government banned the first two issues of *Cosatu News* (circulation 200,000) and ordered *SASPU National* and *Free Azania* to show censors issues before dissemina-tion (fourteen issues of the South African Student Publications Union paper had been banned in its first five years). Police detained and then banned the first two *SASPU National* editors and were detaining other employees; the editorial office had been destroyed by fire soon after the second Emergency. In March firebombs caused R20,000 damage to the office of Ravan Press. Government banned two February 1987 issues of the *New Nation*.[27] *Saamstaan* (Stand Together), launched in Oudtshoorn in 1983, published six issues in 1984. At the end of the year the government charged employ-ees Derek Jackson and Humphrey Joseph with attending an illegal gathering, although they were acquitted eleven months later. In 1985 its offices were burned three times. In September government detained Jackson, Joseph, and treasurer Louis Noemdoe under ISA §29. They were acquitted of subversion in February 1986. The next day government charged Joseph under the Police Act; he was found guilty in May 1987 for stating that police had shot three children when they had only shot two. The Department of National Health and Population Development was investi-gating the paper's foreign financing.[28]

Governments curtailed criticism in other ways. The bi-weekly Zulu-lan-guage *Ilanga* sold 105,000 copies and reached over 1.2 million readers. In April 1987 threats forced three reporters who had written about KwaZulu government corruption to flee with their families. Three days later Natal Newspapers sold *Ilanga* to Inkatha, whose general secretary, Oscar Dhlomo, became its managing director. When the South African Society of Journalists chapel said many of the twenty editorial staff opposed party ownership, feared for their lives, and wanted to move to another Argus paper, the Natal Newspaper managing director told them to resign. All staff, even Inkatha supporters, stopped work, leaving KwaZulu employees to produce the first edition. Buthelezi attacked the strikers, calling the chapel father the ANC's "fetch and carry boy."[29]

Although government had broad powers over the media, as this incom-plete synopsis demonstrates, it promulgated an even more restrictive regime on June 11, the beginning of the third year of the Emergency.[30] This prohib-ited publication of information about security forces or any restricted gathering, boycott, illegal organization, people's court, restricted person, or detainee, any blank space, any subversive statement, including anything discrediting compulsory military service, and anything encouraging people to

participate in an illegal gathering or attack the security forces,

oppose any member of the Cabinet of the Republic or of a homeland or any member of the security forces,

take part in a boycott against a business, product, or school,

engage in civil disobedience by refusing to obey any law [such as conscription] or pay for rent or services,

stay away from work,

attend any restricted gathering,

join or support any unlawful organization or take part in or support the organization's campaigns,

participate in people's courts,

commit any other act named by the Commissioner of Police in the Government Gazette.

The Home Affairs Minister and Commissioner of Police could seize any publication violating these regulations; and for the first time the Minister could ban it for three months if "necessary in the interest of the safety of the public, the maintenance of public order, or the termination of the state of emergency." Before doing so he had to gazette a warning, find a subsequent issue in violation of the regulations, notify the publisher he was contemplating suspension and state his grounds, and give an opportunity to reply. Violation was punishable by a R20,000 fine and ten years imprisonment.

Two months later in a Parliamentary debate over the State President's budget, he accused the "alternative media" of "blatant distortion and stage-setting," "misrepresentation and the creation of negative perceptions." They "unashamedly support the leftist and radical groups." They engaged in "conspicuous omission of positive event," "repeated use... of the most negative examples on record," "careful selection of... material which benefit leftist and radical organizations," "selective application of facts," and "the calculated use of editorials... to propagate a leftist and radical message." Some newspapers "were out to urge the spirit of revolution along." He concluded his defense of government policies, "with all due respect and apologies to the late Sir Winston Churchill," by declaring: "Never in the history of a country did so few do so much for so many without acknowledgment by the international community."[31] Home Affairs Minister Stoffel Botha denounced the alternative media for showing "complete contempt for the hallowed Press values" and "fuelling a revolutionary climate."[32] Within days he promulgated further regulations allowing him to suspend a daily newspaper on the basis of six issues, a weekly on three, and other publications on two. He also added as grounds material

> promoting or fanning revolution or uprisings or other acts aimed at the overthrow of the Government,
>
> promoting, fanning, or sparking unrest or the breaking down of public order,
>
> stirring up feelings of hatred toward a local authority, security force, or any population group,
>
> promoting the public image or esteem or any unlawful organization.

His opinion did not have to be based on anything outside the publication. Both sets of regulations were made retroactive.[33]

The Minister targeted the "revolution-serving media." "[I]n order to be successful on the violent level, revolutionaries rely on the media... to mobilise the masses." The ANC had declared that "the press is one of those weapons we are using in the struggle against apartheid." "The critical point in the promotion of revolution lies in... praising its leaders, its flag and other symbols... dealing with the revolutionary organisations and their symbols in an ennobling and propagandistic way." "The existing order is condemned as being repugnant.... A whole string of negative appellations are associated with the Government and its leaders." Enforcement of the regulations, however, would aim "at the optimum maintenance of democratic practices." "The rules of natural justice are duly taken into consideration. The *audi alteram partem* rule... is respected. A comprehensive administrative process is being created." He and his office "will be available at all times for discussions." Because he expected compliance by "the organised conventional media," the regulations were designed for "the unconventional revolution-supportive Press." Freedom of the press was not absolute, as even the U.S. Supreme Court had held. The South African "system of publications control is one of the best in the world."[34] The PFP rejected the Government's " 'commitment' to Press freedom with contempt." The "State President has shown signs of having reached the stage at which he can actually no longer stand criticism, of whatever nature." Government was "once again bypassing the courts of our country, allowing of [sic] a politically motivated subjective ministerial opinion to hold the power of life and death over the Press in a manner in total conflict with natural justice." A Nationalist replied with a demand for an investigation of the funding of the "revolution-supportive Press and licensing or registration of news agencies and mechanisms "to bring freelance journalists under control."[35]

Several months later Stoffel Botha conceded that "in normal circumstances," it was better for courts to review offensive material.

But we are not living in normal circumstances.... Since 1985 we have experienced severe uprisings; we have experienced a sustained propaganda campaign. ...

[O]ur courts will be overcrowded if we follow this particular procedure. ... [T]he very reason why the legal system is such a sound one, makes it also a very drawn-out system.... And that will not meet the situation which the government has to face.[36]

Deputy Information Minister Stoffel van der Merwe distinguished between the "promotive" and "reportive" media.[37]

Well, it is of course a fact, not policy but a fact, that if one would take each of those cases to court it would mean long drawn-out court cases. Because, in fact, it is a very fine distinction and in fact the law against which the courts will have to test it is not actually so refined to be that very sharp cutting instrument. ... [T]herefore it will in fact overburden the court system because one must bear in mind that the court system is created and maintained for the ordinary run-of-the-mill type of cases that it has to handle....[38]

In a contemporaneous interview Stoffel Botha claimed to be a "media man" because he had been legal adviser to the Afrikaans Pers in the 1960s.[39] "I know exactly the way media people think, and I have much sympathy for the difficult task they perform." Although it pained him to wield such powers—"As a lawyer I do not like it, as a media man I do not like it"—they were necessary.

South Africa's developing people do not share a tradition of representative democracy... such people are also exceedingly vulnerable to simplistic ideology, agitation, inflammatory speech and pamphleteering. Critics of the government conveniently forget that most of the countries of today's industrialised West were themselves most undemocratic in their earlier development. ... [T]he people who wish premature full democracy and all its freedoms upon the country, must be considered to be either naive, or they must have other motives. The leftist radicals want a total takeover of power....

Many other countries had "similar rules and regulations. But nevertheless we have more democracy here than, for example, Zimbabwe...we know what the situation is in Africa."

That is not to say that the government does not believe in Press freedom. The fact is, it does. And those who doubt that commitment need only read the opposition newspapers to see how government is constantly under attack and endlessly criticised for almost every deed.

The media regulations were "part of our efforts to stabilise the situation so that we can carry on with our reform programme."

Asked why Zwelakhe Sisulu had been detained for over a year, he replied "Every country has a set of laws, whether you like them or not. ... I am sure that very careful consideration has been given to his case." "[I]n any profession, there are restrictions on the way people may practise. A lawyer also has to act within certain confines, so does a doctor, and so forth."

The media was forbidden to report on township unrest because "it has been found that newspaper reporting, and particularly television reporting, does not simply involve reporting on events, but in fact stimulates the unrest situation." "[T]he media have become more than observers of the scene. They have become participants, as someone said…'on the great battlefields of perceptions where modern conflicts rage as much as they do in steamy jungles or shantytowns.' They are the field commanders."

> The new regulations included procedural safeguards. ... [T]he publisher is given the opportunity to make representations and even though my decision is not subject to appeal, a court can still review any decision I make if I fail to apply my mind to the matter or act without *bona fides* or if I do not follow correct procedures. ... I cannot merely say: "*New Nation*, I dislike you; I now close you down." I must indicate right from the start to the publisher that "that article, and your next one, and your next one incited violent action." ... If a particular article did not incite violence, and I based my decision on such an article, then he can take me to court....

Although he could not "at this stage" define objectionable articles, he stressed the importance of "a balanced view."

> *Interviewer:* If I interviewed Oliver Tambo, if I critically examined him on such issues as Press freedom under another government, and I then went to the State President for his comments and I wrote a balanced story, would that be acceptable?
>
> *Botha:* No, it will not be. It will elevate Tambo to a status he doesn't deserve.

He concluded with paternalistic admonitions.

> Some journalists and editors tend to lay claim to the sole right to prescribe what people may read and what not, even if it favours self-acknowledged revolutionaries. They are quick to voice the people's right to know. Surely, if the alleged right to know rests with the readers, they should have a say in what is not printed. This would mean a representative readers' body in every editorial office. Democracy cannot thrive without a responsible Press. However, Press freedom must be earned by an honest Press.

> Those sections who do not earn it must be curbed. In present circumstances, only government is capable of deciding on and enforcing the ncessary curbs.

Botha used *The Star*'s October 9 centennial celebrations as a third occasion to justify censorship.

> [T]he Government and the press are not ends in themselves—they both have to serve people. Both of them are in positions of power. ...
>
> I was asked to reflect on the "line" between government interest and public interest and the question of whom [sic] should draw it. This theme presupposes that there is a difference of conflict between government and public interest. That however, is not necessarily the case. When a government acts in the interest of the state in the context of ensuring the state's existence for the common good, then the interest of government and the public is indivisible. ...
>
> The press's role as one of the watchdogs is therefore a qualified one. It must "watch" how the Government governs, but in doing so, it must accept government's right to govern in the first place.

He located South Africa's "social responsibility concept" of freedom of expression between the "extremes" of "totalitarian control over the media, such as behind the Iron Curtain and in many African countries" and the "'all or nothing' liberal press approach." "We all seem to agree, however, that freedom of expression—freedom of the press—cannot be absolute." The Media Council created by the establishment press in the early 1980s had promulgated a Code of Conduct mandating "due care and responsibility" with respect to "matters that may detrimentally affect the peace and good order, the safety and defence of the Republic and its people; the presentation of brutality, violence and atrocities." But when government asked "that the Press should effectively implement its Code of Conduct..this was eventually declined." He concluded ominously, "[I]f I have failed to convey to you a perception of there being substance in South Africa's case, that will not deviate me from my course and my obligation to my country."

The Black Sash demonstrated against the regulations, declaring: "The press is threatened, the universities are threatened, the Government's own severely flawed constitution is threatened, the funding of the opposition organisations is threatened, the organisations themselves are threatened and we seem to be sinking into a dark age of ignorance and mailed fist control." The SACBC agreed.

> The Government, which is running scared, is fitting larger and tighter blinkers over the eyes of the white electorate to shield them from the ugly realities of South Africa today. ... [T]he new

measures will prevent the oppressed from making their voice heard as they cry out against the injustice and inhumanity to which they are subjected by the structures and agents of the apartheid system.

The U.S. Embassy was "saddened to see that the South African Government does not trust its own citizens with information about the happenings in their country. We are sorry to note the action further removes South Africa from the code of Western values to which it professes to adhere." The International Press Institute in London called the regulations "a slap in the face" of free speech and "a total violation of human rights." Even the South African Media Council chairman acknowledged they would have "an additional inhibiting effect on the free flow of information reaching the public," while welcoming the "safeguards against arbitrary banning" and the invitation to discuss.[40]

In early September Stoffel Botha admonished thirty-one editors not to "praise the existence of an extra-parliamentary committee, say they are doing a good job and are better... [or] praise the illegal organisation that is part of the revolutionary process." He would not allow "the free play of revolution-mongering." He distinguished between "criticism which is fully justified against existing government and existing order" and "other criticism which entails the overthrow of the existing order by way of violence." Inkatha exemplified the former and the ANC the latter. However, he could not define what was outlawed "by way of describing it in legislation." Instead he had created a Directorate of Media Relations headed by Andries Engelbrecht, who had an M.A. degree in "human motivation" from the University of Pretoria. It would make "scientific evaluations" advised by a panel of experts; he would not name them but promised that "they will not be fly-by-night and prejudiced experts." His actions would be "reviewable" by the courts, which could overturn them if he acted in bad faith.[41]

Engelbrecht's staff of five to ten would be mostly lawyers, although he planned to add sociologists, psychologists, and communications and journalism specialists. Although discretion was unavoidable "the whole idea is to give as objective a view as possible." Rather than being a "super censor" he aimed at "establishing good media relations."[42]

> If anybody thinks that South Africa has developed to that extent of intellectual development whereby we can say the majority of people in South Africa are so informed that we can afford the luxury of absolute freedom of the press, then they should look again at the realities.

> South Africa is a country where you have a very small input of Western values, but by and large the Third World is with us. They are among us and live with us.

Those [journalists] dedicated to and qualified for their mission and profession now have to suffer a measure of statutory control...on account of the hijackers of the journalistic profession or the newspaper method for their partisan objectives; the protagonists of subversive propaganda; the manipulators of copy, headings, captions and camera material; the instigators and promoters of a revolutionary climate by publicising acts of terrorism, intimidations by stage managing if they can't get their material any other way, biased highlighting and misinformation; by bias and band wagoneering—in short, the abuse of communication in order to further their own digressive views or the views of their misguided mentors.

... If I read of intimidation I feel intimidated as well.

... No government can be expected to accept that freedom of speech goes that far that freedom of speech be totally ruined by the misuse of freedom of speech.

The emergency regulations... proved to be insufficient to curtail the subversive propaganda... [because of] the diversity and scope of the manifestations of relevant printed propaganda and publicity and the frequency of volume of same. Propaganda and publicity per se cannot be adequately dealt with in terms of definitive criminal law and criminal procedures during a state of emergency.

...

Finally it is [the Minister's] decision, and his decision alone. If the Minister decides to take action, it is done in the prescribed manner.[43]

The Citizen predictably applauded: "There had been scientific studies which enabled one to determine whether criticism was permissible or whether it was part of a multifaceted plan to overthrow the government by force and to encourage violence."[44] But the first appointments to the advisory panel did not inspire confidence in science: Dr. Isaak de Vries (a Rand Afrikaans University political scientist who had testified for the state in twenty political trials), Attie Tredoux (Botha's chief legal adviser), and Koos de Vries (a state legal adviser).[45]

While the government was creating and justifying this new regulatory structure, it continued to use the old. Publications Committees banned two issues of *South* in July and August and a third *New Nation* issue in August.[46] But the PAB demonstrated independence by reversing the *South* decision— one reason why Stoffel Botha wanted to bypass it. The "cumulative effect" of a publication, the PAB said, had to be documented in detail. "Support for the objects of the ANC" meant more than a "brief biographical sketch of Nelson

Mandela," calling a terrorist a guerrilla, seeking clemency for thirty-two convicts, or describing the Dakar meeting between South African businessmen and ANC officials. Writers could praise the Freedom Charter. Exposition of the views of Swapo's Sam Nujoma was not "a scarcely disguised call to terrorism and violence." "[M]uch as this newspaper is one-sided, biased and would be regarded by many as deplorable journalism," the Board held, "it can, nevertheless, not be concluded to be prejudicial to the safety of the State...."[47] It reversed the ban of an issue of the English-literacy journal *Learn and Teach* because its summary of a speech in mitigation of a convicted terrorist "does not seek to eulogize or improve the image of the ANC." "In interpreting a publication, the adjudicator must be careful not to draw the most sinister inferences from the articles...."[48] Yet the PAB upheld bans on two UDF journals, a black power journal, and a union journal, and limited another to bona fide bookshops and lending libraries.[49]

Closing the <u>New Nation</u>

The new Directorate of Media Relations lost no time in ordering *South*, *Work in Progress*, the *Weekly Mail*, *Learn and Teach*, and *Upbeat* to send it free copies.[50] On October 1 Stoffel Botha informed the *New Nation* he had found that three recent issues represented "systematic and repeated publishing of matter which has or is calculated to have one or more of the effects contemplated in regulation 7A(1)," whose language he quoted at length. He was considering issuing a formal warning and gave the paper two weeks to reply. The threat elicited surprisingly little media comment.[51] Four years later the then acting editor Gabu Tugwana recollected the paper's response.

> We knew that they were going to close us but we were determined to make it as difficult as possible. We had taken many precautions. For instance, our lawyers will tell you that all the stories that went into our paper—be they concerned with culture, sport, or news—they were extremely careful. They had to look at the stories and show that we are not breaking any principle in the laws of the day. ... [T]hey would come back to us and say: look, we know you feel very strong about this story but we think there is trouble or would create problems. And half the time we disputed with them and we would say we want to take a chance. Therefore you as lawyers can tell us how we can reduce the risk. ... [W]e saw ourselves as a bridge where people can vent out their frustration, where they can control frustration and expose it so the government can have an opportunity to address these issues. ... [After the first notice] we went out of our way to try and please the government. If we had the facts we double checked them.

Soon thereafter Botha issued similar notices to the *Sowetan, South, Work in Progress, Die Stem* (a right-wing journal), and the *Weekly Mail. South* editor Rashid Seria denounced the charges as "ludicrous to say the least" but submitted a thirty-eight-page response.[52] *Work in Progress* replied that publication was unpredictable, its readership small, intellectual, and skeptical, and its content "highly theoretical and analytical." Botha warned the *Sowetan* for quoting an ANC leader condemning necklacing because it "tends to legitimse a revolutionary leader." *The Star* asked rhetorically: "Must one deduce that the Minister would have been quite happy had the paper quoted the ANC in *support* of such acts?"[53] But perhaps because the *Sowetan* was owned by Argus (one of the two largest English newspaper groups), had a wide circulation, and supported black consciousness rather than the UDF and ANC, Botha met with its editors and lawyers and took no further action. Robert van Tonder, leader of the Boerestaat Beweging and editor of *Die Stem*, was contemptuous: "I'm not wasting my time with the government. If they come with such silly objections it shows they have ulterior motives." He refused to make representations because the government "appoints their own judges and they tell them beforehand what to decide."[54]

A day before the deadline to reply Bishop Reginald Orsmond issued a placatory statement on behalf of the SACBC. "The *New Nation* does not have any sinister aims of fomenting revolution or encouraging uprising or in any way threatening public safety."[55] The eighty-eight-page reply reiterated that "*New Nation* is completely committed to a peaceful resolution of the conflict which besets South Africa" and sought a personal meeting. The applicant made several legal arguments. The Minister had not properly exercised his judgment. "No person honestly applying his mind to the matter could conceivably have come to the conclusion that the *New Nation* falls foul of the regulations." In assessing the publication's actual or probable effect, he had to consider how its readership would understand it. The Minister had "not questioned the veracity of a single article." The regulations were excessively vague. The first issue cited appeared before the regulations were promulgated.

The paper invoked leading South African cases upholding free speech. In the 1930s *Usembenzi* had been acquitted of crimen laesae venerationis after denouncing King George as "the figurehead of the English and Boer Imperialists... [who] are robbing and exploiting the poor people and workers of South Africa.... Do not kiss the boot that kicks you."[56] In 1950 government lost two prosecutions for language far more inflammatory than anything in the *New Nation*. A speaker at an ANC meeting had declared: "White civilisation is bound to go down—that is a certainty. ... The day will come when we will simply defy the discriminating laws of the land... and those unfortunate enough to have White skins will suffer...."[57] A cartoon ridiculing Prime Minister Malan showed a European "gripping the throat of a native; in his right hand, which is raised high in the act of striking, there is a heavy blunt instrument.... Immediately to the rear of the European there is the prone figure of a native who has either been killed or rendered insensible."[58] In 1964 the Appellate Division acquitted a speaker who incited 200 Indians to defy the Group Areas Act: "Fascists know no respect for any moral standards recognised in the civilised world. ... The nationalists must be made aware of the fact that the attack against these people is an attack against the Indian people as a whole and will be met by the organised strength of the entire community."[59]

Nearly a month after this reply Botha wrote the *New Nation's* attorneys that "your clients did not appreciate the true import of regulation 7A." The issue was "systematic or repeated" publication of objectionable matter. "Your clients, however, dealt with the matter on the basis of a separate response in respect of each individual article...." Because of the "gravity of the matter" he was giving them two weeks for a further reply.[60] To assist them he offered a "prima facie evaluation" of the offending material, reminding them that "the articles referred to above should be read in conjunction with one another and regard should be had to the cumulative effect...." The following is a synopsis of the articles, the paper's justification, Botha's evaluation, and the paper's reply.

1. An advertisement by the Release Mandela Campaign, UDF, COSATU, and SAYCO calling for the release of long-term political prisoners and prisoner-of-war status for Umkhonto we Sizwe combatants and quoting the Freedom Charter.

New Nation justification. "The matter contained in this advertisement is part and parcel of the general political debate for at least the past five years." Other politicians and newspapers had made similar proposals.[61] The Freedom Charter was lawful, and calls to unban the ANC "could hardly be thought to be subversive of state security."

Botha's evaluation. The article promotes the public image of the ANC and PAC and calls central figures "our leaders." It "brings into disrepute the existing judicial order which is a mainstay of the public order" by calling such people "patriots" and claiming prisoner-of-war status for them, suggesting that death sentences were prompted by mere "political opposition" rather than "violent capital offences."

New Nation reply. Many Afrikaner leaders were associated with "organisations that regarded violence as a means to their political ends." Opinion polls show that many South Africans regard Mandela as their leader.[62] The regulations do not proscribe statements bringing the judiciary into disrepute.

2. A photograph of thirty-two people on death row with the caption "Save These 32 Patriots" and call for an end to hanging political prisoners.

New Nation justification. There had been numerous publicized calls for clemency.[63] Photographs arguably were not covered by the regulations.

Botha's evaluation. The photograph was "part of the systematic or repeated attempts... to fan revolution or uprising."

New Nation reply. "This does not appear from the photo or the caption." Furthermore, "it is a well documented fact that the death penalty...generates deep emotional reactions...."

3. A subsequent report on "'Save the 32' launched in W Cape."

New Nation justification. "The report is purely factual and unemotional."

4. A poem entitled "To My Son," including the lines "This son's nose will be/Baptised by the sweet/Smell of teargas/The healthy odour of Gunpowder, Ai! the/Caress of the sjambok."

New Nation justification. "We cannot believe that the security of the South African state is so fragile as to be incapable of tolerating a poem of this nature."

Botha's evaluation. "[P]eople who have partaken in resistance are inter alia depicted as 'selfless sons of the soil'; and a further attempt is made to stir up or foment feelings of hatred toward security forces...."

New Nation reply. "We submit, with respect, that the Minister's interpretation is exaggerated and hypersensitive and not borne out by the text."

5. A long report on a conference of the National Education Crisis Committee, detailing government closure of schools and the NECC success in reopening some.

New Nation justification. The article is "merely a restatement of historical and notorious fact." No one could be "ignorant of the problems associated with black education," which is "historically unequal." "To suggest that the article could conceivably have or be calculated to have the effect of promoting the public image or esteem of the ANC borders on bad faith." The minister "has utterly misconceived the nature of his powers...."

Botha's evaluation. The article gives "credit to the ANC's attitude to education." References to and photographs of the Soweto uprising tend "to create the perception that breaking down of the public order is necessary to achieve these goals."

New Nation reply. The "mere statement of historical fact" could not "threaten public safety" or else it would be impossible to write history. The photograph was previously published.

6. A call by the Natal Student Congress to "Lift ban on COSAS," alleging that there still were "detentions, harassment of progressive organisations and deaths of students and community leaders by vigilante hit squads, while the SADF is still occupying our schools." It urged implementation of the Freedom Charter.

New Nation justification. The report was factual. NASCO used "the rhetoric of politics. A prediction of further violence should not be confused with a threat or incitement to violence." It was "preposterous" to suggest that the article could foment hostility to the SADF.

Botha's evaluation. "A categoric statement is published that *no peace* will exist until certain conditions are met...." The reference to "the *occupation* of schools by the SADF...seems to be an attempt to stir up or foment feelings of hatred...." It also promotes the image of COSAS, an unlawful organization.

New Nation reply. Many lawful organizations have made similar statements. SADF occupation of schools has been much debated in Parliament.

7. "Crazed 'Omie' Is a Reality of SA," a review of Ian Fraser's one-man show "Bring me Gandhi," about a racist brute. The reviewer says "there are such omies all over the country."

New Nation justification. "We are at a loss to see" how the review could violate the regulations. It "warns of the dangers of racial intolerance." A similar review appeared in a pro-government paper.[64]

Botha's evaluation. "The 'omie' is linked to the SAP having the effect of stirring up or fomenting hatred towards a security force."

New Nation reply. "[T]he play is a piece of fiction…no reasonable person could conceivably suggest that a review of a fictitious work could have the effect of fomenting hostility…." It was "quite incongruous" to object to the review when the play itself was permitted.

8. "Victory for Potwa," describing pay raises ending a one-month strike by the Post & Telecommunication Workers Association.

Botha's objection. An international union condemned police action.

New Nation justification. "[T]he only reference to the police is at the very end of the article…." Other papers covered the strike.[65]

9. "Arsonists strike at UDF offices" and SAAWU.

Botha's objection. A SAAWU official said he did not plan to report the incident to the police because "nothing ever happens."

New Nation justification. It described efficient police work. The "lack of confidence" by the SAAWU official "cannot be elevated into a statement which has the effect of fomenting hostility…."

10. "Cosatu offices broken into."

Botha's objection. COSATU said "we can expect no protection from the authorities."

New Nation justification. The article "amounts to nothing more than the view of an individual."

11. "New fear grips Hambanathi" about the recurrence of violence if the government transferred the township to KwaZulu.

Botha's objection. A township spokesman said police criticized and took action against street committees. "This is why we informed the council and police about our plan. When you mention street and area committees, the police see red and think it's the M-plan. We'll give the defence units a different name, but we'll use the same tactics we used in the past."

New Nation justification. The article described "cooperation with the police."

Botha's evaluation of articles 8-11. They stir up or foment hatred or hostility toward the SAP and contain "derogative or negative statements with regard to the Police."

New Nation reply. "It is invalid to suggest" that such statements can have that effect. If they did, nothing could be published "which reflects 'negatively' on the activities of the SAP regardless of the truth of such statements."

12. An advertisement by West German Catholic Services urging an end to detention, with the epigraph "The Lord does not forget His people in Prison."

Botha's evaluation. The exhortation that government should "abolish torture throughout the country" "infers" its existence.

New Nation reply. The Minister was displaying unwarranted "hypersensitivity." "It is difficult to believe that the call for the abolition of torture can be thought to constitute the fomentation of hostility towards the perpetrators of such torture." The advertisement was aimed at detention, not the security forces. Other papers had reported torture allegations.[66]

13. "Youth: 'Church is bogged down by tradition.'"

Botha's evaluation. Rev. Joseph Tshawane said "detentions, harassment and imprisonment of young people have become the order of the day in South Africa."

New Nation reply. Young people are detained and imprisoned. "[W]hile these violations of human rights continue in South Africa there will always be allegations of torture...." Botha appeared to claim "that one may only report on security force actions... insofar as they reflect positively on those institutions. This could scarcely have been the intention of the legislature."

14. "'Church's duty to oppose system in SA.'"

Botha's evaluation. Rev. Frank Chikane, South African Conference of Churches general secretary, referred to "victims of the unjust system," which Defence Minister Malan's forces were defending.

New Nation reply. "That the SADF is perceived by many to be defending the apartheid system is surely a matter of historical record." The article reflects "the views of an individual... [which] are by no means controversial and have been articulated in many guises by a wide variety of people."

15. A photograph of Oliver Tambo announcing the opening of an ANC office in Nairobi.

New Nation justification. It was "inconceivable that the Minister could honestly have concluded" that publishing a photo promoted the ANC's image. The practice was "well established in all countries," and other papers had done so.[67]

16. "ANC women hold major conference" about past and future meetings, radio broadcasts, and calls for action.

New Nation justification. The Minister's assumption "that the mere mention of the ANC, its activities or office-bearers" could promote its public image "is self-evidently incorrect." The ANC was "one of the facts of political life in South Africa," mentioned by government spokesmen "on a daily basis," usually in connection with "acts of violence." The paper described the ANC in "objective terms."

Botha's evaluation. The article promotes the ANC image "by publishing the activities of this unlawful organisation."

New Nation reply. The article is "a factual, unemotional news report." The Minister's objection would preclude "reports of acts of sabotage by that organisation." Government publicity of such acts arguably has "the same effect of promoting the image of the organisation."

17. "'No' to offer," describing the NUM turndown of the Chamber of Mines last offer and mentioning an SACP pamphlet.

New Nation justification. The strike was covered by other papers.[68] The article did not seek to "glorify the SACP," especially since "communism is incompatible with the Catholic views upheld by the SACBC."

Botha's evaluation. Mention of "a pamphlet said to be issued by the SACP" further promotes "the image or esteem of an unlawful organisation."

New Nation reply. "If a pamphlet was in fact issued and it purports to have been issued by the SACP then it is 'said to be issued' by the SACP."

18. "Tambo visit" to Yugoslavia and ANC campaign for stronger sanctions.

Botha's evaluation. "[M]ore publicity is given to the revolutionary leader Tambo. Furthermore certain campaigns and aims of the ANC are depicted, thereby reinforcing the promotion of the image of an unlawful organisation."

New Nation reply. "Mere publicity" does not violate the regulations; "it is the public image which must be enhanced."

19. "'Sellouts' offered new IDs," describing advertisements in a Swaziland newspaper offering political refugees a new life and good job if they returned to South Africa. The ANC said South Africa was trying to recruit agents and urged the Swazi government to protect refugees.

New Nation justification. It had merely printed the comments about the advertisement.

Botha's evaluation. Quoting an ANC spokesman promoted the organisation's image.

New Nation reply. "[T]he regulations do not prohibit quoting a spokesman of the ANC."

20. "'No' to council," reporting ANC rejection of a proposal that blacks elect nine members to an advisory "National Statutory Council."

New Nation justification. Many legal organizations had rejected the proposal.

Botha's evaluation. "A further example of a tendency to reinforce the ANC's image."

New Nation reply. The statement "cannot conceivably have the effect of 'reinforcing the ANC's image' (a concept not covered or even implied in the regulations) let alone threatening public safety."

The *New Nation* concluded that "some of the objections border on the frivolous." The Minister "failed to appreciate" that he had to form an opinion about the effect of the articles on public safety, order, or the termination of the emergency. One of its advocates commented later: "there was no contrition expressed on behalf of the papers I acted for. ... [The representations] were designed, let me put it bluntly, to embarrass."[69] Believing that the best defense was an offense, acting editor Gabu Tugwana said "we decided to launch a local campaign by calling all mass-based community organizations in the trade unions, the community, the churches. We even went to the foreign ambassadors. We held a press conference...."

Botha replied on November 26, refusing to meet and warning that he was prepared to take the next step. The paper's attorneys telexed back the next day, reminding Botha of his "public undertaking to entertain verbal representations" and seeking "an opportunity to canvass detailed particulars." The same day, however, Botha gazetted a formal warning.[70] The paper was defiant, criticizing his objections as "vague and unsubstantiated."[71] Displaying new solidarity, *The Cape Times* noted that it and other established papers frequently published similar matter and thus were threatened as well.[72] On December 5 Botha wrote the *New Nation* that he had examined another issue (December 3), as required by the regulations, and was considering suspending the paper. He again enclosed an evaluation, to which he invited representations within two weeks, urging that the articles be read "in conjunction" and for their "cumulative effect."[73] The *New Nation* warned readers to "brace themselves for possible suspension of their favourite newspaper— or the appointment of a government censor to vet its contents."[74] Several days later a full-page advertisement by foreign anti-apartheid organizations, media unions, and parliamentarians warned that "the South African State has declared war on the South African Press and on Press freedom."[75] *The Star* carried denunciations of press censorship by the Black Sash, and *The Sunday Star* expressed sympathy for the *New Nation* and Zwelakhe Sisulu, detained for eighteen months.[76]

The *New Nation*'s representations again criticized Botha for overlooking the effect on public safety, contested his insistence that the articles be read in conjunction, and demanded that he explain their "cumulative" effect if he intended to rely on it. His "evaluation," they said, "amounts to little more than the Minister's conclusions without an adequate statement of the reasons underlying" them. The paper also invoked its recent victory before the Publications Appeal Board, which had approved one of the issues to which Botha had objected.[77] "As a specialist tribunal," the Board's reasoning should be heeded.

The Publications Committee had objected to the *New Nation*'s criticism of government for invoking the "rooi gevaar" (red menace), which it found real. The paper's allegation that government propagated a "swart gevaar" (black threat) was a "filthy lie which led to racial animosity." The PAB replied that the Supreme Court required it to give comprehensive reasons for its decision, not merely advance vague or speculative views or draw conclusions that were "too remote" or based on trivia. It would not adopt the most sinister possible interpretation or engage in a microscopic or hyperanalytic investigation. Although the *New Nation* exhibited "blatant partiality," this was "typical of the press and politics and not, as such, undesirable" unless it endangered the existence of the state.

The Board approached individual articles very differently from Stoffel Botha. An article about street committees did not encourage anarchy but rather presented various perspectives about vigilante attacks. A story about violence against Emergency detainees noted that police had denied the allegations. An article defending the ANC and SACP against government charges that they had planned a bloodbath in 1986 did not promote the aims of those organizations. Where the Committee had interpreted a cartoon as depicting a *white* man as a "zombie" who wanted to murder a black infant, the Board interpreted it as saying that the state was turning *blacks* into passive instruments. The Committee had condemned an illegal quotation by the ANC, but it was not illegal to quote the ANC. The Committee had complained that two-thirds of the captions expressed grievances and none was positive, but the Board declared that "the law does not require a newspaper focusing on politics to contain 'positive' material." Appeals for clemency in another article were not illegal, nor was the call for prisoner-of-war status. Although some resented references to "comrades and compatriots," those words had lost their power to incite through overuse. The Board concluded by warning the *New Nation* about the cartoon and about calling those sentenced to death "patriots."

Fearing the worst, the paper again sought a personal audience and made three other requests. It wanted time to seek Supreme Court review of the validity of the regulations and Botha's notices. It invited pre-publication censorship as an alternative to suspension.[78] And it "unreservedly" offered to submit to the Media Council, thereby gaining exemption from the Emergency regulations. Gabu Tugwana explained later:

> We were seen as a wild bull with horns and we thought we would look for certain compromises. ... The name of the game is to continue to exist. We were still going to fight the government. If those people tried to dictate what we are supposed to write then we would let the world know it.

He gave a contemporaneous press conference in London, predicting that Botha would suspend the *New Nation* or impose an in-house censor and fearing that this was "just the beginning of the blacking out of all the news about South Africa."[79]

The following synopsizes the objectionable articles, Botha's evalution, and the paper's reply.

1. "What Govan Mbeki Would Have Said," since government had banned publication of his utterances on release from prison, and what Albertina Sisulu planned to say by way of welcome.

Botha's evaluation. The article depicted "one of the leaders (symbols) of the ANC and SACP in a positive light."

New Nation reply. The Law and Order Minister allowed Mbeki to be quoted at a press conference, where he declared his continuing membership in the ANC and SACP. Many papers covered this. "[T]he government itself went out of its way to give publicity to Mr Mbeki's release and to his comments at the press conference." After twenty-three years in prison "it is far-fetched to suggest that his release has elevated him to the status of a symbolic figure." The regulations say nothing about "positive" publicity.

2. An SACBC "Clemency plea" for the Sharpeville Six, asserting that "killing people who are perceived as collaborators with apartheid is seen as a political, not a criminal act."

Botha's evaluation. The article foments hatred toward "collaborators."

New Nation reply. Collaborators are not a "section of the public."

3. "Rent raids give lie to boycott flop claims." The UDF condemned joint operations against boycotters by the SADF, the SAP, and local councils and their police.

Botha's evaluation. The article foments hatred toward security forces by referring to their action as "raids."

New Nation reply. The South African Broadcasting Corporation, police, judges, and the Oxford English Dictionary used the term. It could not conceivably have stirred up hatred.

4. "Anti-Apartheid Movement plans huge offensive against Thatcher" as well as meetings and demonstrations for Mandela's 70th birthday.

Botha's evaluation. "[F]urther positive publicity to an unlawful organisation and a leader (symbol) thereof."

New Nation reply. The reference was "entirely factual and unemotional," and few people have not heard of him. "[T]he bland statement of notorious facts cannot promote the public image or esteem of the ANC."

5. "CPSA [Church of the Province of South Africa] stand 'a move to just ministry,'" describing its acceptance of the Lusaka Document of the World Council of Churches, which "recognises that the liberation movements are 'compelled' to use force as a means of achieving political change in South Africa."

Botha's evaluation. It "promotes or fans revolution or uprisings in the Republic by legitimising the use of force to achieve political change."

New Nation reply. The article made three references to the commitment to peaceful change. A year earlier Chris Heunis, Minister of Constitutional Planning and Development, said that ANC violence in the 1960s was understandable because there was no outlet for black political participation.

6. "A lifetime in the struggle," a biography of Govan Mbeki in the English literacy "Skills for Learning" section.

Botha's evaluation. Using the article for educational purposes gave "positive publicity to a leader (symbol) of such revolutionary organisations."

New Nation reply. The article was bland, stating the facts of his life "tersely and unemotionally." Similar articles appeared in pro-government papers.

This issue also was banned by a Publications Committee and then reprieved by the PAB.[80] Govan Mbeki's release and speech were covered by other papers, and his biography and views well known. Although Albertina Sisulu had used "emotionally loaded words" like "oppressed and fighting people," these were not undesirable per se. The reference to "martyrs who have fallen in the fight against injustice" did not necessarily refer to the ANC.

The Committee had misread "resolution" as "revolution." Gabu Tugwana later complained that the Directorate

> did not select the entire article...[which] meant something different. They selected paragraphs in articles. I can find fault, if I can do that, to any of the innocent statements. ...We were not surprised. And we knew that there was nobody that could escape that selective out-of-context editing.

In mid-December Botha sent formal warnings to the *Weekly Mail*, *South*, *Work in Progress*, and *Die Stem*.[81] The *Weekly Mail* submitted a 174-page reply but had a "genuine problem and a genuine dilemma" understanding and complying with the regulations. Since the objectionable material constituted less than five percent of its content, the paper urged Botha to consider the effect on

> a reasonable, rational and balanced reader...[without] a myopic and obsessive and stuttering attention on some phrase in the middle of a lengthy analysis through which obsession everything else in the newspaper dissolves from his brain and his mind becomes singularly concentrated on the manner in which he could endanger the safety of the public.

The reply appended fifty-five similar articles from established papers, including "two very positive descriptions of an ANC camp" in pro-government Afrikaans newspapers.[82] *Die Stem* closed rather than respond to Botha, but *Die Volkstem* immediately appeared in its place, continuing to support the Boerestaat Beweging, the AWB, and the Conservative Party, while denying any connection with Robert van Tonder.[83]

Two days after submitting the second set of representations, the *New Nation* anticipated its imminent closure in a long article denouncing the government's actions as "not entirely unexpected, given its 'proud' record of media bashing" and the closure of seven other newspapers. The attack was part of "the suppression of broad democratic activity at every level." The government had even "outlawed large sections of the English vocabulary." On January 10 Gabu Tugwana declared: "[T]he only way to keep going is to carry on as though the threat did not exist...." Three days later, however, the paper sought an interdict against closure. A special edition the next day carried a front-page editorial promising readers "that their favourite newspaper will continue to uphold the highest standards—despite concerted efforts by various Government officials to phase us out."[84] An advocate who worked on the case explained:

> The name of the game quite honestly was staying alive. And we felt that we wanted to adopt legal strategies which were designed to achieve that result. To allow the newspaper to remain on the streets for as long as was humanly possible, in the

knowledge that we were up against very drastic emergency powers coupled with an immensely restrictive interpretation, which had been placed on those powers by the Appellate Division. ... [W]e launched the application at what we thought was the last possible minute.... [T]he Minister had already made up his mind to close down the newspaper...two days previously. ... [W]e bought something like six months of time for the *New Nation*....

The following week the government issued additional regulations (back-dated a year) explicitly relieving Botha of any obligation to meet newspapers affected by his warnings or "disclose any grounds for such action to any person."[85]

The *New Nation*'s founding affidavit declared it was "completely committed to a peaceful resolution of the conflict which besets South Africa." It printed 60,000 copies and sold the twenty-four-page issue for thirty cents (about $.10). The threatened three-month closure would deprive it of advertising revenue while compelling it to pay the full complement of editorial and printing staff; lost readership might never be regained.

The paper made several legal arguments. The first issue criticized appeared before the regulation; the legislation did not authorize the State President to "make punishable any act or omission," and closure was punishment. The State President delegated more power to the Minister than he enjoyed himself; the delegation was so grossly unreasonable that the President had acted in bad faith or for ulterior motives or failed to apply his mind. The regulations were unacceptably vague. The notices failed to allege the requisite threats and raised irrelevant objections. Stoffel Botha had sub-delegated authority to the Directorate of Media Relations and denied the promised personal audience.

In response, the State President declared that he had been "convinced in good faith that the said measures were not only advisable but necessary to make provision for the security of the public and the maintenance of order and to make satisfactory provision for the termination of the state of emergency...." Stoffel Botha acknowledged that he had intended to close the paper two days after the application was filed and would do so unless prevented by the court.[86] He appended a pamphlet by Young South Africans for a Christian Civilization—Tradition, Family and Property, which revealed its politics by describing the homelands as "self-governing territories within the Republic of South Africa, inhabited by the same Black race-group. Four of them... [enjoyed] full autonomy." For nearly forty pages it castigated the *New Nation* for adopting "Liberation Theology censured by the Vatican for its acceptance of criteria of analysis borrowed from Marxism" and showing "unveiled sympathy toward Frelimo, the MPLA, SWAPO and the ANC" and no "reservations about the communist ideology or the political objectives of [Zimbabwe's President] Mugabe." "Frequently, the focussing of African historical subjects...coincides with those of communist theoreticians." The paper's treatment of "work/capital issues and social problems in general, is in our assessment consistent with the revolutionary line." It "promotes certain poets...as 'cultural leaders of the people,'" whose work contains "heavy doses of the spirit of class struggle." The pamphlet's influence on Botha's "prima facie evaluation" was undeniable.

> [I]t is common for modern journalism not to limit itself to the academic presentation of theses and arguments but to present its own views in a variety of ways. These stretch from the way the news items are selected for publication, to the manner of placing them on the printed page...a) in the headlines...b) in poetry...c) in the formulation of questions for an interview...d) in the ease with which the term "comrade" is used to designate worker leaders...e) in far-fetched affirmations from readers, printed uncritically....

The New Nation reply criticized the Home Affairs Minister for claiming good motives (which were irrelevant) and invoking information he refused to disclose. His affidavit "suggests that the [Minister] would have been satisfied had the applicant acknowledged some form of wrongdoing and adopted an apologetic and subservient approach." He met with papers that made concessions and gave undertakings. Having publicly promised to grant such an audience "he was not at liberty to break this promise." Newspapers could not make representations without knowing the charges. The first notice failed to communicate them. The Minister urged that it be read with the second, but the two were inconsistent and even together did not reveal his objections. Perhaps acknowledging this, the Minister insisted that the New Nation knew his grounds. But "this is surely fundamentally unfair and not in conformity with the requirement to state the 'grounds of the proposed action.'" "It is not competent now for the [Minister] to give details of the nature of his complaint" since the New Nation could no longer respond. The Minister appended to his affidavit something he presented as the New Nation published abroad but which clearly stated that it was produced by the Catholic Institute for International Relations. The paper also objected to the appended pamphlet, which "contains scurrilous and unsubstantiated attacks...[and] can only be described as a 'smear.'" The Minister accused the New Nation "of the grossest opportunism for assuming that [he] did not dispute the factual accuracy of the articles specified by him...it is this sort of observation which is the unmistakable hallmark of the spirit in which the so-called representations were made."

Argument scheduled for January 26 before Justice van Niekerk was postponed when he secured the appointment of a full bench. Stoffel Botha agreed not to close the paper before judgment. The New Nation's advocate was Jules Browde SC, former chair of the Johannesburg Bar Council and judge pro tem; a colleague said he was "taken seriously by judges because he has an unbending rule of not arguing rubbish."[87] In the face of the threat, the *New Nation* published a cartoon by a reader showing Stoffel Botha as a traffic cop stopping the paper

> from collecting and spreading the truth in and about South Africa and its homelands. He wants [the people] to be fed with his propaganda only. ... [If the paper survived] you would be able to compare it with what Fatty says in his sources of information. Then, between them and the *New Nation* you would know which is dirty propaganda.[88]

On March 8 the U.S. State Department and a group of senators called for the release of Zwelakhe Sisulu, "a leader in efforts to resolve South Africa's political problems peacefully. He's the type of black leader the South African Government should be talking to, not repressing."[89]

The same day Justice Curlewis delivered an oral opinion (Justices Spoelstra and van Niekerk concurring). An advocate who observed the argument was surprised that despite Curlewis's reputation for being "intemperate on the bench, or of being short-tempered, of constantly interrupting counsel" he "listened with interest for two days, hardly interrupted Jules in argument at all." He found retroactivity "the most attractive of all the arguments." But the Minister had not punished an act occurring prior to the regulations since the paper could "cease" or "continue with innocuous material." The objection to retroactivity was fairness, and "it is not unfair...to tell a person that what he has heretofore been doing innocently is now considered offensive." The discretion granted was not too broad since it "was considered expedient by the State President... [which] is of paramount importance." It "sets out in some detail what the Minister must form an opinion about." That opinion was not restricted to the contents of the paper, without reference to conditions in South Africa. "To suggest that the words of the regulation make him read the article as if he were sitting on Mars is absurd."

The paper's alleged "confusion" about the Minister's objections was gainsaid by its detailed representations and affidavit. In any case, the objections were "abundantly clear" in the regulations and notice, which "speak for themselves." The court also found that the "concept of promoting revolution is perfectly clear." "The meaning of [fomenting, feelings, hatred, and hostility] are clear to any person, and there is no difficulty at all in giving them a meaning." "Public image" and "esteem" had a "perfectly clear meaning." The paper's complaints were "a mere semantic quibble." "We are not engaged in compounding a dictionary or in a lecture on semantics." Even if publication of similar articles by other papers "indicated a certain lack of consistency," "this is not something that this court can deal with" and "does not affect the Regulations or the bona fides of the Minister in regard to *New Nation*."

The court could not make its own factual findings. "[W]hether there has in fact been systematic publishing in the periodical is a matter of the Minister's opinion, whatever anyone else's opinion may be."

> The problem for [the applicant] is not the words used in the Regulations but that he does not know what will be the opinion of the Minister. Or, if he suspects what it will be, it will appear to him totally unacceptable and indeed unreasonable.

Opinions are "dependent in the first place, [on] where the person stands in the political spectrum, and whether he is black or white." "But this is not something that arises out of any ambiguity or vagueness as to the object of the opinion."

> [T]he real deficiency in part of Applicant's representations...[is its] failure to understand that [it] was dealing with the opinion of a politician and not a judgement of a court of law. It is of course clear that censorship on the grounds set out in the Regulations is a political act.

The court would not address the fundamental question whether "so unfettered a discretion... should not be given." Nor would it expose the Minister's subjective opinion to any review.

> It is no use asking rhetorically, would the call for the release of Mandela constitute promotion of the public image of the ANC. I decline to give any view on it because whatever I said or anyone else said, would be entirely irrelevant. If the Minister's opinion was in the affirmative, then that is enough and it would be offensive. ... That is the reason why the reference to certain cases which laid down that there must be certainty in the regulations is somewhat misplaced. How can there be certainty where the opinion of a politician is involved; the converse would be the case.

The court rejected the argument that the Minister's failure to give reasons violated the basic principle of audi alteram partem.

> The short answer is that the Minister does not have to give "reasons" why he formed an opinion that certain matter offended. ... The "grounds" for the proposed action... are precisely what it says—his opinion that certain disclosed matter offended.... If deponent did not agree with the opinion of the Minister, all he could do is say so. If there was a factual error... he could say so. It might be said, if this is the whole purpose of the representations then very little can come out of it. Well, I am inclined to agree. ... [T]hat arises because of censorship and the discretion of someone, in this case a politician. And of course, censorship is very like a guillotine, and there is very little use in growing honeysuckle over a guillotine.

Judge Curlewis adamantly refused to discuss the merits.

The fact that one may be somewhat astonished by the vast apparatus that has been put up to deal with this matter has no bearing upon the legal aspect at all. So I leave that there. ...

It is not our function to pass an opinion, favourable or unfavourable, on what the State President appeared to think necessary or upon the Minister's opinion. On the other hand, it need only be said that as far as the first is concerned, lack of bona fides has not been established.

The Supreme Court dismissed the application with costs.

Jules Browde immediately sought leave to appeal, opposed by J.D.M. Swart, the state's advocate, on the ground that there was no reasonable prospect of reversal.[90] Curlewis now confessed uncertainties he had previously suppressed: "we think another court might come to [another conclusion]—you know on words and phrases...." Denying the stay, he worried, would "put [the *New Nation*] out of production for three months, and the financial consequences would be enormous, whereas what would happen if they were to continue [publishing] until the appeal?"

> *Swart:* [T]he minister...does regard it as a matter of urgency—he wants the matter disposed of, and as a matter of fact he reserved his right to proceed with an order should there be any undue delay. Now let me make it quite clear that this was in no way intended as any (inaudible) of contempt of the court at all.
>
> *Judge:* No, no.
>
> *Swart:* But it does illustrate that in his opinion the matter had progressed to the stage where, from a viewpoint of the public safety, general order and terminating the state of emergency, that something should be done.

The court adjourned for lunch, urging Swart to seek further instructions from the Minister (which he did not obtain). After the recess, under pressure from Swart, the court conceded it could not simultaneously grant a stay but noted that the same bench probably would hear that application. Browde promptly sought a temporary stay.

> *Judge:* No, there I cannot help you unfortunately, I know that it is very difficult for you.
>
> *Browde:* Well my lord, otherwise it could be rendered (inaudible) [presumably "moot"] tomorrow by an extraordinary gazette, and that would put us out of business for ever, my lord. ...
>
> *Judge:* You see, my trouble is, that as far as I know the law, one—I do not know that I have the right to—well I suppose

there will be no harm (inaudible). Well you know we are anxious not to of course—because, let me put it this way. We are anxious of course, because of what will happen, if it just comes out tomorrow.

Curlewis asked Swart to "try and assist us here," but the state pointed to the "insuperable difficulty" that the *New Nation* had to apply for a new interdict rather than a stay; denial of the original application had rendered the court "functus officio." The court seemed inclined to grant a two-day stay to allow the parties to prepare for a hearing on a permanent stay.

Judge: I do not know if I am making bad cases make hard law or hard cases make bad law, but it sounds to me a practical matter.

Swart: Yes. I am willing to go along as far as that. [But he immediately reversed himself.] I have a very grave difficulty in principle.

The application had been brought before the Minister had acted, and the court found he had a right to act. Curlewis was unimpressed.

Judge: You see the problem I have is just this, if we believe, as we do, that the Appellate Division could come to a different conclusion, it is not going to help them an awful lot if they have already gone bankrupt.

Swart: [Quibbled about the difference between bankruptcy and closure, reiterating that the Minister viewed the matter as of the utmost importance.]

Judge: I do not know if he still does. I do not know if he has seen subsequent [issues]—he might be happy with the way they are now publishing?

Swart: I do not know at all.

Judge: Well, you see this is what to me is a whole in [read "new"] reality. There were things that constrained him to come to the opinion that there was then.... Public safety was endangered in August/September, was—how serious that could have been when, on the way the matter is framed, and with no attempt to be dilatory on either side, by the middle of the end of December there still has not been a conclusion reached. So that what we are concerned with, but it does, I must say—extraordinary. The point is that if he now says—and that is gone, it is finished. I do not know whether—there has been no revolution fortunately, so obviously nothing catastrophic has happened. It is a different matter if he now says, that I have taken note—I have no doubt he has, I mean his people have been sifting—of other applications, and really I am not satisfied. He does not have to give detail. He is not going to talk about a banning again—I am not telling him what to do. If he says that look, this is a matter affecting the question of a stay, I am not satisfied with the way they are publishing, and it is in my opinion, and my opinion I have already dealt with—that is a different matter. That is why I felt at the very outset that I cannot just let your client be bound, or just go on these papers. But in the absence of that, if on the other hand he turns round and says to you, that you know really Mr Swart I am satisfied that—like I was—that this matter is not really all that urgent, it is not all that dangerous, then what is the problem? That is why I wanted to know what your instructions— but I suppose you cannot get instructions from him over lunch.

The court granted leave to appeal and issued a two-day stay pending a hearing on longer stay. On the basis of the state's affidavit that the paper would not be harmed by suspension because it operated at a loss, however, the court denied the second stay. The Minister promptly closed the *New Nation* from March 22 to the annual end of the Emergency (June 10).[91] Anticipating this, its March 17 issue contained a front-page editorial about "The threat facing all of us."

> If our [application] fails, you will effectively be denied your right to know. ... The interesting coincidence is that the government chose to suppress basic freedoms and silence dissenting voices, while claiming it was in the process of "extending democracy." ... "Reform", for us, has become synonymous with repression.... What credence do the handful of hand-picked pawns, partners of "reform", enjoy in the community?

Many papers condemned the ban.[92] The *Sowetan* headlined "*Nation* Is Silenced," editorializing on its front page: "the Government is not prepared to test the cases it has made out against newspapers in a court of law, and outside of the media regulations."[93] *The Star* concurred: "The Minister's whim is now mightier than the pen."[94] *The Cape Times* deplored "a new phase of authoritarian rule in South Africa... it is plain that the government has grown impatient of the judicial process and Western ideas of freedom and democracy."[95] *Business Day* declaimed: "SA can no longer claim to have a free Press and in this respect, as in others, it has left the ranks of civilised nations."[96] Even the center-right *Daily Dispatch* regretted that "the National Party government has again shot the messenger."[97] The South African Council of Churches denounced the "blatant suppression of the freedom of expression," while Black Sash called the ban tantamount to a death sentence.[98] Journalists demonstrated, students held a rally, the South African Society of Journalists and the Media Workers Association of South Africa condemned the closure, the International Press Institute protested, and the United Nations special committee against apartheid expressed deep concern.[99] *The New York Times* described the *New Nation* as "the most authentic voice of South Africa's blacks" and quoted Archbishop Tutu: "It is only a Government which is very close to being totalitarian which behaves in this way."[100]

Trying to convey an image of even-handedness, *The Citizen* headline declared "Govt Monitoring Press: Warns AWB," revealing only in the subhead that "*New Nation* Banned."[101] Deputy Information Minister Stoffel van der Merwe explained that government had to prevent the "sort of propaganda" that leads people "to overthrow [it] by violence." After "months and months" of study, officials had concluded that the *New Nation* identified with communism. The ban had been demanded by Bishop Isaac Mokoena of the United Christian Action network, representing fourteen organizations and four million people.[102]

Repression Under the Emergency, 1988–89

Censorship continued much as before. In February the government tabled the National Supplies Procurement Amendment Bill, which would allow the Minister of Economic Affairs to ban reports on the effect of sanctions.[103] Stoffel Botha reiterated his warning to the *Weekly Mail* and warned *Grassroots* (a Cape Flats community paper), *Out of Step* (the ECC magazine), and *Saamstaan*.[104] After *South* denounced "the arrogant Botha regime" and asked EC countries backing the alternative press to pressure the government, Stoffel Botha issued a second warning.[105]

The *Weekly Mail*, most of whose 35,000 readers were educated whites in South Africa and abroad, was able to mobilize more support than papers directed at blacks or small audiences. On May 8 Sunday newspapers carried an open letter to the State President from editors, writers, and media people in thirty-three countries. The Inter-American Press Association (representing more than 1,300 newspapers), the vice chancellors of the Universities of the Witwatersrand, Cape Town, Natal, and the Western Cape, businessmen, ambassadors, readers, and the editors of twenty-six South African newspapers expressed solidarity.[106] *Business Day* offered the ambiguous defense that *Weekly Mail* readers were marginal and more likely to emigrate than attack. The warning "proves what we have suspected all along: that the Minister and his advisers have neither the general education, nor the wit, to distinguish between revolution and radical chic."[107] The paper's co-editors were equally contemptuous. Anton Harber declared "we have broken no rules because if we had done so, the Government would have prosecuted us" and predicted an "international and local outcry" if banned. Irwin Manoim said Botha's warning letters "showed so little sign of a mind actually engaged in examination of the contents of the objectionable publication that they tended to produce guffaws rather than alarm."[108] "Mr Botha accuses us of promoting revolution. He cannot, surely, believe this. Our real crime is the telling of awkward truths which the Government would prefer not to hear."[109]

Deeply angered, Stoffel Botha issued a statement "to alert the general public not to be misled by the hysterical campaign in certain circles against the emergency media regulations."[110]

> The false impression is being created that I want to close down or place restrictions on publications indiscriminately; that freedom of speech and the free flow of information are unnecessarily restricted and that the emergency restrictions pertaining to the media have no other purpose than to shield the government against criticism. All this is untrue.

During the May 17–20 debate on his departmental budget the Minister faced strong criticism in the ("Coloured") House of Representatives from the Labour Party, which deplored that "since the imposition of the state of emergency in 1986 the news media have been practically paralysed by more than 1,000 laws and the whole range of emergency regulations." "[T]he policy of the Government of the day... is to eliminate people or newspapers who seem to inform the community of what is happening in South Africa."[111] Botha retorted that the "'media terrorists'... provide these revolutionaries' cause with publicity...by proclaiming the revolutionary message and by providing deeds of terror with publicity." They "present terrorists as 'freedom fighters' or 'guerrillas.'" They carry the "false message that the days of the established order in South Africa are numbered." Whether the *Weekly Mail* will be banned "is up to the editor[s]." If they "decide to continue publishing the matter which is referred to in this document they have taken the decision in their own hands."[112] In the (white) House of Assembly the PFP condemned the Minister for exercising powers "without reference to Parliament." "[A]uthority to render Press freedom meaningless is given to the subjective opinion of one man." "We must be one of the few countries in the world where so much pain is taken to clad authoritarianism in the elegance of legalistic jargon." "[A]fter almost three years of emergency rule [the government] obviously learnt some lessons on how to avoid the embarrassment of Supreme Court censure."[113] A Nationalist responded that the speaker was "extremely soft on the ANC." "[T]he Government is intent upon the highest possible maintenance of the freedom of the South African Press and the media." Another asked why foreigners were allowed to be newspaper editors and journalists.[114] Botha replied:

> For how long must the Government, and I as a responsible Minister, continue to caution in a friendly way and ask the Press for its co-operation in these matters of national importance? ... [T]he negative press... [is guilty of] the venomous suspicion-mongering, the over-emphasising here and the under-emphasising there and the creation of a distorted image.[115]

This prompted Jan van Eck (Independent) to compare him to Josef Goebbels, provoking J.J. Lemmer (NP) to call van Eck a "sick man," a comment the chairman made him withdraw. Van Eck declared that "by closing down the newspapers the hon the Minister wishes to prevent the most heinous atrocities that are being committed by this regime from being revealed." When Dr. J.T. Delport (NP) claimed the government was protecting "the safety, the continued existence, the orderliness and the very survival" of the country, S.S. van der Merwe (PFP) retorted "Every tyrant in history has made that statement." Botha maintained that "a newspaper can actually promote revolution"

> when a publication predominantly gives positive publicity to the revolutionaries... by building up their image and by reporting favourably... mentioning how he is honoured...popularising him by publicising slogans... publishing photo's [sic] of the ANC leaders...reports creating sympathy for ANC detainees and prisoners; and by pointing out, with a great flourish, the recognition which the ANC enjoys abroad.

He offered a statistical analysis of the 188 reports on which he had based warnings: forty-seven percent promoted the public image of unlawful organizations, twenty-eight percent stirred up hatred against security forces or sections of the community, fourteen percent promoted revolution, five percent discredited the judiciary, four percent promoted boycotts or civil disobedience, and two percent propagated people's courts or street committees. Boasting that "they have failed to prove me wrong in the other two Houses," he warned the (Indian) House of Delegates about

> the media terrorists... the people who do not have the guts... to be terrorists themselves as it is too dangerous. They hide behind the protection of an editorial office to motivate others to do the dirty work for the sake of their selfish aims.... It is an ego trip by dropouts from other fields of endeavour. ... Government is doing its best to bring about: Peace and tranquility where we live; the opportunity to share in what this country has to offer; to use our God-given talents; and—it sounds simple—just to be happy.

He explained once again that he had used the Emergency regulations rather than prosecuting the *New Nation* because "it would take at least a year before a case was brought to court and a decision taken." He reassured members "that the Government and I respect freedom of the press as much as anyone else. ... democracy is what we stand for."[116] But even the establishment media expressed alarm about the "ominous threat,"[117] "press curbs,"[118] and the "Death of the truth."[119] The *Sunday Tribune* offered space to Mansoor Jaffer of *Grassroots*, while the *Sunday Times* championed the *Weekly Mail*.[120]

Hoping to anticipate the now inevitable suspension, *South* printed a special edition four days early, which reached the newsstands at noon but had sold only twenty percent of the press run before the ban was enforced at 2:30 p.m. Editor Rashid Seria promised that the press would survive underground.[121] *The Cape Times* warned: "Freedom at risk for everyone."[122] Joe Thloloe entitled his *Sowetan* column "Death of truth."[123] The closure was condemned by the Media Workers of South Africa and the South African Society of Journalists.[124]

Government intensified harassment of *Saamstaan*. Because no printer within 500 kilometers of Oudtshoorn would handle it, the paper had to be printed in Cape Town; one entire edition disappeared in transit. No local white lawyer would represent it; no local shop would sell it. Reggie Oliphant, a journalist, had his car burned and received threatening phone calls every night. Umbulelo Grootboom, another reporter, was arrested for cattle theft; government dropped the charges but banned him. Both of them and Derek Jackson were under nightly house arrest. When reporter Patrick Nyuka tried to pass his notes and film to a young woman to avoid seizure by the police, they shot him and the woman, seriously wounding both, and charged Nyuka with public violence.[125] In May the South African Society of Journalists conferred the Pringle Award on the paper for its commitment to press freedom.[126] Two months later the paper reported that repression had nearly doubled its circulation.[127] Mbulelo Linda and Mike Loewe of the Port Elizabeth News Agency were detained, restricted on release, and suffered three burglaries in which the recently installed alarm was silenced and documents, negatives, and phones were stolen but no money.[128]

In response to these threats forty-five organizations launched the Save the Press Campaign at the end of May, spanning the spectrum of English papers from conservative to alternative. The next month 120 Transvaal journalists created the Association of Democratic Journalists to replace both the mainstream South African Society of Journalists and the alternative Media Workers Association of South Africa, establishing branches in Natal, the Border, Eastern Province, and the Western Cape. Within two weeks police posing as plumbers searched the apartment of a newly-elected officer.[129]

Government was no more tolerant of the foreign media. Stoffel Botha reported in February that he had rejected 186 visa applications by journalists the previous year.[130] In the May budget debate he had declared that South Africa had a duty to exclude or expel foreign journalists who produced "more negative than positive results." "The foreign political correspondent is usually a nomad with no allegiance, accountability or responsibility towards the host country…[who] commits many communicational and other misdemeanours." He particularly condemned CBS for its documentary "Children of Apartheid."[131] Three weeks later Law and Order Minister Adriaan Vlok threatened to expel the BBC for televising a London rock concert celebrating Nelson Mandela's seventieth birthday. When SAP Commissioner Brig. Mellet asked why reporters had not sought his department's comment on "Suffer the Children," a program about child detainees, he was told "quite frankly, the BBC does not believe the South African government." Vlok fulminated: "If this is the BBC's attitude, then why should the South African government continue to host their representatives in our country?"[132] Government prohibited all employees from talking to foreign journalists unaccredited by the Bureau for Information and ordered them to report all approaches. It also planned to inform public officials of the "attitude" of accredited journalists.[133]

In mid-June government gazetted Emergency regulations, requiring most "news agencies" to register and empowering it to deregister those threatening public safety and law and order or delaying the termination of the emergency. Media Relations Director Engelbrecht increased fears by announcing that established papers supplying news to others were included. The outcry by the United States government, the American and German Chambers of Commerce, and the Inter-American Press Association persuaded Stoffel Botha to repudiate this interpretation and then withdraw the regulations.[134]

On orders of the Wits Divisional Commander, police raided the literacy magazine *Learn and Teach* in July, seizing 14,300 copies of "The Historic Speech of Nelson Rolihlala Mandela at the Rivonia Trial." They copied the names and addresses of purchasers and even detained a man who was fumigating the office, taking his name and address before releasing him. Continuing the raid at Exclusive Books, they confiscated three unsold copies and demanded descriptions of the man who had bought copies the day before and the photographer accompanying him. When the publisher applied to the Supreme Court for return of the issue, state counsel denounced Mandela's speech for being unbalanced and incorrect and placing the South African legal system in a bad light! Acknowledging his powerlessness, Justice G. Gordon complained: "This kind of legislation excludes the courts from things no court is happy to be excluded from. ... [The state was objecting to] a quotation from court proceedings, proceedings that were held in the open."[135]

In December 1987 a Publications Committee had passed Richard Attenborough's movie about Steve Biko, "Cry Freedom": "the unconditional approval of this film despite its one-sided viewpoint, publicly demonstrates that South Africa is politically mature, unbiased and fair by allowing all points of view for public screening." United International Pictures postponed the opening for seven months, trying to learn if government would accept the ruling. Four days before the announced screening Stoffel Botha directed the Publications Appeal Board to review it. Justus Tshungu, a thirty-year employee of the South African Broadcasting Corporation and organizer of Radio Pulpit, testified for banning.

> [Youths will] completely lose their heads... rivers of blood will flow... there will be uprisings. [There] had never been a better recipe for revolution than showing [it] to black kids.... [T[hey

> would stone every car nearby. And if they saw police—I cannot
> say what they would do.

They would view the film as "gospel," seeing Biko as Christ and Donald Woods as John the Baptist. Minutes before the July 29 opening the Board approved the movie (for those over nineteen) because it contained no "incitement to racial hatred, violence, civil disobedience, and the like." This "somewhat mediocre product" "fails dismally to evoke a revolutionary response." The caricatures of the security forces "as unfeeling, inhuman and brutal" were so "blatant" that "even a foreigner would realise, or at least suspect the extent of this bias and 'over-kill.'" Furthermore, "the airing of grievances is legitimate and overreaction also poses a threat to security."[136] The PAB chairman received death threats as a result, and theaters showing the movie were bombed. Within hours of the first screening, however, Information Minister Stoffel van der Merwe banned the film on the ground that Donald Woods was a "listed" person, whose words could not be quoted, complaining that government had hoped the "censor board would do its job" but the board functioned as if times were "normal."[137] Police confiscated all copies. About the same time a Publications Committee banned "A World Apart" (about Ruth First) at the *Weekly Mail* "Cinema under Siege" festival, finding that "it propagates the ANC and the basic message is that there is no alternative to violence for the black man in South Africa." The Board denied the appeal because "the film seems to lack the dramatic or artistic merit which one has come to expect of a 'film-festival' film." An award at Cannes was unpersuasive because the Board had not been told its basis. The film lacked sufficient "historical and political interest" because it fit a well-known genre: "brutal police action, raids, rioting, inflammatory speeches, questioning by the security police and suffering by those affected." Having banned it after seeing a video, however, the Board watched the film on a large screen; persuaded by the "difference in format" that it was a "docu-drama of some excellence," the Board allowed a single screening.[138]

On October 12 government issued a fourth warning to the *Weekly Mail*. Co-editor Anton Harber responded that "Stoffel Botha is trying to win votes" in the forthcoming municipal elections. Many papers protested,[139] as did the American Society of Newspaper Editors, the International Press Institute, the World Press Freedom Committee, and the Committee for the Protection of Journalists.[140] The *Weekly Mail* contacted "virtually all the embassies in South Africa," made representations to Botha and vainly sought a meeting.[141] The Save the Press Campaign organized a Stand by the *Mail* meeting on October 29.[142] The paper appeared at the end of October with a full-page article boldly proclaiming "Not Guilty."[143] But on November 1 Botha suspended it for a month.[144]

This produced predictable denunciations from newspapers, church and human rights organizations, and foreign embassies (including the U.S.).[145] Within days co-editor Anton Harber defiantly addressed an IDASA conference.

> We no longer see the courts as a useful arena in which to fight
> the state. ... It is now a question of having a good defence, quick
> feet and trying to slip nimble punches in between raised fists.
> ... [I]t happened this way because, and only because, Botha
> decided it *should happen* this way. He has acted as prosecutor,
> judge and executioner—and the whole case was heard in cam-
> era. ... His action appears to be punitive—the act of a petty and
> petulant schoolmaster rather than a Cabinet Minister dealing
> with a total onslaught on his country. ... Although Stoffel Botha
> still dresses up his action in legalistic finery, this is only a thin
> cover for his naked power. The law is now based on his whim,
> his personal intolerance and his individual narrow-mindedness.
> ...The fight against censorship is a fight for people to take con-
> trol of their situations.... That is why *Weekly Mail* will be back
> on the streets on December 2 as strong, as determined and as
> outspoken as ever.[146]

The same weekend Foreign Minister Pik Botha, sounding even more like
Harber's "petulant schoolmaster," dressed down the Foreign Correspondents'
Association.

> I am sick and tired of a lot of foreign representatives descend-
> ing on my country and picking up on all the dirty work instead
> of all the beauty, promise and goodwill. You don't understand
> Africa. You don't understand African aspirations. You don't
> understand African history. I accuse you of being superficial. I
> accuse you of glibly gliding over the African realities of which
> you know nothing, absolutely nothing.

The *Weekly Mail* had been suspended because it was one of the most
"vicious" newspapers he had ever seen and responsible for "more violence
in this country." Refusing to accept the thanks of his host, he recalled the
opening words of a speech by former president Paul Kruger: "Friends, citizens, thieves and enemies." "That is how I look at you this evening." When
the audience responded with boos, hisses, and shouts of "go home," he
stalked out.[147]

Days after the *Weekly Mail* suspension *Vrye Weekblad*, the first Afrikaans
alternative paper, appeared with a front-page picture of SACP leader Joe
Slovo, the most hated white South African exile. Government first refused to
register it, then demanded a R30,000 security deposit (the highest ever), and
finally prosecuted editor Max du Preez for quoting Wits academic Mark
Swilling paraphrasing Slovo. Heeding the prosecutor's argument that the
Internal Security Act sought to "silence the voice of a listed person altogether," a magistrate sentenced du Preez to six months imprisonment
(suspended for five years) because he had committed "such a serious
offence." In March 1990 he was convicted for publishing six subversive state-

ments about conscientious objectors, one being Charles Bester's statement from the dock (see chapter four).[148]

Government began 1989 by issuing a first warning to *Al-Qalam* (the four-teen-year-old organ of the Muslim Youth Movement, with a circulation of 13,000) and final warnings to *New Era, Work in Progress,* and *Grassroots. Al-Qalam* editor Mahomed Faizal Dawjee was vitriolic:

> Cowering under the fig-leaf of Emergency regulations, the Minister has again assumed the responsibility for hiding the shame and crimes of the apartheid state. We will not compromise on truth. The limits of what we will or will not report will be determined not by the apartheid state or Stoffel Botha, but by our commitment to the divinely-guided principles of truth and justice.

The following month government suspended *New Era* and *Grassroots* and issued a final warning to *Al-Qalam.*[149]

Stoffel Botha returned to the attack in Parliament in February, condemning the alternative press for

> confrontation...sophistic journalism, vitriolic journalism, journalism that pays no attention to any code...that takes its refuge in unbridled, extravagant, insulting, presumptuous and even slanderous language. ...Sometimes it is so banal that I cannot repeat it here.

He denied vehemently that "publications have no protection in courts of law."

> No discretion, including my own, is unrestricted. Any publication objecting to my action against it, has the right to test the validity of my decision in court. This has, in fact, happened in the past. The court has the power to set aside my decisions in accordance with established legal principles. I must exercise my discretion honestly and in accordance with the rules of reasonableness and fairness. ... the Government holds our legal system in the highest esteem.

Under "ideal circumstances, no person, including the State, ought to be prosecutor and judge of his own case." "We live in abnormal times," however, which call "for abnormal measures to combat the propaganda campaign," which "cannot be effectively dealt with by means of the normal criminal procedure. Firstly, it is impossible to define propaganda fully." "What the Government views as propaganda, is often seen by its critics as acceptable viewpoints and criticism. This is a pity." "It also does not help to punish propaganda. Propaganda must be prevented." Not only were courts too slow. If they tried to stop propaganda

> the high esteem enjoyed by our courts as institutions functioning independently of the legislature and the executive would be seriously jeopardised. Whether a statement constitutes propa-

ganda or not, whether the publication of material is contrary to public interest and security, is a matter of opinion. If courts of law had to give a ruling on such opinions, the courts themselves would inevitably be drawn into the political arena. ... [Interjections] I would like to remind hon members of the wide publicity given to recent treason and terrorism trials which have already unjustly been labelled "political trials."[150]

A month later PFP MP David Dalling moved a resolution on "Restrictions on Free Press," condemning

the Government's use of arbitrary executive powers during the past two years to—

(a) muzzle the free press in South Africa;

(b) suspend and/or close down publication of newspapers and periodicals opposed to it; and

(c) harass, restrict and detain journalists doing their jobs.

"Perhaps the worst feature of the exercise of this power is that the hon the Minister's decision is not subject to appeal to an independent court. The hon the Minister, God-like, can prosecute, judge, sentence and execute any publication...." Botha dismissed the speech as "generalisations, emotional words, exaggerations and innuendo." Coming to his defense, a Nationalist denied that the government was "guilty of authoritarian action." "The very presence here of these hon members of the PFP who are making snide remarks, and the freedom of extra-parliamentary opposition groups proves that the emergency measures make it possible for political parties as well as a legal divergence of opinion to continue to exist within this democratic state." But the alternative press was

as much a part of the onslaught as the murdering gangs of the ANC...it is not an informant or watch-dog, but an instigator and advocate of violence. ... The fact that any government has the fullest right to take action against this sort of Press, is stated unequivocally in section 20 of the UN's Declaration of Human Rights.

Another Nationalist noted that "a full Bench of the Witwatersrand division declared that regulation seven of the media Emergency regulations and the implementation of the regulation were valid." Botha's decision not to take further action against the *Sowetan* and *Work in Progress* showed that he "maintains a very high standard as far as the principle of fairness is concerned." There were approximately 3,000 opposition publications and only about two dozen pro-Government. "[W]hen it comes to the security of the State we must take into consideration that the State, with its security and intelligence services, is in a much better position to make judgements...." The CP asked rhetorically whether a case "should be taken to court every time and that the entire background of the South African political climate, state security and so on should first be submitted to court by way of evidence"?

PFP MP David Dalling replied that Botha really should have said "that he and his party would not be able to stop anti-NP propaganda if they had to rely on due process of law as no court would construe information of public concern as subversive merely because that information painted the NP Government in a bad light." This member had been in the United States when the *Weekly Mail* was banned, which "did more damage to the image of South Africa than any other single act of oppression." Dalling concluded:

> If the hon the Minister is so sure that these newspapers are fomenting revolution, why has there been no prosecution of those newspapers? ... [Although a Nationalist MP] mentioned that [the] question of the banning of *New Nation* was tested in court[,] all that was tested in court was the hon the Minister's power to act as he does in terms of the regulations. The merits of the hon the Minister's action and the merits of his opinion were never and was not capable of being tested in courts.
> ...the only major and important guardian of democracy in South Africa is a free Press coupled with the independent courts of our country.

Having made his point, he withdrew the resolution to avoid inevitable defeat.[151] Two months later the Minister reassured Parliament that "in administering and implementing the media emergency regulations, I take the utmost care and the process which I devised and which I am obliged to adopt, is a pain in the neck. I have to give so many notices and listen to so many representations, which I do...I rather feel inclined to throw them away, but I think that after a couple of years of administering these regulations, some success has been achieved."[152]

The government complemented seizures, bannings, and dirty tricks with other tactics. For years it had threatened criminal charges without following through: fourteen times against the *Natal Witness*, seven against *New Nation*, three against *The Star*, and eleven against the *Weekly Mail*.[153] Now it actually prosecuted reporters and editors at the *Weekly Mail*, the *Sowetan*, *South*, the *Sunday Times*, the *New Nation*, and *The New African*.[154] The Association of Democratic Journalists estimated that more than a hundred reporters were arrested in the month before the September election.[155] The police also succeeded in placing Gregory Flett as a "coloured" photographer for *South*, giving him a cover for taking photos for police at political meetings and press conferences and helping police copy the paper's computer files. When activists grew suspicious his handler made him become an agent provocateur, inciting crowds to throw stones. When he tried to quit, his handler threatened to expose him to the UDF, who would kill him. It was police violence in Cape Flats on election night and its criticism by Gregory Rockman, a "coloured" lieutenant, that convinced him to break cover. Brig. Leon Mallet of the Department of Law and Order confirmed that Flett had been a paid informer since 1987.[156]

The <u>New Nation</u> Appeals

The *New Nation* and *South* reappeared immediately after the annual expiration of the Emergency (government not having used a new regulation allowing it to extend *South*'s brief suspension by two months). Many papers cheered their return.[157] The *New Nation*'s inaugural issue included dummy front pages from the banned issues and a front-page editorial denouncing Botha's "secret media 'watchdogs'" and broken promise to meet the press. "This has been our experience with the Nationalist Party 'media hit-man' who has been given power by government to subjectively decide which material in newspapers is a threat to the apartheid system in this country." The second issue summarized its appeal against the Supreme Court decision, and the third recapitulated the past three months' news.[158] Government released Zwelakhe Sisulu in December after nearly thirty months in detention but prevented him from working or being quoted.[159]

The *New Nation* filed 104 pages of heads of argument in December 1988, reiterating its earlier position. The Appellate Division heard oral argument on August 29, 1989, and gave judgment on December 1.[160] Chief Justice Corbett found that a "temporary prohibition on the publication of a periodical" was not punishment according to several legal dictionaries. The State President had not delegated more power than he possessed because the Public Safety Act "confers upon [him] powers of the widest possible character." Nor had he unlawfully subdelegated legislative powers since the Home Affairs Minister's "powers and the procedures for their exercise, are specified in detail...." The ouster clause prevented the court from testing the regulations for vagueness.[161] An earlier case requiring government to state the reasons for detention did not impose an equally extensive "duty to state grounds" for other action.[162] Any defect in the first notice was remedied by the supplementary notice, which included Botha's prima facie evaluation of the objectionable articles. Another reading of the regulations would be "unduly technical," and anyhow the *New Nation* had not "been prejudiced in any way." Even if the notices "are not models of lucid draftsmanship," "the publisher concerned is adequately apprised of the 'case' against him so that he can make appropriate representations...." Although the Minister had not always given reasons for his opinions, they were "self-evident." Any promise he had made in September 1987 to meet with the affected papers had no legal force. The court unanimously dismissed the appeal.

The End of Censorship?

This was the zenith of censorship. The *New Nation*'s circulation nearly doubled in 1989. Editor Gabu Tugwana exulted: "It is the government's action that gave more credence to our ability to fight against our government." In November, however, the new Home Affairs Minister, Eugene Louw, warned it again about promoting the image of the ANC and threatened immediate suspension. The paper called a press conference to condemn his action, and journalists and media workers marched to Department offices in support.[163] While filing 111 pages of representations about twenty-eight articles in eleven issues it claimed to be mystified why "displays of support and solidarity for the ANC…on television…which apparently received government approval, do not, for example, 'promote the public image or esteem of the ANC.'" An advocate familiar with the case "could not believe what that newspaper was publishing. The closure…had precisely no effect whatsoever on the editorial content…[which] displayed to me an attitude of what I can only describe as open defiance." Still, the representations were not "as aggressive," "more subtle," designed really to embarrass the minister…to expose at every available opportunity the arbitrary nature of what was being proposed and to contrast it with what was permissible in some cases and not permissible in other cases."

The opposition celebrated the freeing of Mandela and unbanning of organizations by launching the Campaign for an Open Media (reviving Save the Press), which included all the alternative press as well as Black Sash and COSATU.[164] The *New Nation* greeted this with a front page displaying ANC and SACP flags and a back page declaring "Freedom Now" above the ANC flag and emblem; it sold an unprecedented 73,000 copies. With the lifting of most Emergency regulations Zwelakhe Sisulu returned to his post as editor (and the suspension threat evaporated).[165] Two weeks later the state abandoned two judgments upholding the Emergency regulations against Sisulu's challenge and agreed to pay his costs, estimated at R100,000. But though government withdrew charges against the *New Nation* for quoting Harry Gwala (a listed person), it continued to pursue civil and criminal actions against *Vrye Weekblad*.[166] And though "Cry Freedom," "A World Apart," and "A Dry White Season" were approved, as well as other films and plays, government banned four movies at the annual *Weekly Mail* film festival.[167] In the May debate over the Home Affairs budget Eugene Louw, the new Minister, regretted it was not possible to unban all the publications of the unbanned ANC because they "may still contain matters of a nature that is dangerous to the State."[168] When de Klerk reimposed the Emergency in September 1990, security forces barred the press from Vaal and East Rand townships because people were inclined to "give a show for journalists."[169]

As state censorship diminished, private action against the media increased in importance. Young South Africans for a Christian Civilisation—Tradition, Family, and Property, whose attack on the *New Nation* had been a foundation of the government case, published an eleven-page open letter asking "Is It Licit for a Catholic to Support the Communist Party?" and demanding that the SACBC disavow its organ. Two months later it sent a second open letter, deploring the Church's silence. In January 1991 the SACBC announced that it would transfer ownership to an independent company now that government no longer threatened the paper.[170] Journalists suffered increased threats and attacks, and bombs damaged the *Vrye Weekblad*, *The Namibian*, and the movie theater hosting the *Weekly Mail* film festival.[171] Government officials now responded to criticism by suing for defamation.[172] With his costs paid by government, Gen. Lothar Neethling, SAP Deputy Commissioner of Scientific Technical/Services, sued the *Weekly Mail* for R500,000 and *Vrye Weekblad* for R1 million for reporting Dirk Coetzee's allegations that Neethling had provided knockout drops and poison for assassinations (see chapter seven). In January 1991 Justice Johann Kriegler found for both defendants, awarding them costs, but Neethling obtained leave to appeal. Nearly three years later the Appellate Division entered judgments for the full amount against both papers.[173] Threatening defamation actions, Chief Buthelezi forced several university libraries to remove a critical biography, although his lawyer insisted that the KwaZulu leader was committed to "genuine academic freedom as well as open and honest political debate."[174]

Government used subpoenas to threaten and harass reporters for *The Star*, the *CP Patriot*, and the *Weekly Mail*.[175] But the established press was gaining courage. In March 1991 it unanimously withdrew from agreements granting preferential access to official sources on condition of self-censorship.[176] When police investigated the *Weekly Mail* for reporting police violence in Alexandra, editor Anton Harber refused to cooperate: "The Police Act is a throwback to the dark days of the State of Emergency."[177] Yet government initiated a prosecution under the Prisons Act against a *Weekly Mail* team investigating allegations that Leeuwkop Prison inmates were forced to make weapons for hostel dwellers.[178]

The very liberalization that reduced government repression accentuated the economic vulnerability of the alternative press—a grim reminder of the death of the *Rand Daily Mail* in 1985. *New Nation* editor Gabu Tugwana complained:

> The mainstream newspapers have moved more like opportunists or hawks. Given the conditions now they are the ones that want to be seen as this big human rights paper. ...[O]ur market has been sort of eaten. ...Big business could actually support our existence through advertising, but they seem to be very, very reluctant—for good reasons...because we stood through thick and thin to our policies and principles and they were one of the people we fought for exploitation.

The Newspaper Marketing Bureau confirmed that companies refused to buy advertising space in the *New Nation* because of its earlier support for the ANC and economic sanctions.[179] The external anti-apartheid movement curtailed funding for the *Weekly Mail*, *New Nation*, *Umafrika*, *South*, *Vrye Weekblad*, and *The New African*, all of which operated at a loss.[180] *Grassroots* had already closed in 1989.[181] In early 1994 *Vrye Weekblad* closed, and even the *Saturday Star* and *Sunday Star* merged into a *Weekend Star*.[182]

In anticipation of taking power, the ANC displayed its own intolerance of criticism. Condemning "malicious attacks" by the *Eastern Province Herald* and *Evening Post*, it launched a boycott by burning old copies outside Newspaper House. Spokesman Phila Nkayi declared: "The media is at liberty to criticise the ANC-led alliance, but we could not take the vilification and bossy stance that appears to have been adopted by the *Herald* and *Evening Post*." Editor Derek Smith replied that the *Herald* had a tradition of opposing apartheid but would not be dictated to by the ANC or "become an ANC paper."[183] In July 1992 the ANC disclosed that it was considering publishing a daily newspaper with its partners the SACP and COSATU. Six months later a rumor surfaced that billionaire Nigerian press magnate Chief M.K.O. Abiola (later the successful presidential candidate in the aborted presidential election) was considering providing the capital.[184] Political involvement in the press was particularly sensitive in light of the 1970s "Muldergate" scandal (in which government money launched and supported *The Citizen* in competition with the anti-apartheid *Rand Daily Mail* and sought to buy foreign newspapers), Inkatha's purchase of *Ilanga* and attempt to buy *City Press*, and recent revelations that government had secretly spent R12 million on *Newslink* in Gaberone.[185] Echoing the past, the new SABC director, Dr. Ivy Matsepe-Casaburri, criticized the media for dwelling excessively on violence and ignoring the "good" news.[186]

Journalists, regardless of race or politics, increasingly were threatened by mob violence. SABC-TV reporter Calvin Thusago was stabbed to death in Sharpeville in April 1993 and his colleague Dudley Saunders critically injured. Worldwide TV News cameraman Sam Msibi was shot five times in Katlehong. Radio 702 reporter Brett Hilton-Barber was struck by a rock at Chris Hani's funeral. *Daily Dispatch* journalists George Galanakis and Mkhululi Bolo were stoned by a crowd attacking the South African embassy in Umtata after a memorial service for Hani. *Eastern Province Herald* journalist Jack Dewe's car was stoned in Uitenhage on the way to an ANC media conference. And Visnews journalist Mike Vincent was harassed in kwaZakhele.[187]

Analysis

Two of white South Africa's proudest boasts have been a free press and the rule of law. These events tested both pretensions and found them empty. Government attacked and ultimately suspended the few papers brave enough to assert their freedom. The judiciary offered little protection against this assault.

Even without the Emergency regulations government exercised extraordinary control over the media. It banned and seized periodicals, books, movies, and plays and punished readers for possessing them. It used the Police, Prisons, and Defence Acts to frighten and prosecute. It silenced opponents by "listing," "banning," and detaining them. It had a monopoly over television and hegemony over radio. It secretly invested in newspapers. It sought to reach printers, news services, and foreign reporters. It required shoestring operations to post large bonds. It subpoenaed journalists to disclose confidential sources and trumped up other charges against them. Officials sued for defamation. Security forces failed to prevent or punish assault, burglary, and arson and may have been complicit.

Unable to reach the anti-apartheid movement in exile or underground, government attacked the internal opposition through detentions, police and vigilante violence, treason trials, and censorship. UDF, COSATU, and the alternative media, though legal, were just as anathema because they embraced the same revolutionary end—democracy—if not the violent means. Government was determined to silence the alternative press, by either cowing it into submission or bankrupting it through suspensions. Botha mocked foreign correspondents as "nomad[s] with no allegiance"—a slur resembling anti-Semitic taunts of Jews as "rootless cosmopolitans." He openly identified the *New Nation* as his bête noire. By intensifying repression, however, he increased solidarity between the previously compliant establishment press and the beleagured alternative media.

Like other forms of regulation, censorship inevitably becomes a game, if one with unusually high stakes. Each time government proscribed, the alternative media sought a loophole; and each successful evasion prompted greater repression. Government responded to the Vaal uprising and persistent unrest, growing strength of UDF and COSATU, and intensified international condemnation and sanctions by changing the rules of engagement. Working two variations on the maxim "de mortuis nil nisi bonum," it commanded: about living opponents say nothing unless evil, about security forces nothing unless good. Just as prosecutors and judges equated treason trialists' failure to condemn violence unequivocally with tacit condonation (see chapter nine), so government insisted that every mention of the ANC express revulsion. Neutral description constituted endorsement (a perversion of the media ethic of "objectivity"). Predictions of violence became exhortations to violence. The press could say nothing negative about security forces, not even call massive searches and arrests "raids" or imply a negative pregnant by urging an end to police violence. It had to limit itself to repeating police public relations—and a little praise for "our boys" would be welcome.

Government seemed to believe that if the anti-apartheid struggle were not publicized it would not exist. It argued (with some truth) that coverage of organizational launches, demonstrations, funerals, boycotts, and stay-aways encouraged them. It portrayed blacks as politically naive and the alternative and foreign press as agitators—dupes of the total onslaught if not conscious allies—exaggerating media influence to strengthen the government case.

All too aware of its own marginality, the alternative press responded with justifications rather than apologies, thereby aggravating its offense. The *New Nation* protested it was just telling the truth. For government, however, the greater the truth the greater the subversion. The media's real crime was lèse majesté. Stoffel Botha found the *New Nation*'s representations "pugnacious, contemptuous," bordering on "bad faith." Government demanded an admission of wrongdoing, acknowledgement of its authority, and promise to reform.

Government revealed its guilty conscience by protesting too much the legitimacy of censorship. Home Affairs Minister Stoffel Botha, who gave three lengthy interviews when the scheme was launched, was master of the well-turned empty phrase. "Every country has a set of laws whether you like them or not." "In every profession there are restrictions on the way people may practise." The issue, of course, was whether these laws and restrictions were good or bad. His henchmen, Deputy Information Minister Stoffel van der Merwe and Media Relations Director Andries Engelbrecht, parroted more of the same. South Africa should be compared not with the advanced capitalist world (to which it aspired) but premodern Europe or contemporary Africa (which it constantly contemned). South Africa claimed both that it was more democratic than black Africa and that its own blacks were not ready for democracy. Western liberalism was just as extreme as communist totalitarianism; South Africa, by contrast, took a "moderate" position. Government claimed to dislike the Emergency powers it had been forced to assume. Disregarding circularity, it justified the media regulations as essential to end the Emergency, which government had declared in order to authorize those regulations. It claimed to have shown great restraint in exercising its powers, refraining from closing the *New Nation* until after the Supreme Court decision, tolerating the *Sowetan*, and demonstrating even-handedness by suspending *Die Stem*. It thus invoked press criticism to justify silencing it. Inverting the media claim to represent citizens against state oppression, Botha claimed to protect readers from media autarchy. Only establishment papers had earned their freedom—by demonstrating that they would not use it.

Today the last refuge of a scoundrel is more likely to be science than patriotism. Botha presented the Directorate of Media Relations as a mechanism for "scientific evaluation" and later offered a statistical analysis of the objectionable articles; Engelbrecht promised "to give as objective a view as possible"; *The Citizen* invoked "scientific studies which enabled one to determine whether criticism was permissible." Yet Botha concealed the membership of the Directorate's advisory panel, identifying only a few government yes-men. And his reliance on the Tradition, Family, and Property smear of the *New Nation* was hardly scientific.

Although the *Sowetan* may have saved itself through contrition and assurances, the alternative press was defiant. As the voice of the anti-apartheid movement it could not publicly capitulate to threats. *South* editor Rashid Seria denounced the government's "superficial case" as "ludicrous." Under suspension, *Weekly Mail* co-editor Anton Harber called Botha "a petty and petulent schoolmaster." The *New Nation* indulged in sarcasm and irony, telling Stoffel Botha how to read his own regulations and denouncing his interpretations of its articles as hypersensitive, exaggerated, proposterous, incongruous, invalid, far-fetched, self-evidently incorrect, inconceivable, frivolous, and in bad faith. Such behavior must have been partly expressive, since few would see the representations other than Botha. But it also may have reflected incomprehension of government motives. The alternative media were incredulous that accurate reports about the ANC were prohibited. How could government proscribe discussion of the central issue of the day? Refusing to accept that Botha was impervious to persuasion, it invoked the classic free speech arguments: truth, objectivity, history, factuality, lack of emotion or bias. It invoked precedent—even without a bill of rights, South African courts had upheld press freedom. It demanded consistency: other papers were allowed to publish similar articles. It defended the merits of each article, refusing to acknowledge that the individually innocuous could become obnoxious through cumulation. It argued that the regulations required Botha to make findings about the publication's effect, which he had not done and could not do. Words were inherently ambiguous and consequences unpredictable. When Botha's implacable determination to close the *New Nation* became clear it offered to submit to pre-publication censorship or join the Media Council and respect its code. But these accommodations were too little and too late.

If government would not tolerate press freedom, would the "rule of law" and an "independent judiciary" protect it? Tragically, no. There had been some reason for hope. Courts had interpreted the Police, Prisons, and Defence Acts narrowly, acquitting journalists of violations. They had quashed subpoenas to reveal sources and held that Inkatha could not sue for defamation. The Supreme Court had invalidated other Emergency regulations as overly broad, ultra vires, or vague. But the outcome seemed to turn on judicial personality. Occasional victories did not alter the fundamental facts of Parliamentary supremacy and no bill of rights. Government simply promulgated new regulations—often within twenty-four hours—and made them retroactive. Courts submitted to a clause denying them authority to review regulations for vagueness. Even when the media won, it lost: enormous energy was diverted into fighting government; all journalists engaged in self-censorship; like treason trialists, some were forced to compromise their beliefs; and the empty forms helped preserve the facade of procedural fairness.

Government openly acknowledged that the reputation of its legal system was at stake. Stoffel Botha prefaced the new regulations with assurances: "[A] court can still review any decision I make"; "if a particular article did not incite violence, and I based my decision on such an article, then he can take me to court." He promptly qualified this, however. Although government preferred to use the courts, they were too slow and overburdened. It pained Botha to circumvent the courts: "as a lawyer I do not like it." When the *New Nation* actually sought judicial protection, the court acknowledged its impotence. Botha had protested: "I cannot merely say: *New Nation*, I dislike you; I now close you down." But Curlewis ruled that the *New Nation* "was dealing with the opinion of a politician and not a judgement of a court of law." "The Minister does not have to give 'reasons' why he formed an opinion." "It is not our function to pass an opinion upon the Minister's opinion." Yet Botha had the nerve to reassert a year later:

> The impression is created that when action is taken against publications, they have no protection in courts of law. This is not true. No discretion, including my own, is unrestricted. Any publication objecting to my action against it, has the right to test the validity of my decision in court. This has, in fact, happened in the past. The court has the power to set aside my decisions in accordance with established legal principles. I must exercise my discretion honestly and in accordance with rules of reasonableness and fairness.

A Nationalist backbencher chimed in: "[A] full Bench of the Witwatersrand division declared that regulation seven of the media emergency regulations and the implementation of the regulation were valid." Another Nationalist invoked the UN Declaration of Human Rights to justify censorship! When critics pointed to the government's failure to test its actions in court, however, Botha hedged again. "Propaganda" could not be defined legally. If government prosecuted offenders

> the high esteem enjoyed by our courts as institutions functioning independently of the legislature and executive would be seriously jeopardised. Whether a statement constitutes propaganda or not, whether the publication of material is contrary to public interest and security, is a matter of opinion. If courts of law had to give a ruling on such opinions, the courts themselves would inevitably be drawn into the political arena.

South Africa preserved the rule of law by eviscerating it.

Lacking both political power and substantive arguments, the *New Nation* had no alternative but to make highly legalistic objections, such as the overlap of annual Emergencies and inconsistencies between the two notices. Neither the Supreme Court nor the Appellate Division chose to use the available administrative law grounds to overturn the suspension. The *New Nation*'s contention that existing legislation was adequate fell before the State

President's opinion that the Emergency regulations were expedient. Its alleged inability to understand the Minister's objections was belied by its detailed representations. Its criticism of the regulations' vagueness was dismissed by Justice Curlewis: "[H]ow can there be certainty where the opinion of a politician is involved?" Its plea for consistency in the treatment of alternative and established papers was simply ignored. Three months after de Klerk's accession accelerated reform, the Appellate Division rejected a plausible objection to retroactivity with the retort that closure was not punishment and in any case was not retroactive, since the paper could correct the error in later issues. The AD went out of its way to approve the Emergency regulations: Botha's "powers and procedures for their exercise, are specified in detail." By relying on technical arguments and procedural issues, the *New Nation* relinquished the moral high ground of principled opposition to censorship without gaining any strategic advantage.

The Supreme Court was uncomfortable about being reduced to a rubber stamp (as it was when denied the power to grant bail, shape evidentiary rules, or determine sentences). Justice Gordon protested that "this kind of legislation excludes the courts from things no court is happy to be excluded from. I am hit by the legislation." Having given government all it wanted, Justice Curlewis tried to evade responsibility. He asked the state's advocate to take further instructions, hoping the Minister had changed his mind. He immediately granted leave to appeal, hoping the Appellate Division would resist the government. And he flirted with granting a stay pending the appellate decision, which would have protected the *New Nation* almost as effectively as the interdict he denied. But though he expressed sympathy for the paper's plight (like judges sentencing conscientious objectors to long prison terms), he lost his nerve, accepting government's flimsy argument that public safety and general order would be endangered by allowing continued publication. As he said in his own inimitable language: "I do not know if I am making bad cases make hard law or hard cases make bad law."

The failure of judicial review contrasts sharply with the protection sometimes afforded critical publications by the PAB, even though members lacked lifetime tenure and professional status. The PAB approved two *New Nation* and two *South* issues that grounded Botha's suspensions. Unlike courts, furthermore, the administrative agencies gave reasons for their actions. They sought consistency, predictability, and certainty. They accepted the defense of truth. They tolerated bias and criticism. They acknowledged ambiguity, refusing to choose the worst of several possible interpretations. They looked at effects rather than potential.[188]

In the end, however, government always worked its will. When both a Publications Committee and the Board approved "Cry Freedom," government simply seized the film. Stoffel Botha did not wait for the PAB to rule before warning the *New Nation*. He did not wait for the Appellate Division before suspending it. And the judges accepted their powerlessness. The "rule of law" was form without content. Like a witch, priest, or lawyer, the State President and his Minister only had to utter magical words according to a precise formula to effect their ends. Those words did not reflect or describe reality—they constituted it. "Whether there has in fact been systematic publishing in the periodical is a matter of the Minister's opinion, whatever anyone else's opinion may be." Because the Minister's opinion was political, so were the *New Nation's* objections. "[T]he opinion that is formed will be dependent in the first place, [on] where the person stands in the political spectrum, and whether he is black or white." Courts could not choose between political opinions. Form (procedural regularity) triumphed over substance (press freedom and judicial authority). There was no need to evaluate the adequacy of the notices; since the Minister could ignore the newspaper's representations, the opportunity to make them was virtually meaningless. As Justice Curlewis was forced to conclude: "[I]f this is the whole purpose of the representations then very little can come of it."

Yet sometimes the opposition won by losing. Forced removals displayed the worst face of grand apartheid. Treason trials exposed the bankruptcy of its political theory. Prosecutions of conscientious objectors highlighted the exemplary morals of anti-apartheid whites. And censorship revealed a government afraid of both the truth and its own courts.

CHAPTER 9

THE ALEXANDRA TREASON TRIAL

> Treason is a crime in a very special category. Where the ideas and political aspirations of those charged are part of the issue... and given the spectrum of the politics of our citizens from Black to white and from far left to far right—with their grievances and aspirations—in most cases legitimate, and the often intemperate and exaggerated language and liberally spiced with current political cliches, most of these citizens just striving for a better South Africa—a charge of treason should be very carefully considered and reconsidered before it is brought before the court. (Justice van der Walt giving judgment in April 1989)

A Brief History of Alexandra

In 1905 a Mr. Papenfus registered his farm "Cyferfontein" as township land for whites and sold it to the Alexandra Township Company Ltd (named after his daughter). Because the company was unable to find any whites willing to live thirteen kilometers from downtown Johannesburg, it had the land reclassified for Black and "Coloured" residents in 1912 and further subdivided the 338 lots for sale as freeholds. To serve the 900 residents the Administrator of the Transvaal established a Health Committee in 1916: three nominated whites and two nominated Black and "Coloured" representatives; the latter were replaced by four informally elected in 1917 and eight formally elected in 1921.[1] In 1926 Johannesburg rejected a recommendation by the Secretary for Native Affairs that it incorporate Alexandra; because of its uncertain status the township was nicknamed "Nobody's Baby." Four years later the Transvaal Provincial Administration was unable to persuade the

Native Affairs Department to assume responsibility. In 1932, when the population had reached 12,000, the Transvaal Administrator replaced the eight elected Black representatives with three nominees. Three years later white residents of the North Eastern Suburbs strongly resisted expansion by Alexandra, which now contained 20,000. In 1936 a government commission rejected white demands to abolish the township, because it would cost too much to compensate landowners and resettle the entire population. Yet two years later whites persuaded the Johannesburg City Council to prepare an estimate of the cost of removal. That year the TPA again allowed Black standholders to elect two representatives to the Health Committee.[2]

A penny increase in bus fares in 1940 provoked the first boycott, which forced its repeal. A second boycott two years later curtailed a proposed increase. In August 1943, 15,000 people walked for nine days, again securing a reduction. Another penny increase in November 1944 led to a seven-week boycott, coordinated by an Emergency Committee of local leaders, black trade unions, white sympathizers, and the SACP.[3]

In response to demands by the white Federation of Ratepayers Associations to abolish the township, now containing 50,000–60,000 people, the Alexandra Vigilance and Protection Standholders Committee was established in 1942; the rival Alexandra Native Tenants Association emerged four years later.[4]

With the National Party electoral victory in 1948 and the appointment of Verwoerd as Minister of Native Affairs in 1950, Alexandra became a pawn in the scheme of grand apartheid. In 1952 a committee recommended reducing its population to 30,000 and surrounding it with a buffer zone. In 1955 the Peri-Urban Areas Health Board began expelling those who worked outside the northern suburbs, stopping unlawful immigration, and increasing taxes. It began the first hostel, provoking riots, in 1957. Another bus fare increase launched the Alexandra People's Transport Action Committee, which led a three-month boycott by 15,000 riders. By 1958 the population was nearly 100,000, making it by far the densest settlement in South Africa. Over the next four years, however, government moved 44,000 people to Soweto.[5]

In 1963 the Minister of Bantu Administration and Development announced that the township would be converted to eight hostels, housing 20,000 single workers. In pursuit of this plan the Better Administration of Designated Areas Act 1964 extended to freeholds the pervasive regulation of African tenants, and government spent R4.2 million to buy 2,539 plots by 1972. Over opposition by the white liberal Citzens Hostel Action Committee, government opened the second hostel in 1970 and the third in 1981. In 1972 a Peri-Urban Board committee published a plan for another twenty-three hostels divided into sections of 100 to 150, separated by steel doors, with a toilet for every twenty, bath for every twenty-five, and shower for every thirty-five. To prevent deracination it suggested dividing inmates along ethnic lines, painting "bantu motifs" on the buildings, and giving them "bantu names." Unless both parents had §10 rights they were separated from their children and sent to hostels. When Selma Browde objected to taking small children from their parents, the Manager of Bantu Administration replied: "Africans like living away from their children. It's a custom, you know. Bantu women prefer leaving their children with their grandparents because they don't like children around them while they're working."[6]

In 1973 the newly-created West Rand Administration Board predicted that Alexandra would be eliminated within a decade; its population already had been reduced to 40,000. The following year, however, it was estimated that expropriating the remaining 887 freeholds would cost R6.2 million and other townships could not accommodate those removed. Although WRAB began evictions for nonpayment of rent, the number dropped from 2,284 in 1974 to thirty-five in 1976, and it lacked sufficient funds to expropriate houses. The 1976 Soweto uprising led to twenty deaths and numerous injuries in Alexandra. NGK minister Sam Buti organized the Alexandra Liaison Committee, which gained government recognition in 1979. In May the Minister of Co-operation and Development reversed the 1963 decision, allowing families to remain, and promised to redevelop Alexandra. This announcement may have been timed to help Buti's Save Alexandra Party (SAP), which won all thirty seats in the first ALC election, making Buti mayor.[7]

Under the motto "Through Development We Reach the Sky," the ALC took credit for improvements and created the Alexandra Development Corporation to build factories that would employ residents. The SAP youth wing established the Thusong youth center, which operated a junior town council. In July 1980 government approved a master redevelopment plan, which would demolish all existing structures to house 65,000 family members and 8,000 hostel-dwellers. When the remaining 300 standholders refused to sell, the ALC supported expropriation. Although SAP councillor Harry Makubire had promised "to help those people [without residential rights] become lawful residents of the township," the ALC now insisted illegal residents had to leave.[8]

In the second ALC election in September 1981 two opposition parties challenged the SAP. The Alexandra Action Committee was chaired by Mike Beea, an Ethiopian Church minister and production manager, who had resigned from the SAP over the expropriation of a stand. Buti dismissed them as a "handful who... barked like confused puppies in a shebeen.... It is strange that now that we have saved the township, an opposition party should emerge.... Whoever opposes us will be against Alexandra." Although the SAP again won overwhelmingly, the turnout was less than half that of the first election (and less than twenty-five percent). When a hundred squatters were evicted in November 1981, the ALC dismissed them as "not bona fides of the township [but] people who had just streamed to Alexandra from nowhere." In 1983 those evicted for urban renewal were housed "temporarily" in twenty buses (twelve were still occupied three years later) and an abandoned tuberculosis hospital, where they feared attacks from the neighboring hostel and danger to their children from falling in the Jukskei River. Few residents could afford to rent, much less buy, the new accommodation.[9]

In 1981 a group of Alexandra residents, Wits students, and white Sandton suburbanites formed Ditshwantso tsa Rona to discuss and document township conditions. In September 1983 it led a protest at Buti's home, composed of evictees in "temporary housing." Allegations of corruption in the allocation of trading licenses to councilors' relatives repeatedly surfaced. When the ALC celebrated the seventieth anniversary of Alexandra in 1983, only 2,000 participated, perhaps because the Alexandra Youth Congress (AYCO) called a boycott. The ALC became the Alexandra Town Council in November 1983. As a result of boycott calls by AYCO and the Congress of South African Students (COSAS) the SAP candidates were returned unopposed. At the end of 1984 the Council had accumulated a R1,225,000 deficit (twenty percent of its budget). Ditshwantso formed the Phase One Neighbourhood Committee (tenants who refused to pay the increased rents), Bus and Zinc Committee (evictees housed in buses and huts), and Sewer Committee (247 families threatened with eviction). At the beginning of 1985 these joined into the Alexandra Residents Association (ARA), a "workerist" organization that refused to join the UDF. It had hostile relations with the charterist AYCO and the Alexandra Civic Association (the former Alexandra Action Committee), whose leaders included teachers, shebeen owners, and businessmen.[10]

In late 1984 the Department of Co-operation and Development authorized Alexandra and fifteen other local authorities to establish police forces. When the ARA denounced this, Buti said the Council had only done a feasibility study; but in April 1985 the Council newspaper reported that hiring police was a top priority. The Council responded to the ARA rent boycott by suspending increases but attacked it as impractical and obstructionist.[11]

In February 1985 Vincent Tshabalala, a former AYCO member and ANC guerrilla, was killed by a hand grenade in a shootout with police. At the funeral two weeks later 3,000 people heard Buti denounced as a sell-out, and mourners stoned his house. Early in March two firebombs caused R80,000 damage to Buti's home. Later that month a mob of pupils attacked his children (who had been forced out of school), burned his shop, and burned three buses and damaged others. At the end of the month police arrested two AYCO officials, Paul Mashatile and Jacob Mtshali, for organizing a memorial service for Langa victims. In mid-April AYCO held a rally of 3,000 to launch International Youth Year; youths leaving the meeting broke windows in the homes of Buti and town clerk Arthur Magerman. Two days later 500 Alexandra High School pupils marched to the Wynberg police station to demand the release of a youth arrested in front of the school. Their arrests provoked further demonstrations and arrests, including that of Mike Beea.[12]

At the beginning of May, Beea chaired a meeting addressed by representatives of COSAS, AYCO, the ARA, and the Alexandra Women's Organisation (AWO), as well as trade unionist Moses Mayekiso. It called on pupils to return to school and stop attacking buses. At the end of the month thousands of pupils participated in a township cleanup organized as part of International Youth Year. Following the June commemoration of Soweto, 300 youths attacked the houses of Buti, Magerman, and a policeman. The entire AYCO leadership was detained at the beginning of the Emergency in late July. Nevertheless, AYCO launched an anti-crime campaign in August, alleging police indifference to victim complaints. Youths searched and disarmed residents, stopped other youths from drinking, and closed the shebeens at 9 p.m. By December, however, the "comtsotsis" (hoodlums masquerading as comrades) had diverted the campaign to criminal purposes. The AYCO executive, released soon thereafter, reasserted authority and regained popular support by January 1986.[13]

In August the Johannesburg City Council announced a R200 million redevelopment project for Alexandra, including the transfer of 250 acres of land; this immediately elicited protests from neighboring whites. When the ARA demand for rent decreases was not met, it called a general rent boycott. On December 6 Mayor Buti and the Alexandra Town Council were elected unopposed, one of two out of thirty councils still operating. The previous day government had announced a gift of 200 acres, full autonomy, the promise of 1,500 houses and 1,000 flats, and freehold rights.[14]

The Alexandra Uprising, January–June 1986

Richard Padi, twenty-one, was shot to death by Alexandra Council police on New Year's Eve, allegedly while he was enforcing the UDF "Black Christmas" boycott. Although police banned an outdoor funeral, 3,000 people attended, some of whom stoned a Casspir and firebombed a police car, badly burning an occupant; four residents were wounded. On February 1 a store security guard shot to death Michael Isaac Dirading, nineteen. At the funeral on Saturday, February 15, an estimated 6,000–13,000 heard speakers condemn police shootings and Mayor Buti. When police teargassed mourners engaged in the ceremonial washing of hands, youths threw firebombs, burning a policeman and destroying a beerhall and ten white-owned factories, supermarkets, service stations, and other businesses adjoining the township. The next night an eighty-three-year-old woman suspected of being a witch was necklaced and died in hospital. The same day a white family was attacked driving their maid home, an event graphically described in *The Citizen*. Police excluded television crews and promulgated new restrictions barring photographers from telephoto range, although the events were the top story in British newspapers and television.[15]

On Monday residents began a massive stay-away, boycotting schools for the entire week. The next day AYCO organized a meeting of 30,000 at the football stadium, which demanded immediate withdrawal of security forces, release of all prisoners, and suspension of the Emergency. Police barred Beyers Naudé and Allan Boesak from the township but allowed Bishops Desmond Tutu and Manas Buthelezi to speak. Police refused to meet a delegation of ministers, however, insisting they would speak only to Mayor Buti. That day a white policeman jumped from a Casspir and shot to death Jerry Mthembu, eighteen, at point blank range. The next day police detained Moses Mayekiso and John Grant (a leader of the "coloured" community). The Metal and Allied Workers Union (of which Mayekiso was secretary general) organized a stay-away on March 5; he was released two days later with the end of the Emergency. Estimates of the number killed in the "Six-Day War" ranged from nineteen (by Deputy Law and Order Minister Vlok) to eighty (by Beyers Naudé). The National Medical and Dental Association accused security forces of ordering the Alexandra Health Centre to identify those it treated. When it refused, police obtained a subpoena, then withdrew it and, armed with a search warrant, seized 175 medical records. Mike Beea declared: "Our people are being shot by young and inexperienced soldiers and policemen, most of whom are gun crazy." But Sam Buti attributed the uprising to "agitators" from other townships. "The political elements are taking advantage of the situation, and this is definitely one aspect of the violence."[16]

Some papers condemned "the ham-handed way in which security forces handle funerals" and commented that "far from bringing peace to the townships, the state of emergency is another irritant to an already considerable sense of grievance."[17] But *The Citizen* accused "radicals" of having "deliberately set fire to a powder keg of suppressed feelings...." Their aim "is to make the townships ungovernable and to take over themselves. The African National Congress has broadcast instructions to set up street committees and kangaroo courts...."[18] The SABC condemned "the ANC and its affiliated organisations" for fostering "the law of the jungle." Without "effective police protection against violence [people would be left] to the mercy of the revolutionary clique and its hooligan storm-troopers... the justice of the kangaroo court and the 'necklace.'" Two weeks later the anti-apartheid *Sunday Tribune* portrayed these institutions in another light.[19]

> Because many activists are detained and subjected to alleged harassment once they become known to the police, community organisations have decided that street committees should run—more or less—the affairs of the townships.... Each committee member knows how many people live in his street. The committees liaise with bereaved families and keep records of everyone who is killed, missing, injured or detained. ...Township sources say courts have been introduced in Alexandra to do criminal cases and determine "sentences", but this has been difficult to confirm.

Church leaders Manas Buthelezi, Allan Boesak, Beyers Naudé, Desmond Tutu, and Lionel Louw and ACA chairman Mike Beea met Deputy Law and Order Minister Vlok and others in Cape Town on Thursday, February 20, and were given permission to report back. Tutu addressed a crowd of 45,000 the next day. Contrary to rumors, State President Botha did not snub them. "He sent a message that he was busy." Tutu told Vlok "we are on the winning side...there is no doubt that apartheid was immoral, unjust and that it was collapsing." Vlok said police would "facilitate" burials. The "request to release all detainees would be given the necessary attention." He would "welcome further discussion with the churches" about lifting the Emergency "seeing that even on the side of the Government this was the wish." The audience booed Tutu, and many left early. Youths stopped him outside the stadium and asked where they should sleep because "the police harass us and raid our homes every night. As soon as you leave here we will deal with the police in our own way because they are merciless."[20]

On Monday, February 24, the ACA reported that seventeen dead had been identified. Mike Beea announced that Black Sash, Detainees Parents' Support Committee, Johannesburg Democratic Action Committee, and Lawyers for Human Rights were helping the ACA open a Crisis Centre to trace the missing, transport relatives to the mortuary, and provide legal advice. The ACA rejected the Council's message of solidarity. The next day Beea denounced self-styled "comrades" who claimed to be collecting money for the funeral. On Wednesday he announced a mass funeral a week later. At a UDF conference that week he denounced the killing of forty-five people and said police were still harassing residents. On Thursday Wilson Molepo, fourteen, died of a police gunshot he had received ten days earlier. His father, Rev. Thomas Molepo, resigned from the Council the next day and asked that his son be included in the mass funeral. Mike Beea commented: "Mr Molepo has realised that no man can fight a crocodile in the river because he has little chance of winning. All those who are saying they will fight the system from within have been misled. We urge all our brothers and sisters who are still in such bodies to reconsider their positions and resign."[21]

The Mass Funeral Coordinating Committee, composed of the Alexandra Youth Congress, Students Congress, Traders Association, Taxi Association, Funeral Undertakers Association, Women's Organisation, Voice of Priests, and Parents Crisis Committee, worked with the Alexandra Ministers' Fraternal to identify nineteen bodies at the mortuary. Mike Beea persuaded police to stay away, but they still banned all audio-visual equipment, and government deported three CBS television journalists for defying the ban. At a mass meeting at Wits on Tuesday, March 4, the presidents of the National Union of South African Students and the Black Students' Society urged 2,000 students to attend the funeral; an estimated 700 did so. A vigil that night at Alexandra stadium drew 25,000, and churches held other vigils. Two youths were shot to death driving to attend one of them, while community leaders and marshalls saved a suspected informer from the crowd's anger.

The March 5 mass funeral attracted a crowd estimated at 12,000–100,000. The U.S. acting consul general sent Mike Beea his "profound sympathy and condolences." Representatives of the United States, Britain, West Germany,

France, the Netherlands, Australia, and Canada attended. Speakers included the SACC Secretary General, the Catholic Bishop of Johannesburg, and the UDF president, national chairman, and Transvaal vice-president. The Secretary General of the Catholic Bishops' Conference conducted the service. UDF, ANC, AZAPO, ECC, and Soviet flags were displayed. The crowd shouted "Vivas" for Mandela, Tambo, and Slovo. Winnie Mandela's speech was read for her because she was banned. The only violence was the burning of two cars as mourners returned from the cemetary. Two days later community organizations announced plans for a second mass funeral for the thirteen victims still at the mortuary, but it was aborted when eleven bodies disappeared. Mortuary officials would not say who took them, but police had earlier warned families to bury them separately.[22]

On March 10 Darkie Rametse, former SAP chairman, resigned from the Council. "The whole community of Alexandra was one in telling me to quit." Albert Maphala followed suit two days later. "My students told me that, as a middleman, I was standing in the way of the liberation struggle." Buti persuaded the others to remain, but a policeman resigned the same week because "I cannot raise arms against my younger brothers and sisters." On March 18 an Alexandra Junior Councilor resigned because "the people" were still "calling him names," and he wanted them to accept him back into the community. When Paul Mashile resigned on March 26, the nine-person Council lacked a quorum and could not function (one had resigned the previous year and another been removed because of a criminal conviction). Mashile wrote: "Members of my church and the entire community have urged me for a long time to resign." Another policeman quit the next day. "The community asked me to resign and my parents told me to leave the police force. The job I had been doing for 12 years was hated by everybody."[23]

Mayor Buti replied in *The Sunday Star* on April 6. "We are not stooges." He had saved Alexandra and initially refused community council status. "The council, as any other council, has municipal police who patrol the township." Housing was the "most important single issue." "So, when I concentrate on building a town, I am also involved in liberating my people." It was "all right to mobilise people to boycott but not to the point where authority—parental, school or otherwise—is undermined." But he was "all for" civil disobedience. "Government authority can be undermined.... I don't stand in opposition to any other liberation group.... unban the ANC and give it recognition.... I don't even accept the concept of reform." He favored "selective sanctions" on South Africa. He and his family had "not been intimidated in any way." But despite these brave words, the entire Alexandra Junior Council resigned on April 15. According to its mayor, Harvey Phalatse, "the people of Alexandra...took us as if we were being sponsored by the Government." The Town Clerk also resigned that day and a week later was joined by Buti and the three remaining councilors. Buti insisted "we were not intimidated."

"Our Government is applying modern slavery.... Reforming apartheid is like shifting the furniture around in the same house. We want transformation, not reform." The ACA newspaper greeted this "people's victory," and UDF welcomed the "fall of the Alexandra Town Council."[24]

On April 12 a gang of youths dragged Theresa Maseka, twenty-two, from her home, and accused her of being a police informer. She escaped at 7th Avenue, taking refuge in a house, but was caught, necklaced, and burned to death. The same day a thousand youths attended an AYCO congress, which was dispersed by police. The day after several youth organizations held a workshop at Thusong Youth Centre, at which an AYCO activist presented a paper entitled "Governability within ungovernability." He recalled that "this meant being ungovernable to the state, but being governable within our own organisations. ... I spoke of the emerging rudimentary structures of people's power." Two weeks earlier *New Nation* editor Zwelakhe Sisulu had given the keynote address at the National Education Crisis Committee conference, declaring that "in a situation of ungovernability, the government does not have control."[25]

Although the ACA had condemned a boycott call in March, the Alexandra Consumer Boycott Committee launched rent and consumer boycotts on April 18-21 and asked all students to leave multi-racial, boarding, and homeland schools. Youths patrolled the twenty-five shops targeted; observers differed about whether they used persuasion or intimidation.[26]

On the night the Council collapsed, dozens of vigilantes wearing riot police uniforms and balaclavas attacked the township. Most were Black, but a few whites had blackened faces. Although they shouted the slogans of comrades, they were accompanied by a police Hippo. They burned the houses of leading activists, including Mike Beea, Linda Twala (chairman of the Alexandra Crisis Committee), Tex Zwane, John Grant, Richard Mdakane, Moses Mayekiso, and Jeanette Yekwa (the neighbor of UDF leader Popo Molefe, probably the real target). Zwane recognized some of the attackers as police. Beea's wife Rebecca and his young children and mother were assaulted. Rebecca said the attackers accused Mike of having "instigated the children to kill the police and move them from the townships." Spent cartridges and full magazines were found in Mayekiso's yard. ACA executive member Billy "Ace" Hlongwane was burned to death and his girlfriend beaten. His yard contained the ACA headquarters; the attackers asked his girlfriend for the association's minute book. Two of the dead were Alexandra Action Committee (AAC) and ACA activists. The PFP denounced the attack in Parliament. The same week vigilantes attacked activists in Soweto and three other Vaal triangle townships.[27]

The next day residents staged a massive stay-away from work and school to meet in the stadium (estimates ranged from 7,000–50,000). They resolved to continue the rent and consumer boycotts (having identified shopkeepers among the vigilantes), called for the withdrawal of all police, and built barriers and tank traps against security force vehicles. After the rally 10,000 people

confronted the police, leading to an exchange of gunfire in which one resident was killed and fifty residents and a policeman were wounded. Police
searched the township, detaining AAC vice-chair John Grant, AAC executive
committee member Sarah Mthembu, and AYCO member Obed Bapela.[28]

The Star attributed the attack to abuses at a people's court, describing a
"presiding officer's desk," a "judge's gavel," and "two motor car tyres, painted
red and white—reminders of the awful necklace death which awaited collaborators with the 'system.' The sentences meted out ranged from beatings
to death, sometimes by burning." Both it and the *Sowetan* reproduced photographs of the tires. The next day Mike Beea explained that the court only
resolved family disputes, dismissing the tires as "just decoration." Other residents agreed, including those accused before the court. But two days later
the *Sunday Times* offered a sensationalistic account.

> [T]he "comrades"—the faceless group of hard-line militants who
> aspire to rule the township—were quick to exploit the gap left
> by the resignation of Mr Sam Buti and his councillors. They
> called on Blacks to "isolate collaborators socially", to refuse to
> serve councillors and their families in their shops and "to end all
> personal relationships with police and other collaborators."
> Wide-eyed township dwellers talk of "people's courts" where the
> comrades dispense their medieval justice—often condemning
> victims in absentia, with the dreaded "necklace" as the symbol
> of their revolution.

A newspaper noted that seven cars outside the court had been destroyed by
the vigilantes and that John Grant (whom it called chairman of the court) was
in detention and Moses Mayekiso (whom it called his deputy) was hiding.[29]

Police killed Orlando Pirates soccer player Vusi "Fire" Silango two days
after the vigilante attack and two others a day later. An hour-long gun battle
at 37-10th Avenue the following day wounded two white security police and
killed Zephaniah Mdakane (an AYCO member and brother of Richard) and
Emanuel Ngubeni. The AAC claimed that police had killed eighteen people
since the vigilante attack.[30]

Transvaal vice-chairman Samson Ndou declared: "The UDF calls on people to form self-defence committees on every street, on every block, in every
township...." At a press conference on April 29 the AAC claimed "grassroots control of the township." Chairman Moses Mayekiso said "residents
have now successfully been mobilised so that they can defend themselves
against the police." "The police and the army are the enemies of the people."

> We are not against law and order. In fact, we have introduced
> what police and their emergency powers could not.... What we
> did was organise the youth and form the AAC. We had to set an
> ideal for them and continuously remind them that they should
> respect a human being. People who disregard law and order are

called to our place and we talk with them in an amicable and encouraging manner to have respect for the community.... We patrol our township day and night. [Residents would not hand suspects over to the police] as we believe we can solve our problems by ourselves.

Street committees mediated family problems and dealt with crime; those they could not resolve were sent to the 7th Avenue people's court, which had not imposed any punishment and could not sentence people to death. "Necklace burnings will not help the community solve its problems."[31]

The next day David Dalling, PFP MP for neighboring Sandton, submitted affidavits to Law and Order Minister le Grange detailing police involvement in the vigilante attack, which he compared to the killing fields of Cambodia. When Helen Suzman accused le Grange of tacitly condoning police abuses in townships and prisons he called her a mouthpiece for the SACP, ANC, PAC, and UDF (but was forced to apologize). He rejected criticism of his restrictions on funerals, which were political meetings used to display the Russian and ANC flags. "We have now had enough and these people must take what they get." The Director General of Constitutional Development and Planning refused to acknowledge the AAC, even if it controlled the township, because "government has provided mechanisms and structures for communities to elect representatives to deal with the development of their towns." Mayekiso retorted that residents rejected them.[32]

On May 4, 5,000 people attended a mass funeral for Vusi Silango, at which an AAC representative spoke. Two days later the second Alexandra Crisis Committee began planning a mass funeral for victims of the vigilante raid. On May 8 firebombs burned the home of a white anti-apartheid activist, the Alexandra Medical Centre, and St. Catherine's Anglican Church Sanctuary in Bramley (which had been damaged twice before, after meetings devoted to Alexandra). Popo Molefe's house was firebombed at 1:15 that morning, and a white man was seen fleeing from the scene. Although the AAC had to cancel a press conference that day because police had raided their homes the previous night, Moses Mayekiso declared that the people refused to accept Buti back as a leader. At the press conference the next day AAC publicity secretary Naude Moitse blamed vigilantes for the fire bombings and said they had also attacked the 3rd Avenue people's court. "For about three weeks now, troops have been present 24 hours a day in the stadium, our major venue of meetings and funeral gatherings.... Alexandra is a war zone. You won't see people on the streets after 8 p.m. when there are massive searchlights over the township. Every day you hear shots." The AAC and PFP planned to ask the courts to order police out of the township.[33]

Instead, 1,670 security forces surrounded the township on May 10 and conducted house-to-house searches and body searches. They called it a "normal crime prevention campaign" but arrested only twenty-eight people, mostly for minor offenses. They handed out leaflets asking for "information concerning people who are preventing your children's education... keeping you from work... stop[ping] you to buy where you like." They warned that "no further lawlessness will be tolerated" and "regret[ted] any inconvenience." Mayekiso replied that "the security forces are the ones who have made life difficult."[34]

Two days later *Business Day*, usually a government critic, published a full-page "exclusive report" on an Alexandra people's court.[35] An unnamed comrade declared "a decision has been taken to form an alternative administrative structure to govern the township, because the residents rejected any government-appointed administration." The article claimed that "highly politicised youths brandishing AK47 rifles stalk the township on days of mass prayer meetings and funerals of unrest victims." Government collaborators were stoned to death or necklaced. An "astonishing" development was the people's courts, about which residents told "hair-raising tales." One said "there are tyres hanging on the walls of these 'courts' ready to be used as 'necklaces' around the necks of those who have been found guilty."

Reporter Sipho Ngcobo observed a trial on May 3, after "days of shadowy contact with people whose names and faces I did not and still do not know." The court dealt with "cases of all kinds—rape, theft, housebreaking, family disputes." The prosecutors were four young men wearing red, black, and white caps with the slogan "Aluta continua." The judge was about thirty-two. All belonged to the AAC. The silence was "deafening," the tension "frightening," and the accused "shaking like a leaf." But the lengthy "transcript" presented a much more attractive picture. The sixty-four-year-old complainant accused a young man of theft and demanded he be sjambokked. Both were given ample opportunity to talk and an interpreter was provided. Prosecution witnesses explained that their "uncle" drank up his wages and then stole from neighbors. They agreed to accept him back if he stopped drinking. At the judge's request a prosecutor offered "political education."

> 'Ntate' [Daddy], one of the Alexandra Action Committee's major objectives is to build the community, and you will notice that crime has decreased considerably since we started running our own affairs after the fall of the local town council and our resolution to build the wall separating us from the police.
>
> We do not believe the accused is beyond redemption. He can be rehabilitated and then join the struggle for freedom of the oppressed people.... Sjamboking a man does not necessarily mean he will change.... We will work hard to make the accused a good person and we will also ask you to help us change this man. What do you say? Can you help us?
>
> *Complainant:* My children, I am very pleased. If only that was possible and if he could give up liquor. You know, I like this boy.

The accused agreed not to drink. The judge persuaded the accused's "nephews" to let him live with them because "you cannot hope to rehabilitate a renegade, a vagabond who does not even have a place to stay." They, the complainant, and the AAC would monitor his drinking and spending. The article concluded: "There is laughter and shaking of hands. All faces are bright and radiant. Even the young, scruffy accused is no longer shaking." The accompanying editorial said it was "clear that an alternative to the constitutional system of justice now functions in black society...." But the sentence was "reasonably fair." Despite the "appalling dangers that lie in the emergence of kangaroo courts... the striking thing about the alternative structure of local government is the degree to which it mimics the system that whites have been trying unilaterally to impose...."

The *Pretoria News* found such alternative structures "chilling" because they revealed the lack of "confidence in the State and its instruments of power.... the 'committees of the streets' in so many black areas have convinced sizeable chunks of the communities that true power resides with them and not with 'our' South Africa." The *Financial Mail* asked whether they were "an ambitious experiment in grassroots democracy, or vicious rule by intimidation?" It described the AAC yard, block and street committees, capped by a twenty-two-member executive. "Accountability is of primary concern, making regular report-back meetings a necessity." Mayekiso claimed the AAC had organized about sixty percent of Alexandra and declared "the court's intention is to educate, not punish." "The court teaches offenders that they have been manipulated by the system. We understand how poverty drives people to steal, but we encourage the offender to look for a job instead. In addition, he is assisted by employed residents...." Courts did not try serious offenders, like informers, but even they could be redeemed. "Informers are sick. You can not heal them by killing them. People inform either because they are hungry, or are pressurised by the police after being arrested."[36]

On May 12 a magistrate rejected the AAC application to hold a funeral for eight unrest victims in the football stadium, which security forces had occupied for three weeks. Businessmen offered to intercede with the magistrate if the AAC would stop residents from displaying ANC and SACP flags, but the AAC replied: "We don't order the people to wave flags, how can we tell them not to wave them?" The Law and Order Ministry said permission for the funeral had been denied because "radicals wanted to turn it into a political forum." The magistrate rejected a second application but allowed an indoor funeral on Saturday, May 17. Three youths were wounded by police the night before, one on his way to the vigil. The eight coffins were covered by ANC flags and followed by two youths carrying a larger one. A thousand people crowded into the church, while another 3,000–4,000 remained outside. Transvaal UDF president Curtis Nkondo told them: "Either you join the struggle or you join the police. There is no such thing as the politics of neutrality."

Mourners chanted slogans supporting Umkhonto we Sizwe. Although police surrounded the cemetary, following the procession in Casspirs, armored personnel carriers, trucks, and horses, they arrested only three. The next day the Johannesburg Democratic Action Committee brought 300 to 500 whites, who defied police threats of arrest to lay flowers on the graves of unrest victims and meet community leaders. They were greeted by thousands of singing residents. A white leader said they had come as "friends and comrades," "conscious participants in the struggle," not mere "sympathetic onlookers." Police gave them ten minutes to disperse and lobbed a tear gas cannister after five. Two days later, after a Hippo visited the cemetery, residents found offensive messages on the graves: "If you live by the sword, you die by the sword;" "Fuck Black Sash."[37]

On May 15 the ACA newspaper claimed responsibility for establishing street committees and persuading the Council to resign, called for a "people's alternative administration," and concluded with a rousing "Viva the Civic!" During that week youths renamed township streets ANC, Tambo, Mbeki, Sisulu, Madhiba (an honorific for Mandela), and Tshabalala and a school after Solomon Mahlangu. On May 19 Steve Burger, appointed township administrator after the Council's collapse, thanked residents and community organizations for their cooperation and said he could "see the withdrawal of the Defence Force in the near future." Yet two days later police detained AAC organizers Richard Mdakane, Godfrey Msizane, Mzwanele Mayekiso and Naude Moitse for fourteen days. On May 22 AYCO president Paul Mashatile announced that AYCO, ASCO, the ACA, and the AAC would meet four days later to form a liaison committee to hold democratic elections for a single body to govern Alexandra.

> We don't just want money, we want control. [The liaison committee] should be seen as a continuation of our programme of setting up community structures and taking control of our destiny. Our attitude remains the same: we don't want any Government organisation or people to run our lives.

On May 24 the AAC met at Thusong Youth Centre to elect an interim executive. Two days later publicity secretary Obed Bapela appealed to Law and Order Minister le Grange to stop "harassing the people" by confiscating the AAC bank book, minutes, other documents, and t-shirts and "going around taking the names and addresses of youths in the street." A mass meeting at Thusong on June 7 chose the AAC as sole representative of the township, dissolving the ACA and subordinating AYCO and ASCO to the AAC. The AAC suspended the two-month consumer boycott (but not the rent boycott) and planned a commemorative service on the anniversary of Soweto, June 16.[38] Sandton councilor Ricky Valente met with community organizations, including the AAC. That day youths (returning from a UDF meeting that called for unbanning the ANC) captured a suspected informer, put a tire around his neck, and made him drink gasoline. He escaped while they went looking for his employer, whom they necklaced and stoned to death. Five days later the AAC executive condemned the killing, promised to discipline the youths, appointed a committee to protect the victim's family, and offered to help with funeral arrangements. The same day AAC members interrupted a carjacking. The youths returned with guns and shot at AAC members but missed. That evening youths (presumably the hijackers) shot into a meeting, killing the ASCO president and wounding two children; seventy others were injured trying to escape. Police redetained Obed Bapela the next day.[39]

On June 12 the State President re-declared the Emergency (which had lapsed in March), condemning the ANC, UDF, and other "radicals and anarchists" who planned Soweto commemorations. "They further intend to undermine Government institutions and to establish so-called 'alternative structures' on a wider basis... [including] so-called 'people's courts' and actions by the 'comrades.'" Police redetained AAC activists Mzwanele Mayekiso that day and Richard Mdakane a week later. Government reported that the day after the Soweto anniversary (June 16) Addis Ababa Radio Freedom broadcast:

> [We] can assert our will over that of the oppressor. We have now reached the stage where our will counts. Now we have to move to a stage where our will rules, where we decide in our own country.... The enemy is resorting to the state of emergency not because it is demonstrating its strength but because we have reduced its capacity to govern.... We have to move from the recent stage of ungovernability to people's power—combine mass activities with armed struggle.

When MAWU recalled Moses Mayekiso from Sweden on June 28 he was detained at the airport, an event reported in *The New York Times*. COSATU called a stay-away on July 14 to protest the detention of 245 union members, including Mayekiso; on the Witwatersrand it succeeded only in Alexandra. The International Metalworkers' Federation organized its members around the world to send postcards to Botha demanding Mayekiso's release.[40]

Alexandra's new administrator, Steve Burger, began to fulfill his promise of development, immunizing 10,000 children against polio and organizing youths to clean up the township. Government appropriated R7 million to build 300 apartments, and Johannesburg City Council donated 250 acres for a 60,000-person stadium. At the same time security forces sealed off the township with barbed wire, diesel drums, boulders, and concrete slabs to stop carjacking. At the end of November a store security guard was convicted of the February murder of Michael Dirading, the disruption of whose funeral by police provoked the Six-Day War. By the following March government had built a post office and clinic, installed pay telephones, tarred the main road, erected street lights, begun six new schools and planned two others.

In July Burger claimed there was no more unrest. ACA president Mike Beea agreed; his was the only functioning community organization, as the AAC, AYCO, and ARA had gone underground. Yet residents boycotted the October 1987 commemoration of the development plan and continued withholding rent. Alexandra did not participate in the October 1988 local elections.[41]

The UDF Treason Trials

The Alexandra treason trial followed two others. Police arrested fifteen UDF and South African Allied Workers Union (SAAWU) leaders in Natal between August 1984 and February 1985 and indicted them for treason in April.[42] Their trial in Pietermartizburg was observed by a U.S. Court of Appeals judge, prominent lawyers from the U.S. and U.K., and diplomats from Australia, Sweden, Britain, Italy, the U.S., Canada, and West Germany.[43] Justice Milne took the unprecedented step of appointing two Black assessors: an Indian lawyer and one of the first African magistrates. The prosecutor, Gey van Pittius, relied heavily on fifty-three videotapes, which turned out to be virtually inaudible. Watching the first, Milne commented: "we're not hearing what has been said…was he speaking in English?" Three police contradicted each other, forcing the prosecution to admit that dates on documents had been altered. The state's star witness was Isaak de Vries, doctoral candidate and senior lecturer at Rand Afrikaans University and expert witness in nineteen previous trials, who had been preparing for two years to prove a conspiracy among UDF, SAAWU, and the Transvaal and Natal Indian Congresses. He testified for almost a week, boring the judge by interminably reading from documents.

> *Milne:* What is he doing that we can't do for ourselves?

> *Van Pittius:* Yes. No, I agree with that M'Lord. It's just because—well we consider him as an expert and in view of his evidence…and…for the court to know at this stage what the State thinks is applicable to his evidence on the revolution and the revolutionary movement in South Africa.

> …

> *De Vries:* No you see in these passages which I've read…I…thought the State would…argue at the end…. So I'm still not supposed to refer to the meaning of sentences….

> *Milne:* You must lead your witness, Mr van Pittius. You know what you want from him, get it from him.

> *Van Pittius:* That is what I'm trying to do M'Lord.

> *De Vries:* Could I perhaps ask M'Lord, as a witness…[for] a ten minute adjournment for me to have consultations with Mr van Pittius?

De Vries deteriorated further under cross-examination by defense counsel Ismail Mohammed SC, becoming flustered, switching between Afrikaans and English, and admitting fundamental mistakes, such as ignorance of the fact that the Natal and Transvaal Indian Congresses had not existed in 1960 and 1971. After an adjournment to allow him to refresh his memory, he conceded his evidence could never be conclusive. The state was given another adjournment to decide whether to retain him as an expert. Losing patience, the judge intervened.

> *Milne:* Did you form such an opinion—that there were certain individuals who were apparently committed to violence? And certain organisations?
>
> *De Vries:* No, not a final opinion on that. I have only indicated the revolutionary directed actions.
>
> *Mohammed:* M'Lord, then I don't know the value of this whole evidence and of this witness.
>
> *Milne:* That's why I'm asking the questions.

He adjourned the case to allow prosecution and defense to confer. Two days later the Attorney General invited the defense team to supper and said he was dropping the charges against all but the four trade unionists.[44]

When the trial resumed the prosecution withdrew thirteen of the twenty-five transcripts of recordings of SAAWU meetings because of numerous errors, many identified by the two Black assessors. The judge described one transcript as untrustworthy, an "extremely slovenly piece of work." Defense counsel Marino Moerane used his linguistic expertise to challenge translations. The judge observed that a word the state used to link SAAWU to the outlawed SACTU was not on the tape. The prosecutor conceded the translation was sloppy. A new state expert witness admitted in cross-examination that the tape contained "portions where changes had been made," including an "obvious interruption" when an alleged co-conspirator was denying any knowledge of ANC meetings. The witness confessed that his earlier statement that "there had been no attempt to edit" the tapes was "ill considered." When Milne issued a 143-page judgment excluding all video and audio tapes the prosecution dismissed all charges in June 1986, ending a trial estimated to have cost R2 million.[45]

In June 1985 the state indicted twenty-two Transvaal activists for treason, notably UDF secretary Popo Molefe and publicity secretary Patrick "Terror" Lekota. Defendants in each case were unindicted co-conspirators in the other. The trial began in January 1986, after the state had changed the venue from Pretoria to the Eastern Transvaal town of Delmas to reduce both publicity and the number of Blacks in the audience. This was Justice Kees van Dijkhorst's first political trial. When the state rested in October, after producing 8,000 pages of testimony, he dismissed charges against three and granted bail to six. In March 1987, three months after the defense began, its fourth witness testified about the UDF Million Signatures Campaign. Although both assessors had assured the judge they had no relationship to UDF, Dr. W.A. Joubert now said he had signed the petition. Joubert was the most respected legal academic in the country: former dean of the Unisa law faculty, a verligte critic of apartheid and founding member of the Progressive Federal Party. Joubert had known van Dijkhorst for years and given him his first academic position. After consulting the Judge President of the Transvaal Provincial Division, van Dijkhorst dismissed Joubert. When defense counsel requested a week's adjournment to respond, van Dijkhorst gave them fifteen minutes. Joubert refused to accept dismissal, sending a report to the State President, Minister of Justice, Chief Justice, Transvaal Judge President, van Dijkhorst, Transvaal Attorney General, General Council of the Bar, Association of Law Societies, and the defendants.

> It was manifest throughout the period of the trial in discussions which I had with the presiding judge that there continued to be very great differences in our political perceptions and in our approach to political issues in the country. ... [T]he contribution I was making in these debates acted as an important counter-vailing influence to balance the orientation of the judge towards various issues of great importance. ... If my political dispositions, expressed openly to the presiding judge and to others, constitute a reason why I should recuse myself then, for the same reason, the presiding judge should recuse himself.

Van Dijkhorst called Joubert's statement "an attempt to justify his refusal to recuse himself by attacking my integrity." The defense declared: "We have gained the clear impression that [van Dijkhorst and assessor W.F. Krugel] have formed opinions adverse to our case." Krugel belonged to the Afrikaner Broederbond and served as state liquidator of anti-apartheid organizations to which some accused belonged. Declaring they had lost faith in the fairness of the trial, they applied to quash the prosecution and recuse the judge and the remaining assessor. Van Dijkhorst denied those motions, commenting that the atmosphere of the court was "reasonably relaxed." "I am at a loss to understand the allegation that I by tone, gestures or otherwise favour the state." "At no stage has the Afrikaner Broederbond in any way attempted to influence the course of the administration of justice." When defense counsel Arthur Chaskalson persisted, van Dijkhorst threatened him with contempt. Ruling that Joubert's second report on the dismissal contradicted the judge's own account, he struck out one paragraph and refused to admit Joubert's third report. In July 1987 he moved the trial back to Pretoria and granted bail to all but three accused, whom he kept in custody because of their counsel's earlier statement "that they had no belief in the impartiality of this court."[46]

The Alexandra Treason Trial

The State's Case

Obed Bapela, Mzwanele Mayekiso, Richard Mdakane and Moses Mayekiso were detained June 10–28, 1986, and Paul Tshabalala on January 22, 1987. (Mike Beea was charged with sedition and subversion at the end of February but released on bail and never prosecuted.)[47] Bapela recollected his seven months in solitary confinement without access to a lawyer.[48]

> You are not allowed to talk to any of the neighboring cells. … You would be taken from the cell handcuffed to be interrogated. They would ask you the ordinary things like to see if you would deny everything. You do have to be careful that what you say will not implicate others or yourself. [He was interrogated four or five times.] … You just don't know what to do. Sometimes they brought food with these plastic containers and we would play with them. Or read the same book from page one and it wasn't boring to you. Or you sit there wondering what to say at an interrogation. Or you sleep and wake up and sleep and wake up. By the time it is night you are no longer sleepy. Some criminals would sing to themselves and you would just sing with them.

Interrogation focused on the AAC yard, block, and street committees and people's courts. Bapela and Tshabalala were severely beaten during questioning.

On January 26, 1987, the police charged them with sedition and subversion, observing that "it results from your involvement with the 'people's courts' in Alexandra."[49] Now they shared a common cell with others. Bapela recalled:

> Some came in and out. Others were sentenced. It was a long trial. The comrades that did come in told us about the life outside and how they were arrested. We also had access to the prison library. And as the trial progressed people would give us papers and magazines. During the important days like June 16th we had dramas, music and dancing. During exercises we had teams so we would get together. It's quite interesting how you get used to it. You begin to forget about the outside world. You get a visitor and after they have left you are satisfied. We also applied for reading time. We had chess.

When the Attorney General filed a certificate denying bail under the Internal Security Act the Steel and Engineering Industries Federation of South Africa rebuffed a request by the Metal and Allied Workers' Union to lobby for Mayekiso's release: "[I]t was wrong in principle for an employer body to give character references for trade union officials.... it would be improper for SEIFSA to interfere in the normal processes of law."[50] Justice Strydom rejected the bail application on October 12.[51]

The April 15 indictment added the charge of treason, accusing them of seeking to "seize control" of Alexandra or render it "ungovernable" by establishing "so-called organs of people's power": the Alexandra Action Committee; yard, block, and street committees; People's Courts; and "a group known as the Marshalls and/or Comrades," which investigated misbehavior, discussed and executed discipline, liaised with block and street committees on "heavy punishment," carried out AAC decisions, and acted as a people's army. The accused allegedly campaigned against the SAP and SADF, Alexandra Town Council, and "so-called collaborators" and boycotted rent, shops, and manufacturers to "coerce the State into meeting their demands." They changed street names. They "assailed" the authority to administer justice. They sought to promote constitutional, political, social, or economic change. They conspired with the AYCO, ASCO, ACA, AWO, ACC, Transvaal Youth Congress, COSATU, the ANC, and the SACP. In response to a defense request for further particulars the state named seventy more unindicted co-conspirators. It accused Mdakane and Mzwanele of belonging to the people's court at 31-7th Avenue. It based the conspiracy with the ANC and SACP on shared goals. Mayekiso's commitment to a "socialist dispensation" was revealed by his words:

> [T]he unions and the progressive organisations should strive to take over the control of all the means of production and our residential areas. The capitalists must be squished out and be pushed to a position where they are unable to control.... South Africa and people are ripe for social, economic and political revolution.

Richard Mdakane was detained with a note in his handwriting:

> the totally isoltion of the police in all spheres of life.
>
> the rent boycott must be intensified
>
> the resignation of Bantustan puppets, like Lucas Mangope—other councillors
>
> The youth must became more militant.

The international press denounced the prosecution. The *Guardian* headline called Mayekiso "Trade unionist we must save from South Africa's hangman." *The Times* reported his May 1987 election as general secretary of the National Union of Metalworkers of South Africa: "Leader of new black union faces treason trial." The British *News on Sunday* published a cartoon about South African justice and British ignorance. *The Age* (Melbourne) headlined "Pretoria pushes 'treason' to the limit." "The trial of a leading black trade union official, Mr Moses Mayekiso, and four others is an attempt to determine whether peaceful—as well as violent—activities against apartheid can be identified legally as treason." *The Times* noted: "The judge and the prosecuting and defence counsel are white; the accused are Black. Nothing unusual there. Nor are treason trials anything out of the ordinary these days."[52]

Many foreign groups demonstrated support for Mayekiso. In May 1987 the UAW announced a picket of the South African Embassy: "The UAW will not stand idly by while the racist, apartheid government of South Africa keeps a leader of our counterpart trade union in prison facing possible death sentence." It distributed a pamphlet entitled "Don't Let South Africa Hang This Labor Leader." UAW President Owen Bieber visited South Africa in August, meeting the Minister of Justice, though not Mayekiso. The UAW formed a Jurists Committee to monitor the case, including a former Attorney General, Secretary of Transportation, Supreme Court Justice, three Court of Appeals judges, a District Court judge, a Representative, the EEOC chair, and the president of Yale.

The South African Embassy responded: "Our judicial system is an open one. When people go to court… it is in public like in any civilized country." The UAW Jurists Committee issued a press release after a month of trial, questioning "whether the alleged actions of this well-known labor leader and community activist actually occurred and whether the charges truly constitute treason, subversion and sedition." "Through the Mayekiso case the Jurists Committee will assess the extent to which 'justice' and the 'rule of law' can prevail for the Black majority still repressed by the white minority in South Africa."[53]

The City of London Anti-Apartheid Movement formed a Friends of Mayekiso group, taking full-page advertisements in British newspapers signed by MPs, shop steward committees, unions, the Labour Party, local councilors, writers, artists, and performers. This aroused the ire of the British Anti-Apartheid movement, which viewed the City group as Trotskyite and the focus on Mayekiso as a "personality cult."[54] The General Council of Trade Unions of Japan telegrammed the South African government: "[T]he arrest and detention of Brother Mayekiso and four others is a symbolic case of the inhumane oppression against the South African Trade Union movement by the South African Government." The beginning of the trial was observed by officials from the TUC and International Metalworkers' Federation, as well as officials and members of South African unions. Lord Hoosen QC, a member of the House of Lords, visited South Africa while the trial was in recess but met the judge. The secretary-general of the International Congress of Free Trade Unions flew to South Africa in February 1988 to observe the trial, and ICFTU prepared pamphlets in 100 languages to mobilize support.[55]

Justice Piet J. van der Walt presided. He was fifty-seven years old, had been on the bench for over a decade, and since 1979 also was Advocate-General (charged with investigating government misconduct). In 1983 he had granted bail to Methodist minister Cedric Mason, who fled the country.[56] In 1986 he had tried Marion Sparg, the first white woman charged with military training for the ANC, who had pleaded guilty to setting off limpet mines at

John Vorster Square (SAP headquarters) and the Cambridge police station in East London, causing R40,000 damage but no injuries. She expressed no regret, declaring that "even as a white South African I do not owe any loyalty to a government which is clearly not based on the will of the people." Condemning her as a Marxist and a revolutionary—traits he would understand in a Black but not a white—he sentenced her to twenty-five years.[57] Yet van der Walt took three surprising actions at the start of the Alexandra trial: Unlike judges in the two other treason trials he ruled out the death penalty by sitting without assessors; unlike van Dijkhorst, he conducted the proceedings in English (although he and the prosecutor were Afrikaners) to make them visible to the world; and he accepted a defense invitation to tour the township.[58]

The prosecution case lasted from October 19, 1987, to May 2, 1988 (with a December-January adjournment), producing 1,768 pages of record. At the state's request, forty-six witnesses testified in camera; another two dozen were identified, mostly security force or local government employees or whites. The state introduced two circulars, one handwritten "By the Comrades" and the other printed by "Alexandra Consumer Boycott," which ended "Starting from 21 April The People Shall Govern." A dozen shopowners testified about intimidation during the boycott; but none implicated the accused, and the defense induced many to portray the terrible living conditions in Alexandra. They also lost credibility by denying knowledge of security force killings and mass funerals. One well-educated witness claimed he had stopped reading newspapers and talking to people in 1985. A Council employee, sounding like Dr. Pangloss, asserted that police stopped enforcing pass laws in 1979. Others strengthened the defense case: business dropped because of police killings, long before the boycotts; councilors resigned because of family pressure, not intimidation; people voluntarily took problems to the yard committees because police had withdrawn assistance.

Several witnesses told of appearing before people's courts for domestic disputes or petty theft within yards. Although courts tried to reconcile the parties, they also sjambokked defendants. On cross-examination, one anonymous witness agreed that the 3rd Avenue court was formed by adults as well as youths. Residents respected it and brought complaints about tribalism, young girls leaving home, and assaults. Anyone could observe and ask questions. When his testimony resumed the next day, however, he claimed that the court forced him and others to participate by threatening to burn them.

One witness sought to implicate Mayekiso. When IC34 (witnesses who testified in camera cannot be named) told his employer, Michael Giddins, that two workers were late and disobdient, Giddins fired them. Comrades from the 31-7th Avenue court told IC34 to warn Giddins to rehire the women or MAWU would strike. When IC34 responded that Giddins refused, the court ordered him to quit. Giddins testified that he resisted a letter from the union and then a phone call from Mayekiso, who said IC34 was in danger. When

Giddins suggested Mayekiso call the police, he replied: "So you do not care about IC34's life?" On cross-examination, however, he admitted he did not know Mayekiso and could not identify him as the caller, conceding it was unlikely the national secretary would be involved in such a trivial matter.

IC44 described Obed Bapela presiding in two cases at the 53-19th Avenue court: a quarrel between yard residents and a complaint by a woman who would not sleep with her husband (which Bapela refused to hear). He behaved well and opposed lashing. When a youth started lashing defendants at that court, residents asked Bapela to talk to him. People took problems to the court because police stopped accepting them after the Six-Day War.

IC45 testified that his son, A, summoned him to appear before Paul Tshabalala at the 31-7th Avenue court. Inside the mkhukhu (shack) he found two women and three men. There was a smell of gasoline, two tires against the wall and three on the ground. A complained that IC45 thrashed him and expelled him from home for seducing a girl. IC45 claimed Tshabalala said: "It is the tyre," but a woman objected: "You are not supposed to put the tyre on this man before you have asked him if all that is alleged is true." IC45 admitted thrashing A because he seduced the girl and stole. A woman said: "It is A who is supposed to be given the tyre," but Tshabalala reiterated that IC45 should get it. The parties were asked to return but never did. IC45's story broke down under cross-examination. He had difficulty identifying Tshabalala in court, describing him as fifty-two rather than thirty years old. He admitted having complained to the police when the comrades threw *him* out of the house at his son's behest. When he sought to divorce his wife the latter accused him of trying to seduce her daughter; in the ensuing row he had thrown all his children (including A) out of the house and tried to stab his wife. IC45 now said he returned to the court after the first hearing and amicably settled the dispute with his wife, not in the mkhukhu but the house, where Tshabalala and three women sought to mediate to save the marriage.

Several witnesses described the vigilante attack, identifying the assailants as police, although IC25 said the police investigation was inconclusive and police uniforms had been stolen when their houses were burned (implying the attackers had impersonated police). A white SADF colonel testified that looking through a telephoto lens from outside the township he saw marshalls coercing people to attend the March 5 and May 17 funerals. Several witnesses claimed that some of the deceased buried during mass funerals were not killed by police. Finally, Brigadier H.D. Stadler (a frequent "expert" witness) maintained that the AAC conspired with the ANC, submitting *Sechaba* and other ANC and SACP publications to show that the AAC had followed the ANC call to render the townships ungovernable, create organs of people's power, and destroy the Council. In four-and-a-half days of testimony, however, he could show no connection between the ANC and AAC, nor did he know anything about Alexandra.

South African papers reported the evidence extensively, appearing to credit the allegations: "Mayekiso treason trial is told: Boycott led to Alex man leaving council," "Court hears of police isolation," "Court told of fear and death in Alex," "People's court orders witness: Mend marriage or be sjambokked," "Comrades kicked me out of my house."[59] The *International Herald Tribune* published an op-ed piece by the general secretary of the International Metalworkers' Federation entitled "Moses Mayekiso: His Crime Was to Lead His People."[60] Toward the end of the state's case supporters staged further protests. On March 18, 1988, 800 union members marched in Chicago, and eight were arrested for sitting-in at the South African consulate. A week later, 500 unionists rallied in New York. The UAW took full-page advertisements in three South African papers explaining "Why American Jurists Are Monitoring the Mayekiso Trial." They concluded: "The case is an unparalleled test for South Africa's legal system beneath the spotlight of international opinion."[61] The City of London Friends of Moses Mayekiso took full-page advertisements in the *Guardian* and the *Independent* and double-page ads in the *Weekly Mail* and *South* and described solidarity committees in the Netherlands, Belgium, Brazil, and Australia.

Three weeks after the prosecution rested the defense argued an application to dismiss the sedition and treason counts because the state failed to allege violence. Van der Walt asked if violence were not implicit in overthrowing the state with hostile intent and pointed to the alleged conspiracy with the ANC: "Surely to a great degree their acts involve violence." The issue turned on the interpretation of Justinian's Corpus Iuris Civilis by Matthaeus, a seventeenth-century Dutch author, particularly the phrase "id est rebellio sumtis armis, initave factione adversus patriam vel principem." The critical question was whether the two definitions of rebellion—"taking up arms" and "forming a faction against the fatherland or emperor"—were to be read together (so that violence was necessary) or separately (so it was not). Van der Walt concluded that the comma between the clauses showed they were to be read separately. He then turned to two South African cases construing "oproer" or sedition as a crime of laesae maiestatis, requiring hostile intent but not violence.[62] He rejected the defense argument that they arose in the unique circumstances of the two World Wars. Invoking the language of "total onslaught," he noted that "in many cases the warfare takes the form of insidious rebellion with hostile intent to unlawfully overthrow a particular state by any number of means." Although the defense argument was "novel and interesting," he denied the motion on June 1. "We are not busy with games here, it is a serious criminal matter."[63]

The Defense Case

The defense case lasted from August 1, 1988, to February 9, 1989 (with a December-January adjournment), producing 1,997 pages of record. Obed Bapela said of defense counsel David Soggot SC: "I think he is one of the greatest advocates I have ever met. He's a hard worker. He was consulting every day but Sundays. He would come at eight in the morning until the prison closed. He prepared us for every little point." Soggot's opening statement announced his theory of the case. "[T]he intention of the accused was at all stages free of the faintest of treasonable purposes." "Their purpose was to create in Alexandra…a community organisation which would organise members of the community and represent them in the manner that a trade union organises…." They "were not inspired by a general strategy a la ANC to demolish municipalities and other institutions of government with a view to setting up so-called people's organs of self-government." The yard committees were "a sort of neighbourhood watch." The AAC soght "to create soup kitchens for the poor, self-help centres for the unemployed and advice centres." "They also set out to participate in the struggle for political rights, for a non-racial democratic society," but "their political strugle was…non-violent, aimed not towards coercion of the government." "Their aim on the economic front…extended…in a long-term perspective towards the creation of a mixed economy." The press on both sides of the spectrum sympathetically reported this portrayal: "Council defects, not ANC, motivated treason accused," "Intentions 'free of treason,'" "Action Committee condemned 'courts,'" "Committee's aim to encourage."[64]

Then Soggot dropped a bombshell. The state had seized and introduced "Minutes of the AAC of 9 March 1986."[65] But this was just a draft for the official minute book kept by Richard Mdakane. Despite exhaustive searches, the police had missed it because Mdakane had given it to Mayekiso's wife Kola to type, and she had left it at her office. According to Soggot, the minutes demonstrated the accused's "distress at the unrest, their pre-occupation with the township's needs and their wish to represent the community in their communication with government servants…[and] the co-ordinating committee's unqualified disapproval of people's courts." The judge showed particular interest in the last claim, but Soggot postponed further inquiry. He concluded that the events could only be understood against the background of "widespread and intense bitterness" toward the police caused by the Six-Day War and the vigilante attack. This "crisis without precedent in Alexandra's history" had "inflamed the rhetoric of many in the community, especially the youth."

Although Mayekiso was the first named defendant and principal target of the prosecution, Mdakane testified first to introduce his minutes. Mzemeni Richard Mdakane was born in Dundee, Natal in January 1958, the oldest of five children of a laborer and a housewife. He herded livestock as a youth, began school at nine, and passed his matric in 1980. Unable to find work he moved to Alexandra in 1982, where he started as a laborer but was promoted to storeroom checker after three months. He tried to organize his plant, which had a terrible safety record. There was a strike the next year, during which he resigned, preferring to be self-employed in construction work. He supported a wife and son, her parents, his parents, and two younger sisters on his R400/month income.

After hearing Mayekiso address 150 to 200 people on 8th Avenue (where Mdakane lived) on February 10 about efforts to create yard committees on 7th Avenue, he reported back to his own yard "that we should form committees in order that we should have harmony, because we had problems in our yard... only one washing line... people were locking their toilets... during the weekends when people were doing washing one would put the bucket for the whole day" under the single tap. The yard elected two representatives, passing over Mdakane, who was only a "youth."

When the judge asked for clarification of the word "conscientising," Mdakane defined it as making "people understand and know the problems which they come across and the way of solving." Van der Walt objected that "explain" would be sufficient; "does it not go a bit further... if a man is conscientised you... involve him in the problem to the extent that he wants to do something about it?" Mdakane agreed but stressed that "people elected would work collectively and... report back and get a mandate from the people who had elected them," contrasting this with Mike Beea's ACA, which "was not mass controlled."

Mdakane was tear gassed with other mourners at the Dirading vigil on the night of February 14 and during the ceremonial washing of hands the next day. After the stadium rally on February 17 he attended the meeting that launched the Alexandra Action Committee and selected Mayekiso as chair, John Grant vice-chair, Kola Mayekiso treasurer, Mapule Morale vice-treasurer and himself secretary until the AAC's formal inauguration. Although street meetings had been held on 3rd, 4th, 6th, 7th, and 8th Avenues by then, the Six-Day War halted further organization. Van der Walt interrupted.

> *Judge:* [W]hat concerns me is that you said you were not elected a yard representative because you were still concerned [sic] a youth by the members of the yard. ... Where did you get your sudden maturity from?
>
> *Mdakane:* The organisation concerned the whole community. It brings all the people together, young and old. ...
>
> *Judge:* Why I am putting these questions, because this election of the execution [sic], if only temporary, does not seem to have taken place democratically. ...
>
> *Mdakane:* Democracy is always needed, but there we were volunteers.

His minutes described the yard, block, and street committees and the inadequacy of the ACA and ARA and then listed the community's problems, emphasizing councilors and impimpis (informers). The judge pointed out the inconsistency between blaming the Council for failing to make improvements and refusing to pay rent or accept increases. The meeting, which adjourned because of too much police activity, resumed at 4 p.m. and decided against approaching the police commander "because of the sensitivity of the situation," deputing Father Cairns instead.

The AAC acting executive met at 31-7th Avenue the next day, after the detention of Mayekiso and Grant, and decided to contact other organizations to demand their release. It had already approached the SACC "to defuse the situation" and found it forming a delegation "in order to talk to the people and the police, to stop the fighting that was taking place." Pending confirmation by the inaugural convention, the meeting chose the logo "The struggle must continue" for their t-shirts and red for their flag "to symbolise the workers' struggle." They suspended street meetings "because of the tense situation in the township."

The AAC acting executive met on March 9, two days after Mayekiso's release. According to the minutes, yard committees

> need guidance of how to settle their disputes.... [T]he meeting wanted [information] about the progress in the drafting of the constitution. Moses presented the structures and the proposals of the constitution and he apologised for the structure was not typed because of the detention. The copies were circulated to the people present. The meeting decided that the draft should be finished and given to the lawyers to make corrections.... It was decided that the community organisation should not have marshalls because they were already being used by youth in conducting the funerals, being cause [for] confusion with the youth organisation and it would be difficult to control the youth.

His explanation of the role of marshalls at funerals suggested an analogy to van der Walt: "In the same manner, if one has a big society wedding, you have ushers in the church to show people to their seats?" Mdakane agreed, but they did not want marshalls within their organization because "they would then abuse those powers and claim to be members of the AAC." He had seen youths "tearing up articles" during boycotts of shops, hijacking taxis, and demanding food from storekeepers. Marshalls could be controlled at funerals, however, because "we go there with sadness and we try to be respectful. Even the youth can also behave at the funeral."

The minutes recorded relations with other groups. The AAC had withdrawn from the Alexandra Crisis Committee (formed to organize the first mass funeral) "because of the lack of democracy." Although the ARA proposed a merger, the AAC responded by inviting ARA members to join its own structures. The AAC warned the ACA not to pretend to organize yard committees on its behalf. Concerned about the financial irresponsibility of the first ACC, "the house made the following proposal for the coming mass funeral: The copies of collection forms should be numbered. No photocopies should be used. We should get reports from our delegates about general donations." They decided to have membership cards, fees, and a bank account, and recommended that the treasurer take bookkeeping courses. Because t-shirts were missing they bought a trunk for storage and entrusted the key to the treasurer. "It was decided that all the suggestions raised above should be discussed by the Alexandra residents."

When a woman complained to Mdakane that his cousin Lucky had lashed some people and threatened her, he and others told Lucky

> to stop harassing, disciplining, lashing people. The meeting condemned the corporal punishment as unacceptable to the community and resolved to stop people practising this, especially at the number 31 Seventh, the youth grouping headquarters. They were also reports of people being lashed at the so-called people's courts at youth quarters.

Mdakane explained that the court began when

> youth used to come there to console [Sarah Mthembu] as a person who had lost a son [Jerry, killed by police on February 17]. She in turn gave them food and they also loved her.... [One day] her sister-in-law came in the company of another woman. They said they had gone to the police station to go and report their husbands who had assaulted them. When they got to the Wynberg Police Station she said they were told they must go to the stadium to Tutu and one said they must go to 11-Eighth Avenue.... After Sarah had seen this and the youth nearby, Sarah then said she is now going [to] open up to solve people's problems.

Youths held a people's court in the mkhukhu that had been Jerry's. "There was the screaming of people, which was an indication that people were being assaulted." Sarah mediated family problems in her house. The trunk with the t-shirts was at Sarah's house because vice-treasurer Mapule Morale had moved there in March. "The meeting raised the problem of the people's court not clearly under any organisation's control, which caused some individuals to lash offenders." It asked Mzwanele (the youngest executive committee member) to investigate; he reported that "the youth who were controlling the people's court at number 31 were very aggressive and they did not like any person who was criticising or condemning the lashing of the people."

At the same time, the meeting encouraged yard committees to discuss minor disputes, such as children's fights, the single water tap, the theft of clothes from wash lines, cursing, and deliberately spilling water in front of doorways. When the judge asked how they solved problems of serious assaults, such as stabbing, Mdakane said they did not deal with crime, except petty theft. "We were trying to teach the people that stealing is not required and gave them education, but we were doing all that in mediation.... The crime, such as killing of people, raping, that had to be taken to the police." At the behest of residents, influential whites had persuaded the police to accept cases again by June. Mdakane agreed with the judge that until then residents felt bound to go to the people's court but insisted that the AAC condemned all lashing, even of an "impimpi." "Lashing a person does not stop him from doing mischief." Indeed, the minutes stated: "Corporal punishment never be used, but people should mediate and educate people about the causes of their disputes and problems and discourage misbehaviour."

The acting executive met on March 11 to discuss adult literacy programs, family housing for hostel dwellers, helping the unemployed earn money by hawking goods, a soup kitchen, first-aid training, after-school day care, worker cooperatives, and other self-help projects. Mdakane's minutes continued:

> 2.4 To make people govern themselves. The house felt that the proposals was good. It decided to take the proposals to the inaugural congress for further discussions and decisions.
>
> 2.5. To form people's courts the house decided against the proposal since there were people's courts initiated by the youths. The house felt that it could not involve AAC to projects like people's courts as it was not clear who controlled.

Asked by Soggot why the AAC did not stop the people's court, Mdakane replied: "There was going to be fighting between us and the youth, which would endanger our lives, because we did not know where these youth came from in the township."

The acting executive joined other organizations in planning the April 13 Thusong meeting. Mdakane explained that the youth were disturbed they "were unable to control themselves in the community. They were stealing cars and driving them in any manner." They also objected to the failure of the AYCO executive to "be democratic and be mass based." Mdakane rejected the judge's equation of youths with "comrades." "I personally think a comrade is a person who respects discipline and can control himself and has love for people." The workshop invitation, signed by Mdakane, concluded "Viva Socialism." Mdakane testified: "It did not worry me because at meetings people used to shout it. It was something popular with the people in the township and the trade unions also usually shout that." He recalled the workshop:

> One man stood up... and said that Alexandra township is a liberated zone. Whilst he was on the floor another stood up and countered that and said to him he thinks like a child.... Alexandra township cannot be a liberated zone in South Africa... [while] we ask that the police get out of the location and the army should get out of the township.... Some were talking about insurrection and some were disputing that and said that cannot happen....

The workshop broke up into commissions, which returned with proposals. Van der Walt again expressed interest in process.

Judge: Well, if this were a democratic workshop, the chairman would formulate what the majority of the people there felt.

Mdakane: Yes.

Judge: So, must I accept it that these views were expressed by a minority of the people at the workshop?

Mdakane: All the rejected suggestions were made by the minority in the workshop. The chairman was accepting something that he had consensus in and was accepted by the majority.

The workshop recommendations had to be approved by the groups that had organized it, which would take about a month. "Some were grumbling that this is rather too conservative."

Two days later the AAC interim executive discussed the Thusong proposals, accepting the single civic association, rent and consumer boycotts, and ostracism of police and councilors. Unhappy with the demand that students return from schools outside the township, they asked ASCO to consider it further. Mdakane, Mzwanele, and two others had heard yard representatives object to the consumer boycott. "[T]hey were saying the youth were going to interfere in their affairs when they buy. ... the business people were saying it is not good...." The anonymous boycott call was disseminated on April 22, before any decision was taken. The same day the vigilantes attacked. The minutes of the next AAC meeting, on April 24, recorded that Mayekiso had met Father Cairns and asked him to arrange a meeting with Ricky Valente of the Sandton Management Committee. They also directed Mapule Morale "to make research at the youth headquarters, more specially on the resolving of the disputes of the people and the reported problem of sjambokking of people and to report back to the organisation." And they circulated "the draft typed constitution."

Mdakane's younger brother Zephaniah was killed in a shoot-out with police on April 28 and included in the May 17 mass funeral. Although each bereaved family held a separate vigil the night before, youths defied the magistrate by bringing the eight coffins draped in flags to St. Michael's Anglican Church.

Mdakane: The flags had no names on them, but they were green, black and gold in colour.

Soggot: The ANC flag?

Mdakane: I would say it is of the same colour as that of the ANC.

Soggot: Do you know how those coffins came to be draped with ANC flags?

Judge: He has not conceded they were ANC flags.

Soggot: Yes, but now, just tell his lordship, what did you understand those flags to mean?

Mdakane: I thought they were just flags to show respect to the deceased.

Judge: Yes, but the flag is not merely a piece of cloth. ... What did the flag represent to you?

Mdakane: Although I cannot know about all the flags, but I know that certain flags represent certain countries and the people. And that a flag is something that is respected in any country.

Judge: Well, no doubt you are right. Would you have been agreeable to the South African flag being draped over these coffins? That is a country's flag, and showing respect to the flag and to the people concerned?

Mdakane: As a South African citizen I would not oppose it.

Judge: Why did you not then ask: "My brother is being buried. I would like the South African flag over his coffin, not these strange flags I do not know where they come from?"

Mdakane: I realised that what they already had done, I had no way of opposing it, because I only saw it there when they were brought.

Judge: Now, did you not relate that flag to any particular country or organisation?

Mdakane: It is a flag that we heard that does come to various funerals in the country. My impression was that it is a flag that people like.

Judge: All right, thank you. Is that your last word on the topic?

Mdakane: That is what I can say about flags.

Soggot: Do you know the colours of the ANC?

Judge: He said it is similar to the ANC colours, he said that, but he has not said it was an ANC flag.

Mdakane: Yes, if it was written I would know that it was the ANC flag, but the colours are similar to that of the ANC, but there was nothing written, it was only colours.

Judge: So, you do not accept the guarantee of genuineness of a flag unless something is written on it?

Mdakane: Mostly I believe that on a thing that has been written that it is what it is which, but in colours it is all the same.

Mdakane was detained from May 22 to June 4, missing the May 25 meeting at which more than 100 people elected another interim executive and appointed a committee to resolve internal and external disputes and maintain discipline. They agreed to "extract some passages of the constitution on duties of yard, block and street committees and make a pamphlet which would be circulated to the yard committees to guide and inform the representatives of their duties." There was a report back on the May 8 meeting with Ricky Valente and a decision to confer with Steve Burger, the new township administrator. Mapule Morale reported "that there was still many problems at the [7th Avenue youth] headquarters. That there was still sjambokking and the people concerned did not want to stop it." Although the vigilante attack on 31-7th Avenue had temporarily suspended the people's court, the youth wanted to revive it. Mdakane added:

> Vuyesile Mayekiso did go to the headquarters at Nineteenth Avenue to go and tell the people to stop all that. Mr Obed Bapela also discouraged. Myself and Mzwanele went to Fifteenth Avenue, number 64, where we told them that they must stop what they are doing and the people at Seventh Avenue were also told. I believe the people at Third Avenue were also told.

Early in June the AAC, ACA, AYCO, ASCO, AWO, the 3rd, 7th, 8th, 12th, and 19th Avenue youth groups, Alex Traders Association, (Wynberg) Indian Traders Association and block representatives met to respond to the April Thusong proposals. They decided that the AAC would absorb the ACA to become the entire community's representative. The consumer boycott was lifted in response to objections from residents and merchants. So was the isolation of police and councilors: "70 people in a bus, when one policeman enters they all get out. This thing was a great disturbance and... caused people to arrive late at work." But they retained the rent boycott to press for improvements in the township.

Mdakane: It was because the youth were not meddling too much concerning rent and the entire community was supporting it.

Judge: Is the obvious answer not that it suited the community not to pay rent, whereas all the other boycotts affected their personal lives?

Mdakane: I do agree with that.

He concluded with disavowals of treasonous intent.

Soggot: Did you ever wish to create a situation of ungovern-ability?

Mdakane: No, we never have. We were trying to bring love and harmony to all the people. ...

Judge: If the evidence were to show... that in fact the early part of 1986 conditions in Alexandra developed which made it virtu-ally ungovernable... did you do anything to solve that problem?

Mdakane: Yes, with our yard committees and our own commu-nity system it was helping to solve all that.

Judge: Yes, but ungovernability as I understand it is that Alexandra could not exist in an encapsulated or in a community of its own. It is still part of a larger community in this country.... How would your community system help that?

Mdakane: Everything we did was localised in Alexandra, but we had hoped that other people would like to copy... so that the whole situation must come back to normal.

Soggot ended direct examination by asking whether the AAC was pre-pared to work with the ANC.

Mdakane: Seeing that the ANC is a banned organisation... we would not be able to work with them.

Judge: That is not quite answering the question.... Were you sympathetic to the views of the ANC and had they not been a banned organisation, would you have worked with them?

Mdakane: I personally sympathise with certain aspects of the ANC, such as their fighting for a non-racial democratic unitary South Africa, but I do not sympathise with the way they want to do it in violence.

State counsel A. C. Human obtained a postponement of cross-examina-tion because he had assumed that Mayekiso would be the first witness and "Exhibit JJJ [Mdakane's minutes] caught us by complete surprise." Although cross-examination lasted almost as long as direct examination, much of it was an uninformed fishing expedition, which often backfired, as in this colloquy about the location of the first AAC street meeting.

Human: Did this open space have a name?

Mdakane: Yes, I later saw that it was given the name Freedom Park.

Human: Who gave it that name?

Mdakane: I do not know who gave it the name, but I think it was the youth, as they were the people who were busy building up parks in the township.

Human: Did you ask them why they named it Freedom Park?

Mdakane: I did not ask them.

Human: Were you not curious about this name?

Mdakane: Well, when I read it I just saw it was called Freedom Park and I had no problems with that.

Human: Well, why did you not have any problems with it?

Mdakane: Well, I did not have a problem about it because apparently the author thereof is maybe one of the persons who is interested in having freedom in South Africa.

Human had somewhat more success pursuing the judge's concern with proper procedures. "Why did you not work in the system, the existing legal system, namely the town council?" Mdakane's response that "in the polls some were getting a two percent and some were getting six percent of the votes" did not satisfy van der Walt.

Judge: [W]hy... did you not involve yourself in the council by being elected? ...

Mdakane: The institution has its own regulations. The regulations are the cause that it should not be well-funded.... [T]hey work under racists and apartheid and all the people are opposed to it.

Judge: I am talking about upliftment of people and bettering your own community. I do not know whether you have a chance to see the papers while you are being detained at present.

Mdakane: They are being sensored [sic] by the prison authorities.

Judge: What is happening now, the Johannesburg City Council wanted to take the government to court because of toll roads... if you had been elected, could you not have done the same... on behalf of Alexandra?

Mdakane: We would not be able to do that because the institution itself has got no funds. It is just people who just sit there and do nothing and just become the administrators. ...

Judge: This is the first time you have said that the system itself... makes the town council bad.

The judge re-entered the conversation soon thereafter, when Human got Mdakane to repeat that local government was racist.

Judge: Is that your complaint? ... because the town council of Alexandra is part of a structure of apartheid systems....

Mdakane: ... [W]e were not against it as established by the government. We are against it because it is a bad institution. ... If tomorrow morning when we get up we find Mr Nelson Mandela and the others released, no one will say because the government has released him, let him go back to jail. ...

Judge: More questions, Mr Human?

Van der Walt asked why the AAC responded to the Six-Day War by visiting the bishops at Khotso House.

Judge: Was it not equally important to go informally as responsible leaders of the community to see the town council and say: "This is what the people feel, this is what we feel"?

Mdakane: That did not come to our minds.

Judge: Is that not a glaring omission in your thinking?

Mdakane: Even if I do not say it is a mistake, but if it did not come to mind it just did not come to mind.

Judge: Yes, I accept that.

The judge's skepticism was directed at the prosecutor almost as often as Mdakane. When Human questioned the justification for public outrage over the Dirading killing, van der Walt countered that "people believe what they tend to believe," especially since no official had publicly declared that a suspect had been arrested. When Human argued that the Council could have obtained money for improvements from abroad, van der Walt reminded him of the economic boycott. When Human insisted that "no reasonable person would expect to pay R7.70 for a six-roomed house," van der Walt retorted "whether it is reasonable or not...that is the perception." When Human ridiculed Mdakane's statement that the AAC were afraid to go to the police, van der Walt interposed: "They foresaw difficulties for themselves. They went through intermediaries. That is the answer." And van der Walt did not hide his impatience when Human dwelt interminably on inconsistences among the papers seized by police.

Judge: Mr Human, I do not want to stop you, but are we getting any further?

Human: It does not appear to be so. I just want to point another, just one more.

Judge: Certainly.

Human: If the court will allow me.

Judge: Certainly.

Human: I know it is getting a bit tedious, my lord.

Finally, it was Mayekiso's turn. His testimony, the longest by far, attracted the only press coverage after the initial flurry of interest.⁶⁶ Workers from the factory he had organized filled the gallery.⁶⁷ He was born in Cala, Transkei, in 1948, the oldest of twelve children. His father was a migrant worker in Cape Town; the family were sharecroppers. Mayekiso left school during standard 8 in 1968 to work for two years in a Cape Town cafe for R5–6/week. He ran out of money again before he could take his matric. Unable to return to Cape Town without a pass he became a mine worker for R7/week. He decided to desert after seeing others accidentally injured and killed but feared arrest for breaking his twelve-month contract. Abandoning his luggage, he escaped by pretending to visit another mine and fled to Johannesburg, staying illegally at a hostel, where he and seven other men shared three beds. He moved to a room in Alexandra but had to sleep in the veld because the Peri-Urban police conducted pass raids two or three times a night. After several arrests, from which he was released by bribing police, he got his passbook endorsed. He married in 1975 and began working for Toyota Marketing the next year, filling shipping orders for R15/week. He organized the work force for MAWU, being elected shop steward and then chairman of their committee. After many strikes in 1978 and 1979, Toyota fired the work force and rehired all but the shop stewards.

Mayekiso became an East Rand organizer for MAWU at R160/month. Because he spent so much time on the road his marriage dissolved in 1982. He was elected to the MAWU executive in 1978 and became treasurer in 1979. When MAWU joined the Federation of South African Trade Unions that year, Mayekiso was named to its central committee. FOSATU believed that "workers must involve themselves in community issues."

> Community organisations were being led by people whom we regarded as populists, like the Civic Association of Alexandra, which was led by Mr Mike Beea…. A populist is a person who wants to be famous, to be conspicuous…. the populists are educated people who want to use the masses in order to further their own interests….

Mayekiso was drawn into Alexandra politics when youths consulted him during the November 1984 stay-away about their critique of Bantu education. "The final decision was that these students must be helped, because they are children of the workers and that FOSATU should involve itself with anything that concerns the people in the community." Although Mayekiso attended the stay-away committee's first meeting, union business kept him from others. Tammy Mahli of the Soweto Civic Association, who drafted the stay-away pamphlet, declared "We want to make the townships ungovernable." After the entire committee was arrested, Mahli jumped bail and fled the country, while the state dropped charges against the others. Mayekiso was "pulled over the coals" by MAWU for allowing Mahli to take an adventurist position without consulting the committee.

In March and April 1984 Mayekiso traveled abroad for the first time (with Geoff Schreiner, who organized BTR SARMCOL—see chapter five) to learn about and develop contacts with trade unions. In London he met ANC representatives, which rang alarm bells for van der Walt.

> *Judge:* Why the ANC?

> *Mayekiso:* …They wanted to hear as to what was happening within the unions, as well as what was happening inside the country…. I did not regard it as wrong. When you meet a person he is not an animal. You just have to hear what he has to say.

After his 1982 separation Mayekiso married Kola, with whom he had four children. On his R650/month salary as MAWU general secretary he supported the six of them, her two children by a former marriage, her parents, his parents, his three unemployed brothers, and his first wife's child.

As Soggot took Mayekiso through his many public statements, van der Walt repeatedly intervened.

> *Judge:* [W]hat do you understand by the analysis of the situation requiring mass mobilisation to challenge the legitimacy of the state internally?

> *Mayekiso:* …[O]ur struggle was that we should get the vote and thereafter there would be a mixed economy. In that we would say it would evolve up to socialism. I can rather refer to it as utopia. I can therefore not set a definite time…. I believe this term "powerful enemy" it was referred to the example that is set there of the guerilla and the worker. With the worker he is referring to the bosses. About the guerilla I think there is referring to the army.

> …

> *Mayekiso:* When I used that word ["fight" and "forced"] the intention was that we must work honestly and very hard, so that the workers must be provided with accommodation.

> *Judge:* That is not answering the question. The question is why did you use the word "forced" and what did you mean by the word….

> *Mayekiso:* By "force" we mean that there should be strong negotiations….[He was asked about the sentence: "We should

challenge the employers to give all workers proper family accommodation."] [T]he challenge would be a challenge at table. ...

Judge: Does that term also not make a person feel strong to do something more than go to the table? Is that not the danger?

Mayekiso: It is possible that another person may issue a violent challenge, but our use of "fight," "challenge" and "enemies" was based on negotiations.

Judge: Yes, but this is a press statement.... As a responsible trade union should one not try and temper your language not to incite people?

Mayekiso: When we organise at the factory, the workers have their common language that they get used to.... They would say "We are challenging the employer," but not meaning that they are going to use spears. ... [They discussed other inflammatory words: black muscle, black power, revolutionary explosion, Leninist vanguard party, revolution.] I am not used to making use of that term, but I do sometimes use it....we would say "revolutionary change," which would mean "fundamental change."

Mayekiso gratefully accepted less threatening interpretations of his words suggested by the judge. He had embraced the two-stage theory of revolution, first nationalist and then socialist.

Judge: So, you want a mixed, socialist and capitalist state or to put it another way, a capitalist state in which the worker has more say?

Mayekiso: Yes, it is so and the model that I saw when I went to Sweden is the one that seems to be giving something to the worker and there would be no super exploitation.

Some words were hard to explain away: "workers have seen that they are a vanguard and the bomb of any liberation struggle."

Mayekiso: I used the term bomb as a phrase, which I would call a metaphor, to try and show as to what the workers, what is their part in the struggle.

Soggot: The word bomb does imply destruction?

Judge: Explosion?

Mayekiso: Yes, that is so.

Judge: Mr Mayekiso, you use English very well. What did you mean by using the word bomb? You have not explained that yet.

Mayekiso: Bomb meant the way the workers were going to work.

Judge: They are the explosive force in the liberation struggle, is that what you want to say?

Mayekiso: Not that way. It means they are the people who could work effectively towards liberation.

Judge: In other words, if they did not explode and act, there would be no liberation struggle.

Mayekiso: Just to explain.

Judge: I am waiting for that.

Mayekiso: As I said before, that is a metaphor. It does not mean an explosion in the way of a bomb....for instance, an athlete ran like a bomb. He did something in a complete way, determinedly.

Judge: He exploded from his starting blocks like Ben Johnson?

Mayekiso: It could be so.

But van der Walt resisted some evasions. When Mayekiso said "profits stolen from the workers" meant they were "not being well paid," the judge asked: "Are you accepting responsibility for your choice of words in this address or not?" And when Mayekiso argued that "the capitalists must be squished out and be pushed to a position where they are unable to control" merely meant workers should have "participatory control," the judge objected: "Where words are written, they must be taken as written and expressed in their normal ordinary meaning." But Mayekiso explained that "English is my second language," and van der Walt agreed that "'participatory control' is not a phrase which readily lends itself to use in Xhosa."*

Mayekiso turned to his involvement in Alexandra politics. He had rebuffed requests to join existing organizations. "My opinion was...the civic [ACA] was not really democratic." Although two MAWU organizers invited him to ARA meetings, "I realised that they were also not working properly, because they were against the students' organisation, as well as the youth organisations...[and were] merely referring to workers." Around Christmas 1985, however, his neighbor John Grant asked Mayekiso's help in opposing the efforts of MP J.A. Rabie to move all "Coloureds" to Rabie Ridge. And when Kola returned from a Christmas visit to Queenstown, she enthusiastically told her husband about its street committees. Mayekiso and Grant met four or five times toward the end of January with groups of ten to fifteen and decided to call a street meeting to create a democratic structure to deal with

---

*All the accused testified in their first languages, although all spoke English, some with great fluency. They gained two things by insisting on interpreters: more time to prepare their answers as the questions were being translated, and dilution of the effect of hostile prosecutorial comments. See Gilbey (1993: 260).

Alexandra's numerous problems. The judge expressed unhappiness that Grant was "trying to do something undemocratic and unconstitutional by bypassing their representative and bypassing parliament."

The minutes of that first street meeting, on February 5, stated that the purpose

> is to Unite the people of Alexandra and to look at peoples problems in order that they be solved. The struggle in Alex is backward, & therefore the street Co. is a step toward conscientising & building unity amongst residents, to fight their problems.

Van der Walt again drew attention to the inconsistency between ideology and practice.

> *Judge:* [Y]ou wanted something mass based and democratic, you discussed and got problems from a few people in the informal meetings and then suggested a structure of an organisation which you…"imposed" upon the residents, not leaving them much choice and certainly not democratic.… where does the minutes show a vote in favour of this organisation… because that is certainly the best way to show democracy at work.

> *Mayekiso:* In our meetings we mostly discussed about things. … it is difficult to go to a general meeting of 500 people and seek a vote.

> *Judge:* Are you afraid that in the 500 meeting you would not get agreement for your ideas?

> *Mayekiso:* The person chairing the meeting, as soon after the people had risen and discussed, without anybody opposing them, he would then say what has been said, is it perhaps what the whole meeting is agreeing upon and ask is there anyone opposing it and the opposer will then come forward, but should there be no one opposing, there is no need for voting.

This was not yet "full democracy" because they were still "building up levels," trying to persuade people to form yard committees and planning for an inaugural congress "where a final decision would have been taken about everything." The judge kept returning to "political struggles beyond Alexandra" because "it seemed to me the concern was greater with fighting apartheid than in improving the conditions of the people of Alexandra."

Mayekiso played a prominent role during the first half of 1986, whenever he was in the township. He spoke at the Padi vigil and funeral on January 9 and 10. He attended the Dirading vigil and saw the confrontation between police and mourners. He led the funeral and watched police disrupt the ceremonial washing of hands. "[T]he police were acting as if they have no leaders of their own, because the way people were dying. They were dying like birds." Two days later he had to tell Sarah Mthembu that police had killed her son. Mayekiso's description of the AAC February 9 decision to adopt a flag provoked van der Walt.

Judge: Now it is not said "a red flag," but "the red flag."

Mayekiso: I will try to explain. Although in our language the article "a" and "the" does not always appear and we do not always make a difference there.

Judge: ... Why not a blue flag?

Mayekiso: If we take Numsa for instance, they use red. It is a colour that is regarded as a workers' colour internationally, red.

Mayekiso was arrested that day and detained until the end of the Emergency on March 7. The next day he asked Father Cairns to seek a reduction of the aggressive policing. The day after that the AAC executive met to discuss the constitution, withdraw from the ACC because of financial irregularities, and gain greater control over the sale of t-shirts. It also discussed the people's courts being held by youth in the mkhukhu and by Sarah Mthembu in the house at 31-7th Avenue.

Mayekiso: The majority of women were in favour of it, because they were the people who had problems with fathers, sometimes with children.

Judge: When you say "fathers" I take it you mean husbands?

Mayekiso: Yes, my lord, naughty men who sleep out.

Judge: And what else?

Mayekiso: As well as other problems faced by the community, mainly women.

Judge: Hell hath no fury.

Soggot: That is so, my lord, whip them back.

Mayekiso: My feeling was, seeing that it was handled by untrained people, some of the decisions made there could be wrong and be harsh and it would not be in keeping with fairness at times. There was also a rumour that some of the youth took advantage of this...as if there are now bribes that are being used. Now, the tsotsis also got involved in it.

The AAC had sent Mapule Morale and Mzwanele to stop it, prompting the judge to ask if he ever intervened himself. "I realised," said Mayekiso," that should I go there myself it was possible because of my presence people would link me with it...."

Mayekiso was abroad when the April Thusong meeting was planned and unable to attend it because of a conflict with the MAWU AGM. On the night of the vigilante attack he was returning to Alexandra with his wife and others.

> When we were at First Avenue, next to the clinic in Alexandra, we came across a group of people in police uniforms.... They had knobkierries and iron rods. Some had firearms. They had powder blue shirts and blue trousers. Some were in civilian clothes. When we were near them they stood in the road and blocked it and they started striking the car with sticks they had and demanded the driver to open the window. He opened it. They asked us where we came from and they were rough in their speech. We told them we were coming from town. Some at the time were forcing to open the door of the vehicle and it did open, and they shone a torch inside. They started swearing and asked us why we travel at that time. They started hitting people inside the car and the driver drove from there, took off very fast to get away.

After hearing this account, van der Walt asked:

> [Y]ou are a responsible person. You had your wife with you. You came from a meeting. You were not driving, but was it not irresponsible to chase away at speed from the police?

> *Mayekiso:* We pressurised the driver to pull out, because we realised that we were being attacked..... What we got was hostile language and the assault and we realised that now we were being assaulted.

Neither he nor his wife ever slept at home again. He spoke at the mass meeting the next day, where the audience was urged to be patient and return to work and school. After it he stopped youths from attacking a photographer, whom they accused of being a police informer.

The June 6 meeting of yard and block representatives elected Mayekiso chair and Paul Tshabalala vice-chair. (The two, who were charged with conspiring, had never met before.) With Mdakane in detention, Mzwanele took the minutes of the discussion of people's courts.

> It was raised that there were problems encountered by people at 31 Seventh Avenue, lashing and vigilante attacks. It was decided that since there was no organisation responsible for the activities of PC it should be discouraged. The residents are discussing and solving their disputes and problems in the yards. ...If they cannot resolve the matter, it should be referred to the block committee.

They decided to postpone the AAC inauguration until August, partly because their attorneys were still redrafting the constitution. Mayekiso missed the June 8 meeting of community organizations because he was preparing to leave for Sweden the next day. He was arrested on his return.

Mayekiso sought to explain his more radical public statements. After the vigilante attack *Business Day* reported that "the AAC yesterday claimed it had established grass roots control of the township." Mayekiso testified:

> [T]he youth and people in general were enthusiastic about our committees and they were regarding these committees as in fact they now have a certain control and some people were already referring to it as our self-government.... it was difficult for me to say, no, we do not control, these are not the alternative structures. Because we wanted publicity for our committees, that they should be accepted in Alexandra and that they should be accepted by Steve Burger who was coming, and that the world should also see that these committees are responsible committees. What I would say is that it was mostly an exaggeration.

He was quoted as saying "Each yard has its own court in which trials are held and community problems discussed."

> *Mayekiso:* I did say words to that effect, but I did not talk about trials. I explained that broadly, how our committee system works by way of mediation..... When I talked about the people's court, which was 31 Seventh Avenue, I said there are trials, but there is no necklacing there, but there is mediation there.
>
> *Judge:* You told them there were trials and so this is a factually correct report....
>
> *Mayekiso:* That is why I say there is a confusion, because it is not so.
>
> *Judge:* You just said it is so.
>
> *Soggot:* No, my lord, with respect, he tried to explain the difference, my lord.
>
> *Mayekiso:* ...What I said about the yards, they deal with people's problems and they also act as people's courts. I was referring there to the situation where the people were dealing with their little problems. I was trying to say it in the direction that there should be no reference about number 31 in order to justify the attack.
>
> *Judge:* Mr Mayekiso, with due respect to your council [sic] and attorneys' protests, that is exactly what I put to you. You said that in each yard there were trials and settlement of domestic

squabbles. ... Gentlemen, I am not going to argue about this.
You can play back the record. The court is adjourning.

When they resumed Mayekiso sought to explain the *New Nation* account
of his press conference.

"[H]e said it is the people who will decide how much to pay [for
utilities] and what housing structures suit their pockets."

[Mayekiso explained they would negotiate these issues.]

"We are not going to replace the councillors. We do not want to
work within the apartheid created structures."

Mayekiso: [W]e would not join and work in that council as it is
now... the municipality that we favoured is the one that has
money and possible it should be non-racial.

"The proposed appointment of an administrator by the government will fail according to Mayekiso because such a person or
body must first get a mandate from the Alexandra people."

Mayekiso: If he wishes to have success in his duty, he must come
in contact with Alexandra people....

Sometimes his contemporaneous statements served to exculpate. In the June
1986 MAWU journal *Metal Worker* he declared: "We do not believe in corporal
punishment.... We have been discussing punishment for the person that does
not listen, but we have not reached a solution. However, the necklace will never
be used, because we believe that the courts have an educational function."

The most embarrassing language appeared in the (British) *Socialist
Worker.*[68] After a half-day interview during his March visit to London the
reporter gave him twenty-four hours to correct a twenty-eight-page transcript, which he now tried to explain.

"[W]e decided to form street committees to organise people from
the group up, from the grass roots. And they also have to discuss the social problems and also because people are sick and
tired of the courts system. They do not want to take their cases
to the state."

Mayekiso: [Explained people were sick and tired of being driven
away by the police.] The people in Alexandra, they still wanted
the courts to take their matters.

Judge: No, but Mr Mayekiso, I have great difficulty with your evidence in this regard. [Why would the journalist write courts if
you said police?]

Mayekiso: I think there was some confusion, because that interview took a long time.

Judge: Yes, it may be, but he is a Britisher and he may be a socialist, but I think even British socialists have respect for the British courts system. So, he would not think that it is normal to be disrespectful or be sick and tired of the courts system....

"It was at the meetings that we held...that we told people they must defy the law and so on."

[Mayekiso indicated that this was wrong and he had "cancelled" it.]

"I think the South African government has got problems... with the militancy in the townships that has made them ungovernable.

Mayekiso: It was obvious that there was ungovernability in the locations, but we did not see it as something that would free us, that the location should become ungovernable. We were, therefore, not in favour of it.... Yes, the ANC was talking of ungovernability, liberated zones, up to insurrection, but as we saw it it was something that we realised could not be done in South Africa, because one cannot create a liberated zone, say for instance like a place in Soweto, because all the people in Soweto depend on coming to work in town.

"[The Alexandra uprising] was a victory because the police were driven out and also the councillors, because they are a threat to society."

[Mayekiso explained the people saw it as a victory.]

"People believed that what they are fighting for they will not get easily. It will not come on a platter. They will have to fight heavily. There will be bloodshed and harassment, so they have to be determined."

Mayekiso: When the people demonstrate and exact pressures to the government, it does happen that there should be bloodshed. Sometimes in strikes we have seen that when the police kill people, kill the workers.

By the end of Mayekiso's testimony, van der Walt seems to have understood the absurdity of connecting him to the ANC.

Mayekiso: ANC, I regard it as a political organisation which wants to control the whole country. AAC was a community organisation which wanted to deal with the community wishes only. ...[W]e had no co-operation with them concerning Alexandra problems.

Judge: ...[Y]ou were very much concerned about the worker and being workerists that was a different philosophy as far as you were concerned to the philosophy of the ANC?

Mayekiso: Yes, our aims were different.

Human's cross-examination occupied 570 pages but again achieved little. Mayekiso asserted his opposition to underground methods and structures, armed struggle, mass strikes and industrial action, and a Leninist party. Van der Walt's numerous interventions often displayed impatience with the prosecutor and sympathy for the accused. At one point Human argued that underlining in materials seized from Mayekiso demonstrated agreement with those passages.

Judge: Mr Human, I have difficulty with this line of cross-examination. These are not the ideas of the witness. ... If each of us be examined as to documents in your library or books or passages therein, you will have difficulty answering many of the questions.

(Soggot demonstrated in re-direct that most of the marginal notations emphasized the ANC and violence; these had been made by the police, not Mayekiso!)

Human grabbed at another straw.

Human: Mr Mayekiso, is it correct that this morning you gave a sign to the audience in the form of a clenched fist and outstretched thumb?

Mayekiso: Yes, I did greet the workers with that fist. I do not know how the thumb was standing.

Human: Is it not true that that is the ANC sign or the ANC greeting?

Mayekiso: What I know is that at meetings and many other places people do greet one another with that fist.

[In the early 1960s the ANC distinguished its salute (clenched fist with outstretched thumb) from the PAC's (open palm). By the 1980s, however, all opposition movements had adopted the clenched fist of American Black power.]69

When Human sought to conflate the views of COSATU, the ANC, and SACTU at a Lusaka meeting in March 1986, van der Walt demurred: "common ground is mentioned and differing ground is mentioned, and each is holding his idea, keeping to its identity, whilst still co-operating in other respects." The judge interrupted the prosecutor's interminable examination of Mayekiso about everyone he met during the March 1986 trip to England, asking: "Are we going to get somewhere, Mr Human?"

Van der Walt acknowledged that context could distort speech. The announcement of the May 17 mass funeral for victims of the vigilante attack contained an ACC statement "Building Organs of Self-Government." "Our challenge of government-created bodies remains our programme. With the collapse of the town council formation and strengthening organs of self-government are vitally important to involve the people in matters affecting them."

> *Mayekiso*: [A]lmost everybody, out of excitement was also saying "We want self-government and control".... Now, if a person sees it he will not really say "Let me object or do something about it"....

> *Judge*: Did it suit you at the time to increase your support to follow the popular line and say you are attacking government created bodies or go along with the idea? ...

> *Mayekiso*: Yes, it is so, my lord.... Now, if we went out and criticised it outright and said this is incorrect, it is wrong, the people, especially the youth, would look at us badly.

When Human reverted to the embarrassing British interview, van der Walt again rescued Mayekiso: "[W]ere you flattered by the attention you received in Brittain [sic] on your visit? ...And if a long...report of an interview with you appears in the *Socialist Worker*, that also...tends to flatter you, does it not?"

At another point Human attributed Mzwanele's minutes to an AAC meeting.

> *Mayekiso:* You have already seen the minutes of the AAC and in myself as a person who is used to taking minutes at union meetings I would not let the minutes be written like this.... [When Human persisted the judge told him to question Mayekiso and then preempted this.]

> *Judge:* If one takes the page and turns it around you find on the back the balance sheet of the Cool Gang, who bought, have a fondness for Amstel beer and six Lion beers and a collection was made in this regard. We have not discovered this fondness for beer yet at the Alexandra Action Committee.

Sometimes, however, the judge refused to let Mayekiso off the hook. Although he had written about "taking over" factories and "workers' control," he testified that he meant merely participatory control.

> *Mayekiso:* [T]he reference towards this take over, as I have explained that it is participatory control, it is the way we are discussing that the workers must get a say in the factories.... [W]hen we talk about the vote, such as the one man one vote, a person can refer to that as a take over, on language. Not neces-

sarily that he is going to take everything for himself, it would mean that he would have a very high influence in the matter.

Judge: The highest?

Mayekiso: Highest.

Judge: The highest or very high?

Mayekiso: High influence.

Similarly, van der Walt showed little sympathy for the rent boycott: "Any resident of an urban area...would realise [that] to have services costs money. To upgrade services costs more money. So, if you withhold rent, then even the current services cannot be supplied because there is a lack of money."

By this point in the trial the state's case seemed very weak. Mdakane's minutes had nullified most of the documentary material seized by the police, and the prosecutor had failed to implicate Mayekiso in any significant illegality. The state's only hope was to show that the other accused had committed serious crimes, in which Mayekiso was a co-conspirator. The next witness was its best chance.

Paul Tshabalala was born in Alexandra in 1956. Because his mother was a live-in domestic worker in Rosebank and his father disappeared when he was young, he and four siblings were raised by his mother's mother (born in Alexandra in 1912). He left school in standard 7 because of poverty and took a series of jobs, but his real energies were directed elsewhere. He became a soccer referee in 1977, qualifying as a professional in 1983. He ran a delivery service and hawking business in his pick-up truck. And he had a daughter Pretty with Gertrude Mhlangu, a daughter Semongele with Maria Mogako, a daughter Portia with Rita Modau, a son Vusi with Cynthia Segonyela, and a son Donny with Xoliswa Gaba. He supported these children and their mothers and paid the R200/month school fees of his two younger sisters. At the age of thirteen he had been arrested for assault, convicted, and given four lashes—all on the same day. On other occasions he was fined R120 for assault and acquitted of stealing money from work.

He had never been involved in political activity before 1986 and did not even attend the vigils or funerals for Padi or Dirading. But after his friend Stephen Sithole was shot to death by police while returning from a party at Tshabalala's on February 16 he attended the mass meetings on February 18 and 21. Because people liked Mike Beea's idea of yard committees to fight tribalism and build democracy Tshabalala called a meeting in his own yard on February 23, at which his mother was elected chair and another woman vice-chair; neither was political. Tshabalala collected R2 for the bereaved from each family and delivered it to Beea's house, where he was asked to make bookkeeping entries and issue receipts, something he continued doing daily. On one occasion he watched Beea mediate a domestic dispute. Interrupted by a telephone call, Beea asked Tshabalala to complete the hearing. He persuaded the wife to give her husband another chance and got him to agree to look for work and cease drinking.

On February 28 several youths came to Beea's for help in stopping a fight. With a minister Tshabalala went to 31-7th Avenue, where he met Sarah Mthembu for the first time. The minister criticized both groups of youths. Tshabalala gave the injured boy R10 to visit the clinic and persuaded the leaders to shake hands. Sarah thanked him and asked him to return. That evening he found Sarah and three women mediating a domestic dispute; the next day he learned that the youths had a people's court in a shack. He visited 31-7th Avenue frequently until the week before the vigilante attack; one of the attractions was Mapule, who lived in the yard (but turned out to be married). He assisted Sarah by talking to husbands who neglected their families (a subject about which he had some expertise) and sometimes saw youths inflict corporal punishment in the shack. Police seemed aware of those activities.

He heard a woman complain that her neighbor called her a witch and struck her. In order to pacify her he wrote that the accused was guilty of "ungentlemanly conduct" and sentenced him to five heavy lashes. When she asked to observe, he said she was not supposed to see a man's buttocks. After she left he told the accused to say he had been beaten. Tshabalala gave a very different version of the case about which IC45 had testified. The witness's wife and son appealed to 31-7th Avenue to allow the boy to return home. When IC45 claimed his son smoked dagga and had seduced a neighbor's child, his wife responded that IC45 tried to have sex with her child and, when she refused, threw them all out of the house. Tshabalala and Sarah Mthembu asked IC45 to give his son another chance and discouraged the couple from divorcing. He recorded Sarah hearing a complaint by IC35 for abandonment. Tshabalala said the husband asked him to take notes to ensure he would stop seeing other women. Then he stood up, waved his hands in the air, and said "Viva Action Committee." "I was writing and also was excited as to the easiness of this whole thing. I therefore wrote 'Viva Action Committee.' What I have written there has no meaning."

Tshabalala represented his mother in forming a block committee. He became a member and represented it at the May 25 meeting, which decided to abolish people's courts, a decision he supported. He claimed political naivete. "I personally did not have a stand on apartheid or any political ideology.... I was never a member or supporter of the ANC.... I first heard about liberated zones from Brig. Stadler....I do not know much about people's power and regard it as merely a political slogan." He saw Bapela when the latter was arrested on April 23 and met Mayekiso on May 17, Mzwanele on May 25, and Mdakane on June 5.

Although Obed Bapela, the fourth defendant, was the most active in township politics, he was uninvolved in the people's courts and thus added little to the prosecution case. He was born in Alexandra in 1958, the oldest of six children. When he was 18 a close friend was killed by the police in the Soweto uprising. He left school to support his family after his stepfather was arrested. In the late 1970s he joined the youth committee of Buti's Save Alexandra Party and worked on the 1979 UNISA survey of Alexandra. He also joined the youth branch of the Lutheran Church and the Thusong Youth Centre, serving as deputy mayor of the junior town council until 1983. Although briefly chair of the Alexandra steering committee of AZAPO, he resigned out of disaffection with black consciousness. When Thusong and the church youth clubs formed AYCO in February 1983, Bapela was elected to the six-person steering committee, serving as vice-president the next year. In March 1984 he began a full-time job with Media and Resource Services, working first for student organizations and the UDF and then for unions, supporting his mother and five siblings. He was detained in August 1983 and January and November 1984. Hearing that the police had begun looking for him when the July 1985 Emergency was declared, he stayed out of Alexandra. He was hospitalized following an automobile accident in December and spent February 1986 at a Cape Town workshop.

Bapela helped organize the night vigil before the March 5 mass funeral. The next day he was called to 53-19th Avenue, his brother Titus's youth group, and introduced as someone long involved in the struggle. He gave weekly lectures to the youths about movement history until his April 23 detention. The next week, at a mother's request, he lectured them for nearly an hour about proper behavior toward their parents. He also warned them that their people's court could provoke revenge and urged them to stop lashing. Following the May 25 AAC decision to abolish people's courts he told another youth to stop, without effect. At the same time, he mediated family disputes.

Mzwanele and Naude Moitse asked him to speak about the history of civic organizations at the April Thusong meeting. This was his first encounter with Mzwanele. When the meeting agreed to form the second ACC he became a member of the publicity subcommittee. After his release from detention on May 2 he attended the May 9 meeting to secure Ricky Valente's help in obtaining a funeral permit. After Moitse's May 22 arrest, Bapela gave the report on the ACC to the AAC on May 25 and was appointed AAC publicity secretary.

Mzwanele Mayekiso arrived in Alexandra in December 1985 to live with Moses and look for work. He met Mdakane in January or February, Bapela in April, and Tshabalala just eight days before being arrested. Although he was closest to the youths in age, he did not belong to any youth group or AYCO. He helped organize the April Thusong workshop, adding "Viva Socialism" to the invitations because it was a popular slogan. The original draft agenda had been revised to substitute "Present State of the Township" for "ungovernability," "Popular organisational structures" for "People's organs of power," and "non-participation campaign" for "anti-collaboration."

"Freedom charter," "police," and "councillors" had been eliminated. After being released from two weeks of detention on June 4 he and Mdakane warned the 15th Avenue youth group to close their people's court. He also spoke to the 31-7th Avenue youths, but Sarah Mthembu defended them for having controlled crime.

The defense called five other witnesses. Riccardo (Ricky) Valente, a Sandton councilor from 1982 to 1988 and chair of its management committee for much of that time, had long been involved with Alexandra. He established refuges during the Six-Day War and persuaded the security forces to allow Rev. Buthelezi and Bishop Tutu to address the February 18 mass meeting and permit the March 5 mass funeral. At the May 8 meeting Mayekiso had urged liaising with authorities to return the township to normality by ending army patrols, persuading police to accept complaints, restoring normal services, and resuming upgrading. In a private conversation, Mayekiso expressed disapproval of the people's courts, especially corporal punishment. The judge asked if Mayekiso intended to overthrow the state.

> *Valente:* Absolutely not.... The main purpose of the meeting with me was to seek cooperation and dialogue....

> *Judge:* Did you get the idea that the purpose was to work within the existing system or to put up structures alternative to the existing system or in opposition to it?

> *Valente:* Can I say work within the existing system, very much the acknowledgement of the system, the acknowledgement that the State has power and is in control.... I definitely did not get the impression that the AAC were behind the people's courts. ...We never discussed the ANC.

Refilwe Mashigo, born in Alexandra and a social worker at Thusong from 1981 to 1983, described township conditions, the emergence of yard committees, and police refusal to accept complaints. Belinda Bozolli, a Wits sociology professor, described the 1985 anti-crime campaign as a form of moral purification, whose success gave youths a moral advantage over adults. The people's courts became their second institutional base. Together they reflected a "local cultural revolution," evidenced in the booing of Bishop Tutu at the February 21 report-back and the youths' defiance of the magistrate by bringing together the coffins at the May 17 mass funeral. Community leaders like Mayekiso feared that denouncing the people's courts would undermine their influence with youths and perhaps provoke physical retaliation. In response to the judge she denied that events in Alexandra were caused by outside agitators. Colin Bundy, a UCT history professor, described how consumer boycotts shifted from economic to political goals during the 1980s. Finally, Father Ronald Cairns, a Catholic priest in Alexandra since July 1981, testified that he had suggested establishing the first ACC. Mayekiso approached him in March to help persuade police to reduce aggressive patrolling and accept residents' complaints. Mayekiso was strongly opposed to violence and entirely unconnected with the people's courts. Cairns described the township mood during the first half of 1986.

> At the time when the town council had fallen from favour and there was antagonism towards the police force... I found a kind of utopia mentality developed amongst certain idealistic youth who thought they now could have freedom and run Alexandra as a separate entity... we can now run our own affairs, we don't need the council or the government, we are completely free. Phrases like organs of people's power... viva liberation, viva Samora Machel... viva socialism—they didn't know what socialism was.

On December 12, 1988, toward the end of the defense case, the accused were unexpectedly released on bail. Four papers reported the event, including UAW President Owen Bieber's reminder that "the spotlight of international scrutiny is shining very brightly on the Mayekiso trial."[70] Four accused had been in jail two-and-a-half years and the fifth two years. They had to report to the police daily and stay out of Alexandra and could not address press conferences or gatherings of more than ten. The City of London Anti-Apartheid Group held rallies outside the South African Embassy in October and November 1988 and January 1989. The defense rested on February 9, 1989, after nearly sixteen months of trial. Although press attention had lapsed since Mayekiso's testimony, the white defense witnesses received sympathetic coverage: "Alexandra's state of siege was 'provocative,'" "Alex council 'not undermined,'" "Priest describes treason trialist as peaceful man: Mayekiso 'tried to negotiate,'" "'Chaos bred people's courts.'"[71] Benno Schmidt, Yale president and member of the American Jurists Committee, attended the end of the trial, met van der Walt, and issued a harsh statement, reported by six newspapers. The trial

> is being watched closely in legal circles, in trade unions, church groups, the human rights community and by the public.... If the defendants did, in fact, commit the alleged actions in the indictment, would they have committed treason by the norms of international law and by standards applied in other countries? ....Is the South African Government, through these treason prosecutions and convictions, criminalising what would be considered legitimate political dissent in the context of international norms?[72]

The Other Trials Conclude

Judges decided two related cases as the Alexandra trial was ending. In July 1986, less than a month after detaining four of the Alexandra Five, police also detained eight Alexandra youths, seventeen to twenty-eight years old. In March and April 1987, contemporaneously with the Alexandra Five, these eight were indicted for sedition, subversion, and treason for operating the 15th Avenue people's court. In September 1988 Justice Grosskopf found all eight guilty of sedition.[73] Although much of the evidence resembled that offered against the Alexandra Five, his interpretation was uniformly unfavorable. The March 5 mass funeral "became a political rally. The coffins were draped with ANC flags...people carrying a large red banner with the hammer and sickle and others carrying an ANC flag also formed part of the funeral procession." The "so-called vigilante attack" of April 22 was an "unfortunate incident," but there was "insufficient evidence...to come to a definite conclusion as to the identity of the attackers." He credited the testimony of Brig. Stadler (again the state's expert witness) that "the ANC called upon the people in South Africa to attack the police and to drive them out of the townships with a view to making those areas ungovernable. That call was apparently heeded by some people in Alexandra." Because the police found a fourteen-page document entitled "Organising for people's power!" in the house where the accused were detained, the judge had "no doubt that at least some of the accused read the document and that the information contained therein was made available to the other members of this group."

This youth group called themselves the Vincent Tshabalala section after the ANC guerrilla killed by police in Alexandra in February 1985. They renamed local streets Grenade, AK-47, and Bazooka and local schools Solomon Mahlangu ("an ANC terrorist sentenced to death for murder"), Oscar Mpetha ("the president of the ANC for the Western Cape"), and Oliver Tambo (ANC President). They addressed each other as "comrades," which he equated to "members of radical organisations," and encouraged the formation of yard committees, which "were not so innocent as the accused made them out to be." He did not believe their "sanctimonious assertions" that the anti-crime campaign was "merely 'educating' the youth." If they had "truly regarded" it "as their civic duty" they would "have sought the sanction and assistance of the police." Instead they "made use of whistling to warn the comrades against the presence of the police." Far from being "a local neighbourhood watch," these were "seditious gatherings...they deliberately seized the opportunity to arrogate to themselves some of the functions of the police... thereby intend[ing] to defy the authority of the state."

After the 31-7th Avenue people's court was closed by the vigilante attack, they established their own, thereby "co-operating" with the March 4 and 5 call to stop taking cases to the police. Residents "were obliged to take their problems to a group of youngsters... [who] dealt with those matters in their own peculiar way."

> The alleged wrongdoers or offenders would be summarily tried
> by the comrades...[who] would reach a decision or make an
> order.... Punishment would comprise a number of lashes with a

> sjambok which would be executed summarily by the comrades on the premises. A person who was not willing to make the required admissions...would receive lashes. The same thing would happen when the comrades were of the view that a person was not telling the truth....
>
> There were no formal rules of procedure for the people's court. Alleged wrongdoers had virtually no rights. It is really an insult to the people of Alexandra and to courts of law in general to call such a distorted structure a people's court....
>
> [T]he whole process was in defiance of the authorities right from the acceptance of complaints up to the execution of the orders of the people's court.

He imprisoned seven for three or four years, giving the youth under eighteen a suspended sentence.

In December 1988, Justice van Dijkhorst decided the Delmas treason trial on the basis of a record of 24,637 pages and 15,000 pages of exhibits.[74] He convicted eleven of the twenty-two accused, sentencing Patrick Lekota to eleven years, Popo Molefe and Moss Chikane to ten, and Thomas Manthata to six (all for treason and terrorism) and Amos Malindi to five (for terrorism) and giving two-year suspended sentences to another six on condition that they attend no public meetings, make no public statements, give no interviews, hold no offices, engage in no public protests, and meet with no more than twenty people at a time. Van Dijkhorst appreciated "that the demise of the UDF may leave a void which may take a number of years to fill...[which] will slow down the process of reform." But "the UDF has itself to blame."

The accused smuggled a statement out of prison:

> We view the present trial as an interim affair. Somewhere in the future lies a date when Black and white South Africans will take a second look at these moments of our history. They will evaluate afresh the events now in contention and our role in them. And since the privilege will belong to them, they will pass final judgement.... They will vindicate us.

The defense applied for leave to appeal, citing procedural irregularities and the judge's bias, revealed in his frequent interventions and obvious animus toward defense counsel. He had said in judgment: "[T]he record will show that I was evenhanded in my treatment of counsel on both sides. They all came in for the criticism which was due to them. Where tediousness or repetitiveness of some led to exasperation, my remarks were sometimes caustic. I offer no apology therefor." He initially refused to allow the application to include an affidavit by the dismissed assessor because its disputation of his own version of events was contempt of court. At the end of January 1989, however, he allowed its inclusion and granted leave to appeal.[75]

Judgment

The state began its heads of argument by dropping the treason charge—ostensibly because essential witnesses had been frightened out of testifying.[76] It sought to link unions and community organizations.

> The aim of [Mayekiso] and MAWU was for the workers to gain control of the government of the country which would eventually become a socialist state. ... To be more effective in their struggle it was also decided that the workers and their families should be mobilised in the townships and conscientized about the national liberation struggle.

The ANC's guiding role was revealed by subsequent events.

> In 1984 the ANC called for the destruction of government organs such as the army, the police, the judiciary and the community councils. During the first half of 1986 60 policemen were killed and the houses of 900 policemen were set on fire countrywide. Due to intimidation councillors and policemen resigned during the first half of 1986.... 14 [out of 18 police sections] had in total more than 400 people's courts.... Rent boycotts, consumer boycotts as well as funerals were used to further the aims of the ANC.

Since most of the illegal acts were committed by anonymous youths, the state argued "that there was a close relationship between the youth groupings and the AAC... [which] acted as overall leaders of the youth of Alexandra." It emphasized Tshabalala's participation in the 7th Avenue people's court, connected AYCO to the 3rd Avenue court and argued that Bapela led the youth group operating the 19th Avenue court. It depicted the April Thusong meeting as the heart of the conspiracy because it called for illegal acts. The rent boycott, which it blamed for the forty-five percent drop in rental income from April to May, sought

> to ensure the withdrawal of the police and the SADF from Alexandra, the resignation of the police, the dissolution of the Town Council, the unbanning of COSAS, the ANC and other political organisations, the unconditional withdrawal of charges against political prisoners, the release of detainees and the changing of government policies.

It also blamed the meeting for the consumer boycott, isolation of the police, and collapse of the Council.

The defense heads of argument divided the state's case into three categories: the yard, block, and street committees and AAC; the people's courts and marshalls; and the campaigns. The accused organized the community in order to make representations to authority. Their preoccupation with a constitution reflected "a common outlook imbued with notions of legality, accepted and regular procedures and openness in all their dealings." They also were concerned with "the proper handling of funds and donations." The defense sought to explain inflammatory language as "a general political vocabulary which was apparently fashionable and widespread in the townships at the time especially amongst the youth." Police and media efforts to justify the vigilante attack as provoked by the people's courts prompted Mayekiso's press conference and what may have been his "exaggerated rhetoric." Civic organizations like the AAC were "endemic in South Africa and...long preceded ANC calculations as to their usefulness in the political and military struggle." Mayekiso, "far from being a supporter of the ANC," was rather "in a state of tension with them," having defied their insistence that South African unions channel outside contacts through SACTU.

The marshalls and people's courts expressed the heady experience of youths in the anti-crime campaign; the AAC repudiated both. The consumer boycott was the work of anonymous youths. The rent boycott was a spontaneous response to police violence and the Council's unpopularity. Rent payments had already declined sixty-one percent from February to March as a result of the Six-Day War, well before the AAC called for a boycott. The Thusong workshop was "a 'Talk Shop' in which a considerable volume of hot air was expended especially by certain of the youth." The state's failure to demonstrate the use of coercion to enforce the rent boycott was surprising in light of "the thousands of potential witnesses." The defense concluded boldly.

> [T]he Accused were not revolutionary or radical leaders imbued with revolutionary ideologies.... They were not adventurists setting out to seize power in any shape or form, but men of sound judgment and moderation who sought to apply the manifestly successful techniques of the trade union struggle to the township... to represent the community of Alexandra in negotiation with the authorities.... They created an organisation which had no economic policy and expressed no wish to link up with other political ideologies or parties.... They did not preach ideology, they did not promote a spirit of confrontation, they acted without a trace of clandestine purpose, they did their best to defuse a state of extreme crisis and tension in Alexandra, they sought the help and intervention of priests and eminent public figures, they sought the restoration of normality, they wanted the police to accept criminal complaints and the judicial system to operate normally.

In April 1989, after oral argument but before judgment, Kola Mayekiso spoke at more than 200 meetings in Britain, accepting trade union awards for her husband, before proceeding to Dublin, New York, Chicago, Detroit, Washington, and Stockholm. She addressed trade unionists and met the chairs of the House and Senate subcommittees on Africa. The UAW's Mayekiso Trial Update welcomed the dropping of the treason count but repeated Benno Schmidt's criticism that the conduct charged "would be considered clearly legitimate political action in my country and elsewhere."[77]

Justice van der Walt had revealed his sympathies during the two days of oral argument.

> The difficulty one has with a case like this is that you have white perceptions and you have Black perceptions. I am sitting as a judge. I am white. I view it in a certain way. A Black person might view it differently. Politics comes into it. Nationalism comes into it. You have a whole minestrone of ideologies.[78]

He began reading his fifty-seven-page judgment on April 24 by asking the audience not to disrupt "by any overt show of emotion or demonstration of any kind." He saw Alexandra as an example of what the American author Allen Drury had called the "very strange society" that is South Africa. The failure of development to alter the squalid township conditions "clearly is the reason why the community was dissatisfied and developed a lack of trust and faith in the authorities." "The physical features and lack of amenities were only too apparent to me when with counsel I drove through Alexandra during the course of the trial." Although the lives of urban Blacks "are beset with problems and difficulties of various kinds, not experienced by their white fellow citizens," he agreed with Professor Bozzoli that those in Alexandra "have problems and experience living conditions that are found nowhere else or are intensified to a degree far greater than anywhere else." The extraordinarily dense settlement had "led to the yard comprised of several families developing into an important unit of community life peculiar to Alexandra."

Next van der Walt offered some political observations that would have been commonplace elsewhere but were extraordinary under the circumstances. Although Afrikaner nationalism had achieved its goal in the establishment of the Republic in 1961, black nationalism had not.

> [T]he Black citizens of the Republic do not have a vote in the process of election of members of parliament... who are the legislators of the laws that govern the actions, the lives of all the citizens of the Republic.... While white South African citizens may have a democracy, Black South African citizens certainly have no share in it.

"For obvious reasons," the 1983 Constitution giving the vote to "Coloureds" and Indians "was a cause of resentment among the Black citizens of South Africa."

He largely adopted the defense summary of events during the first half of 1986. Although it was "common cause" that the "outspoken intention of the

African National Congress is to overthrow the state by violence," there was no evidence that the accused conspired with the ANC. Nor had the state shown the accused's responsibility for the consumer and rent boycotts. "It does indeed call for comment, as submitted by the defence, that out of some 100,000 or more residents of Alexandra" only a few witnesses with little credibility "could be found to link the accused to certain events...."

The judge remarked on the fact that, despite the existence of other community organizations like the ACA, ARA, and ACC, "the state has singled out the Alexandra Action Committee and the five accused...as being responsible for whatever took place in Alexandra." But it was the ACA's Mike Beea who represented Alexandra in the Cape Town meeting with Adriaan Vlok and the ACC that organized the March 5 mass funeral. It was an overstatement to call the AAC "an umbrella organisation for the whole of Alexandra." The residents' belief in police involvement or complicity in the vigilante attack "had a great deal of substance." It was "a matter of regret and concern that those responsible have not been identified and prosecuted." "This certainly did not facilitate amicable co-operation of residents with the police," especially in view of the perception "that the police were refusing to accept complaints in criminal matters." Although the AAC "played a prominent role" in the May 17 mass funeral, this "highly emotional occasion" was "not necessarily subversive or seditious."

Because the people's courts were "an important factor in the state's case," he dealt with them at length. Bapela and Tshabalala were not members of the AAC acting executive during their involvement with the courts. Furthermore, both dealt with family disputes and had nothing to do with corporal punishment by youths in the shacks. The sedition charge rested exclusively on the April Thusong workshop. But it merely made recommendations to the constituent organizations, which reported back on June 8.

Finally, the judge turned to the legal requirements of subversion. Although Internal Security Act §69(5) created a presumption of the requisite intent, the state still had to prove each element beyond a reasonable doubt. It made a "persuasive" case of subversive intent, especially based on Mayekiso's statements.

> However, taking into account the conditions in Alexandra, the desire for political support sought by the accused and the AAC and the need for propaganda and publicity, the amount of perceived provocation of the residents of Alexandra because of what they subjectively saw as unwarranted police action...the evidence placed before the court by the accused...refutes any suggestion of a subversive or seditious intent.

Although the judge had "no knowledge whatsoever of what actually took place in Alexandra during the first half of 1986," his task was to determine whether the state had proved guilt beyond a reasonable doubt. "In my view the state has not." Not content to acquit the accused, he condemned the state for having charged them with treason in the first place.

> Treason is a crime in a very special category. Where the ideas and political aspirations of those charged are part of the issue— in this very strange and complex society of ours as set out at the beginning of this judgment—and given the spectrum of politics of our citizens from Black to white and from far left to far right— with their grievances and aspirations—in most cases legitimate, and the often intemperate and exaggerated language and liberally spiced with current political cliches, most of these citizens just striving for a better South Africa—a charge of treason should be very carefully considered and reconsidered before it is brought before the court.

Although most Blacks in the audience had openly defied the bailiff's command to "rise in court" when van der Walt first entered, at least half did so when he resumed after lunch and acquittal was clear. After his final words

> the packed gallery began cheering and stamping their feet while shouts of "viva" sounded.... The crowd stamped and chanted down the passages to the front door of the Supreme Court when several policemen with sjamboks and a loud hailer let them out of the building 10 at a time and told them to disperse in different directions.[79]

The Aftermath

At least ten South African papers covered the acquittal in more than twenty articles. Most front-page headlines called it a major victory for anti-apartheid forces: "Landmark acquittal may affect the prosecutions of other activists," "Judge attacks treason charge," "Rebuke for A-Gs may stem flood of treason trials."[80] The *New Nation* warned that "government plans to charge Eastern Cape leaders with treason could be in jeopardy."[81] Several editorials condemned the state for bringing the charges: "Political goals don't have to be treason," "Listen closely when these judges speak."[82] "[T]he state's action in subjecting these men to a prolonged trial...[is] reminiscent of the worst excesses of the Soviet Union."[83] The judgment was a "setback for the State in terms of... seeking to criminalise the township protests of the mid-eighties, the most bruising period of unrest in South Africa's history." The Witwatersrand Attorney General, who initiated the prosecution, denied the imputation of ulterior motives and insisted the acquittal signified only inadequate evidence.[84] Two papers praised the judge for "appealing for tolerance of other political viewpoints and an end to prosecution for political purposes" and for making "personal contact with the type of environment the accused came from."[85] At least three asserted that the judgment would enhance respect for the judiciary.[86] The American press was equally enthusiastic; and the U.S. State Department welcomed the verdict, hoping the government would allow Mayekiso to resume his trade union duties.[87]

The opposition was triumphant. Both the SACBC and Lawyers for Human Rights took advertisements in the *New Nation* to congratulate the accused and denounce the government.[88] COSATU General Secretary Jay Naidoo called the trial a test case of the state's atempts "to criminalise our activities." The National Union of Mineworkers hailed the acquittal as "a victory for the entire mass democratic movement." UAW President Owen Bieber called the prosecution "malicious and outrageous," declaring that "the acquittals are a victory for the defendants, but also for those who helped shine the spotlight of international scrutiny on this trial." He telexed the Minister of Law and Order opposing further restrictions on Mayekiso.[89]

When the accused returned to Alexandra that night, for the first time in nearly three years, there was dancing and singing in the streets.

> A second kombi arrived shortly behind them, carrying youths chanting slogans and singing freedom songs. They climbed out of the kombi, formed a group in the middle of the street, and danced the toyi-toyi.... The sounds of "Viva Nelson Mandela, Viva Oliver Tambo" and slogans about other leaders of the ANC filled the air...

Mayekiso declared: "We are back and we will start where we stopped. I want to hear that the street, yard and block committees are meeting tomorrow. The court said they are not illegal. We must begin restructuring."[90] But repression continued: government banned a welcome home party for him; Obed Bapela's house had been firebombed the previous December, making him and the others fear further attacks; and the accused consulted their lawyers before accepting invitations to resume leadership positions in community organizations.[91]

Township conditions had seriously worsened during their absence. More than 10,000 squatters had arrived and were erecting shacks at the rate of 1,000 a month. "Freedom Park," where the AAC had held their first street committee meeting, was full of them. Thirteen families of about ten people each lived in Mayekiso's yard, sharing one tap and three portable toilets. Some 7,000 families were on the waiting list for older housing; new houses cost R46,200—far beyond the range of almost anyone. Land originally subdivided for 338 white families now housed 200,000 Blacks.[92]

Bapela recollected their attempts to revive political activity.

> Less fear was there as we had just been acquitted and there was a less likelihood of us being arrested again. We started organizing nonpolitical campaigns to clean up the township. For the

very first time since 1986 people saw us singing while we cleaned. An escort of soldiers and police were alongside us as we sung. Wearing a t-shirt was an offense in the township. The police said you can wear a t-shirt in town or in Soweto but not here. All of a sudden all of us are coming down the street wearing t-shirts and singing songs joined by students.

A month after the judgment NUMSA re-elected Mayekiso general secretary, conferred an honorary presidency on Harry Gwala (an ANC and SACP leader, recently released from a life sentence for terrorism), and reiterated its commitment to socialism. A month later Mayekiso reaffirmed that "our aspiration is a socialist society." Mzwanele, Tshabalala, and Mdakane were detained after leading a march for better housing on November 30 and released only after a two-week hunger strike. Mayekiso launched the Alexandra Civic Organisation in December. Although government prevented him from obtaining housing in the township and seized the ACO's papers, the organization began negotiations with the Transvaal Provincial Administration early in 1990, expanding them to include Black and white local councils, utilities, and lenders. In February 1991 the ACO, TPA, and Alexandra City Council signed an accord, ending the five-year rent boycott.[93]

At the end of 1989 the Appellate Division overturned the eleven Delmas convictions on the ground that van Dijkhorst had improperly discharged the assessor, freeing the five after a year on Robben Island. Joubert's affidavit, released for the first time, revealed that the judge had bet him a bottle of whiskey none of the accused would testify in his own defense.[94]

A year after the Alexandra acquittals history appeared to repeat itself but under the very different circumstances following de Klerk's February 1990 release of Mandela and legalization of opposition groups. In July Meshack Kunene, twenty-three, was shot dead by police during an Alexandra rally honoring ANC secretary general Alfred Nzo. At the funeral Walter Sisulu, head of the ANC Interim Leadership Core, denounced the "unprovoked attack" and declared the ANC "will not stand by and watch the cream of our community slaughtered. We reserve the right to defend ourselves in these extreme circumstances." Mayekiso, now ACO president, announced a meeting at the stadium, from which people would march to the police station to present demands to Law and Order Minister Adriaan Vlok. Mayekiso urged: "Let us build organs of people's power."[95]

Less than a month later Mayekiso appeared among the leadership of the South African Communist Party at its formal launch. He acknowledged that he had been a member "for a long time" and had met party leaders outside South Africa. In November, as president of the Civic Associations of Southern Transvaal, he announced mass action, isolation, and boycotts to force Black councilors and "coloured" and Indian management committees to resign by the end of December and merge their townships with Johannesburg to form a single nonracial city. The same month, as NUMSA general secretary, he urged COSATU, the ANC, the SACP, and government to spend R4 billion to replace single-sex hostels with family housing, in response to the first wave of fighting between the ANC and the Inkatha Freedom Party (IFP) in August and September.[96]

In March 1991 IFP-ANC violence in the township left at least sixty-one dead. The new mayor, an outsider from the East Rand and an Inkatha member, had contracted with developers to build expensive houses, allegedly telling Mayekiso "Now we are going to hit you." Angry residents forced him into hiding and threatened and attacked councilors. The ACO and TPA later agreed to abolish the Council and suspend the development. Inkatha killed ANC members in the hostels and expelled others. ANC youths retaliated by necklacing Inkatha members. After the police had refused requests to protect a vigil for an ANC member, Zulu-speaking men armed with automatic rifles attacked, killing at least fifteen. By the end of April at least twenty more died in fighting. Insignificant in Alexandra in 1990, the IFP now controlled a quarter of the township. In the beginning of 1992 the violence escalated into open warfare. The township formed an Interim Crisis Committee on April 1, with Mike Beea as the ANC representative, which managed to eliminate political murders between December 1992 and March 1993.[97]

People's courts, which had grounded the prosecution of the Alexandra Five (and led to the imprisonment of seven youths in the companion case), were the basis of long sentences for twelve in Witbank in 1988.[98] In 1990 a magistrate sentenced an Alexandra resident to two years for giving five lashes to a witness who disrupted a people's court proceeding. "[I]n an organised society no government, no police force, no court of law can allow a position to develop in a state whereby private gangs, private individuals serve functions of the state, of the police force and of the courts. The authority of the state to maintain and to enforce law and order must be supreme and unchallenged."[99]

But the state's attitude was changing. In June 1991 a prosecution of residents of Missionvale, the "coloured" township of Port Elizabeth, for establishing a people's court ended in suspended sentences. The Regional Court president noted that "witnesses and even the investigating officer simply do not turn up at court and the cases are withdrawn. It is quite possible that residents do, in fact, feel desperate [about the failure of police to respond to complaints]."[100] The Wits Centre for Applied Legal Studies and the National Association of Democratic Lawyers established the Community Dispute Resolution Resource Committee to assist communities in mediating disputes. Their first pilot project was located in Alexandra with the blessing of the Minister of Justice and the professional associations of attorneys and advocates. Communities throughout South Africa eagerly sought to emulate it.[101]

Just as people's courts shed the stigma of necklace and sjambok to become "community dispute resolution" and the darling of the legal establishment, so the renaming of streets and schools after revolutionary heroes was transformed from an act of symbolic defiance—one of the allegations against the Alexandra Five and Eight—to an emblem of the "new" South Africa. In 1992 Mvuzemvuze Comprehensive in Khayelitsha became Joe Slovo High School, Sizamile in Nyanga became Oscar Mpetha High, Sabenza in Crossroads became Dr. Nelson Mandela High, and Simon Hebe Secondary in Paarl became Desmond Tutu High—with the approval of the Department of Education and Training. The following year government created the National Place Names Committee to consider renaming John Vorster Airport and Kafferstad and even changing Johannesburg to Egoli or Rhawutini (place of gold in Zulu and Xhosa).[102] Plus c'est la même chose, plus ça change.

Analysis

The Alexandra Five was the last treason trial.[103] The defense victory there (and in Pietermaritzburg just before it began and Delmas eight months after it ended) terminated a strategy of repression the state initiated in 1955, abandoned after the ignominious acquittal of all 156 accused, but reembraced in 1979, prosecuting 190 people for treason in forty cases between 1980 and 1987.[104] Begun under P.W. Botha but decided after his stroke, the Alexandra trial offers an excellent opportunity to evaluate the attempt to criminalize opposition politics.

Criminal law is ill-suited to repress mass action. Although the state believed that a few troublemakers coerced the otherwise obedient masses into action, the reverse was closer to the truth: the people led and leaders followed. Alexandra was a highly politicized township, with seventy years experience of self-government and nearly fifty of organized resistance. But the actors were anonymous and innumerable; every time one was eliminated—arrested, charged, prosecuted, and convicted, or more summarily shot—others took his place. The Alexandra Eight convictions did little to eradicate people's courts. The only way to put down a mass uprising is through equally massive force: saturation policing, detention without trial, and torture—i.e., the Emergency. But this admits that the state has lost control.*

The focus of the Alexandra treason trial was Moses Mayekiso and through him MAWU (later NUMSA), COSATU, and the entire labor movement.** At the end of the 1970s capital's demand for a more predictable labor supply had convinced the state to legalize black trade unions. With their rapid success in organizing, securing recognition, winning material gains, and uniting under COSATU, they increasingly challenged government. Unable to outlaw

---

*It is noteworthy, and somewhat mysterious, that the state detained Zwelakhe Sisulu for two-and-a-half years for declaring during his keynote speech to the NECC on March 29, 1986, that "in a situation of ungovernability, the government does not have control."

**Defense attorneys Norman Manoim and Amanda Armstrong rather emphasized civic organizations and Alexandra—a relatively small township, surrounded by white suburbs and chosen for urban redevelopment by the Joint Management Committee (the local organ of the security apparatus). Interview (July 1990).

the unions, the state sought to discourage links with community organizations, remove a militant leader of the second largest union, and encourage a return to economism.

But Mayekiso was an unlikely target. A notorious "workerist" critic of bourgeois populists, he refused to link his AAC to the UDF. He had been hurt by his association with Tommy Mahli's adventurist statement in 1984 that "we want to make the townships ungovernable." He had been publicly rebuked for criticizing the ANC and bypassing SACTU to forge direct links with the international labor movement. This prosecution was another instance of the state's ignorance of or indifference to the complexities of black politics, its insistence on lumping together all opposition under the slogan "total onslaught" (just as elsewhere it conflated the nonracialist UDF and ANC with the black consciousness AZAPO).

The only way to get at Mayekiso was to connect innocent local initiatives with national campaigns, the AAC with the ANC, trade unions with community organizations, grassroots democracy with socialism. Alexandra must have seemed the ideal place to find the dirt (figurative as well as literal). It teemed with illegality. Heightened political activism following the 1984 Vaal uprising inevitably was accompanied by petty illegality: the anti-crime campaign, intimidation to enforce boycotts and stay-aways, coercion to attend funerals, and attacks on security forces, local government, and shops.

The prosecution's weakest argument was that the AAC did not prevent illegality, restore order, and disavow or denounce criminal acts—as though it were responsible for cleaning up the state's own messes.[105] (This virtually acknowledged the "dual power," which the state was prosecuting the AAC for claiming.) Next the prosecution pointed to incendiary language by the accused, the AAC, and other organizations. Then it objected to the creation of alternative institutions, which challenged the Council and the police. The capstone was the people's courts, first mentioned in the press as early as February 19, 1986. Their demonization by government and the media fueled whites' worst fears that Blacks were savages who defied state authority and disregarded legality. (Similar prominence was given to Winnie Mandela's notorious April 13 speech—"Together, hand in hand, with our boxes of matches and our necklaces we shall liberate this country"—and her involvement in the kidnapping and murder of "Stompie" Mokhetsi.)[106] The vigilante attack on yards with people's courts may have been intended to highlight their activities.

People's courts had emerged in other townships in the 1980s. Although their reliance on mediation followed the traditional makgotla, brought to the city by elders, they differed dramatically in three ways. The personnel were youths. They attacked traditional values like patriarchy. And they used, often abused, corporal punishment.[107]

When the security police seized people's court records they must have felt the participants had handed them irrebuttable evidence of guilt. Two days later *Business Day* devoted a full page to an "exclusive" on people's courts, a journalistic coup reported by other papers. The May 10 house-to-house search uncovered lists of cases, parties, and witnesses. The state must have felt confident that those punished would be eager to testify, breaking the conspiracy of silence that had frustrated other prosecutions.

They were disappointed. Witnesses were vague and inconsistent, unable or unwilling to identify their "judges." Some fabricated or distorted their stories, presumably under police pressure. Others portrayed the courts as mediating between parties eager for help. Paul Tshabalala and Obed Bapela were partly successful in distancing themselves from the youths who inflicted corporal punishment in the mkhukhu. The AAC documented its efforts to halt the lashing and ultimately close the courts, although it could not publicly repudiate them without risking a backlash.

In order to hold the AAC responsible for everything that happened within Alexandra in the first six months of 1986, the state exaggerated the Action Committee's power, mischaracterizing it as a quasi-military structure that tightly controlled residents' behavior. Perhaps the state was projecting onto the enemy the authoritarian structure of its own security apparatus. Perhaps its cultural ignorance, accentuated by apartheid, misled it to reify the opposition, transforming "youths" and "comrades" from rhetorical labels into organized entities. The AAC contributed to this misunderstanding: creating charts representing organizational aspiration rather than actual lines of authority, fostering township unity by obscuring and denying divisions. (Oppositional groups always run the risk that boasts to followers will be turned against them by the state.)

In reality, of course, a multiplicity of organizations competed for power: the AAC, ACA, ARA, ASCO, AYCO, and AWO, as well as official structures like the Council and Save Alexandra Party. Newspaper accounts of Alexandra during the first half of 1986 barely mentioned the AAC. Conflict within the two Crisis Committees also exposed differences. The fluidity of boundaries appeared in shifting allegiances: Mike Beea moved from the SAP and Junior Council to the ACA; Obed Bapela started in the same place and tried AZAPO before joining the AAC; Paul Tshabalala began 1986 with Beea but moved to the AAC. Larger animosities further divided Alexandra. Mayekiso and the AAC were workerist, Beea and the ACA populist. Charterist ASCO and AYCO criticized black consciousness AZAPO for the infantile tactic of carjacking; in response AZAPO members killed the ASCO president. The AAC hoped to reduce tribal tensions, which first emerged in hostility toward hostels in 1957 and escalated to open warfare between the ANC and IFP in 1990. Van der Walt seemed surprised that "coloured" residents would work within the AAC rather than use the House of Representatives created specially for them. The people's courts aligned youths against elders, women against men. The consumer boycott pitted youths against shopkeepers and shoppers; the rent boycott highlighted differences between plotholders and shack tenants.

The state insisted that the accused fomented, or at least heightened, unrest. The prosecutor, and initially the judge, saw "conscientizing" as stirring up trouble. But Alexandra had a long history of resistance, beginning with bus boycotts and opposition to removal and conversion to hostels. The rent and consumer boycotts and school and work stay-aways antedated the founding of the AAC and were endemic to black townships during this period. Aggressive policing, disruption of funerals and other gatherings, detentions, and shootings provoked the isolation of and attacks on security forces and local government. Buti and the other councilors resigned because the entire community repudiated them. Furthermore, the fundamental ethos of oppositional politics (not just in Alexandra) was grassroots democracy and accountability, particularly in the trade unions, which inspired the AAC.

The AAC had little or no influence over much of the resistance. The youth anti-crime campaign antedated it by more than six months. Car hijackings were carried out by "comtsotsis," juvenile delinquents posing as comrades. The AAC could not remove the trunk of t-shirts because Sarah Mthembu's moral stature as a bereaved mother was reinforced by youths assembled at her deceased son's shack. Youths took over the May 17 funeral. They had their own organizations—AYCO and ASCO—which initially were suspicious of Mayekiso. Within these constraints the AAC could point to its efforts to curb "left-wing adventurism, an infantile disorder" (to paraphrase Lenin). It urged the people's courts to moderate punishment and later to disband. It decided against recognizing marshalls. It organized the Thusong meeting to seek control of the youths. It rejected the consumer boycott because youths abused their power. After the vigilante attack Mayekiso counseled against revenge and rescued a suspected informer from possible necklacing. Like any mediating institution, the AAC felt it could do no more without driving the youths into opposition.

Because the state's monolithic power had silenced open defiance, it now sought to criminalize the whisper of dissent. The indictment charged such crimes as "promoting change" and "pressuring the state"—the essence of politics in any normal society. It argued that organized *inaction* was criminal: declining to vote, attend school, complain to or associate with the police, work, pay rent, or shop. It sought to criminalize community self-help: yard, block and street committees, civic organizations, marshalls, and especially people's courts. The state's central grievance was the affront to majestas: the refusal by Blacks to recognize its authority, their creation of rival institutions, even dual power. Days before the trial began Law and Order Minister Adriaan Vlok vowed to dismantle "alternative governmental structures—people's courts, protest education, street committees and para-police groups," which posed the "most serious threat to law and order."[108] The state endowed the AAC with the very authority government had lost through racist repression. For purposes of majestas, rhetoric is reality. Van der Walt repeatedly asked the accused whether they condemned the entire system. The month that four of the Alexandra accused were detained Botha denounced "alternative structures" in his speech redeclaring the Emergency. About the same time a Nationalist MP warned Parliament: "If one is not on the side of the judicial authority of the people's courts, one is executed in the cruellest possible way."[109] Two years later the State President again insisted "it's subversive to create alternative organizations in South Africa for the education of people, for local government, for proper economic development."[110] People's courts challenged the legitimacy of the judge himself, who was naturally disturbed by Mayekiso's statement that "people are sick and tired of the court system." A magistrate sentenced a people's court member to two years, declaring "no government, no police force, no court of law can allow a position to develop in a state whereby private gangs, private individuals serve functions of the state."

The problem with such blanket proscriptions, however, is their failure to discriminate. Law consists of drawing boundaries. If everything is prohibited, moral judgment becomes impossible. Before the state can effectively stigmatize actions as criminal they must inspire moral revulsion. By the 1980s it was hard to generate outrage against *all* oppositional activity, even among white South Africans.

In response to the prosecution attempt to criminalize all politics, the defense sought to depoliticize its behavior and goals. Taking a cue from the judge, who repeatedly distinguished between blanket condemnation of apartheid (which he associated with the ANC) and criticism of particular institutions and actions, the AAC emphasized its localism. It was just the township equivalent of a white ratepayers' association, interested in toilets, sewers, and garbage collection. Far from opposing the police, the AAC sought to persuade them to accept complaints. The youth anti-crime campaign resembled suburban crime watch programs or private security companies. People's courts engaged in family mediation. No one ever discussed national issues. Mayekiso minimized his encounters with ANC members abroad, although white South African business leaders, clergy and politicians were conducting highly publicized meetings with the ANC in Dakar and Lusaka. The AAC even refused to join the legal UDF. It sought out contact with white officials. Mayekiso bowdlerized his own political philosophy: he was not a communist or even a socialist but just a Swedish social democrat, and even that was a utopian aspiration. Where the AAC had exaggerated its unity, power and radicalism to local supporters, rivals, and foreign sympathizers, it now stressed division, impotence, and moderation.

Such repudiation of achievements, ideologies, and loyalties may be one of the most insidious attributes of treason trials. Whereas punishment affirms moral purity and confers martyrdom, strategic denials are a degradation ceremony.* Obed Bapela recollected painful discussions with defense counsel,

---

*Garfinkel (1956). When Breyton Breytenbach pleaded guilty under the Terrorism Act in 1975 he declared: "I accept the responsibility for what I have done. …the methods…were wrong…my behavior was foolish…." He apologized for having hurt people and particularly "for a crass and insulting poem" addressed to Prime Minister Vorster. He thanked the security police "for the correct and humane way in which they treated me." Despite this he was sentenced to nine years without possiblity of parole. Weschler (1993: 92).

naturally preoccupied with outcome: "Certainly in some areas we would dis-agree completely with the lawyer. He is a lawyer and not a comrade. It should not be done at the expense of undermining our objectives. We want to agree with the ANC but not their methods." The residue of hypocrisy can taint subsequent victories, as when township residents displayed ANC colors to welcome home the accused after acquittal, or Mayekiso, the self-styled reformist, joined the SACP executive at its public launch the next year. (Similarly, the Delmas defendants became high ANC officials when the Congress was legalized little more than a year after their convictions in a trial where they had protested that the UDF had nothing to do with the ANC.)

Although the state sought to convict the accused of violating positive laws whose legitimacy was unproblematic, this trial, like all political trials, inevitably became a contest between competing conceptions of legality and democracy. The very attributes that provided the state with what it hoped was damning documentation—detailed minutes, agendas, and organization charts—also demonstrated the AAC's respect for regular procedures. Indeed, the formalis-tic insistence on typing the minutes preserved them from police seizure. The AAC began drafting a constitution almost as soon as it was formed, repeatedly sought advice from its attorneys, and delayed the formal launch to make fur-ther revisions. It mimicked parliamentary jargon, self-consciously referring to the executive committee as "the house." It quit the first Crisis Committee because of fiscal irresponsibility and political unaccountability. The AAC was concerned about recording donations, opening a bank account, and educating its treasurer in bookkeeping. Because many residents were only partially liter-ate and the organization lacked access to the mass media, it could only enroll and retain members through public meetings. Since whites retained political hegemony, it had to use white intermediaries. If the state's principal goal was to delegitimate the labor movement through contamination with township unrest, the result was just the opposite: Trade unionism imbued community politics with maturity, caution, democracy, and legality. The defense made a strong case that security forces bred anarchy, whereas the AAC fostered order.

Both prosecutor and judge contested the defense on this terrain, faulting the AAC for its undemocratic and irregular procedures. They denounced the peo-ple's courts, criticized the AAC for shunning local elections and the Council, questioned why John Grant had not approached the House of Representatives, and noted that the executive was self-selected. These criticisms reflected deep cultural ignorance. Most Blacks long ago repudiated the South African state as morally bankrupt. Contact with officialdom condemned Sam Buti and the entire Council. Because van der Walt identified democracy with voting he could not understand the boycott of local elections or the practice of creating consensus through discussion and report-backs rather than head-counts. His criticism of the AAC executive as oligarchic demonstrated that he had never tried to organize people. Human's ignorance of black experience, constructed by the very apartheid he defended, seriously impaired his efficacy as a litigator. Once he questioned Mayekiso about the initials "CPSA" on a letter the accused had brought from England. Human assumed they stood for Communist Party of South Africa; every Black knew the correct acronym was SACP; CPSA stood for the (British) Civil and Public Servants Association![111]

The state displayed moral arrogance as well as political naivete. How could it demand legality from opponents when it killed without justification and tortured indiscriminately? When its security forces assisted and may have engineered the vigilante raid, for which no one was punished? All the accused personally suffered state violence; all had been detained. During the first half of 1986 police killed Richard Mdakane's brother Zephaniah, Paul Tshabalala's friend Stephen Sithole, and Sarah Mthembu's son Jerry. Vigilantes attacked Mayekiso's home and would have injured him and his family had they been present. Most outrageous was white officials, in the only country disenfranchising Blacks, criticizing the AAC for not holding elections.

Because the accused committed no illegal acts, much of the debate concerned the meaning of inherently ambiguous actions and words. The state employed a tactic it had used successfully in the 1970s trials of NUSAS leaders and the Delmas prosecution of UDF leaders: tainting behavior through association with illegal organizations. In his 1984 New Year's message, ANC President Oliver Tambo had declared: "To march forward must mean that we advance against the regime's organs of state-power, creating conditions in which the country becomes increasingly ungovernable." A year later the National Executive Committee again called for ungovernability.[112] This must have inspired the AAC. The Thusong workshop, sponsored by the AAC, discussed consumer boycotts and therefore was responsible for the one that ensued. Although van der Walt rejected these arguments, Justice Grosskopf concluded that "at least some" of the Alexandra Eight had read the ANC pamphlet "Organising for people's power" and communicated the information to the rest.

Opposition movements compensated for their powerlessness with symbolic challenges, like renaming streets and schools after resistance heroes. In a society with limited literacy and numerous languages, flags and slogans played an important role.[113] Both the Save Alexandra Party and the AAC had them. Once adopted, however, they could be used against the organizations, which sought refuge in ambiguity. Green, black, and gold were the colors not only of the banned ANC but also of Inkatha, which government praised for its "moderation." A red flag might be associated with communism, but it also was the traditional workers' color. "A luta continua" might be borrowed from revolutions in Angola and Mozambique, but government could not prohibit people from calling for continued struggle. The raised fist might be an ANC salute, but it was ubiquitous; Justice Milne joked during the Pietermaritzburg trial that "it seems to be used exclusively by football players!"[114]

The accused had more difficulty extricating themselves from incautious rhetoric. Mayekiso could invoke language differences, translation errors, and linguistic incompetence (each accused testified in his first language). But his eloquence in interviews and on the witness stand (from where he corrected the interpreter) belied such modesty. Even Mzwanele, his much less experienced younger brother, carefully replaced revolutionary slogans with bland euphemisms in the Thusong conference agenda. And Mayekiso composed a virtual dictionary of hypocrisy during his testimony: "fight" = "work honestly," "take over" = "participate," and "dictatorship of the proletariat" = "let worker voices be heard." (There were uncomfortable parallels to the regime's own newspeak, in which the bureaucracy that repressed Blacks was called the Department of Co-operation and Development and the law requiring them to carry reference books was titled the Abolition of Passes and Co-ordination of Documents Act.) Van der Walt clearly preferred the superficial exactitude of legal phraseology; but he also recognized that politics used rhetoric for its power to evoke and move rather than its precision in communicating or analyzing. Nor were inflammatory words peculiar to the accused. Even Mayor Buti was against "apartheid" and for "liberation," demanding transformation not reform, calling for unbanning the ANC, and advocating boycotts and civil disobedience.

Despite the trial's preoccupation with fundamental issues of political authority, the outcome turned on more mundane strategic weaknesses (just as Pietermaritzburg failed because of expert witness and transcription errors and Delmas because of the assessor's improper dismissal.) Although the state charged conspiracy, only the Mayekiso brothers cooperated closely (and Mzwanele, indicted after the other four, may have been an afterthought). Mayekiso had known Tshabalala only three weeks before leaving for Europe and returning to detention. Tshabalala met Mdakane and Mzwanele even later. Bapela had been an AAC officer for only two weeks before being detained. State witnesses lacked credibility: some were complicit in the acts charged, others closely associated with the state. Many offered vague conclusions or patent lies, changing their stories and denying knowledge of notorious facts.

Silence was almost as damaging. Although the indictment alleged a massive conspiracy affecting the entire township, the state could persuade few residents to testify—not even most "victims" of the people's courts. Key accomplices were never charged or called: John Grant, Mapule Morale, Sarah Mthembu, and youth leaders Jacob Mtshali and Victor Kgobe. The state was particularly ambivalent toward Mike Beea, who publicly demanded that councilors resign, claimed credit for the street committees, called for "peoples' alternative administration," and involved Tshabalala in mediating disputes. He and the ACA dominated township politics during the first three months of 1986; he accompanied the delegation of church leaders to Cape Town and organized the mass funeral after the Six-Day War. His prominence was recognized when vigilantes attacked his house and he was charged with sedition and subversion. There is some evidence the state hoped to turn him: He worked closely with Burger, was never prosecuted, and was quoted by Human against Mayekiso. But he was not called to testify and ultimately rejoined Mayekiso's ACO, as well as the ANC.

Whereas the common law requires the state to make its case without help from the defense, this prosecution obviously counted on cross-examining the accused, who could not refuse to testify without arousing suspicions in the judge's mind. But Human's interrogation often seemed an uninformed fishing expedition, which sometimes lapsed into legalistic objections—that Mayekiso was relying on "hearsay," for instance, in believing that councilors were corrupt. By contrast the first two accused, who bore the brunt of the defense case, made a very good impression.

The state's ruthless determination to crush the opposition paradoxically impaired the prosecution. The Six-Day War ended street meetings. The vigilante attack created sympathy and support for the AAC, which thereafter dominated township politics. The state's moral standing was damaged by its brazen complicity: Attackers did not bother to shed their police uniforms; several were recognized by victims; they demanded and seized organizational records valuable only to the security police; and they targeted leaders of the AAC, ACA, youth organizations, and UDF (including Popo Molefe, a Delmas treason trialist). That attack and subsequent saturation policing suppressed overt resistance and closed most people's courts. Detention of four of the accused and reimposition of the Emergency in June aborted the mass launch of the AAC. Thus the prosecution had to rely on plans rather than achievements, and the accused could protest that everything remained tentative pending the inaugural meeting.

Much writing about South African law and politics has focused on whether judges are verligte or verkrampte, liberal or executive-minded. Observers retrospectively discovered signs of liberalism in van der Walt: He granted bail to treason trialist Cedric Mason (who fled) and excluded his confession as coerced; he condemned the "improper" and "unethical" actions of a cabinet minister; and he called for investigation of torture allegations against the Brixton Murder and Robbery Squad.[115] The judge dominated the trial in ways surprising to common lawyers, if not unusual in South Africa. He often interrupted the prosecutor, redirecting or cutting off questions, sometimes answering for the witness. He seemed to enjoy playing with witnesses, showing off his skills as a cross-examiner at the expense of both sides. Obed Bapela saw him as "a gentleman who was quite accommodating." Van der Walt knew he was being closely scrutinized in the courtroom, through the domestic press, and abroad (later expressing resentment of the international campaign). Determined to show the world the quality of South African justice (perhaps in contrast with the people's courts), he conducted the proceedings entirely in English and met with British and American observers. It is noteworthy that he began and ended his judgment by quoting an American author's characterization of South Africa as "a very strange society."

He seemed unusually open to defense efforts to educate him about black life, accepting the invitation to tour Alexandra (which Grosskopf refused in the companion case). His judgment acknowledged the impact of that intimate exposure to black misery—probably his first ever. He quickly mastered the ideological differences between workerists and populists. He tried to understand what he heard by assimilating it to his own experience—analogizing marshalls at black funerals to ushers at white society weddings—while conceding that race colored his outlook.* Emphasis on the larger sociopolitical context in his judgment contrasted sharply to his legalistic refusal to dismiss the treason and sedition charges at the end of the state's case. Similarly, he effectively nullified the statutory presumption of intent by requiring the state to prove it beyond a reasonable doubt. He adopted the defense summary of the evidence. Even more striking, he conceded that South Africa was undemocratic and black pride was frustrated—perhaps the first time a government official publicly stated what the rest of the world always maintained.

The importance of judicial personality emerges clearly from comparison with other cases. Justice Grosskopf interpreted similar evidence very differently to convict the Alexandra Eight. He blamed township unrest on youths, who attacked police without provocation and politicized funerals. He refused to implicate the police in the vigilante attack. He rejected any analogy between the anti-crime campaign and a white neighborhood watch, asserting that the accused should have sought the "sanction and assistance of the police." He was convinced by Brig. Stadler that parallels between the accused's actions and ANC propaganda demonstrated conspiracy. Similarly, van Dijkhorst convicted eleven Delmas accused and sentenced five to prison on evidence no stronger than that proffered in the Alexandra Five trial.

There were limits to van der Walt's empathy, however. Where the accused saw the Council as black puppets, the judge analogized it to the Johannesburg City Council. Where the accused saw the tricameral parliament as racist exclusion, the judge saw it as a gracious concession to the "coloured" community. Where the accused feared and hated the security forces, the judge experienced them as helpful and protective. Where the accused justified the rent boycott because payments were high and amenities poor, the judge saw rents as ridiculously low and the only source from which local government could make the improvements residents demanded. Where the accused saw state complicity in the vigilante attack, the judge initially saw it as "Black-on-Black" violence expressing political differences.

Acquittal on the merits after an exhaustive hearing represented a dramatic denouement to the use of treason trials to suppress resistance to apartheid, especially when the judge bluntly criticized the state for having brought the charges at all. The accused, the township, anti-apartheid groups, and the

---

*In the 1980 trial of the "Soweto Eleven," Judge Hendrik van Dyk could not understand why Blacks complained that primary school classes contained eighty children; his own son attended classes with 100 students at the University of Pretoria. Nor could he comprehend why migrant workers objected to single-sex hostels; when the judge was at university he had lived in an all-male residence hall. Halberstam (1980: 82). Three years later the judge dismissed the pleas of the Magopa to stay on their land, see chapter ten.

press were triumphant, perhaps because there were so few other occasions. A judicial victory is particularly sweet because it confers moral vindication. Should it also be seen as a celebration of the rule of law? Only in part. The Alexandra community was deprived of leadership for three crucial years. The trade union movement (domestic and foreign) was put to enormous expense in mounting a defense that included two counsel, two attorneys, and three researchers. The accused languished in jail for up to two-and-a-half years. They were kept in solitary confinement for more than six months and repeatedly interrogated. The Attorney General denied bail and refused to explain why. If the treason charges were unjustified at the end of the case they should never have been filed, and the judge should have dismissed treason and sedition at the end of the state's case. The rule of law governs the prosecutor as well as the judge, but he gave no reason for targeting these accused. The rule of law presupposes that a trial will reveal what actually happened, but the minimal conditions for truth-finding were not met. The state refused to allow its witnesses to testify in open court, where their evidence could be scrutinized by the audience, media, and public. Prosecution witnesses mouthed patent falsehoods and changed their testimony overnight, strongly suggesting police pressure. The in-camera hearing prevented the community from openly expressing support for the accused during the long first half of the trial.

The rule of law has substantive content as well as procedural criteria. The accused were prosecuted for engaging in behavior that would have been praised anywhere else (and was widely lauded abroad). They were charged under laws they had no role in enacting. The case was prosecuted and heard by men they had no say in appointing. Acquittal was an act of grace, not recognition of a right. Blacks dependent on white mercy do not enjoy the rule of law.

CHAPTER 10

BAKWENA BA MAGOPA: THE LAST FORCED REMOVAL

Whereas I consider it in the public interest that you, the members of the black tribes...must move...so it is that I, by virtue of the power vested in me...hereby order that you...must move...and I order further that you...may not at any time return. (M. Viljoen, State President, November 10, 1983)

[N]obody was wronged because this action was undertaken with the greatest caution and acknowledgement of human dignity. All transactions were legal and the necessary provision was made that the removal and reimbursement were undertaken for the good of the community. (Report to the Nederduitse Gereformeerde Kerk, May 1984)

We don't have power with guns. All we have is the right that the land belongs to us.

We've got our "gun," which is Christ. He is more powerful than an ordinary gun. (Two elderly Magopa, August 1987)

Forced removals are the iron fist of apartheid. Like security force killings and hangings of "patriots," such acts of state terror reverberate around the world. The Surplus People Project's estimate that government forcibly removed 3.5 million evoked comparisons to genocide and deeply embarrassed the regime.[1] In an effort to improve its image, Co-operation and Development Minister Piet Koornhof declared in 1981 that "as far as is humanly possible and as far as is practical" there would be no more forced removals.[2] Two years later he reiterated that "everything possible is also being done to ensure that [resettlement] is carried out with consideration and compassion."[3] Magopa is the tragic story of the government's last vain effort to hide its iron fist within a velvet glove.

Expulsion

The Bakwena Ba Magopa (hereafter the Magopa people, who live in Mogopa) include farmworkers from the Orange Free State, peasants from Lesotho, and Tswana from Mogale.[4] They bought two farms of nearly 20,000 acres in the Western Transvaal in 1913 and 1931, selling their cattle to raise the more than £15,000. The Minister of Native Affairs held the land in trust for the group, which he recognized as a separate tribal entity subordinate to its chief at Bethanie. The community prospered; by the early 1980s it contained more than 420 families, who had built a primary and a secondary school, a clinic, four churches, shops, a reservoir, and 332 stone houses. They sold their surplus production to local white co-operatives.[5]

A newspaper announced as early as 1969: "The 2,500 strong Bakwena Ba Magopa tribe will soon be moved from the land which they have owned and developed since 1912. Their place will be taken by diamond prospectors who will be allocated claims during an old-fashioned 'diamond rush.'" The prior owner had retained mineral rights. The Department of Bantu Affairs had decided to move the Magopa to Swartruggens, thirty-five miles away. "A Government official said this morning that the tribe was being moved, not only to make room for the prospectors, but also in accordance with general Government policy."

Throughout this period the Department of Native Affairs (and its increasingly euphemistic successors—Bantu Affairs, and Co-operation and Development) had respected the community's recommendation in appointing headmen, who lacked authority to allocate land or resources. In 1979 the Magopa replaced Simon More but soon became disillusioned with his successor, Jacob More, a former policeman.[6]

> It is hereby noted that the above tribe is not satisfied of certain things which arise against our ex headman Mr J.L. More during his headmanship from 1978. The tribe would like to know what happens to the monies collected for different reasons and fines which were imposed to different people and handed to Mr J.L. More during his headmanship. [It enumerated fines, taxes, and water receipts.]...
>
> The land as it stands, is the tribal land. There is no one who can say he or she got better shares than the other one, individual inheritance and rights are the same, now the point is Mr. J.L.

> More is claiming that the tribal land is his. So the tribe would like
> to know where does he got that idea from. ...

They reiterated these complaints in another memorandum, adding that Jacob refused to meet with the tribe on six occasions between May 1978 and February 1981, purporting to act unilaterally. On September 20, 1981, at a meeting attended by migrant workers, the tribe replaced Jacob by Shadrack More, disestablished the council, and informed the magistrate, P. de Villiers, who immediately called another meeting to confirm the decision. On October 7 the community did so overwhelmingly, only seven people supporting Jacob. The magistrate solicited suggestions for new councilors. Later that month, however, he called a third meeting and rebuked the community: "I am a white man and as magistrate of this district I am telling you that Jacob More will rule until he dies."[7]

Refusing to accept the decision, Isaac More wrote the magistrate on behalf of the community in November, "politely and respectively" seeking return of the tribal stamp, which Jacob was hiring out for R20 a time. The Ventersdorp magistrate appointed his colleague in Klerksdorp to conduct a commission of inquiry, which sat in January 1982. Although the community participated, its skepticism about the proceeding was confirmed when the magistrate refused to reveal the evidence or publish his report.[8]

Less than a month later government told the Magopa they might be "resettled" at Pachsdraai. "At that meeting," according to a later tribal memorandum, "members of the Tribe left no bones in explaining to the Officers that were present the irrelevancy of their request and they left." (The idiomatic mistake ironically inverted what became the Magopa's trump card against removal.) On Saturday, June 27, Jacob More mentioned removal to some migrants home for a wedding, who replied that the tribe had to decide collectively, with adequate notice to other migrants. Several hundred people attended such a meeting at Rapitse's Old Hall, the traditional venue, on July 10. Jacob, however, stayed in his house with ten community members and three government officials, rebuffing two invitations to address the tribe. Instead he selected a "Planning Committee" of ten Magopa and five officials, whose identities were not revealed for more than a year. In the following months Jacob held secret meetings with this committee, excluding others who sought to attend.[9]

On September 19 the tribe reiterated its grievances about Jacob's continuing financial misconduct, adding more ominously:

> [S]ince he was deposed from his headmanship on the 20th
> September 1981, he has with his few followers started to hold
> private secret meetings and make decisions without the concern
> of the tribe. These they take to the native commissioner as if
> they had consulted the whole tribe and agreed.... For instance,
> they held private meetings with the Bophuthatswana officials

and talked over tribal rights without their concern to the extent that they had already arranged to move the tribe without their concern. They are breaking up the tribe by moving them against their will yet in addition to this they have not got the status.

Despairing of direct appeals to the magistrate, the tribe retained the Johannesburg law firm of Bowman, Gilfillan and Blacklock. They wrote to the Chief Commissioner of the Western Transvaal, who referred them to the Ventersdorp magistrate, who told them he did not keep the tribe's book. On September 15 they wrote Jacob More, seeking "access to all the books, records and documentation pertaining to the administration of the tribe's funds" so they could be audited. He replied a day before the two-week deadline, referring them to the Ventersdorp magistrate. A request for the report of the January commission of inquiry was referred to the Director-General of Co-operation and Development. After additional requests the Chief Commissioner replied in February 1983 that, though government regulations required an annual audit of all tribal accounts, "[T]he Department is therefore not prepared to accede to your request. A copy of the record of the inquiry into the affairs of the tribe can likewise not be made available to you." The same month Jacob More also failed to reply to a demand that he convene a tribal meeting to hear complaints and open his financial records.

The community issued another memorandum making clear that the real issue was not Jacob More's corruption but his lack of authority to negotiate removal.[10]

> The standing order in the Administration of the Tribe is constituted on the bases of the Chieftainship order by Kraals in the form of seniority, for peace and good administration we have as a rule Tribally constituted Kraals which has to respect each other in all the fundamental issues affecting the Tribe.... The Tribal constitutional procedure is that any major question or case that involves the whole Tribe, must be discussed at a general meeting, where every member of the Tribe has got the right to come up with his opinion, and to the satisfaction of everybody....
>
> Our opinion is that, not even the Magistrate, has the right to deny us of, our birth right property.

Eight men signed it "most humbly yours for the humble and weak members of the Swartkop Bakwena Ba Mogopa Tribe."

The community replaced Bowman Gilfillan with the Legal Resources Centre, which wrote Louis Pretorius, Assistant Director of the Department of Co-operation and Development, in January that its clients were "willing and anxious to discuss the details of the proposed resettlement" but denied the authority of the planning committee. Since the two groups were at "loggerheads" and actually in litigation (they were not), "it seems to us that it would be in the interests of all concerned if both groups were to participate in the planning committee." The Department stalled, responding in March only to ask for "the names of your clients and the letters of authority whereby you have been appointed."

During the year following its secret formation the "Planning Committee" and the government sought to "persuade" the tribe to move to Pachsdraai, threatening the reluctant with forcible removal and denial of compensation. On June 23 Jacob More moved with about ten families, including committee members and former councilors. He occupied the former white owner's farmhouse and allocated his supporters brick houses and land. Some of those arriving later had to pay R400 for access to land; shopkeepers were required to obtain trading licenses from Jacob. Government demolished the houses of those who left (and four others by mistake, leading to civil actions for damages). Andrew Mpshe, a migrant laborer, had a long-standing marital conflict; after his wife followed her family to Pachsdraai his house was destroyed without notice to him. Enoch Rathebe, who opposed removal, fought with his brother and sister-in-law, breaking her arm. During his trial his house was demolished.[11] Government also destroyed the school (whose teachers had already been withdrawn by the Bophuthatswana government), medical clinic, and churches. All the building materials were deposited in Jacob's yard. The magistrate terminated bus service to Ventersdorp and ordered the removal of the community water pumps, charging the resident who had custody with theft. He threatened to withhold pensions and refused to endorse reference books for migrant laborers. When white farmers began cutting fences and allowing cattle to graze on Magopa land, he declined to intervene. By August 170 families had left, but more than 300 remained.[12]

The threatened removal finally hit the papers in September. Under the headline "Bulldozed out of their church," 85-year-old Isaac More bemoaned the fact that "our children are without schooling and our churches are gone," and Bishop Tutu denounced the government action as "high-handed and careless."[13] Five days later another paper described the removal as a mystery.[14] "The Department of Co-operation and Development knew nothing of the removal and was unable to trace any information on the property, a department spokesman said after investigation." The story revived the myth of untapped diamond mines. That weekend a feature focused on the conditions of those who had moved.[15]

> Forlorn people in a resettlement camp at Pagsdraai [sic] near Zeerust have been shattered by the suicide of a male member of their community who hanged himself this week. His death focused attention on the appalling living conditions in the camp, which its inhabitants—moved there against their will—ironically call "the promised land." … At Pagsdraai, conditions are dry and primitive. There is no food, no grazing—and no water. Pagsdraai is nothing more than a crusty dustbowl.

> There is no tap water—in fact, when I visited the settlement this week, the only water I found were the bitter tears of the people of Pagsdraai....
>
> After three months, the people are regretting their move. They say they want to return to the peace and prosperity of Mogopa where drought was unknown, work was more easily available and the community united.

The interview was interrupted by four whites, who ordered the reporter to leave and demanded to know whether the photographer had taken pictures. The local office of the Department of Co-operation and Development told the reporter (falsely) that permits were necessary to enter trust land because "the area can be dangerous." Another Department spokesman said the tribe had been told of the move five years earlier and government had bought their farm "many years ago." Assistant Director Louis Pretorius had another story: the removal began in 1981; Mogopa probably would be expropriated; the schools had been demolished because Bophuthatswana had withdrawn its teachers; and he could not discuss the stolen water pumps because the matter was sub judice.

The following week the *Sowetan* described "Mogopa's lasting agony" through the words of Isaac More, whom it misidentified as the headman.

> Our parents bought this land. It is ours. Now we are told that we have to move. Why? The fact that we still have the title deed to this land is ignored. We dug the water holes, built the schools and churches and to see all these achievements now just rubble pains my heart.... We will not move until we are addressed by the paramount chief, Chief Lerothodi Mamogale.

A companion story headlined, "Village weeps: Mogopa laid waste in prelude to land grab," retold the apocryphal story that the farms were "reputedly rich in minerals, particularly diamonds. There are currently a number of white diamond prospectors in the area." The Director-General said "people must realise that they will have to move at some stage." Government did not recognize Mamogale as paramount chief of the Bakwena but had consulted with Bophuthatswana, into which "Pargsdraai" would be incorporated. The churches must have requested demolition.[16] Two days later Pretorius revealed for the first time that government had paid R688,831 to 182 families but refused to disclose Jacob's share or discuss the suicide beyond insisting that the motive had been "entirely personal."[17]

The *Sowetan* renewed the attack that day, describing the "Village the govt broke." "Today what was once a proud village is a spooky rubble; children have no schools to go to, worshippers no churches, and the sick no clinics—because they have all been demolished on instructions from the South African Government." Kgotla member Jacob Moloatsi insisted "we were never consulted or even officially informed about the removal. We heard rumours and the next thing we knew there were bulldozers coming to destroy the village. Further we are being taken to a strange place we do not even know." In a companion article Frans Swanepoel, who had bought 100 claims for a rand apiece when the farm was opened to prospecting in 1970, said: "I have done quite well for myself. The biggest diamond I sold fetched R25,000." Although he would miss some of the Magopa "like Ou Johannes here,"

> I don't blame the Government for moving them. These people can hardly grow mealies for themselves, let alone for us and you people in the cities. We are a growing nation and we need farmers who can grow food. These people have not been able to utilise this land meaningfully in spite of being on it for a hundred years.[18]

Columnist Aggrey Klaaste repeated the canard a week later: "The trouble with Mogopa is not that it is a black village in a so-called white area, but it has wealth stored under its belly—diamonds."[19] The literacy magazine *Learn and Teach* ran an illustrated story about "When the bulldozer came."[20]

On October 21 Nicholas Haysom of Cheadle Thompson & Haysom (the tribe's third law firm) wrote Dr. Piet Koornhof, Minister of Co-operation and Development, on behalf of Shadrack More (whom the tribe had chosen to replace Jacob as headman) and four others, demanding that further homes not be destroyed like those of Andrew Mpshe and Enoch Rathebe and the bulldozers be removed. Threatened with an interdict application, the Department complied in November. Haysom then sought compensation for the damaged property.

Government would not stop, however. On November 10 State President Viljoen secretly issued the removal order.

> Whereas I consider it in the public interest that you, the members of the black tribes, the black communities and the black people living in the Released areas of Zwartrand and Hartebeeslaagte, district of Ventersdorp, province of Transvaal, together with the members of your families, must move to the Pachsdraai district .... So it is that I, by virtue of the power vested in me in Section 5(1)(b) of the Black Administration Act 1927 hereby order that you... within the period of 10 days from delivery of this order to you, must move.... And I order further that you... may not at any time return.

The press reported this for the first time a week later, under the headlines "300 families must go" and "'Apartheid with a velvet glove?'"[21] The Department had told the Magopa a few days before that it would formally order the removal at a meeting on November 18.

On the appointed day, in the presence of Jacob More, Ventersdorp Mag. de Villiers told 150 residents that those who had not moved by November 29 would be "loaded up by force and moved." Trucks would arrive in three days. When they objected Danie Smith told them for the Chief Commissioner: "There is only one item on the agenda. You are here to listen to the order of the State President—that's all." Some said they had never been properly consulted; others reverted to the alleged diamonds. But de Villiers dismissed their complaints: "When we held talks you sat to one side. Today you come crying."[22] Under the headline "Govt will 'force' Bakwena out," *The Star* published photographs with captions like "The children of Magopa..their school in ruins, they now share the household chores." Lazarus Kgatitsoe asked "how can we go to a place where we hate the people and they hate us? Does the Government want bloodshed?" A companion article entitled "Elderly face the order to go with fear and dismay" pictured "World War 2 veteran Mr Elifas Pooe" displaying his medals. "I fought for this country. I don't get involved. But if I must go, then they must build me a nice house in Pretoria." Jemima Lepa said of her mother Martha Matlae: "She's nearly 100 but still active. She doesn't want to go. This is her homeland—she grew up here." A day later it pictured six large trucks and described lawyers' efforts to stop the move.[23]

At a "pitso" on November 20 more than 285 adults authorized Shadrack More to represent them. Haysom wrote Koornhof the next day that "in the absence of reasonable negotiations and consultations" the tribe would remain on the land as they were entitled to do since Parliament had not approved the removal. They could not wait until "your Department has committed irreversible and unlawful acts" and "demanded" an undertaking that they would not be evicted. If that did not arrive by nine the next morning they would apply for an interdict.[24] Koornhof did not reply, and the application was filed.[25] Shadrack More, supervisor of the Mapatla Hostel in Soweto, attached a petition with 270 signatures to his founding affidavit. The government ignored seventy years of peaceful residence. He made a casual observation that later became crucial.

> There is situated on the land a cemetery which has been used for the burial of tribal members. This cemetery is not only considered sacred to the tribe but in terms of tribal custom is regarded as the source of well being for the tribe and must be cared for. In terms of the orders made by [de Villiers] no provision has been made for the care of the cemetery nor the right of members to return to the village to look after the cemetery themselves.

The next day *The Star* repeated its feature story on the elderly and continued the countdown. Danie Smith again admonished the tribe: "I want to tell you negotiations have been going on for all of six or seven years. You didn't want to walk the same road." [26]

The interdict application began inauspiciously. Philip More, a tribal councilor, tried to serve Mag. de Villiers, whom he knew. The defendant "informed me that there was no one at the magistrate's office by the name of de Villiers. He told me rudely to get out of his offices....He kicked me on the calf of my left leg and I left a copy of the application at his feet." Three days after it was filed (and four before the removal deadline) Justice Hendrik van Dyk summarily rejected the application on the ground that removal was authorized by a 1975 Parliamentary resolution recommending "the withdrawal of the Bantu tribes, Bantu communities and Bantu persons residing in the area set out in Schedule B in terms of the provisions of Section 5 of the Bantu Administration Act." Rejecting the argument that Parliament had to specify the destination as well, he quoted a 1977 decision:

> It is clear that what was intended was that Parliament should have the power to decide the area from which Bantu committees [sic] should be withdrawn, and that [when] the time came to implement the withdrawal, the State President should specify the area to which such withdrawal should be made....[27]

Five days before the deadline Black Sash officer Ethel Walt organized a press conference at which Magopa told their story to more than twenty-five local and foreign journalists and five diplomats.[28] This had the desired result. On Sunday, November 27, two days before the deadline, the two most influential American papers ran articles. (The Sunday after Thanksgiving, which launches Christmas shopping, typically sees the thickest newspaper of the year.) Under the headline "Pretoria Moves to Erase 'Black Spot,'" *The New York Times* related the seventy-year history of Mogopa, described "homes in cut stone of a permanence rare in Africa," and pictured Elizabeth Katitswe (Kgatitsoe), who had lived there for thirty years, farming and running the Swartkop General Dealers Store, and had built a new three-bedroom house.[29] It exposed Jacob More's treachery and described the destruction wreaked by bulldozers. "A walk around parts of the village these days resembles a stroll through an archaeological site: here the ruins that must have been the Methodist church, there a straight dirt road running through the rubble of garden walls, further on the debris that might once have been a school." The *Washington Post* carried a front-page story by South African journalist Allister Sparks.[30]

> This trim little African village 120 miles west of Johannesburg is under sentence of death this weekend. Its 300 peasant families, who have built one of the most stable and prosperous rural black communities in South Africa, have been ordered under the country's segregationist apartheid laws to evacuate the village by Sunday night. If they refuse to go, the government will remove them by force Tuesday.

He also featured the sixty-one-year old widowed Elizabeth Kgatitsoe, describing her "modern ranch-style home with 10 rooms, tiled bathroom, carved front door and attached garage with an Alfa-Romeo inside." At Pachsdraai she would be reduced to a tent and tin toilet.

The *Post* devoted its lead editorial to the subject the next day.[31]

> Those wonderful people who brought you the South African government's idea of racial and electoral reform earlier this month (a "reform" that made things worse for the 70 percent of the population that is black) have another terrific project in the works. It is the evacuation and destruction of a village called Mogope [sic].... [Sparks's article] should serve as a useful antidote to all the cynical propaganda that is being put out about how the Botha government's heart is really in the right place, but it can only move so fast, etc., etc.

> Why did the authorities decide to mow down this village in the first place and to dispossess its several hundred families? Well, you don't have to be told: because these villagers are black people.... Mogope constitutes an unauthorized "black spot," being 80 miles from where it should be according to the plan to establish racial purity.

> So what is to be done? Simple. You just kick the people out and destroy what they have spent decades building up and compel them to go somewhere else—somewhere terrible....

> It is disgusting. But, importantly, it is also what is really going on in South Africa—the hard, irreducible essence of the apartheid system. The next time someone talks to you of savagery and a want of civilization in Africa, don't be so quick to take offense at the language. It is a fitting description of the people who are perpetrating these acts.

PFP MP Helen Suzman was in the United States Thanksgiving weekend. Alerted by Ethel Walt she talked to Chester Crocker, Assistant Secretary of State for African Affairs, on Monday. That, together with the two articles, elicited an immediate official denunciation of the threatened removal.[32]

In South Africa that weekend *City Press* carried two articles.[33] One pictured an old man sitting on the ruins of a destroyed house with the caption "Next week we'll use force" and the explanation "Devastation, sadness and anger...a family man turns his back on the rubble that was his home before Government bulldozers flattened it in an attempt to get the Bakwena BaMogopa people to 'volintarily' [sic] leave their ancestral lands near Ventersdorp." Another warned that "Mogopa move 'may lead to violence.'" The accompanying editorial was scathing.

The tragedy being forced on the Mogopa people exposes us all.

It exposes the nonsense spoken by Dr Piet Koornhof when he says there will be no more forced removals.

It exposes the nonsense spoken by the Government when it claims that it is embarking on reform.

It exposes the gullibility of Western governments prepared to give Prime Minister P W Botha the benefit of the doubt.

It exposes the true role of the homeland governments and their collaboration with the forced removal of people from ancestral land.

It exposes the collaboration of these men and women standing for the new Black authorities with a system which is premised on the homeland system and people being deprived of their birthright.

It exposes the reality of apartheid....

Stop this madness now, or accept that we are bent on suicide.

The same day Bishop Tutu and other leaders of the South African Council of Churches (SACC) met some twenty Magopa in the Black Sash office in Johannesburg.[34] Anticipating government complaints about outside agitators, Tutu stressed that "the SACC would respond only to specific requests from the tribe." The Magopa wished to remain but were prepared to leave if government compensated them and negotiated the destination. That night Tutu telephoned Koornhof, who seemed willing to talk. He also told Koornhof that church leaders would hold a vigil at Mogopa Monday night to observe and oppose any removal. Koornhof referred Tutu to his subordinate, Koos Celliers, who referred him to his subordinate. On Monday Tutu met Solly Vermaak, Deputy Director of Land Affairs, who said removal could not be postponed "because it was both a State President's and Court Order." The Magopa would be moved "gently" on Tuesday. The Department could not negotiate further because "there was no alternative land available other than the Pachsdraai." Celliers telephoned Tutu later that day to the same effect. Archbishop Philip Russell and Rev. Fremont Louw tried unsuccessfully to intervene with both Koornhof and the Department.

That night representatives of the Methodist, Anglican, Presbyterian, Evangelical Presbyterian, Congregational, Dutch Reformed, Lutheran, and Catholic Churches and the SACC, Black Sash fieldworkers, diplomats, and newspaper and television reporters waited for removal. The media offered vivid accounts. Dr. Allan Boesak condemned it as "the ultimate blasphemy." Tutu asked why it had to occur "just before Christmas—a feast which celebrates family and community life? Why should violence be done to a peaceful people just before the feast that commemorates the Prince of Peace?" The *City Press* feature story was entitled "'Oh Lord, Deliver Us From Evil.'"

> "Tell your children how they stole your land. Tell your children how they broke down your churches and schools."... The young preacher, Shun Govender, spoke as though he was conducting a funeral to the material past...but also at the baptism of the determination that would carry people into a new and difficult future.

Although the police never came, rumors frightened a group of residents to pay whites to move them in five thirty-ton trucks to their paramount chief in Bethanie.[35]

International pressure continued to mount. The World Council of Churches, World Alliance of Reformed Churches, and several Dutch churches protested. The Dutch government issued a strong statement on Thursday. U.S. Undersecretary of State Lawrence Eagleburger summoned South African Ambassador Brand Fourie that Tuesday to express displeasure. A State Department spokesman declared: "The United States has consistently made clear its view that South Africa's problems cannot be addressed constructively by the arbitrary relocation of peoples on an ethnic or racial basis." Two U.S. Embassy officials visited Mogopa on Friday. Even Republican Congressman Gerald Solomon, who had strongly supported South Africa, wrote Prime Minister Botha in dismay.[36] Under the headline "Eviction Awaited By South Africans," *The New York Times* warned that government would resort to force as soon as the media left.[37] U.S. National Public Radio broadcast on the following Saturday, juxtaposing two quotations.

> *Matthew Kgatitsoe:* We didn't want to go to Pachsdraai. We couldn't understand why we had to go to Pachsdraai. Pachsdraai is not a place we can stay at. It's a dry place. There's no water, there's nothing.

> *George de Villiers Morrison* (Deputy Minister of Co-operation and Development): You do get to a stage when for certain reasons you have to move these peoples. And then you are left with no other option but to move them by force. But generally that is a minority of people. We never reestablish them in an area that has no viability.

In England the *New Statesman* denounced the "Death of a Village," quoting Bishop Tutu saying that apartheid was "as evil as Nazism" and removal its "final solution." "You don't need gas chambers if you put people in places where they will almost certainly starve." The *Sunday Express* declaimed: "The forced removal of the Ba Mogopa people is an atrocity. Note the names of those who do it."[38]

Black Sash chairperson Sheena Duncan was realistic about what the opposition had accomplished.[39]

> It is probably a failure as far as preventing the removal goes but I don't think we had any illusions about how difficult it is for people to resist successfully. It has, however, been a great success as far as "raising the political costs" to the government is concerned.... [I]t was easy to get the press etc., interested because of the State President's order with its time limit.... Another lesson, of course, is that the promises of reform which were believed in the West regarding the new Constitution have raised expectations overseas which have now been confounded and that makes their reaction that much stronger.

Yet government clearly was uncomfortable with its public image. On Friday the newly appointed Deputy Information Minister, Louis Nel, organized a helicopter tour of Mogopa and Pachsdraai for nine correspondents, including *The New York Times* and the *Washington Post*.[40] Sweeping down unannounced on a meeting of 250 Magopa, Nel shook hands and climbed on a chair to address them. "Dear friends, it is nice to be here with you. It is nice to see people who sing so nicely and who are so joyful. I'm from the government and the government's attitude is that we must help the people to have a better life in this beautiful country of ours. With that I will say goodbye, and may you stay well." After villagers applauded Philip More replied "We are not against the government. But, since the government say they are going to take us away, the people start shivering and getting scared." Nel reassured them: "It is not the Government's intent to suppress people. If you think the Government wants to throw you into the street, that is not going to happen." But the removal was irreversible. "A white man cannot always solve the problems between Black people. We must bring you and Jacob More together so you can solve your problems." He concluded: "I am very glad I came. It is good for me to listen and to hear what you have in your hearts." He would be glad to meet with them in Pretoria. On the way back to the helicopter the elders accused the magistrate of lying; he responded that the chief elder had been "so drunk he couldn't stand" during the crucial meeting at which the tribe was informed of the removal.

At Pachsdraai Nel continued to justify the removal to the press. "It is basically a Third World situation, which cannot be judged by New York or London standards." "If it wasn't for this Black on Black conflict, the whole tribe would have moved without any problem whatsoever. Not one single person has been forcibly removed." Although government wanted to raise everyone's standard of living, it was not possible to do so at Mogopa, which "was not planned. It was a sort of informal living together of people, so that if you had wanted them to stay there you would have had to demolish and start afresh anyway." Land at Pachsdraai was better and more plentiful. They would benefit from being incorporated into Bophuthatswana, which South Africa was helping develop. Pachsdraai had a staffed health center (he conveniently forgot that government had destroyed the Mogopa clinic). It had three schools (costing $1.6 million) compared with Mogopa's two. Government had spent another $5.2 million on the move, paying households an average compensation of $1,700. The headmaster of the new primary school agreed: "The school buildings are much better, people can grow gardens here and I am very much happier." Out of Nel's hearing, however, several families expressed serious reservations.

Although Koornhof had rebuffed reporters the day after the deadline, saying "I don't intend to make further statements to complicate the issue," he also succumbed to the compulsion to justify on the same day as Nel's public relations exercise.[41] Many families were moving voluntarily because Mogopa had few buildings, no planned residential area, only three faucets, and barren rocky soil unsuitable for cattle or crops. Pachsdraai, an "attractive part of the Transvaal bushveld," was "anything but arid." The move would provide "better living conditions and prospects" and unify Tswana speakers. Government made similar arguments in a press release the following Monday, to counteract critical reports in the German press.

This campaign did not go unchallenged. Black Sash issued a press statement rebutting lies on Radio Setswana, Afrikaans Radio, and the SABC English Service.[42] And the day following Nel's visit, the *Sunday Tribune* carried another three-handkerchief story, appropriately titled "The Tears for Paradise Lost."[43]

> As the early morning mist lifts over Mogopa, it reveals soft green rolling hills dotted with stone houses and kraals.... It would be a rural paradise but for the weeping of its people. There's a soft sobbing in the community's neat graveyard as a young woman leans on the cairn of stones marking her father's grave. A toddler whimpers at her side.

A companion article, entitled "From dream to nightmare: Gone... the house that Phillip built in 27 years," described the "four-bedroom home that would not look out of place in any white middle-class suburb." Inverting the comparison advanced by Nel and Koornhof, it stressed the startling "contrast between the semi-arid bushveld of Pachsdraai and the arable grasslands of Mogopa." Originally called Sebatlani (the place of dust), Pachsdraai had "no grass, not even under the trees." Only "a couple of streets have taps." There was "no livestock apart from chickens." The nearest town was a R5 trip.

Although Koos Celliers rebuffed Nicholas Haysom's request for a postponement while the tribe sought another place to live, the Magopa took up Nel's Saturday invitation and arranged a six-hour meeting with him, Koornhof, Celliers, and seven other officials the following Monday. They were angry that they were allowed only six representatives and Haysom was excluded, while Jacob More and other Pachsdraai residents attended.[44] They restated their position in a memorandum.

> The question of Pachsdraai and the facilities there does not concern us. The tribe deposed Jacob More in 1981 and since then he had had no right to represent us…. The "negotiation" of the Removal to Pachsdraai was kept secret from us and so has nothing to do with us…. According to Tribal Law and statute, an open meeting of adult members of the tribe must be held before land transaction can take place.

They asked several questions. Could they remain? If not, could they choose their destination? Could it be Bethanie? Could they stay through Christmas? the August 1984 harvest? "We need urgent replies to these questions because the tribe is living in terror and the old people cannot stand the strain." They received no answers.

The following day the community agreed to inspect Pachsdraai but asserted their independence by refusing to accept government transport or allow their houses to be appraised for compensation until they had agreed to removal.[45] The Friday visit again coincided with a helicopter tour, this time organized by the Deputy Minister and Deputy Director of Land Affairs.[46] The local journalists who took it seemed more credulous. They reported that Alex Pooe, a tribal councilor, declared that the government and the Bible ordained that each tribe should go to its own homeland. Council secretary Johannes Andrews warned them not to defame the tribe and the government by writing that the removal was coerced. A *Sunday Times* report under the headline "Mogopa tribe bows to 'The Law' " took the government line.[47]

> Facilities at Pachsdraai and future development prospects are better than at Mogopa. The government is handling the removal with far greater circumspection and sensitivity than preceding ones. Opinions of the original Mogopa people seem genuinely divided…. A long-standing leadership squabble in the tribe presaged major difficulties…. Genuine conflicts of economic interest between the Mogopa factions could lie at the root of the refusal by some to move.

The problem was not "the ethics of being made to move" but intra-tribal and economic conflict. It concluded by quoting Johannes Andrews: "The Government must be obeyed. It is the father and the mother. It is the giver of things." The *Pretoria News* concurred that "Fate of Magopa is sealed."[48] Jacob More maintained that the tribe was "not forced" to move but did so because "we must obey the government." Pachsdraai was "95 percent better." The paper also quoted councilor Alex Pooe that "the resettlement was in fact a move from Egypt to Canaan" and agreed that "the majority of people chorused these sentiments" and were "fat and happy."

The Magopa delegation saw things differently. When they reported back on the visit and showed samples of soil and vegetation the community decided not to move. Haysom recalled the reaction three years later.[49]

> They were amazed to see that Jacob More was installed in a large house with a sign post referring to it as a "G G Office." They were concerned to see the materials from their demolished schools in his yard. Miss A Claassens of the Black Sash asked Mr L Pretorius of the Department how it was that the "Planning Committee" had all the substantial structures at Pachsdraai and Mr Pretorius replied that the headman and his councilors had the power to allocate resources as they saw fit.

They authorized Haysom to ask the Supreme Court for leave to appeal, which he did on Monday, and they drafted a letter to Koornhof (delivered Tuesday) stating their objections to Pachsdraai. It was remote from the Witwatersrand (where many were labor migrants), local employment, and shopping (69 kilometers to Zeerust). It lacked water, the soil was poor, there was little grass for grazing, and cattle were thin. They had no capital for irrigation and house construction. Land was distributed unequally and unfairly. They could not live under Jacob More. If they had to move, they wanted adequate compensation in the form of land and money for improvements at Bethanie. They wanted the minutes of the last meeting and assurances that future meetings would include Haysom and as many Magopa as officials and exclude Jacob More. They concluded: "We hope and trust that it is possible to negotiate this matter in a way that befits human dignity. We have faith that you as a Christian will approach this matter in a way that takes account of our terrible suffering."

Jules Browde SC, chairman of Lawyers for Human Rights, wrote Prime Minister Botha the same day, quoting a famous Appellate Division judgment that "the individual citizen, provided he obeys the law of the land, is not liable to have his personal freedom restrained by executive action." Perhaps Botha was unaware of the community's long residence, self-sufficiency, contributions in World War II, and tribal cemetery. "For humanitarian reasons alone" he pleaded for a delay "until the legality of the removal has been decided by a court of appeal." This request was reiterated at a press conference the same day by LHR, Professor John Dugard (Director of the Centre for Applied Legal Studies), Helen Suzman (PFP spokesperson on Black affairs), Black Sash, and Magopa.[50] When government officials indicated their willingness to await a court ruling the community sought to reconstruct Mogopa, buying a pump and collecting money for a school. On behalf of Shadrack More, "duly elected as the headman by tribal law," and seven other elders, Haysom sent the Ventersdorp magistrate a letter reiterating their legal right to remain, complaining about his behavior, and threatening to sue if he did not begin performing his duties within fourteen days. In January he resumed paying pensions and issuing and endorsing registration books.[51]

Mogopa remained in the spotlight in the new year. *The New York Times* ran a feature entitled "How Apartheid Uproots and Transplants Millions," discussing removals in Mathopestad, Badplaas, and Mogopa, illustrated with photographs of men destroying a building in Mogopa and an eighty-year-old woman told she had to relocate.[52] During the January-February no confidence debate Helen Suzman warned of the country's increasing economic and political isolation.

> [N]othing could be more damaging to the pro-South African lobby than the sort of headline stories that appeared in the *New York Times* and the *Washington Post* shortly after the [constitutional] referendum, while these very [boycott] measures were having their passage through the House of Representatives, about forced removals in South Africa…. A sharp editorial in the *Washington Post* described [the Magopa removal] as disgusting and part of the "hard, irreducible essence of the apartheid system", which of course it is…. [T]hanks to the Press, thanks to the Black Sash and thanks to the efforts of certain concerned PFP members the old days of stealthy removals with police, dogs and lorries are gone…. [I]t is no easy task to talk in, say, the United States on campuses against disinvestment, against isolation, against economic sanctions…the task is impossible when we get the sort of stories such as the Mogopa removal.[53]

PFP MP Colin Eglin condemned Foreign Minister Pik Botha for denying that the threatened removal was forced. "To hold a pistol to somebody's head and say: If you do not move voluntarily we are going to force you to move, is in fact a forced removal." Botha responded with "the facts." Mogopa "was not planned. The conditions were undesirable…. There were squatters in that camp with no fresh water. The schools…could only be described as shacks or dilapidated slums. No proper hygiene measures were taken…." "[T]he main chief, the man in charge there who was recognized as the leader of the people," moved voluntarily with 230 families to Pachsdraai, which "has scenic beauty and is well vegetated." Government built primary and secondary schools, roads, and clinics, for R8 million. The "other brother of the chief" refused to follow with the remaining 130 families because he "saw in this the chance to exert his own chieftainship…this was purely an African tribal matter." The Deputy Minister of Foreign Affairs took a group of reporters to Mogopa, where he was invited to address the people. "Thereafter he was cheered and applauded. Each came to sake [sic] his hand…." When Koornhof tried to reconcile "the two brothers," Shadrack More took aside the Deputy Minister and said "Look, this has nothing to do with Whites, with the Government, with your politics or your policies; it is just that I hate that Bastard."[54]

Matthew Kgatitsoe, chairman of the Bakwena Ba Mogopa Town Committee, issued a press release rebutting Botha's statement. "We were amazed and furious to see the things Pik Botha said about Mogopa in Parliament. There is not one accurate point in his statement." It was not an "African tribal dispute between two brothers": Shadrack and Jacob were not brothers. "He said the problems at Mogopa were a 'purely African tribal matter.' There were no problems at Mogopa until a purely white commissioner imposed Jacob More on us....'The chief is the chief by the people'...[but apparently] according to S A law the chief is the chief by the State president." Botha "says the conditions at Mogopa were unsatisfactory. Maybe he is talking about the rubble...the ruins of our schools and churches and houses." As taxpayers they considered the R8–10 million spent on Pachsdraai "a complete waste of money." Only a "small group of people" agreed to the move, bribed by white farmhouses. The others left under threat after demolition started.

A week later a front-page article in *The Star* entitled "Mogopa school rises from the rubble" suggested the possibility of a reprieve.[55] It quoted Timothy Rathebe, who had lived in Mogopa since its purchase seventy years earlier: "It won't be so easy to get us out. This is our place, this ground is my heritage." The article noted, however, that the Supreme Court was to decide whether to grant leave to appeal the next day. On Friday, February 10, Justice van Dyk refused. *The Times* (London) headlined "Village stays doomed."[56] Haysom telegrammed Koornhof indicating his intention to seek leave to appeal from the Chief Justice and requesting a stay until that decision. Lawyers for Human Rights backed him.

At 4 a.m. Tuesday (St. Valentine's Day), however, police arrived with two buses and eighty-five trucks, sealed off the village, and ordered people to remain in their homes. Jacob More led them to Isaac More and George Rampou, who were handcuffed and put in police vans. Shadrack's daughter Adele said: "They kicked in the door of our house at 4 a.m. and shouted— 'Okay, where are the Black Sash now?' I was surrounded by four men with guns and made to get onto the bus." Someone telephoned Black Sash, and Ethel Walt and Gill de Vlieg rushed from Johannesburg.[57] A police spokesmen told them the SAP was there to "stop people running away into the bush" and said they needed a permit to enter. When they sought one at Ventersdorp, however, the magistrate said the area was closed and the removal had nothing to do with them. De Vlieg and two reporters evaded police roadblocks and walked the 20 kilometers cross-country to find "an unnatural stillness" and empty houses, "as though we had come in after a neutron bomb attack." "It was very obvious that people had left in a rush because their animals had been left behind and there were dog bowls and washing basins left lying outside." That evening Koornhof declared that government was seeking to "persuade" residents to leave voluntarily and all were being "fully remunerated for their buildings and other improvements."[58]

By the next morning thirty-five families had arranged their own transportation to Bethanie, thirty-nine had been moved to Pachsdraai, and the rest were to go there the following day. The same day the Bophuthatswana government announced that Pachsdraai would be incorporated shortly. Representatives of the British and American governments had arrived at Mogopa. Black reporters were allowed to enter the village, but white reporters were referred to the Ventersdorp magistrate, who refused permission. SAP Maj. Scheepers announced: "Right now the people are moving peacefully and voluntarily and we keep in the village in case they need our help. And up till now we have not demolished any of the people's properties because the department concerned will deal with that." The village had *not* been declared an operational area. Nevertheless, journalists were stopped, expelled, and threatened with arrest, and film was confiscated. Houses were broken open, and white farmers granted access to buy whatever the Magopa could not take with them.[59]

At a protest meeting at Khotso House Dr. Nthatho Motlana, chairman of the Soweto Committee of Ten, reported that police had taken children from their parents and sent them to Pachsdraai alone. Sheena Duncan proudly admitted the accusation of Deputy Development Minister Ben Wilkens that Black Sash had tried to prevent the removal. She denounced the police for diverting private trucks from Bethanie to Pachsdraai. "We also state categorically that the removal of the people of Mogopa has not been voluntary. [It was] a forced removal and Dr Koornhof can go on repeating the word 'voluntary' as often as he likes." Bophuthatswana television interviewed several women, who complained of police violence.[60]

The Times (London) carried reports of the handcuffing of Isaac More and George Rampou.[61] The *Sunday Tribune* entitled its feature story "Pack up and get out! The day the police came for the people of Mogopa. First they lose their birthplace...and now their South African citizenship is on the line."[62] They had lost their harvest and had to sell many of their thousand cattle. For Shadrack Madibikane "it means they want us to live in a location." A white farmer who had been his father's friend was sympathetic but silent. "There are some who would call me a coward for not speaking up for these people...but when they have gone I will have to stay and live in the community of Ventersdorp." Under the headline "Cry the Beloved Mogopa," *City Press* described "their bitter and bewildered faces and...cries that went straight to the heart." Its editorial called the removal "yet another blot on this country's professed Christian heritage."[63] Helen Suzman observed in Parliament that "at the very moment that the hon the Prime Minister was telling us that 22 February...was to be declared a day of prayer and atonement, one of the nastiest aspects of NP policy was being revealed....So much then for all the big talk of reform and change which we heard so much about last November...."

The Deputy Minister of Development repeated earlier justifications. Jakob [sic] and Lazarus [sic] More were "half-brothers and...regard themselves as brothers." "[A]ccording to tribal custom the chief of a tribe cannot be deposed." "If hon members of the PFP want to act in the interest of that group of people, then they must ensure that they act in accordance with local customs...." The 1982 investigation of Jacob More "found that the book-keeping left something to be desired, but that no irregularities had occurred." "The findings were made known to the tribe and they accepted them as such." The dissidents did not even live in Mogopa but in Johannesburg. "[T]here are certain resettlements that have to take place," which whites also find "extremely difficult." "[T]he co-operation of the people who have to be moved is obtained as far as possible and they are consulted from time to time in this regard." The PFP and Black Sash "do everything in their power to make matters difficult for those people...using those Black people as a means to other political ends." Lazarus More and Phillip More "who live in Johannesburg, and who, for all purposes of our discussion, are urban Black people," have no "claim to their tribal links and their tribal rights in this specific matter."

When Helen Suzman interjected that this negated the very foundation of forced removals—ethnic consolidation and the preservation of tradition—the Deputy Minister responded: "Very well, we are not arguing about that. We are not denying it. It is a basic fact. The fact that they are urbanized, still does not mean that they are entirely free of their tribal and ethnic links." "The principle with regard to the resettlement of these people is...that it must be a development-oriented action." When Suzman interrupted that they did not want to move, the Deputy Minister replied: "Is it because you indoctrinate them not to go?" "The hon the Minister displayed a degree of patience and willingness to take trouble the like of which I have never encountered in any other person."[64]

Many of those forcibly removed to Pachsdraai immediately sought to flee to Bethanie. With the assistance of the Witwatersrand Council of Churches the first truck picked up three households the following Monday. The *Rand Daily Mail* headlined "We want out, say Bakwena people." Although Bethanie offered little land for grazing or cultivation and few places in schools and was part of Bophuthatswana, they could not tolerate Jacob More.[65] Pachsdraai's tin shacks were suffocatingly hot by mid-day and too small to store personal belongings. Ezekiel Pooe, eighty-eight years old, had lived in Mogopa since 1911 and raised five children there.

> My children, only God knows why He made it possible for the Government to take us from our land. But I believe that God will punish those who throw His children around like stones. They will one day pay heavily for their sins in purgatory and those they had forsaken will be glorified in heaven.

Jacob More, who refused to allow his "imposing homestead" to be photographed, "sold" a field to one woman, who got neither a receipt nor land. He told Mogopa general store owner Elizabeth Kgatitsoe she would never get a license.[66]

In the Wilderness

With the forced removal complete the pace of events slackened. Somewhat belatedly, the Nederduitse Gereformeerde Kerk (NGK) came to the government's defense (getting most of the facts wrong).[67] The Magopa had to move because "it was difficult to supply the area with services and conveniences—as a result of the fact that it was a Black area in a white territory." Whites also had to sacrifice for apartheid by leaving "farms which have been owned and cultivated for many generations." Even if some Magopa preferred Bethanie "truly, it cannot be expected of the government to fully develop two areas simultaneously." Pachsdraai was clearly superior to Mogopa, especially in view of "the likely consolidation with Bophuthatswana—which in the long run will be only to the advantage of all." But the report denied having any "opinion about the government's policy of homelands and independent states. It is not the task of a church to do so." It concluded: "Nobody was wronged because this action was undertaken with the greatest caution and acknowledgement of human dignity. All transactions were legal and the necessary provision was made that the removal and reimbursement were taken for the good of the community."

On May 11 the Chief Justice granted leave to appeal, three months too late to save the Magopa.[68] For a while the press remained interested. The *Washington Post* put "Uprooted S. African Blacks Defiant" on its front page. Allister Sparks noted that Bethanie was no refuge; Paramount Chief Mamogale allowed only eighty families to settle there, forcing another 125 to squat at Berseba and Midikwe, eight miles away, and prohibiting meetings in his absence. A companion editorial, "In Sunny South Africa," called the removal "a typical instance of apartheid in action, part of the whites' giant sorting out of the Black population, physically and politically, into tribal 'homelands' that, chances are, the Blacks have never seen...."[69] A *City Press* reporter found that no one in Pachsdraai would speak to him without Jacob More's permission, but one old woman pulled the reporter aside and hoped "we could return to our homes. This is no place for a person to live."[70] The policy of forced removals received unwanted international attention when it was condemned by Britain, Germany, Italy, and the Vatican during P.W. Botha's European tour in May and June.[71]

Shortly after removal the Department of Co-operation and Development had promised that the Mogopa graveyard would be excised from the farm and preserved for the community. Relying on this, several Magopa returned in August to unveil six tombstones.[72]

On January 15, 1985, Deputy Minister of Land Affairs B.H. Wilkens wrote Cheadle Thompson and Haysom, disclosing for the first time that government had expropriated Zwartrand and Hartebeeslaagte ten months before (a month after removal). Since the land had been held in trust by the Department of Co-operation and Development, notice had been served on it but not the tribe! Two weeks later Dr. Gerrit Viljoen, the new Minister of Co-operation and Development, announced at a press conference that government was suspending forced removals. The decision would affect hundreds of thousands but not communities whose leaders "agreed" or illegal squatters. The action showed that "the Government is sensitive to the general critical attitude towards resettlement." PFP Black affairs spokesman Ray Swart said "for the first time one could look to announcements by Government on Black affairs with less cynicism and the expectation that something real would be done to improve the lot of Blacks."[73] But when foreign correspondents asked "Does that mean there will be no more Magopas," Viljoen replied: "Oh no. Magopa wasn't a forced removal. It was a negotiation."[74]

Although expropriation mooted the appeal, government tabled a bill in May, targeted solely at the Magopa, retroactively foreclosing legal challenges to removal on the ground that Parliament had not approved the new site.[75] It justified the bill as "merely a formulation of the existing interpretation of the legal position" by "two Supreme Court judgments."[76] Black Sash denounced the proposal, echoed by an editorial in *The Star*.[77] PFP MP Nic Olivier called it "utterly unacceptable" and "a ham-handed way of dealing with the issue."[78] Asserting that the Magopa's appeal had a "better than 50%" chance of success, their attorney, Nicholas Haysom, denounced the bill as "one of the most extraordinary breaches of the rule of law I have ever encountered."[79] During debate in the House of Assembly Helen Suzman condemned it as retrospective and thus bad.[80] Three weeks later government dropped the provision—not because of criticism by white opponents and the English press, which it consistently ignored, but because neither the "Coloured" House of Representatives nor the Indian House of Delegates would approve it. Bypassing them through the President's Council would have exposed the 1983 constitutional "reform" as a sham in its second year.[81]

A contemporaneous feature story described the plight of the 250 families who had fled Pachsdraai. Divided into three communities, subjected to hostile Bophuthatswana authorities, they were fast exhausting the compensation for their demolished houses. The local labor bureau would not register them as migrant workers, they had lost most of their cattle, and they could not be sharecroppers. Elisha Kgatitsoe declaimed:

> We were taken in the dead of the night by force to a place where the Devil lives. Our way of life was to plough. Now we can't plough. I feel just like Jeremiah. He cried for the people of Jerusalem who were moved to Babylon. Even when we are dead our tears will stay on the face of the earth.[82]

Two months later *The New York Times* published a follow-up of the Mogopa shopkeeper, under the headline "In a Broken Community, Hope Fades." She had moved from "a home of stone with many rooms, and a store stocked with everything" to a "home of tin…[and] a new store built of brick that the authorities will not permit her to operate."[83]

There were signs of change, however. Senior government officials told a UCT political scientist that they were considering opening white agricultural land to black settlement, although they feared electoral gains by the Conservative Party.[84] And in August, for the first time, government reprieved two "black spots," Driefontein and KwaNgema.[85]

The Magopa appeal was argued on August 29 and decided on September 19.[86] The only question was whether the statutory requirement of "a resolution approving the withdrawal" had been satisfied by resolutions adopted eight years before the removal naming the Magopa but not their destination. The statute "purports to be…for the better control and management of Black Affairs," "a form of social engineering, namely the enforced removal of people (in this instance Blacks) from any area to any other area…[for which] purpose it confers some quite extraordinary powers on the State President."[87]

> There can be no doubt that the enforcement of such an order may have grave and far-reaching consequences for the tribe concerned, and it may also impinge on the rights of personal liberty of its members. The instant case provides a striking example of the drastic inroads that such an order could make upon a tribe and its members residing on tribal lands. In a case such as this it is, therefore, necessary that the court should carefully scrutinise the terms of the order issued, and the procedure adopted for its enforcement, in order to ensure strict compliance with the provisions of §5(1)(b).[88]

The statute required that the tribe be notified of its destination; if it refused to move, the order had to be approved by Parliament. "It follows, as a matter of logic and common sense," that Parliament could not fulfill its role meaningfully unless "apprised of the terms of the order and the reasons for the tribe's refusal or neglect to withdraw." "This proviso is obviously intended by the Legislature to provide a check on or curb of the exceptional powers vested in the State President." The court invoked the common canon of statutory interpretation that when "two meanings can be given to a section, and the one meaning leads to harshness and injustice, while the other does not, the Court will hold that the Legislature rather intended the milder than the harsher meaning." It would not allow government to argue for the first time that the tribe had not refused the move to Pachsdraai or that the order was directed only to some members, not the whole tribe. Yet all this solicitude was empty.

> We have been informed by counsel that, save for the question of costs, the dispute between the parties has become academic because the farms in question have, in the meanwhile, been

expropriated by the State and vacated by the appellant and the
members of the tribe who supported his application.[89]

Marge Brown of the Black Sash welcomed the decision as "one step
toward going back."[90] The *Sowetan* took the opportunity to rehearse the sad
record of government atrocities, repeating the apocryphal claim that "the
land is rich with diamonds, metals and minerals."[91] In response to a letter
from Haysom to Viljoen, Deputy Minister Wilkens instructed the Department
of Agriculture not to alienate the farms "pending further discussions."[92]

Despite Viljoen's proclamation of an end to forced removals, government
continued to oust Blacks from their land. In October it sought to move 20,000
as part of the KwaZulu consolidation.[93] In November it tried to evict 426 families from Langa to KwaNobuhle and moved 4,800 families within the next
ten months.[94] It moved the inhabitants of Leandra to KwaNdebele and subsequently incorporated Moutse into that homeland (see chapter eleven).[95]
Sometimes homelands retaliated. In February 1986 Ciskei evicted 7,000 residents from Kuni and threatened 10,000-12,000 in the Potsdam squatter camp;
in September it evicted another twenty-seven families.[96] Under pressure from
neighboring whites South Africa sought to move Oukasie to Lethlabile (see
chapter twelve) and demolished 400 shacks in KwaNobuhle.[97] In October
and November 1986 it moved 200 families from Despatch to KwaNobuhle
and tried to move another 450 from Red Location to Motherwell.[98]

Government disregarded the Magopa's persistent pleas for more than a
year, until Viljoen restated his position on November 26 (replying to a letter
from Haysom four months earlier). The move had been voluntary. "Your
clients, as dissident individuals who were conducting a boycott action were
nevertheless bound by the agreements reached and decisions made." Viljoen
reiterated the argument the Appellate Division refused to consider—that the
State President's order was directed at "dissident individuals" rather than the
tribe (and hence did not require Parliamentary approval). He went further:
the AD had overruled the 1977 Supreme Court decision but *not* the decision
in this case. The dissidents had been given every opportunity to inspect
Pachsdraai; if they "refused to investigate or to participate in the tribal decision-making process they have only themselves to blame." Because they "do
not have any legal interest in the Magopa farms" after expropriation, they
have "no right to return." Although "discussion is obviously advisable in
order to attempt elimination of prolonged confrontation," Haysom first
should clarify "the factual situation."

Haysom's thirty-five-page reply on December 2 welcomed the opportunity to correct factual errors.[99] He represented 249 families at Bethanie, "the
clear majority of the tribe," who "are now preparing to return to Magopa."
"At the outset it is necessary to stress that my clients are not militant radicals,
dissident boycotters or the like. They are conservative, rural, mostly elderly
folk." Haysom was pleased that Viljoen acknowledged the "forcible nature"
of the removal, which other officials had characterized as "voluntary." He

contested the validity of the expropriation because Koornhof had breached his fiduciary duty to the tribe. Not only had the Appellate Division explicitly invalidated the Presidential Order, but Parliament also had repealed its alleged statutory authority. The situation demanded "a more generous and creative" approach to the Magopa, "the last people moved in terms of this procedure." His clients were desperate and deeply convinced they had been wronged. Nothing could compensate for their hardships. They had planned to return on November 28 but were dissuaded by Viljoen's letter on November 26; they still planned to return in the new year.

This produced a meeting with Deputy Minister of Development Aid Hendrik Tempel three days later. "Let the past be forgotten," he urged, "and let us look forward." Since neither Bethanie nor Pachsdraai was satisfactory and the tribe could not return to Mogopa, the Department would offer other land. Haysom replied on December 18 that the proposal had to be "significantly attractive and concrete" and suggested, instead, that they be allowed to return to one of their Mogopa farms. Tempel responded on February 2 that this was "unfortunately not possible." Instead he offered land adjacent to Bophuthatswana, which would be incorporated into the homeland and held in trust for them. Since President Mangope had denounced the Magopa for defying him, they found this unacceptable.[100] Negotiations broke down after the Magopa visited one of these alternative sites on March 20.

Aided by the Transvaal Rural Action Committee (TRAC), the Magopa turned to the South African Council of Churches, which raised R2.8 million to buy a farm named Holgat, to be shared among 270 Magopa families, thirty-five Machavie families (who had been in "temporary" accommodation since their removal sixteen years earlier), and twenty families of former farmworkers. After R2 million had been paid and the deed signed and title was about to be registered, the government expropriated Holgat on July 7.[101] The PFP condemned the government for behaving "in a really sordid manner...because [the Magopa] won an action in the Supreme Court [sic], the Government is punishing them by not allowing them to settle on the land of their choice...."[102] The Minister responded that Government "do not find acceptable the concept...of reintroducing a Black settlement area in that vicinity. This would be contrary to the policy that has been carried out in the past."[103] Media reaction was predictably vitriolic.[104] At a workshop that was to have formulated final plans for moving, the Magopa expressed despair.[105]

> We tried to achieve our just aims in a peaceful way by buying a new farm. The government has now closed this door of peaceful action, as it has closed all the other doors we tried to use. Now we have no choice but to go and claim our own farms. We know that the government will treat us as criminals for this whereas we are just South Africans fighting for our birthright. We believe that all our suffering has been caused by the way in which the government treats black people, as though we are not

people but animals to be herded around or birds that can live in the sky with no home on earth. Yet we know that in the eyes of God all human beings have rights.

At a press conference called by the urban committee three weeks later Lucas Kgatitsoe used even stronger language. In Bethanie women worked for R3 a day clearing stones from cornfields. They waited three hours to pay R2 for water, or walked 3 km to drink from the river and get sick. The Magopa were "missionaries appointed by God" to obtain "our rights to our father-land...our birth land." "Home is the best place on earth." Without it "we would rather die." Desperation had driven them to a "suicidal course." On September 12 some 300 trucks would transport 2,000 people back to Mogopa, accompanied by church officials, diplomats and white students.[106] Government warned that "if the Mogopa people go back to their farms, they are exposing themselves to prosecution." Strangers appeared at Bethanie asking about the planned return.[107]

On August 4, a month after the expropriation, Viljoen offered the justification that the Department of Education and Training needed to expand Bethel Secondary School at Holgat. Black Sash and TRAC promptly rebutted this: the land they bought had been for sale for three years and excluded the school. Even Viljoen acknowledged that the real reason was grand apartheid: "The Government is not in favour of the establishment of a black community such as the Magopas in an area which has not been earmarked for this purpose and which does not form part of the Government's consolidation programme." Some believed it was wooing local whites, who had elected a Conservative Party MP.[108]

On August 23, some 200 elderly people in Bethanie agreed with the urban committee. One man said "We don't have power with guns. All we have is the right that the land belongs to us." A woman agreed: "We've got our 'gun', which is Christ. He is more powerful than an ordinary gun."[109] Perhaps fearful the Magopa would carry out the threat, Viljoen telexed Haysom four days later to reopen negotiations. He again offered land adjacent to Bophuthatswana but now was negotiating for full title and preservation of South African citizenship. He was willing to explore sites proposed by the Magopa—especially if they furnished the money to buy it. Haysom telexed back, rejecting one site proposed by Viljoen because "the history of negotiations have led to suspicion and a hardening of attitudes" and again suggesting Holgat. "Unless flexibility is introduced" his clients would maintain their current position. Viljoen quickly disabused Haysom about reopening Holgat but offered to meet.

On Saturday, September 5, twelve Magopa, Haysom, and TRAC fieldworker Aninka Claassens met with Viljoen and eight other officials for four hours. Viljoen offered two sites near Bethanie; to reassure them about neighboring Bophuthatswana he pointed out that Oukasie had been removed to Lethlabile, also adjacent to the homeland, but not incorporated (see chapter twelve). He rejected Mathopestad because it was not designated for black settlement. The Magopa responded passionately that the present situation was intolerable; children were not learning, and the elderly were dying. They refused land next to Bophuthatswana and again proposed Mogopa; "black spots" had been preserved elsewhere, and for decades the Magopa had lived peacefully with their white neighbors, one of whom was Andries Terre'Blanche, brother of AWB leader Eugene. Haysom warned that the community would return unilaterally unless government made an acceptable offer. Viljoen rejoined that such action would "politicize the situation and there will be conflict." He offered two temporary sites. The committee promised to consult the community on Sunday and reply on Monday. When Haysom asked how government would react if the community returned to Mogopa in a week, Viljoen said that "such a move would lead to confrontation and that it would bedevil ways and means to find a workable solution for the problem."

A news story the next day recounted the people's travails, reported the joint press release, and reiterated their determination to return. "This is not a suicide mission," explained Lucas Kgatitsoe, "We are just going home." Henry More declared: "We have no choice. Our people are dying in the wilderness. Like the Israelites of old, it is time to return to the promised land." The cemetery had become "ruins and rubble." "We do our best, but it is difficult because we are now so far away."[110] After consultations at Bersheba and Bethanie, Haysom telexed a response on Monday. The Magopa understood that government would give them freehold title to South African land. They proposed Mathopestad and Ventersdorp. Government would answer by the end of November. Because of social dislocation and fragmentation, it would move them to Onderstepoort on September 12, providing temporary housing, bus service to town, schooling, and pensions. Viljoen replied the same day, accepting the proposal but insisting that they explicitly acknowledge that the resettlement was "voluntary."[111]

This mollified the critics. PFP MP Peter Soal commended government for negotiating while deploring the long delay and describing the offer as a "pill [that] had been sweetened" because government had "cheated" the Magopa of their land.[112] The National Committee Against Removals called the sad history "one of the most serious indictments of the forced removal policy of the last 10 years" but saw the offer as a "sign of hope."[113] The government's "common sense," said The Cape Times, "set a healthy precedent which could be applied elsewhere in the country with advantage. What about District Six, for example?"[114] The Argus applauded government for showing "more common sense and less ideology."[115] Black Sash credited the Magopa, whose "saga will go down in history as an apartheid classic—and as proof that organised resistance can achieve results."[116]

On September 10, state trucks moved 2,000 people from Bethanie to Onderstepoort (a site ironically designed for the Mathopestad people, who successfully resisted removal six years earlier).[117] While Haysom was on extended leave, Geoffrey Budlender of the Legal Resources Centre prepared the Magopa proposal and sent it to Viljoen on October 5. They sought at least 9,700 acres in the maize triangle, not adjacent to Bophuthatswana. "To return Mogopa to its original owners would be a gesture of good faith rather than a material concession. Mogopa is the only community with a Supreme Court judgment in its favour. In this context, the return of the Mogopa community can be explained as respect for the rule of law rather than as the beginning of a new trend."[118] The same day *The Star* published an article headlined "Businessmen will welcome return of Mogopa community."[119] Chris Botha, retiring local organizer of the Rural Foundation (a farmers' self-help group), said, "I can't see that there would be problems because there was never any animosity between them and the farmers. Every person has a right to a place in the sun—where he can raise his children and have his church." Ventersdorp funeral parlor proprietor J.M. du Plessis lost substantial business because two-thirds of his clients had been black. The owner of the largest store in the Indian shopping center agreed that "the town would come to benefit from the population increase." Farmers were more cautious, but none strongly opposed a return.

The Magopa, Budlender, and Claassens met with Viljoen and five officials on November 28. The full Cabinet had rejected Ventersdorp and Mathopestad as designated for whites. If an exception were made other removed communities would advance similar demands. Government offered different land and reiterated its promise to excise the Mogopa cemetery when the farm was sold to whites. The Magopa were adamant. Viljoen stressed the political realities; returning land to Blacks would drive whites into the Conservative Party; a by-election was imminent in nearby Schweizer-Reneke. The parties deadlocked but agreed to negotiate further. Two months later officials took the Magopa to six potential sites, but the tour was so perfunctory that Budlender had to write for more information. Several papers commemorated the fourth year in exile under headlines like: "Return our land,"[120] "Mogopa people still in limbo,"[121] and "My people want to return home."[122] Repeated government delays postponed a visit to additional sites until May. All were unsatisfactory: poor soil, little water, hostile whites, and threatened incorporation into Bophuthatswana. The two sides finally met again on July 2 but quickly stalemated. The Magopa emphasized the inadequacies of the land government offered; Viljoen categorically prohibited a return to Mogopa; they would just have to learn new agricultural techniques.

Perhaps despairing of negotiations, the Magopa adopted a new tactic. The Director General of Development Aid wrote the Hartebeesfontein Town Manager on August 24 confirming Deputy Minister Tempel's December 1986 ruling that the Magopa could maintain their graveyard. This issue occupied a November 19 meeting between six Magopa and Viljoen and three officials.[123] Government would retain title to the graveyard and an access road and provide water. It would tolerate the Magopa's "temporary structures" until the graveyard had been cleaned and "the ox has been slaughtered" but would build a house for the workers to minimize the area they occupied. At this point disagreement emerged.

> Mr Matthew Kgatitsoe re-affirmed their commitment of co-oper-ation with the RSA Government. They have no intention to settle at Zwartrand and will do nothing of which the Minister does not approve. *They, however, want to discuss the proposals of the Minister regarding the isolation of the graveyard within the com-munity.* The structure erected by the Department is not suited for their circumstances. They are used to living in separate struc-tures. The structures must be further away. *They also want to discuss these issues with the community.*
>
> The Minister asked the Magopa Committee to indicate (a) *how far the structures must be from the graveyard* and (b) *how many structures they have in mind.*

Although Viljoen promised to present new land proposals by the end of November, Budlender received a letter from him on December 12 asking for another three months.

Conflict over the graveyard soon intensified. Viljoen wrote an angry letter to Budlender (undated, misdirected, and never received) denouncing the cemetery cleaning as "a smoke screen to start a process of resettlement." This was "completely contradictory" to the "good spirit of co-operation." He asked Budlender to intercede "as Legal Representative of the community" and warned that "although not preferable, legal steps will nevertheless have to be taken...." Haysom (who had resumed representation of the community) telexed Viljoen on January 16 that a local policeman and an official had ordered the Magopa to demolish their shacks. He asked that this issue be post-poned to their next meeting and promised no further construction. Instead, the new Director General of the Department of Development Aid wrote Matthew Mpshe and Matthew Kgatitsoe at Onderstepoort the next day to complain that families were settling at Mogopa in violation of their agreement. The Minister therefore ordered that all structures built since December 9 be removed within twenty-four hours and work on the cemetery stop.[124] Haysom telexed Viljoen on January 31 that he had met the forty men cleaning graves, who had built nothing since January 16. They wished to continue until Viljoen submitted his proposal for a permanent settlement. He enclosed a proposal that the Botshabelo Trust buy Mogopa and urged a prompt meeting.

Viljoen responded with more threats on February 7. "[T]he erection of 43 completed and 4 partly completed structures at Zwartrand and the presence of 70 persons on the property are contrary to the negotiations...." Government planned to sue for eviction. The Cabinet had decided irrevoca-bly that the Magopa could not return. It now rescinded the December 1985 promise not to alienate the farms and would do so soon. Viljoen agreed to meet on February 18, but the parties quickly stalemated. Without waiting for the meeting, government filed suit on February 10.[125] The opposition press reacted with outrage: "Mogopa families could be evicted yet again,"[126] "On the fifth anniversary of Mogopa, a new attack,"[127] "Govt seeks to re-evict Magopas."[128]

Dirk Jacobus Minaar filed the founding affidavit.[129] When he visited the farm on January 30

> it was clear to me that the members of the Magopa-tribe were busy with a secret attempt at trying to re-establish themselves on the farm Zwartrand....[O]nly about one third [of the cemetery] had been cleaned up in spite of the fact that members of the Magopa-tribe had already been there for a period of three months....
>
> [T]his unhappy re-establishment of the Magopa-tribe...has received worldwide news coverage. Such news coverage was virtually always negative and as a result the image of the Government of the Republic of South Africa was seriously damaged. In fact, there were television teams and reporters at or in the vicinity of the cemetery and also at the entrance.

Police patrolled the entrance but could not secure the farm.

> It is also untenable that the South African Police should be used for this purpose.... [A]n explosive situation started developing. The television teams and reporters spied on every movement in anticipation that much money could be made out of the situation and to the detriment of the South African Government.

The Magopa at the farm attracted others. Because government planned to sell the farms soon eviction was urgent.

On the basis of this and three other affidavits and oral argument on February 14—the fifth anniversary of the forced removal—Justice Human issued an interim order on February 24 prohibiting the erection of new structures and the entrance of new people and gave the respondents a month to reply. His lengthy judgment adopted the applicants' affidavits verbatim. *The Citizen's* report also took the government line: "An end was put to litigation when the state expropriated the farm in 1986, and members of the tribe vacated the farm, with one section settling at Pachstraai [sic] and another at Onderstepoort. Members of the tribe were compensated by the state in the amount of more than R1.4 million."[130]

On March 15 Haysom telexed Viljoen to follow up the February 18 meeting. The community did not "see its way clear" to resolving the controversy over the cemetery until they reached "a satisfactory conclusion" about alternative land or a return to Zwartrand.

[T]he community would like to be advised for what reasons the Cabinet has decided that they cannot return there. In all negotiations and discussions to date the only reason given by yourself is that "it is a Cabinet decision." If the community is advised on what grounds this decision is based they will be able to make a realistic assessment of what their prospects are of ever returning there. Until this issue is cleared up they cannot abandon their hopes of returning to Swartrand.

Daniel Molefe filed a forty-page answering affidavit on March 17. After reviewing the injustices and hardships he turned to the cemetery, which government had promised to the tribe in December 1986 and August 1988. During four years of neglect erosion had created a large donga (gully). "The Magopa tribe has never given up hope of returning to their land," which they believed was "fair and reasonable" since the expropriation was unlawful. They denied "any secret attempt to re-establish the tribe on the farm." Only a third of the graveyard had been cleaned when government stopped their work. There could be no urgent need to sell land that had been vacant for more than five years. The police were unnecessary, "provocative and intimidating. They did little to enhance the image of the South African government." They fouled the community reservoir by swimming in it. When they withdrew, reporters and television teams also left. The respondents also submitted a physician's affidavit attesting to adequate sanitary and health conditions.

Minaar replied on March 29. The court could not consider the legality of expropriation because this had been conducted by the Minister of Community Development, who was not a party. The Minister of Co-operation and Development's fiduciary duty to the Magopa was irrelevant since he had not performed the expropriation. The respondents could question it only by a Rule 53 application, which was no longer timely. Reopening the Zwartrand claim would unsettle the rights of those at Pachsdraai, violating the important values of stability and certainty of title and disrupting state administration.

Francois Gerhardus Johannes Wiid, Director of Community and Ethnological Services in the Department of Development Aid, offered expert testimony. After earning a BA in African Studies at the University of Pretoria in 1957 he had been with the department for a quarter century; he spoke fluent Northern Sotho and had "an intimate knowledge of the habits and customs of the Tswana." They traditionally buried inside the kraal to minimize the danger of desecration. The Zwartrand cemetery was a western innovation. No custom barred men from working in it after noon. There was a customary aversion to living near the graves of "strangers," however, which would have justified building temporary residences some distance away.

Jules Browde SC argued that the expropriation was invalid because it was not for a public purpose and was effected in bad faith and for an ulterior motive. Although government sought to justify it under the Development Trust and Land Act, the notice referred only to the Expropriation Act. Furthermore, the former act applied only to unscheduled land, whereas these farms were in a scheduled area. The former act required expropriation by the Minister of Agriculture, whereas the title deed referred to the Minister of Community Development. The act referred to Schedule B tribes, but Mogopa was in Schedule A. The Minister of Co-operation and Development had violated his fiduciary duties to the tribe by destroying houses, schools, and churches, dealing with a deposed headman, and seeking to thwart adjudication. He had engaged in racial discrimination by allowing white farmers but not black to buy the land.

The media displayed its usual partisanship in reporting oral argument. *The Citizen* echoed the government line.[131] The *Sowetan* headlined "Lawyer accuses govt of racism,"[132] while *City Press* said "Govt told to return land to Magopas."[133] *Business Day* quoted Browde's denunciation of the expropriation as "one of the most flagrant violations of human rights conceivable."[134] Just before judgment the *Washington Post* published another tearjerker by Allister Sparks.[135]

> At 84, Ephraim Epooe is thin and grizzled. He wears a tattered brown bonnet pulled low on his head as protection against the chill of the approaching Southern Hemisphere winter. He does not look strong, but for three days last week Epooe retreated into the mountain behind his small tin shack to fast and pray for a cause that he says is dearer to him than life...that his small Magopa tribe would win a court battle it is waging and "the Boers will be chased from our land"....

Justice W.J. van der Merwe gave judgment on May 2. He declined to "go into everything that they did on the farms" or "go into detail" about the conflict over Jacob More. He noted the Appellate Division judgment but emphasized that the court found the dispute moot because the farms had been expropriated. Although the tribe invested "great and intense emotion" in cleaning the cemetery, government had withdrawn permission on January 13. The Minister of Community Development was a necessary party to any challenge to expropriation. The judge evicted the Magopa and asked the Ventersdorp police to execute the order.

The Citizen headline could not conceal its satisfaction: "Squatters get seven days to leave land." Government intended to sell the farms to whites within two or three months.[136] Other papers were more sympathetic: "Mogopa tribe loses battle to stay on farm,"[137] "D-Day for tribe that refuses to leave land of their forefathers."[138] The *Sunday Times* photographed Ephraim Pooe, who declared his refusal to budge, and it editorially condemned the "bad move," which "makes a mockery of the Government's much-vaunted new approach to the question of forced removals."[139]

Despite this decision, the government's commitment to grand apartheid was weakening. Potsdam residents removed to Ciskei in 1983 fled to South Africa in 1988. In January 1989 the Supreme Court affirmed their South African citizenship, although it declined to award them a place to live. Two years later Ciskei offered to transfer their land back to South Africa, which promised R500,000 to rebuild their homes.[140] In January 1989 the Cape Supreme Court denied a white municipality's application to evict 500 blacks from the Port Nolloth salt flats. Justice H.L. Berman warned that the "mass deportation" of a relatively stable community would have "mind-boggling" consequences. Reflecting the Magopa Appellate Division judgment, he noted that every removal specified the destination.[141] In November 1989 Lawaaikamp convinced the George town council to abandon its four-year effort to remove the community and upgrade it instead.[142] In December government reversed its August 1988 decision to incorporate Peelton into Ciskei.[143] The same month the Supreme Court invalidated an attempt by the House of Representatives to subdivide Namaqua common grazing land.[144]

The eviction order was not the end of the Magopa saga. A dozen European governments strongly protested. The West German embassy first secretary declared at the farm: "The destruction of the Mogopa village in a clandestine night raid showed clearly how the South African Government treats peace-loving people who had lived on their land for more than 70 years." When the Magopa applied for leave to appeal the next day, Judge van der Merwe refused a stay pending action on their application. But though the state attorney would not delay eviction until the appeal was resolved, the *Sunday Tribune* found twenty defiant Magopa at the graveyard more than a week later. First respondent Daniel Molefe proclaimed: "We are not going anywhere. The Government can shoot us or take us to jail, but we will not give up the rights to our own land."[145] On October 2 Justice van der Merwe granted leave to appeal and stayed the order of ejectment. In mid-November a TRAC fieldworker met the Magopa Planning Committee at Onderstepoort. Four families had already returned to Mogopa, but the truck was too small. People had to be patient and leave quietly without their livestock while the community looked for a larger one.

On February 16, 1990 (two weeks after government released Mandela and the sixth anniversary of removal), TRAC fieldworkers and lawyers visited Mogopa. Haysom read a Department of Development Aid telex denouncing rumors that Magopa were returning by truck and building shacks and asking him to persuade them to go back to Onderstepoort. The community responded with laughter. They were happy to be back, even without resources, and would never leave. Government would have to shoot them and throw them into the diamond mine. Residents carried whistles to summon assistance and wanted to construct a security fence around the cemetery to show they would never be moved. They asked Haysom to try to arrange a meeting with Minister of Development Aid Stoffel van der Merwe. Three

months later van der Merwe announced that government would sell no agricultural land expropriated from black communities and would revise the
Land Acts.

On July 3 Haysom sent the "Magopa Land Proposals 1990" drafted by
TRAC to Deputy Minister of Development Aid Piet Marais, reiterating familiar arguments and adding:

> [T]he issue need not involve a major debate of principle....[T]he
> return of the Mogopa community can be explained as respect for
> the rule of law rather than as the beginning of a new trend. The
> return of the Mogopa would greatly benefit the Government's
> image both in South Africa and internationally. It would be seen,
> not as a reform handed down from on high, but as the result of
> a negotiated settlement with a widely respected black group. In
> this era of negotiations, it would set a positive example of what
> the process of negotiations can achieve.

Marais's secretary replied four days later, seeking time to consult the Cabinet,
secrecy, and Haysom's cooperation in stopping more Magopa from returning. Three weeks later the Department announced a reprieve from removal
for 160,000 people in 180 communities in the Natal Midlands.[146]

Hundreds of Magopa attended the August 24 Appellate Division argument,
as they had each of the three earlier hearings. But the court declined to adju-
dicate. Acting Chief Justice Christiaan P. Joubert declared: "Before we begin
this case, I want to ask what is at stake here? These events deal with the past,
and I am looking to the future. Is there no prospect of finding a solution to
this matter?" He urged the parties to settle. During a brief adjournment the
state's lawyers telephoned the Minister, who agreed to meet the Magopa on
September 20. The parties asked the court to rule if they had not reached a
settlement two months later. In the meantime those at Mogopa could remain,
but no one else could come nor could there be any further building.[147]

The small number of people who defied the March 1989 order had grown
to only about seventy by the end of 1989, but many others arrived early in
1990. By August there were at least 250 families with 800 people. The community was rebuilding the school for the third time. It had a medical clinic
staffed by two nurses, whose wages were paid by a $2 levy on every house-
hold. Both the domestic and international press described the situation in
reporting the AD hearing.[148] By late September Piet Marais had conducted
negotiations in a "very good spirit." On September 23, however, police
alerted by an informer dispersed a meeting in Onderstepoort because magisterial permission had not been granted.[149] At a second meeting three days
later ten of the remaining families decided to return, four to stay, and twenty-
five were undecided. Many feared retaliation if they returned. In mid-October
representatives from Pachsdraai and Mogopa met with lawyers to discuss title
to both lands, the threat that Pachsdraai might be incorporated into
Bophuthatswana, and reunification of the Magopa. At the end of the month

Marais revealed that government wanted to "clear" the Magopa out of Onderstepoort but would not provide transport. The parties agreed to allow the November 20 deadline to pass on the understanding that the case had been adjourned sine die. Government allowed the Magopa to resume work on the school but not to move furniture from Onderstepoort as long as children were attending there.

The Promised Land?

The Magopa victory and de Klerk's public commitment to reform inspired other exiles. Just before Christmas 1990, twenty elderly Baralong Ba Modiboa returned to Machaviestad, from which they had been expelled almost twenty years earlier. Others had returned to Roosboom, Charlestown, and Cremin in Natal. Three hundred and fifty had returned to a settlement near Ladysmith from which they had been evicted in 1975.[150] In February 1991 a thousand of the 20,000 removed from Doornkop in 1975 met to plan their return; so did the Mfengu people removed from Tsitsikamma in 1977.[151] In March government published a White Paper on Land Reform, promising repeal of the Land and Group Areas Acts but warning that "a programme for the restoration of land…would not be feasible." Communities should accept this "in the interest of peace and progress."[152] No one did. In May twenty families who had taken refuge in nearby Allendale after being removed from Elandskloof in 1962 were given notices to vacate when they sought to return. In August 1992 the eviction proceedings were postponed indefinitely while the Advisory Commission on Land Allocation (ACLA) considered their claim.[153] In July 1992 Andries Radebe, one of those removed from Cremin in Natal fifteen years earlier, sued for title on grounds of lack of notice and no public purpose for the expropriation.[154] Blacks became increasingly impatient with ACLA, demanding an independent body with decisional powers.[155] The Majeng community in the Northern Cape had been removed in the 1970s. After repeal of the Land Acts they lodged a claim with ACLA, but before it was heard the government sold their land to six white farmers and then argued that ACLA lacked jurisdiction. By November the Commission had collapsed before challenges by thirty-nine communities threatening unilateral occupation if their demands were not satisfied.[156] In December government agreed to restore Roosboom and Charlestown to their original black owners.[157]

The most dramatic attempt to emulate Magopa was the reoccupation of nearby Goedgevonden. The community had settled on Native Trust land in 1947, building stone and brick houses, developing water resources, producing a surplus, and constructing a school, two churches and graveyards. In 1978 they were forcibly moved to smaller, less fertile farms adjacent to Bophuthatswana and never compensated for their improvements. They returned regularly to maintain the cemetery. Breaking a promise, government incorporated them into Bophuthatswana five years later. Angry at the community's opposition to incorporation, the homeland detained its leaders, banned meetings, and forced some residents to take citizenship in order to collect pensions. In 1990 South Africa offered Goedgevonden for sale. When the Pretoria Legal Resources Centre protested and sought a meeting, Deputy Minister Marais replied on August 7: "As your clients live in the independent country of Bophuthatswana, it would be inappropriate and totally irregular for me to agree to meet them for discussions."

During the next eight months the people discussed returning and reached a decision on Easter weekend 1991. On April 9 Levy Segopolo led a group of fifteen families, who found the land empty aside from 400 cattle. One white farmer welcomed their return and asked Segopolo to arrange farm labor. Two days later LRC attorney Carrie Kimble wrote Dr. A.I. van Niekerk, Minister of Agricultural Development, confirming their phone conversation that he was aware of the situation and intended "to deal with the matter objectively [which] encompasses adherence to the principles of natural justice." The following day government closed the area with a roadblock, preventing some of the group from returning from Ventersdorp (including mothers whose nursing infants were on the farm) and barring later arrivals, as well as Kimble. She told Mr. Smit, a Ministry official, that 3,000 planned to return. At his request she offered to try to stop them but only if he promised to admit those already waiting and not evict anyone. Over the next two days Afrikaner Weerstandsbeweging (AWB—Afrikaner Resistance Movement) leader Eugene Terre'Blanche and some of his followers drove around Goedgevonden intimidating Segopolo, who reported this to the police.

On April 13 Smit and Kimble reached an agreement. Government would allow those waiting outside to enter the farm "for humanitarian reasons and without admitting the legality of the occupation," while Segopolo would "undertake to stop the influx." The agreement worked, but the Ministry rebuffed every community request to meet. On April 23 the Minister and seven white farmers brought an eviction proceeding against against Segopolo and the others.[158] Three days later D.J. Minaar (first applicant in the action to evict the Magopa) wrote Kimble that her clients "are occupying the relevant state land unlawfully by squatting thereon and thereby depriving the State as owner of the land and the lessees, of the free and unhindered use thereof," which government views "in a very serious light." It therefore rescinded the agreement and prohibited any vehicles from entering the farm "to prevent the squatters strengthening their position."

On May 3 the State Attorney's office refused to allow Operation Hunger to deliver a water tank. Kimble wrote State Attorney Coertze four days later: "Is it your clients' intention to deprive our clients of access to water?" This not only violated the agreement but was "an inhuman act unbecoming of a government which has a duty to all its citizens." "In view of the threatening statements allegedly being made by certain right wing organisations in the area," her clients were "extremely concerned that your clients, by their actions, are allying themselves with this behaviour." Coertze replied that his clients did not "want to make it as difficult as possible for the squatters on the farm." But because his clients "do not view the people as a 'community', but as squatters" they had no "duty to supply the said squatters with creature comforts." Any attempt to install a water pump would be a "flagrant contravention of the Court order." The contractor who moved the people told police he was paid R1 million. "You will agree that this does not seem to be a free and unvoluntary [sic] move....It does seem more likely to be an orchestrated (and maybe even forced) removal...." His clients were "losing a considerable amount of money each day." He demanded confirmation that she had written instructions from all eighty-seven respondents. "I do not agree with you that a legalistic approach to this matter will exacerbate the matter, but am of the oppinion [sic] that any other approach will do exactly that." Kimble replied on May 14, asking why proceedings had been instituted despite the agreement and whether government had decided to oust her clients. Coertze denied that government had ever entered any agreement.

On the evening of May 10 Lt. Palmer, the Ventersdorp Station Commander, warned the community to remain in their houses but not sleep because "the AWB are coming to attack you." A reinforced patrol of twenty-five men would guard the farm. Between 1 a.m. and 2 a.m. some 180 armed whites chanting "AWB" and wearing its neo-Nazi insignia attacked people standing outside Mrs. Mogape's house, damaging her car and belongings and twelve other shacks. Lt. Palmer and another policeman recognized Eugene Terre'Blanche. The AWB left to attack Tshing, the Ventersdorp township, injuring fourteen people, before returning to Goedgevonden, where police repulsed a second assault, wounding two attackers and arresting three. The SAP press release stated: "Appropriate legal steps were taken against the squatters...and it was totally unnecessary for anybody to take the law into their own hands. The SAP has a duty imposed by law to act against anybody who transgresses the law and will not hesitate to take appropriate steps to maintain law and order." On May 17 Segopolo and his community sought an interdict against Terre'Blanche and the AWB, which was granted on June 25.[159] Segopolo and six others were convicted of trespass on May 20.

The community replied to the eviction proceeding on May 24, asking the court to set aside the Minister's decision to oust them, invalidate Proclamation 189 of 1984 (thereby revesting title in the South African Development Trust), and recognize their right to exclusive occupation. Their affidavit documented the government's new attitude. In March Minister de Villiers declared his flexibility and willingness to discuss the claims of dispossessed communities. "A programme for restoration is not feasible, but there is a spirit of cooperation and a willingness to speak. I have large ears and they are open."[160] The next month he added that, though government did not intend to buy land for redistribution, "it does not mean we would never do this; we have a negotiating stance."[161] While urging the Goedgevonden community to return to Bophuthatswana, he was always willing to talk: "Our doors are open to help sort out problems that have arisen because of past events."[162] Early in May de Klerk had qualified the White Paper's assertion that restoration of land "would not be feasible." "That does not mean the government is unapproachable. Government's general approach to this issue is to address the cases concerned with sympathy and reason."[163] The community planned to challenge the original removal under administrative law. They also offered evidence by an agriculturalist that the land they had been given in exchange for Goedgevonden was grossly inferior and by the Ventersdorp District Surgeon that there was no health threat.

U.S. Ambassador William Lacy Swing wrote Agriculture Minister van Niekerk on May 15, endorsing the LRC request for negotiations. He expressed "concern about the negative repercussions that could result from a highly-publicized forced removal" and hoped the Cabinet could "find a solution which defuses the situation, and does not put your government in the position of appearing to enforce the policies of an earlier era."

Justice Goldstein gave judgment on June 3.[164] Although the respondents invoked the agreement with Smit, he was not the agent of the seven white farmers. Since a defendant could not raise issues of ultimate right in a spoliation action, Goldstein struck the respondents' counter-application. The government had failed to establish possession, but the seven private applicants' claim was uncontroversial. "[T]heir peaceful occupation of the ground has been invaded without due process by large numbers of people and that is a most serious wrong." Turning to the applicants' claim for costs, however, he addressed the real issues, accepting the respondents' affidavit, which the applicants had not controverted. "No court can fail to be profoundly moved by what has happened to the respondents and their community." Government was the "real litigant" and was paying all the costs. It had "committed an error of judgment" in refusing the community's offer to negotiate. He sought to "soften" the effect of his order by denying costs for two counsel.

> Given the profoundly tragic history of this matter no court can grant an order for eviction in the present circumstances affecting hundreds of people without feelings of distress and anguish. But the principle at stake here is the cornerstone of the rule of law. The principle that no man may take the law into his own hands as the respondents have done is sacrosanct. Respect for it is absolutely necessary for human society to function in conditions of peace, serenity and security. The principle is an ancient one of our common law. It existed long before the misfortune which dispossessed the respondents was conceived of, and hopefully, it will continue to exist and be respected long after that misfortune is corrected, and it and their pain are no more than a blot on the pages of our history books.

Goldstein granted leave to appeal, automatically suspending the eviction order. The respondents remained on the land as virtual prisoners surrounded by barbed wire and a roadblock opened only to residents during the day.[165] As the hearing approached the parties agreed to postpone it pending further negotiations. The community presented evidence to the Advisory Commission on Land Allocation in December 1992, which awaited the government's response. In October 1993 a Potchefstroom magistrate convicted Eugene Terre'Blanche and ten others of public violence for the attack two years earlier. After the AWB leader expressed remorse, the magistrate imposed a R10,000 fine and suspended prison sentence. As he left the courtroom, Terre'Blanche shouted "Long live the struggle." [166]

The Magopa also sought to normalize their situation. On January 10, 1991, they asked that the school they built be opened. In mid-February Haysom wrote Deputy Minister Marais, reminding him of their November 1990 request to begin plowing and building and inviting him to a feast to celebrate the completion of the school. Marais temporized: The land question could not be resolved until Pachsdraai and Onderstepoort were incorporated into Bophuthatswana. But he assured the community in March that the school was registered, five teachers would be provided, and government would assume full responsibility by 1992. After many further inquiries, Marais met the community on July 24 and granted permission to plough, plant, rebuild their houses, and construct a secondary school.

Analysis

The Magopa removal exposed the government's need and inability to justify the use of force, illuminated the strategic choices on both sides, and highlighted the significance of timing and publicity.

Government felt strongly obligated to justify uprooting thousands of people from their home of seventy years and dumping them in a distant wasteland slated for incorporation into a brutal and corrupt Bantustan. The dialogue with the Magopa and other critics constantly shifted ground. The principal government strategy here, as in all colonial regimes, was to co-opt pliable leaders who purported to represent the tribe. Bophuthatswana State President Lucas Mangope could not serve this purpose until the Magopa were incorporated into the homeland. Bakwena Paramount Chief Lerothodi Mamogale seems to have betrayed Magopa hopes for protection. Jacob More brought the legitimacy of tribal selection to the puppet role. The state repaid him by ignoring corruption, retaining him after the community ouster, allocating the best houses and land at Pachsdraai to him and his followers, and granting him revenge against his enemies. His follower Johannes Andrews faithfully told reporters: "The Government must be obeyed. It is the father and the mother. It is the giver of things."

The strategy was fatally flawed, however: The Magopa claimed they had lawfully removed Jacob. The Ventersdorp magistrate responded: "I am a white man and as magistrate of this district I am telling you that Jacob More will rule until he dies." But though government had the power to disregard the community, doing so destroyed the traditional legitimacy of the office. Having justified the exclusion of blacks from national politics by arguing that they were empowered locally, the apartheid regime then violated traditional democratic practices by autocratically imposing puppets, who quickly became corrupt and petty tyrants. "[A]ccording to African tribal custom," said the Magopa, " 'the chief is the chief by the people,' " but "according to S A law the chief is the chief by the State President."

The government's next line of defense was to portray resistance to Jacob as mere factionalism, a fight between brothers (although Shadrack and Jacob were not brothers), the equivalent among elders of "Black-on-Black violence" (both of which government had fomented). This was another instance of the divide-and-conquer strategy minorities always use to subordinate majorities. Government also propagated the big lie that the Magopa had consented. It exaggerated the number who moved with Jacob in July 1983, dismissing the rest as a "dissident minority" who willfully boycotted discussions of the removal. Many of the latter "chose" to move to Bethanie. Government was shameless: the Zwartrand churches requested demolition; Deputy Minister Wilkens imputed any reluctance to move to PFP "indoctrination"; Minister Viljoen continued to insist that the move was voluntary long after the Appellate Division invalidated it; State Attorney Coertze called the return to Goedgevonden a "forced removal" because outsiders helped defray the cost of transportation.

The Magopa responded by exposing the myriad forms of coercion: threats of no compensation, withdrawal of teachers, demolition of schools, termination of bus service, removal of the water pump, white farmers' cattle trespassing on their land, the magistrate's refusal to pay pensions or endorse reference books. Worst of all was the constant uncertainty about whether and when government would use force. Under these circumstances, those who moved before February 14 hardly consented. Nor had they acquiesced in the decisions of Jacob More and his "Planning Committee." Jacob excluded *them* from his secret conclaves and boycotted tribal meetings, violating the consensus decisionmaking required by the traditional authority on which government relied.

Compelled to admit the removal was forced, government retreated to other rationalizations. Some were circular: Apartheid's requirement of separate facilities made black spots "inefficient"; since negotiation had not secured tribal consent, government had no choice but to use force. In 1969 it invoked "general government policy"—presumably grand apartheid. Fifteen years later it hid apartheid beneath the euphemism of the "public interest" in consolidating all Blacks inside the homelands. This was explicit in the planned incorporation of Pachsdraai and Onderstepoort into Bophuthatswana, government persistence in offering the Magopa only land adjacent to the homeland, and its expropriation of Holgat. Several apologists portrayed apartheid as a "neutral principle" because it demanded sacrifices from whites as well as blacks. Removals became increasingly difficult to justify, however, once government declared an end to them.

The second meaning of public interest was development. Where Zwartrand had been chaotic and small, Pachsdraai was planned and large. (This also justified moving the people of Oukasie from the outskirts of Brits to Lethlabile, see chapter twelve.) By borrowing the western rhetoric of "urban renewal," South Africa sought to disarm foreign criticism or at least expose its hypocrisy. The NGK found that Mogopa lacked churches and "the general condition is one of neglect." The community responded: "This rubble is the ruins of our schools and churches and houses. Before these were demolished the conditions at Mogopa were quite satisfactory to us, the people who built them." Government generously paid for the move and compensated Magopa for all losses (just as it compensated victims of police violence) and promised money for development. The Magopa responded that the R8-10 million cost was "a complete waste of money." If Pachsdraai's virtues were so obvious, moreover, force would be superfluous. Eventually acknowledging the deficiencies of land outside the maize triangle, government simply responded that the Magopa would have to learn new agricultural techniques.

With the removal accomplished, government offered new reasons for resisting Magopa claims. It suddenly needed Holgat for an agricultural college—although the farm had been on the market for years. Local whites near Holgat and Ventersdorp would react to black neighbors by electing the Conservative Party, thereby endangering all of P.W. Botha's "reforms." The Magopa may not have seen much difference between Conservatives and Nationalists. Nevertheless, they responded that local farmers and businesses welcomed their return. Furthermore, both they and the Goedgevonden community could point to the fact that the land remained uncultivated.

Because South Africa was uniquely susceptible to Proudhon's equation of property with theft, government feared that capitulation to the Magopa would expose the illegitimacy of grand apartheid, inviting others to reclaim their land. Such a prediction (which was quite prescient) could only strengthen the community's resolve. To allay white anxiety, however, they stressed their uniqueness: The Appellate Division had upheld their claim, and Parliament had repealed the statute under which they had been removed. The government riposte showed real effrontery: Allowing the Onderstepoort Magopa to return would endanger the rights of those at Pachsdraai—and title had to be secure and certain! (Similarly, Justice Goldstein rebuked the Goedgevonden community for reoccupying land from which they had been forcibly removed thirteen years earlier because the "rule of law" was "absolutely necessary for human society to function in conditions of peace, serenity and security"!) But though Haysom argued that a government concession "need not involve a major debate of principle," the regime could not admit that forty years of apartheid had been wrong. Even de Klerk has never managed such an unqualified mea culpa.

Sometimes government lapsed into ipse dixits. Magistrate de Villiers declared that he would choose the headman. Solly Vermaak "explained" that the removal could not be postponed "because it was both a State President's and a Court Order." George de Villiers Morrison was equally tautological: "You do get to a stage when for certain reasons you have to move these people. And then you are left with no other option but to move them by force." Gerrit Viljoen insisted that the Magopa could not return to Zwartrand because "it is a Cabinet decision." To which Haysom replied: Until "the community is advised on what grounds this decision is based...they cannot abandon their hopes of returning to Swartrand."

Although government felt the primary need to justify its exercise of power, the Magopa also argued their case. They had bought Zwartrand, which should not be expropriated without notice or sold without their consent. The government replied that it held title and had "exchanged" Zwartrand for Pachsdraai. The Magopa cited both traditional and modern legality. Jacob More had violated the tribal constitution through his corruption and unilateral decision making. Given the Appellate Division decision, a concession could "be explained as respect for the rule of law." They defeated the bill retroactively validating the removal, which Haysom excoriated as "one of the most extraordinary breaches of the rule of law I have ever encountered." In common with most rights strategies, these pleas for special treatment emphasized the uniqueness of the Magopa rather than solidarity with the millions removed earlier. Like Moutse (see chapter eleven), the Magopa even adopted the language of apartheid, arguing that proximity to three black settlements would allow efficient administration along racial lines.

Perhaps because occupation of the graveyard was their one means of self-assertion, the Magopa invested much rhetorical energy defending it. They declared their obligation to preserve the cemetery even before physical removal; they returned six months after removal to unveil tombstones. Their attachment to the graves was spiritual rather than material, grounded in a religiosity that whites also boasted. Agricultural land might be fungible but not their ancestors' graves. The government conceded access to the cemetery as early as December 1986—one of the few promises it felt unable to break. It could forcibly remove, imprison, torture, even kill—but not interfere with burials, in townships or even rural areas (as Sophocles wrote of Creon more than 2,300 years earlier).

Both sides made inconsistent, even opportunistic, use of the warrants of tradition and modernity. Because the ineradicable uniqueness of "tribes" was the cornerstone of apartheid (which somehow disregarded the contradiction inherent in forcibly moving people to "homelands" they had never seen), government had to rely on tradition (see chapter eleven). When it recognized Jacob More as "traditional" headman, the Magopa deposed him by traditional means for violating traditions of consultation and consensus—to which government responded: "According to tribal custom the chief of a tribe cannot be deposed." Paradoxically, Magopa tradition was democratic and thus modern, whereas government modernity was autocratic and thus traditional. Government maintained that Magopa working in Johannesburg were "urban Black People" who had forfeited their "tribal links" and "tribal rights." Helen Suzman seized upon this acknowledgement of deracination as an abandonment of the ideology of grand apartheid underlying forced removals. To which the Deputy Minister could only reply lamely: "Very well, we are not arguing about that....[but] the fact that that they are urbanized, still does not mean that they are entirely free of their tribal and ethnic links." When the Magopa insisted they were traditional farmers who could survive only within the maize triangle, however, government responded that younger farmers could learn modern techniques. When the Magopa argued that custom dictated how they must clean ancestral graves, government produced an Afrikaner who claimed to know their customs better than they did (just as BTR SARMCOL invoked its white Zulu-speaking labor relations officer's insights into the minds of its black employees—see chapter five). Wiid testified the Zwartrand cemetery was modern, not traditional (which would render his expertise irrelevant).

Other rhetorical exchanges revealed similar contradictions. The legitimacy of Afrikaner hegemony rested on three basic premises: history, paternalism, and religion. The Magopa turned each against the government. Afrikaners claimed they had been on the land for years; so had the Magopa. Afrikaners claimed they had been tragically wronged (by the English); so had the Magopa (by the Boers). If Afrikaners were devoted to the well-being of Blacks they should heed the protests of the Magopa.

Religion was the most hotly contested arena. The Biblical names of many actors reflected its centrality: Jacob, Shadrack, Isaac, Elisha, Enoch, Lazarus, Johannes, Lucas, Matthew, Elifas, Ezekiel, and Ephraim among the Magopa; Tempel, Christoffel, and Christiaan among the Afrikaners. Place names like Bethanie and Berseba echoed the Holy Land. Jacob's follower, Alex Pooe, said the Bible ordained that each tribe should go to its own homeland; the move from Mogopa to Pachdsraai was like the flight from Egypt to Canaan. Justice Goldstein evicted the Goedgevonden community because the principle that no man may take the law into his own hands was "sacrosanct." The NGK, which had endorsed apartheid, commissioned a lengthy exoneration of the removal. But the opposition was on firmer rhetorical ground. Virtually every other church and church organization in South Africa and abroad vocally condemned the removal. *City Press* headlined "Oh Lord, Deliver Us From Evil" and called the event "yet another blot on this country's professed

Christian heritage." The Magopa declared their faith that Koornhof would approach the issue "as a Christian." Like his namesake, eighty-eight-year-old Ezekiel Pooe prophesied: "God will punish those who throw His children around like stones. They will one day pay heavily for their sins in purgatory and those they had forsaken will be glorified in heaven." Elisha Kgatitsoe (named after another prophet) denounced Pachsdraai as "a place where the Devil lives." "I feel like Jeremiah. He cried for the people of Jerusalem who were moved to Babylon." For Lucas Kgatitsoe the Magopa were "missionaries appointed by God" to obtain "our rights to our fatherland." Henry More protested that "our people are dying in the wilderness. Like the Israelites of old, it is time to return to the promised land." An elderly woman called Christ "our 'gun.'" The Magopa claim that "in the eyes of God all human beings have rights" was echoed by Chris Botha, a leader of the local farmers: "Every person has a right to his place in the sun…where he can raise his children and have his church." The media constantly reported and photographed the destruction of the four churches. Rev. Allan Boesak called the removal the "ultimate blasphemy." Bishop Tutu deplored that it was taking place just before Christmas, which commemorated the Prince of Peace.

In choosing among strategies, both sides preferred negotiation to direct action and legal forms. The Magopa postponed a legal challenge to the expropriation of Zwartrand so as not to jeopardize negotiations for its return. Aware of their powerlessness, they threatened self-help more than they engaged in it. Government twice made significant concessions within days of an impending return to Zwartrand. Powerlessness also made the Magopa and Goedgevonden communities prefer to be reactive, forcing government to take the initiative—remove, evict, starve. They sought to turn weakness into strength, constantly equating exile with death. (Government replied it was not starving Goedgevondon but just denying them the "creature comforts" of food and water.) Despite its monopoly of political power, government also refrained from enforcing the ejectment judgment in favor of continued negotiations. Even the Appellate Division shrank from adjudicating and ordered the parties to negotiate a solution. As the successful struggle against apartheid reduced the power disparity, strategic positions inverted. Government could forcibly remove the Magopa in February 1984 but not five years later. In 1984 the Magopa could only threaten injury to themselves— illness and death, suicide, fratricidal strife, uneducated children, unproductive adults; five years later they could return unilaterally and declare they would not leave without a "satisfactory conclusion."

Each side preferred negotiation for different reasons. Lacking legal rights, political clout, economic leverage, and physical power, the Magopa had no real choice. Negotiation allowed them to appear reasonable—the antithesis of township youth. Unable to make substantive demands, they could still advance procedural claims: equal numbers of negotiators, legal representation, the minutes of previous meetings. Yet this posture may also have

perpetuated their dependence and allowed government to appear conciliatory. Government also could delay by missing deadlines and making patently
unacceptable proposals. Furthermore, the Magopa found it much harder to
mobilize themselves and others around the relative merits of different farms.
Negotiation minimized publicity, especially since government often
demanded secrecy. The importance it attached to negotiation was visible in
the prominent role played by Cabinet Ministers Koornhof and Viljoen. Yet
even they disclaimed authority, allowing Viljoen to appear the "good cop"
undermined by the "bad cop" Cabinet (behind whom loomed the threat of a
Conservative Party government).

Both sides treated negotiated agreements as obligatory and strenuously
protested their breach. When government believed the Magopa had abused
their limited permission to clean the graveyard, it repudiated its earlier
promise not to sell the farm. But though it adopted a tone of moral outrage,
it could only point to the interference with grazing by Magopa walking on
the grass and drinking the water, thereby subordinating the rights of Blacks
to the needs of cattle owned by whites. The government felt that concessions
from its plenary legal power should have particular weight. For the Magopa,
by contrast, agreements were the only way to participate in lawmaking.

Despite its centrality, however, eight years of negotiation produced no
resolution because the parties' positions were fundamentally irreconcilable.
Government insisted the Magopa acknowledge its authority to decide their
fate and agree to relinquish Zwartrand. Everything else could be negotiated:
other land, compensation, development aid. The Magopa insisted on their
birthright; once this was recognized they would again be loyal and reasonable subjects. The outcome turned on neither eloquence nor strategy but
power, which gradually eroded during the 1980s—partly because of challenges like these.

Both sides periodically resorted to legal forms. The Magopa consulted
four different lawyers, who challenged the authority of Jacob More, threatened an interdict if government did not remove the bulldozers in October
1983, sought an interdict against the removal, sued for compensation, and
defended the eviction action. But though law influenced timing and secured
compensation, it could not divert government from its course. The National
Party, by contrast, controlled the executive and (for part of this period) the
legislature. Parliament passed the 1975 resolution that constituted the
(flawed) legal foundation for removal. The Department of Co-operation and
Development instructed the Klerksdorp magistrate to hold a commission of
inquiry into the conduct of Jacob More—but then suppressed the results. The
State President ordered the removal. Government sought to neutralize a
potentially adverse appellate decision in two ways: secretly expropriating the
farms and introducing a bill to validate the removal retroactively and oust the
courts of jurisdiction. Yet it withdrew the latter: The political costs of losing
in the Houses of Representatives and Delegates and having to overrule them

in the white-dominated President's Council were too high. Government showed little respect for the courts, refusing to postpone the removal while the Chief Justice decided whether to grant leave to appeal, and continuing to assert its legality after the Appellate Division had invalidated it. Government used expropriation again to prevent the Magopa from buying Holgat. Yet rather than take executive action, legislate, or simply resort to brute force to oust the Magopa from their cemetery in 1989, government initiated an ejectment action. This time the Magopa would have preferred to confront the police, whom they hoped to neutralize through their numbers and media observers.

The two Magopa cases illuminate the complex, contradictory relationship between law and politics. Law did not determine the first case: the Supreme Court thought government clearly was entitled to execute the removal, while the Appellate Division thought it obviously lacked authority. Yet the Magopa argued legalistically that the Black Administration Act required Parliamentary approval of their destination, and government replied legalistically that the "tribe" had agreed to move and the order was directed at only a fraction. The Appellate Division purported to engage in conventional statutory interpretation: A tribe could not respond nor could Parliament decide whether to overrule them without knowing the destination. (The court cleverly purported to be respecting Parliament while limiting it.) Such formalism verged on hypocrisy: *no* tribe moved voluntarily; and Nationalist Party control of Parliament assured approval. The court invoked an interpretive canon favoring the less harsh of two possible constructions (which it conveniently ignored in upholding the Emergency regulations). Yet the court also acknowledged the hardship of removal, the tribe's resistance, and the need for thorough governmental deliberation about such a draconian measure. And it declared the removal illegal. (It may be significant that government reprieved Driefontein and KwaNgema three days before oral argument.) All this was superfluous, however, since the court found the substantive issue moot. Perhaps its gratuitous rebuke was a politically cheap form of sympathy; the Appellate Division could be generous with rhetoric precisely because it was stingy with results. Justice Goldstein did the same for Goedgevonden. Having decided for the white farmers, he made a point of rebuffing the government on procedural grounds (although this had no consequences) and used the application for costs to address the merits. Both courts gave government all it wanted and then sought to show solicitude for the communities by awarding them costs.

The second lawsuit was similar in everything but outcome. Both parties were legalistic: The Magopa argued that government had invoked the wrong statute and failed to give formal notice to quit the cemetery; government responded that the expropriation could not be challenged in an ejectment action, such a challenge was no longer timely, and the Minister of Community Development was a necessary party. Legalism channeled evidence toward two peripheral issues: the number of people and huts, the time devoted to cleaning graves. Both courts decided the case on technical grounds, but neither granted government the relief it sought. Thus, the Magopa won the first action but could not enforce it, and government won the second but could not enforce it. In each instance, law bowed to the shifting constellation of political power.

Goedgevonden also illuminated the complex relationship between law and power. Although the police were sympathetic to whites (perhaps particularly to the AWB) they felt obligated to enforce the law and were furious at open defiance: "It was totally unnecessary for anybody to take the law into their own hands." May 11, 1991, may go down in South African history as the first time white police shot fellow whites trying to attack blacks. It prompted the far-right to join its sworn enemy, the ECC, in opposing conscription (see chapter four). But fidelity to law cut both ways. Justice Goldstein not only granted the ejectment but also dressed down the black community for committing "a most serious wrong" by depriving white farmers of "peaceful occupation" "without due process." Just as the police invoked the "duty imposed by law to act against anybody who transgresses the law," so Goldstein declared that "the principle at stake here is a cornerstone of the rule of law. The principle that no man may take the law into his own hands as the respondents have done is sacrosanct. Respect for it is absolutely necessary for human society to function in conditions of peace, serenity and security." The community's "misfortune" would be "corrected" and dwindle to "no more than a blot on the pages of our history books." While rhetorically generous to government, however, Goldstein also granted the community leave to appeal, staying his eviction order. Once again government had won a victory it could not consummate.

If legal forms were not decisive, they significantly influenced both timing and publicity. Government generally controlled the former. Sometimes it acted with great expedition, as when police removed the Magopa without warning in February 1984 (preempting the Chief Justice's grant of leave to appeal) and when it expropriated Zwartrand (mooting the appeal) and Holgat (preventing its purchase at the eleventh hour) and offered Zwartrand for sale (in retaliation against the cemetery occupation). More often, however, it was master of delay. Years passed between the first rumors and the removal. What was proposed as a two-month stay at Onderstepoort dragged out to more than two years. Government constantly passed the buck up and down the bureaucratic hierarchy and laterally across departments. All this reflected government's plausible but erroneous belief that time was on its side. In fact, the endurance of subordinated peoples always exceeds the tenacity of their rulers. Gross power imbalances are inherently unstable; the greater the numerical disparity, the more difficult for few to repress many.

Although it held the initiative, government sometimes miscalculated badly, most dramatically in giving the ten-day notice to leave. This transformed a war of attrition, which had persuaded many to move, into a frontal assault, attracting the media and effectively paralyzing government. The mistake was not repeated; two-and-a-half months later police acted secretly and without warning. Dispossessed, the Magopa were at a pronounced disadvantage. It was a brilliant piece of strategy to infiltrate back to clean the cemetery, thereby compelling government to remove them all over again. Government made another fatal error in allowing the settlement to expand for several months before acting. As the political environment began to change, delay favored the Magopa. Furthermore, they controlled the speed with which the task proceeded, invoking custom to exclude women and limit work to morning hours.

Information was even more valuable strategically than timing. Lacking political and economic power and therefore legal rights, the Magopa's only hope was to mobilize opinion, at home and abroad, in the churches, through the media, and from foreign governments. They had several advantages in this project. Black Sash was an invaluable ally, issuing press releases, guiding reporters, informing outsiders, and organizing meetings. The Magopa ordeal was highly newsworthy and ideally suited to generate sympathy. Forced removals are almost as hard to justify as the Holocaust—an analogy Bishop Tutu drew. Government no longer was willing to take the political heat of dragging people out of their houses in front of television cameras. Foreign governments sent consular officials to observe; even the Reagan Administration expressed disapproval. Trade embargoes and disinvestment intensified. Hence the threat of publicity did make government abort the removal in November. One reason both government and judge later gave for evicting the Magopa from the cemetery was media attention.

Press reports consistently presented the events as an atrocity story. After millions of people had been forcibly removed for decades, something more was needed to grab attention and arouse sympathy. Photographs of demolished houses, schools, and churches highlighted the community's industry and prosperity. The deteriorating cemetery also offered good visuals. Although physical removal was a transitory event, anniversaries presented occasions to mourn it again. Some of the commonest atrocity stories were apocryphal: the Magopa were being robbed of their diamond mines; a man committed suicide in Pachsdraai because of the removal. Deaths at Bethanie or Onderstepoort, even of natural causes, could be blamed on government. The media focused on the plight of women, children, and the elderly, who happened to preponderate demographically but also were more innocent, unthreatening, sympathetic, and vulnerable. For the same reason there were several references to military service and financial contributions during World War II. As Haysom emphasized, these were not township youths engaged in necklacing but conservative, rural, land-owning, church-going farmers. After removal the press stressed the intolerable conditions of exile. The Magopa were the Biblical Israelites (whose names they shared), condemned to wander the (almost literal) desert for forty months (if not years) until they could enter the Promised Land. Or, to modernize the metaphor, they were the latest exiles from the Holy Land—Palestinians in the refugee camps. In a country obsessed with water resources (flooding in Natal, drought elsewhere), the community was depicted as moving from the green pastures of Mogopa to the parched lowveld, watered only by their own tears. Media rhetoric steadily escalated: death of a village, atrocity, final solution, as evil as Nazism, the ultimate blasphemy, sentence of death.

Government was much less successful in managing information. It was unable to speak convincingly. Koornhof initially admitted this—"I don't intend to make further statements to complicate the issue"—and later declared that the removal was voluntary at the very moment police were breaking down doors and arresting those who resisted. Deputy Information Minister Louis Nel also told bare-faced lies: "If you think the Government wants to throw you into the street, that is not going to happen.... Not one single person has been forcibly removed." It disseminated disinformation about the numbers who had left for Pachsdraai, the date of the proposed removal, and the legal status of the farm. It courted the media in vain, taking them on two helicopter trips to Zwartrand and Pachsdraai; but these tended to backfire, as the Magopa reiterated their refusal to move. It sought to implicate the Magopa in its own hypocrisy, demanding that they characterize the move to Onderstepoort as "voluntary." It tried to enhance its image by dramatic proclamations: the end of forced removals in 1985, repeal of the Black Administration Act, the reprieve of Driefontein and KwaNgema. Yet these only accentuated its gratuitous cruelty toward the Magopa. It minimized publicity by acting when the media were absent. It berated the media for distorting the truth and inflaming public opinion, a convenient justification for secrecy. Sometimes it concealed potentially damaging information, such as the appointment and identity of Jacob More's "Planning Committee" and the expropriation of Zwartrand. When all else failed, it used force to silence critics, barring reporters and television cameras from Zwartrand and Pachsdraai.

The struggles over information and image, like the legal conflict, consisted of battles won and wars lost. In both arenas the Magopa felt entitled to demand, and government felt obligated to offer, reasons for the exercise of power. Inside and outside South Africa the media sided with the Magopa. Yet adverse publicity did no more than delay the removal for two-and-a-half months. It could not bring the Magopa home or even secure them another acceptable farm. Together, however, physical endurance, legal resistance, and media embarrassment denied government the ultimate victory. Courts refused to place the imprimatur of legality on the removal. Media kept the atrocities fresh in the public mind. Both allowed the Magopa to keep reiterating their claim until the changed political climate forced government to concede.

CHAPTER 11

MOUTSE AND KWANDEBELE: ETHNICITY AND GENDER IN THE CHALLENGE TO GRAND APARTHEID

We started this homeland with only R16.40 in our coffers and only 240 Ndebele people with one school to our credit. We are now able to count our money in millions. I cycled all over getting our people together. Now that we have built expensive schools people want to burn them. Mbhokoto will deal with such people. (KwaNdebele Chief Minister Simon Skosana, January 1986)

Government is not exercising any pressure on any resident in the Moutse area to move elsewhere. Consequently it is not dependent upon a possible Parliamentary debate on the Proclamation incorporating Moutse into KwaNdebele. (Minister of Education and Development Aid Gerrit Viljoen, February 1986)

[The government denial that this was a removal] was like telling people sitting in a truck that you are not taking them anywhere. (Maredi Chueu, Moutse member of the Lebowa Legislative Assembly, January 1986)

[T]he excising of Moutse from the jurisdiction of the Lebowa Government took place by statute....The loss of rights associated therewith, consequently, is not caused by Proclamation R227 and the incorporation into KwaNdebele, but by Parliament. Insofar as unreasonableness is the issue, it therefore drops out of consideration. It is not for me to pass judgment about whether that decision was good or bad, desirable or undesirable, wise or unwise. (Justice T.T. Spoelstra dismissing Moutse's challenge to incorporation, December 1986)

It is not for the purposes of effective administration that self-governing territories are created—the aim is...the political development of the various peoples. (Justice Grosskopf allowing Moutse's challenge to incorporation, March 1988)

For a long time, it has been reasonably accepted in South Africa that women are no less eligible than men to express themselves politically. There also is no reason why women are less eligible than men to hold elective office. I believe that the inequality...is unfair and therefore not authorized by the 1971 Act. (Justice Eloff granting KwaNdebele women the vote, May 1988)

As the political cost of forced removals increased, especially in the aftermath of Mogopa, government pursued grand apartheid by incorporating black communities into homelands and seeking to persuade the six "self-governing" territories to accept "independence." None had been willing to do so since Ciskei in 1981. The incorporation of Moutse into KwaNdebele illustrated both strategies.

Removal by Incorporation: 1977-86

The 140,000 acres of Moutse District in Northern Transvaal contained about 120,000 people, just under half of whom were North Sotho (or Pedi) Bantoane, who settled there in 1780. The Ndebele minority (twenty-five to thirty percent) sought land from them in 1924. The district was well developed: forty-six primary and twelve secondary schools, the Philadelphia hospital, churches, tarred roads, and telecommunications. One area was said to be rich in minerals, which JCI had begun to explore.

Government established the Bantoane Tribal Authority in 1956, upgrading it to a Regional Authority five years later.[1] Chief Tlokwe Gibson Mathebe was head of both. In 1970 Mashung Tribal Authority was added and the entity renamed Moutse.[2] When government created the Lebowa Territorial Authority in 1962 for the North Sotho it included Moutse, which had two elected and two nominated members in the Legislative Assembly.[3] Lebowa became a self-governing homeland in 1982.[4] All Moutse chiefs were Sotho, as were twenty-six of the thirty members of the three community authorities and sixteen of the twenty members of the Moutse Regional Authority. North Sotho was the dominant language and medium of instruction in forty of the forty-six primary schools.

During this period South Ndebele labor tenants were being forced off white farms and moving to Bophuthatswana and Lebowa.[5] In 1967 I.J. Mahlangu launched an organization to seek an Ndebele nation. Simon Skosana also began talking to Ndebele leaders about founding their own homeland.[6] Instead, government created the Ndzundza Tribal Authority within Lebowa in 1968, recognizing as leader David Mabhogo (King Mapoch).[7] Under further pressure, government met with Ndebele in March 1972 and drafted plans for a homeland. In 1974 it upgraded Ndzundza to a Regional Authority, excised it from Lebowa, and made Skosana chairman.[8] In 1975 it announced plans to add 128,000 acres to the original 126,000.[9] Two years later it excised three Ndebele tribal authorities from Bophuthatswana, merged them into the Mnyamana Regional Authority and added it to Ndzundza to create the Ndebele Territorial Authority.[10] In 1979 it established the KwaNdebele Legislative Assembly (KLA), consisting of forty-six nominated members chaired by Skosana.[11] During the opening ceremonies Skosana said "full independence is out of the question at the moment" because of the total lack of infrastructure.[12]

The same year government expropriated nine farms in the Nebo district of Lebowa, thereby excising them from the homeland. Chief Andries Mahlangu, an Ndebele leader who owned part of the land, opposed the action. Solly Mahlangu, a rival (and later KLA speaker), approved it and sought incorporation into KwaNdebele. The two groups fought, and Andries was murdered in January 1981. KwaNdebele Interior Minister Piet Ntuli was charged with instructing Moses Skosana and three others to commit the murder. Ntuli's son Samuel sought state protection to testify against his father. But all were acquitted in August 1984.

In September 1977 Greyling Wentzel, Deputy Minister of Co-operation and Development, first raised the possibility of excising Moutse from Lebowa. Lebowa Chief Minister Cedric Phatudi and his cabinet met with Minister of Co-operation and Development Piet Koornhof in November 1979 and June 1980. When Moutse community leaders first learned in October about the possibility of incorporation into KwaNdebele, they flatly rejected it. The next day government excised Moutse from Lebowa, telling Dr. Phatudi it was for "administrative reasons" and would not lead to incorporation into KwaNdebele. Indeed, Moutse retained its four representatives in the Lebowa Legislative Assembly.[13] On November 6 Chief Mathebe and two of those representatives (Godfrey Mathebe and Maredi Chueu) repeated Moutse's position to Koornhof.

A year later Koornhof defended the government's policy to a hostile crowd of 6,000. "There should be no doubt" in their minds about the "legal fact" that Pretoria had taken over administration. "According to the 1975 consolidation proposals the Moutse district had to be excised...." The decision had been taken long before Koornhof became Minister. Opposition by Moutse leaders "hampered good administration and in fact confused the people." "[T]he people of Moutse could for the present continue to live here in peace and harmony and...their interests would be catered for...." "[N]o decisions affecting the lives of the citizens of Lebowa living in Moutse would be taken without prior consultation and deliberation with the leaders of Moutse and the Lebowa Cabinet." But he offered those opposing incorporation 143,000 acres of "highly developed farms" in Immerpan/Saliesloot, reassuring them that "the whole resettlement action will be undertaken in a compassionate manner....With your co-operation the whole action can be carried out with a minimum of disruption and inconvenience." He brushed off their warnings: "If you are going to invoke trouble and violence and bloodshed you are only absolutely foolish. Who will be killed? Black people."[14]

At its request, KwaNdebele became self-governing in April 1981.[15] The previous February Skosana denied he was seeking independence. At the same time, however, he was negotiating to open a casino, which could only operate outside South Africa. The KwaNdebele Legislative Assembly formally expressed interest in independence in May 1982. After a meeting with Skosana and his cabinet, Koornhof appointed his Director-General, Gilles van der Walt, to chair a commission to prepare for it, a process expected to take five years. KwaNdebele Interior Minister Ntuli declared there was no need for a popular vote because self-government implied independence. At the same time, KwaNdebele demanded more land, including Moutse, as the price of independence.[16]

When Skosana sought support among Moutse residents, Maredi Chueu turned to Professor John Dugard, Director of the Centre for Applied Legal Studies, who replied in October 1982 that Skosana's activity was lawful. Dugard also interpreted an Appellate Division judgment the previous month invalidating the excision of Ingwavuma from KwaZulu as possibly giving Lebowa but not Moutse standing to challenge the threatened incorporation.[17] Instead of exploring legal action, however, Chueu gave an interview to the *Rand Daily Mail*.[18] The Bantoane had settled Moutse first.

> According to African custom, they [the Ndebele] were assigned land by the Bantoane—and by virtue of that, they owe allegiance to the Bantoane. That makes it difficult for the Bantoane to recognise the (adjacent) state of KwaNdebele, let alone the fact that they will be incorporated into KwaNdebele.
>
> Dr Koornhof has been informed that nothing short of bloodshed will subdue the Bantoane and make them subjects of KwaNdebele.

KwaNdebele was "crude" and uneducated: the kgotla (council of elders) administered corporal punishment; Skosana had left school at standard six. Lebowa Chief Minister Phatudi had complained to Koornhof about Skosana's agitation within Moutse. "The meeting was tactlessly handled and had the effect of annoying and irritating the Lebowa people in the extreme." He warned of violence. Koornhof rebuffed Phatudi's request to visit Moutse: "[A]t present, as a result of commitments, I am unable to hold such a meeting." Chief Mathebe also failed to secure a meeting.

In February 1983 the van der Walt commission proposed to incorporate Moutse and other land into KwaNdebele as a preliminary to independence.[19] In April Lebowa sent a 100-man delegation, including all the Moutse leaders, to express their opposition to Koornhof, who promised not to act without further discussion. The following month Dr. Phatudi and Chief Mathebe addressed a meeting of thousands opposing incorporation. At the end of May, however, Phatudi learned that the South African Cabinet had decided in favor of incorporation. A month later Koornhof claimed that incorporation had been "envisaged" in the 1973 and 1975 consolidation proposals and would be "conducive to more effective overall planning" and "more effective expenditure of development capital." "Are the Black peoples of Southern Africa generally, and the South Ndebele in particular, to be denied the fulfilment [sic] of their national aspirations merely because there are enemies of the Republic of South Africa...?"[20] Phatudi promptly instructed his lawyers to initiate a legal challenge, rejecting the offer of compensatory land.[21] Chief Mathebe added that his grandfather had granted land to King Mapoch in 1925, making Ndebele in Moutse his subjects. He also rejected Immerpan. "This is our home and we shall stay here, even if the court case goes against us." At an August 2 meeting Prime Minister Botha reiterated the promise not to incorporate Moutse into KwaNdebele without further talks, and Phatudi postponed legal action.

Later that month Parliament affirmed the 1980 proclamation removing Moutse from Lebowa and stripped it of representation in the Lebowa Legislative Assembly.[22] When Helen Suzman denounced as nonsense the government's desire "to unite those who belonged together" because "these people are not Ndebele," Koornhof responded: "Of peoples you understand sweet Fanny Adams."[23] Criticized by the PFP for trying to avoid the legal challenge that had invalidated the KwaZulu excision, Koornhof replied that government was "bent on trying to resolve the matter in a friendly and amicable way." Since Moutse had been effectively under his jurisdiction for years "the *status quo* is being maintained." He promised to amend the law so it did not automatically apply to Moutse. It was necessary to resolve these matters "to bring about stability, certainty and assurance."[24]

On November 18, Skosana again requested independence, although he admitted later he did not know its meaning.

> How can my people know what independence is all about when
> I don't even know myself. But we're learning.... [M]aybe I am

stupid, but independence for me became a logical step when I accepted territorial authority. It's either you agree or you don't. There is no middle ground and people who don't agree with this system should be with Mandela or Sobukwe.[25]

The same day Botha met a forty-five-person delegation of Moutse leaders and the Lebowa Cabinet. Lebowa would have to resolve its differences with KwaNdebele because government was only a "third party." He refused a referendum on incorporation. Ministers of the two homelands met without Moutse representation in December 1983 and February and March 1984. Government drafted a proposal in April, which it discussed with the two chief Ministers twice in May. Phatudi again asked for a referendum. On June 28 Botha (now State President) signed legislation declaring that any proclamation requiring prior consultation with a homeland would be "deemed to have been preceded by consultation" whether or not it had occurred. This retroactively immunized the excision of Moutse from legal challenge. The PFP deplored that Parliament was being asked to "legislate a lie" by passing a "cynical provision to cover the government in the event of its having issued proclamations without compliance with the law." In October Gerrit Viljoen, the new Minister of Co-operation and Development, announced plans to incorporate Moutse into KwaNdebele and compensate Lebowa with Immerpan/Saliesloot.[26]

Government remained cautious about KwaNdebele independence. In January 1984 Louis Nel, Deputy Minister of Foreign Affairs, expressed concern that the failure of one homeland could endanger the others. In May Koornhof told Parliament, "We must take these people by the hand and try to train them, so that when eventually they take that step the necessary spadework will have been done to enable them to govern KwaNdebele competently."[27] The same month Botha said independence would be granted only to homelands that had shown an ability to run their affairs smoothly. He therefore shelved plans to confer independence that December.[28] KwaNdebele chose its second Legislative Assembly in November: fifty-six nominated members (forty-eight by tribal chiefs, eight by Skosana) and sixteen elected by men (only 600 voted). Skosana explained that "women have first to be taught by their husbands how to vote."[29]

In February 1985 Viljoen announced the incorporation of Ekangala into KwaNdebele, despite earlier promises that only the Ndebele portion of the township would be affected (forty percent of the population). Chris Heunis, Minister of Constitutional Development and Planning, explained in May that residents had not been consulted because incorporation had been decided "before the planning of the town and, therefore, before there were any residents." It was "necessary for good management to have the town administered by only one authority." Residents burned the East Rand Development Board (ERADEBO) office in protest and assaulted a KwaNdebele official. Toward the end of February the Ekangala Action

Committee (EAC), formed the previous May, organized a rent boycott. Some residents prepared to return to the East Rand townships from which they came, fearing loss of §10 rights and South African citizenship despite government reassurances. On March 23 police shot at a peaceful demonstration of 4,500, killing one. Government banned all EAC meetings and appointed a community council dominated by KwaNdebele representatives, including Information Minister F.K. Mahlangu. Vigilantes attacked anyone opposing incorporation. On March 30 they beat a woman and her daughter for holding EAC meetings in her house, and a group including F.K. Mahlangu attacked a man, warning him that Ekangala was "not a place for dogs from the East Rand." EAC vice-chair Peter Kose was a primary target. His house was damaged on March 30; the next month a member of the community council tried to abduct him. In June men driving a car with KwaNdebele license plates searched his house and kidnapped him; he was tortured for two days by many men, including F.K. Mahlangu. He was abducted again in July and assaulted at Mahlangu's home. When Kose complained to the police he was arrested and charged with assault (but never prosecuted).

Later that year the EAC decided to support a collective move back to the East Rand. But in September it submitted a petition against incorporation signed by almost 1,000 people, seventy percent of all householders.

> We are location people…used to location law where each man is equal according to his property. There is a Mr [F.K.] Mahlangu at Ekangala who acts as a chief. He has set up a tribal "court". This "court" fines people and gives sentences of corporal punishment. We are not a tribe and we do not accept the system of being fined, asked for money and controlled by chiefs. This is the homeland system…which we as location people long ago left behind….

> We think that non-Ndebeles would have problems with pensions, jobs and houses under KwaNdebele…. Already representatives of the KwaNdebele government are telling us to leave Ekangala….

> Ever since the incorporation issue came up we have been assaulted by KwaNdebele government supporters. If they behave like this while Ekangala is still under the [government] we fear that they will become much more violent when Ekangala is incorporated into KwaNdebele, or KwaNdebele becomes independent.

They got no reply.[30] A year later the government explained that it refused to speak with the EAC because it was not elected, dealing instead with the Coordinating Committee (thirty-one of whose thirty-three members were white!).[31]

Opening the new KwaNdebele Legislative Assembly on April 24, Skosana said he expected independence by the end of 1986. Soon thereafter Parliament amended the Laws on Co-operation and Development Act for the *third* time to frustrate any legal challenge by redefining Lebowa as though it had never contained Moutse.[32]

On August 14 Botha and seven ministers, deputy ministers, and permanent secretaries met for two hours with Phatudi and seven other Lebowa officials and several Moutse representatives. Chief Mathebe said Moutse "stood firm, that they were Lebowan people." Maredi Chueu urged a referendum, noting that Moutse originally had been included in Lebowa because of cultural similarities. Botha replied that he had been personally involved with the problem for more than six years. He did not know why the parties could not settle it among themselves. He had visited Moutse and appointed a mediator, but nothing worked. If a referendum were held in Moutse it would have to be held every time there were changes in the boundaries of the "national states." "If it was expected of him to declare that Moutse was to form part of Lebowa, he had to disappoint them. He could not do so." When L.C. Mathebe asked whether Botha was prepared to accept responsibility for the repercussions, he complained that Moutse was "pointing the pistol to his head." There was no alternative to incorporation, but he would give Lebowa and KwaNdebele two more weeks to reach a solution. He had had to transfer land "of his own people" to "other people." Phatudi and another proposed to amalgamate the two homelands. "[H]e did not want to threaten the State President…[but] his people…would not put a foot in KwaNdebele. Everything would be beyond control." Ignoring this, Botha told Viljoen to brief the Lebowa Cabinet on the government's secret consolidation proposals but warned "if anything should leak out, he would never be prepared to interview a delegation of this nature again."

Viljoen detailed the consolidation, which he called "a package with sweet and sour ingredients." Phatudi then asked about the 61,000 acre Nebo farms, which he wanted for Lebowa. Although Botha would not promise, he declared that insistence on the return of Moutse would eliminate any chance of getting them. Phatudi said some of the proposals were "very good news indeed." He was particularly delighted by the planned railway: "Generations to come would put that to the credit of the State President." Botha replied, "He was fair to Lebowa. He appealed to Lebowa Government to be fair to him on the Moutse issue." Phatudi said he did not want bloodshed and would see what he could do. Botha replied he did not like to be threatened; any blood would not be on his head. *"He would give his decision on Moutse on 1 September 1985. He could not wait any longer as the consolidation proposals have to be made known."* Phatudi promised to reply in two weeks and thanked Botha "for the amicable spirit in which the discussions took place."

Maredi Chueu later accused Phatudi of acceding to bribes, although government may also have disregarded Lebowa's protests. In any case, Heunis announced the final consolidation scheme on September 25, giving Bophuthatswana and Lebowa some land originally scheduled for KwaNdebele but giving it Moutse and other land. Some 6,000 people protested in Moutse and started a legal fund, which had collected R42,000 by November. On November 18 Maredi Chueu led a nineteen-man delegation seeking a referendum. Heunis refused, saying the decision was "in the best interests of all concerned." At a press conference Chueu declared: "We feel like John the Baptist's head being served up on a platter."

Two meetings to report back were planned on November 30, but the first was banned and the second dispersed by police. Hundreds marched to the home of a Moutse man violating the boycott by operating a shop in KwaNdebele. The homeland anticipated incorporation by starting to supervise Moutse police, sending income tax forms to Moutse taxi drivers, and requiring Moutse businessmen to obtain loans in KwaNdebele. On November 21 Moutse teachers sent a protest to the Moutse Circuit Inspector; a week later they were summoned to meetings and told to register with the KwaNdebele Department of Education or request transfer. On December 3 the chairman of the Moutse Principals' Council transmitted an elaborate resolution denouncing the politicization of education and urging negotiation. It received no response.[33]

Government issued a press release on December 5. It had to "end the consolidation tug of war." Moutse had been incorporated "for the purposes of meaningful consolidation and orderly government, as well as in the interests of the inhabitants of the further development of the Moutse district." Heunis had listened to "divergent opinions" on the incorporation and had secured the promise of the KwaNdebele Cabinet "to listen to the leaders and inhabitants of Moutse with regard to fears some of them had." Government offered alternative land to those "prepared to move voluntarily." "No forced relocations will take place." Incorporation would occur on January 1 "and the inhabitants of Moutse are requested to accept the South African Government's decision as it is in the interest of the prosperity and development of the area." Black Sash vice-president Ethel Walt denied that the action was "in the interests of the inhabitants" and called for a referendum. TRAC and the National Committee Against Removals warned that government would have to "take full responsibility for the violence and terrible suffering that will result." CALS Director John Dugard said the incorporation "will create an ethnic minority a third of the size of the population of KwaNdebele."[34]

Several papers denounced incorporation. *The Cape Times* declared that "grand apartheid is alive and well....The wishes of the people involved are irrelevant, as are the 'consultations' we have been assured have taken place over the years."[35] "One wonders what the Government's reaction would be," the *Sowetan* asked, "if they tried to do the same thing to a white community.... The Government must stop pursuing its homeland policy, because even they have realised that this is not a viable option in trying to find a solution to the problems of this troubled land of ours."[36] "In order to convince black and white South Africans—as well as the rest of the doubting world—that reform is more than a mere word," said *The Argus*, "the Government would do well to scrap these incorporation plans."[37]

Chief Mathebe made another attempt to report back on Maredi Chueu's November 18 meeting. He rejected a permit that only allowed him to recite Heunis's message without discussing any "counter-action regarding the incorporation of Moutse into KwaNdebele" but then obtained unconditional permission for a meeting at the royal kraal on December 15. After he addressed a thousand people, youths burned the shops of two suspected KwaNdebele supporters and stoned a bus. The SADF was called in and fourteen youths arrested. The detention of two local journalists working for Worldwide Television News in London was covered by the American press; the British Embassy sent two representatives to investigate the violence; and twenty-six members of Congress protested to the South African Ambassador. Police dispersed a meeting of youths at Chief Mathebe's kraal on December 17, arresting and beating many. The next day vigilantes assaulted members of the Dennilton Youth Congress. Police attacked another demonstration on December 22, killing one man and arresting eight.[38]

When Chief Mathebe and Godfrey Mathebe sought police protection in anticipation of incorporation, Major Malan of the Dennilton Police Station declared that his only responsibility was the police station and magistrate's court and faulted them for not seeking his help on behalf of KwaNdebele businessmen attacked by youths. Early on New Year's Day a car with KwaNdebele license plates drove to Chief Mathebe's kraal. The five armed men announced Moutse was theirs and they had come to take over the kraal and kidnap the chief. Four attackers were killed and the fifth seriously injured. Men in trucks with white crosses on their foreheads, armed with pangas and axes and shouting "Mbokotho" (millstone), attacked two Moutse villages adjacent to KwaNdebele, abducting more than 380 men to the Siyabuswa community hall. A victim recollected:

> Mr Skhosana was standing next to a strongman at the door of the hall. Skhosana had a whip in his hand and as we were marched in he asked us where we were from. Those from Johannesburg—whom he considered to be outsiders and troublemakers—he flogged heavily. After we were all in the hall, the door was shut and Skhosana addressed us. He said he was not fighting us, provided we accepted his rule. He said we must fight the whites, not each other. After he left we were asked to strip naked, a hosepipe was put through the window and soap powder sprinkled on the floor. Then Skhosana put his head through the window and said we must put underpants on in case the children see us naked. We were made to lie down in the water while the vigilantes flogged and kicked us so that we slipped

around the floor, unable to hold onto anything. We were made to do physical jerks while the vigilantes hurled insults at us. When we were released, we were given petrol bombs and told to use them against our chiefs and leaders.

The next day more than fifty were treated for sjambok wounds at the hospital, one of whom died from his injuries. When a reporter asked about the incident, Skosana said "that is a secret of the government" and hung up. Women and children fled to the bush. During the fighting seventeen vigilantes were killed and the cars of suspects burned. Although a hundred riot police had been seen at the Dennilton station they took no action. Maredi Chueu's accusation that they "have taken a very indifferent attitude towards our situation" elicited the usual response: "Should any person be of the opinion that there is legal cause for complaint, such allegations can be made available to the police in the form of affidavits." But despite complaints against Skosana, Ntuli, and two other Ministers, they were not prosecuted.[39]

Meetings to protest incorporation were held in three Moutse villages on New Year's Day. Two black policemen driving a car with KwaNdebele license plates tried to disrupt one, taunting residents and shooting without provocation, killing one person. They were caught and their "mutilated" bodies found the next day. Police responded with five days of house-to-house searches, beating and torturing people, breaking doors and windows, and stealing property. When hunger finally forced people out of the bush, police paraded them in front of hidden informers, arresting eighty-nine and charging thirteen with murder. Maredi Chueu denounced the experience as "an invading army" but feared it was "only the beginning if incorporation goes through." Although government said this was not a removal, "it was like telling people sitting in a truck that you are not taking them anywhere." On January 3 police tear gassed some 7,000 mourners at the funeral of a victim killed by police during the December 22 meeting. Chris Heunis reiterated that incorporation was in the "interests of all concerned" and government had shown the "greatest understanding and compassion"—claims that Black Sash president Sheena Duncan called "astounding and ludicrous."[40]

The press agreed with her. *The Star* urged government to "re-think Moutse."[41] *The Cape Times* called for reassessment of "the disastrous homelands policy."[42] Although the *Eastern Province Herald* accepted "government stewardship of less advanced peoples...it was the very antithesis of stewardship to force incorporation on the unwilling people of Moutse." "This is a mass removal in another guise...."[43] *The Argus* condemned Heunis for failing "to explain why such a step was necessary at all at a time when the whole Verwoerdian fantasy of homelands and partition is widely discredited and when constitutional options such as federation are being debated."[44] The *Evening Post* attacked "the Government's enduring obsession with racial division and ethnic control. Whatever it says about reform, it is still wedded to apartheid as the basis of government."[45] *The Natal Mercury* asked, "Why is our

Government looking for trouble? Why does it go out of its way to outrage the few friends it has in a hostile world?"[46] The *Pretoria News* was most emphatic.[47]

> Moutse is a name that will be etched into South African history as deeply as Magopa and kwaNgema—more knots in the rope to finally hang apartheid. It is classic evidence that in spite of vehement and repeated protestations that it has reformed, that it is holier, the government is doing exactly what it said it has stopped....
>
> [T]he government makes great play of ethnicity, when it is convenient. In this case it has deliberately and cold-bloodedly ignored its favourite segregationist tenet and thrown together people of unsophisticated level and known tribal enmity....
>
> Ethnicity can never be a justification for apartheid at either local level or in some grand federal plan but it is a fact of life which cannot be realistically ignored.

PFP MP Helen Suzman, touring Moutse the following weekend, called the government's actions "scandalous." Acting UDF publicity secretary Murphy Morobe denounced "another atrocious act by the SA Government. It is treasonous and hypocritical for a government to raise such an outcry because landmines have been found on the borders, yet they continue to forcibly remove settled communities." Black Sash sent the Transvaal Attorney General and the press affidavits by eighty victims of the New Year's Day abduction.[48]

Mbokotho ruled KwaNdebele with terror, beating children for not attending school and forcing adult men to be circumcised even if they were not Ndebele. (The previous year the Kwaggafontein magistrate had fled his post when it was learned he was uncircumcised, going to a private physician to avoid having the operation performed in the bush.) When Chief Makhosana Klaas Mahlangu (a royal family member popular with youth) had opposed the homeland constitution proposed by South Africa in 1975, he was ousted by Skosana and seriously wounded by Skosana supporters. Because his wife was the sister of Zulu King Goodwill Zwelithini, he spent seven years in KwaZulu (some of it in a "rebellious chiefs camp"). In 1984 his cousin Cornelius Mahlangu asked him to return to KwaNdebele, where he won election to the Legislative Assembly in 1985. But on December 19 he and his mother and wife were dragged from their kraal by 100 armed men, allegedly Skosana supporters, and taken to Mbokotho headquarters in Siyabuswa. Although police were called, they hesitated to intervene "because the Mbokotho are dangerous people and therefore they could not open a docket"; instead they helped him escape to KwaZulu. He returned in January but soon resigned from the Legislative Assembly. On March 16 he was shot; he identified three Mbokotho, who were arrested. In April his wife was moved from GaRankuwa Hospital after vigilantes tried to force their way into the ward.[49]

The violence attracted international attention, if also miscomprehension. *The Times* quoted the police blaming the deaths on "faction fighting."[50] A front-page *New York Times* article denigrated it and a Zulu-Pondo clash near Durban as "tribal fighting." The paper wrongly attributed the excision of Moutse from Lebowa to the interests of white farmers and miners and explained incorporation into KwaNdebele as an attempt "to give it the appearance of a legitimate nation."[51] The *Washington Post* focused on the real issue: Moutse resistance and vigilante violence. "The government decision not to reconsider will be recorded by history as one of those fateful and fatal moves that causes a war because that is what is now beginning—a full-scale war." Three days later it reported the mass abduction and torture.[52] Even the staunchly Reaganite American Ambassador asked aloud (in a speech criticizing economic sanctions) why "the decision to force 120,000 Sotho-speaking Moutse people to become part of KwaNdebele before that homeland gains a dubious independence is allowed to put the South African Government's commitment to reform in doubt."[53]

On January 6 Skosana declared that eighty percent of Moutse favored incorporation. "The impression being created, among others by the Black Sash, that Ndebeles are instigators, is devoid of all truth and can rather be subscribed to revolutionary elements who represent only a small minority in Moutse." He promised that "the needs, wishes and aspirations of all the people will be taken into consideration." Education Minister Placid Kunutu admitted that people had been captured in revenge for the seizure of KwaNdebele taxis and conceded that "traditional Ndebele ways of information extraction might have been used." Victims testified that Kunutu participated in the mass abduction and assaults. Skosana issued a second statement on January 9 reassuring Moutse residents that they would not have to take KwaNdebele citizenship after independence, their property would be respected, trade licenses would be issued, Sotho would be used in their schools, and their representatives would serve as chiefs and in the Legislative Assembly. "To discriminate in any way against the people of Moutse will only mean that the government will boycott itself in its economic development."[54]

This did nothing to allay anxiety. On behalf of Moutse teachers, Nicholas Haysom telexed Deputy Education Minister Sam de Beer on January 10, urging postponement of the transfer "until the status of Moutse has been finalised" and seeking a meeting. M.L. Shaku, chairman of the Moutse School Principals' Council, wrote the Moutse Circuit Inspector on January 15, denying radio and television reports that a majority of teachers had accepted the transfer. De Beer curtly rebuffed Haysom on January 22: "the constitutional status of the Moutse District is a fait a compli [sic].... Arising from this fact the DET no longer has any jurisdiction over schools in Moutse.... I wish to emphasise that no coercion has been applied in any way on teachers in excercising [sic] their free choice."[55]

On January 10 Chief Mathebe and Godfrey Mathebe met Dr. Phatudi in Lebowa. On his return, Godfrey was detained for fourteen days under the

Internal Security Act, transforming him from "collaborator" into hero in the eyes of youths. The police subsequently fired tear gas into his bar lounge. On January 16 the Lebowa Legislative Assembly held a special session on Moutse, defying Heunis's request that they discuss this privately between governments because public debate "could conceivably cause more harm than good." The gallery was packed with eighteen busloads of Moutse people singing freedom songs and dancing. Phatudi warned: "The Pretoria government is making a big mistake by treating Lebowans as children or slaves who are ordered about at the bidding of the master." The Assembly unanimously rejected the incorporation, reaffirmed the seats of Moutse representatives Godfrey Mathebe and Maredi Chueu, and resolved to demand the withdrawal of Pretoria's Commissioner General until Moutse was returned, Godfrey released or tried, and Skosana reprimanded. But this facade of unity concealed deep divisions. Even Chueu accused Phatudi of having colluded with Pretoria.[56]

At a meeting of 400 people on January 25 Skosana officially launched Mbokotho; he was president, Ntuli vice-president, and Assembly Speaker Solly Mahlangu a member of the executive committee. Skosana defined its functions as "protecting the interests of the community, dealing with people who enforce boycotts...[and] any trouble-maker who may be arrested. They can fetch such a person from the police and hit him."

> I have been told some people say they will see to Mbhokoto's downfall. I will keep this position for a year or two to see who will bring about the organisation's downfall....
>
> We started this homeland with only R16.40 in our coffers and only 240 Ndebele people with one school to our credit. We are now able to count our money in millions. I cycled all over getting our people together. Now that we have built expensive schools people want to burn them. Mbhokoto will deal with such people.

By the end of May the organization contained 800-900 people, he claimed, and operated like "ordinary tribal police." "I am satisfied with Mbokotho. They have nothing to do with political matters.... They just keep the peace." They were armed with sjamboks and did not have to file reports when using them.[57]

In mid-February Skosana promised independence on December 4; A committee was planning the capital at KwaMhlanga, and construction of the "independence" stadium at Siyabuswa was proceeding. This was confirmed by the South African Commissioner General for KwaNdebele. *The Cape Times* editorialized against "partition again" just after the State President had pledged an undivided nation and the restoration of citizenship to all who wanted it. *The Argus* also said the contradiction "simply doesn't make sense." At the end of February the British government again protested the incorporation.[58]

Violence, disorder, and uncertainty had their intended effects. Ndebele began leaving Moutse on January 8. Police escorted government trucks carrying 600 families on the weekend of January 18-19; further removals occurred on February 6, allegedly at gunpoint. The following day twenty-two Moutse families moved to the compensatory land at Saliesloot. Residents said that three unpopular families who asked to move were told by government to produce at least twenty names. They persuaded elderly men and women caring for the houses of labor migrants to sign forms under threat that the move was inevitable and those refusing would not be compensated. (Three hundred families had moved by September.) Viljoen announced on February 7 that

> the present moving of about 107 families…is taking place at the voluntarily request and insistance [sic] of the residents…. The Government is in duty bound to provide the necessary assistance to people asking for help and in particular also to provide them with protection against intimidation…. I wish to give the assurance that the Government is not exercising any pressure on any resident in the Moutse area to move elsewhere. The whole operation is a completely voluntary one. Consequently it is not dependent upon a possible Parliamentary debate on the Proclamation incorporating Moutse into KwaNdebele.

The last comment referred to a petition Helen Suzman presented to Parliament on February 5 on behalf of Chief Mathebe and Maredi Chueu, who sought leave to ask the House of Assembly to disapprove the incorporation resolution. Petitioners had asked to be heard at the Bar of the House only three times before. Mrs. Suzman herself moved to disapprove the "idiotic," "utterly reprehensible and incomprehensible" incorporation, "the sort of callous action which totally disregards the views of the people concerned and which earns Pretoria the condemnation of the whole world." "Is it not amazing how easily the Government discards the sacred principle of ethnicity and group identity when it suits them to do so, and hangs on to it desperately when it does not?"[59]

In response to Parliamentary questions, the government conceded that Moutse chiefs were opposed to incorporation and unwilling to move to Immerpan, but "there is a difference of opinion among the inhabitants of that area." Because of "intimidation," a referendum would not achieve "the correct testing and opinion." Instead, government had engaged in "extensive consultation" and taken "the best decision with the total package in mind."[60]

On February 13, after a futile meeting with Heunis and Viljoen, Phatudi asked that the Commissioner General be withdrawn. Heunis telexed the next day that the "problem of Moutse" had "caused the South African Government great anxiety." Conscious of the "sacrifice" required of Lebowa he was determined it would be "adequately compensated" "as far as is humanly possible." It stood to gain Saliesloot/Immerpan, the Zebediela citrus estates, other "very valuable land" expropriated from whites "in the face of fierce objection by the farming community," and the Nebo farms despite the "very strong historical and emotional claims" of KwaNdebele. If the Moutse issue were reopened, "the rest of the package will also have to be reconsidered." He again refused a referendum. Since the decision had been "preceded by a 10 year period of consultation and investigation by the Commission for Co-operation and Development and by virtue of the report of Dr P S Rautenbach DMS, the Government was fully aware of the views of the residents of Moutse." He reminded Lebowa that government also had rejected Ndebele residents' request for a referendum about joining KwaNdebele. He deplored the recall of the Commissioner General, which would have "serious repercussions." "The Lebowa Government must take full responsibility for all disruption arising form [sic] its action."[61]

On February 17 Moutse also submitted its petition to the (Indian) House of Delegates and the ("Coloured") House of Representatives. The majority parties in each (National People's Party and Labour Party) introduced resolutions opposing incorporation—the first time they had jointly challenged grand apartheid—and agreed to hear the petitioners on March 6. Somaroo Pachai declared: "It is a white initiative and we didn't come to Parliament to support relics of the past." Desmond Lockey tabled a motion in the House of Representatives calling for repeal of "all legislation which determines the reservation of public premises for the exclusive use of certain persons."[62]

The liberal press continued to berate government. The *Daily News* criticized its "senseless pursuit of ethnic policies [which] created yet another unnecessary trouble spot." Incorporation "rivals the bulldozing of squatter camps," said the *Pretoria News*. "Moutse has become a test case of the honesty of our State President and his government." *The Cape Times* reiterated that "a government which talks hollowly about negotiation and power-sharing is still riding roughshod over the wishes of a large section of the population to try to implement a failed ideology." *The Star* observed: "The minor Houses are playing shrewd politics. How the Government responds will say much about its own view of its own institution: the tricameral Parliament."[63]

It responded by finding a loophole. On March 4 the Assembly Speaker announced that Lebowa had asked the Supreme Court to void the incorporation. "I accordingly rule that as [the proclamation] is now going to be adjudicated upon by a court of law, the matter is sub judice...." The other Houses followed suit. Although Lebowa vehemently denied any intent to torpedo Moutse's petition, it did want to regain the initiative. Deputy Development Minister Ben Wilkens again rejected a referendum on the ground that there was a difference of views and intimidation.[64]

Despite this procedural defeat Chief Mathebe, Godfrey Mathebe, Maredi Chueu, and their legal representatives (John Dugard and Dolly Mokgatle) visited Cape Town on March 5 and 6 to meet with members of all three Houses, as well as American, British, and West German diplomats. Chief Mathebe declared: "We will fight to the very end. We are not prepared to be part of KwaNdebele and we will not move." Chueu opposed incorporation because KwaNdebele flogged adults in public, denied women the vote, and might interfere with property and language rights. Dugard added that incorporation would violate the "old Verwoerdian dream" of ethnic states. Believing they had been betrayed by Lebowa, the delegation declared their preference for South African rule.[65]

In April the State President's attempt to claim that his action was compelled by the failure of Lebowa and KwaNdebele to agree led to an exchange with Helen Suzman.

> *Botha:* Eventually I had to make a decision and the Government had to take a stand because we cannot simply let things go. That is when I am accused of not acting. Whatever we do is wrong.

> *Suzman:* Why don't you just leave them where they are?

> *Botha:* One cannot simply leave people in the air.

> *Suzman:* They were not in the air!

> *Botha:* They were. From a planning point of view it was quite wrong to leave them where they were. ... I want to put the questions now and the hon member must listen very carefully. Firstly, did the Black Sash interfere?

> *Suzman:* No, I was asked to go and see myself.

> *Botha:* Very well. Did the hon member see the Black Sash in this connection?

> *Suzman:* Certainly.

> *Botha:* ... Did she also get in touch with the British Foreign Ministry in this connection?

> *Suzman:* Yes, indeed. I will do it again.

> *Botha:* I now leave it to the House to judge. The hon member is a busybody and she is creating trouble throughout the country.[66]

The Struggle Against Independence: 1986

At the opening of the KwaNdebele Legislative Assembly on April 4, the South African Minister of Transport Affairs reaffirmed the commitment to independence on December 4 and promised R37 million for the celebration. Early in May Botha reiterated the promise of independence by the end of the year. The Minister of Constitutional Development and Planning denied it was "the responsibility of the RSA-Government to consult the citizens of KwaNdebele. It is the prerogative of the Government of KwaNdebele to decide on such a matter." He had not received "any representations from any citizens of KwaNdebele in which objections were raised to independence."[67]

By early April an estimated twenty-three people had been killed in Moutse and a thousand arrested. Within KwaNdebele resistance to independence intensified. At the end of February the Mmashadi High School principal called in police, who tear gassed and sjamboked pupils and made teachers instruct the wounded; five pupils and five teachers were arrested and delivered to Mbokotho. In April a boycott at Benginhlanhla High School provoked an invasion by Mbokotho, who captured and tortured ten pupils for two days, sending three to the hospital. Later that month Mandlethu High School pupils sent Skosana a list of grievances against Mbokotho. On the day he was to reply Mbokotho searched the village, capturing thirty pupils and beating them in Skosana's presence. The vigilantes returned that night and murdered a man for siding with the students; they also raped his wife. Although thirty-four men were arrested, the most prominent were released on bail and never charged. Police raided an Mbokotho prison camp, freeing fifty-four men, most of whom had been deprived of food and water for six days. By May eighty schools were closed by boycotts.[68]

On May 12 a meeting at the royal kraal, chaired by the king's younger son, Cornelius, was attended by all the chiefs and some 20,000-30,000 residents, many arriving on Putco buses hijacked by youths. It asked Skosana to withdraw his acceptance of independence, disband Mbokotho, dissolve the Assembly, and dismiss his cabinet. One of the two Ministers present said Mbokotho had been suspended for three weeks and the other requests would be considered. In the same village that day an Mbokotho member shot dead a thirteen-year-old boy sent to buy bread at his shop; residents retaliated by burning the shop, and houses and shops of other Mbokotho. The funeral of an Mbokotho victim a week later attracted thousands, again transported in buses hijacked by youths, although police had postponed it for three weeks and the magistrate restricted attendance to fifty. Police declared the gathering illegal, and they and the army fired tear gas, bird shot, and rubber bullets. A nineteen-year-old girl was killed when she fell under a bus whose driver had been tear gassed. Youths again burned shops of Mbokotho and MPs (including Piet Ntuli) and battled police and soldiers throughout the homeland. That day Skosana said independence could "again be discussed in full" if the Assembly wished. Prince James Mahlangu, oldest son and heir of King Mapoch and chairman of the Ndzundza tribal authority, asked Mag. J. Theron for permission to meet the next day to hear the response to the demands at the funeral. Theron refused, but 25,000 people arrived at the royal kraal, nevertheless, after the entire bus fleet had been hijacked. Before the meeting started security forces fired tear gas and rubber bullets from Casspirs and a helicopter. A driver leaped from a bus, which ran over and killed a child. Two other bodies were found in the royal kraal. Fighting between youths and security forces raged for two days, killing four or five youths and causing an estimated R4 million property damage. Police refused to comment because "KwaNdebele is not in the SAP's jurisdiction."[69]

Two papers interpreted the conflict as a power struggle between the royal family and Skosana.[70] The *Sowetan* deplored the amazing "inability—or sheer hard headedness—on the part of the Government and its puppets to learn from past lessons." *The Argus* warned that the government "is looking for still more problems that will cause it even greater anxieties and consequent turmoil unless it backs away from implementing further figments of the Verwoerdian fantasy that have landed the country in such a mess." The *Evening Post* said the decision "defies logic." Newspapers in the United States and Britain reported the violence. The American Embassy found the decision "puzzling and inconsistent" with Botha's declaration that apartheid was outdated. "In our view KwaNdebele is and will continue to be an integral part of South Africa."[71]

Neither violence nor criticism had any effect. On May 15 Deputy Development Minister Wilkens condemned those who "belittle steps directed at extending participation of communities." The following month Heunis explained that South Africa had not consulted the people about independence because "it is the prerogative of the government of KwaNdebele to decide on such a matter." At least two more people were killed on the weekend of May 17-18. The next Monday the KwaNdebele Cabinet made all chiefs and headmen swear loyalty, in an effort to isolate the royal family. Although a Minister, Cornelius Mahlangu was not invited. Following the meeting Piet Ntuli exulted: "No one can stop independence now." He refused to disband Mbokotho because "with the riots their work has only just begun. The imbokhoto are being used against the comrades."[72] On the weekend of May 24-25 youths burned the homes and shops of several Ministers and MPs, including Piet Ntuli. The KwaNdebele Youth Congress (KWAYCO) called a stay-away for June 2-4. Clashes between youths and security forces the night before caused many injuries, and Mbokotho kidnaped some youths. Partly because youths stopped buses on June 3 the stay-away was very effective, including all 2,000 civil servants. At least five people were killed during this period, but Skosana still insisted that "the Ndebele people will be celebrating their independence." On June 11 youths attacked security guards at shops, killing three. Piet Ntuli led an Mbokotho retaliation the next day, in which seven to sixteen people died, some shot by Ntuli. The same day South Africa reimposed the Emergency; the KwaNdebele Commissioner of Police added restrictions on June 26, under which more than 300 people were detained. On July 8 a Minister, an MLA, and Mbokotho abducted seven people accused of burning shops and held them for two days. A week later police found the bodies of nine pupils at Kekana Secondary School in Mamelodi. Two survivors described being approached by alleged ANC members offering to take them across the border, who hid them at a "safe house."

When the alleged ANC members returned they shot into the house and burned it. Virtually the entire civil service went on strike that day to protest independence. Security forces raided the royal kraal the same night and interrogated King Mapoch and his son James.[73]

On July 17, Skosana demanded that South Africa withdraw its Commissioner General, apparently because he had talked to Prince James in an attempt to make peace. On July 26 James organized a meeting of youths and headmen, which decided that the stay-away of civil servants and primary school pupils should end in two days. He also sued to bar Piet Ntuli from the Assembly. By this time neighboring whites were sufficiently upset at the disruption of their labor supply that the Elands River Farmers Association approached the government. On July 21 religious leaders declared their opposition to independence. The PFP called for a commission of inquiry. The majority parties in the Houses of Delegates and Representatives threatened to block legislation granting independence. A local priest kept a diary of 160 deaths in the homeland between May 12 and July 25, which he attributed in equal parts to security forces, Mbokotho, and the comrades. The Bureau of Information estimated that only eighteen people had been killed in the first four weeks of the Emergency, which it blamed on urban "radical elements" motivated by "no purpose other, apparently, than to stimulate unrest." Yet the Commissioner General was still promising independence in December and characterizing the situation as a "purely domestic power struggle."[74]

Although both governments appeared impervious to pressure, the tide turned significantly when Piet Ntuli was murdered by a car bomb as he left Skosana's residence on the night of July 29. The next day 200 youths marched on Ntuli's Bar Lounge; his relatives responded with gunfire, killing one and wounding sixteen. Another ten were injured when they tried to burn a government car. A front-page article in the *Washington Post* vividly described the jubilation.

> For four heady days cattle have been slaughtered for huge bar-
> becue feasts. People have danced in the streets with slogans
> pinned to their clothing saying things such as, "Liberty, freedom,
> equality—the tyrant is dead." Bus drivers have taken groups of
> singing, chanting youths on free rides around the territory.[75]

Although the ANC took credit for the assassination, many attributed it to the KwaNdebele Cabinet or Pretoria. Ntuli had been charged with murder and assault; during a recent arrest police had found fifty stolen cars and many weapons at his house. He was buried secretly at a farm on August 1. Police concluded their investigation on September 11 without charging anyone.[76]

The press used the occasion to lambaste South Africa. The *Guardian* wrote that "the imminent, induced delivery of KwaNdebele at this highly sensitive stage...proves that the ruling Afrikaner Nationalists are lying in their teeth when they claim apartheid is on its way out." The *Sowetan* asked "why it is so desperately imperative to grant independence to the ridiculously tiny KwaNdebele?...Ironically, elsewhere people die to gain independence, while in KwaNdebele people die while fighting against independence." The *Sunday Times* warned: "The area is destabilised, divided and increasingly lawless. Worse, it is in danger of offering a first base for revolutionaries intent on rural insurgency." *The Argus* called it a "divisive and self-defeating exercise which South Africa can ill afford." The majority parties in the Houses of Representatives and Delegates again vowed to reject independence. Although the President's Council had passed new security legislation in June over their opposition, Labour Party constitutional spokesman Desmond Lockey said "I don't think they can afford to make that a convention rather than an exception." Helen Suzman said independence "was a rotten idea to begin with but now it has caused a lot of bloodshed." The UDF denounced the "sham independence scheme" as "totally unacceptable." Local white farmers sought an end to the violence, according to Abraham Viljoen, Pretoria District chairman of the Agricultural Union and twin brother of the former Army Chief of Staff.[77]

The assassination deepened rifts within the homeland. Prince Cornelius changed his mind about independence: "I can see now that the people are totally opposed to it. I don't know how the other ministers feel, but I know that Piet Ntuli's death has shaken them." Skosana's more than twenty sons and daughters (by five wives) all strongly opposed independence. Peter, nineteen, a leader of the "comrades," said Mbokotho had beaten him for eight hours without any intervention by his father, whom he had not seen for months. Ntuli had dominated his father. "Now that Ntuli is dead I think my father will back away from independence." Following a meeting between the Cabinet and the chiefs on August 1, Skosana conceded: "If possible, we will go for independence on 11 December, but we are now trying to get a second mandate from the people." Minister of Citizen Liaison and Information F.K. Mahlangu insisted that "the feeling was not one of rejection but of the need to inform the people of the issues." On August 7 the Legislative Assembly voted to disband Mbokotho. Indeed, F.K. Mahlangu claimed it had already been dissolved and conceded that some Ministers now opposed independence "because of pressure." "If the independence issue is the cause of the unrest—and that is debatable—I personally would agree to the postponement of independence if it meant saving souls."[78]

King Mapoch, who controlled twenty-one of the seventy-two Assembly members, declared:

> There can be no independence without seeing a constitution first.... [The Cabinet] should have consulted the people first and not forced them to take what they don't want....If they do not listen to my counselling, they are declaring war on my people.

> To me it looks as if they are fighting me through my people for refusing independence.

He rejected UDF support, however: "this was an internal matter and we would solve it in our own way." On August 8 Prince James convened a meeting of 120 headmen and youth and community leaders to persuade pupils to return to school. When the group inevitably discussed independence, James expressed his anger at being ignored. "The royalty is more respected by the people than the KwaNdebele or the South African governments." Three days later 200 independence opponents were released from detention.[79]

On August 12 the Legislative Assembly met beneath a gallery vocally opposed to independence. During the discussion of unrest Prince James proclaimed: "The people have sent me to tell the meeting that they were not consulted and would not accept independence, which they do not want." Some MPs tried to block discussion on the ground that independence was not on the agenda (which listed the police and raises for civil servants). Works Minister K. Mtsweni moved postponement, but the audience was determined, and Paradise Mahlangu (the new Interior Minister) urged discussion. Every speaker said his constituency opposed independence. This prompted all the Ministers to disclaim responsibility for the idea and blame each other. Skosana sat silently until the end of the meeting, with his head in his hands. "I am a messenger of this house. I ran as instructed and executed all duties I had to perform. Today I am damned to be a criminal. Today even young children point their fingers at me. If nobody wants it, I can't force it on them." Assembly Speaker Solly Mahlangu closed the debate.

> Not one of you said independence was all right and should go ahead. Independence is being uprooted and eradicated with all its roots and thrown into the deep ocean. I am of the opinion that the house is quite unanimous with regard to independence. It can now be reported to Pretoria that the KwaNdebele legislative assembly has indicated that the KwaNdebele people do not agree with independence and will not opt for it.

He outlawed Mbokotho because it lacked both a constitution and royal approval. "I do not want to hear anything about this organisation anymore because I am disbanding it and I am not going to allow anybody to say anything about Mbokotho in this assembly." The Assembly instructed Justice Minister A. Mahlangu to draft a law making it a criminal offense to mention the word.[80]

A broad spectrum of South African opinion rejoiced. Helen Suzman advised that "the wisest thing for the Government to do is to drop the whole absurd project," while on the right-wing, HNP leader Jaap Marais agreed that it was wrong to force independence on reluctant people. Chief Buthelezi said he had always opposed the homeland policy, while the UDF called it "a resounding victory against Pretoria's scheme of tearing our country apart," and AZAPO deputy president Nkosi Molala said it "underscored the fact that black people are one."[81] *The Cape Times* hoped "this will end the Verwoerdian dream of independent homelands surrounding a white South Africa" and reverse the incorporation of Moutse. The *Sowetan* was "sure that KwaNdebele has set a precedent that will be joyously followed by other homeland people." *The Natal Witness* expressed relief that "sanity had prevailed" and hoped "that the Government now will relinquish, once and for all, any other schemes for homeland independence." *The Argus* said KwaNdebele had "suffered enough from the burden of National ideological traumas." The *New Nation* called it "a watershed in the fight against apartheid in all its forms." *The Sunday Star* noted the irony that "on the day President Botha was preaching the virtues of mini-states such as Liechtenstein and Andorra, South Africa's new bantustan administered some timely cold water to the further fragmentation of the country." *City Press* declared triumphantly: "Apartheid is a lie. And no lie lives forever."[82]

But the real situation was more ambiguous. The Department of Constitutional Development and Planning liaison officer refused to comment until Skosana made a formal statement, and Minister Heunis expressed doubt that the decision was final. F.K. Mahlangu (acting Chief Minister as Skosana's diabetes worsened) agreed that "good leaders listen to their people." But he was pleased that the homeland would retain R6-8 million originally earmarked for independence celebrations. He denied that government was responsible for the "unwarranted actions" of the "privately owned" Mbokotho.

Skosana fired Police Commissioner C.M. van Niekerk, blaming the security forces for Ntuli's murder and angry that van Niekerk refused to arrest the royal family. His replacement, Brig. Hertzog Lerm, had a different style.

> One of my first aims is to get the entire area in order, foil lawlessness and make the homeland governable again.... I want to issue a firm warning to the elements of troubleshooters. No intimidation, incitement, dissoluteness, hooliganism and thuggery will be tolerated. I am prepared to listen to residents' problems and grievances, but will root out violence with all the power and machinery at my disposal.

He issued orders prohibiting non-residents from entering KwaNdebele, school-age children from being in KwaNdebele unless their parents were residents or they were enrolled, ownership of tires and fuel, travel on public transport without payment, and the delivery of any goods to the homeland without government permission. He imposed a 9 p.m.–5 a.m. curfew. He forbade anyone to "play, loiter, or aimlessly remain on any public road." He severely restricted funerals of unrest victims: only on weekdays and indoors, speeches only by ordained ministers, no political speeches, flags, banners, placards, pamphlets, posters, or public address systems, only one deceased, no more than 200 mourners, and no longer than four hours. All gatherings other than church services and government meetings required permission.[83]

KwaNdebele soon began equivocating. F.K. Mahlangu reaffirmed on September 8 that it had abandoned independence "in accordance with the wishes of its people." "The whole situation also demonstrated to us that people are very good judges of their own needs. It is only in a democratic society that a government can heed the wishes of its people. What happened here proves that KwaNdebele is such a society." At a meeting seeking investment in Ekandustria the same week, however, three Ministers denied there had been a final decision because independence had not been put to a vote. Skosana was seeking legal advice about this interpretation. Violence in KwaNdebele was part of the unrest throughout South Africa and not attributable to independence.[84]

After meeting Heunis on September 17, Skosana sent him a memorandum of complaints against the Ndzundza royal house. Chief Mapoch was a "man of advanced age," whose sons James and Cornelius were "taking advantage of this situation." Cornelius had left school after Standard 6 and joined a gang of car thieves. He assaulted his father and supported M.K. Mahlangu against Piet Ntuli. James had developed "strong radical tendencies" at Turfloop and Ingoya Universities and was "spiritual leader of the Comrades." Cornelius sought to establish a Ndzundza kingdom, even though it was only one of six chieftainships and junior to Manala. KwaNdebele had remained peaceful through the first quarter of 1986, despite the absence of a homeland police force, because vigilante groups maintained "strict discipline." Unrest was caused by "UDF, ANC and other radical movements," which "plan to substitute the National State Government structure with 'People's rule, People's courts, People's education and Village Committees.'" The comrades held mass meetings under King Mapoch. "Cabinet attempts to ban these meetings were unsuccessful because of the intervention by the Commissioner General Mr van der Merwe and the Commissioner of Police, Brigadier van Niekerk, who were supporting the meetings." The Cabinet "is strongly opposed to being prescribed to in conducting politics."

The new Police Commissioner soon followed regulations with actions, raiding the royal kraal in the first week of October and arresting M.K. Mahlangu and Tim Skosana, one of Simon's sons. Later that month Heunis failed to persuade Simon Skosana to talk to King Mapoch and Princes Cornelius and James. The following month police detained James and Andries Mahlangu and ten others, including the homeland's deputy sheriff and the secretary general of the Ndzundza tribal authority, and seized six years of tribal records. The Pretoria Supreme Court ordered their return a year later, but some were never recovered. This initiated the campaign to substitute Manala for Ndzundza as the royal house.[85]

On November 16 Skosana denied PFP charges that the detentions were an "ominous sign" of the continuing commitment to independence. "Should this be the case I would be misleading the people of KwaNdebele and nothing is further from the truth." The next day he died of diabetes. The civil service protested the detentions by launching its third major strike that day. The state funeral was guarded by a large security force but attracted few mourners. Klaas Mtsweni, Minister of Works and independence proponent, was appointed acting Chief Minister. Ten days after Skosana's death the Assembly elected Majozi George Mahlangu as the new Chief Minister by forty-one votes to twenty-five for Prince James, who had been released from detention only two days earlier. George was a thirty-five-year-old businessman with a law diploma from the University of Zululand. The Transvaal Attorney General was investigating him for shooting a youth to death and participating with Piet Ntuli in the January mass abduction and shooting eight youths to death from their car. But George said he "had no attitude" toward Mbokotho since it "was banned... and no longer exists." He was silent about independence.[86]

Moutse in the Supreme Court: 1986

At the end of February 1986 Lebowa had challenged the excision of Moutse on the grounds that South Africa had failed to consult Lebowa, any meetings had omitted its Cabinet and Chief Minister, the State President had made up his mind in advance, the operative resolutions invoked the wrong laws, and retroactive attempts to cure those errors failed.[87] On May 28, 120 Moutse residents travelled to Pretoria to hear the case argued before Justice H. van Dyk (although most were excluded from court). Police dispersed a silent protest in Church Square by a dozen men holding placards opposing incorporation of Moutse into "any part of the homeland system," arresting two.[88] Justice van Dyk (who had rejected the Magopa challenge to removal three years earlier) dismissed the application on June 27, ruling that Moutse had been properly excised in 1980 and the excision had been retroactively validated in 1983 (rendering superfluous the second retroactive validation in 1985).

In July the Department of Foreign Affairs produced 20,000 copies of a twenty-four-page glossy pamphlet on "The Moutse Issue," at a cost of more than R12,000, to correct "the distortion of the facts and misrepresentation." The 1986 incorporation decision was of "at least ten years' standing." Government acted because the parties "had failed to reach agreement after negotiations stretching back for many years. Finality had become urgently necessary for stability and sound regional government." North Sotho and Ndebele were two of "South Africa's many minority communities," which had "migrated several centuries ago into what is today South Africa." Their dispersion and intermixing "prompted the South African government to suggest political cohesion or amalgamation in one form or another in the interests of effective local and regional government. The Ndebeles would have none of it, however." Moutse was adjacent to KwaNdebele but separated from

Lebowa by 30 kilometers of farms "owned and cultivated by Whites for generations." Because of its proximity "administration from Siyabuswa would be
more direct and therefore more practical." "To allay any fears they might
have about their rights in the new dispensation," Government assured that
Moutse people would retain South African citizenship, be able to use North
Sotho in schools "where appropriate," and suffer no discrimination in the
issuance of trading licenses. It sought "to avoid any unnecessary disruption
of national life in the territory during and after the transfer." The Supreme
Court had rejected Lebowa's objection to the excision.

On May 19 Chief Mathebe sued South Africa, KwaNdebele, and Lebowa
to invalidate the incorporation.[89] His founding affidavit stressed Moutse's
long settlement, prosperity, and ethnic composition. The Northern Sotho
were much more closely related to Sotho than Ndebele, who required male
circumcision, flogged adults in public, and denied votes to women. John
Dugard, his advocate, recalled being criticized for invoking apartheid ideology, but TRAC fieldworker Joanne Yawitch said the few leaders who
understood the argument did not care, so desperate were they to leave
KwaNdebele.[90] Moutse feared Ndebele would replace their language, they
would lose South African citizenship when the homeland took independence, and businessmen would be denied licenses. Incorporation and
impending independence had increased violence. Because the only reason
for incorporation was to reward KwaNdebele for accepting independence,
the State President had been guided by an ulterior purpose.

The applicant submitted several supporting affidavits. A Wits regional
planning lecturer described the ethnic composition of Moutse. The chairman
of the Principals' Council asserted that ninety-nine percent of the 770 Moutse
teachers refused to accept transfer to KwaNdebele. The author of the definitive history of the Pedi documented the absence of any Ndebele claim to
Moutse. Joanne Yawitch listed forty-two violent incidents over the previous
six months involving more than 1,150 people, at least twenty-seven of whom
had died. R.F. Magolego, a Moutse attorney, described the dramatic increase
in criminal prosecutions for political activity. The last affidavit detailed a
shooting directed by Skosana and Ntuli.

Dugard argued on November 25 before a gallery full of Moutse chiefs,
elders, and youths and Lebowa MPs. Government could not rely on "geographic contiguity," which had been disregarded in constructing other
homelands. The first priority in consolidation was ethnic units. Education had
been disrupted by incorporation; fewer than five percent of Moutse teachers
accepted transfer to KwaNdebele. Violence was new to Moutse and entirely
attributable to incorporation. I.W.B. de Villiers responded for the state that
"one of the inevitable consequences of the consolidation of the homelands
was the violation of certain basic rights," including suffrage and citizenship.
KwaNdebele had never been exclusively Ndebele. The boundaries of
national states took account of factors like tribes, communities, and territorial authorities.[91]

Justice T.T. Spoelstra took just a week to dismiss the action.[92] Ethnicity, language and custom did not determine the composition of self-governing areas. He refused to review the State President's proclamation. The National States Constitution Act anticipated that "it would be necessary for the State President to sacrifice the principle of ethnicity to the requirements of suitability and effective administration." *Legislation* had excised Moutse from Lebowa. "Insofar as unreasonableness is the issue, it therefore drops out of consideration. It is not for me to pass judgment about whether that decision was good or bad, desirable or undesirable, wise or unwise."

> The dissatisfaction of the North Sotho population in Moutse is understandable. I do, however, agree with Mr de Villiers that in any case where one ethnic group is placed under the authority of another majority group, who differ from them ethnically, it could lead to dissatisfaction. It is apparent that one is forced to come to the conclusion that the legislature should have taken those facts into consideration when it placed Article 1(2) in the law books and that the legislature, in spite of this real possibility, granted the State President very wide powers.

Recognizing the importance of the case, he immediately granted leave to appeal. To show they were undefeated, the Moutse Civic Association, Moutse Youth Congress, and KwaNdebele Youth Congress held a press conference in Johannesburg declaring their determination to remain part of South Africa and rejecting the policy of separate development.[93]

The Struggle Against Independence: 1987

In January KwaNdebele expelled St. Oliver's Catholic Mission (whose priest had documented the previous year's violence). The Chief Minister seized documents and vehicles at the Ndzundza Tribal Authority and closed it, assigning its functions to a magistrate. Prince James successfully challenged this in court on February 17, but as he left the courthouse, KwaNdebele police arrested him for holding an illegal gathering. At his trial police detained Prince Cornelius (who had been dismissed from the Cabinet) and twenty-five tribal leaders and MLAs. Government removed Solly Mahlangu as Assembly Speaker. In April Nicholas de Villiers of the Legal Resources Centre was detained while seeking bail for the detainees. Andries Kuhn, divisional commissioner of police, accused him of entering the homeland with a view to bringing about the violent overthrow of the governments of KwaNdebele and South Africa. He was released after three days when the LRC sought an interdict.[94]

At the end of the month the Assembly (supported by a majority of Ndzundza members) dismissed Prince James and Solly Mahlangu from their positions in the Tribal Authority, automatically expelling them from

Parliament. They had been in detention for six weeks. Prince Andries was in hiding to avoid being detained a third time. On May 4 the Assembly unanimously dismissed Prince Cornelius for refusing to discuss his letter warning the South African government against independence. Two days later it unanimously endorsed independence, rescinding the (equally unanimous) decision nine months earlier on the ground that independence had not been on the agenda that day and there had been no formal vote. The Chief Minister prepared to reopen discussions with South Africa, hoping to backdate independence to December 11, 1986. Work continued on the capital and a R3.75 million "independence" stadium.[95]

UDF acting publicity secretary Murphy Morobe called the decision a declaration of war on the people of South Africa. The South African Institute of Race Relations denounced it as "sheer madness... the height of political irresponsibility... dangerous nonsense." But Chris Heunis replied that "the government is prepared to consider the wishes of the people of the territories." Information Minister F.K. Mahlangu said the people had been asked to speak against independence but no one had done so. This was a time of "rejoicing" for residents "scattered for years striving for their own country," who now would take their "rightful place in the row of nations." "Let me assure all who have any interest in the right of nations to decide for themselves, that this decision in the Legislative Assembly followed weeks of consultation with the people themselves, by means of public meetings held throughout KwaNdebele." "The threat of unrest and agitation against KwaNdebele's proposed independence came not from Ndebeles, but from outsiders," especially Black Sash, which "lives in Parktown yet they want to speak for the citizens of KwaNdebele."[96]

Violence escalated after the declaration of independence. Civil servants went on strike. Pupils boycotted schools, three of which were burned. Vigilantes responded by raiding five villages and beating any pupils they found. Victims identified the Information Minister and two MLAs among the attackers. Vigilantes also destroyed the bar of an anti-independence advocate. A week after the decision thirty-five South African and KwaNdebele police attacked the royal kraal, arresting Prince Cornelius's wife (daughter of the Swazi king), beating Prince James's brother-in-law, arresting and beating Andries's younger brother, and forcing King Mapoch to flee. Some 2,000 people had been detained, including a *Sunday Star* reporter, photographer, and driver, who publicized the brutality they witnessed. There was a general stayaway two days later. The international press picked up the story, although information was hard to obtain. On May 26, however, the Chief Minister reaffirmed the decision. The people demanded "independence, self-respect and self-realisation." "We see ourselves as an independent nation and all that remains to be done is to celebrate our independence."[97]

Later that month Prince Cornelius told a press conference that he sought to meet the State President on behalf of his father. On May 28, however, the

SAP detained him and Andries outside the British Consulate in Johannesburg, where they had just briefed western diplomats, and handed them over to the KwaNdebele police. Britain filed a formal protest. Soon afterwards anti-independence activists erected a roadblock at the KwaNdebele border. When police ordered commuter buses to proceed the drivers refused, fearing recognition; three were arrested, and the others went on strike.[98]

Opening Parliament on May 19 the State President said George Mahlangu and his cabinet were the "legitimate leaders and representatives" of KwaNdebele. "The Government will not stand in the way of communities that seek greater autonomy or even independence." Chris Heunis added: "The further handling of the matter will be dealt with through negotiations between the two governments."[99] Perhaps embarrassed by *Weekly Mail* and *Sunday Star* articles implicating Mahlangu and the KwaNdebele police in violence, however, Botha backed away. After meeting Mahlangu on June 9, Botha declared that "the government of KwaNdebele must consider some or other acceptable method of demonstrating that it has the support of the broad population in its striving for independence." Helen Suzman called for a "free and fair referendum including women," angering Information Minister F.K. Mahlangu, who told her to "concern herself with her White voters and not with the affairs of KwaNdebele." "She was against us when we wanted a homeland and now she is against us when we seek independence. Does she want us to be slaves forever?"[100]

On June 19 KwaNdebele Police Commissioner Lerm prohibited James and Cornelius Mahlangu from participating "in any campaign, project or action aimed at disrupting or delaying the contemplated independence of KwaNdebele" or attending any "gathering organised, convened or held to resist or oppose any action or proposed action of any member of the Cabinet or the Government of KwaNdebele." Under threat of litigation he withdrew the regulations. The KwaNdebele police had returned Cornelius to the SAP, who were detaining him. By the end of June KwaNdebele released all but twenty-seven detainees on condition that each sign a statement that "I…undertake, voluntary [sic] and without being subjected to any compulsion" not to oppose independence. Early in July Cornelius and James were charged under the Internal Security Act for speeches allegedly made at the royal kraal (although the Attorney General later dismissed charges against Cornelius). Released on R2,500 bail, Cornelius was redetained within hours for allegedly attending an unlawful meeting. Brig. Lerm also served them with an order prohibiting the actions in the withdrawn regulations. In the first ten days of July eight people were detained at the royal kraal. On July 21 Justice Roux ordered KwaNdebele to release Cornelius. The "somewhat erratic behaviour towards the detainee in the past of having arrested him and released him and rearrested him and then released him" required explanation. The claim that new information justifying detention emerged in the two hours after his last release "strikes me as being such an improbability as I must reject it." The police had "not seen fit to give instances and dates which would enable the applicant to dispute [their reasons]....I feel that if a discretion is exercised on no facts which justify it, it is a decision which is subject to attack on review." More than eighteen months after the mass abduction and torture, the Transvaal Attorney General finally charged George Mahlangu and two other Ministers with a trivial offense, allowing them to avoid trial by paying R50 admission of guilt fines.[101]

George Mahlangu pursued his attack on the royal family by ordering the Ndzundza Tribal Authority (NTA) to replace the nine dismissed for anti-independence activities. Many likely candidates were in detention. King Mapoch, however, refused to convene the Tribal Authority without holding a general meeting, which was impossible because its chairman, Prince James, was barred from any event at which the government was criticized. The nine remaining NTA members then held their own meeting, nominated K.S. Mahlangu to replace James as chair, appointed nine more to create a quorum, and appointed nine pro-independence members to the Assembly. Andries Mahlangu briefed lawyers to challenge this. Solly Mahlangu sued to reverse his removal as Speaker and expulsion from the Assembly on the ground that those actions were taken in committee stage, not general session; he won reinstatement four months later.[102]

During the July budget debate, PFP MP Peter Soal declared that the reign of terror prevented KwaNdebele from satisfying Botha's condition of free choice and detailed the abuses. Gerrit Viljoen called this characterization "deplorable, irresponsible and in many ways mean" and condemned Soal's comparison of George Mahlangu to Idi Amin. The Chief Minister was a "well-educated, responsible person who has impressed" the government. A few weeks later Mahlangu signed the KwaNdebele Public Safety Act authorizing himself (as Minister of Law and Order) to "order the removal of any tribe," "restrict the presence of any person to a particular place," and "prohibit any organization or membership of such an organization; the furtherance in any manner, of the objects of such an organization; and the publication or dessemination [sic] of the contents of any speech, utterance, writing or statement."

In early September Princes James and Cornelius were tried on charges of intimidation and public violence. Immediately after the hearing their lawyer, Nano Matlala, was charged with intimidation and ordered not to participate in any activity opposing independence. Threatened with an interdict, KwaNdebele agreed to stop enforcing the Emergency regulations.[103] When the PFP again asserted in Parliament that "the majority of the people are not being given a fair opportunity to express their opinion" about independence, the Minister questioned "how many people that hon member could have met in two days with a view to forming an overall impression of what the people of KwaNdebele want." "The Government belives that states have the right to opt for independence. KwaNdebele expressed such a wish. The Government accepted it." The only dispute concerned whether the president would be a nominal head of state or have executive authority.[104]

At the end of the month the Chief Minister invited the South African press to lunch at the Carlton Hotel and asked them to report fairly. He acknowledged that he restricted pensions, residential sites, and trading licenses to KwaNdebele citizens. The people had demonstrated their desire for independence when the Assembly accepted it in principle in 1982 and in the 1984 election. "The opposition to independence was perpetrated by only a few individuals....everything is now done. We are only waiting for the South African government." In response to the press, Botha's office reiterated the earlier condition. Nevertheless, Mahlangu appeared on television the next day to advocate independence. A day later, however, his opponents launched the UDF-affiliated Congress of Traditional Leaders of South Africa (CONTRALESA). The founders were mostly Ndebele and Moutse chiefs opposed to independence, including Cornelius, Andries, and M.K. Mahlangu; the interim chairman was the son of Moutse Chief Mathebe. In a surprising alliance Peter Mokaba, president of the South African Youth Congress, helped organize the group.[105]

Moutse in the Appelate Division: 1987-88

On September 7 the Appellate Division heard Lebowa's challenge to the excision of Moutse, rejecting it three weeks later.[106] Lebowa complained that the Prime Minister had not consulted it when excising the territory in 1980, as the National States Constitution Act required? The 1983 legislation made consultation superfluous. Lebowa claimed that the 1983 legislation amended the wrong proclamation? The 1985 legislation retrospectively corrected this. Lebowa claimed that punctuation in the 1985 statute subverted this effect?

> [It] quoted no authority for the proposition that words in parenthesis were to be differently interpreted depending on whether the parenthesis was indicated by brackets rather than by commas or semi-colons.... [P]unctuation is a matter to which little or no regard is had in the interpretation of statutes.... [A]n interpretation supported only by the use of a particular punctuation mark must inevitably yield to one based on the intention of the Legislature as it appears from the meaning of the words used read in their context.... Assuming that in linguistic theory brackets can have such an effect on the meaning of words, I can do no better than to quote the following dictum by Fry LJ in Duke of Devonshire: "Now, whether brackets can or cannot be looked at if they appear on the Parliament Roll, I express no opinion; but...in the present case...I must read through them and pay no attention to them, for the sense is too strong for me to pause at these miserable brackets."

The defeat attracted little media attention.[107]

This left Chief Mathebe's appeal as the only legal challenge to incorporation.[108] He had been denied permission to hold a meeting the previous April to report on its progress. At the end of August he joined the secretary of the Moutse Civic Association (a migrant laborer) and a white reporter in challenging the Emergency regulations, persuading the homeland to withdraw them.[109] Moutse teachers had been compelled to accept employment by KwaNdebele; businessmen, taxi drivers, and car owners had been ordered to obtain licenses in KwaNdebele; pensioners were told they had to have KwaNdebele citizenship. When Chief Mathebe and other leaders refused to attend the opening of the KwaNdebele police station in Dennilton, kitskonstabels hijacked buses and forced their passengers to attend. The senior KwaNdebele policeman, Lt. Fourie, and his son were assassinated near Dennilton, and the police station was attacked. Many people were detained and some tortured. Three members of CONTRALESA and two executive members of the Moutse Civic Association were abducted, among others; the Supreme Court rejected their application for an interdict. In February 1988 the Moutse magistrate banned all indoor and outdoor meetings until the end of March.[110]

Discontent with "homeland consolidation" was expressed by another constituency, more difficult to ignore than Moutse. Sixty-three Rust der Winter whites were angered when government appraisers appeared without warning in early December in anticipation of expropriating their farms for incorporation into KwaNdebele (another bribe for independence). The Deputy Director of Land Affairs rejected a protest by the Transvaal Agricultural Union, even though its chair was the twin brother of the Army Chief of Staff. In one of the stranger political alliances, the Boers were championed by the Progressive Federal Party, which condemned the "government's juggling with land and people for ideology" and invoked apartheid principles: "Many of the farmworkers in Rust der Winter are not Ndebeles and they have no desire to live in a homeland controlled by Ndebeles." The PFP was joined by the Conservative Party, which excoriated the Nationalists for "progressively" giving away South Africa and opposed the incorporation of Moutse, complaining of "democracy utterly destroyed, I could almost say violated." Gerrit Viljoen expressed amazement that "the farmers of that area…are the kind of people who represent the PFP's standpoint" and asked why the CP opposed making KwaNdebele economically viable "if, according to the CP's partition policy, Black people from the existing metropolitan areas have to be resettled in Black areas."[111]

Government won approval for the incorporation over substantial resistance in the other two houses. When the opposition leader in the House of Representatives declared his party's opposition to "ethnic regional government," Viljoen called it "an experience" to hear him "as champion of the interests of White land-owners." "Almost like the Jews, the Ndebele have actually lived as a widely dispersed people, and when a national state was created for them, they 'came home', as it were, in large numbers to an area which had previously been the historic KwaNdebele area."[112]

Fearing interference with the many Moutse residents who planned to attend oral argument on Tuesday, March 9, Chief Mathebe had his attorney, James Sutherland, write the KwaNdebele police on February 26. Receiving no reply, he telephoned the State Attorney on February 29 and was told to deal with SAP Col. Stopforth, who demanded the names of every participant. The State Attorney asked Sutherland "why persons other than myself should attend the appeal because…the people would not, in any event, understand the proceedings." On Friday, March 4, the KwaNdebele police refused to allow the departure of more than a single bus containing chiefs, headmen, and councilors. Sutherland filed an urgent application in Pretoria on Saturday morning.

At 4 p.m. Justice de Klerk ordered the police to allow Sutherland to enter Moutse, permit four busloads to leave, and demand no names.[113] Sutherland and Stephen Langbridge, another attorney, served the order on the police in KwaMhlanga. When they had driven Chief Mathebe home about 7 p.m. they learned that the Police Commissioner had issued another order eight hours earlier. They asked a local policeman to contact him but were instructed to return to KwaMhlanga. Reaching it at 10:30 p.m. they were told by Lt. Jones to contact Col. Stopforth, who had heard about the court decree but doubted its effect given the new order. The Commissioner now allowed no one except Chief Mathebe and ten others to leave Moutse. Sutherland telephoned Denis Kuny SC, who had argued the first application, and arranged to meet at his Johannesburg home that night. He also telephoned the Pretoria Supreme Court Registrar to schedule a judge to hear another application on Sunday morning. Langbridge phoned Stopforth at 1:35 a.m. to warn him of the 8 a.m. hearing. Justice de Klerk invalidated the second police order.[114] Before argument began in Bloemfontein on Tuesday both applications were lodged with the Appellate Division. Because there were only forty places in the public gallery, the 200 spectators rotated during the day-long argument. Those outside had no toilet facilities. All wore traditional dress, even the young comrades who otherwise detested it (making do with synthetic leopard skins and nothing else).[115]

Three weeks later the Appellate Division allowed the appeal.[116] The Prime Minister had acted for impermissible purposes. "It is not for the reasons of effective administration that national states are created; the purpose is completely different, namely the political development of national units." Only an eighth of Moutse people were South Ndebele, and more than sixty percent were North Sotho. The vast majority opposed incorporation. Government had disregarded ethnicity in the expectation that dissatisfied Moutse residents would move to Immerpan/Saliesloot. Deputy Development Minister Wilkens had disclosed that the primary reasons for incorporation were geographic proximity and infrastructure. But "if administrative considerations make it impracticable to establish or expand a self-governing territory in a particular area, there is nothing in the Act which obliges the State President to proceed none the less...."

Chief Mathebe said the decision was "too wonderful to be true." His nephew John added: "We were about to be swallowed by KwaNdebele. The court took us from its very throat." Godfrey Mathebe said "the people will have to decide" about reincorporation into Lebowa. Sheep and goats were slaughtered in celebration. John Dugard politely declined the people's traditional expression of gratitude—another wife. A *Sowetan* cartoon showed a white judge protecting Moutse women and children from a bearded George Mahlangu. "The country can be truly grateful for the Supreme Court," said the *Evening Post*. "However much its authority has been whittled down by Government statutes, it stands as a beacon of truth and justice."[117]

This was not the end of the matter. Less than a month later Chris Heunis announced that government would introduce new legislation to effect the incorporation but refused to reveal the bill's content to avoid judicial challenge. TRAC denounced the move as a "flagrant disregard for the decision of the highest court of the land." Lebowa, which had invited Moutse to rejoin it, condemned the "mockery of justice." The *Sowetan* called it "cynical," an "insult...to the courts and the people of Moutse."

> All that courts can do now is give judgments on the technicalities of writing laws—nothing more. And immediately the courts point out that a law is badly written, the Government simply goes back to its drawing board to rewrite it, following the court's prescriptions.

The Labour Party opposed the legislation (suggesting it would not pass the tricameral Parliament). John Dugard urged the State President to respect the court's judgment. Botha replied that Dugard, a longtime critic of the courts, was the last person to insist that their judgments be followed.[118] In the House of Representatives the majority Labour Party also hoped that government would "heed the Appeal Court decision and that Moutse will remain part of South Africa."[119] And the Deputy Minister of Environment Affairs told the House of Delegates that Moutse preferred to be governed by South Africa.[120] Viljoen appeared to concede Moutse's objection: "The tensions between the Pedi-orientated and the Ndebele-orientated people living in Moutse serves as further evidence of the antipathy existing amongst different ethnic groups."[121]

Three weeks later a PFP member of the House of Delegates asked whether the government "plans to ride roughshod over the wishes, not only of the people of Moutse, but also over a decision of the Appeal Court?... [T]he Government... has had a history of riding roughshod over the decisions of appeal courts."[122] The next day an opposition member of the House of Assembly warned of the "crisis of legitimacy that our courts are facing, particularly after the pronouncement on the Sharpeville Six [whose death sentence was upheld]....[T]he courts do not enjoy high legitimacy amongst urban Blacks." "[A]mong rural Blacks they do still have considerable authority," but if government overruled the AD decision "the confidence they still have in the courts, will then be lost."[123] Helen Suzman took up the attack on J.C. Heunis, Minister of Constitutional Development and Planning.

> *Suzman:* I want to warn the hon the Minister that if he goes ahead with the announced plan of introducing legislation—and he would make it retrospective—in order to reverse the effect of the favourable court decision which the Moutse people obtained against their incorporation into KwaNdebele, he will deliver a real death blow to any hope of true negotiation.... The Government has said on many occasions that people who do not agree with their policy have recourse to the courts of law. The Moutse people took the hon the Minister at his word.... Moutse is a very high profile case.... [The Minister] accused me of taking information to the British Prime Minister, and that is true....
>
> *Heunis:* You assisted in making it a high-profile case.
>
> *Suzman:* Of course! That is the way to stop such actions. I will do so on every possible occasion....
>
> *Heunis:* No one disputes, not only the right, but also the responsibility, of Parliament to take the necessary remedial steps to put matters right when courts interpret Parliamentary legislation in ways which Parliament does not regard as being in accordance with its own objectives.... [W]hat is to become of [Suzman's] party's opposition to foreign interference in the domestic affairs of South Africa?... Quite probably she spoke about that in Moscow too [Interjections.] I am sure she also spoke about it in Red China.[124]

The Minister reiterated this position in the House of Representatives.

I accept the finding of the court and therefore also the right of the court to interpret laws of Parliament. If any court gives an interpretation of a law, however, other than that contemplated by the legislature, it is the legislature's duty to rectify that law so that its intention is clear.... The legislative authority in the country is sovereign.... [I]f this were no longer the case...we would then no longer be able to leave democracy in the hands of the people who sent us here. We would be placing it in the hands of appointed people and this would be fatal.[125]

Two months after the judgment the State President appointed Justice F.L.H. Rumpff to conduct a commission of inquiry into the "constitutional and political future of Moutse and into the appropriate method to determine and amend the boundaries of the self-governing territories." Rumpff, who had earlier chaired a commission that recommended against incorporating KwaNgwane into Swaziland, invited written submissions within three months. After the deadline the Moutse Anti-Reincorporation Committee convened a secret meeting of 200 people, who denounced the inquiry, refused to participate, and threatened to return to court. But Chief Mathebe and the Moutse Civic Association submitted a lengthy memorandum, relating the unhappy history.[126]

At the same time, however, government suffered another rebuff. The previous December it had incorporated the Bloemfontein township Botshabelo into QwaQwa.[127] Government claimed that a thousand inhabitants had attended a July 19 meeting "and enthusiastically supported the incorporation."[128] The township—the second largest in South Africa—had more than twice the homeland's population and was 330 kilometers away, which undermined the geographic contiguity argument invoked for incorporating Moutse. A majority were South Sotho and another fifteen percent Xhosa, whereas eighty percent of QwaQwa was North Sotho speaking. About seventy percent of Bothsabelo residents were under thirty and far less traditional than those of QwaQwa. A survey found three-fourths opposed to incorporation; the threat had stimulated school boycotts. Within weeks a school teacher applied to the Supreme Court to invalidate the action, arguing that the power to "amend" the area of a homeland did not contemplate doubling its population.[129] Because the matter was sub judice, Heunis refused to tell Helen Suzman whether residents had been consulted. During the May 1988 budget debate on agriculture, the PFP opposed incorporation, deploring Botshabelo's miserable living conditions.[130] So did the majority Labour Party in the House of Representatives.[131] Viljoen responded that anyone who chose to settle in Botshabelo should have known it was going to be incorporated into QwaQwa. Furthermore, "it would not have been appropriate for the South African Government to go back on the word it had given the QwaQwa government."[132]

On August 26, 1988, a full bench of the Orange Free State Supreme Court invalidated the incorporation.[133] Although the State President was not required to consult the people being incorporated, his failure to do so was relevant to determining whether he was pursuing the purposes of the National States Constitution Act. Botshabelo was "an artificial town…which came into existence less than a decade ago as a catchment area particularly for urbanized surplus Blacks." The two differed in ethnicity, lifestyle, and culture. QwaQwa lacked any historical claim to Botshabelo. The State President's action was ultra vires because he was promoting the political development of Botshabelo. Although Justice Findlay, concurring, did not wish to

> express any view on underlying policy, the fundamental and far reaching consequences flowing therefrom call for an exercise by this Court of the utmost vigilance and careful scrutiny. Since no

other effective legitimate avenue may be available to safeguard the rights of those so affected, this Court would be failing in its duty if it did not do so. Recognition of this obligation is to be found in those canons which require a strict construction of language used in such enactments where existing rights may be affected....

The state indicated its intention to appeal, prompting more than 50,000 people to demonstrate in Bloemfontein against the incorporation six weeks later.[134] The following year Viljoen maintained that the appeal had "stabilised the *status quo*" and Botshabelo remained incorporated into QwaQwa.[135]

On April 6, 1989—a year after the Appellate Division had invalidated the incorporation of Moutse and six months after the Supreme Court had invalidated the incorporation of Botshabelo—government tabled the Alteration of Boundaries of Self-Governing Territories Bill. "To obviate uncertainty," it empowered the State President to excise any area and incorporate it into a homeland "if he deems it expedient." "[N]o court of law shall be competent to inquire into or pronounce upon the validity of any proclamation." Any prior proclamation, "which would not otherwise be valid, is in point of fact valid." The Joint Committee on Constitutional Development was "unable to reach a consensus on the desirability of the Bill." Deputy Minister of Constitutional Development R.P. Meyer explained that court judgments invalidating legislation "create legal uncertainty" through their "retrospective effect." "In various court cases various criteria have been elevated to become the decisive consideration," such as ethnicity in Moutse and political development in Botshabelo. The "finalisation of the consolidation process" required "a clear criterion being... laid down as the decisive factor." The bill made this "clear criterion" the State President's decision that incorporation was "expedient." Although the press had criticized the bill for "empower[ing] one person, namely the State President, to add any land...this allegation is not correct." Only "a Black area" could be added after "a long process...during which representations may be heard from interested parties" and with the concurrence of all three Houses. The bill would retroactively incorporate Botshabelo into QwaQwa because "the Government of the RSA would be breaking its word if it did not now give effect to this solemn undertaking" to both that homeland and Bophuthatswana; without incorporating Moutse into KwaNdebele, the bill made it far easier for the State President to do so.

The majority parties in the other two houses opposed it. The Labour Party leader urged government to await the outcome of the Botshabelo appeal. J.T. Delport (NP) replied that "a court cannot judge merely on the basis of some or other vague feeling of what is just or fair." "The decision that has to be taken is a political one... but we cannot expect the courts to become involved in political decisions or to answer yes or no to political statements." P.H.P. Gastrow (DP) exploded: "Hypocrites! To hell with the courts! That is exactly what you are saying." The Chair forced him to withdraw "hypocrites."

A DP member of the House of Delegates declared: "There is a court judgment which the NP is attempting, though this Bill, to subvert. That is subversion of the law. That is immoral. It is thoroughly disgusting and we are not prepared to support that kind of cynical, utterly indecent measure."

When his turn came, Gastrow returned to the attack on the Deputy Minister, who "is a lawyer." "[I]n this Bill he is responsible for deliberately undermining the standing of our courts. It is a deliberate attempt to circumvent our Supreme Court…. It is a vote of no confidence in our Supreme Court." He had called the Nationalists "skynheilig" (hypocrites) "to illustrate the fact that those people, who on the one hand pretend to espouse the independence of our courts and support our judiciary, on the other hand come up with legislation which runs directly contrary to that and undermines our whole legal system." Citing a 1985 report by the Human Sciences Research Council, he asserted: "With this step the Government is contributing to the present legitimacy crisis in our judiciary…this hon Deputy Minister is contributing his share to ensure that our Blacks see our judiciary as part of the apartheid state which the Government can use as it chooses to enforce its will on people." The Deputy Minister replied that the courts had produced "two conflicting judgments," showing that they found themselves "in an uncomfortable situation." He did not "in any way want to criticise the judgments of the courts." But their divergence demonstrated that the Bill was necessary to "create legal certainty."

When debate resumed four days later P.G. Soal (DP) emphasized the "outcry from within and without South Africa against the courts losing their competence to inquire. I am aware that certain embassies made representations to the Government on this issue. Within South Africa there were lawyers, pressure groups from commerce and industry and many others…." The Assembly passed the bill 113-20, but the House of Delegates rejected it. The State President asked the House of Representatives to act on it before the dissolution of Parliament on June 12; when they failed to do so, it died.[136]

The Botshabelo appeal was heard on February 15, 1990. Less than two weeks earlier, on the day de Klerk legalized the ANC, he signed an affidavit urging the court to consider new evidence and expressing support for the homelands. During argument the judges suggested the government withdraw the proclamation and issue a new one under other legislation. Nevertheless, they dismissed the appeal on March 1.[137]

As the threat of incorporation into KwaNdebele diminished, Moutse's fragile unity dissolved. Godfrey Mathebe, businessman and former member of the Lebowa Assembly, wished to rejoin that homeland. In April 1989 Chief Gibson Mathebe declared his support before a meeting of 3,000 people. The Moutse Civic Association and Federation of Moutse Youth Congresses resisted.[138] The Rumpff Commission completed its work in January 1989. At the end of 1990 government accepted its recommendations that Moutse 1 and 3 remain under central government control for ten years but Moutse 2 be incorporated into KwaNdebele.[139] John Dugard called this contempt of the Appellate Division decision. In any case, it was hopelessly anachronistic.

Women Join the Struggle Against Independence

The battle over independence had been fought in the streets, political arenas, and media. Now opponents tried a legal strategy. Geoffrey Budlender, of the Legal Resources Centre national office, believed that KwaNdebele disenfranchisement of women was unlawful in the absence of explicit statutory authority (even though white women did not get the vote until 1930, and "coloured" and black men had voted in the Cape when "coloured" and black women could not). The Pretoria office sounded out the many violence victims who sought its protection. After obtaining the support of Ndebele leaders the lawyers interviewed fifteen to twenty women, choosing as plaintiffs those actively involved in local governance. Warned of the risks, they told Budlender: "Our sons are being arrested, our husbands are being arrested…we have to do this." Shots later were fired at their houses. The goal was a new election to turn the Assembly against independence. Lacking any precedents on sex discrimination, Budlender relied on cases about race discrimination. Although he asked the court to invalidate all homeland legislation, he did not expect such relief.

On October 26, 1987 six women sued the State President and the sixteen elected members of the KwaNdebele Legislative Assembly.[140] The founding affidavit described Paulina Machika as a fifty-year-old housewife who was "assisted in bringing this application" by her husband Petrus, a bricklayer. After a 1984 proclamation added sixteen elected members to the KLA the first and only election occurred on November 15–17. Machika had been an elected member of the Morwe Lower Primary School Committee for four years and regularly attended tribal meetings. She was very surprised when she heard on the radio that she could not vote. "I nevertheless went along to the polling station at the tribal office on the day of the election. I saw that young men, who on any basis were junior to me in responsibility and status, were nevertheless allowed to vote." She detailed the cycles of violence following the declarations and retreats from independence, which she strongly opposed because it would deprive her family of South African citizenship, relegating them to "the small impoverished state of KwaNdebele" and subjecting them to "an arbitrary government which does not tolerate any opposition. South Africa is the country in which I was born, and to which I owe allegiance."

The proclamation denying women the right to vote for or be elected to the Assembly was ultra vires. The National States Constitution Act did not empower the State President to discriminate against women. The definition of "voter" was unreasonable because it was partial and unequal; "it involves such oppressive or gratuitous interference with the rights of those subjected to them as could find no justification in the minds of reasonable men [sic]." The democratic goal sought by adding sixteen elected members was defeated by excluding half the population from voting. The other plaintiffs filed similar affidavits. Two married women had been elected to school committees; a widow objected that her twenty-two-year-old son could vote.

The defendants made two arguments: Women traditionally were excluded from politics; and the Assembly demanded that this be included in the constitution. Machika replied that the constitution reflected efforts by nominated Assembly members to maintain their power. No other national state disenfranchised women. The State President had refused to accept the Assembly as representating popular wishes about independence. Because the interests of men and women diverge, an all-male Assembly could not serve women. Two elected Assembly members, named as defendants, supported the plaintiffs. Prince Andries Mahlangu said he always believed there was no justification for excluding women from the franchise or the Assembly. M.K. Mahlangu agreed, adding that he had resigned at the beginning of 1986.

Former Speaker Solly Mahlangu argued that the Assembly franchise never reflected Ndebele custom. When a boy was initiated at about sixteen he became an adult, with all the attendant rights, including marriage and children, and should therefore be able to vote. Since women became adults at initiation, they too should vote. Women traditionally had been excluded from decision-making at the tribal level and thus from territorial authorities based on tribes. As men became labor migrants, however, women assumed greater authority over non-traditional issues, such as schools. Tribal authorities disregarded school committees at their peril. Women also participated in decisions about water, land, agricultural production, roads, clinics, and tribal levies. They were even more essential to national decisions, playing an equal role with men in the May 1986 mass meetings about independence and Mbokotho. Although the fifteen-member Constitutional Committee had recommended that women vote, Skosana had strongly opposed this in the Assembly, silencing the opposition. "From my experience as Speaker, I can state that this reluctance to contradict a senior-ranking person was not unique or unusual. Debate has been very rare in the Legislative Assembly. Once the senior-ranking person has expressed a view, that has generally settled the matter."

Professor W.D. Hammond-Tooke of the Wits Department of Social Anthropology noted that all Bantu-speaking South Africans treated women as inferior in customary matters and excluded them from tribal councils, yet all but KwaNdebele allowed them to vote. Even the government's expert admitted that Ndebele culture had changed radically. Traditional tribal government, more concerned with dispute resolution than administration, could not be the basis for national states, composed of heterogeneous people, many of whom had been moved to their present sites. Homeland governments performed mostly non-traditional functions: schools, pensions, development, markets, labor, police, and road traffic. Because men were working in cities or mines, women, who also were better educated, dominated rural decision-making. Since elections were alien to traditional politics, custom could not be the warrant for modern elections. Non-Ndebele women (more than a quarter of the homeland's population) were disenfranchised by the geographic accident of inclusion in *this* homeland rather than the one to which they belonged ethnically. Conversely, Ndebele women in other homelands enjoyed a franchise their KwaNdebele sisters were denied. Professor Belinda Bozolli of the Wits Sociology Department narrated the history of women's suffrage. Denied the franchise until the end of the nineteenth century, they gained it almost everywhere soon after World War II. The 1952 UN Convention on the Political Rights of Women mandated equal suffrage. By 1978 only four Moslem countries excluded women from the electorate and legislature: Jordan, Kuwait, Saudi Arabia, and Yemen.

During the seven months the lawsuit was pending the struggle continued outside the courtroom. Prince Cornelius was rearrested on October 16, 1987, for intimidating people seeking to attend the KwaMhlanga agricultural show. Justice Myburgh refused to release him. The police had formed a

> genuine opinion about the desirability of the arrest of the detainee... [who] makes no suggestion as to why this police officer would be acting mala fide against him, and he cannot say that the information at his disposal was not sufficient for him to form an opinion genuinely. Then, I have noted that he fails to give any reasons for his alleged absence after the dramatic events from KwaNdebele from 7 to 27 May 1987 when he was arrested. And he really in substance makes no suggestion why the people would be making false affidavits against him disclosing his involvement in these disturbances.[141]

In early November there were reports of increased violence by Mbokotho, which had merely gone underground or joined the KwaNdebele police. Most youths in Uitvlught village had been arrested, and more than 100 were in detention; parents were assaulted for refusing to disclose the whereabouts of their children.[142]

Two incidents exposed the sham of grand apartheid. Four armed white KwaNdebele policemen entered Dawson's Hotel in Johannesburg on November 18, demanded the keys to two rooms, unplugged the hotel telephone, and kidnaped three KwaNdebele members of the South African Youth Congress. Two weeks later Justice Spoelstra (who had rejected Moutse's challenge to incorporation) held that KwaNdebele police had no powers beyond their borders and ordered the men released. The following week KwaNdebele police seized a Pretoria Council of Churches field worker at Jan Smuts Airport and abducted him to KwaMhlanga, where he was detained and tortured.[143]

Within the homeland police showed no restraint. In January 1988 they disrupted a shareholders' meeting of the Siyabuswa Bakery, seizing documents and detaining Sam Skosana (son of the late Chief Minister) and Prince James. In February they abducted Senior Magistrate M.J. Mahlangu from Northern Transvaal, former school circuit inspector E.S. Matjiu, former MLA Charlie Skosana, and four CONTRALESA chiefs. The Police Commissioner ordered King Mapoch and his family not to leave the homeland, talk to reporters, or prepare anything for publication; but the Supreme Court invalidated this two weeks later. Another fifteen chiefs fled the homeland after being threatened with loss of office for opposing independence. In April the KwaNdebele Assembly again followed its South African mentor by passing the Indemnity Act, immunizing from liability Ministers, police, and anyone acting under their authority.[144]

Despite the Appellate Division decision in March invalidating the Moutse incorporation, Chris Heunis opened the KwaNdebele Assembly on April 8 by declaring that the State President was "well-disposed" to independence because he sympathized with the national aspirations of minorities. "[I]ndependence can unite the people so that the country can be developed to the benefit of all." But KwaNdebele would have to "create a favourable climate," "cultivate the right disposition," and demonstrate "orderly government, an effective and purposeful civil service and the maintenance of law and order." Addressing the House of Representatives during his May budget vote, the State President hedged:

> We have moved away from the policy of independent states. We established self-governing regional areas which are now asking for more autonomy and more powers, which are being granted to them. No one, however, is being forced to take independence. In the most recent instance of a community asking to become independent, I warned them to be careful and to make sure that before they accepted independence they had the sense of responsibility and the ability to be independent.[145]

In order to comply the homeland paid R343,000 to a former Atteridgeville mayor and Pretoria businessman, who had performed similar functions in Venda and Transkei, to motivate people to "joyous anticipation of independence." Complicating the situation, M.N. Ramodike, the new Lebowa Chief Minister, proposed to merge with KwaNdebele, perhaps facilitating independence. Heunis denied suggesting this (as Ramodike told his Assembly) but offered to mediate between the homelands. KwaNdebele Information Minister F.K. Mahlangu, however, appeared hostile to the proposal.[146]

The women's suffrage case was argued on April 28. I.W.B. de Villiers SC, appearing for the state, contended that women attained the vote only when the West reached the pinnacle of development. The Bible, Aristotle, and feminists agreed that women remained second-class citizens. It would be wrong to impose Western ideas at the expense of tradition. R.S. Welsh SC, the leading commercial advocate, replied that the court was not being asked to consider religion or philosophy but only whether the State President had validly exercised delegated power. Where de Villiers was florid, theatrical, and long-winded, Welsh was brief, direct, and soft-spoken. The KwaNdebele women who attended were disappointed that their advocate had not been more flamboyant and wanted to speak for themselves.[147]

On May 20 Justice C.F. Eloff upheld the right of women to vote for and serve in the KwaNdebele Assembly and invalidated the 1984 election.[148] He invoked a 1950 Appellate Division case (citing an 1898 British case) holding that "regulations may be declared to be invalid on the ground of unreasonableness... if they are found to be partial and unequal in their operation as between different classes, unless of course the enabling Act specifically authorises such partiality and inequality." Government argued that the National States Constitution Act authorized the male franchise. KwaNdebele initially resisted any elections. Its constitutional committee first recommended that only a minority of Assembly members be elected by men over twenty-three, but its final report gave women the vote. When this was presented to the Assembly, Skosana said: "I feel we shall not go astray if we follow the path of our ancestors, which is known to us.... According to our tradition, the husband is above the wife and in that respect I believe that even God is on our side." The Assembly, therefore, was responsible for disenfranchising women.

Justice Eloff noted that the Bantu Authorities Act, establishing local government, authorized the State President to respect black traditions, but the National States Constitution Act did not.

> I do not think there is a traditional model of a political system for a national state like KwaNdebele when it comes to the question of voting rights. The fact that women have a subordinate status compared with men and in the community is not of real consequence when it comes to stipulating voting rights in public life, which is alien to the whole tribe. I also do not think there is room for a sort of cosmetic mixture of the old views and the new dispensation.

Even if progress toward democracy must follow a "gradual evolutionary outgrowing of third-world government forms... such an evolutionary process must take place without discrimination between men and women."

He accepted the applicants' arguments that women were more knowledgeable about local affairs, their interests were not identical to those of men, women everywhere were gaining equality, they voted in other black communities, and one had briefly been Chief Minister of the Transkei. "For a long time, it has been reasonably accepted in South Africa that women are no less eligible than men to express themselves politically." The inequality of disenfranchisement was "unfair and therefore not authorized by the 1971 Act."

Some fifty women in traditional dress cheered when their lawyer explained the judgment. The state promptly obtained leave to appeal. At a news conference five days later Solly Mahlangu said he had asked the State President to dissolve the KwaNdebele government and call an election "to test the feelings of the people for independence." Andries Mahlangu said all the detentions were now illegal. But Prince James said KwaNdebele had told the people "that everything was normal and that they should ignore press statements on the matter." About the same time the State President met the Lebowa Chief Minister and Cabinet and gave them two weeks to start negotiations to merge with KwaNdebele, failing which he would introduce legislation to incorporate Moutse into KwaNdebele.[149]

A month after the decision Chris Heunis introduced a bill retroactively validating KwaNdebele legislation, ensuring early elections, and enfranchising women, warning that "the rights of 1.7 million people will be threatened if the legislation is not accepted." In the House of Assembly the PFP refused "to accept responsibility for the maladministration of KwaNdebele or for the failure of the Government to get its proclamation correct in the first instance." But a Nationalist backbencher asked if the PFP wanted "total disorder and chaos, to the detriment of everyone in KwaNdebele?" With the backing of the Conservatives the bill passed 124-16.[150] In the House of Representatives Heunis insisted the bill "has nothing whatsoever to do with the independence or non-independence of KwaNdebele." Its purpose was "to maintain legal certainty... to give effect to the Supreme Court ruling... to stabilize the political rights of the Black people who live there." He failed to persuade the majority Labour Party, which opposed it "to reiterate and confirm our opposition to the creation of homelands based on ethnicity and/or tribalism." "We will not soil our hands by having any association with any of the legislation which was passed or with any of the steps which were taken by this legislative assembly of KwaNdebele over the past four years."[151] The House of Delegates passed it over the dissent of the two PFP members.[152] The President's Council overrode the House of Representatives, despite opposition by the Conservative Party (which invoked Ndebele tradition) and the three anti-apartheid parties (PFP, LP, and NDM).

Government also tabled a bill retroactively legalizing any action taken by KwaNdebele in Moutse. The PFP opposed it as "chutzpah.... There is no apology, no explanation." Viljoen sought comfort in the fact that "the Transvaal Division of the Supreme Court, which dealt with the case in the first instance, rejected the objection and regarded the incorporation as being valid.... There was consequently nothing obviously invalid or illegal in the situation...." He expressed amusement "that the members who normally would have nothing to do with ethnicity, language difficulties and group context are here becoming filled with excitement and indignation because the Government did not adhere strictly to the concept of ethnicity in deciding on Moutse." The CP supported the NP in the House of Assembly, but the government decided not to take it to the President's Council after being *unanimously* defeated in the other two Houses.[153]

On September 15 South Africa decreed that the KwaNdebele Assembly would be dissolved on December 7 and elections would begin the next day.[154] In anticipation, Police Commissioner R.J. Ihubane issued an order on November 11 prohibiting

> the taking part of the debating of the following issues at meetings...
>
> (a) identifying and the associating of election candidates with the "Mbokoto" and "Comrades" organisations;
>
> (b) the defamation of the public image of the KwaNdebele police;
>
> (c) justifies, defends or commends any campaigns, projects, programmes, actions or policy of violence or resistance against, or subversion of the authority of the Government or any tribal authorities or of violence against, or intimidation of any person or persons belong to any particular category of persons.[155]

By mid-November, fifty-three candidates were seeking the sixteen seats. Pamphlets supporting Chief Minister George Mahlangu declared: "We do not need a Sotho-speaking person under the guise of the UDF to tell us not to exercise our democratic right....We do not want the sons of chiefs who hold no elected positions to govern us." Those supporting Solly Mahlangu warned that "the present government knows it wants to opt for independence."[156]

On the first day of balloting women constituted ninety percent of voters in the homeland (although many men voted at their urban residences). Anti-independence candidates won all sixteen seats, one of them trouncing George Mahlangu 6,130 to 1,938. Nevertheless, he engineered retroactive nomination by the Sokhulumi Tribal Authority and sought to persuade the seventy-two other nominated members to re-elect him Chief Minister. A Supreme Court application was still pending to invalidate the replacement of the twenty-one nominated members of the Ndzundza Tribal Authority by his supporters. Mbokotho reappeared, driving underground the victorious anti-independence MLAs. Independence advocates planned to challenge the election in court on the ground of balloting irregularities. On January 11, 1989, several hundred KwaNdebele women set out for Pretoria to protest harassment of King Mapoch and demand the immediate expulsion of George Mahlangu from the Assembly. About half were intercepted and detained by KwaNdebele police. On January 14 thousands demonstrated against independence in Moutse. At the beginning of February Jonas Mabena became Chief Minister, defeating Prince James.[157]

From September 1989 to April 1990 the Parsons Commission of Inquiry took evidence about KwaNdebele violence during the campaigns against incorporation and independence, documenting extensive involvement by homeland officials.[158] In November 1989 George Mahlangu (now opposition leader) and 13 Mbokotho were charged with murder, attempted murder, arson, and assault for a June 1986 attack.[159]

At the beginning of May 1990 the Assembly replaced the government of Jonas Mabena with that of the Ndzundza royal family, including Chief Minister James Mahlangu, Minister of Works and Water Affairs Cornelius Mahlangu, Minister of Interior and Manpower Solly Mahlangu, and Minister of Justice Johannes Mahlangu. The new Chief Minister promptly declared: "We rejected independence and will strive for a new SA."[160]

Challenging Other Incorporations

Encouraged by the Moutse and Botshabelo victories, Braklaagte sued at the end of 1988 to interdict its incorporation into Bophuthatswana. The Bahurutshe Ba Sebogodi had purchased their farm in 1907. South Africa announced the incorporation in press releases in June 1983 and October 1984. In July 1983 the *Government Gazette* announced that the Commission for Co-operation and Development would hear evidence in August and September.[161] The community, however, claimed they first learned about the threat in July 1986 and immediately voiced opposition. When Parliament debated the Borders of Particular States Extension Amendment Bill in September, the PFP expressed concern about the lack of consultation. A Nationalist MP defended the "meaningful rounding off and consolidation of four independent and national states."

> If an open invitation is addressed to someone and he has the opportunity to appear before the commission and he does not make use of that opportunity... the hon member for Berea cannot now complain, after the process has been completed, that the people were not consulted.... The department, through its officials and the old commissioners, had constant contact with all Black people.... There is a third channel... namely the recognised authority of the relevant Black people... the government of Bophuthatswana.... We cannot simply abandon the process of turning the national states into viable territories—a home for their own peoples.

The CP also opposed the bill because government violated its "solemn agreement" to consult with white farmers and agricultural unions. Nevertheless, the bill passed by a comfortable majority of 79-32.[162]

The community wrote the State President: "We cannot believe you would make us foreigners in the land of our birth, without speaking to us first. ... We will be punished by President Mangope for resisting incorporation and applying for South African Citizenship.... He has already tried to depose our chief, who has ruled us since 1949."* Deputy Development Minister Wilkens replied two months later that the legislation "cannot be withdrawn." When their lawyers protested in May 1987 that the community had never been consulted, Gerrit Viljoen insisted in August: "On a previous occasion your clients were informed that it is not possible for the Republic of South Africa government to deviate from the agreement entered into with the Bophuthatswana government." When the PFP complained in Parliament that the "Standing Committee on Foreign Affairs and Development Aid was misled into believing that this matter was non-contentious," the NP reprimanded the opposition for "run[ning] riot on the strength of one individual case...one cannot, after all, obtain complete unanimity among 15,000 people." And Viljoen reiterated that there "was ample opportunity for everyone concerned to address the Commission." The dissidents had "the support of the Black Sash and similar organisations and access to certain legal organisations [which] are always immediately ready, when a decision has been taken by this Government, to see whether they cannot upset it."[163]

When Chris Heunis removed John Sebogodi as chief in May 1988, the community elected his son, Pupsey Sebogodi, in July and asked the Director General of Constitutional Development Services in September how to arrange the appointment. He answered in November that "by Tswana custom the appointment of a headman is the function of the chief of the tribe." South Africa had appointed Joseph Godfrey Moilwa, a Bophuthatswana citizen and resident, as chief of Braklaagte and Leeuwfontein, and he had appointed his relative Edwin Moilwa as headman of Braklaagte.[164]

The community requested a meeting with Viljoen in October and obtained one two months later. They invoked the reprieves of other "black spots"—Driefontein, KwaNgema, Mathopestad, and Motlatla. The government's minutes recorded: "As [Viljoen] has previously promised to their representatives and also said in Parliament he has now listened to them so that he understands what is in their hearts and minds...." But he wrote on December 27 that they had failed to make timely objection and "the government is unable to rescind or renegotiate its decision. In order to remove the cloud of uncertainty to which delegates from Braklaagte referred, the Government has decided to finalise the position as a matter of urgency." Incorporation would occur in four days. "I trust that the fears and concerns expressed by your clients will be fairly taken care of after incorporation." Their attorney telegrammed Viljoen and Botha seeking a postponement, but when they did not reply he sought an interdict on December 29; the next day Justice Spoelstra granted a rule nisi, and the incorporation was gazetted.[165]

*Abram Moiloa, chief of the Bahurutshe, was deposed in 1957 for refusing to make women carry passes. Hooper (1989). Lucas Mangope (the future president of Bophuthatswana), appointed in his place, told the Minister of Bantu Affairs: "Lead us and we shall try to crawl." Lodge (1983: 273).

Pupsey Sebogodi's application argued that the State President should have considered the people's fears (as he had promised) and had concluded the agreement with Bophuthatswana before he had the power to excise Braklaagte. (Botha had relied on the Borders of Particular States Act, which contained no criteria for incorporation, rather than the National States Constitution Act, whose criteria courts had used to invalidate the Moutse and Botshabelo incorporations.) Mangope's reply expressed anger at their ingratitude. His government had built schools in Braklaagte and welcomed their children to its schools. The homeland did not discriminate against non-citizens, and its services and benefits were equal to those of South Africa. Sebogodi was motivated by pique at not being made headman. During Mangope's regular consultations with John Sebogodi about incorporation his son Pupsey had often been present. John was such a good friend that a street in Mmabatho was named after him. But John had no real claim to the headmanship; he was merely a regent for Edwin, who had been too young in 1948 to assume the position. The "election" of Pupsey was irrelevant because "it is foreign to the tradition of this tribe to elect leaders."

Pupsey Sebogodi, supported by his eighty-eight-year-old father, joined issue about his claim to the headmanship, based on an elaborate genealogical reconstruction. "It is clear that the authorities are merely attempting to suppress opposition to incorporation into Bophuthatswana...by favouring members of the Moilwa family who are supportive...." South Africa justified incorporation on the ground that the Bahurutshe were a single tribe, which had to be united within Bophuthatswana, but they actually were three tribes, and "there can be no such turning back of the clock." Mangope had expressed his anger at non-citizens two years earlier:

> [W]e have attained these successes without any help from those "Tswana", that is South African Batswana, who are opposed to our existence. We have never thought of them as anything but South Africans...we insist upon knowing exactly who is throwing in their lot with us and who is not.

The two governments did not await trial to effect the incorporation.[166] South Africa began transferring telephone service and expelling high school pupils. By the end of January homeland police were patrolling the village, arresting and charging residents, while the SAP rebuffed complaints. Bophuthatswana refused to grant permits to sell cattle or admit patients to hospital. The community's attorney protested that this violated the rule nisi, and Justice Spoelstra had threatened to award damages, but the State Attorney noted that the court had granted no interim relief.

Justice van der Merwe gave judgment for the respondents on March 10. After adopting the historical summary from their affidavits he quoted the statutory language giving the State President unlimited discretion. Incorporation "is an involved process affecting many people and involving vast amounts of money... having taken such a decision... it cannot be lightly tampered with." Nevertheless, Viljoen "was prepared to have further discussions and consultations with aggrieved people." He had not "closed his eyes" to them, nor had the State President's discretion been "fettered by the history of the matter." Sebogodi obtained leave to appeal in July.[167]

Immediately after judgment Bophuthatswana security police established a permanent post in Braklaagte. On Wednesday, March 22, they stopped a bus carrying pupils home from Zeerust and beat them for attending a South African school. The next day heavily-armed police fired tear gas at random and assaulted residents. When labor migrants returned for the Easter weekend that night, the homes of four pro-incorporation residents were attacked. Early the next morning homeland police began assaulting and arresting residents, including Pupsey Sebogodi (later charged with murder), and continued through the weekend. When the community's attorney arrived on Sunday, police constantly interfered with his consultations. The Motswedi police commander refused to accept complaints about abuse or allow medical care to detainees for two weeks. Only six of the 106 arrested were convicted. In April the PFP condemned the incorporation. Although the government "claim to have abandoned their policy of forced removals...they now have a policy of forced boundary changes." The Labour Party added: "The goings-on in the Border Corridor have been the subject of communications to foreign embassies. South Africa, for so long the polecat of the world, faces further condemnation and scorn." Viljoen replied that "the Supreme Court found in favour of the incorporation and confirmed it." Furthermore, "the President of Bophuthatswana gave assurances in connection with the goodwill of his government in relation to the residents."[168]

Police repression increased after November 1990, and a vigilante group calling itself Inkatha also kidnapped, assaulted, and destroyed property. Arrests, assaults, and murders escalated in January 1991, forcing 5,000-6,000 of the original 9,000 residents to flee to Ikagaleng township, Zeerust.

The Appellate Division dismissed the appeal in May 1991, finding the applicant's arguments "manifestly unsound," based on a "fallacy," and "devoid of real substance." "There is nothing on record to indicate that the State President considered his statutory discretion to have been fettered by the Government's 'final decision' on 15 October 1984." He exercised his discretion in the five days between Viljoen's December 15 meeting with the community and his own signing of the proclamation. The court was convinced of "the bona fides of Minister Viljoen" by his willingness to meet the community. The "careful consideration" given their memorandum and arguments "belie the submission that the State President had failed to apply his mind."

In August 1989 Leeuwfontein also challenged its incorporation into Bophuthatswana the previous January, despite Braklaagte's Supreme Court defeat in March.[169] Nkgokoloane Dadelik Majafa, senior elder of the 15,000 member Bahurutshe Ba Ga Moilwa, claimed that at meetings of elders and the entire tribe in January and May his ill, seventy-four-year-old half-brother, Chief Moswana David Moilwa, deputed him to bring the application. Like Braklaagte, the tribe had bought its farm in 1906 and developed a strong infrastructure of schools, churches, shops, and a clinic. They successfully interdicted a removal to Driefontein in the late 1950s and forestalled another to Bergvliet in 1975. When the Commission for Co-operation and Development took evidence in August 1983 it personally invited white farmers and informed the Bophuthatswana government but not the tribe. Although the Commission recommended in 1984 that both Leeuwfontein and Braklaagte remain within South Africa, the Director General urged incorporation in August 1987. The community sought to distinguish itself from Braklaagte, arguing that it had no notice or opportunity to consult.

In addition to the usual arguments against incorporation, Majafa related recent acts of repression. In March homeland police confronted a group of children and beat those who expressed loyalty to South Africa. On April 19 nearly 4,000 residents fled police violence to an adjacent white farm, returning only after a pledge of police restraint. Three weeks later the South African Ambassador lectured residents for ten minutes that they were now "children of Bophuthatswana." Following another confrontation with police on May 15 youths again fled to South Africa. This time the SAP handed them back to homeland police, who tear gassed them in vans and arrested 131, denying them access to lawyers for three days and then releasing all but six without charge. The next day President Mangope addressed a meeting, which security forces made 150 attend. He warned them not to retain attorneys, whom he had not invited to the meeting, but a black attorney sitting in the front row secretly recorded the speech.

> Beware that Bophuthatswana is like a prickly pear…very tasty, but…also dangerous. I warn you strongly not to abuse me. I am not your dustbin. Do not play games on me. If you do I will prick you and pierce you like a prickly pear…. [A]lthough Bophuthatswana is a very peaceful and interesting country, we do have laws in Bophuthatswana. I shall start by informing you that I have heard that you do not want to see my police force in this place. Know that I actually love them. I love them for carrying out my instructions. They are the ones who see to it that all people of Bophuthatswana obey the laws to the letter. I am going to order them to come to this place. They will see to it that there is order in this place…. Even if you engage the services of attorneys you will not accomplish your wishes. I am not afraid of Johannesburg attorneys or any attorneys.[170]

On July 1 members of both communities opposing incorporation met at the Braklaagte football grounds. When police dispersed the crowds with tear gas and shots, they retaliated by fire-bombing a hippo, in which five police burned to death, and hacking to death another four. Police killed two residents there, and then stopped a bus at a roadblock and beat a sixty-five-year-old man to death. They conducted house-to-house searches in both villages, beating people indiscriminately and arresting thirty-four, some of whom had to be hospitalized. The nine police were buried in the largest state funeral ever held. The homeland prevented public funerals for the residents and banned Black Sash and TRAC.[171]

South Africa opposed the application on the ground that it had consulted Leeuwfontein. It submitted an affidavit by Chief Moswana David Moilwa, who asserted that he still performed his functions and had not appointed a substitute. When the tribe was first threatened with removal he and the diKgosana (a council of fourteen elders) sought the help of Mangope, who offered incorporation. The homeland had operated its schools and clinics since 1976, at the chief's request. "It was public knowledge that our farm was actually under the control of the Bophuthatswana Government." He contested Majafa's genealogy: Although his mother once lived with Moilwa's father, they never married. Majafa was her son by a non-Tswana. Furthermore, Majafa had not lived in Leeuwfontein for many years, and presently was in Johannesburg. Anti-incorporation forces had intimidated many people, attacking the chief himself in March and June. Three elders supported his story.

Majafa's 151-page reply claimed that the homeland police forced him to flee in July. He was the product of a customary marriage between his mother and Moilwa's father. The chairman of the lekgotla, seven diKgosana, and four other senior representatives of kgoros in the lekgotla denied being notified of incorporation and opposed it. One of the three elders supporting Moilwa had taken his kgoro back to South Africa, and the other two were not members of the lekgotla. Moilwa never reported any meetings with Mangope to the lekgotla.

The nine-page 1983 government press release referred to scores of farms (Eighty in the Marico corridor alone), was directed to the Transvaal and North-Western Cape Agricultural Unions, and was reported only in *The Citizen* and the *Rand Daily Mail*. This was not the way to reach Tswana-speaking communities. Newspaper reports of Parliamentary debates did not name Leeuwfontein. District Commissioner Bam said in front of the South African Ambassador that he had not told the community about incorporation. Mangope could not represent the community since his interests were clearly adverse. The white neighbor, on whose farm the tribe took refuge from homeland police, provided an affidavit in their support. The professor of indigenous law at Rand Afrikaans University confirmed that the grundnorm of Tswana politics was: "A chief is a chief through his tribe and a tribe is a tribe through its chief." Moilwa could not consent to incorporation without the tribe's agreement. The case was scheduled for oral evidence in August 1991.

As the Nationalists tried to find a formula that would maximize white power while paying lip service to democracy the status and boundaries of the homelands remained a critical issue. In May 1990 the Minister of Development Aid, C.J. van der Merwe, declared that "the basic law for these areas, the National States Constitution Act... is geographically based and not ethnically, despite its title. Not one of the present national states consists of or comprises a single ethnic unit." But when a Labour Party member quoted this back, he insisted "in any country like South Africa, with so many different peoples, groups, languages and cultures, it would be sensible to decentralise and then probably give the various groups some or other form of local self-government." "The basic principle we are dealing with here is that as far as possible we must create specific units with homogenous interests...language and culture—culture in particular—play a major role." [172]

Analysis

Grand apartheid sought to rid white South Africa of its black majority by creating ten "independent" statelets, which would provide labor power and care for the unproductive. These homelands also perpetuated the moral division of labor.[173] While South Africa proclaimed its fidelity to the rule of law, corrupt, autocratic, often vicious rulers controlled the masses, confirming Blacks' unreadiness for democracy (as did necklacing, people's courts, and "Black-on-Black" violence in the townships and political abuses throughout Africa).[174] This strategy of delegating dirty work carried two risks, however. Homeland governments had to maintain a plausible facade of autonomy, but apperance might become reality (just as the Houses of Delegates and Representatives could refuse to rubber-stamp the white government's actions). Half the homelands demonstrated their independence by rejecting it. Lebowa fought the excision of Moutse, suing South Africa and expelling its representative. Even Simon Skosana could become refractory, dismissing both the South African Commissioner General and the Police Commissioner seconded from the SAP, warning that the Cabinet "is strongly opposed to being prescribed to in conducting politics." When South Africa sought to assert control over the latter's replacement, Brig. Lerm simply threatened to resign from the SAP.

The opposite danger was contamination. Homeland leaders had to avoid direct involvement with illegality, which might dirty the white hands manipulating the puppet strings. But Chief Ministers Simon Skosana and George Mahlangu, Interior Minister Ntuli, and Information Minister F.K. Mahlangu were deeply complicit in violence, especially against Moutse. The Transvaal Attorney General was reluctant to prosecute them for fear of implicating his government. What should have been an argument against democracy in South Africa became an argument against KwaNdebele independence. Compliant homelands held an embarrassing mirror up to white South Africa.

To repress their black citizens, rulers assumed Emergency powers, detained, authorized their own forced removals, and indemnified police from civil and criminal liability. Such imitation was not the highest form of flattery.

Unlike the physical removal of millions, described in chapter ten, incorporation moved boundaries rather than people, generating far less publicity. Viljoen maintained there was no need for Parliamentary debate since there had been no "forced relocation" and everyone had "moved voluntarily." Yet government still felt compelled to offer justifications. Like all propaganda, these contained kernels of truth. The first was consent. Simon Skosana and George Mahlangu embraced independence in exchange for Moutse, Rust der Winter, development aid, the prospect of a casino, and wealth for them and their cronies. Lebowa could not demand a referendum in Moutse without drawing attention to territory it had incorporated over the objections of residents; it also bowed to excision in exchange for land and money. Because South Africa had created homeland governments to express black political aspirations, it refused to look behind them. Bophuthatswana represented all Tswana, even those outside the homeland. The KwaNdebele Assembly represented all residents, although more than three-fourths of its members were appointed and the rest elected by just 600 men.

Information Minister F.K. Mahlangu exemplified the quality of that representation. In September 1986 he affirmed that the homeland had rejected independence "in accordance with the wishes of its people…. The whole situation also demonstrated to us that people are very good judges of their own needs. It is only in a democratic society that a government can heed the wishes of its people." Less than a year later he declared that Ndebele, who had been "scattered for years striving for their own country," would now take their "rightful place in the row of nations…. Let me assure all who have any interest in the right of nations to decide for themselves, that this decision in the Legislative Assembly followed weeks of consultation with the people themselves, by means of public meetings held throughout KwaNdebele." Heunis promised to "consider the wishes of the people of the territories." But Police Commissioner Lerm prohibited James and Cornelius Mahlangu from attending any meeting to "oppose any action or proposed action of any member of the Cabinet or the Government of KwaNdebele."

Internal divisions facilitated the charade of consent. Some Ndebele living in Moutse favored incorporation; some KwaNdebele residents supported independence. Yet opponents also could employ the government's favorite strategy of divide and conquer. Consent was flawed because of divisions between Moutse and KwaNdebele, Lebowa and KwaNdebele, and especially within KwaNdebele between government and the royal family. Neither South Africa nor the homelands saw any contradiction between coercion and consent. Braklaagte and Leeuwfontein "chose" incorporation into Bophuthatswana to avoid physical removal. Moutse teachers "chose" to work in KwaNdebele rather than be transferred elsewhere at the government's whim.

Moutse residents unhappy with incorporation "chose" to move to Immerpan/Saliesloot, protected by security forces from "intimidation"; lest there be doubt, government required them to sign forms saying they agreed to move. The KwaNdebele Police Commissioner only released detainees who signed a statement that "I... undertake voluntary [sic] and without being subjected to any compulsion" not to oppose independence.

Yet the fiction of consent was untenable; South Africa may be the only country in the world where oppressed peoples died resisting independence, declaring their allegiance to a white racist regime rather than an ethnic homeland. Government fell back on the surrogate of consultation. Resources expended on making the decision distracted from the unpalatability of what was decided. Of course, government controlled timing and content, promising further consultation to stave off resistance or legal action and allow it to act secretly. Consultation did not obligate government to modify its plans, because its black subjects were irresponsible fractious children who could not perceive their own good. In any case, government often acted first and consulted later.

Government reified autocratic actions into external compulsion; it was "unable to rescind or renegotiate its decision." Having created homelands, installed puppets, and foisted "treaties" on them, South Africa claimed to be bound by international law. Government invoked the time it had invested in "consulting" and seeking "consent" as reasons for not budging. The older the decision, the more irreversible. Popular resistance (not government autocracy) created "uncertainty," which had to be eliminated by more autocracy. Botha could not just "leave people in the air." Civil servants blamed Ministers, Ministers blamed their predecessors and the full Cabinet, and the executive blamed the legislature. Officials endowed with awesome power used the passive tense: Moutse "had to be excised." A Commander-in-Chief whose military outgunned the rest of sub-Saharan Africa protested that Moutse was "pointing a pistol to his head" by warning that incorporation would lead to violence.

In the era of "reform," government could no longer exalt apartheid as its inspiration. Instead it offered bland technocratic justifications: "good management," "good administration," "the best interests of all concerned," "meaningful consolidation," "orderly government," "development," "prosperity." Given the patent incompetence and corruption of homeland governments and their woefully impoverished populations, these were transparent rationalizations.

Finally, government sought to portray the conflict as a power struggle among blacks rather than a liberation struggle against whites. Mangope attributed the controversy over Braklaagte to Pupsey Sebogodi's unwarranted claim to the headmanship. South Africa dismissed Leeuwfontein's resistance to incorporation as a challenge by Nkgokoloane Dadelik Majafa to the chieftainship of Moswana David Moilwa. Moutse was the unfortunate object of a squabble between Lebowa and KwaNdebele. Resistance to KwaNdebele independence expressed the Ndzundza royal house's resentment of the homeland leadership. This characterization shifted responsibility from whites to Blacks, further demonstrating their political immaturity. And their inability to resolve the issues compelled the white government to act unilaterally. With some success South Africa sought to conceal its pivotal role in constructing, exacerbating, and manipulating these conflicts, breaking up peaceful heterogeneous communities into ethnic adversaries competing for scarce resources.

Because the Nationalists monopolized political power, opponents had no alternative but to appeal to the judiciary. South Africa's much vaunted respect for the rule of law was not just an empty boast. Executive power, though extraordinarily broad, derived from and was limited by legislation. Although courts could not invoke a written constitution or natural law, they did apply administrative law doctrines of ultra vires, reasonableness, and discrimination. Their invalidation of the excision of Ingwavuma from KwaZulu for incorporation into Swaziland offered some hope to Lebowa and Moutse. But administrative law placed no restraints on Parliamentary supremacy. Parliament retroactively validated the excision of Moutse from Lebowa, foreclosing the judicial challenge that had succeeded in Ingwavuma. As Justice Spoelstra bluntly declared: "The loss of rights…is…caused…by Parliament. Insofar as unreasonableness is the issue, it therefore drops out of consideration. It is not for me to pass judgment about whether that decision was good or bad, desirable or undesirable, wise or unwise."

The Nationalists made Parliamentary supremacy both a responsibility and a virtue. "If any court gives an interpretation of a law…other than that contemplated by the legislature, it is the legislature's duty to rectify that law so that its intention is clear." Judicial review was usurpation of power by "appointed people" violating "democracy in the hands of the people." Because court judgments were "retrospective," they created "uncertainty." Instead of the "uncertainty" of judicial criteria for incorporation, like ethnicity and political development, government proposed the "clear criterion" of the State President's decision that it was "expedient." Such an inescapably political decision could not be entrusted to courts (just as censorship could not be, see chapter eight). Frustrated by the constraints of the National States Constitution Act, which led to the invalidation of the incorporations of Moutse and Botshabelo, the State President relied on the Borders of Particular States Extension Act to incorporate Braklaagte and Leeuwfontein and was rewarded by the Appellate Division's confirmation of his unfettered discretion. Parliament could retroactively remedy defective legislation or administrative acts and even tell courts how to interpret statutes. If government had failed to consult Lebowa before excising Moutse, Parliament could legislate that the excision be "deemed to have been preceded by consultation." If Moutse remained part of Lebowa despite the excision, Parliament could legislate that it had never been part. Like Soviet historians (and as sat-irized by Orwell in "1984"), South African legislators blithely rewrote their past.

As a two-edged sword, legal formalism could be invoked by the state as well as against it. Although its lack of formal political power usually com-pelled the opposition to choose the judicial arena, Moutse decided to appeal to the recently created tricameral legislature, where it hoped to embarrass the government in the white House and win the support of the "Coloured" and Indian Houses. Government frustrated this by playing the opposition's strongest suit—judicial autonomy. Respect for the courts, in which Lebowa had just filed its application, prevented Parliament from debating the matter. Such deference was more than a little hypocritical, given the government's readiness to overturn judicial decisions through retroactive legislation, yet all three Houses accepted the argument.

Both parties and courts opportunistically used and ignored legal formal-ism. In August 1986 the KwaNdebele Legislative Assembly initially refused to discuss independence, which was convulsing the homeland, because it was not on the agenda. In 1987 the Assembly disregarded the previous year's unanimous repudiation of independence, again because it had not been on the agenda. A court invalidated the Assembly's removal of its Speaker on the ground of lack of notice. Yet both the Supreme Court and the Appellate Division summarily dismissed Lebowa's challenge to the excision of Moutse based on the use of brackets rather than commas or semicolons: "Punctuation is a matter to which little regard is had in the interpretation of statutes." Government readily constructed or dispensed with legal forms to work its will, detaining thousands under the Internal Security Act and Emergency regulations. Some of the legal system's most important decisions were unconstrained by law. The Transvaal Attorney General long refused to prosecute Simon Skosana, Piet Ntuli, and George Mahlangu for notorious kidnappings, torture, and murders—and then charged them with common assault, accepting R50 fines to foreclose judicial exposure of their crimes. Courts generally failed to stop or correct executive illegality: expulsions from the KwaNdebele Legislative Assembly, interference with the Ndzundza Tribal Authority, violations of personal freedom under the Emergency regulations, access of detainees to lawyers and doctors. They did nothing about police terror or Mbokotho violence.[175]

When courts did review executive action, the outcome was unpredictable. Moutse lost its challenge to incorporation in the Supreme Court but won on the same grounds in the Appellate Division. The Supreme Court judge who approved Moutse's incorporation also released anti-independence activists, angrily condemning government illegality. Justice Roux ordered KwaNdebele to release Prince Cornelius in July 1987, commenting that the "erratic" con-duct of the police "creates a suspicion in my mind as to whether there was any real reason for their behaviour." They had offered "bald allegations" but no "instances and dates which would enable the applicant to dispute them." When KwaNdebele redetained Cornelius three months later Justice Myburgh refused to release him. The police had formed a "genuine opinion about the desirability of the arrest." Cornelius could not demonstrate that the information available to the officer "was not sufficient to form an opinion genuinely," nor had he offered reasons "why this police officer would be acting mala fide." The Appellate Division upheld Moutse's excision from Lebowa but invalidated its incorporation into KwaNdebele. The Orange Free State Supreme Court followed the Appellate Division decision about Moutse on the different facts of Botshabelo. Both the Supreme Court and the Appellate Division upheld the incorporation of Braklaagte into Bophuthatswana. Yet KwaNdebele women won the right to vote, relying primarily on natural law arguments for sexual equality.

Despite the strongly positivist tradition in South African jurisprudence, the logic of ideology proved more powerful than written law. Government could not justify the incorporation of Moutse as a means of uniting the Ndebele minority with its KwaNdebele homeland without violating the right of the North Sotho majority to remain in South Africa or join its homeland, Lebowa. Ethnic self-determination for some inevitably became ethnic oppression of others: non-Tswana in Bophuthatswana, non-Ndebele in KwaNdebele. The Conservative Party embarrassed the Nationalists by quoting their Programme of Action: "The ideal dispensation would be one in which every nation could rule itself as it pleased, preferably within its own geographic area." The CP championed "the course of true freedom" for KwaNdebele in order to demand its own white homeland.[176]

Yet South Africa could not abandon the rationale of ethnic homogeneity in favor of geographic contiguity or administrative convenience without utterly betraying grand apartheid, nor could it reconcile geography or efficiency with incorporating Botshabelo into QwaQwa (or the fragmentation of other homelands). Government promoted grand apartheid as essential to black self-determination, yet it refused to hold a referendum in Moutse (about incorporation) or in KwaNdebele (about independence). It disregarded the wishes of one homeland (Lebowa) in favor of another (KwaNdebele). Government argued that ethnic heterogeneity bred violence; yet incorporation provoked even more. Government deplored the disruption of education; yet Moutse, untouched by the Vaal uprising, lost months of schooling following incorporation. Grand apartheid was supposed to foster tradition; yet incorporation subordinated North Sotho hosts to Ndebele guests, their traditional inferiors. Government's argument against KwaNdebele women voting—the uniqueness of Ndebele culture—undermined its argument for subordinating Moutse to that alien culture. Government touted homelands as a vehicle for political development, yet the "location people" of Ekangala resented subordination to such KwaNdebele "tribal" customs as chiefs, arbitrary fines, and corporal punishment. Although many criticized the 1983 constitutional "reforms" as window dressing, they did constrain government. The Houses of Delegates and Representatives could not destroy apartheid, but they refused to give government more power or correct its mistakes. Overriding them in the President's Council was politically costly.

In the women's vote case it was the plaintiffs who initially ran up against ideological consistency. In the only country in the world that legally mandated racial discrimination, how could they argue that natural justice demanded sexual equality? After the Nationalists had made apartheid a religious dogma for four decades, the court had to portray sexual discrimination as so evil that only explicit legislation could disenfranchise women. Whereas critics of apartheid could point to a mass movement, South African feminism was very weak, especially among blacks. Indeed, the married women plaintiffs acknowledged patriarchy by declaring they had their husbands' support.

Yet women were able to employ the tension between tradition and modernity. Grand apartheid was supposed to foster evolution toward democracy. Government promoted KwaNdebele independence as "extending participation of communities." South Africa had insisted that sixteen members of the KwaNdebele Legislative Assembly be elected. In return, reluctant traditional leaders demanded the exclusion of women from voting and holding office. Modernity created pressures for democracy. Local school committees played an essential role in creating an educated workforce. It was embarrassing that Ndebele women enjoyed more democratic participation in the "traditional" tribal council than in the "modern" Assembly and that Ndebele women could vote in other homelands, while non-Ndebele women could not vote in KwaNdebele.

Government encountered other problems if it reverted (inconsistently) to the goal of preserving ethnic tradition. Homeland governments were alien institutions, which could claim no traditional warrant. The KwaNdebele franchise already violated tradition: Boys became men when circumcised at sixteen but could not vote until twenty-one; allowing youths to vote but not their mothers mocked traditional respect for age. Apartheid seriously undermined traditional patriarchy by relying on black male labor while excluding black families, thereby enlarging the role of women in homeland politics. Urban Ndebele women, although not traditional, were denied political participation. Finally, the strongest advocate of disenfranchising women was the brutal, corrupt, violent upstart Simon Skosana, not the Ndzundza royal house, two of whose members switched sides to back the women.

If ideology offered powerful arguments, politics determined outcomes. The black community contained complex divisions. The rivalry between Lebowa and KwaNdebele reflected tribal loyalties, as did Moutse's preference for Lebowa. But Lebowa showed little interest in Moutse until it was about to be incorporated, and then Lebowa was bought off; and Moutse preferred South African rule to that of Lebowa. Both Moutse and KwaNdebele were divided internally: urban and rural, modern and traditional, more and less formally educated, youths and elders, women and men, businessmen and consumers, rulers and subjects, new and old elites. While Braklaagte's case was pending before the Appellate Division, Leeuwfontein argued that its claim was stronger because it had not been notified or consulted. At the same time, conventional adversaries formed strange alliances. Moutse pupils and teachers strongly opposed incorporation. Comrades joined traditional elders in opposing KwaNdebele independence. Peter Mokaba, the fiery leader of the South African Youth Congress, helped launch the Congress of Traditional Leaders of South Africa. Civil servants, often detested as government collaborators, struck three times against independence. Businessmen, often the victims of arson attacks, boycotted KwaNdebele licensing authorities. Detention turned Godfrey Mathebe—Lebowa MLA and bar owner—into a hero of youths. Conservative rural women grew into outspoken champions of democracy. Even white farmers, backbone of the Nationalist Party, opposed government, fearing disruption of their labor supply and angered by expropriation of their land, and found surprising support in the PFP. Within KwaNdebele, one main fault line divided the Ndzundza royal house from Skosana, his successor, and their henchmen. In this struggle, ironically, "tradition" was progressive and democratic, while "modernity" was regressive and autocratic. Individuals and groups changed sides. Members of the royal house turned against independence and even became champions of women's suffrage. Solly Mahlangu, Assembly speaker and Mbokotho executive committee member, did the same. Even KwaNdebele followed the prevailing political winds, shifting from support for independence to opposition to support to opposition, all within four years.

The conflict constantly oscillated between legal and political forms. Moutse's petition to be heard at the Bar of Parliament, a unique appeal by disenfranchised Blacks to address the seat of power, was frustrated by the Assembly Speaker's legalistic ruling that the matter was sub judice. The KwaNdebele Assembly almost failed to debate independence because it was not on the agenda; a year later it ignored the earlier decision against independence on the same grounds; and it abolished Mbokotho not because of its atrocities but because it lacked a constitution and had not been approved by King Mapoch.

Political institutions rested on shaky foundations. White rule was built on the crime of apartheid. The Houses of Delegates and Representatives had been elected by minorities of "Coloured" and Indian voters who defied the mass boycott. The KwaNdebele Legislative Assembly was dominated by nominated members, and women could not vote or serve. Its tenuous legitimacy was further weakened by blatant manipulation: detention of the royal family just before elections; expulsion of Cornelius and Solly Mahlangu from both the government and the Assembly. The only popular political actions, such as mass meetings and boycotts, were illegal. Ironically, the formally undemocratic processes of litigation and adjudication expressed the people's will far better than such formally democratic processes as the franchise, legislature, and executive. The notorious violence mobilized on behalf of incorporation and independence may have turned the courts against them.

Judicial decisions enjoyed striking legitimacy with the masses, media, and opposition parties. Blacks made great sacrifices to attend oral argument, even though they understood little, and triumphantly celebrated victories. The opposition effectively used government embarrassment about overturning judgments. Defeating a bill that would retroactively approve KwaNdebele legislation, a member of the House of Representatives declared: "If the courts made a decision to invalidate the action of the KwaNdebele Government we do not feel we can disagree with them. It would be immoral and illegal." A member of the House of Delegates called it "subversion of the law," "immoral," "disgusting," "cynical, utterly indecent." Government "had a history of riding roughshod over the decisions of appeal courts." And a DP member of the House of Assembly accused government of saying "to hell with the courts." It was "undermining the standing of our courts," "circumventing our Supreme Court," casting "a vote of no confidence in our Supreme Court," and "contributing to the present legitimacy crisis in our judiciary." "[C]ourts do not enjoy high legitimacy amongst urban Blacks." If government overruled judicial decisions the residual confidence they retained among rural Blacks would be lost. Even government sought comfort in the fact that the Supreme Court accepted the incorporation of Moutse, showing there was "nothing obviously invalid or illegal in the situation" (which conveniently ignored the AD's reversal).

In the last instance, however, politics was determinative. Government tabled the Alteration of Boundaries of Self-Governing Territories Bill to incorporate Moutse and Botshabelo over judicial resistance, although it was unwilling to use the President's Council to overrule the Houses of Delegates and Representatives. Government circumvented those judicial decisions by using the Borders of Particular States Act to incorporate Braklaagte and Leeuwfontein, eliminating meaningful judicial review. After being ousted by women enfranchised by the Supreme Court, George Mahlangu and his supporters threatened to challenge the election in court, sought to control the nominated members, and again resorted to police and Mbokotho violence. Yet South Africa did not succeed in incorporating Moutse into KwaNdebele, disenfranchising KwaNdebele women, or foisting independence on the homeland. The political climate changed—partly through these and other struggles, partly because Botha had a stroke. Accepting the inevitable, all the homeland leaders except Mangope and Buthelezi embraced a unitary South Africa. Grand apartheid was dead.

CHAPTER 12
DISESTABLISHING OUKASIE

[T]he Brits "location," which has been a
local eyesore and abuts one of our smart
suburbs, will shortly no longer blight our
town. (*Brits Post*, April 10, 1970)

Take this letter and go to your lawyer and
tell him to stuff it up his ass and tell him
not to bother me any more. (Oukasie
superintendent M.B. de Beer rejecting
Moshe Jan Mahlaela's request for a house,
January 1986)

In the light of the respondent's unwarranted and boorish conduct, the vulgar
and abusive language he used in telling
the applicant not to waste his time and not
to return to the office again with a similar
application, I have come to the conclusion, on the balance of probabilities, that
the respondent is hostile towards the
applicant. (Justice Stafford granting
Mahlaela's application and ordering de
Beer to allocate him a house, April 1986)

[F]rom the point of view of services the
inhabitants of Oukasie were "homeless"
and slum conditions existed. Even persons
who dwelled in "homes" could be
described as "homeless" in view of their
living conditions. (Government heads of
argument justifying its declaration of an
emergency camp, August 1989)

The overwhelming majority of inhabitants
of Oukasie live in dwellings of a permanent or semi-permanent nature which
shelter them against the elements and provide some of the comforts of life. They can
truly be called homes and are in fact home
to their inhabitants. (Justice van Dijkhorst
invalidating the declaration of an emergency camp, August 1989)

Oukasie, the "old location" of Brits (an industrial city north of Pretoria), was formally established in 1928.[1] Located just 2 kilometers from the city center and 4 kilometers from the industrial area, it grew slowly at first. When Brits was designated a decentralization point for economic development in 1970, Firestone, Alpha Romeo, Bosch, and Ciba-Geigy established factories. Hurt by the recession and economic sanctions in the early 1980s, however, many plants closed or relocated to Bophuthatswana to avoid unions.

In December 1985 some 16,000 people were living in an area 2,000 by 300 meters, served by two primary schools, a secondary school, about ten churches, nine shops, a clinic, and a child care center. Among those under thirty, ninety percent had been born there. The community built three parks, maintained roads, and sought to improve drainage, with almost no help from government, which had constructed no housing since the 1930s. There was no electricity, only fifty water taps, and buckets for human waste.[2]

Brits city council had sought to remove Oukasie for decades and won the agreement of the Transvaal Provincial Administration in 1953. In 1971 several hundred families were moved to Mothutlung, about 20 kilometers northeast, and subsequently incorporated into Bophuthatswana. The local paper reported on the front page that "the Brits 'location,' which has been a local eyesore and abuts one of our smart suburbs, will shortly no longer blight our town."[3] White hostility intensified as the two communities expanded to just 150 meters apart. In 1975 the city council approached the Department of Bantu Administration and Development. Mayor Japie Steenkamp later remarked: "At that stage forced removals were a common thing. We didn't work through negotiations."[4] The next year the Department bought 400 hectares for this purpose, 24 kilometers away and just across the Bophuthatswana border from Maboloka. Every annual mayor's report until 1982/83 declared: "The Council has, during the year, continued its efforts to have the Brits Black township, which constitutes a hindrance for the development of white suburbs, removed." In 1981/82 the mayor asserted that "the Department of Co-operation and Development has decided that the residents of the present Black township shall be moved." Government closed the Oukasie cemetery in 1980, forcing residents to bury their dead in the new township.

Government named it Lethlabile ("sunrise" in Setswana). Under intense pressure it abandoned its plan to incorporate the township into the homeland. By 1982 government had spent R20.2 million to develop Lethlabile, at an average cost of R6,380 per plot, each of which had a tap, flush toilet, and optional electricity. But government built only 175 houses, which sold for R4,000-8,000 and rented for fifteen times as much as in Oukasie. Whereas Oukasie residents could walk to work and shops, the bus from Lethlabile cost R1.40 round trip. There was no secondary school.[5]

Dr. Jan Grobler, elected Nationalist MP for Brits in 1977, strongly advocated removal, correctly fearing that the right wing would gain from the issue. In 1981 he defeated the Herstigte Nasionale Partie candidate by only

5,362-3,517. In 1987 he lost to the Conservative Party candidate, Andrew Gerber, 5,644-7,311. But in June 1983, responding to domestic and international criticism, Deputy Minister Hennie van der Walt had declared that henceforth people would be consulted before being moved "voluntarily." And on February 1, 1985, Co-operation and Development Minister Gerrit Viljoen had declared an end to forced removals.

On November 11, 1985, *City Press* reported that Oukasie had been declared a "black spot," threatening 350 families with removal to "Lechabile" in Bophuthatswana. Less than a month later the black community council confirmed this. Councilor Sam Khumalo, who moved immediately, maintained that the council had been consulted earlier. Jan Grobler even claimed the council had requested the move. Critics responded that the decision had been presented to the council as a fait accompli. Furthermore, only 390 of the more than 10,000 residents participated in the November 1983 election, and four of the six seats were uncontested. On February 25, 1986, the council voted to dissolve because all members had moved to Lethlabile. About forty of the 1,000 plot-holders eagerly accepted the R5,000–10,000 compensation government paid for improvements. Once they left, officials demolished the houses of their far more numerous tenants, forcing them out. A government bus took residents on free daily visits. By early 1986, 4,000 people were in Lethlabile.[6]

Many others resisted, however. The day after the council announcement 800 residents elected the twelve-member Brits Action Committee (BAC), chaired by Marshall Buys (formerly active in the National Automobile and Allied Workers' Union) and including three of his close friends. It immediately obtained 1,000 signatures on a petition against removal and collected another 3,000 by the following March, demanding that the land be sold to residents, drainage improved, roads tarred, and schools built. Complaining that the Lethlabile cemetery was waterlogged and graves had caved in, they asked that the bodies be reinterred in Oukasie. The Brits Women's Federation and Council of Churches offered support.[7]

After several peaceful gatherings, government banned a BAC meeting scheduled for February 8-9. Violence erupted by the end of the month. Claiming that a crowd of 200 had stoned them, police opened fire with 9mm pistols, wounding one person. Fire destroyed a shop and the Central Transvaal Development Board office. Police virtually occupied the township for two days, raiding the homes of community leaders, who went underground. The houses of Marshall Buys and Young Christian Workers president Jacob Mohatshe were firebombed on March 7. That evening police tear gassed a meeting at the Roman Catholic church hall; many were cut by glass trying to escape. The next day Buys was arrested for arson, although the charges were soon dropped. On the night of March 10-11 the house of Sello Ramakobye (BAC secretary and NAAWU chief shop steward at Firestone) was firebombed and the home of the parents of activist Leonard Brown was damaged by a hand grenade. Brown was detained on April 15 and charged with intimidation and attempted murder but acquitted. The police tear gassed another meeting of 2,000 at the Roman Catholic church hall on March 11. Although this violence persuaded some to move, an estimated 11,000 remained.[8]

At the end of February Constitutional Development Minister Chris Heunis replied to a PFP question that "all the residents of the black town at Brits may be resettled in the SA Development Trust town Lethlabile, with the understanding that Lethlabile will not be incorporated into Bophuthatswana." At the same time he reprieved thirteen other townships. "Each case is considered in view of its particular circumstances and with the aim of improving living conditions." Early in March he reiterated that it would "be to the advantage" of residents to "force them to relocate."[9]

With the assistance of NAAWU and the Metal and Allied Workers' Union (MAWU), the BAC commissioned a feasability study, which estimated it would cost just R3 million to upgrade Oukasie. Later that month the two unions sought the support of local employers and employer organizations. They also criticized Firestone for donating $15,000 to a day care center in Lethlabile and making loans to employees wishing to move there; the company promised to reconsider its position.[10]

Residents decided to take legal action as well.[11] Moshe Jan Mahlaela, BAC treasurer and former NAAWU shop steward at Alfa Romeo, was left homeless when his father moved to Lethlabile. He applied for permission to build on one of the many vacant lots. On January 20, Geoffrey Budlender, an attorney with the Legal Resources Centre in Johannesburg, wrote on his behalf to Oukasie superintendent M.B. de Beer.

> Our client has always lived in Brits Location, and is qualified in terms of section 10(1)(a) of Act 25 of 1945 to remain in the area....
>
> Our client wishes to remain in Brits with his wife, Elizabeth Mahlaela, and their minor daughter. He is temporarily unemployed, and will find it much easier to obtain employment, whether casual or permanent—if he is resident in Brits Location nearby the local industrial area.
>
> Our client is in a financial position to build his own house if a vacant site is allocated to him....
>
> On behalf of our client, we now make application for a residential site to be allocated to him, *alternatively* for a vacant dwelling to be allocated to him.
>
> If you have any practical difficulties in this regard, would you kindly advise the writer so that we may take the necessary steps to deal with them.

Mahlaela presented the letter two days later.

> The respondent read the letter, showed it to another official, and then gave it back to me, saying [in Afrikaans]: "Take this letter and go to your lawyer and tell him to stuff it up his ass and tell him not to bother me any more." He also told me not to come to his office again with such a letter.

When the TRAC fieldworker accompanying Mahlaela recounted this later that day, Budlender surprised him by bursting out laughing and saying: "It's fantastic, wonderful, isn't that terrific!" He had expected a more subtle rejection. Budlender telephoned another government official, who confirmed that Oukasie was a proclaimed township, to which the usual regulations applied.

On February 6 Mahlaela asked the Transvaal Supreme Court to order de Beer to allocate a site or dwelling and issue a residential permit. He alleged that de Beer had failed to apply his mind, acted mala fide, and had a fixed policy against allocating sites. In his reply affidavit on March 20 he rejected de Beer's suggestion that he move to Lethlabile and become a farm laborer because he was a skilled industrial worker. He accused the Central Transvaal Development Board (CTDB) of demolishing every vacant house "with the deliberate intention of frustrating the attempts of unhoused Brits residents, including me, to obtain housing in the Brits location." He also denied that government sought "to improve the living conditions of the residents of Brits," since it had done nothing to develop the location for years. Because de Beer was legally obligated to allocate a site, the relative merits of the townships were irrelevant. Nevertheless, he asserted on behalf of the BAC that the overwhelming majority of residents preferred to remain. De Beer was misusing his nondiscretionary function of allocating permits for the unauthorized goal of disestablishing the township.

> I respectfully submit that the Respondent's hostility towards me is most clearly indicated by the manner in which he dealt with my initial application (which he does not deny) and by his allegation...that I am simply trying to obstruct the attempts of the Development Board to improve the circumstances of the Brits black township.[12]

Justice E. Stafford granted the application on April 23.[13] Mahlaela had not failed to exhaust his administrative remedies.

> If the respondent's contention that he was entitled as it were to throw the letter of application back in the applicant's face, is wrong in Law, then the refusal to allocate a house has been made without applicant having been given an opportunity of being heard. This would be a fundamental irregularity.

There was no point in appealing to the Development Board because it had "laid down a fixed policy that houses are not to be allocated in light of their view that the Brits Black Town ought to be disestablished." The regulations governing Oukasie "do not deal with or confer any power on the respondent...or in fact on anyone else to disestablish a Black Township." Only the Minister could do that. "The Central Transvaal Development Board has in this case pre-empted the Minister's discretion." Mahlaela maintained that 10,000-12,000 people still lived in Oukasie; de Beer conceded 4,000-5,000. "I mention these figures to indicate that I am dealing with a real problem which may effect [sic] thousands of people in the presently existing township...."

> [T]o use a power to allocate housing in order to achieve the disestablishment of the town, is not sanctioned by the legislation and a decision given to achieve such a purpose, is invalid. It is an abuse of that power. Powers given for one purpose cannot be used for obtaining other objects.

Stafford saw no reason to remand Mahlaela's application. During argument he had revealed his anger at de Beer's vulgarity and refused to allow respondent's counsel to deny it had occurred.

> In the light of the respondent's unwarranted and boorish conduct, the vulgar and abusive language he used in telling the applicant not to waste his time and not to return to the office again with a similar application, I have come to the conclusion, on the balance of probabilities, that the respondent is hostile towards the applicant.

> I am also of the view that the respondent's past conduct, influenced by his applying an invalid policy in refusing to hear the application, is calculated on the probabilities to impair the prospects of respondent applying his mind fresh, unbiasedly and objectively. These factors have persuaded me to exercise my judicial discretion in favour of the applicant and to allocate him the home he should have been allocated months ago.

Stafford seriously considered Mahlaela's request that costs be awarded against de Beer personally but concluded that "his high-handed disregard of the applicant's rights and the consequent demolition of the houses which were available at that time, pending this action, derives, as I see it, not from an individual malice against this particular applicant, but from a bureaucratic or an official disregard for people's rights." However, he strongly rejected the respondent's claim that Mahlaela was to blame for de Beer's "disgraceful behaviour" because he applied for a house "knowing that there was a general policy to refuse to allocate houses." "The applicant's behaviour on the papers before me was above reproach. He was an individual exercising his legal rights, seeking to obtain a home for himself and his family in the Brits Township where he has always lived."

Newspapers were sympathetic: "Super ordered to give resident a home," "Court awards Brits man 'a long overdue home,'" "Court rules Brits removals illegal."[14] They quoted extensively from Justice Stafford's harsh criticism of de Beer. The latter did not carry through his threat to seek leave to appeal.

Budlender followed this legal victory by urging Heunis not to disestablish Oukasie, invoking the government's promise to end forced removals and its white paper recognizing the need for black urban housing. Two weeks after the judgment the CTDB gave Mahlaela a house: a single room, three meters by six, with a cracked floor, no glass windows, leaky roof, lockless door, and holes in the walls. Water was thirty meters away, and the bucket latrine had no door. But demolitions had ended, and government removal trucks disappeared. The Board allocated six more homes that month. The Steel and Engineering Industries Federation of South Africa (SEIFSA), the Federated Chamber of Industries (FCI), and the Northern Transvaal Chamber of Commerce all declared support for residents. The Brits Industrial Association (BIA) offered to help fund the upgrading of Oukasie.[15]

Local whites were outraged. Brits MP Jan Grobler had invited the Cabinet to see the support Nationalists enjoyed. But when Deputy Information Minister Louis Nel sought to address a meeting on May 21 opponents from the Afrikaner Weerstandsbeweging, Herstigte Nasionale Partie, Conservative Party, and Afrikaner Volksweg shouted him down for an hour and took over the stage when he left.[16]

Early in the morning of May 29 a powerful bomb killed Joyce Modimoeng, severely injured her husband David, a MAWU organizer, and destroyed their house. Just before the blast David's younger brother Joseph heard men debating in Setswana whether to destroy cars or the house. David later said that SAP Capt. Java had warned that continued opposition to removal would have unfortunate consequences. At the night vigil before Joyce's funeral police tear gassed and arrested mourners—the fifth violent attack on removal opponents. The Northern Transvaal region of COSATU responded with a two-week boycott of white businesses and workers' canteens. When government declared the second Emergency on June 11 it detained all BAC members not in hiding.[17]

In June the Department of Constitutional Development wrote in its propaganda sheet *Informa*:

> The old town (Brits location) is the epitome of decline. Conditions are unhygienic because the draining system has ceased to function effectively. Houses collapse because they have been built on clay soil. Furthermore, there are not enough houses for the 2,500 residents, with the result that squatting is on the increase.... [It is] impossible to construct a sewerage system.[18]

Residents responded in October with a plan to improve Oukasie, prepared by engineers and social scientists. An initial outlay of R1,115,000 would double the number of water outlets, upgrade storm drains, erect ten communal flush toilet blocks, and grade roads. Another R1,911,000 would deliver water to each household, extend sewers to every plot, complete the storm drains, and tar the two primary roads. If government provided a subsidized loan at 7.5 percent, at least eighty percent of households could afford the R6 per-month for the first phase and fifty-five percent could afford the R16.70 for both phases.[19]

Without further warning government disestablished Oukasie on October 17.[20] As part of its attempt to cultivate a reformist image, however, it had abolished the pass laws earlier that year, repealing legislation that authorized summary eviction and demolition and allowed police to remove residents forcibly.[21] Consequently, disestablishment had no immediate significance. Heunis claimed "the move followed several years of negotiations with the former community council of the township after it had been decided that the poor hygienic conditions there and the astronomic costs involved in upgrading the town did not make its continued use a viable proposition." ("They say this place can't be upgraded," a resident rejoined, "but as soon as we move they will do that and move whites in.") Heunis offered free transportation "to assist these people in moving to the better conditions offered by Lethlabile without delay...." More than 1,500 families had already moved "voluntarily." The rest would be eligible for loans up to R5,000. He promised to pave the road to Brits in 1987 and subsidize transportation. Government prohibited further burials in Oukasie and dug more than 500 graves in Lethlabile, which filled with water while awaiting their occupants.[22]

Wealthier families did benefit from the move. The wife of a liquor store manager had a three-bedroom, two-bath house with an outside garage. "Oukasie was dangerous. There was a necklacing in the location while we were there...we are glad to have left all that behind." Her neighbor had bought a plot for R54 and borrowed R38,000 to build a similar house. A shop owner enthused: "In Oukasie I was locked inside a cocoon.... I was unable to expand my business because I did not have enough land. I think Lethlabile will give me a new lease on life and enable me to concentrate on my business."[23]

But most residents remained defiant. Many feared Lethlabile would be incorporated into Bophuthatswana to undermine the strong unions Brits workers had organized. The elderly heard rumors their pensions would be stopped if they did not move. Sello Ramakobye spoke for the BAC: "We are going to challenge Heunis all the way. [We are] not going to take it lying down...even if it means violence." The bereaved David Modimoeng said: "Our experience here is proof that apartheid is as alive as ever. If they try to force us, that will be the end of peace in this area. We will fight." Levy Mamabolo declared to 800 residents at the Catholic Mission on October 19: "We want to tell the world: If we go to Lethlabile, it's not voluntarily. We've been forced to go there." The audience voted to stay away from work on October 22. But on October 21 MAWU, NAAWU, SEIFSA, FCI, BIA, and local employers sought a meeting with Heunis to protest the removal. Grateful workers cancelled the stay-away.[24]

Newspaper headlines remained sympathetic: "Oukasie is dead," "Digging community's grave," " 'Forced removals in a new guise,' " "New ploy to force people out." The story of a black reporter denied service in Mollani Hotel while covering the removal was entitled "Baas rules at Brits, OK!" A *Sowetan* cartoon showed a fat Heunis erasing Oukasie from the map. It interviewed seventy-nine-year-old Bertha Mokua, who helped found Oukasie in 1935 and swore the location would never die in the hearts and minds of the people. The *Weekly Mail* described the ten-room villa built by a seventy-year-old former policeman, who moved to Oukasie in 1946.[25]

Black Sash, the Transvaal Rural Action Committee, and the Legal Resources Centre condemned disestablishment. Budlender immediately telexed Heunis, questioning his reasons and seeking an opportunity to present the plan to upgrade Oukasie; there was no response. Tom Boya, deputy president of the generally conservative Urban Councils' Association of South Africa, said it was "shocking and unreliable of the government to renege on its stated policy on the issue of forced removals, especially in the light of their recent announcements on reforms." He warned against repeating the KwaNdebele-Moutse disaster. The "inhuman" removals were an "ill-fated effort by the government to appease the verkrampte White constituency of Brits." MP Jan Grobler lent support to this view when he declared that disestablishment was a high point in his term.[26]

The removal attracted attention abroad. *The New York Times* published four stories in five weeks with headlines like "South African Town Vows to Resist Order to Move," "Long-Built Dreams Crushed as Pretoria Razes Township," and "Uprooting of Blacks Resumed in South Africa."[27] The *Washington Post* carried one, and the *Christian Science Monitor* headlined a front-page story "Pretoria under fire for removals."[28] Britain and Germany urged South Africa to reconsider; on November 14 the European Community delivered a démarche deploring both the removal of Oukasie and the threatened incorporation of Lethlabile into Bophuthatswana.[29]

In response to panic among residents, soldiers drove through the township in Casspirs on Wednesday and Thursday, October 23 and 24, distributing a notice in English and Setswana.

> Office of the Director of Local Government
> Transvaal

> The rumours which are being spread that the township will be demolished during the coming weekend are totally false.

> It is the work of instigators with evil intent who want to cause confusion.

No forced removals are contemplated before proper consultations with residents have taken place.

On October 31, however, a bulldozer began destroying empty houses, stopping only when the LRC threatened to sue. The CTDB claimed that 1,400 residents had moved "voluntarily" between October 17 and November 4 and an average of thirty families were doing so weekly. The BAC called the statement "malicious and misleading," insisting that only four families had moved. TRAC and NAAWU put the total at no more than ten, most of them forced out by rent arrearages, which the Board promised to forgive if they went to Lethlabile. BAC member Abel Molokoane warned that the return of the bulldozers would produce a riot: "I'm not saying this to incite people—I'm telling you, this is what people are saying."[30]

Marshall Buys announced at a November 16 prayer meeting that internal and external pressure had persuaded government to meet the management-labor delegation. More than 2,000 adult residents signed affidavits saying they had not been consulted and did not want to move. Daveyton Mayor Tom Boya and Atteridgeville Mayor Matthew Mahlangu also met Heunis, who merely reiterated that the decision was final. Meanwhile the Brits Women's League used materials from demolished houses to repair roads and planned to weed the Oukasie graveyard. Two papers carried heart-rending pictures of Mrs. Emily Mabiletsa, who had lived in Oukasie for more than fifty years, breaking rock for the road while leaning on crutches because of a disabled leg.[31]

In preparation for removal, government sent officials into the township, guarded by security forces, demanding house permits and pass books. Although they did not tell residents their purpose, they informed lawyers and reporters they were conducting a census, since CTDB records had been destroyed when the office was burned. They vanished when foreign television crews appeared but returned as soon as they departed.[32] On Christmas Eve Heunis reasserted to Budlender that Oukasie must go. *Business Day* reviewed the year's removals despite government's declaration of a moratorium.[33] In May vigilantes protected by police had driven 70,000 residents out of Crossroads, and security forces moved others in July and August. Government served eviction notices on 4,000 Lawaaikamp residents in July and moved nearly 30,000 people to KwaNobuhle in October.

The Bureau of Information published a lengthy feature on "Oukasie vs Lethlabile" in the December 1986 issue of *Light/Khanya*, rehashing the government line. Because it "was never intended to be a township government had been consulting with the leaders of the people of Oukasie for the past 30 years to find an alternative and better area to establish a permanent township." It was the Oukasie Advisory Board that first approached the Brits Town Council in 1945 seeking another site. "Lethlabile was chosen in consultation with the people who served on the Advisory Board." Its name signified " 'Sunrise'—after the long and 'dark' search for a suitable place."

Oukasie was a "slum," with land for only forty-four families, whereas "living conditions in Lethlabile are very attractive." "[A]n official job-creation programme is envisaged for Lethlabile where people will be engaged to establsh lawns in the parks, a soccer stadium, and tennis courts. At R4.00 a day one could in a relatively short period earn enough money to buy a stand." The article contained testimonials from happy residents, under the heading: "This is mine! This is mine!" Advisory Board member M.W. Matolane moved in November 1985 and had almost finished building a home. Another Advisory Board member had a four-room house and was building a shop. S.S. Khumalo was principal of a new primary school. The new shop of Paul Maye "has reached an advanced stage."

Two papers republished this propaganda without disclosing the source.[34] One was headlined "They love Lethlabile."

> In a snap interviews [sic] with residents, it came to light that negative reports about Lethlabile were badly exaggerated by the popular press. Not one of the residents interviewed showed a negative attitude to their new place.... Mr S.S. Khumalo who is principal of the local Molelwaneng Primary School was oozing pride when he talked about educational development in the new place.... A local businessman, Mr Paul Maye, said that despite having lived in Oukasie since 1952, he had no second thought [sic] when Lethlabile was available.

The other story was headed "The mood is calm at Letlhabile [sic]: Residents do not regret moving and are happy with conditions." Those interviewed had strangely stilted diction. For Mrs. Elsie Dlamini, "Letlhabile [sic] is a far better place than Oukasie as it offers most of the basic facilities which were lacking in our former township. The conditions here are hygienic and we have proper toilets, electricity and roads which are in good condition." The foreign press was less credulous. *The Times* headlined "Oukasie awaits Botha's bulldozers," characterizing the threat as a "forced removal" by a government fearful of losing the Parliamentary seat to the far right. Oukasie remained "a well-knit community" despite the miserable conditions, violence, and detentions.[35]

Government followed its public relations campaign by demolishing a hundred homes in the first two weeks of January. The Department of Education and Training (DET) closed the Itumeleng primary school, forcing its 300 pupils to crowd into the only other school, whose fifteen teachers now had to deal with a thousand students. A DET spokesman condemned the fact that children from outlying areas were being sent to the school "in an orchestrated attempt to cause problems." The DET also transferred most Oukasie teachers to Lethlabile and stopped issuing stationery and textbooks. After a crèche for 200 children closed when its management committee moved to Lethlabile the BAC sought funds to run it and restore the Itumeleng school.[36]

At the end of February Heunis defended his resettlement policy in response to a PFP question. The seven planned removals were not politically motivated but directed only at "unorderly squatting" and "poor health conditions." "Voluntary relocation" at Oukasie had been gaining momentum; if a "few" residents refused to move "it will be to their advantage to force them to relocate. It will not be feasible to upgrade Oukasie for the sake of a few persons." The party organ *The Nationalist* listed the fact that "forced removals have been halted" as one of the government's "20 proud landmarks on the reform road."[37]

The BAC replied that an average of only two families were leaving a month. *The Star* noted that "every visit [it] has made to the township has confirmed an overwhelming resistance to resettlement." "Removals embitter the affected communities and spread uncertainty to many thousands of other black people who fear they may be next." *Business Day* urged government to abandon "its meddlesome social engineering and let people live and work where they want to.... [N]one of this would be possible in the first place if the vested voting interests to which the government responds included the black people now shunted around the country at government's whim." The South African Catholic Bishops' Conference expressed their "deep concern at the continuing forced removal of people" during what the United Nations had designated as "international year of the home for the homeless." To rebut the government claim that the cost of upgrading Oukasie would be "astronomic," the Legal Resources Centre obtained an estimate from consulting engineers Ove Arup Inc. that the direct cost would be similar to that of developing Lethlabile, which would have much greater indirect costs. More than "a few persons" remained at Oukasie; Budlender had affidavits from 2,500 adults, and a July survey found 6,300 people. He asked Heunis to meet with the engineers.[38]

Government efforts to eliminate Oukasie did not save the Brits seat, which the Nationalists lost to the Conservative Party in May. Five months later Heunis reiterated "that I am not prepared to reconsider my decision to disestablish Oukasie and that I regard the matter as closed." He refused to meet with Ove Arup or "enter into further correspondence with you on matters concerning Oukasie." Couched in more polite language, this is just what de Beer had told Mahlaela. In September the government could not tell CP MP C.J. Derby-Lewis when Oukasie would be removed, but the next month it assured the new Conservative Brits MP Andrew Gerber that "the Transvaal Provincial Administration is already taking steps in terms of the Prevention of Illegal Squatting Act, 1951, to effect the establishment of an emergency camp" to contain 136 illegal squatters "until they can settle elsewhere." And the following day it told Derby-Lewis that the decision had been taken to eliminate Oukasie.[39]

Gerber was not satisfied: "To establish an emergency camp for illegal squatters next to the white town is deplorable." Oukasie was "an eyesore," and "the white residents" expected deproclamation to be followed by removal. On October 17 more than a thousand residents met at the Roman Catholic church hall to oppose removal. A TRAC fieldworker told them that lawyers had concluded that the Act could not be invoked. TRAC and the BAC had conducted a health survey, which found that the death rate among Oukasie infants was low. On the anniversary of disestablishment two weeks later *The Star*'s feature story "Bustling life in a 'ghost town'" showed pictures of happy children in the BAC crèche. Marshall Buys declared: "disestablishing the township officially meant more unity among the people." Volunteers were repairing roads, cultivating gardens, and cleaning the cemetery.[40]

On January 11, 1988, Heunis sought to reconcile reform with removal. "Government has never said there would not be any more forced removals. After all people will squat illegally wherever and you cannot accept they will stay there forever. What government said was there would be no forced removals for political reasons." Provincial Administrators were now responsible for removing squatters.[41]

A week later Oukasie tried to elicit international support by becoming the sister city of Berkeley, California, an event covered by South African and American newspapers. Telephoned by Berkeley Mayor Loni Hancock, BAC chairman Marshall Buys said: "As Americans, you have a lot of influence. ... We are of the opinion that international pressure will force the South African government to change its decision." A South African Embassy official in Washington insisted his government had ended forced removals in early 1986. Oukasie residents left "voluntarily because of immense squatter problems. How have they managed to stay there if we wanted to move them?"[42] Nevertheless, Helen Suzman visited Oukasie and raised the issue in Parliament.[43]

In mid-February police detained seventeen community leaders, and vigilantes attacked residents. Marshall Buys and other leaders fled the township, and the homes of two suspected vigilantes were burned. On March 9 the U.S.-South Africa Sister Community Project placed an advertisement in a Berkeley newspaper naming sixteen detainees, who could not be identified in South Africa under the Emergency, and urging readers to write Heunis and Ambassador Koornhof.[44]

Toward the end of March Heunis told CP MP C.J. Derby-Lewis: "It was decided that only those persons who of their own free will so request, will be resettled at Lethlabile." Helen Suzman welcomed the decision, which *The Star*'s editorial called "Sense at last." The same day the *Wall Street Journal* strongly criticized government plans to move 600 Black families from Koster township in the Western Transvaal to a site 500 meters away in order to appease whites, whom it quoted.

> We need a buffer area for the same reason every other town has one. The Blacks' standard of living isn't the same as ours. Their culture isn't the same. (Town Clerk)

> They're different. They aren't on the same level as us; they aren't as developed. In the United States, you don't understand. Your Blacks are more cultured and educated, just like the whites. our Blacks aren't. (Farmer)

A few days later TRAC held a press conference for Moutse to celebrate its Appellate Division victory and Oukasie its reprieve. But Heunis quickly corrected the misapprehension. He "did not mean that the decision of the Government in respect of the de-proclamation of Oukasie had changed in any way." Rather than using force "it has been decided to negotiate a more attractive incentive with these inhabitants." Suzman denounced Heunis for backtracking and wondered whether he was responding to the Conservative Party by-election victory in Randfontein the previous week. The *Pretoria News* editorial headlined "White man speaks with..." noted that "government 'persuasion' in the past has involved closing schools and water supplies...." *The Star's* cartoon showed a piggish Heunis telling an Oukasie family "naturally, we wouldn't move you before you were ready," while concealing a can dripping repulsive insects in their house.[45]

In April government passed legislation precluding the incorporation of Lethlabile and Soshanguve into Bophuthatswana on the ground that their "strong inter-ethnic composition" rendered it "both impractical and inadvisable." The only opposition was from the Conservative Party, especially Brits MP Andrew Gerber:

> How ironic! Of all the political parties in South Africa, the NP bases the incorporation or non-incorporation of these two towns in an independent state on ethnicity. The Republic of South Africa, the Whites of this country, including the Afrikaner, have to be willing to accept all and sundry as citizens of this country, with all the political implications that this entails. However, when it comes to a country like Bophuthtaswana, such a town must consist only of a Tswana population in order to qualify to be incorporated in that state. What kind of logic is that?

Fearing the implications of this argument for the government's continued efforts to incorporate Moutse into KwaNdebele (see chapter eleven), the Minister of Education and Development Aid replied:

> The point is precisely that we cannot deal with the complexity of our situation in South Africa merely with theoretical logic. We also have to deal with realities.... When the Government in this case excludes multi-ethnic released areas because it no longer intends including them in a self-governing or independent state, it does not wish to imply that it now intends including only pure uni-ethnic communities in the self-governing areas or the national states. There are many examples of multi-ethnicity

> working well in practice in a predominantly Tswana, Pedi or
> Swazi area.... [L]arge numbers of Ndebele, especially North
> Ndebele, live in Lebowa.... In western Lebowa there is even a
> whole area in which chiefly Tswanas live.... In the same way
> there is a large number of people in KwaNdebele, with Pedi-
> speaking ethnic ties, whom one could call Lebowans and who
> live peacefully under the rule of the KwaNdebele government.

If Gerber were serious about ethnic purity, the Minister suggested, "the entire
Brits area should be gone through with a fine-tooth comb and... all who are
not Tswanas should be removed." But he warned that this would have serious side effects on the labor force. Government policy was "to make the
development in Lethlabile as attractive as possible for the purpose of persuading the population of Oukasie to move as quickly as possible."[46]

On April 26 government took the next step. Transvaal Administrator
Willem Cruywagen declared Oukasie an "emergency camp for the accommodation of homeless persons." Budlender had been warned a few days
before by an anonymous phone call in Afrikaans setting up a cloak-and-dag-
ger meeting in Pretoria, where an unidentified "deep throat" gave him
minutes of the Transvaal Provincial Administration and Brits Town Council
and a TPA strategy paper expressing concern that the disestablishment had
been invalid. Cruywagen issued regulations for the "Brits Emergency Camp"
authorizing the appointment of a superintendent with extraordinary powers.
The regulations allowed only registered occupants and their families to enter
the township, empowered the superintendent to suspend registration, barred
all house construction and improvement, banned all livestock, and raised service charges more than fifty percent.[47] The TPA also distributed a two-page
"Information Bulletin" to employers explaining that it had declared Oukasie
an emergency camp to keep it "well organised" and ensure "basic community services such as water supply and refuse removal," which "the high
population density in a relative [sic] small area" had precluded. Despite
"intimidation by radical elements" more than 2,000 families had voluntarily
moved to Lethlabile.

Early in the morning of the proclamation a hundred security personnel
camped in the soccer field, blocked Oukasie's main entrance, and searched
every house in an effort to prevent squatting, list all residents, and mark the
houses. That night they imposed a 9:15 p.m. curfew. The BAC denounced
this "pretext for the state to establish a permanent military and police presence at Oukasie so as over a period of time to totally demoralise the
community.... We reject with contempt the notion that we are squatters."
The *Pretoria News* called "the Government's appalling handling of Oukasie
township" "the seamy side of apartheid." The *Sowetan* said: "[W]e have been
plunged back to the ugly old days of permits and permit raids."[48]

Budlender wrote Cruywagen three weeks later, asserting that the declaration was invalid but deferring litigation in the hope of negotiating a solution

and asking about the compensation promised those who moved. A month later he learned that an average of R4,865 would be paid for the 349 permanent structures and R2,000 for the 250 temporary structures (substantially less than the R5,000-10,000 paid the first wave of emigrants). His request that residents be allowed to improve the roads was ignored.

Answering a PFP question on May 10, the Deputy Minister of Constitutional Development reiterated that the camp was declared "to gain control," "prevent further squatting and influx of persons," and "improve the living conditions as far as possible." He rejected Helen Suzman's accusation that "this is an indirect method of forcing removals for political reasons." When Parliament debated the report of its Committee on Transvaal Provincial Affairs at the end of the month she reminded members that Viljoen had declared in 1985 "that there were to be no more forced removals in South Africa" and Heunis had said the same thing. "When is a forced removal not a forced removal?" she asked rhetorically, detailing the "various forms of pressure and harassment." "One might well ask whether that is Russia. The climate is different but not much else." Heunis "has betrayed these people. He gave me his personal assurance that he would not force the removal." She returned to the attack a week later.

> *Suzman:* The hon the Minister told me face to face, eyeball to eyeball—he will remember this—that he was not going to move those people who did not wish to move.

> *Heunis:* That's right!

> *Suzman:*...What he does is to allow the Administrator of the Transvaal to issue regulations which make life unbearable for those people who remain at Oukasie. Shifting around in his bench like that will not help.

Shortly thereafter Marshall Buys told a meeting of more than 100 residents not to be intimidated. The regulations went into effect on June 1, immediately raising the service charges.[49]

On June 23 Oukasie residents and Budlender met with J.S.A. Mavuso and other senior TPA officials. Mavuso had been an ANC member when it was legal, an organizer of the Alexandra bus boycotts, an accused in the 1956 treason trial, an Inkatha member, and the first black on a provincial executive committee. About this time he told an American reporter: "The government has concluded that the participation of blacks in central government is inevitable and the question is how. President Botha is waiting at the table."[50] Budlender had worked with Mavuso when the LRC represented Inkatha in protests against bus fare increases. Impressed by Mavuso's flexibility, Budlender wrote Cruywagen commending the spirit of the negotiations. Within days, however, government increased rents in Oukasie by seventy to eighty-eight percent. At a second meeting the TPA refused to allow residents to build a church following their minister's departure to Lethlabile because this would draw people to Oukasie, which was only a "temporary" emergency camp and would be disestablished. The next day a mass meeting denounced the increased charges as a device to drive out residents and refused to pay them. The LRC notified the TPA a few days later, and Mavuso promised to stay any legal proceedings against residents. The community also submitted detailed proposals for extending the graveyard, expanding the child-care center, and improving the clinic.

Government efforts to remove Oukasie, never a unified community, deepened its fissures, initially between those staying and leaving. Police tried to recruit residents. Moshe Jan Mahlaela, plaintiff in the lawsuit and BAC treasurer, testified that the security branch warned he would never find work in Brits. During detention in 1986 and 1988 Capt. Java threatened him with death if he remained in the BAC but promised a house in Lethlabile if he joined the police. In February 1987, when many BAC leaders were detained or hiding, a rumor spread that they had misused money donated by foreign embassies. Unable to contest it, they gradually lost support. When the old leaders were released or resurfaced in August 1988, a new Brits Action Committee headed by Leonard Brown challenged them. Supporters divided into the Vark (Pig) Squad, following the older leaders, and the Comrades, following Brown. When the two groups fought, police refused to respond to complaints, telling residents to move to Lethlabile, where crime was low. The following March attackers killed Marshall Buys and seriously wounded Moshe Jan Mahlaela.[51]

The BAC sought to counteract government propaganda and appeal for support by commissioning a demographic survey and a public health evaluation of Oukasie, completed in September and disseminated soon thereafter.[52] The community was ethnically diverse, and its gender and age distribution was more representative than those of most homelands. More than two-thirds of adults had lived there more than fifteen years. The average number of people per household (four) was less than a third that of all black townships. Almost all those employed worked in Brits, men in skilled or semi-skilled industrial jobs, women as domestics. They did all their shopping there, most by walking or bicycling. Two-thirds had close relatives in other housholds, and all belonged to churches, burial societies, trade unions, savings clubs, sports clubs, and women's and youth organizations. Virtually all wanted to stay because Oukasie was close to Brits, it was home, and the cost of living was low. The health survey found that only a fifth of the plots were dirty. The most significant health hazards were the rubble caused by government destruction of houses and its failure to collect garbage. Health, morbidity, and mortality compared favorably to other townships and homelands.

Answering a PFP question about removals at the end of September, Heunis assured the House that "resettlement [to Lethlabile] is in progress and takes place at the rate residents apply voluntarily to be moved." Removal had cost R2.5 million thus far.[53] To encourage it the TPA rejected all of Oukasie's proposals a week later, conceding that the reason was not lack of money but a policy against improvement. Budlender persisted in urging meetings with accountants on both sides to reach agreement on increased service charges. Mavuso visited the township in October and provided some documentation of the R500,000 allegedly required to administer the "emergency camp."[54] Having consulted an actuary, accountant, and water engineer, the LRC asked for greater detail. Mavuso replied on November 11 that the earlier information represented estimates based on previous experience. He could find "no justification for the provision of more details for each item" and demanded the residents' memo by the end of the month. On the basis of the inadequate data available, the LRC submitted its representation about service charges on November 25. Mavuso replied angrily on December 9.

> The great number of enquiries and requests originating in your office tend to create the impression that Fabian tactics are being applied to the detriment of the residents of the emergency camp whose arrears are accumulating to the point where they will shortly be totally unable to meet their commitment. In order to ensure that the people are not further embarrassed by the unnecessary accumulation of debts, we will now have to proceed with the application of prescribed procedures for the normal debt recovery process.

The LRC wrote a long letter to Mavuso on December 23, narrating all the events and attributing any insufficiency in their November 25 letter to his refusal to provide information "of a public nature to which our clients...are surely entitled." They regretted negotiations had failed and were preparing to initiate litigation but remained willing to meet at any time. On December 27 M.B. de Beer (demoted to deputy superintendent) wrote Joseph Makama, refusing his request to revise the new service charge, informing him that he owed R225, and threatening a fine of R500 and three months imprisonment.

The next day Makama and three other residents, who had lived in Oukasie twenty-seven to forty-four years, sued the Administrator of the Transvaal to invalidate the declaration of the emergency camp and the regulations promulgated. They acted on behalf of 1,063 residents whose signatures had been collected in just three days but who had not joined the lawsuit because of the cost (South Africa does not allow class actions). Few papers reported the lawsuit.[55]

Makama rented three sites, on which he had built brick houses for himself and his son and a brick shop. He recounted government efforts to remove residents, including de Beer's vulgar rebuff to Mahlaela and the successful lawsuit. He paid his site rent, which the superintendent accepted, even late, until the amount increased in August. Movement to Lethlabile had virtually stopped, leaving 6,000–7,000 people in the township. Residents were not homeless, the prerequisite for an emergency camp. Most "squatters" were people whose parents had moved to Lethlabile or tenants who built homes on vacant plots after their landlords left; a few had moved to Lethlabile and returned. Declaration of the emergency camp had actually worsened living conditions: five of the water taps had been closed, garbage collection became less frequent, and telephone service deteriorated. As hardship drove out residents, government destroyed their houses rather than giving them to the homeless.

In his reply affidavit Makama documented government pressure to move. The vice-chair of the Community Council had threatened him with demolition, and her husband threatened another plaintiff. Makama also controverted the government's flimsy evidence of intimidation. De Beer claimed that tires and stones in newly constructed parks encouraged necklacing and rock-throwing.

> There was only one tyre in these parks, which was a large tractor tyre. It was half buried in the ground. The tyre symbolised movement, and the fact that it was half buried in the ground was intended to symbolise that Oukasie residents would not be removed. The stones were an attempt to build rockeries and beautify the area.

The only incident government described was ambiguous. Joanna Rantho decided to leave, using compensation for her mother's house to buy land in Lethlabile. Joanna claimed to have been threatened. Her mother chose to stay, and Joanna soon returned to Oukasie.

While the case was pending two papers that had supported residents ran glowing articles about Lethlabile.[56]

> Luxury German cars stand in the driveways of sprawling mansions with manicured lawns. There is a scattering of doctor's rooms, the roads are paved, the place is electrified and comfortable, multi-storied school buildings, sports fields, shops, service stations and a regular bus route make Lethlabile totally self-sufficient.

Replying to Parliamentary questions, Heunis again defended the emergency camp as necessary to exercise "formal control" and deal with the "potential health risk" created by 1,230 "squatter structures."[57]

The case was argued on August 2.[58] Arthur Chaskalson, representing the applicants, was dismayed to find himself before Justice Kees van Dijkhorst. For nearly three years he had jousted with the judge in the Delmas treason trial, the longest in South African history (see chapter nine). When Chaskalson moved to recuse van Dijkhorst for improperly dismissing an assessor, the judge threatened him with contempt. Relations in the courtroom distinctly cooled. The previous November van Dijkhorst wrote a thousand-page judgment sentencing the accused to long prison terms. Now Chaskalson was appealing the judgment because of the dismissed assessor.

He argued that government could not characterize residents as homeless because Oukasie lacked water, sewers, electricity, and storm drains since this was true of many other townships. Government had ample powers under the Health, Slums, and Prevention of Illegal Squatting Acts to improve services, enhance health, and control squatters. A TPA official admitted that "Oukasie was merely a temporary 'emergency camp' which would in due course be disestablished and the residents required to move out of it." This illegitimate purpose rendered the government's action ultra vires.

Government responded that during World War II it had declared a Johannesburg shantytown an emergency camp, creating infrastructure and providing services. The Appellate Division had upheld the conviction of a resident who refused to pay rent "because I have no house."[59] The Prevention of Illegal Squatting Act authorized similar regulations. Government argued that "as a result of the disestablishment of the town no rules applied there which would ensure that conditions in Oukasie would not worsen." Although the parties disagreed whether squatters arrived before or after the declaration of an emergency camp, "the application must be decided on the basis that the information contained in the memorandum was placed before the respondent.... [I]t is not the function of the Court in a matter of this nature to decide whether the facts placed before the respondent are correct or not." "In our submission the discretion conferred upon a local authority... is a free, unfettered, unbound and subjective discretion."

Although the Act authorized the declaration of an emergency camp to provide accommodation for homeless people, "it was specifically decided that the said phrase did not import an obligation to erect adequate dwellings. Furthermore, that any improvement in the conditions of the living of the persons residing in the emergency camp would be a realisation of the aims and objects of the measure." At the same time, "from the point of view of services the inhabitants of Oukasie were 'homeless' and slum conditions existed. Even persons who dwelled in 'homes' could be described as 'homeless' in view of their living conditions."

Van Dijkhorst gave judgment on August 7. He agreed he could not evaluate the facts on which the Administrator based his decision but only whether the Administrator had acted "for the purpose of the accommodation of homeless persons." Government contended that "a homeless person is not only one who has no roof over his head and no place to live, but also a person who does have a roof over his head but whose amenities are below standard." The judge replied that the "ordinary meaning" of homeless "is lacking a home and though the concept 'home' is of wide and varied nature when applied to persons, it does connote a shelter against the elements providing some of the comforts of life with some degree of permanence." "The overwhelming majority of inhabitants of Oukasie live in dwellings of a permanent or semi-permanent nature which shelter them against the elements and provide some of the comforts of life. They can truly be called homes and are in fact home to their inhabitants." "It follows that the decision of the respondent was substantially for an ulterior purpose and is thereby rendered invalid." He set aside the declaration of the emergency camp and invalidated the regulations, although he also granted leave to appeal.

More than 2,000 people celebrated victory at the Dutch Reformed Church that night, singing "Oukasie, freedom is coming." Budlender urged them to tell the authorities to reestablish and develop the township. BAC leader Leonard Brown called for unity with those who wished to return from Lethlabile, unable to afford its high rents. The Transvaal Administrator denied ever having intended to remove people forcibly. Because government had obtained leave to appeal, however, the regulations remained in force and the higher service charges continued to accumulate. The township superintendent refused residents permission to improve the roads. Budlender replied that the invalidity of the declaration would be raised in any prosecution under the regulations.[60]

The Star called it a "reprieve, but no cause for celebrations," noting that "the people's hopes have been dashed before." It urged government not to appeal.

> The National Party has a new leader [F.W. de Klerk] who says he is seeking a fair deal for all. The Planning Department has a new Minister [E. Louw] who needs to prove his even-handedness. Oukasie is the challenge for them, to match the spirit with the letter on policy. Let the court decision stand unchallenged.

The *Pretoria News* condemned the appeal as an instance of "when morality gives way to legality." DP MP Peter Soal said the appeal was "old-style apartheid." "In spite of reform rhetoric it is clear that the state does not intend to abandon its policy of forced removal."[61] Before the judgment the National Party leader in Cape Province noted that "past experience had shown that it cost between R12,000 and R19,000 to move just one black family consisting of about 6.5 people. Furthermore to move 3,000 people would cost R6.9 billion [sic; he meant million]."[62]

At a church service the following Sunday the community thanked representatives of the Canadian government, TRAC, and the press for support. TRAC fieldworker Lydia Kompé declared: "Oukasie is going nowhere. One day we will flush our toilets and turn on taps like people everywhere in the world. This is a right and not a favour they're doing us." Rev. P. Moatshe of the South African Council of Churches asserted: "We cannot obey Botha or Mangope because they are only looking after their own interests and deprive people of their rights. The church is also there to struggle for peace and justice." Residents of Braklaagte and Leeuwfontein resisting incorporation into Bophuthatswana also attended (see chapter eleven). The *Sowetan* declared support for all three groups, who "have shown that such unilateral decisions over their lives should not be tamely accepted." The government's defeat may have helped the Conservative Party nearly double its majority over the Nationalists in Brits in the September elections.63

Government refusal to withdraw the appeal fueled further conflict. Divisions within the BAC led to the expulsion of several executive committee members, provoking fights that seriously injured four people and drove the leadership into hiding. Government banned a December demonstration demanding that it drop the appeal, upgrade Oukasie, eliminate the color bar in Brits buses, hospitals, and sports grounds, publish the inquest into the deaths of Joyce Modimoeng and Marshall Buys, and remove the security forces. Residents responded with a five-week boycott of white shops, supported by the Brits Taxi Association.

At the beginning of 1990 Rev. Morote Makhanya of the Pretoria Council of Churches held a meeting to unite residents against vigilante violence. Unrest in Oukasie and Lethlabile schools, heightened by the suspension of thirteen teachers in May, effectively disrupted education during the first half of the year. On June 14 Abel Molokoane, a member of the Pig Squad, was shot to death by vigilantes while protesting a hit list containing his name. Shortly thereafter the United Democratic Front appointed Lawyers for Human Rights to conduct an inquiry into the violence. Its April 1991 report blamed the police for tolerating and perhaps encouraging vigilante terror.64

Toward the end of 1990 the Chief Justice asked government to file the heads of argument in its appeal by February 8. On New Year's Day the Oukasie Civic Association (the former BAC) sent a memorandum to de Klerk threatening to "seize authority of this township and develop it on our own" and to "canvass for national and international mass action" unless government resumed negotiations within a month. On January 25 Transvaal Administrator Danie Hough announced:

> During December 1990 the Cabinet decided that Oukasie will remain to be a residential area.
>
> As a result of this decision, the Cabinet decided earlier this week that Oukasie must be upgraded.
>
> Such upgrading would mean that the present residents may live there permanently....
>
> As the upgrading process will be very expensive, groups and organisations that propagated the reservation of Oukasie are asked for financial support....
>
> A recent threat by the Civic organisation of Oukasie did not influence the Cabinet's decision as the policy decision was already taken last year.

The Conservative Party MP for Brits denounced this as evidence that government could no longer withstand pressure from blacks or be trusted with the interests of whites.65

The OCA sought to cooperate with the Brits Town Council to create a single nonracial municipality. Residents were particularly concerned that new housing remain affordable, since Lethlabile was so expensive that some had abandoned their homes for a squatters camp "Re Swabile" (We are sad). The Oukasie People's Delegation (including representatives of OCA, NUMSA, the ANC, and the SACC) joined with the TPA to establish the Oukasie Development Trust, a majority of whose trustees were residents. In May the TPA appointed as project manager the engineering company Bouwer Viljoen, which obtained a R13 million loan from the Independent Development Trust to upgrade the 1,200 existing stands and provide 872 additional serviced stands (doubling the area of the township). It planned water at each stand and communal flush toilets and was negotiating for electricity. It proposed to expand the number of crèches from one to four, primary schools from one to three, and secondary schools from one to two. The anticipated price of a site was R7,500.[66]

The Oukasie Development Trust was launched on March 1, 1992, with an hour-long parade concluding in a meeting addressed by Geoff Budlender, Rev. Peter Moatshe (SACC), and Levy Mamabolo (ODT chair). ANC representative Rocky Malebane-Metsing declared: "Together we have a country to rebuild—a country savaged by war and experimental policies, the likes of which were never implemented anywhere else in the world." Residents moved into the first twenty plots by the end of November.[67]

Analysis

Government failed to remove the 15,000 residents of Oukasie because the underlying political situation changed. When the original decision was made, according to Brits Mayor Japie Steenkamp, "forced removals were a common thing. We didn't work through negotiations." By the time van Dijkhorst invalidated the emergency camp two decades later, however, F.W. de Klerk had replaced P.W. Botha as State President and set the stage for an ANC government in less than five years. Hindsight clearly reveals the contradictions dooming grand apartheid. The South African economy depended on cheap black labor. As decentralization dispersed blacks from the major cities, however, it expanded townships around regional growth centers like Brits. Commuting from the homelands wasted time and money. Furthermore, it was hard to justify destroying homes, especially the many substantial structures in Oukasie, when most blacks were so poorly housed.

Because liberal political theory holds government more accountable for its actions than private entities, officials must justify the exercise of power. South Africa could not sustain a credible explanation for removing Oukasie. In 1970 whites shamelessly demanded its elimination because it was "a local eyesore and abuts one of our smart suburbs." During the following decade the white Council repeatedly called it "a hindrance for the development of white suburbs." But because Chris Heunis had declared an end to forced removals in February 1985, he had to justify the move a year later as enlightened paternalism. It was "to the advantage of residents" to "force them to relocate." Unfortunately, ordinary whites constantly exposed such hypocrisy. In the Western Transvaal they demanded a "buffer area" around the township of Koster because Blacks' standard of living was lower, their culture was different, and they were less developed. The Oukasie superintendent told Mahlaela to "take this letter and go to your lawyer and tell him to stuff it up his ass and tell him not to bother me any more." (Scatological images pervade the struggle against apartheid. Overflowing buckets of excrement symbolize the degradation of townships; Lydia Kompé declared: "One day we will flush our toilets...like people everywhere in the world.")

Several months later the Department of Constitutional Development claimed that "conditions are unhygienic...[and] there are not enough houses." (The language of urban renewal, which cleared American inner cities of its poor, is embarrassingly familiar.) Next Heunis invoked "the astronomic costs involved in upgrading the town." At the same time he reiterated that "no forced removals are contemplated before proper consultations with residents have taken place." The Bureau of Information belatedly remembered that the township Advisory Board had requested the removal to Lethlabile. While maintaining that the removal was a "voluntary relocation," Heunis warned that a "few" recalcitrants could not frustrate the plan. Several days later the Nationalist Party hailed the end of forced removals as one of the government's "20 proud landmarks on the reform road." But Heunis promptly backtracked: "Government has never said there would not be any more forced removals. After all people will squat illegally wherever and you cannot accept they will stay there forever. What government said was there would be no forced removals for political reasons." Two months later he reassured Parliament that "only those persons who of their own free will so request will be settled at Lethlabile." But when others construed this as a reprieve he insisted that incentives would make relocation attractive and declared the emergency camp to create them. It was justified as a means of ensuring "basic community services" and preventing "even more deterioration." "It must however be made clear, that no additional residents will be allowed in the abovementioned area."

These rationalizations were mutually contradictory: residents had to be removed first because Oukasie was overcrowded, and then because it was underpopulated. More important, they permitted rebuttal. Government maintained the Community Council embraced removal? Residents replied it lacked legitimacy: only 390 people had participated in the election, two-thirds of the candidates were unopposed, and all the councilors had moved to Lethlabile. The removal was voluntary? But thousands refused to go. They were intimidated? Removal opponents suffered far more violence than advocates. Health conditions compelled the removal? They were better than average for urban blacks. Oukasie could not be upgraded? Engineers showed it was feasible and cheaper than removal. Homelessness and squatting required declaration of an emergency camp? The homeless could be housed on vacant plots; and most "squatters" were residents displaced by removal.

Government attempts to justify the unjustifiable sometimes descended to Orwellian newspeak. It declared the emergency camp because living conditions were worsening? But government had caused that deterioration by withdrawing services and prohibiting improvements, and the declaration accelerated that decline. It declared the emergency camp because of homelessness? But government had created homelessness by destroying houses and prohibiting construction. Government maintained that Oukasie residents living in homes were homeless because of slum conditions it had caused. (If *they* were homeless, government had rendered virtually all Blacks homeless.) Government claimed the declaration had furthered the statutory purpose of "accommodation of homeless persons" even though it provided no accommodation; it did so by claiming improvement in living conditions despite the fact that it had declared the camp precisely to worsen those conditions as an incentive to move. Government declared Oukasie an emergency camp to obligate itself to provide services it no longer provided because it had disestablished the township. It declared the emergency camp to forestall the anarchy that would ensue now that the disestablished township no longer was governed by rules. Government declared the emergency camp so it could terminate the emergency camp, since disestablishment of the township had not achieved the removal.

Conceding the impossibility of justifying its actions, government retreated to denying it had to offer reasons. In defending the declaration of the emergency camp it insisted "it is not the function of the Court in a matter of this nature to decide whether the facts placed before the respondent are correct or not" and that its discretion was "free, unfettered, unbound and subjective." Pretensions to the rule of law founder when a court cannot find facts or test behavior against legal criteria.

Government retained power, if not authority. Like a New York landlord trying to empty a rent-controlled apartment, it adopted a policy of malign neglect (as it had in Mogopa). It reduced services: collection of garbage and human waste, maintenance of water taps. It allowed bad roads to deteriorate and prevented residents from repairing them. It eliminated bus service. It closed one of two primary schools and withdrew funding for the crèche. It moved the community council, which lent its limited legitimacy to removal. It frightened resisters with loss of their pensions. It prohibited burials. It demolished every house when a plot-holder moved and prevented new construction. It raised rents and service charges. Security forces harassed, arrested, and detained resisters and tolerated, perhaps conspired in, vigilante violence. The thin veneer of legality always hid an underworld of force. Declaration of the emergency camp gave government the kind of absolute control over residents it sought nationally through declaration of the emergency.

Government accompanied these sticks with carrots. It handsomely compensated plot-holders who moved early and offered little or no compensation to resisters. In Lethlabile, those with means could buy land (which they could not own in Oukasie) and build much larger houses and shops. Loans were advanced to those who could make the repayments. Only Lethlabile offered electricity, running water, flush toilets, paved roads, new schools, and recreational facilities. Government moved people without charge and subsidized transportation to Brits. When some accepted its offer, government could invoke "choice" and blame violent radicals for intimidating others, who must share the same preferences.

The government's resolve was impaired, however, by divisions among whites. Brits employers needed Black labor, especially skilled workers, at the same time that they wanted to destroy Black unions; and industry feared that bad publicity would intensify international economic sanctions. But many Brits residents did not want Black neighbors. The Nationalist Party was threatened from the right, first by the Herstigte Nasionale Partie and then more effectively by the Conservative Party, which won the Brits constituency and displaced the PFP as the official opposition. National leaders wooed domestic and foreign audiences with promises of reform, while local demagogues pandered to their racist supporters by championing the status quo. High officials spoke pretty words, while their underlings were arbitrary, rude, and violent (although one broke ranks to tip off Budlender).

Oukasie residents developed numerous means of resistance. They induced government to commit atrocities, which they used to generate support, both inside and outside South Africa. Government was all too cooperative, overreacting to the least defiance. The greatest embarrassment was not the removal so much as routine official behavior. During both oral argument and his judgment, Justice Stafford voiced his anger at de Beer's insulting rebuff to Mahlaela, quoting the "vituperation" and "vulgar and abusive language" and condemning it as "high-handed disregard of the applicant's rights," "unwarranted and boorish conduct," and "disgraceful behaviour." He criticized the state's transparent attempt to portray Mahlaela as a troublemaker for asserting his rights. Helen Suzman denounced Heunis for breaking his word: "There is no ambiguity in what the Minister said...and indeed he conveyed to me personally that the inhabitants of Oukasie would not be moved against their will."

Residents secured support from the media (national and international) and foreign governments, assisted by the clarity of the issues and the accessibility of the township to embassies in Pretoria. Trade unions pressured employers, who spoke to government. The BAC commissioned social surveys to disprove government claims and demonstrate the feasibility of upgrading the township. Perhaps the ultimate weapon was endurance: Because the stakes were so high, Oukasie residents could outlast the government. Their obligation to ancestral graves signified the strength of their attachment to the land—even an urban location created by the apartheid state. Blacks had displayed equally strong loyalties to more wretched slums:

District Six and Crossroads in Cape Town, Sophiatown, Alexandra, and Soweto in Johannesburg.[68] This is another of apartheid's ironies. Just as Moutse residents preferred direct rule by white South Africa to the "ethnic" homeland of KwaNdebele, and KwaNdebele and the other five "self-governing" homelands rejected independence, so residents of the miserable black townships preferred them to such scientifically planned communities as Lethlabile and Khayelitsha.

Like whites, however, Oukasie also had internal divisions, as shown by the fact that two-thirds of residents moved. Local councilors were prepared to do the government's bidding, if they had few supporters. Yet the conservative Urban Councils Association of South Africa opposed the removal. Some plot-holders were persuaded to move by the prospect of compensation, but few tenants had such claims. Those with money could enjoy better living conditions in Lethlabile; those without would be worse off. Those with jobs could pay the higher transportation costs; those without could not look for work. Government exacerbated these divisions with bribes, detention, selective prosecution, spies, agents provocateurs, and violence. Yet the animosities pre-existed such intervention and survived it.

Law played a vital role in the struggle. Unlike private persons, most government can act only through law, which constrains even a regime endowed with almost unlimited power. Functional divisions between executive, legislative, and judicial branches and national and local government can lead to divergent attitudes. Personal differences among legislators, judges, even Ministers can hobble action. An omnipotent government is not infallible, and South Africa made more than its share of mistakes. As long as Oukasie was a township, the superintendent lacked authority to refuse permits for vacant buildings and sites. Even lowly officials must obey the law and treat citizens politely; at least they should deny their misdeeds. Disestablishment did nothing to eliminate the township because government, perhaps inadvertently, had repealed the law authorizing force. Prosecuting thousands of individuals under the Prevention of Illegal Settlement Act would have been slow, cumbersome, and embarrassing. Government should not have relied on a statute directed at homelessness to deal with those living in homes. The state could not simultaneously promote its reformist image and cultivate the loyalty of racist whites. Judicial decisions enjoyed considerable legitimacy. De Beer threatened to appeal but never did so; the Transvaal Administrator obtained leave to appeal but was criticized for persisting and settled before filing heads of argument.

Law did not compel the outcomes in the two cases. Stafford appears to have been equally influenced by outrage that a white official behaved so boorishly. Van Dijkhorst was a staunch Nationalist, who convicted and harshly sentenced UDF leaders in the Delmas treason trial and certainly had no love for Chaskalson's co-counsel George Bizos. He found that 10,000 Oukasie residents had moved "voluntarily" and agreed that he could not review the government's factual findings. Yet even he could not swallow the argument that those whose homes the government wanted to destroy were anticipatorily homeless. He followed the statute's "plain meaning" to rule against the executive. Both judges relied on procedural grounds, avoiding more fundamental challenges to government policy. Yet Stafford could have found a technical flaw in Mahlaela's application. And van Dijkhorst could have held that the presence of some squatters, which Makama admitted, justified the declaration of an emergency camp.

Law dealt the government only temporary reversals. Soon after losing the first case it resumed destroying vacant houses, although forced to desist by the threat of further litigation. It continued to drag its feet in allocating houses and sites. When Stafford held that government had to disestablish Oukasie it promptly did so. And though van Dijkhorst invalidated the declaration of the emergency camp, he immediately granted leave to appeal, thereby staying his decision. Service charges accumulated, and the appeal was still pending thirty months later. (A criminal prosecution for violation of the emergency camp rules almost certainly could not have succeeded, however.)

Yet these temporary defeats became permanent as the political climate changed. Law slowed the project of grand apartheid until politics could reverse it. Residents who held out at Oukasie won the right to remain and the chance of better housing. By 1991 they were strong enough to issue an ultimatum. The vision of a post-apartheid society, however, appears to be the perpetuation of separation, now structured in terms of class rather than race and enforced by the market rather than the state. Demand will price most blacks out of white areas and even out of the more established townships, and color-blind laws against squatting will control informal housing.[69] The judiciary was a surprising ally against apartheid; will it be equally effective against institutional racism?

CHAPTER 13

THE ROLES OF LAW

Recent theoretical discussions of law tend to end where this book begins—by acknowledging that it is "relatively autonomous," influenced by economic infrastructure, pressured by political forces, shaped by the social system, but not fully determined by any of them. Although extreme positions have the seductive attraction of elegant simplicity, they quickly founder on uncomfortable facts. A pure theory of law—logically coherent, universally valid, uncontaminated by the messiness of life—is a misguided dream. At the same time, we cannot simply "read off" a superstructural element like law from the material base. And even in a polity like South Africa, where state power was highly concentrated and minimally constrained, law (like all social institutions) is autopoetic; its structures, processes, personnel, ideology, and history all offer resistance to external constraints. The question is not whether law is relatively autonomous but how autonomy is manifested.

The answers have political as well as theoretical significance. The centrality of law in the American labor, civil rights, feminist, welfare rights, consumer, environmentalist, and gay rights movements can tempt observers to parochial and ahistorical exaggerations of its capacity to effect social change. We should not overreact, however, by dismissing law entirely. Sometimes it is the only meaningful source of influence. Political institutions may be corrupt, paralyzed, or inaccessible, economic pressure limited, the media hostile, and foreign sympathizers preoccupied or impotent. South Africa in the 1980s was an ideal setting in which to explore how law could resist and constrain apartheid, offering opponents a protected space for their struggle and unique forms of leverage. In this concluding chapter I gather the insights drawn from the ten case studies. But though I hope they offer lessons to those resisting other oppressive regimes, I deliberately remain at a fairly low level of abstraction. The density of factual detail necessary to understand events of this complexity discourages generalization. These stories should be read more as a method for analyzing the relation between law and politics than as a source of ahistorical, culturally universal theory.

Party Strategies

Although most discussions of legality and rights focus on the behavior of judicial, legislative, and executive officials, the decisions of private parties are more important. Unofficial actors are far more numerous, enjoy greater discretion, and usually initiate the encounter with law.

The threshhold question is the construction of adversaries: who they are and whether individual or collective. Often this is unplanned: neither Black Sash nor the LRC chose Komani to challenge the pass laws, nor was Tom Rikhoto the ideal plaintiff. He was apolitical; indeed, his Zion Christian Church accepted the white regime; and there were questions about the continuity of his employment and the legality of his urban tenancy. Ivan Toms, unlike David Bruce, was the perfect person to contest conscription and had been chosen for this purpose. Toms was deeply involved in collective action through the End Conscription Campaign, while Bruce was the quintessential loner. Both seemed driven by expressive as well as instrumental motives—to gain moral authenticity, cleanse themselves of complicity with apartheid. Wendy Orr—not Cheadle Thompson and Haysom—made the decision to challenge security police torture. The other affiants were only loosely bound together (although union support was essential to the application). Residential communities were strongly solidary, strengthened not only by ethnic ties but sometimes also by ideological affinities and union loyalties (UDF and MAWU in Mpophomeni, MAWU and SAAWU in Oukasie). Yet they, too, contained differences that easily could become divisions: urban and rural, modern and traditional, more and less formally educated, youths and elders, women and men, businessmen and consumers, rulers and subjects.

Government constantly provoked conflict within the opposition (and then condemned black factionalism and violence). It bribed leaders with public office and closed its eyes to corruption. This failed in Moutse (though it drove a wedge between Moutse and Lebowa) but was more successful in KwaNdebele (pitting the Ndzundza royal house against Skosana), Mogopa (Jacob More against Shadrack More), Oukasie (plot-holders against tenants, workers against the unemployed), and Braklaagte and Leeuwfontein (competition for the headmanship, framed in genealogical terms). Government backed Alexandra's councilors only to see the township repudiate them. Sometimes it was surprisingly ignorant of latent tensions: workerist versus populist in Alexandra, ANC versus PAC. It succeeded brilliantly in turning Inkatha supporters against other Blacks (including fellow Zulu), in Mpophomeni and elsewhere. It managed to separate liberal English newspapers from the alternative media, until it started suspending the latter. Yet repression (and especially prison) often intensified unity.

Sometimes the state treated the opposition as monolithic, only to discover it was quite disorganized. The treason trials assumed that eliminating a few leaders would end township unrest; but the Pietermaritzburg and Delmas prosecutions did not destroy UDF; and leadership in Alexandra meant following the masses, not dictating to them. Whites also tended to assume their own solidarity (in the face of the "swart gevaar"). BTR SARMCOL took for granted the alliance of management, government, and capital, while treating workers as individuals and refusing to recognize MAWU as their collective representative. But white unity was not inevitable: A prison doctor with a guilty past might seek protection against new accusations at the expense of security police; the SADF and SAP might blame each other for hit squads. Large capital seeking greater productivity to compete in the global marketplace might clash with the white middle and working class, concerned about electoral power and social status. National and local politicians appealed to different audiences.

Once constituted, parties must choose the mode of engagement. It is not surprising that the South African opposition generally preferred negotiation to more public confrontation—a recognition that the law usually favored the government, which could always rewrite it. Centuries of oppression had inculcated a colonial mentality, especially among the older generation, a need to believe in the benevolence of whites, particularly employers and government officials; this was the stimulus for the black consciousness movement of the 1970s. Weakness compelled the opposition to appear reasonable, moderate, in the hope of persuading superordinates who could not be coerced. Negotiation carried certain procedural advantages: an opportunity to be heard, legal representation, minutes.

The opposition, therefore, often deployed its limited leverage to commit the government to negotiate. After the Magopa had been removed to Bethanie and then Onderstepoort, they threatened to return home unilaterally unless government agreed to discussions. Although they probably could not have penetrated the security cordon, the force necessary to stop them would have been an embarrassment. The government also preferred negotiation, but for different reasons. Private talks allowed it to shape publicity—preserving secrecy when it was exerting pressure or stonewalling, drafting and issuing press statements when it got what it wanted. Negotiation allowed it to control timing, offering endless opportunities for delay. Like others operating from a position of power, officials used the good cop/bad cop ploy: Talk to us or you will have to deal with our much less reasonable superiors, inferiors, or successors (a Conservative Party government). Agreement, once reached, carried considerable weight, even with a regime possessing extraordinary power.

But negotiation presupposed the possibility of compromise. Because the root of the struggle was indivisible authority, even honor, positions were fundamentally irreconcilable. BTR SARMCOL would not share control over the workplace with MAWU; conscientious objectors and the SADF could not decide whose moral criteria would prevail; the UDF, SAAWU and the Alexandra Action Committee could not agree with the state about the limits of legitimate resistance; the *New Nation* and other alternative media would not allow government to establish the boundaries of dissent; black residents would not accept forced removals or incorporation into homelands; victims of violence would not submit to police brutality or Inkatha domination.

After negotiation, government preferred executive action: deploying police, bulldozing homes, seizing newspapers, banning meetings, promulgating regulations, unilaterally incorporating Blacks into homelands, transferring Moutse teachers who refused to accept employment in KwaNdebele. This also gave it considerable control over timing and publicity. Next it resorted to legislation to achieve its ends. This much slower, more public process risked embarrassment by the miniscule Parliamentary opposition. After 1983 the (infrequent) resistance by the Indian House of Delegates or the "Coloured" House of Representatives required the President's Council to expose the charade of constitutional reform by over-ruling those talking shops. Even an omnipotent government could make mistakes—as the government repeatedly did in drafting legislation or engaging in ultra vires executive action. Adjudication was the government's least favorite alternative—for reasons vividly illustrated by its inability to evict the Magopa and Goedgevonden even after obtaining civil judgments against them. Its preference for detention (under the Internal Security Act or Emergency Regulations) over prosecution was fully validated by the dismal failure of the three treason trials of the 1980s: Pietermartizburg, Delmas, and Alexandra.

Courts themselves sometimes chose negotiation over adjudication, as when the Appellate Division urged the parties to resolve the claims by the Magopa and Goedgevonden communities to remain on their land (claims the Supreme Court had rejected). Even if government knew it could win, litigating individual cases was slow, cumbersome, and inefficient. It would take too long to prosecute thousands of Oukasie residents under the Prevention of Illegal Settlement Act, or punish the *New Nation* for each offending word. In South Africa, as everywhere, state regulation bred evasion rather than compliance. Just as closing tax loopholes stimulates lawyers and accountants to find new ones, so Alexandra residents and the alternative media took advantage of the inherent ambiguity of language to find new ways to voice resistance.

These rights-based strategies did not exhaust the government's arsenal. It was fully prepared to use its virtually unlimited power—withholding services and benefits to drive the residents of Mogopa and Oukasie from their homes, detaining tens of thousands during the Emergency, killing hundreds and wounding thousands more, using the SADF to occupy the townships, and torturing detainees. As the hearing of Wendy Orr's application showed, the purpose of torture was less to extract information than to humiliate opponents and frighten them into submission. But torture had perverse consequences. Most activists were too committed to be discouraged. The cost of killing them—intentionally or inadvertently—was high. Neil Aggett,

Steve Biko, Griffiths and Victoria Mkenge, and David Webster were almost as potent as dead martyrs as they had been as living leaders.

Indeed, the opposition could turn physical weakness to its advantage (as Gandhi had shown at the beginning of the century): Mass hunger strikes threatening death forced the government to release a thousand Emergency detainees in Spring 1989. Even lengthy imprisonment could become an embarrassment, as shown by de Klerk's release of Mandela and others. Rank and file might be incapacitated, discouraged or killed, but millions were ready to take their places. Indiscriminate state violence transformed the stigma of arrest, detention, and punishment into badges of honor. This experience also educated cadres and intensified their commitment: "graduation" from Robben Island became the revolutionary equivalent of an Oxbridge or Ivy League degree.[1]

The opposition also used violence but with even less effect. For all the talk about Umkhonto we Sizwe by both government and the ANC, the bombings had little impact on white society. And though acts of intimidation were commonplace within the black community, they hardly explained the overwhelming support for boycotts of elections, schools, shops, and workplaces, or the appeal of mass democratic organizations like UDF, COSATU, and the outlawed ANC. If the government had firepower, the opposition had numbers, which it wielded effectively whenever it could put bodies on the line: demonstrators on the streets, mourners at funerals, MAWU members in SARMCOL's factory, rural farmers in "black spots," detainees on hunger strikes. As always, however, possession was nine-tenths of the law; that advantage was lost once the Magopa had been ousted from Zwartrand or MAWU members locked out of the SARMCOL factory.

A party has to choose not only the mode of engagement but also whether to seek it or respond to an adversary's moves. Proactivity offers strategic advantages in political arenas, both Parliamentary and extra-parliamentary: control of timing, content, forum, and publicity. This may reflect the proactive nature of executives and legislatures. In courts, which are inherently passive, reactivity may be the stronger posture. When the opposition sought judicial confrontation, government often defused the situation through strategic concessions: paying damages to torture victims or the families of prisoners who died in custody, consenting to an interdict against further state violence, promising to postpone removal, offering conscripts noncombatant status. Litigation is more effective as a shield than a sword. After the Magopa had been forcibly removed from Zwartrand, an Appellate Division judgment invalidating the action was virtually worthless (especially since the government had already expropriated the land). Once the Magopa had reestablished a foothold in the cemetery, a hitherto omnipotent government found it difficult to expel them; even a favorable Supreme Court decision in the eviction action did not help. In each instance, therefore, the party obtaining a legal remedy found it politically unenforceable. Oukasie residents prevailed in their two lawsuits partly because they maintained a physical presence in the township.

By contrast, all forty-three accused in the three show trials of the 1980s won acquittals or dismissals, as did many activists charged with ordinary crimes (such as public violence). Indeed, the 1989 Defiance Campaign (like its 1952 predecessor) invited prosecution by seeking access to public amenities: parks, beaches, hospitals, and transportation. In the changed political climate of the de Klerk administration, the later campaign succeeded. Conversely, the opposition was singularly unsuccessful in securing arrest, prosecution and punishment of white racists, security force members, or black vigilantes who assaulted or murdered blacks, as Mpophomeni illustrates (though these outcomes also were influenced by politics, as the conviction of Chris Hani's killers showed). Reactivity can transform weakness into strength. The state could not publicly attack the women, children, and old men of Mogopa. Security police torturing helpless prisoners had to worry about killing or permanently injuring them. Government had to release Emergency detainees before they starved themselves to death. But reactivity also could make the opposition deny its strengths. During the first half of 1986 the AAC aggressively achieved political leadership of Alexandra; but the five treason trialists defending against the charge that they had challenged state authority had to minimize its influence. MAWU had to accuse its members of indiscipline for engaging in wildcat strikes at SARMCOL. The *New Nation* claimed to reflect rather than shape black opinion.

Reactive strategies have inherent limits even when successful. The legal shield may protect against particular acts of oppression, but it rarely changes policies. After losing a criminal prosecution the state often charged the accused with another crime or simply resorted to detention. A massive national and international campaign saved the Sharpeville Six from the gallows but could not free them from prison or eliminate the death penalty (which was effectively suspended only when de Klerk initiated negotiations with the ANC). Ivan Toms and David Bruce won conscientious objectors the "right" to be sentenced by a judge (rather than the legislature), but only repeal of the Population Registration Act as part of the repudiation of apartheid could herald the end of conscription. The affidavits of Wendy Orr and dozens of victims temporarily halted torture by the Port Elizabeth security police, but they did not secure the release of detainees or prevent torture from recurring. The Supreme Court could nullify the declaration of Oukasie as an emergency camp, but it could not compel the government to restore services. Courts invalidated the incorporation of Moutse into KwaNdebele and Botshabelo into QwaQwa but not that of Braklaagte and Leeuwfontein into Bophutatswana.

Because government deployed overwhelming military force, monopolized formal political power, and outlawed most extra-parliamentary activity, the opposition rarely enjoyed the strategic advantages of planning. Many of the most momentous mass actions were largely spontaneous: the 1960 pass law protests leading to the Sharpeville massacre, the 1976 Soweto uprising, and the 1984 Vaal rent boycott and subsequent township violence. Even strikes, work stay-aways, and election and consumer boycotts often were reactions to an adversary's initiatives. The government, by contrast, could make effective use of its proactive ability to achieve surprise and publicity. De Klerk was a master of such dramatic flourishes. In February 1990 he announced the release of Mandela and legalized the ANC and other organizations. A year later he promised to scrap the legislative foundations of apartheid (the Group Areas, Land, and Population Registration Acts). And a year after that he won more than two-thirds of the white vote in the referendum on his reforms. Usually, however, government used its control over timing to procrastinate, seeking to wear down the opposition and distract media attention. Officials failed to respond to letters and phone calls, postponed meetings, and endlessly passed the buck—up and down the bureaucratic hierarchy and laterally across departmental jurisdictions. Each time Ivan Toms sought a confrontation over his refusal to perform military service, the SADF canceled the camp.

The government's sense of timing was far from perfect, however. When it finally gazetted the removal of the Magopa, it gave them ten days to leave. On the last night dozens of reporters and television cameras from South Africa and abroad were poised to record yet another outrage, forcing government to back down. Three months later, when the media had lost interest, supporters were dispersed, and the Magopa demoralized by the endless suspense, the government secretly conducted the forced removal. Government control over timing also could be constrained by procedural formalities, which multiplied with the power it sought to wield—executions being an extreme example. The prospect of death concentrates the mind wonderfully—and not only that of the victim. Each time government planned to hang the Sharpeville Six a storm of protest erupted, paralyzing its will. Furthermore, the government controlled timing only in the short run. For decades everyone but South African whites has seen apartheid as an obscene anachronism, clearly fated to collapse. The opposition had inexhaustible powers of endurance because blacks had nowhere to go. Like other long-oppressed peoples—Irish, Poles, Palestinians, Armenians—South African blacks turned atrocities into collective memories whose annual remembrance strengthened resistance: Sharpeville, Soweto, Langa. Indeed, the very delay that was government's favorite strategy worked against it in the long run. Liberal critics reflected this in their obsession with time running out; the opposition proclaimed it in their slogan "victory is inevitable."[2]

Timing was not the government's sole error. Power not only corrupts, it also fosters complacency and carelessness. Government repealed its power to conduct forced removals. It continued to call up Toms and Bruce for military service after they had publicly refused and even while they were in prison. It prosecuted Mayekiso and the AAC for conspiring with the ANC, although Mayekiso was notorious as a workerist, and the AAC had refused to join the UDF. Although the five accused were allegedly the core of the conspiracy, some barely knew the others. The vigilante raid forced underground the "institutions of people's power" on which the state based the charge of treason.

Just as the government preferred the political arena (which it controlled) over the more autonomous judiciary and made its adversaries brandish the legal sword rather than hide behind the shield, so it sought to define the issues in litigation as narrowly and legalistically as possible. It distinguished sharply between law and politics, seeking to portray political opposition as ordinary crime: use of the "common purpose" doctrine against the Sharpeville Six and Upington Twenty-five, prosecutions for "Black-on-Black violence," and the trial of Winnie Mandela for the abduction and death of "Stompie" Mokhetsi.[3] The opposition, by contrast, maintained that apartheid rendered all law political; what government justified as legally mandated was merely naked power. Even the "ordinary" enforcement of criminal law was politically motivated. (Many Americans, especially people of color, view their own criminal law through similar racial lenses: Tawana Brawley, the Central Park jogger, Bernard Goetz, the police beating of Rodney King and subsequent civil disorder.) Such issue definition has obvious strategic significance; but it also is an end in itself, given the visibility of major political cases. When, instead, the opposition acceded to the government's insistence that the issues were legal technicalities—as the *New Nation* did in fighting suspension under the Emergency Regulations or Lebowa in opposing excision of Moutse—it predictably lost.

The opposition was strikingly effective in forcing government to engage its own broad definition of the issues. Absent a jury, South African evidentiary rules are less rigid than American. Even the state sometimes seemed to view lawsuits as a cathartic opportunity for airing the questions tearing apart the country. The treason trials addressed the real goals of UDF and the Alexandra Action Committee as well as the substantive grievances fueling black protest. The trials of conscientious objectors examined SADF repression of township residents and SWAPO freedom fighters and aggression against frontline states. The Magopa educated the Appellate Division about their title to the land. Moutse persuaded the court to consider the ideological foundation of apartheid, and KwaNdebele women advanced a natural law critique of gender inequality. But the opposition was not always successful. MAWU could not make the Industrial Court see the injustice of BTR SARMCOL's refusal to recognize and negotiate. And the *New Nation* could not persuade the courts to look beyond the formal "legality" of the Emergency Regulations to the arbitrariness of censorship.

Although the concept of legitimation raises difficult questions about which audience is being addressed and how to measure the impact of the message, much party strategy does seem directed toward the "court of public opinion" as well as adversaries and formal organs of state power.[4] A favorite tactic of human rights activists is to expose the behavior of repressive governments in the belief that daylight is a strong antiseptic for moral as well as physical infection, unmasking authority as naked coercion and thereby undermining its power (at least temporarily). Legal proceedings offered a loophole in the blanket prohibition against criticizing security forces and prisons. The inquest into the Mpophomeni murders revealed both Inkatha's violence and the government's indifference (and possible complicity). Even though no one was prosecuted, the victims did not die unnoticed, and the suspected killers were publicly named. Justice van der Walt chose to conduct the Alexandra treason trial in English for the benefit of foreign reporters and observers, although he also allowed most state witnesses to testify in camera. The revelation of police torture in Port Elizabeth temporarily suspended it, while also showing *whose* voices counted: Complaints by black victims were disregarded for years until corroborated by a white physician. The watchful eyes of Black Sash, prominent clerics, international observers, and domestic and foreign media delayed removal of the Magopa. In each instance brute force hid under cover of darkness: the Mpophomeni murders at night, torture inside the Port Elizabeth police headquarters, and the Magopa removal three months later, when nobody was watching. And in each, publicity was the opposition's *only* recourse, since the legal system offered no remedy: Government did not prosecute the Mpophomeni murderers, failed to discipline the Port Elizabeth security police, and anticipated the Magopa's Appellate Division victory through expropriation. But the effect of this strategy tends to be ephemeral: Inkatha violence, police torture, and removals all resumed when the spotlight shifted and audience attention waned. Furthermore, South Africa—perhaps inured to its status as international pariah—consistently flouted world opinion. At the same time there is *no* evidence that resort to the legal system legitimated the regime in the eyes of critics, black or white, domestic or foreign.

If each side sought support from both sympathizers and the uncommitted, it also hoped to educate its adversary. Harold Berman has characterized Soviet law as parental—an attempt by judges to mold citizens into the new Soviet man.[5] The South African opposition inverted this, seeking to educate judges about township life, SADF atrocities in Namibia, unemployment, long-distance commuting, police violence, rural agriculture, obligations to ancestors, and the nature, tactics, and goals of anti-apartheid organizations. Judges, in turn, lectured parties about democracy, the imperative of social order, and the government's good intentions. Although blacks remained unconvinced, some officials may have broadened their horizons. All the magistrates and judges who heard Ivan Toms and David Bruce fully accepted their bona fides. Justice van der Walt was unlikely to have visited a black township before he toured Alexandra during the treason trial and was predictably appalled by what he saw.

In order to get, hold, and sway the audience, the opposition characterized government actions as atrocities, highlighting the most egregious behavior, imputing the worst motives. The pass laws divided husband from wife, parent from child, in ways damningly reminiscent of American slavery. Hanging, never easy to justify, became indefensible if guilt was uncertain—as when government used the "common purpose" doctrine to convict members of a mob of murder (although most had struck no blows). Prisoners dramatized and exacerbated the hardship of indefinite detention without trial by staging hunger strikes. The Magopa claimed that the government was stealing their diamonds and other valuable minerals, despite documentary proof that they had alienated those rights decades earlier. Oukasie residents made effective use of the white superintendent's vulgar reply to a Black who merely asked to be allocated a vacant house (evocative of Mr. Bumble's outraged response to Oliver Twist's naive request for more gruel in the London orphanage). The wanderings of the homeless Magopa remained a constant embarrassment to a devoutly Christian government that constantly likened the Great Trek to the Israelites' flight from Egypt (and restaged it annually). Newspapers pictured houses and churches destroyed and the graveyard untended, focused on the plight of the most vulnerable and innocent (children, women, the elderly—some wearing medals earned fighting for South Africa in World War II), and recorded illnesses and deaths (attributing them all to exile). A defense witness during Ivan Toms's plea in mitigation graphically related SADF atrocities in Namibia. Crimes like the torture of Port Elizabeth detainees needed no exaggeration. The principal problem of this strategy is the limited capacity for moral outrage. Those not suffering often tire of hearing about others (the analogy to donor fatigue in international relief efforts). Guilt turns into indifference, or even anger at having to listen. New and more extreme offenses must be discovered. And the state, too, can play the game, pointing to terrorism, communist ideology, intimidation, necklacing, people's courts, "Black-on-Black violence," and Winnie Mandela's intemperate language and complicity in the abduction of "Stompie" Mokhetsi. In prosecuting Ivan Toms the state stooped to unregenerate McCarthyism by making wholly irrelevant charges of homosexuality and gay activism in an attempt to discomfit Toms's church supporters. (Many criticized Winnie Mandela for accusing Rev. Paul Verryn of sexual misconduct to justify her bodyguards' kidnapping of Mokhetsi.)

Publicity could backfire. Instead of persuading an adversary to concede rather than seem intransigent, it could strengthen the party's resistance for fear of appearing to sell out or display weakness. The government was unwilling to acknowledge publicly the innocence of the Sharpeville Six or even abuses in the prosecution. The State President ultimately granted clemency as an act of grace, without admitting any error. Pressed by the government to admit their crimes and plead for mercy, many black accused refused to compromise their principles. Those tried for treason were torn by the dilemma of minimizing punishment without disavowing ideals, repudiating followers, or questioning tactics. Nelson Mandela's speech from the dock in the Rivonia prosecution put the government on trial.[6] The Umkhonto we Sizwe cadres charged with murder in the Delmas Two prosecution displayed extraordinary courage by refusing to participate in the trial at all.[7]

Since publicity was the opposition's chosen battleground, government usually beat a strategic retreat. When the opposition sought confrontation in order to embarrass, government made limited concessions to defuse the demands and minimize visible injustice. If David Bruce did not want to serve in the military the government would do anything to satisfy him short of affirming his moral scruples. If the Magopa were unhappy about moving to Pachsdraai, government would offer them any site but Zwartrand, while demanding a signed statement that this last move was entirely voluntary. Government was willing to compensate detainees and their relatives but never to admit or stop police torture and killings.

If government could not silence or co-opt opposition voices, it used its totalitarian powers to prevent them from being heard. It excluded the media from the scene of removals, prohibited them from observing or reporting about the security forces or prison conditions, and compelled self-censorship under threat of closure. It disseminated disinformation. It alternated between castigating the media and wooing it with trips, tips, and press conferences. It expelled foreign television camera crews from the townships during the Emergency. Government officials and Inkatha leaders frequently sued critics for libel; even when they lost, the legal cost, time, and anxiety of defending discouraged others.

Finally, government emulated the opposition by claiming the moral high ground. Given the universal condemnation of apartheid outside South Africa, it could do so only by dramatic reform announcements: no more forced removals, repeal of the Black Administration Act, even "the end of apartheid." But promises contain negative pregnants, admissions of past injustice—when did you stop beating your wife, or your citizens? Once given, they exert pressure for performance. When fulfilled, demands escalate. If removals are ended, perhaps the 3.5 million dispossessed should be allowed to return. If conscientious objection is recognized, perhaps conscription can be abolished.

The Rule of Law

Decisions to seek or eschew legal remedies may be influenced by the party's desire to gain or avoid publicity, but the real goal is winning. This section will explore the central question: did law make a difference? The bottom line is an unambiguous yes. The opposition secured victories in court that eluded them elsewhere and did so at least partly because of law. I will begin with those successes before turning to the limitations of legality.

Most judges followed clear statutory language, even when this thwarted the government that had appointed them and violated their own preferences. Justice van Dijkhorst, a conservative, ambitious, irascible Afrikaner, clashed repeatedly with Arthur Chaskalson, defense counsel in the Delmas treason trial, the most momentous of the decade. He threatened Chaskalson with contempt for continuing to oppose the judge's dismissal of an assessor who had signed the UDF million-signatures campaign. Shortly after Chaskalson appealed the convictions on this ground, he asked the judge to hold that the Prevention of Illegal Squatting Act did not authorize government to declare Oukasie an "Emergency Camp." Van Dijkhorst concurred even though this doomed the government's effort to win Brits back from the Conservative Party and frustrated its pursuit of grand apartheid by moving the black residents to the Bophuthatswana border. Earlier in this campaign Justice Stafford had ruled that Oukasie's white superintendent lacked discretion to deny house and site permits to residents. In another blow to grand apartheid, the Appellate Division invalidated the Magopa removal on the ground that Parliament could not give the requisite consent without knowing the residents' destination (although the Supreme Court disregarded this requirement). The AD had earlier invalidated the excision of Ingwavuma from KwaZulu because the latter had not consented.

Sometimes judges transcended the imperatives of plain meaning in ruling against the government. The Appellate Division could easily have upheld the Supreme Court's decision that Mrs. Komani did not "ordinarily reside" in Guguletu because she lacked legal accommodation. It could have ruled that Parliament adopted the "call-in" card system to prevent annual contract workers like Mr. Rikhoto from qualifying for urban residence. Like any complex legal regime, however, apartheid law contained ambiguities, inconsistencies, and lacunae, which created space for innovative lawyers and judges.

Unambiguous facts, like unambiguous law, also could induce politically unpopular decisions. The Supreme Court could not deny an injunction against the Port Elizabeth security police in the face of overwhelming evidence of torture. Some judges construed ambiguous facts to reach conclusions that doubtless angered the government. Justice van der Walt acquitted the accused in the Alexandra treason trial despite the visibility of the case, vigorous prosecution, and evidence that at least two had been marginally involved in people's courts. Magistrate S.M. Niewoudt, a young Afrikaner woman subordinate to executive authority, found that a crime had been committed in the deaths of the three Mpophomeni MAWU activists and named some of the Inkatha members responsible, rejecting their defense as a tissue of lies. The Natal Supreme Court dismissed the treason charges against prominent SAAWU and UDF officials when the defense discredited the state's expert witness and unmasked errors in the transcription and translation of videotaped meetings. One contradiction of mass repression, both public and private, is that the bureaucracy necessary for efficient control also preserves a detailed record of its actions. SARMCOL management kept scrupulous notes of every meeting; prison doctors recorded the wounds inflicted by Port Elizabeth security police.

Some courts would not tolerate procedural irregularities. After the two-year-long Delmas trial had led to convictions and harsh sentences for key UDF leaders, the Appellate Division reversed because van Dijkhorst dismissed an assessor. Justice Didcott (affirmed by the Appellate Division) threw out the Industrial Court decision in MAWU's unfair labor practice action against BTR SARMCOL because the presiding judge had been the keynote speaker at a seminar organized by the defendant's labor consultant. Justice Spoelstra released opponents of KwaNdebele independence who had been kidnaped by South African Police and handed over to homeland authorities.

Sometimes judges clearly exceeded the plain meaning of statutes to address the underlying political issues. The Appellate Division invalidated the incorporation of Moutse into KwaNdebele because it violated not only the National States Constitution Act of 1971 but also the grundnorm of grand apartheid—ethnic homogeneity. The normally conservative Orange Free State Supreme Court promptly followed this reasoning by invalidating the incorporation of Botshabelo into QwaQwa. The Transvaal Supreme Court based its decision that KwaNdebele could not disenfranchise women on natural law, in the absence of any statutory authority.

Occasionally judges even disregarded the plain meaning of statutes. For seven years after its passage everyone believed that the 1983 Defence Act compelled judges to impose a prison sentence of one-and-a-half times the outstanding military obligation on anyone who refused conscription and failed to meet the narrow criteria for conscientious objectors. The legislative history clearly expressed this intent. Two magistrates and two Supreme Court benches reached this conclusion with respect to Ivan Toms and David Bruce. But the Appellate Division created a loophole restoring full sentencing discretion to the judges. The court's resentment of Parliament derogation from judicial authority may have been a crucial factor. Yet similar Parliamentary incursions did not provoke the Supreme Court or Appellate Division to overturn the Emergency media regulations. (Anger at contempt for judicial authority also may explain the severe sentences of the Alexandra Eight for conducting people's courts and van der Walt's initial hostility toward the Alexandra Five.)

Despite its unquestionable value, however, legality had severe limitations in the struggle against apartheid. Since the white legislature wrote the rules, it was no surprise that these favored the regime. Even Laurie Ackermann, one of the most liberal judges (who finally left the bench for academia), felt compelled to reject the Seleke challenge to incorporation into Lebowa because the statute did not require *their* consent but only that of the jurisdiction from which they were being excised—South Africa! When the opposition was able to find statutory language justifying its position (usually because of inept drafting or executive bungling), courts disregarded it, rejecting Lebowa's challenge to the excision of Moutse (which turned on the relative meaning of parentheses and commas) and the Magopa defense to eviction from the Zwartrand cemetery (which argued that government had used the wrong statute to expropriate the land). Both the Supreme Court and the Appellate Division disregarded the *New Nation*'s technical objections to the Emergency regulations: timing errors, vagueness, and retroactivity. If courts engaged the larger substantive issues—as when the Appellate Division invalidated the Magopa removal because Parliament had not been told their destination—the government displayed its contempt by reiterating the discredited argument that there had been no removal because Jacob More (bribed by the headmanship and land) had led a faction to Pachsdraai. Furthermore, courts sometimes gave the opposition empty victories, invalidating the Magopa removal after government had expropriated their land, denying the government the costs of two counsel in the Goedgevonden case while granting white farmers an ejectment decree (an equally empty victory for them because enforcement was stayed pending appeal).

Courts construed ambiguous facts as well as laws against the opposition—and facts almost always are ambiguous. Despite the extraordinary skill and energy of the defense team, Justice van Dijkhorst and the remaining assessor convicted some Delmas accused of treason. If Magistrate Nieuwoudt found that the deaths of the three MAWU activists were criminal and named suspects, Magistrate Scholts did neither in a companion case involving a fourth Mpophomeni murder. The Industrial Court disregarded extensive documentation of BTR SARMCOL's determination to crush MAWU. If Justice van der Walt acquitted the Alexandra Five, Justice Grosskopf convicted the Alexandra Eight. Courts consistently favored some witnesses: whites over blacks, government officials over private citizens, management over labor, the security forces over everyone.

The opposition sometimes turned this weakness—like others—to its advantage. Witnesses for whom English was a second language (or third or fourth) took refuge in linguistic incompetence and incomprehension; as a result, interpreters acquired extraordinary power. Witnesses also invoked the inherent ambiguity of words and symbols and the opacity of motive. Accused who wore the black, gold, and green of the banned ANC pointed out that these also were the colors of the legal Inkatha movement. Accused who sang militant songs argued that singing was integral to African culture. The treason trials were full of inconclusive debates over the meaning of words like revolution, socialism, struggle, democracy, and people's power. Justice van der Walt acknowledged that "you have white perceptions and you have black perceptions. I am sitting as a judge. I am white. I view it in a certain way. A black person might view it differently." But Justice Curlewis dismissed the *New Nation*'s defense of its contents on the ground that its "opinion…will be dependent in the first place, [on] where the person stands in the political spectrum, and whether he is black or white." The law subordinated a black editor's opinion to that of a white Minister.

Some government witnesses were so contemptuous of legality that they blatantly told incredible stories full of internal contradictions and inconsistent with the rest of the state's case, as in Inkatha's account of their Mpophomeni rally or the Port Elizabeth security police version of their treatment of detainees. Police—presumably selected and trained for observation and recall—suffered inexplicable amnesia. Government saw nothing wrong with using torture or other inducements to elicit "truth."

Government was at least as effective as the opposition in manipulating procedural niceties. While insisting on Parliamentary supremacy, the (white) House of Assembly displayed hypocritical solicitude for the separation of powers in refusing to hear Moutse's petition against its incorporation into KwaNdebele because Lebowa's Supreme Court action had rendered the matter "sub judice." The Speaker initially raised similar obstacles to Helen Suzman's motion to impeach Justice Strydom. When government sued to eject the Magopa from the Zwartrand cemetery, Justice van der Merwe rejected the defense challenge to the expropriation of the farm because the Magopa had failed to join the Minister of Community Development as a party. The KwaNdebele Legislative Assembly almost refused to discuss independence in August 1986 because it was not on the agenda—although people were dying almost daily in the struggle over that issue. A year later the Assembly repudiated its unanimous decision against independence—again because it had not been on the agenda and had passed by acclamation rather than formal vote. If magistrates and judges allowed parties considerable leeway to argue and adduce evidence, they often decided cases on narrow grounds—as in the lower court sentences of conscientious objectors.

The government also created "legal" forms that eliminated virtually all procedural constraints: detentions without trial or suspensions of newspapers. Police and prosecutors shirked their obligation to investigate and punish crime, forcing victims to gather evidence and seek legal remedies through inquests, private prosecutions, and damage actions (Mpophomeni, the "Trojan Horse" killings, Port Elizabeth torture). Black Sash offices became reluctant participants in the administration of pass laws. Appeals stayed judicial decrees. Punctilious insistence on legal (and illegal) niceties was a transparent excuse for continuing to deny §10 rights after final judgments in *Komani* and *Rikhoto*. Yet Justice van der Walt effectively nullified the statutory presumption of intent in subversion cases by requiring the state to prove it beyond a reasonable doubt.

Sometimes judicial review of executive action was exposed as a meaningless ritual. Although judges had interpreted some legislation—the Police, Prisons, and Defence Acts—as limiting government power to censor, the Emergency Regulations were a different matter. No sooner was one invalidated than government promulgated another achieving much the same goal.

And though the Home Affairs Minister protested that "a court can still review any decision I make," the court itself conceded that the *New Nation* "was dealing with the opinion of a politician and not a judgement of a court of law." "The Minister does not have to give 'reasons' why he formed an opinion," and it was not the court's "function to pass an opinion...upon the Minister's opinion." Even the Minister argued that it would demean the courts to decide "whether a statement constitutes propaganda or not." If the Appellate Division invalidated the incorporation of Moutse into KwaNdebele because it failed to meet the criterion of ethnic homogeneity inherent in the National States Constitution Act, the Borders of Particular States Extension Act endowed the State President with unfettered discretion to declare incorporations whenever he deemed them "expedient."

As we saw in the discussion of strategy, law is far more effective in defending negative freedom than conferring positive liberty; it can restrain the state but rarely compel it. The LRC might persuade courts to extend §10 rights to migrant workers and their families, but it could not assure them jobs, housing, schools, transportation, or safety. Ouksasie residents might overturn the declaration of an emergency camp, but they could not force government to rebuild the infrastructure. Courts might fault the Industrial Court for procedural error, but they were unlikely to order reinstatement of a thousand employees. They might overturn the Magopa removal and refuse the government's request to eject from Goedgevonden, but they would not grant possession.

State neutrality—a cornerstone of the rule of law—was severely compromised, most significantly by government favoritism of Inkatha. The white regime allowed Inkatha to carry "cultural weapons," vouched for its bona fides, and provided financial support to it and its trade union, UWUSA. Government betrayed legality most flagrantly by using the SADF to train, arm, and pay a 200-man hit squad, subsequently incorporated into the KwaZulu Police.

In South Africa, as everywhere, respect for legality was proportional to the visibility of government action. Courts might extend §10 rights to black workers and their dependents, but local officials still refused or simply failed to endorse passes. The scrupulous procedural regularity of the prosecutions of Ivan Toms, David Bruce, and others who refused conscription co-existed with violent attacks on ECC activists, SADF involvement in the dirty tricks campaign, and a plan by the Civil Co-operation Bureau to assassinate ECC director Gavin Evans. The government refused to delay the Magopa removal pending the Appellate Division decision on leave to appeal. When the AD finally addressed the merits, it may have invalidated the executive order precisely because government had mooted the issue by forcibly removing the people and expropriating the land. Magistrate Scholts issued a permit for the Mpophomeni rally knowing that residents were hostile to Inkatha and violence was inevitable. At the end of the formal inquest Magistrate Nieuwoudt named those responsible for the Mpophomeni murders and recommended prosecution—but the Natal Attorney General took no action. Here, as elsewhere, the police favored Inkatha: escorting them to safety after the murders and returning their "traditional" weapons; stalling the investigation while a key witness died and others disappeared (into the security forces!), recording exculpatory statements by several witnesses in identical language (which suggested the police had written them). Extrajudicial violence and threats intimidated witnesses, severely compromising the pursuit of truth—in the Mpophomeni inquest, the Orr interdict application, perhaps the Alexandra treason trial. Magistrates used their discretion to hold informal inquests, preventing the deceased's family from presenting evidence or questioning witnesses. The Transvaal Attorney General waited as long as possible before prosecuting Simon Skosana, Piet Ntuli, and George Mahlangu for kidnaping and torturing several hundred Moutse opponents of incorporation into KwaNdebele. When he could procrastinate no further he charged only simple assault, allowing them to pay R50 admission of guilt fines without standing trial. The security forces constantly referred complaints about brutality to their internal review procedures, which did nothing to restrain or punish torture in Port Elizabeth. The Oukasie superintendent blithely disregarded Justice Stafford's ruling that he lacked discretion to deny house and site permits. The Ventersdorp Magistrate shirked his statutory obligation to pay pensions, endorse reference books, or protect Magopa against the trespassing cattle of white farmers. The Klerksdorp Magistrate audited the books of Magopa headman Jacob More, as ordered, but then refused to let anyone see them or his report. When the Magopa were on the verge of purchasing the Holgat farm as a new home, the government expropriated it.

Loose coupling between top and bottom—the co-existence of rare conspicuous legalism with pervasive covert illegality—are universal, but South Africa refined this moral division of labor into a high art. Judicial decisions extending §10 rights (like the U.S. Supreme Court's desegregation decisions) were frustrated by lower bureaucrats, who displayed far more deliberation than speed. As Inkatha's escalating violence showed, orders directed at leaders were ignored by followers, while conviction and punishment of followers failed to deter or even contaminate leaders. Superiors claimed ignorance of what inferiors were doing. Judges refused to acknowledge what the police were doing. Although individual police sometimes were punished for isolated acts of brutality, the security forces generally were immune from legal correction for systematic torture. The inaptly-named Justice Human, for instance, convicted the Sharpeville Six on the basis of confessions that clearly had been extracted by force.

Apartheid constructed white ignorance of black suffering. Indeed, South Africa created urban township councils and rural homeland governments partly to be able to blame blacks for the illegality, corruption, and violence indispensable to white rule. High-level white security policemen relied on Black subordinates to conduct the actual torture—partly because they rarely spoke the victim's language. The increasing number of black police, especially kitskonstabels, repressed the townships. The use of vigilantes, the incitement of "Black-on-Black" violence, and the "third force" of military, police, and right-wing civilian assassins and provocateurs served the same purpose. Law was not the rule and violence the exception; rather, law became the continuation of violence by other means.

This racial division of political responsibility not only allowed white South Africa to continue proclaiming its fidelity to the rule of law but also demonstrated that Blacks were unprepared for democracy. The strategy could work, however, only if homeland leaders enjoyed some autonomy, which created the risk that they might act independently. It also required the more visible black leaders to keep their distance from the dirty work. KwaNdebele Chief Minister Simon Skosana and Home Affairs Minister Piet Ntuli seriously compromised South Africa by openly directing the kidnaping and torture of hundreds of Moutse residents opposing incorporation—an embarrassment conveniently eliminated within the year by Ntuli's assassination (which conspiracy enthusiasts attributed to South African security forces) and Skosana's death from diabetes.

South Africa's claim to respect as a Rechtsstaat suffered from another, more distinctive flaw: Parliamentary supremacy unconstrained by a bill of rights, unwritten constitution, or natural law. What does the rule of law mean when government can change the law at will? If the Appellate Division threatened to invalidate the Magopa removal, government mooted the decision by expropriating Zwartrand. If even a faithful Nationalist like Justice van Dijkhorst held that the government could not declare Oukasie an emergency camp, it simply disestablished the township. If the Appellate Division followed its Ingwavuma precedent and required Lebowa's consent for the excision of Moutse, the government passed two retrospective acts, one stating that the consent was deemed to have been given, the other that Lebowa had never contained Moutse—a truly Orwellian rewriting of history. As Justice Spoelstra declared: "It is not for me to pass judgment about whether that decision was good or bad, desirable or undesirable, wise or unwise."

Yet the government did not always wield its plenary legislative and executive powers. After introducing bills to overturn the Appellate Division decisions invalidating the Magopa removal and the Moutse incorporation, it withdrew both of them. It backed off from threats to annul *Komani* and *Rikhoto*. Although it obtained leave to appeal the invalidation of its decree declaring Oukasie an emergency camp, it abandoned the case. Judicial decisions enjoyed support not only from successful plaintiffs but also from the media, the opposition, the legal profession, and the courts themselves. Overruling them consumed more political capital than ordinary legislation— sometimes more than the regime could spare or wanted to spend. The configuration of power, which ultimately determined outcomes, comprised more than formal legislative authority.

Ideo-logic

In the previous section I explored the ways in which a government that purports to rule through law becomes constrained by that ideal. This is just one instance of the universal principle that rulers cannot govern indefinitely through naked force. All forms of domination seek to transform power into authority, eliciting consent by offering reasons for their actions. Lacking political power, legal rights, economic leverage, and military capacity, the opposition had no choice but to contest the government on the terrain of ideology.

Two of the most dramatic instances were Moutse's challenge to incorporation by KwaNdebele and the KwaNdebele women's demand for the vote. Moutse resisted incorporation by invoking the grundnorm of apartheid—ethnic homogeneity. Elsewhere the government had argued that mixing ethnic groups not only destroyed their cultural and linguistic heritage but also provoked violence and disrupted production and education. The months following incorporation amply confirmed these fears. Government justified the reversal of its plan to incorporate Lethlabile and Soshanguve into Bophuthatswana on grounds of ethnic diversity (forcing the pro-apartheid Conservative Party to call for compromising that principle). When the government justified homelands as a vehicle for black self-determination, Moutse responded that P.W. Botha had rejected repeated requests for a referendum and excised it from Lebowa without consultation. When the government invoked geographic contiguity and administrative convenience, Moutse pointed to the government's total disregard of those factors in other homelands, such as Bophuthatswana. Indeed, the government had just incorporated Botshabelo into QwaQwa, more than 300 kilometers away. Moutse also argued that incorporation into KwaNdebele would strip its women of the vote, a right enjoyed by all other South African women, regardless of race. Indeed, it turned the government's central argument in the women's vote case—the uniqueness of Ndebele culture—into a reason not to subordinate Moutse to an alien people.

Ideology played an even more important—and paradoxical—role in the women's vote case. Whereas Moutse could cite statutes and principles of administrative law, KwaNdebele women had to rely exclusively on analogy and natural law. Furthermore, they were in the anomalous position of challenging sex discrimination in the only country whose official policy was race discrimination. They pointed to the internal illogic of disenfranchisement: Ndebele women in other homelands could vote, whereas Ndebele women in South Africa and Moutse women in KwaNdebele could not. When the government invoked African political traditions denying women equality, the plaintiffs responded that Ndebele women played a larger role in traditional tribal councils than in the "modern" KwaNdebele legislative assembly. Furthermore, the "traditional" inferiority of women did not prevent them from voting in any other homeland or urban council. Indeed, it was not the traditional Ndebele leaders who opposed enfranchising women but Simon Skosana, a homeland Chief Minister devoid of traditional legitimacy. In any case, tradition was irrelevant to homelands arbitrarily constructed by the white regime. The government showed its own contempt for tradition by denying KwaNdebele men the right to vote until they became twenty-one, although custom recognized them as adults when they were circumcised at sixteen.

When the government—with an Emersonian disdain for foolish consistency—also justified the homelands as a means of introducing "modern," "western," "democratic" political institutions, KwaNdebele women responded in the same language. African women today played a much larger political role. Apartheid banished men from their homes, either as migrant workers for eleven months at a stretch or as long-distance commuters at work or in transit all week and exhausted on weekends. Women had to manage the farm, household, children's education, and locality.

KwaNdebele citizens could not attack the homeland's independence in court, since that decision was entrusted to the unfettered discretion of a State President able to find, or bribe, a compliant leader. But the successful challenges to Moutse's incorporation and the all-male franchise eliminated essential political support. Without Moutse, KwaNdebele was uninterested in independence and economically unviable. Once KwaNdebele women could vote, they elected an anti-independence majority to the Legislative Assembly. The struggle also revealed the moral bankruptcy of grand apartheid. The "modern" political institutions of homeland governments were supposed to be more democratic and enlightened than "traditional" tribal leaders. In KwaNdebele, however, the Ndzundza royal house (particularly Prince James Mahlangu) was more progressive than the tyrannical, corrupt, and brutal homeland Cabinet. Chief Minister Skosana, whose only claim to legitimacy was his alleged "modernity," had almost no formal education. Once KwaNdebele decisively rejected independence, that cornerstone of grand apartheid disintegrated. Elsewhere blacks paradoxically preferred white rule to black puppets: Like Moutse, Braklaagte and Leeuwfontein desperately wanted to remain within South Africa rather than be subordinated to Lucas Mangope in Bophuthatswana; Alexandra preferred Steven Burger, the white administrator, to Mayor Buti and the black town council.

The warrants of modernity and tradition also played important roles in Mogopa. Shadrack More invoked the traditional claim of being a "chief by the people," while disparaging Jacob More's pretension to the headmanship as resting on the dictate of a white magistrate; headmen in Braklaagte and Leeuwfontein made similar challenges. The Magopa maintained that traditional farming techniques limited them to the maize triangle; government responded that younger farmers could learn to grow new crops or irrigate other land. The Magopa declared that tradition obligated them to maintain the graves of their ancestors; the state's expert witness replied that the cemetery was a modern innovation.

In various settings the opposition sought to heighten the fundamental contradiction of apartheid: whites' determination to retain political domination and social separation while exploiting black labor. Large corporations disliked the pass laws, which divided the loyalties of their black workers between urban employment and rural families. Oukasie residents were able to enlist Brits employers to oppose the removal advocated by white residents. Blacks opposing the incorporation of Moutse into an independent KwaNdebele—the dream of Pretoria politicians—could appeal to neighboring white farmers. In the Western Transvaal some local Boers, including the brother of AWB leader Eugene Terre'Blanche, wanted the labor and purchasing power of the Magopa badly enough to speak against removal.

The opposition's ideological leverage was enhanced by the government's need to appear reformist. In February 1985 it proclaimed the end of "forced removals" and subsequently repealed the Black Administration Act. Botha declared that apartheid was dead. Removals no longer could be justified by white prejudice but had to invoke black betterment. If they were truly voluntary, however, residents could refuse to leave despite the penalties for defiance (reduced services, disintegrating infrastructure, vigilante attacks, denial of compensation) and incentives for compliance (new land and better housing). When government sought to justify "voluntary" removal on the ground that Mogopa and Oukasie were unplanned and undeveloped, residents expressed their readiness to accept government money for improvements. When government claimed upgrading was too expensive, residents commissioned a study that found it far cheaper than removal. When government voiced unprecedented solicitude for the health of Oukasie residents, they conducted a survey showing it was no worse than in other black townships. When government characterized Oukasie residents as homeless, they had three retorts: Government itself had destroyed their homes, terminated their services, and refused to maintain their infrastructure; nevertheless, many holdouts still had perfectly good homes.

Although government sought to frame the Alexandra treason trial as a criminal prosecution, the defense turned it into a contest over who was entitled to the mantle of democracy. The AAC could point to its detailed minutes, consultation with lawyers, obsession with drafting a constitution, public proceedings, grassroots accountability, and repudiation of fiscal irregularities and adventurist criminal conduct. Unabashed by its racist exclusion of Blacks from national politics, the state pointed to the people's courts, boycott of local elections, and failure of "Coloureds" to appeal to the House of Representatives. The defense unambiguously won this contest when van der Walt began his judgment with the unprecedented judicial declaration that South Africa was not democratic.

When conscientious objectors raised religious and ethical arguments against conscription, the SADF, prosecutors, magistrates, and judges all felt compelled to reply in kind. They invoked their own Christian faith, the total onslaught, atheistic communism, the utopian impracticality of pacifism, inconsistencies in the objectors' beliefs, and flaws in their character. When magistrates asked what sentence to impose, Bruce and Torr would not let them evade responsibility, insisting it was the magistrates' decision. Discomfort with the SADF role in Namibia and the townships may help to explain why the Appellate Division ignored what everyone had assumed to be the plain meaning of the Defence Act.

Impelled by its guilty conscience, government kept shifting ground in an attempt to justify censorship. It was necessary. The alternative was media autarchy. South Africa took a responsible middle position between the extremes of communist totalitarianism and the license of dogmatic liberalism. It offered greater liberty than the rest of Africa, but its blacks were not ready for the heady freedom of Western capitalism. South African censorship was "scientific" (just as the planned communities of Lethlabile and Pachsdraai were superior to the organic chaos of Oukasie and Mogopa). But when the *New Nation* sought to defend its contents by arguing that they were true and no different from what the established press was writing, the Minister was unmoved.

The opposition could draw strength from ideology only if the government cared about the coherence and integrity of its justifications. But the South African regime often advanced vague, ambiguous reasons, shifting ground whenever one was demolished, boasting a Whitmanesque ability to contain contradictions. One of the most manipulable rationalizations was "choice." Oukasie residents chose to move to Lethlabile; Moutse teachers chose to work in KwaNdebele rather than be transferred; KwaNdebele chose independence through its Legislative Assembly; Braklaagte and Leeuwfontein chose incorporation into Bophuthatswana rather than physical removal; the Magopa chose to move to Pachsdraai; conscientious objectors chose jail over military or alternative service. Like other oppressive regimes, South Africa took refuge in Orwellian newspeak. The Natives (Abolition of Passes and Coordination of Documents) Act 57 of 1952 required all Africans to carry registration books. The Department of Co-operation and Development coerced and underdeveloped Blacks. The Civil Cooperation Bureau bombed, tortured, kidnaped, and assassinated.

Some government arguments addressed only whites: They had suffered as much as blacks to achieve the shared dream of apartheid; the restoration of land to any blacks inevitably would lead to the return of all 3.5 million removed. Other arguments bordered on the outrageous. Allowing the Onderstepoort Magopa to return to Zwartrand would endanger the rights of those who had settled at Pachsdraai—this from a government that had ruthlessly uprooted millions of blacks over four centuries. The return to

Goedgevonden was a "forced removal" because outsiders contributed to the transportation costs. Tired of giving reasons, government resorted to the exasperated parent's ipse dixit. The Magopa removal could not be stopped because the government had ordered it; government claimed to be bound by treaties it had imposed on homelands it had created. Official decisions increased in value with the passage of time, like fine wines or antiques. P.W. Botha presented himself as national patriarch. I'm a hard man, he told Moutse; you should know better than to ask me to change my mind. In the end, government acknowledged that it wielded naked power, taking refuge in its unfettered discretion to expropriate Mogopa, excise Moutse from Lebowa, disestablish Oukasie, or censor the press.

The Accidents of History

A reader looking for sweeping generalizations about the capacity of law to constrain state power may be disappointed with this conclusion. Most of the observations are specific to a few cases. For each, there seems to be a counter-example. Rather than apologize for the apparent lack of theoretical ambition, I want to argue that such particularity is essential and appropriate to the questions I asked. Major political cases do not resemble the routine microbehavior that is grist for most sociology of law: deviance, penology, regulation, impact, complaints, disputing, professionalization, attitudes, etc. This book concerns large, complex events, extending over many years, involving scores of participants, with repercussions for the entire society. Each case is idiosyncratic and inherently unpredictable, peculiar not only to South Africa in the 1980s but also to the unique conjuncture of time, place, and actors. Historical interpretation must complement, and often displace, sociological generalization.

The inquest into the Inkatha murder of the three Mpophomeni MAWU activists reached its damning conclusions only because the hit squad bungled the job, permitting Micca Sibiya to escape and testify. The death of Inkatha leader Joseph Mabaso before the inquest conveniently allowed the suspects to blame him without fear of rebuttal or retaliation. Although I often feel that South African commentators, like their American counterparts, overemphasize judicial personality, the two Mpophomeni inquests displayed profound differences: J.J. Scholts conducted a perfunctory inquiry, making no findings; Mrs. S.M. Niewoudt castigated Inkatha for intimidation, voiced impatience with the officious ineptitude of Inkatha's counsel, dismissed the suspects' tissue of lies, and forthrightly named those she believed were guilty. The political spectrum among Supreme Court justices was even greater, ranging from a few liberals to a much larger number of party hacks. H. van Dyk displayed a verkrampte consistency in rejecting Magopa's challenge to removal and Moutse's to incorporation (only to be reversed in both cases). Yet van der Walt would not have been called a liberal before acquitting the Alexandra Five—or after.

The security forces have been torturing and killing black detainees for decades, suffering serious embarrassment only when the victim was unusually visible, like Steve Biko. Otherwise the government and most of the media disregarded and discounted the tediously repetitive complaints. The same silence would have greeted the massive repression in Port Elizabeth following the 1985 Emergency but for Wendy Orr. She was no political activist. She had not entered the Prisons Department out of a sense of mission but only to repay the government for her university scholarship and spend some time in her home town. Nor did medical training explain her decision to publicize the systematic torture of detainees. Her superiors, who had practiced medicine for years, routinely protected the security forces. Indeed, it was Dr. Lang's guilt about Biko, whose death was being reinvestigated, that enabled her to copy the prisoners' medical records, which became the foundation for her lawsuit. Her shock at the torture of detainees ultimately assumed a legal form because she confided in a sister in Johannesburg, who happened to encounter a human rights lawyer at a party. Ultimately, however, the decisive factor was Wendy Orr's character—courage, inexperience, perhaps even foolhardiness.

The End Conscription Campaign's support for conscientious objectors confirms sociological theories about collective action. But the ECC had almost nothing to do with David Bruce, a highly visible objector and one of the two defendants who persuaded the Appellate Division to rewrite the Defence Act. A loner by nature, he distanced himself from all organizations after an unhappy experience in Wits student politics. He was not a model CO, like Ivan Toms, and probably would not have been selected by the ECC for a test case. His political philosophy was undeveloped. He had no orthodox religious beliefs and called himself agnostic. He was not engaged in public service. He lacked influential friends who could attest to his character. He vacillated between evasion, flight, and defiance. If he had any model, it would have been Melville's Bartleby the Scrivener. He just preferred not to serve—and was prepared, at twenty-two, to spend the next six years in prison. For him (as for Toms and the handful of other COs), refusing complicity with the military apparatus of apartheid—and suffering the harsh consequences—was the only way to cleanse the moral taint of being a white South African.

M.B. de Beer, Oukasie's white superintendent, was not unusually villainous, nor was he out of character in ordering a black applicant to take his letter back to his lawyer and tell him to stuff it up his ass. His real error was admitting he had said this, thereby transforming the routine (and hence acceptable) oppressions of apartheid into gratuitous individual discourtesy, which could not be justified or ignored. Despite this reversal the government might have succeeded in expelling the residents had it not made the arrogant mistake of arguing that people living in adequate houses were homeless.

The struggle over KwaNdebele independence could easily have ended differently. The Appellate Division's invalidation of the incorporation of

Moutse was a serious blow—but the South African government could have overcome it through legislation (and actually introduced a bill for this purpose). The Supreme Court's extension of the franchise to women was a further government defeat—but many other homeland regimes blatantly flouted the popular will. The assassination of Piet Ntuli (probably by Umkhonto we Sizwe) dramatically demonstrated that the forces of repression were not invincible, while the death of Simon Skosana from diabetes deprived the independence movement of essential leadership.

Chance played an important role in every criminal prosecution. In the Sharpeville Six trial, the personal attorney for a key state witness "happened" to be an associate of the defense attorneys, to whom he revealed that the witness had been coerced into giving evidence, which he later recanted.[8] The state botched the Pietermaritzburg treason trial in two ways. Its transcriptions and translations of allegedly incriminating video and audio tapes were so hopelessly flawed that the court threw them out altogether. And the state's expert witness, who offered to unmask the UDF as an ANC front, instead exposed his own ignorance and eventually abandoned that position entirely. In the Alexandra Five treason trial, the defense surprised the prosecution by producing minutes demonstrating the innocence of allegedly seditious AAC meetings. Although the police had ransacked Alexandra township for evidence, the AAC secretary had given them to the wife of the principal accused, who had taken them to her office to type. And in Delmas, Justice van Dijkhorst need not have dismissed the assessor who signed the UDF million-signatures campaign; even without his concurrence the court would have reached a conviction, which the Appellate Division probably could not have overturned.

A similar error undermined the BTR SARMCOL victory over MAWU. Shortly before the six-month trial ended the Industrial Court judge overruled objections by counsel for the union and accepted an invitation from SARMCOL's labor consultants to speak at a management seminar addressed by all of SARMCOL's attorneys and advocates. This was such an obvious breach of judicial neutrality that Justice Didcott summarily reversed the judgment—which probably would have withstood substantive attack—and was affirmed by the Appellate Division.

The Lessons of South Africa

What lessons can we draw from this history of the roles of law in the struggle against apartheid in the 1980s? First, the uniqueness of South Africa would make it dangerous to generalize to other countries. A minority was oppressing a majority—a relic of colonialism in a continent where Harold Macmillan had warned the South African Parliament of the winds of change as early as 1960. The struggle against apartheid possessed distinctive moral purity: By the 1980s the rest of the world had repudiated de jure racism.

South Africa had become an international pariah. If the ANC (and even more the SACP) drew considerable support from the communist bloc, capitalist nations could not openly befriend the white regime without alienating the rest of black Africa. These characteristics distinguished the South African experience from legal resistance to Nazi Germany, the American civil rights movement, communist dissidents, or opposition to military rule in Latin America.

Second, we must be cautious in extrapolating to the post-apartheid era, which will be characterized by a very different constellation of forces. Most commentators have focused on, indeed been obsessed with, the constitutional framework. A bill of rights and judicial review undoubtedly will make a difference (although there is reason to fear that whites will be more effective in using it to defend the privileges they gained during apartheid). But at least as significant as substantive rules are the organization and composition of legal institutions: the bench, prosecutorial branch, and legal profession. A crucial question will be funding for oppositional lawyering. Ethnic rivalries, which were stoked but contained by the white regime, inevitably will intensify now that national power is at stake. Government will be torn between a commitment to redress more than three centuries of injustice and its fear of white armed resistance, economic dislocation, and capital flight. Law may prove much less useful in attacking the oppressions of class than it did in challenging racism. The devolution of power to regions, in response to both black and white pressures, may lead to centrifugal forces the central government cannot contain and the emergence of a new apartheid. In this, as in other incipient democracies in the third and former communist worlds, the military are likely to play an excessive role for many years. Even without military intervention or influence, the bad habits of decades of a strong executive accustomed to wielding Emergency powers may be hard to reform, especially among inexperienced rulers insecure about their authority.

Law was by no means the only or even the most important factor in the struggle against apartheid. The legal victories of the 1980s were part of an intensified wave of resistance in a cycle of challenge and repression dating back to World War II: the Defiance Campaign, women's refusal to carry passes, the treason and Rivonia trials, Sharpeville, black power, and Soweto. During this crucial decade black workers played an increasingly prominent role, partly because competition in the global economy forced capitalists to recognize black trade unions in the hope of raising productivity. The contradiction deepened between large capital, prepared to relax apartheid, and white working class, civil servant, farmer, and petty bourgeois voters fearful of losing their jobs, political hegemony, social status, and lands. The effect of increasing economic pressure from international investors and traders was heightened by the recession. With the end of the Cold War, the South African government could no longer evoke the threat of communism, with either domestic audiences or western powers. Military reversals in Angola and the cost of repressing SWAPO in Namibia—in both economic terms and body bags—pushed the front line back into South Africa.

The recognition that South Africa in the 1980s was exceptional and law alone was not decisive should not mislead us to deprecate its importance. Human rights lawyers, like other progressives, too often frame the issue dichotomously: Law either makes all the difference or no difference at all. Seduced by the romantic delusion of a decisive rupture, they search in vain for a revolutionary event that will ignite the righteous wrath of the suffering masses and sweep away the evil oppressor. They feel guilty at not sharing the misery of those they champion and fearful that they are betraying democratic ideals by deploying their professional skills. Most paralyzing is the anxiety that limited victories will co-opt the masses. Some activists argue that only progressive immiseration can stiffen resistance. All the evidence contradicts this. Hope is necessary for struggle. Legal victories, far from legitimating the regime, demonstrate its vulnerability and erode its will to dominate. The legal battles described in this book did not win the war by themselves. But they empowered the masses while offering some protection from state retaliation. They strengthened the commitment of the anti-apartheid movement to legality—and also, perhaps, that of the post-apartheid polity. They forged one of the few bonds across racial lines. The handful of lawyers who helped blacks overthrow three centuries of white domination in South Africa should be proud of the role they played.

NOTES

Abbreviations

Newspapers and Journals

A	Argus
ACAG	Anti–Censorship Action Group/Update
B	Beeld
BD	Business Day
BG	Boston Globe
C	Citizen
CH	Cape Herald
CP	City Press
CSM	Christian Science Monitor
CT	Cape Times
DD	Daily Dispatch
DFA	Diamond Fields Advertiser
DM	Daily Mail
DN	Daily News (South Africa)
E	Economist
EP	Evening Post
EPH	Eastern Province Herald
FM	Financial Mail
G	Guardian (London)
I	Independent (London)
ILJ	Industrial Law Journal
JAMA	Journal of the American Medical Association
L	Leader
LAT	Los Angeles Times
ND	Newsday (New York)
NM	Natal Mercury
NN	New Nation
NP	Natal Post
NW	Natal Witness
NYT	New York Times

O	Observer (London)
Obj	Objector
PI	Philadelphia Inquirer
PN	Pretoria News
RDM	Rand Daily Mail
SABC	South African Broadcasting Corporation
SE	Sunday Express
SM	Sunday Mirror
So	Sowetan
SP	Sunday Post
SSt	Sunday Star
St	Star
STi	Sunday Times (Johannesburg)
STr	Sunday Tribune
T	Times (London)
WA	Weekend Argus
WM	Weekly Mail
WP	Washington Post
WSJ	Wall Street Journal

Courts

CPD	Cape Provincial Division
NPD	Natal Provincial Division
SECLD	South-Eastern Cape Local Division
STD	Southern Transvaal Division
TPD	Transvaal Provincial Division
WLD	Witwatersrand Local Division

Foreword

1. E. Thompson (1975: 262-63).

Chapter 1: SPEAKING WITH THE OGRE

1. E. Thompson (1975: 265).

2. Paton (1987: 238, 241, 283) (speeches to the University of Michigan, 1977; University of the Witwatersrand, 1978; and King's School, Natal Midlands, 1981).

Chapter 2: POLITICS BY OTHER MEANS?

1. Paton (1987: 283) (1982 speech to King's School, Natal Midlands).

2. See Hart (1958); Fuller (1958); MacCormick (1978; 1981; 1982; 1985; 1986); Soper (1977; 1984); Raz (1979); Dworkin (1978; 1985; 1986).

3. Bronner (1989) (Bork); Simon (1992) (Bork and Thomas); Higginbotham (1992) (Thomas); Rauh (1993) (appointments generally).

4. Grodin (1989).

5. Fernandez (1985); Bennhold (1989).

6. E.g., Rose (1992) (Tottenham Three).

7. See Teubner (1988; 1990).

8. Reifner (1986: 111); Müller (1991: chap. 7).

9. NYT B9 (12.3.93).

10. E. Thompson (1975); see also Hay et al. (1975).

11. Cover (1975).

12. Fraenkel (1969); Neumann (1972); Fernandez (1985); Reifner (1986); Bennhold (1989); Müller (1991).

13. Franey (1983) (prosecution of welfare "cheats"); Jones & Novak (1985) (denial of welfare to crush miners' strike).

14. Skolnick (1966) (United States); Woffinden (1987) (United Kingdom).

15. Swindle (1993) (Texas police beating black to death).

16 The classic statement is Hay (1975).

17. Müller (1991: ch. 8); Reifner (1982; 1986: 102, 109, 111); Lippman (1993).

18. Bisharat (1989).

19. See the case studies by the Lawyers' Committee for Human Rights.

20. Auerbach (1976: chaps. 8–9) (United States); Halliday (1987: chap. 9) (United States); Shamir (1992) (United States); Weisberg (1984; 1991) (France); Olgiati (1989) (Italy); Osiel (1984) (Brazil).

21. Luckham (1981) (Ghana); Lee (1990) (Malaysia); Tun Salleh & Das (1989) (Malaysia).

22. The large literature includes Hurst (1945); Kirchheimer (1961) (the classic and most comprehensive treatment); L. Friedman (1970); Becker (1971); McConnell (1974); Hakman (1972); Allen (1974); Schafer (1974); Roebuck & Weaber (1978); Ingraham (1979); Belknap (1981); Turk (1982); Sumner (1983); Hain (1984); D. Davis (1985a; 1990a); Barkan (1977; 1985); Christenson (1986); Hariman (1990); Albertyn & Davis (1990); Mitchell (1992).

23. On nineteenth-century United States, see Forbath (1989). On the British miners' strike of 1984–85, see NCCL (1984); Goodman (1985); Coulter et al. (1984); Penny Green (1990); Scraton & Thomas (1985); Jackson & Wardle (n.d.); Fine & Millar (1985). On other British strikes, see Dromey & Taylor (1978) (Grunwick); Bell et al. (1977) (Grunwick); NCCL (1986b) (News International). See generally Geary (1985).

24. Gusfield (1963) (Prohibition); S. Cohen (1972); Hall et al. (1978); Hall (1980); Scraton (1987).

25. Belknap (1978); Schneir & Schneir (1965); Sabin (1993).

26. On the civil rights movement, see L. Friedman (1965); Kinoy (1989); Chestnut & Cass (1990). On the suppression of civil unrest, see Skolnick (1969); Balbus (1973) (Detroit riots); NCCL (1980a; 1980b) (Southall); R. Lewis (1980) (Southall); Okojie (1991) (Tottenham 3); Kettle & Hodges (1982) (Britain); Harring (1983) (American tramps); Vogler (1991) (UK); NCCL (1986a) (Stonehenge).

27. Antonio (1972); Hayden (1970); Major (1973); Lukas (1970); Epstein (1970); Mitford (1969); *New York Review of Books* (1970); Schultz (1993).

28. Kirchheimer (1961: 99–105); Kaplan (1990); Müller (1991: chap. 4); Pattee (1953); Labedz & Hayward (1967) (Sinyavsky and Daniel).

29. Thornton (1987) (Zircon affair); Turnbull (1988) (Spycatcher).

30. Northern Ireland: Boyle et al. (1975; 1980); Gifford (1984); Hogan & Walker (1989); Bonner (1985); Stalker (1988); P. Taylor (1987); Mullin (1990); McKee & Franey (1988); Conlon (1990); Hillyard (1993); Farrell (1986); Mulloy (1986). Italy: Jamieson (1989). Israel: Keren (1993).

31. Peterson & Fite (1957); Baskir & Strauss (1978); Barkan (1977; 1985); Bannan & Bannan (1974); Kadish & Kadish (1973); Useem (1973); Dorsen & Friedman (1973).

32. E.g., Lowenstein (1948); Kirchheimer (1961: 8); E. Davidson (1966); Smith (1977); Müller (1991: chaps. 22–23, 26–30); T. Taylor (1993); on the Japanese war trials, see Ginn (1992).

33. E.g., Finkielkraut (1992); R. Bernstein (1992); on Belgium, see Huyse & Dhondt (1993).

34. Osiel (1986); Amnesty International (1987).

35. For fictional treatments, see Klíma (1993); Barnes (1993).

36. Vose (1959); Casper (1972); Kluger (1975); Freeman (1978); Tushnet (1987); D. Bell (1987); Crenshaw (1988); Branch (1988); Tushnet & Lezin (1991); Rosenberg (1991) (revisionism).

37. E.g., Piven & Cloward (1977); Gaventa (1988); Wellstone (1978); Levine (1982); Bumiller (1988); Upham (1987) (Japan); Schrag (1972).

38. Handler (1978); Abel (1985a; 1985b); Weisbrod et al. (1978); Cooper & Dhavan (1986); Kessler (1987); Aron (1989); López (1992).

39. On law as symbolic politics, see Arnold (1935; 1937); Edelman (1964; 1971; 1977; 1988); Gusfield (1963; 1981); Scheingold (1974).

40. On the Canadian experience under the recent Charter, see Hutchinson & Monahan (1987); Fudge & Glasbeek (1992); on Chile under Allende see Ietswaart (1987); on "strategic lawsuits against public participation" in the United States, see Canan & Pring (1988).

41. Coaker (1972); Davenport (1961); Trapido (1970; 1980); J. Robertson (1971); Dugard (1972a; 1987c); Simkins (1986); Butler et al. (1987); Black (1992).

42. Schreiner (1967); South Africa, Department of Foreign Affairs (1968); Snyman (1970); van Blerk (1982; 1988); for a critical view, see Marcus (1985b).

43. *Hansard* cols. 6747–48 (H.M.J. van Rensburg) (6.4.85).

44. *Hansard* cols. 9640–41 (D.P. de K. van Gend) (5.11.88).

45. *Hansard* col. 9606 (J.H.L. Schleepers) (5.11.88).

46. Barberton Commission (1984); Kannemeyer (1985); Rabie Commission (1981); Harms (1990); Hiemstra (1990); Goldstone (1990; 1992); Parsons Commission (1992); see Suttner (1986).

47. Hellman (1949); J. Lewin (1959); Landis (1961); Turk (1972); Horrell (1978; 1982); van der Horst & Reid (1981); Ormond (1985); Burdzik & van Wyk (1987); Rycroft et al. (1987); Posel (1991).

48. See Sachs (1985); Suttner (1984b); Suttner & Cronin (1986); Marcus (1985a); African National Congress (1989; 1991).

49. International Commission of Jurists (1960; 1962; 1968; 1975; 1978); Bindman (1988).

50. United Nations (1973); Commonwealth Group (1986); Unicef (1987; 1989); United States, Department of State (1989); Great Britain (1991); LAT Pt.I p.8 (7.8.86), Pt.I p.6 (8.16.86); *National Law Journal* 1 (1.12.87).

51. WM 7 (5.18.90).

52. van Manen (n.d.); van den Wyngaert (1986).

53. Gardiner (1957); Blom-Cooper (1959); Millner (1961); Falk (1968); Ream (1970); H. Bernstein (1972); Turk (1981); Goldberg (1985); J. Davidson (1985); Greenberg et al. (1986); Butcher (1986); Rayner (1986); M. Green (1987); Bjornland (1990); Higginbotham (1990); Olson (1991); Caiger (1991); Ellmann (1992).

54. WM 10 (10.30.87).

55. See WM 4 (4.15.88); *Hansard* col. 15217 (6.29.88) (R.S. Nowbath, House of Delegates).

56. Beinart (1962); J. Lewin (1963); Hahlo & Maisels (1966); Randall (1972); Acta Juridica (1979); Brookes & Macauley (1958); Milton (1970); Venter (1973); Kahn (1949; 1961; 1966; 1970); A. Mathews (1964; 1965; 1971; 1978; 1985a; 1985b; 1986; 1987); Corbett (1981); Cameron (1982; 1987); Mathews & Albino (1966); Slabbert (1981); H. Suzman (1968; 1973); van der Vyver (1976; 1980; 1982; 1986; 1988a; 1988b); Sachs (1973; 1975); S. Kentridge (1980; 1981; 1982; 1987); Dugard (1970; 1971; 1974; 1987b; 1987d; 1989; 1992); Riekert (1982; 1985a; 1985b); D. Davis (1980a; 1980b; 1982; 1985b; 1987a; 1987b); Dyzenhaus (1982; 1983a; 1983b; 1984; 1985; 1986; 1991); Corder (1984; 1987a; 1987b; 1988; 1989b); Forsyth (1980a; 1980b; 1985; 1988); Bennett et al. (1988); Forsyth & Schiller (1981; 1985); Rudolph (1979; 1980; 1984); Dean (1976b); Basson (1987); Baxter (1985a); Bennett et al. (1988); Boulle (1987); Norton (1982/83); A. du Toit (1977; 1988); D. du Toit (1986); M. Robertson (1991); Robertson et al. (1990); Thomashausen (1984); Suttner (1984a); Labour Law Unit (1988); Klug (1988); Soggot (1986); Plasket (1986a); Didcott (1989); Mureinik (1987); SAJHR (1987); Haysom & Plasket (1988); van Zyl Smit (1984; 1987; 1988a); Cowling (1987).

57. Murray & Mangan (1987); Murray & Sloth-Nielsen (1988; 1989); Murray et al. (1990a; 1990b); SALJ (1989).

58. M. Mathews (1982/83); Plasket & Firman (1984); Dean (1983; 1984; 1986); Baxter (1984); Boulle (1985); Mureinik (1985a; 1985b; 1985c; 1986); Chaskalson (1985a); Corder (1989a); Davis & Corder (1988); G. Budlender (1988a); Nienaber (1983); Mahomed (1989); Kirby (1989).

59. D. Davis (1987b; 1988; 1990b); Cameron et al. (1980); S. Kentridge (1982); Haysom & Plasket (1988); Cowen (1961); Dyzenhaus (1982; 1983a; 1984; 1991); Ellmann (1991).

60. Wacks (1984a; 1984b); Dugard (1984; 1987a); M. Robertson (1989).

61. van Niekerk (1969; 1978; 1979; 1981); S. v van Niekerk 1970 (2) SA 655 (T), rev'd 1972 (3) SA 711 (A); Milton (1970); Rhadamanthus (1970); Hahlo & Maisels (1971); Dugard (1972b); 87 SALJ 467 (1970).

62. Mihalik (1980); van der Vyver (1988a: 73–74 n.92).

63. Coetsee (1988) responding to Cameron (1987).

64. WM 22 (12.10.93) (L. Esselen suing Lawyers for Human Rights director Brian Currin).

65. See, e.g., Dean & van Zyl Smit (1983); van der Westhuizen et al. (1988); Sanders (1986); Leon (1986); Lemon (1987); D. Davis (1987c); Columbia Human Rights Law Review (1989); van der Merwe (1989); Sachs (1985; 1990b; 1991; 1993); Berat (1991); Forsyth (1991); Lee & Schlemmer (1991); Horowitz (1991); de Villiers et al. (1992); Keightley (1992); Scott & Macklem (1992).

66. E.g., Saul & Gelb (1981); Stadler (1987); Lipton (1985); Cobbett & Cohen (1988); but see Wolpe (1980; 1988).

67. Davenport (1987b); Horrell (1971); Karis & Carter (1972–77); Lodge (1983); Mermelstein (1987); Martin (1988); Price (1991); Albertyn (1991); Kenney (1992). See generally the SAIRR's Annual Survey on Race Relations. For a nineteenth-century case, see Herd (1976).

68. Moller v Keimoes School Committee 1911 AD 635; Sachs (1973: 132–33); Dyzenhaus (1991: 53).

69. Minister of Posts and Telegraphs v Rassool 1934 AD 167; Sachs (1973: 138–40); Dyzenhaus (1991: 53).

70. On the ideology of apartheid, see Moodie (1975); Harrison (1981); L. Thompson (1985); Crapanzano (1986); Sparks (1990).

71. Kuper (1956); Lodge (1983).

72. R v Abdurahman 1950 (3) SA (A); Tayob v Ermelo Local Road Transportation Board 1951 (4) SA 440 (A); R v Lusu 1953 (2) SA 484 (A); Sachs (1973: 142–43); Dyzenhaus (1991: 63).

73. Minister of Interior v Harris 1952 (4) SA 769 (A); Collins v Minister of Interior 1957 (1) SA 552 (A); Sachs (1973: 143–45); Davenport (1987b: 363). It was this outrage that provoked the formation of what became Black Sash. Spink (1991: chap.2).

74. Cassem v Oos-Kaapse Kommittee van die Groepsgebiedraad 1959 (3) SA 651 (A); Minister of the Interior v Lockhat 1961 (2) SA 587 (A); Dyzenhaus (1991: 70–80).

75. R v Pitje 1960 (4) SA 709 (A); Sachs (1973: 145); Dyzenhaus (1991: 76).

76. Forman & Sachs (1957); Sampson (1958); Karis (1961; 1965), Joseph (1966; 1986); Mandela (1960); Kirchheimer (1961: 124–25); Sachs (1973: 215); Dugard (1974); D. Davis (1985a).

77. Sharpeville Commission (1960); Feit (1971).

78. General Law Amendment Act 76 of 1962; Strydom (1965) (an account by a government apologist); Helen Bernstein (1989); Mandela (1964).

79. Rossouw v Sachs 1964 (2) SA 551 (A); Dyzenhaus (1991: 101). The article was Mathews & Albino (1966). For accounts of imprisonment and detention, see First (1965); Sachs (1990); H. Lewin (1981); M. Dlamini (n.d.).

80. §215 bis of the Criminal Procedure Amendment Act 96 of 1965.

81. Dyzenhaus (1991: 106–07).

82. S v Hlekani 1964 (4) SA 429 (E); Schermbrucker v Klindt 1965 (4) SA 606 (A).

83. Nxasana v Minister of Justice 1976 (3) SA 745 (D) (Didcott gave detainee access to lawyer to investigate ill-treatment); Sigaba v Minister of Defence and Police 1980 (3) SA 535 (TkSC) (Rose Innes did the same); UDF (Western Cape Region) v Theron NO 1984 (1) SA 315 (C) (Rose Innes overruled magisterial denial of permit for public meeting); Dyzenhaus (1991: chap. 6).

84. Carlson (1973: chaps. 10, 13–18); Sachs (1973: 234); Gilbey (1993: chap. 4).

85. Gerhart (1978); J. Jackson (1980); Lobban (1990; n.d.).

86. Dean (1976a); A. du Toit (1977); Kane-Berman (1978); Brewer (1987); Davenport (1987a).

87. G. Moss (1979); see also Halberstam (1980).

88. Dreyer (1980); Breytenbach (1984); Weschler (1993).

89. Anon (1972); ffrench-Beytagh (1973); ICJ (1975).

90. A. Mathews (1978; 1986); van der Vyver (1980; 1988a; 1988b); Dugard (1978; 1982a; 1982b); Rabie Commission (1981); Bindman (1988); Baxter (1985a); Bell & Mackie (1985); Bennett et al. (1988); Parry (1981); Seegers (1988); Lawyers' Committee for Civil Rights Under Law (1983).

91. See Lelyveld (1985); Denman (1985); Finnegan (1986); Lonsdale (1988); Hochschild (1990); Dugard et al. (1992); Lodge et al. (1991); Schrire (1991); SAR (1985-date).

92. Wiehahn Commission (1979); Fine et al. (1981); Fine & Davis (1990); Gould (1981); Haysom (1984); Clark (1985); Webster (1985); Finnemore & van der Merwe (1986); Roos (1987); Brassey et al. (1987); C. Thompson (1988); S. Friedman (1987); Maree (1987); Benjamin (1987); Cameron et al. (1988); Benjamin et al. (1989); Bendix (1989; 1992); see generally SALB; *Industrial Law Journal; Institute of Industrial Relations, Annual Review*.

93. S. Davis (1987). On one of the most notorious bombings, see Meer (n.d.); Rostron (1991).

94. D. Budlender (1989); Gosiger (1986).

95. Lodge (1989).

96. Meer (1985); North (1986); Helliker et al. (1987); M. Murray (1987); Johnson (1988); Indicator South Africa (1988); Brewer (1989a); Lodge et al. (1991); Mufson (1990); Price (1991); Marx (1992); see generally SAR. The most notorious killing of a local councilor led to the conviction and death sentences of the Sharpeville Six and the long, ultimately successful, campaign to save them. See Diar (1990).

97. Coleman & Webster (1986); Kruss (1987); D. Webster (1987); Friedman & Webster (1989); Brittain & Minty (1988); Lawyers Committee for Human Rights (1986a; 1986b; 1986c); Human Rights Quarterly (1988); Detainees' Parents Support Committee, Annual Reports; Lawyers

for Human Rights, Annual Reports; Human Rights Commission, Human Rights Updates and Area Repression Reports.

98. *Hansard* cols. 13-14 (1.31.86).

99. Ellmann (1990; 1992); Basson (1987); Haysom & Kahanovitz (1987); Haysom & Mangan (1987); Haysom (1989); Haysom & Plasket (1989); Grogan (1988); Bindman (1988); Forsyth (1988).

100. S v Ramgobin 1985 (3) SA 587 (N); Buthelezi v Attorney General, Natal 1986 (4) SA 377 (D). The opposition PFP condemned the ouster clause: "What…is the use of having an independent judiciary if that judiciary's hands are tied?" *Hansard* col. 6742 (6.4.85) (D. J. Dalling).

101. Nkwinti v Commissioner of Police 1986 (2) SA 421 (E).

102. MAWU v State President 1986 (4) SA 358 (D).

103. Radebe v Minister of Law and Order 1981 (1) SA 586 (W).

104. Bill v State President 1987 (1) SA 265 (W).

105. Tsenoli v State President, Natal Provincial Division (1985) (unreported).

106. Omar v Minister of Law and Order 1987 (3) SA 859 (A); see SAJHR (1987); Dyzenhaus (1991: chap. 7); Ellmann (1992: chap 3).

107. Transvaal v Traub 1989 (4) SA 732 (A) (audi alteram partem); see Ellmann (1992: chap. 5).

108. NYT §1 p 6 (2.12.89); *Sunday Star* (Toronto) A11 (2.12.89), A1 (8.3.89), A3 (8.8.89); Maylam (1990); International Defence and Aid Fund for Southern Africa (1990); Schrire (1991).

109. On the negotiations to transfer power, see M. Ottaway (1993); D. Ottaway (1993); Mkhondo (1993).

110. For overviews of the legal system, see Hahlo & Kahn (1960; 1968). On the judicial system, see Hoexter Commission (1983); Bam (1984); Dugard (1985); C. Hoexter (1986); Dlodlo (1987); Mokgatle (1987); C. Dlamini (1988).

111. STr (8.12.85).

112. WM 16 (8.16.91); NYT §4 p.4 (11.21.93).

113. Sachs (1973: 257).

114. Steyn (1967: 105), translated in Dyzenhaus (1991: 127–28).

115. Ogilvie Thompson (1972).

116. SSt (5.3.87), quoted by D. Davis (1987a).

117. Cameron (1987); Dugard (1987a); Bindman (1988); Ellmann (1992: 60).

118. See Dugard (1973); Spiller (1982–85); Baxter (1985b).

119. 1(1) Black Lawyers Association Review (1.87).

120. Sachs (1973: 209–14).

121. WM 9 (9.5.86), 4 (4.15.88).

122. *Hansard* cols. 8188–90 (H. Suzman, PFP) (6.13.86); WM 8 (7.27.88); NYT 4 (1.28.89); *De Rebus* (4.89).

123. Berat (n.d.); Ream (1970); Legal Aid in South Africa (1974); McQuoid-Mason (1982; 1984; 1985; 1986b); Gross (1979); van Zyl Smit (1988b); F. Kentridge (1982); Fernandez (1984); Bam (1985); Steytler (1988).

124. WM 8 (5.27.88).

125. S v Rudman and Another, S v Mthwana 1992 (1) SA 343 (A); Bruinders (1988); SAJHR (1992); WM 13 (1.10.92).

126. Attorneys like Himan Bernardt, Raymond Tucker, Joel Carlson (1973), and John Jackson (1980); advocates like George Bizos, Ernie Wentzel, Bram Fischer, Issy Maisels, Denis Kuny, David Soggot, and Sydney Kentridge.

127. South African Defence and Aid v Minister of Justice 1967 (1) SA 263 (A).

128. LRT (1981–90); Cooper (1979/80); Farmelo (1984); Budlender (1984; 1988c; 1988d; n.d.); Chaskalson (1985b; 1989; nda; ndb); Pitts (1986); Mgogi (1992); Carnegie Quarterly (1981); Kaufmann (1991).

129. Black Sash (1986a); Geldenhuys (1985); Spink (1991: 64–68).

130. Herbstein (1991); WM 2 (9.27.91).

Chapter 3: CARVING LOOPHOLES IN THE PASS LAWS

1. For vivid narratives of pass raids, see Mathabane (1986); for survey research, see Schlemmer & Moller (1985).

2. SAIRR (1978: 323, 1979: 389; 1980: 301-02; 1981: 234; 1982: 277; 1983: 262–63; 1984: 348; 1985: 208; 1986: 345); Savage (1984). On the trial process, see J. Jackson (1980: 19–20); Monama (1983); Spink (1991: 129–35). For histories of influx control, see Kahn (1949); Sher (1985); Giliomee & Schlemmer (1985); Posel (1991).

3. See, e.g., Sampson (1956); Carlson (1973: chap. 7). For an update, see Amnesty International (1986).

4. See, e.g., Hooper (1989); Lodge (1983: chap. 6); Wells (1994). Winnie Mandela's first arrest was in defiance of the pass laws in October 1958. Gilbey (1993: 50).

5. Marx (1992: 35–37).

6. Chaskalson & Duncan (1984); Hindson (1987a: chap. 4).

7. CPD Case No. I.2628/75. All uncited material is taken from the files in this and related cases.

8. No. 25 of 1945.

9. Komani NO v Bantu Affairs Administration Board, Peninsula Area 1979 (1) SA 508 (C).

10. S v Mapheele 1963 (2) SA 651 (A).

11. §6(p) of No. 76 of 1963.

12. A (3.6.80).

13. Letter to Marion Dixon, Monash University, Melbourne (4.27.80). She had written the first Occasional Paper at the newly-established Centre for Applied Legal Studies, entitled "Do Blacks Have a Right to Family Life?"

14. 1980 (4) SA 448 (A).

15. RDM 1 (8.20.80).

16. RDM (8.21.80).

17. RDM 14 (8.21.80) (editorial).

18. SP 4 (8.24.80).

19. SP 10 (8.24.80); FM (8.22.80), 961-62 (8.29.80).

20. RDM (8.30.80).

21. CSM (8.30.80).

22. 8.31.80.

23. E (8.30.80).

24. SP (8.31.80).

25. *Afrika* 4 (10.9.80).

26. Malubi Nelson Mpofu NO v WRAB, MLO, WLD Case No. 17571/80.

27. 1976 (4) SA 1002 (A).

28. St 2 (1.30.81).

29. RDM 8-9 (2.10.81).

30. Virginia Yapi v State, CPD Case No. A117/81.

31. 4.14.81.

32. Ishmael Moitse v WRAB, MLO, Johannesburg and Chief Commissioner for the Witwatersrand, WLD Case No. 9273/81.

33. RDM 3 (7.23.81).

34. EP 2 (7.22.81).

35. So (7.24.81).

36. 7.25.81.

37. St 30 (7.23.81), 1 (Africa Edition, 7.24.81).

38. St (7.25.81).

39. 7.25.81.

40. St (7.24.81).

41. FM 411 (7.24.81).

42. RDM 1 (7.25.81).

43. Maluroyi David Ncqwangi v WRAB, MLO, and the Chief Commissioner, WLD Case No. 10646 /81; Dlokwakhe Robert Dlamini v WRAB, MLO, and the Chief Commissioner, WLD Case No. 10588/81.

44. Black Sash, "'Pressed Between the Tube and the Tyre': The *Komani* case and its aftermath"; STr (7.27.81).

45. Compare Millicent Nombaso Peter Dyantyi, Ramadimetja Magdeline Thindisa Maponyane, and Priscilla Sebenzile Langa with Mr. E.N. Mjoli (Germiston) and Mapogiso Dorcas Legote (Randfontein).

46. See text accompanying note 30 supra.

47. SE (6.26.83).

48. RDM 1 (10.30.80); St (10.31.80).

49. R v Kula & Others 1954 (1) SA 157 (A).

50. These recollections come from interviews after the court victories. STr (6.5.83); STi 8 (9.27.81), 8 (6.5.83); St 4 (6.4.83).

51. Mehlolo Tom Rikhoto v East Rand Administration Board and Muncipal Labour Officer, Germiston, WLD Case No. 9290/81.

52. RDM (9.3.81); St (9.3.81); So (9.4.81).

53. R v Madlebe 1956 (2) SA 565 (C).

54. R v Silinga 1957 (3) SA 354 (A).

55. So 1 (9.23.81); St 1 (9.23.81); RDM 1 (9.23.81).

56. St 3, 29 (9.23.81).

57. STi 38 (9.27.81).

58. So 10 (9.24.81).

59. RDM 11 (9.24.81).

60. NM 24 (9.24.81).

61. STi 8 (9.27.81); St 4 (6.4.83).

62. CSM (9.24.81); BG (9.29.81); NYT 16 (11.1.81); G 9.24.81, 9.28.81); *South Africa/Namibia Update* 3 (10.21.81).

63. FM 42-43 (10.2.81).

64. RDM 13 (9.24.81).

65. RDM 1 (9.24.81).

66. St 1 (9.24.81); So 1 (9.25.81).

67. FM 1514 (9.25.81).

68. St (10.2.81).

69. St (10.20.81); So (10.22.81).

70. So 5 (11.5.81), (12.2.81, 1.8.82, 4.15.82).

71. Oos-Randse Administrasieraad en 'n Ander v Rikhoto 1983 (3) SA 595 (A).

72. A (5.31.83); RDM 1 (5.31.83); St 1 (5.31.83).

73. NM (5.31.83); RDM 4 (5.31.83).

74. C 1 (6.1.83).

75. DN (6.1.83).

76. St (6.1.83).

77. RDM 8 (6.1.83).

78. STr (6.5.83).

79. So 6 (6.1.83), 6 (6.3.83).

80. NM (6.2.83).

81. G (6.1.83).

82. The author was John Kane Berman. WP (6.1.83); PI 12-E (6.1.83); *The Morning News* (Wilmington, Delaware) (6.1.83).

83. NYT A9 (6.1.83).

84. NYT (6.14.83).

85. RDM 2 (6.7.83).

86. CT 1 (5.31.83).

87. RDM (5.1.83); So 1 (6.1.83); CT 6 (6.1.83); St 1 (6.1.83); 25(16) *Garment Worker* 1 (6.10.83).

88. CP 1 (6.5.83).

89. CT 1 (5.31.83).

90. *Hansard* cols. 5548–49 (Chris Heunis, Minister of Constitutional Development and Planning) (5.2.84).

91. STi 8 (6.5.83).

92. STr (6.5.83); CT (6.3.83); WA (6.4.83).

93. St 1 (6.2.83); NW (6.2.83); RDM 1 (6.2.83); So (6.2.83).

94. STr (6.5.83).

95. St 4 (6.4.83).

96. RDM 1 (6.2.83); FM (6.3.83).

97. CT 2 (6.2.83).

98. WA 3 (6.4.83); CT (6.4, 7 and 9.83).

99. *Hansard* col. 1689 (6.24.83).

100. CP 1 (6.5.83); CT 2 (6.3.83).

101. FM 1245, 1265 (6.10.83).

102. RDM (6.3.83); St 4, 6 (6.4.83); STi 8 (6.5.83); STr (6.5.83).

103. STi 8 (6.5.83).

104. *Hansard* cols. 8644, 8763–68 (6.6.83); CT (6.7.83); RDM 2 (6.7.83); NM (6.7.83).

105. 6.5.83.

106. CT (6.9.83).

107. CT (6.9.83).

108. So 6 (6.10.83).

109. Simkins (1983).

110. The latter figure would increase 3 to 4 percent a year. "How much emigration will there be into the towns and cities outside the homelands following the Rikhoto judgment?" (6.11.83).

111. RDM (6.15.83).

112. RDM 1 (6.20.83); CT (6.20.83).

113. CT (6.22.83).

114. St 1 (6.22.83); CT 4 (6.23.83); NYT A13 (6.23.83).

115. CT 1 (6.23.83); *Hansard* col. 1689 (6.24.83).

116. *Hansard* cols. 10988–91, 11003, 11009 (8.10.83) (Piet Koornhoff, J.H. Hoon, C. Uys).

117. §4 of the Laws on Co-operation and Development Amendment Act, No. 102 of 1983.

118. CT (6.24.83).

119. CT (6.23 and 24.83); A (6.23.83).

120. CT (6.25.83).

121. Mthiya v Black Affairs Administation Board, Western Cape, and Another 1983 (3) SA 455 (C), aff'd 1985 (4) SA 754 (A) (9.16.85). Although the case originated with a Cape Town firm paid by legal aid, they asked Arthur Chaskalson to argue the appeal.

122. CT (6.24.83).

123. RDM 3 (7.8.83).

124. *Hansard* cols. 1845-46 (6.29.84) (response to question by R.A.F. Swart PFP).

125. St (4.16.85).

126. *Hansard* cols. 7432-33 (G. van N. Viljoen, Minister of Co-operation, Development and Education) (6.12.85).

127. *Hansard* col. 7395 (R.A.F. Swart) (6.12.85).

128. *Hansard* col. 7401 (C. Uys) (6.12.85).

129. Black Communities Development Act, No. 4 of 1984; Abolition of Influx Control Act of 1986; Identification Act of 1986.

130. *Hansard* cols. 7658, 7662–63, 7673-75 (J.C. Heunis, A.T. van der Walt) (6.9.86).

131. *Hansard* cols. 8400, 8408 (6.16.86).

132. *Hansard* col. 8423 (A.E. Nothnagel) (6.16.86).

133. *Hansard* cols. 8389, 8392, 8396 (F.A.H. Staden), 8444-45 (L.F. Stofberg) (6.16.86), col. 8708 (F.J. Le Roux) (6.18.86).

134. Identification Act, No. 72 of 1986.

135. The Abolition of Influx Control Act extensively amended the Prevention of Illegal Squatting Act, which is supplemented by the Trespass Act and the Slums Act. See West (1984); M. Robertson (1987); Tomlinson (1988); Sutcliffe et al. (1990).

136. WM 4 (3.19.93).

137. Riekert Commission (1979); Wiehahn Commission (1979). On the gradual liberalization of influx control during this period, see Hindson (1980); Hindson & Lacey (1983).

138. *Hansard* col. 8770 (J.C. Heunis) (6.18.86).

139. See, e.g., Hindson (1987a; 1987b).

140. It highlighted these cases in every annual report from 1980 to 1986, quoting newspaper accounts about their importance and including photographs of Mrs. Komani and Mr. Rikhoto. See LRT (1981: 8–10; 1982: 10–12; 1985: 17–18, 22; 1986: 11).

Chapter 4: WHITE RESISTANCE TO THE MILITARY

1. Cock & Nathan (1989); Cock (1992); Grundy (1983; 1988); Hanlon (1986); Martin & Johnson (1986); Davies (1987; 1989); Cammack (1989).

2. CIIR (1989: 77–78).

3. Forder (1990: 36–42).

4. CIIR (1989: 79); Suzman (1993: 85–86).

5. CIIR (1989: 80).

6. CIIR (1989: 56).

7. CIIR (1989: 61-62, 80, 83-85, 110).

8. *Hansard* cols. 3545-3804, 3901–4087, 4102-52 (3.21–25, 28–29.83).

9. *Hansard* col. 3662 (W.J. Snyman) (3.22.83).

10. *Hansard* col. 4143 (M.A. de M. Malan) (3.29.83).

11. *Hansard* cols. 3914–17 (3.25.83).

12. *Hansard* cols. 3917–18 (G.B.D. McIntosh) (3.25.83).

13. *Hansard* cols. 4006–07 (M.A. de M. Malan) (3.25.83).

14. *Hansard* cols. 4066–71 (C.W. Eglin) (3.28.83) (emphasis added).

15. *Hansard* cols. 407375 (W.V. Raw, NRP; J.H. van der Merwe, CP) (3.28.83).

16. *Hansard* col. 4076 (P.H.P. Gastrow) (3.28.83).

17. *Hansard* col. 4077 (R.B. Miller) (3.28.83).

18. *Hansard* cols. 4079–80 (G.B.D. McIntosh, PFP) (3.28.83).

19. *Hansard* col. 4082–85 (M.A. de M. Malan) (3.28.83).

20. *Hansard* cols. 4150–52 (3.29.83).

21. CIIR (1989: 71, 124); WM 2 (12.20.85); Obj (12.89).

22. WM 14 (11.1.85), 7 (4.14.89); CIIR (1989: 62, 73); *Sash* 40 (9.30.88).

23. CIIR (1989: 61–62, 67, 69); WM 10 (3.11.88), 13 (4.21.89).

24. CIIR (1989: 98, 101, 104); Spink (1991: 219–23).

25. *Hansard* cols. 6418–19 (T. Langley) (5.28.85).

26. CIIR (1989: 90); WM 3 (6.28.85), 4 (9.13.85). For histories of the ECC, see Nathan (1987); Jaster & Jaster (1993: ch.3).

27. WM 4 (8.20.85), 12–13 (10.11.85); STr 7 (9.22.85);   A 5 (9.24.85), 4 (9.25.85), 6 (10.6.85), 3, 10 (10.7.85), 23 (10.8.85), 6 (10.9.85), 5 (10.25.85);   C 8 (9.26.85), 8 (10.3.85); CT 11 (9.28.85), 3 (10.7.85); NW 3 (10.5.85); 7 (10.8. 85); EPH 2 (10.8.85).

28. CIIR (1989: 92–96); WM 4 (1.24.86).

29. CIIR (1989: 96, 98); WM 2 (2.7.86), 6 (3.14.86).

30. *Hansard* q. 59 (reply to P.A. Myburgh) (2.12.86). 7,589 failed to report in January 1985 and 1,596 in 1984. *Hansard* q. 569 (reply to P.R.C. Rogers, NRP) (3.22.85).

31. *Hansard* cols. 2106–10, 2118, 2120–21, 2130 (W. V. Raw, NRP; J.A.J. Vermeulen, NP; P.A. Myburgh, PFP; J.H. van der Merwe, CP) (3.16, 18.86).

32. *Hansard* cols. 5515–20, 5569–73 (P.A. Myburgh, C.J. van der Merwe) (5.14.86).

33. WM 2 (2.7.86), 6 (3.14.86), 3 (3.21.86), 8 (7.18.86), 14 (10.9.86), 3 (11.7.86), 4 (11.28.86); CT (9.13.86), (11.6.86);   EPH (3.3.87), (3.5.87); CIIR (1989: 96, 100, 103, 112–13).

34. *Hansard* cols. 555–56, 1301–07 (L.H. Fick) (2.10, 23.87).

35. WM 6 (1.16.87), 4 (2.20.87), 5 (3.20.87), 3 (4.10.87), 6 (4.24.87), 3 (8.7.87); C (4.14.87), CT (5.14, 15.87); St (4.15.87); CIIR (1989: 117-18, 126).

36. *Hansard* cols. 1259–1303 (W.N. Breytenbach, Deputy Defence Minister; B.L. Geldenhuys, NP; P.H.P Gastrow, PFP; A.L. Jordaan, NP; N.J.J. Olivier, PFP; J.J. Vilonel, NP; R.R. Hulley, PFP; D.P. de K. van Gend, NP) (6.11.87).

37. Mönnig and others v Council of Review, South African Defence Force, and others 1989 (4) SA 866 (C), aff'd 1992 (3) SA 482 (A). WM 1 (12.24.87), 1 (1.15.88), 3 (1.29.88), 1 (2.2.88), 1 (3.11.88), 3 (4.24.88), 4 (6.24.88), 5 (8.18.89), 20 (5.29.92); CT 7 (6.9.89), 2 (8.17.89), (8.18.89); C 10 (8.17.89), 10 (8.18.89); St 5 (8.18.89), 6 (8.22.89); NW 1 (8.19.89), 2 (8.21.89); WA 5 (8.19.89); STr 7 (8.20.89); CIIR (1989: 128-29).

38. ECC and another v Minister of Defence and another 1989 (2) SA 180 (C); WM 1 (3.31.88), 3 (4.24.88), 7 (6.16.88), 3 (9.2.88); SSt 11 (11.10.91).

39. *Hansard* cols. 10117–69 (D.P. de K van Gend, NP; Deputy Defence Minister W.N. Breytenbach) (5.18.88).

40. For a pessmistic account of civil disobedience in South Africa, see Cameron (1988).

41. CIIR (1989: 83-85, 110).

42. WM 3 (3.27.86), 5 (8.29.86). For legal analyses of conscientious objection, see Trichardt & Trichardt (1986); Harris (1987).

43. WM 16 (2.13.87).

44. WM 5 (7.17.87).

45. WM 2 (5.9.86), 4 (8.1.86), 2 (1.23.87), 5 (3.20.87), 5 (3.27.87), 1, 3 (5.15.87); CIIR (1989): 49-50); ECC pamphlet on Wilkinson.

46. Unless otherwise stated, all information comes from the trial transcript.

47. CT 3 (6.29.87), 15 (11.9.87), (11.12.87); NW 2 (11.4.87), STr 10 (7.5.87); St 4 (11.3.87), 4 (11.10.87); A 8, 11 (11.11.87).

48. A1 (11.12.87); CT 4 (11.13.87).

49. NW 3 (2.16.88); St 10 (2.20.88); CT 4 (2.29.88).

50. CT 1 (3.2.88) (apparently the only report).

51. This and other observations come from interviews with Edwin Cameron in August 1990 and July 1991.

52. On the range of community service, see Blaauw (1989).

53. WM 1 (3.4.88); CT 1 (3.4.88). The press also reported the testimony of Toms, A 4 (3.2.88) and Russell, C 7 (3.3.88).

54. DN 3 (3.4.88); A 5 (3.4.88).

55. CT 1 (3.4.88), 8 (3.7.88).

56. St 4 (3.5.88).

57. STi 2 (3.6.88).

58. NW 4 (3.5.88).

59. WA 15 (3.5.88); CT 8 (3.7.88); DN 6 (3.8.88).

60. St 8 (3.14.88); CT 6 (3.8.88).

61. SSt 2 (3.6.88) STr 6 (3.6.88).

62. NYT (3.28.88).

63. CT 3 (3.4.88).

64. NW 2 (3.8.88).

65. CT 3 (3.14.88).

66. St 2 (10.10.88).

67. A 1 (10.24.88); St 8 (10.25.88).

68. 1989 (2) SA 567 (C) (with H.C. Nel); St 6 (11.18.88).

69. C 10 (12.1.88); St 2 (12.1.88); CT 1 (12.1.88).

70. WM 5 (12.2.88); C 12 (12.2.88); CP 6 (12.4.88).

71. STr 8 (12.4.88).

72. NW 2 (7.20.88); CP 11 (7.31.88); CT 5 (7.27.88), 4 (8.16.88), 3 (2.21.89); A 4 (2.21.89); WM 8 (2.24.890.

73. Obj (5.89).

74. Unless otherwise noted, comments and quotations by David Bruce come from a July 1990 interview.

75. Brixton Mag. Ct. Case No 062/00388/889. All the following is taken from the trial record, unless otherwise noted.

76. DP 2 (7.10.88); St 9 (7.16.88).

77. St 2 (7.10.88); BD 3 (7.20.88); CT 7 (7.21.88).

78. SSt 6 (7.24.88).

79. C 3 (7.21.88); St 1 (7.21.88); BD 3 (7.21.88); A 2 (7.21.88); SSt 6, 8 (7.24.88); CP 1 (7.24.88).

80. CT 1 (7.26.88); NN 3 (7.28.88).

81. S 3 (7.26.88), 9 (7.30.88); PN 5 (7.26.88); BD 9 (7.29.88); FM 48 (7.29.88); DN 19 (7.27.88); C 1 (7.26.88); CP 11 (7.31.88); STr (7.31.88).

82. CT 5 (7.27.88); SSt 8 (7.31.88). The few blacks at RAU saw him as a hero.

83. PN 1 (7.26.88); St 1 (7.26.88), 2 (7.27.88); A 3 (7.26.88); C 4 (7.27.88).

84. St 2 (7.27.88); CT 5 (7.27.88); NW 3 (7.28.88).

85. CP 8 (7.31.88).

86. NW 12 (7.27.88); DN 18 (7.27.88); A 26 (7.26.88), 27 (7.27.88); PN 14 (7.26.88); St 10 (7.27.88); CT 6 (7.28.88).

87. A 3 (7.26.88).

88. C 6 (7.27.88).

89. Witwatersrand Local Division Case No 522/88. Several papers reported the proceedings: St 6 (1.10.89); CT 5 (1.10.89). *The Citizen* 5 (1.10.89) displayed its continuing animus in its headline: "Court hears conchie's plea against jail term." The press also reported the judgment: C 8 (3.4.89); SSt 2 (3.5.89); BD 2 (3.6.89).

90. SSt 10 (8.20.88), 3 (3.5.89), 8 (7.30.89); NW 4 (7.19.89); St 16 (8.1.89).

91. *Hansard* qs. 180, 185–86 (N.J.J. Olivier, PFP) (3.1.88).

92. WM 7 (3488), 2-3 (8..5.88); St 2 (8.4.88), 2 (8.6.88); NN 3 (8.4.88); SSt 13 (8.7.88); STi 19 (8.7.88); CIIR (1989: 120-21).

93. C 6 (8.5.88).

94. C 11 (9.10.88).

95. WM 6 (6.16.88), 5 (12.2.88), 7 (12.9.88); C 11 (9.24.88_, 13 (12.7.88); CT 7 (9.26.88); St 7 (10.22.88); NN 2 (12.1.88); T (12.56.88); BD 2 (2.2.90); CIIR (1989: 131).

96. FM 49 (3.10.89); St 2 (1.21.89), (3.15.89), (4.13.89); C 8 (3.15.89); BD (3.15.89); WM 3 (2.3.89), 5 (3.17.89), 7, 17 (4.14.89), 9 (7.28.89); NN (4.13.89); S v Batzofin, Johannesburg Magistrate's Court 8/247/88. For Batzofin's own account, see Jaster & Jaster (1993: ch. 4).

97. WM 7 (9.2.88), 9 (2.10.89); *Sash* 40 (9.30.88); NN 12 (10.27.88); *Frontline* 6 (10.31.88); CIIR (1989: 127).

98. WM 9 (5.5.89), 8 (5.12.89), 9 (5.19.89).

99. Obj (12.89); WM 1, 3 (9.22.89), 13 (3.23.90); CP 2 (8.20.89); NW 1 (8.22.89); EP 6 (8.21.89), 6 (8.22.89), 3 (8.28.89); St 4 (8.23.89), 6 (8.28.89), 4 (8.29.89); CT 1 (8.23.89); PN 2 (8.29.89); C 6 (9.23.89).

100. *Hansard* q. 244 (R.R. Hulley, PFP) (3.7.89), q. 986 (D.J. Dalling, PFP) 5.9.89), q. 30 (Dalling) (2.13.90); WM 7 (4.28.89), 1 (9.22.89), 1 (12.8.89); St 2 (12.10.89); STi 2 (12.10.89); PN 1 (1.30.90); Obj (4-5.90).

101. WM 9 (2.2.90); St 2 (2.9.90); CT 5 (2.2.90); BD 2 (2.2.90); C 9 (2.2.90).

102. St 7 (2.27.90); C 17 (2.27.90).

103. S v Toms, S v Bruce 1990 (2) SA 802 (A).

104. Id. 806–09.

105. Id. at 811–15, 818–19.

106. Id. at 817, 820–21.

107. Id. at 823, 830–31, 834.

108. Id. at 821.

109. CT 5 (3.31.90).

110. WM 1 (4.5.90), 4 (9.27.91); DM 3 (6.20.90); Obj 4 (12.91), 5 (6.92).

111. St 2 (8.1.90), 1 (8.2.90); C 5 (8.1.90); WM 10 (8.18.88), 10 (5.18.90), 2 (5.24.91); DM 2 (8.2.90), 1 (8.8.90); Obj (4-5.90); Torr v State, WLD Case No. 8/1084/90.

112. DM 1 (8.13.90), 1, 2, 8 (8.14.90), 10 (8.15.90), 3 (8.20.90); CT 7 (8.14.90), A 12 (8.14.90); St 3, 12 (8.14.90); BD 2 (8.14.90); C 5 (8.14.90); NW 12 (9.6.90).

113. WM 9 (1.1.90), 13 (3.23.90), 5 (6.1.90); Obj (4–5.90).

114. Obj (4-5.90).

115 WM 3 (10.26.90), 9 (11.30.90), 8 (8.30.901); St 3 (11.29.90); NM 1 (8.30.91); C 8 (8.31.91); Obj 4 (12.91).

116. S v Sangster 1991 (1) SA 240 (O) (Malherbe, with Van Coller; Edeling dissenting), remanded, Bloemfontein Magistrate's Court Case No. H379/90, modified, Orange Free State Supreme Court Appeal No. 7/91.

117. C 20 (2.8.90), 17 (2.27.90), 3 (4.19.90); A 5 (2.19.90), 4 (2.26.90), St 7 (2.27.90), 6 (5.26.90), 2 (6.5.90); BD 4 (3.5.90); CT 2 (3.8.90); SSt 7 (4.15.90); Obj (4-5.90).

118. NYT A1 (5.17.90); DM 8 (8.1.90).

119. *Hansard* q. 1347 (R.H.D. Rogers, PFP) (5.15.90); STi 4 (8.5.90); NW 3 (11.5.90); C 16 (11.7.90); WM 8 (11.16.90); SSt 2 (12.2.90); BD 2 (12.4.90).

120. STi 4 (8.5.90); St 5 5.3.91), 2 (6.18.91); WM 8 (1.11.91), 5 (4.19.91), 2 (5.24.91), 8 (6.21.91); BD 1 (5.28.91), 2 (4.30.91); Obj 4 (12.91).

121. Legal opinion by D.I. Berger for Nicholls, Cambanis, Koopasamy and Pillay (6.28.91); ECC Press Release (7.2.91); St 5 (7.3.91), 2 (7.31.91); C 11 (7.9.91); STi 2 (7.14.92); STr 18 (12.15.91); NM (12.12.91); DN 5 (12.18.91); NW 2 (12.24.91); STi 2 (1.5.92).

122. CT 2 (1.4.92), 5, 8 (1.8.92); DFA 1 (1.8.92), 3 (1.15.92); A 14 (1.7.92); St 2 (1.7.92), 6 (1.8.92), 3 (1.9.92); DD 2(1.7.92), 1 (1.8.92); NM 1 (1.7.92); EP 1 (1.7.92); C 1 (1.8.92), 5, 6 (1.9.92); PN 1, 8 (1.9.92); DN 18 (1.9.92); FM 32 (1.10.92); STr 18 (1.12.92).

123. CT 1 (1.21.92), 4 (1.22.92); C 13 (1.22.92); BD 2 (1.22.92), 10 (1.24.92); NM 5 (1.24.92); Obj 3 (6.92); St 3 (1.23.92), 4 (2.21.92); NW 2 (2.21.92).

124. PN 2 (3.3.92), 3 (3.5.92), 2 (4.2.92); BD 1 (3.5.92), 2 (3.23.92); St 12 (3.5.92), 8 (3.6.92), 1 (3.28.92); WM 9 (3.6.92), 8 (3.27.92); SSt 12 (3.8.92), 1 (4.11.92); A 4 (3.20.92); C 13 (3.21.92), 1 (3.28.92); Obj 3 (6.92).

125. St 1 (5.21.92), 6 (7.8.92), 6 (8.5.92), 7 (8.6.92), 8 (9.2.92), 8 (9.3.92); WM 3 (5.22.92), 4 (6.5.92), 10 (7.7.92); A 2 (5.27.92), 6 (7.13.92); WA 4 (5.30.92); NM 5 (7.18.92); PN 8 (6.2.92); DN 23 23 (6.4.92), 9 (7.7.92); BD 2 (7.8.92), 4 (8.5.92), 2 (9.2.92); C 10 (7.8.92), 8 (9.2.92); Obj 5 (6.92), 3 (11.92).

126. A 4 (9.17.92), 8 (10.9.92); C 8 (9.22.92), 8 (9.24.92); St 3 (9.24.92); BD 1 (9.24.92), 2 (9.30.92); DN 20 (9.25.92); WM 6 (9.25.92).

127. St 2 (10.24.92), 19 (11.5.92), 3 (11.13.92), 3 (12.10.92), 14 (12.18.92); WA 10 (10.25.92); STi 26 (11.8.92); C 9 (12.4.92), 8 (12.15.92); DN 3 (12.10.92), 12 (12.21.92); A 4 (12.15.92); CT 9 (12.15.92); WM 24 (12.11.92).

128. Obj 6 (9.93).

129. See Cover (1975).

Chapter 5: SEEKING RECOGNITION

1. Unless otherwise noted, all quotations and facts are taken from the trial record of the Industrial Court hearing of Metal & Allied Workers Union v BTR Sarmcol.

2. Bonnin & Sitas (1988: 48-49).

3. On the history of the trade union movement in the 1970s and early 1980s, see Maree (1987); S. Friedman (1987); C. Thompson (1988); Benjamin et al. (1989); Baskin (1991); Seidman (1993).

4. SALB (1985a).

5. On the government's policy of dividing workers into racially segregated unions, see E. Webster (1985).

6. O (9.27.81).

7. On union efforts to influence retrenchment, see Jaffee (1984); Jaffee & Jochelson (1986).

8. SALB (1985b).

9. S. Friedman (1987: 398).

10. NW (5.1.85).

11. NW (5.2.85).

12. SALB (1985b).

13. Labour Monitoring Group (1985: 98).

14. Labour Monitoring Group (1985: 99-100).

15. WM 3 (7.5.85); SALB (1985a); Labour Monitoring Group (1985).

16. Work in Progress (1987).

17. WM 3 (7.5.85).

18. WM 7 (7.12.85), 7 (7.19.85); Labour Monitoring Group (1985: 101).

19. WM 5 (7.26.85); SALB (1985a); Labour Monitoring Group (1985).

20. Labour Monitoring Group (1985: 97).

21. DN (7.19.85); Labour Monitoring Group (1985: 101-04).

22. SALB (1985c).

23. SALB (1986).

24. *Work in Progress* (1987).

25. BD 2 (12.17.85); WM 2 (3.21.86); Pippa Green (1986a; 1986b).

26. Radford & Leeb (1986) (sample of 126/1604 households).

27. On the Industrial Court's powers and jurisprudence, see Haysom (1984); Benjamin (1987).

28. Perhaps for this reason it received almost no media coverage. See, e.g., WM 10 (11.28.86).

29. By April 1987 UWUSA claimed 60,000 paid members, two-thirds of them in Natal. See A. Fine (1987).

30. Metal & Allied Workers Union v BTR Sarmcol [1987] 8 ILJ 815 (IC). The end of the hearing occasioned another of the very few newspaper reports. NN 2 (7.22.87).

31. C 5 (9.12.87).

32. FW 34 (9.23.87), 35 (10.21.87).

33. There are striking similarities between the last quotations and language in Roux's judgment.

34. NW 3 (2.21.89), 9 (2.27.89).

35. Mawu and Philip Dladla v BTR Industries (S.A.) (Pty) Ltd, P E Roux, M J Oosthuizen and C C De Witt, NPD Case No. AR 159/88; NW 5 (3.9.89).

36. DN 2 (3.3.89); WM 4 (3.2.89), 4 (3.9.89); CP 10 (3.5.89); C 9 (3.4.89).

37. WM 2-3 (7.26.91), 1, 3-4 (8.2.91), 2-3 (8.9.91), 14 (8.16.91).

38. BTR Industries South Africa (Pty) Ltd and others v Metal and Allied Workers' Union and Another 1992 (3) SA 673 (A) (Hoexter, with Milne, Kumleben, F.H. Grosskopf and Goldstone).

39. Council of Review, South African Defence Force and others v H J Mönnig and others 1992 (3) SA 482 (A) (Cobbett, CJ) (5.15.92).

40. WM 10 (6.11.92).

Chapter 6: MPOPHOMENI AND THE WAR IN NATAL

1. Hlatshwayo (1987).

2. WM 1 (12.11.87).

3. See Meer (1985); Haysom (1986a; 1988; 1990a); Lawyers Committee for Human Rights (1987); Merrit (1988); Atchison (1988); Sutcliffe & Welling (1988); M. Kentridge (1990); Macdonald et al. (1990); Rickard (1990); Lawyers for Human Rights (1991); ICJ (1992); Bennun (1993); Kane-Berman (1993). The Human Rights Commission in Johannesburg and the Centre for Adult Education of the University of Natal-Pietermaritzburg offer the most comprehensive documentation.

4. For histories of Buthelezi and Inkatha, see Mzala (1988); Mare & Hamilton (1987); Mare (1992).

5. Haysom (1986a: 81, 83–86).

6. Haysom (1986a: 88-89).

7. WM 5 (10.4.85).

8. WM 6 (11.22.85), 1 (1.24.86).

9. WM 4 (12.13.85), 4 (1.10.86).

10. WM 4 (5.30.86), 3 (6.6.86), 2 (9.19.86), 3 (12.5.86); M. Kentridge (1990: 182-83).

11. Labour Monitoring Group (1985: 93-94).

12. M. Kentridge (1990: 219-20).

13. *Hansard* q. 437 (reply of Minister of Education and Development Aid to R.W. Hardingham, NRP) (7.29.87). On the rise of UWUSA, see Mufson (1990: 301-08); Mzala (1988: ch.9).

14. WM 5 (12.12.86).

15. Howick CR 22/12/86 for the first three deaths; Howick CR 115/12/86 for the fourth.

16. BD 3 (12.9.86); SSt 2 (12.7.86); NM 2 (12.8.86).

17. NW 8 (12.8.86).

18. NW 1 (12.8.86).

19. BD 2 (12.10.86).

20. NW 1 (12.11.86).

21. St 3 (12.11.86); *Hansard* q. 437 (reply of Minister of Education and Development Aid to R.W. Hardingham, NRP) (7.29.87); Bonnin & Sitas (1988: 42–43); M. Kentridge (1990: 198).

22. WM 5 (6.5.87).

23. Unless otherwise noted, all information comes from the inquest records. On the scope of inquests, see Akerson (1989).

24. M. Kentridge (1990: 191).

25. WM 6 (3.4.88).

26. WM 6 (11.6.87), 1 (1.29.88), 11 (3.24.88); M Kentridge (1990: 184-87).

27. The outcome was reported in the WM 3 (3.25.88).

28. Interview with Brand (July 1991).

29. Case No. CR 84/12/87.

30. WM 3 (12.19.91).

31. WM 10 (3.20.92).

32. WM 3 (4.16.92).

33. WM 4 (6.25.93), 5 (9.17.93).

34. For the cumulative effect on youth, see Straker et al. (1992).

35. WM 3 (3.25.88).

36. WM 1 (1.23.87), 5 (2.6.87), 1 (2.20.87), 2-3 (2.27.87), 1 (3.20.87), 3 (3.27.87), 11 (6.5.87), 5 (9.11.87), 1 (10.9.87).

37. WM 3 (10.23.87).

38. WM 3 (10.23.87).

39. WM 1 (10.30.87).

40. Mandla Mkhize v Ntombela and Others, Natal Supreme Court, Case No. 2877/87; M. Kentridge (1990: 189-91).

41. WM 1 (12.11.87), 5 (1.15.88), 1 (1.29.88), 7 (2.26.88), 7 (7.8.88), 4 (8.5.88); M. Kentridge (1990: 185-87).

42. WM 6 (11.6.87).

43. M. Kentridge (1990: 148-52).

44. This incident immediately preceded the Mpophomeni inquest, which Ntombela attended armed with a pistol. Zondo, Cosatu & Others v Inkatha, Mvelase & Others; M. Kentridge (1990: 56-62, 191).

45. WM 6, 7 (2.19.88), 3 (2.26.88), 11 (3.24.88).

46. WM 6 (3.31.88), 3 (6.7.91), 8 (6.14.91).

47. WM 19 (6.4.93).

48. WM 5 (5.13.88).

49. WM 10 (5.22.88).

50. WM 4 (9.9.88); M. Kentridge (1990: 153, 163).

51. WM 5 (9.16.88).

52. WM 3 (2.3.89); M. Kentridge (1990: 164); Macdonald et al. (1990: 22).

53. WM 6 (2.16.89), 6 (6.5.92).

54. WM 3 (3.2.89), 11 (3.9.89); M. Kentridge (1990: 194, 207).

55. WM 1 (3.30.89), 3 (4.6.89).

56. NW 1 (3.22.89), 2 (3.23.89), 1 (3.24.89), 2 (4.11.89), 2 (4.14.89), 2 (4.15.89); 2 (4.27.89), 7 (4.29.89), 3 (5.24.89), 2 (9.16.89), 5 (9.26.89), 3 (9.28.89); A 1 (4.26.89); NM 2 (4.27.89), 1 (9.27.89); NN 3 (5.5.89); So 3 (5.24.89), 4 (9.28.89); WM 6 (5.5.89); M. Kentridge (1990: 198-99).

57. WM 1 (4.28.89), 1 (6.15.89).

58. WM 7 (6.15.89), 13 (9.1.89).

59. WM 7 (7.14.89), 1 (9.29.89).

60. NW 1 (11.23.89), 3 (11.30.89); WM 3 (11.24.89).

61. Macdonald et al. (1990: 11-14).

62. NW 1 (3.31.90), 3 (5.10.90), 3 (7.12.90); STr 12 (4.29.90).

63. S v Petros Fana Ngcobo (Justice Didcott, 8.15.90); S v Phumulani Derick Mweli (Justice Wilson, 8.20.90); cited in Macdonald et al. (1990: 6-8).

64. WM 7 (9.7.90), 42 (11.23.90), 4 (2.8.91), 3 (6.21.91), 2 (8.7.92); Macdonald et al. (1990: 16). Tsenoli had been the plaintiff in one of the few successful challenges to the Emergency. State President and Others v Tsenoli; Kerckhoff and Another v Minister of Law and Order and Others 1986 (4) SA 1150 (A). See Ellmann (1992: chaps. 2–3).

65. WM 1 (8.14.90), 1 (9.21.90), 4 (8.2.91).

66. WM 1 (12.7.90), 3, 4 (12.14.90), 2 (8.9.91), 1, 2, 4 (12.13.91), 1 (1.10.92), 3 (2.7.92), 2 (2.14.92), 1-2 (2.28.92); Lawyers for Human Rights (1991).

67. WM 2 (11.29.91), 1 (12.13.91), 6 (5.17.91), 1 (7.19.91).

68. STr 20 (10.14.90); M. Kentridge (1990: 195).

69. NM 3 (11.12.90).

70. WM 11 (11.22.91).

71. NW 2 (1.23.91).

72. WM 16 (3.8.91), 1 (7.19.91), 3 (10.4.91), 6 (3.27.92).

73. WM 3 (6.21.91), 3 (7.19.91).

74. NW 3 (7.9.91), 2 (7.11.91).

75. WM 6 (2.14.92), 1 (10.30.92); NM 1 (10.29.92); NW 1 (10.29.92).

76. WM 7 (1.29.93), 12 (2.5.93), 4 (3.5.93).

77. E.g., Brer Rabbit in the Uncle Remus stories, who is taken from the rabbit trickster of West African folklore. On colonized peoples, see Fanon (1982); Memmi (1968; 1984; 1990).

78. On the perception of the police in Pietmaritzburg, see Jagwanth (1992).

Chapter 7: STATE TERRORISM

1. The press reported 161 incidents between 1975 and 1981. WM 12 (10.4.85). For accounts of SAP violence, see H. Bernstein (1972); CIIR (1982; 1988); Riekert (1982; 1985a; 1985b); Foster & Luyt (1986); Brogden (1989); Prior (1989); van der Spuy (1989); Foster & Skinner (1990); Haysom (1992); Brogden & Shearing (1993). On prison conditions, see Naidoo (1982); Pheto (1983); Mihalik (1989); Mbeki (1991); Niehaus (1994).

2. WM 5 (6.14.85); see also Lawyers' Committee for Civil Rights Under Law (1983). One of the most notorious deaths in custody was Neil Aggett, a white doctor and trade unionist. See H. Suzman (1993: 230).

3. *Hansard* cols. 2631-32 (3.21.85).

4. *Hansard* cols. 2791-98, 2819-22, 2854-58 (E.K. Moorcroft, D.J.N. Malcomess, R.A.F. Swart) (3.26-27.85).

5. *Hansard* col. 4172 (G.B.D. McIntosh, PFP) (4.24.85).

6. *Hansard* cols. 4425-34, 4436, 4455, 4473, 4514, 4525, 4527-30, 4532-34 (H. Suzman, PFP; L. Wessels, NP; M.D. Maree, CP; F.A.H. van Staden, CP; Louis le Grange, Minister of Law and Order) (4.29.85).

7. *Hansard* cols. 5370-74 (M.S. Barnard, PFP) (5.13.85).

8. Kannemeyer (1985); Marcus (1985c); Haysom (1986b); Majodina (1986); Nicholson (1986); R. Thornton (1990).

9. *Hansard* cols. 7488-90, 7499, 7504-05, 7510-13, 7522-26, 7528-31, 7539 (H. Suzman, PFP; C. Uys, CP; W.V. Raw, NRP; D.J.N. Malcomess, PFP; T. Langley, CP; P.H.P. Gastrow, PFP; Louis le Grange, Minister of Law and Order) (6.13.85).

10. *Hansard* cols. 1891-96 (reply of H.J. Coetsee, Minister of Justice, to H. Suzman, PFP) (6.18.85).

11. WM 14 (6.14.85), 3 (6.28.85), 3 (7.19.85), 2 (1.29.93).

12. WM 1 (7.5.85), 12 (7.12.85), 3 (7.19.85).

13. WM 12-13 (6.14.85); see Mufson (1990: 106-15, 121-26. 242-44, 266-67).

14. D. Webster (1987: 143); Price (1991: 259).

15. Coleman & Webster (1986: 127).

16. Unless otherwise noted, all information comes from affidavits filed in Dr. Wendy Orr's interdict application.

17. Janet Cherry was detained in solitary confinement for three weeks in July. Spink (1991: 289).

18. Rayner (1987: 41).

19. STi 11 (9.29.85); St 14 (7.11.85), 30 (11.26.85), 4 (1.10.87); WM 4 (11.18.85).

20. GN R2080 of 31 December 1965, promulgated under the Prisons Act, No. 8 of 1959. See Medical Association of South Africa (1983).

21. I am grateful to Farouk Abrahams for translating the Afrikaans here and elsewhere in this chapter.

22. Louis Le Grange Square M.R. 631/8/85, 632/8/85, 633/8/85, 634/8/85.

23. Veriava and others v President, South African Medical and Dental Council and others 1985 (2) SA 293 (T).

24. Interview with Halton Cheadle, Johannesburg (August 1990).

25. SECLD Case No. 2507/85.

26. A 1 (9.25.85); see also SSt (9.29.85).

27. NYT 1 (9.26.85).

28. CH 14 (10.5.85).

29. DN 34 (9.26.85).

30. NM 10 (9.27.85).

31. EPH 9 (9.27.85).

32. So 14 (10.14.85).

33. St 14 (11.7.85), 30 (11.26.85).

34. STi 14 (12.22.85).

35. St 13 (9.26.85).

36. NW 3 (9.30.85); BD 1 (10.2.85); EP 4 (10.2.85). The matter was debated extensively in South African and foreign medical journals, see 68 *S. Afr. Med. J.* 705 (1985); 292 *Brit. Med. J.* 343, 560 (1986); 255 *JAMA* 2794-95 (1986); 257 *JAMA* 3066-69 (1987).

37. A 1 (2.4.86); SSt 16 (2.9.86).

38. SSt 2 (12.1.85).

39. STi 11 (9.29.85); EPH 1 (10.3.85).

40. STr 3 (12.1.85); SSt 2 (12.1.85); C 13 (12.2.85).

41. A1 (1.3.86); EP 1 (1.3.86); C 3 (1.4.86); EPH 3 (1.4.86); St 1 (1.4.86).

42. PN 20 (1.6.86); A 8 (1.5.86), 16 (1.9.86); NYT 18 (10.6.85).

43. WM 2 (12.20.85); CP 1 (12.22.85).

44. Spink (1991: 182-85).

45. CT 3 (9.13.86); DD 1 (9.13.86); WM 1 (9.12.86).

46. CT 10 (3.20.87).

47. STr 20 (3.29.87).

48. WM 4 (5.30.86).

49. St 1 (7.5.90); DM 9 (7.5.90).

50. DN 10 (7.10.90).

51. EPH 4 (7.6.90).

52. NW 8 (7.9.90).

53. CT 7 (7.25.90); A 5 (7.25.90).

54. A 4 (9.28.90).

55. WM 14 (10.4.85).

56. WM 5 (4.18.86), 12 (6.13.86); CP (4.20.86).

57. *Hansard* cols. 4518-26 (Louis le Grange, Minister of Law and Order) (4.30.86).

58. WM 1 (9.4.87). On municipal policing in the Eastern Cape, see Black Sash (1988a).

59. WM 9 (9.19.86).

60. *Hansard* cols. 8188, 8329-30, 8333, 8345-46 (H. Suzman, PFP; Louis le Grange, Minister of Law and Order) (6.13.86).

61. NYT §1 p.6 (2.12.89).

62. WM 2 (7.17.87), 1 (7.24.87), 8 (7.28.89), 4 (8.4.89). Government expressed outrage that the pathologist's findings were published while the matter was sub judice. *Hansard* col. 627 (reply by A.J. Vlok, Minister of Law and Order, to S.S. van der Merwe, PFP) (8.25.87).

63. WM 1 (8.28.87), 3 (4.22.88), 3 (12.9.88), 5 (3.10.89), 4 (3.17.89), 4 (7.14.89); *Hansard* col. 800 (reply by A.J. Vlok, Minister of Law and Order, to S.S. van der Merwe, PFP) (9.8.87).

64. WM 1 (11.18.85); 1 (3.4.88); 5 (8.4.89); 6 (8.11.89), 10 (8.18.89); NYT A3 (12.12.89); LAT A12 (12.12.89); *Hansard* cols. 9506-19, 9636-39 (J.J. Swartz, H. Suzman, PFP) (5.10-11.88).

65. WM 7 (5.18.90).

66. WM 2, 3 (3.16.90), 3 (8.30.91), 5 (10.18.91), 5 (11.8.91), 10 (12.6.91), 6 (3.6.92), 1 (4.24.92), 2 (4.30.92), 24 (5.15.92).

67. WM 9 (9.26.86).

68. WM 5 (6.19.87).

69. WM 2 (12.24.87), 7 (3.11.88), 5 (2.24.89).

70. WM 3 (1.22.88); on community response to kitskonstabels, see Fine & Hansson (1990).

71. *Hansard* cols. 1604-26 (J. van Eck, Ind; A.J. Vlok, Minister of Law and Order) (2.2.88), 10690 (Leon Wessels, Deputy Minister of Law and Order) (5.20.88).

72. WM 1 (2.27.87), 6 (3.6.87), 1 (3.13.87).

73. *Hansard* cols. 2474-76 (reply by State President P.W.Botha to P.H.P. Gastrow, PFP) (9.2.86); WM 5 (9.25.87), 3 (9.2.88), 5 (3.23.89).

74. NYT A6 (2.1.90); WM 2 (2.2.90), 1 (2.23.90). Justice Goldstone found that the cause of death was indeed suicide. Gilbey (1993: 226).

75. NYT A3 (3.27.90), A2 (3.28.90), §1, p.4 (4.1.90), A1 (4.6.90), A3 (5.22.90), A4 (5.23.90); WM 4 (3.30.90), 2 (4.5.90), 3 (5.18.90), 5 (5.25.90), 3 (6.1.90); DM 1 (9.3.90); Goldstone (1990).

76. Rockman & Abrahams (1989). WM 1, 2 (9.8.89), 1, 3 (9.15.89), 7 (9.22.89), 1, 3 (9.29.89), 1 (10.13.90), 11 (11.10.89), 1 (11.17.89), 2 (11.24.89), 1 (5.23.90); LAT A5 (3.23.90).

77. WM 9 (5.4.90).

78. It bore the false return address of Bheki Mlangeni, a human rights lawyer and chair of the Jabulani branch of the ANC, who was killed when he opened it on February 16, 1991. WM 3 (2.22.91), 10 (12.6.91), 2 (11.13.92).

79. De Kock was finally expelled from the police in February 1993. WM 8 (2.2.90), 9 (5.15.90), 5 (1.22.93).

80. WM 1 (10.20.89), 1 (1.11.89), 1 (1.17.89), 2 (12.1.89), 5 (12.8.89), 3 (12.15.89), 3 (1.19.90), 11 (1.26.90), 1, 3 (2.2.90), 3 (5.4.90), 3 (10.12.90), 10 (4.12.91), 16 (6.28.91), 2 (10.4.91), 1 (8.7.92), 2 (8.14.92); NYT §1 p.8 (11.19.89), A1 (11.23.89), §1 p.6 (11.26.89), A10 (3.1.90); LAT A16 (11.21.89); Haysom (1990b); Steytler (1990a; 1990b); Pauw (1991); Amnesty International (1992).

81. *Hansard* cols. 1616, 1620 (B.L. Geldenhuys, A.L. Jordaan, NP) (2.26.90).

82. *Hansard* cols. 1625-29 (M.A. de M. Malan, Minister of Defence) (2.26.90).

83. Harms (1990); WM 1 (12.1.89), 1 (1.26.90), 5 (2.2.90), 2 (3.23.90), 3 (30.30.90), 11 (4.12.90), 1 (4.27.90), 9 (11.16.90), 1, 3 (2.22.91), 4 (3.1.91), 2 (4.12.91), 3 (6.7.91), 6 (4.30.92), 3 (5.8.92), 5 (5.15.92), 2 (8.21.91), 3 (8.28.92), 2 (10.30.92), 6 (11.6.92), 8 (11.20.92), 4 (11.27.92), 4 (12.4.92); NYT A4 (12.1.89), A10 (12.5.89), A4 (12.19.89), A1 (2.22.90), A3 (2.26.90), A10 (2.27.90), A3 (3.2.90), A6 (3.23.90), A7 (6.18.90); LAT A6 (12.1.89), A4 (2.27.90), A12 (3.6.90).

An inquiry into spying by the Johannesburg City Council produced a similar whitewash. Hiemstra (1990).

84. WM 1 (1.22.88), 7 (1.29.88), 6 (2.26.88), 3 (4.29.88), 5 (6.24.88), 11 (2.24.89).

85. WM 4 (3.5.93), 1 (3.12.93), 9 (4.2.93), 12 (6.11.93), 8 (6.18.93), 10 (7.25.93); CT 1 (5.9.92); C 1 (5.9.92); CP 2 (5.10.92); So 11 (5.11.92); St 5 (5.12.92), 12 (8.21.92).

86. WM 9 (5.4.90).

87. WM 1 (9.14.90), 7 (9.28.90), 3 (10.5.90), 8 (11.9.90).

88. WM 3 (1.11.91), 5 (1.18.91), 9 (2.15.91).

89. Laurence (1990: 61-62); WM 2, 37 (5.8.92), 1 (5.15.92), 5 (5.29.92), 4 (6.19.92).

90. Gluckman also discovered that his office was extensively bugged with highly sophisticated equipment. WM 25 (7.31.92), 14 (9.4.92), 2 (12.11.92). He died at 78 on May 26, 1993. NYT B8 (5.27.93).

91. WM 1 (8.7.92), 2 (10.30.92). The government also used its executive authority to release individual police imprisoned for illegal violence. WM 3 (4.30.92), 6 (5.8.92).

92. WM 1 (8.28.92).

93. WM 4 (12.11.92). For proposals to reform the security forces, see Mathews et al. (1993); Brogden & Shearing (1993).

94. Compare Hannah Arendt (1977) on the Nazi perpetrators of the Holocaust.

95. Three decades ago Jerome Skolnick (1966) described the pressure on police to clear complaints and produce convictions while respecting due process.

96. Orwell (1949).

97. Arendt (1977: 106) makes this point about Nazis; quoted in Scarry (1985: 58).

98. McKendrick & Hoffman (1990); Manganyi & du Toit (1990); *Journal of Southern African Studies* (1992).

99. Similar conflicts between police and prison warders revealed that the "confessions" of the Guildford and Birmingham bombers had been coerced. See Mullin (1990); Conlon (1990).

100. See Scarry (1985: 40).

101. See Scarry (1985: 50).

102. WM 3 (7.27.85), 3 (8.2.85), 4 (8.16.85), 4 (8.30.85), 3 (10.11.85), 4 (11.15.85), 5-6 (11.29.85), 8 (12.6.85), 4 (3.11.86), 3 (4.4.86), 7 (8.8.86), 4 (11.7.86).

103. On the legal regime governing security forces, see Haysom (1987a; 1987b; 1989b); Plasket (1990a).

104. See Scarry (1985: 14).

105. Compare the focus on Oskar Schindler in Thomas Keneally's book (1983) and Steven Spielberg's 1993 movie.

Chapter 8: CENSORSHIP

1. On the history of South African censorship, see Kahn (1966); Silver (1979; 1983); Hachten & Giffard (1984); Marcus (1985d; 1988b); Haysom & Marcus (1985); Grogan (1986); Sperling & McKenzie (1990); Louw & Tomaselli (1991a), SAIRR, Annual Reports. On the activities of the Publications Committees and Appeal Board, see Silver (1984); Cheh (1986). On control of libraries, see Merrett (1990). On the additional restrictions imposed during the Emergency, see Grogan (1988b); Armstrong (1987; 1989); HRC (1989); Marcus (1990a); Tomaselli & Louw (1991b); Jackson (1993). See generally 1(14) *SA Barometer* (1987); 2(8) *SA Barometer* 119 (1988).

2. For decades, no newspaper has published anything without consulting the massive "Newspaperman's Guide to the Law" (Stuart, 1986). On the alternative press, see Tomaselli & Louw (1991a).

3 See Moseki (1988); Marcus (n.d.); Finnegan (1988).

4. WM 15 (6.21.85).

5. WM 2 (10.18.85).

6. WM 5 (9.6.85), 2 (9.13.85), 11 (10.4.85), 2 (10.11.85), 1 (11.8.85); see Posel (1990).

7. The maximum penalty was three years imprisonment. Heard (1990: 185–219).

8. WM 5 (12.20.85).

9. *Hansard* cols. 3858-61 (D.J.L. Nel, Deputy Minister of Information) (4.21.86).

10. *Hansard* cols. 4119, 4143-46 (S.S. van der Merwe, PFP; J.C.G. Botha, Minister of Home Affairs) (4.24.86).

11. S v Harber 1988 (3) SA 396 (A); Burchell (1988); WM 3 (4.18.86), 4 (5.9.86), 6 (3.31.88).

12. WM 3 (6.27.86).

13. WM 3 (8.1.86).

14. NYT 4 (6.14.86).

15. Mufson (1990: 261).

16. *Hansard* cols. 256–58 (P.W. Botha, State President) (2.4.87).

17. *Hansard* cols. 323–25 (D.J. Dalling, PFP) (2.5.87).

18. Unless otherwise noted, all Tugwana quotations are from a July 1991 interview.

19. WM 3 (10.3.86), 8 (10.9.86).

20. PAB Case No. 129/86 (10.11.86); WM 5 (10.3.86).

21. Armstrong (1987: 206–08).

22. WM 3 (12.12.86).

23. WM 3, 6 (1.16.87), 2 (1.30.87), 2, 15 (2.6.87), 6 (2.13.87), 2 (4.30.87), 8 (9.25.87); *ACAG Update* 4 (6.87); Munnik Commission (1987).

24. WM 13 (2.6.87), 6 (5.22.87), 5 (8.7.87), 1 (9.18.87).

25. WM 2 (3.20.87), 7 (4.3.87), 3 (6.12.87), 7 (6.26.87).

26. Phila Mgqumba and Mxolisi Jackson Fuzile, who ran Veritas, a small news agency in King Williams Town, argued that they did not intend to use "Inyaniso Media Skills and Research Project" to propagate consumer boycotts, civil unrest, or any ideas or ideologies. The Grahamstown Supreme Court was unmoved. WM 5 (10.9.87).

27. WM 5 (6.21.85), 13 (2.6.87), 1 (2.13.87), 3 (2.27.87), 6 (3.13.87), 11 (3.27.87).

28. WM 6 (5.15.87); on the history of *Saamstaan*, see Louw (1991).

29. WM 1 (4.16.87), 11 (4.24.87).

30. Procl. No. R.97 (GG 10772).

31. *Hansard* cols. 3949-54 (P.W. Botha, State President) (8.17.87).

32. NM 1 (8.18.87); WM 3 (8.21.87); BD (8.24.87); C 1 (8.26.87).

33. Procl. R.123 (GG 10880) (8.28.87).

34. *Hansard* cols. 4679-84, 4750-57 (J.C.G. Botha, Minister of Home Affairs) (8.27.87); WM 1 (8.28.87); C 1 (8.28.87), 13 (8.29.87).

35. *Hansard* cols. 4696-99, 4716, 4747-48 (S.S. van der Merwe, D.J. Dalling, PFP; F.J. van Deventer, NP) (8.27.87).

36. Tyson (1987: 144-45).

37. Reproduced in Tyson (1987: 170).

38. Interview for SABC *Network* (10.11.87), quoted in Marcus (1988a: 85).

39. Schneider (1987).

40. C 13 (8.29.87), 13 (9.2.87); So 4 (9.1.87); St (9.15.87).

41. WM 3 (9.4.87); C (9.3.87); PN (9.3.87); So (9.3.87).

42. St (9.4.87).

43. St (10.7.87).

44. C (9.3.87).

45. WM 1 (9.11.87); St (9.3.87). Isaak de Vries's incompetence contributed to the dismissal of all charges in the Pietermaritzburg treason trial against UDF and trade union leaders (see chapter nine). He apparently had learned his lessons poorly. His teacher at the University of Pretoria, Deputy Minister of Information Stoffel van der Merwe, had been a more persuasive expert witness in the Saso trial a decade earlier, see Lobban (n.d.).

46. *The Cape Times* 3 (9.14.87).

47. *South* (7.23-29, 7.30-8.5, 8.6-12), PAB Nos. 110, 114 and 115/87.

48. *Learn and Teach* (No 4 of 1987), PAB No. 121/87.

49. *Isizwe The Nation*, PAB No. 118/87; *UDF News* (Vol. 4, No. 2), PAB No. 133/87; *Azanian Focus* (Vol. 1, No. 5), PAB No. 130/87; *1987 Cosatu Workers Diary*, PAB No. 176/87; *New Era* (Vol. 2, Nos. 1 & 2), PAB Nos. 177 and 178/87.

50. WM 5 (9.18.87).

51. S 13 (10.8.87); *The Leader* 26 (10.9.87); NYT (10.14.87); NN 2 (10.14.87).

52. CT 2 (11.19.87); S 11 (11.19.87); S 1 (11.19.87).

53. S (11.17.87) (emphasis added).

54. WM 5 (12.4.87).

55. Unless otherwise noted, all materials are contained in the papers filed in the SACBC interdict application.

56. R v Roux [1938] AD 271.

57. R v Nkatlo 1950 (1) SA 26 (C).

58. R v Sutherland 1950 (4) SA 66 (T).

59. S v Nathie 1964 (3) SA 588 (A).

60. CT 7 (11.16.87).

61. SSt (9.19.87) (Daveyton Mayor Tom Boya); S (12.12.84) (*Beeld*), (2.8.85) (PFP).

62. It could have noted that the 1988 *Hansard* index listed Nelson Mandela under the heading "Black, leaders."

63. E.g., RDM (6.10.83).

64. C (9.3.87).

65. C (9.3.87); S (9.4.87); B (9.4.87); CP (9.6.87).

66. St (6.28.87); So (8.26.87); STr (9.9.87).

67. So (8.28.87), (8.30.87); St (10.7.87).

68. CP (8.16.87).

69. This and other quotations are from a July 1991 interview. Rules of professional etiquette prevent me from naming the advocate.

70. R.2676, GG 11049 (11.27.87).

71. CT 3 (11.28.87); STi 2 (11.29.87).

72. CT 10 (12.2.87).

73. So (12.8.87); St 11 (12.9.87).

74. NN 3 (12.9.87).

75. C 4 (12.11.87).

76. St 12 (12.9.87); SSt (12.13.87).

77. PAB Nos. 95, 96, and 143/1987 (in Afrikaans).

78. Botha had hinted at that earlier. St (9.3.87). One of the *New Nation*'s advocates believed that such a scheme would be practically unworkable, while offering valuable opportunities for judicial review.

79. So 1 (12.22.87).

80. PAB No. 173/87.

81. So 1 (12.22.87); CT 11 (12.22.87); St 1 (12.22.87); NYT (1.7.88).

82. *Beeld* and *Rapport*. See CP (1.17.88).

83. WM 1 (12.18.87), 2 (12.24.87), 2 (1.15.88).

84. Catholic Bishops' Publishing Company v State President and Minister of Home Affairs and of Communications, WLD Case No. 421/88. NN 1 (12.23.87), 3 (1.13.88), 1 (1.14.88); CT 1.9.88); STr 5 (1.10.88); NP 5 (1.23.88); So 1.15.88).

85. St 4 (1.23.88).

86. WM 5 (1.29.88); NN 1 (2.3.88).

87. Argument was reported in St (1.28.88); So (2.2.88); WM 4 (2.5.88).

88. Robert M. Ntsuku of Umtata, NN 9 (2.17.88).

89. NYT A13 (3.9.88).

90. BD 4 (3.14.88).

91. GN No. 570, GG 11210 (3.22.88).

92. WM 1 (3.25.88); CP 2 (3.27.88); L 6 (4.1.88).

93. So (1 (3.23.88).

94. St 1 (3.23.88).

95. CT 10 (3.23.88).

96. BD 6 (3.23.88).

97. DD 18 (3.24.88).

98. C 3 (3.24.88).

99. CT 1 (3.25.88); BD 1 (3.23.88).

100. NYT A13 (3.23.88).

101. C 1 (3.23.88).

102. BD 1 (3.23.88); So 8 (4.12.88).

103. WM 1 (2.5.88).

104. C 3 (3.24.88), 9 (3.26.88), (3.29.88), 9 (4.27.88); WM 2 (3.25.88), 3 (4.22.88), 1 (4.29.88); CT 1 (3.23.88); So 2 (3.29.88); St (3.29.88); STr 7 (4.17.88). *Grassroots*, founded in 1980, had attained a circulation of 20,000 by 1982. *Saamstaan* (Stand Together) was founded by *Grassroots* to serve the rural Southern Cape and Karoo. See Johnson (1991); Louw (1991).

105. So 9 (3.28.88), 3 (4.1.88); T 1 (4.1.88); NP 2 (4.9.88); WM 11 (4.15.88); STr 9 (4.24.88).

106. WM 1 (5.5.88), 1 (5.13.88); So 9 (5.11.88); St 9 (5.11.88); CT 7 (5.11.88); CT 7 (5.11.88); NW 3 (5.12.88); EPH 2 (5.14.88). The papers were: The Star, Argus Community Newspapers, Diamond Fields Advertiser, Financial Mail, The Argus, Daily News, Finance Week, The Saturday Star, Weekly Mail, The Sunday Star, Sowetan, Natal Mercury, Ilanga, Sunday Times, Business Day, Post Natal, City Press, Times Media Ltd, Eastern Cape, Natal Witness, Pretoria News, The Cape Times, Daily Dispatch, Evening Post, and Sunday Tribune.

107. BD 10 (4.28.88).

108. So 1 (4.27.88); CT 2 (4.27.88); St 3 (4.27.88); BD 10 (4.28.88).

109. St 1 (5.2.88); So 6 (5.3.88).

110. WM 1 (5.5.88).

111. *Hansard* cols. 10181–82, 10184 (S.K. Louw, C.E. Green, LP) (5.18.88).

112. *Hansard* cols. 10207–10 (J.C.G. Botha, Minister of Home Affairs and Communications) (5.18.88).

113. *Hansard* cols. 10312–13 (S.S. van der Merwe, PFP) (5.19.88).

114. *Hansard* cols. 10331–33, 10341 (P.A. Matthee, F.J. van Deventer, NP) (5.19.88).

115. *Hansard* cols. 10347–82 (5.19.88); see also Marcus (1989: 132-33).

116. *Hansard* cols. 10786–91, 10811–13 (5.20.88).

117. NM 8 (5.21.88).

118. NW (6 (5.21.88).

119. NP 11 (5.21.88).

120. STr 10 (5.29.88); STi 22 (5.29.88).

121. WM 1 (5.13.88).

122. CT 8 (5.10.88).

123. So 6 (5.13.88).

124. NW 3 (5.12.88).

125. WM 20 (5.13.88).

126. CT 1 (5.14.88).

127. SSt 12 (7.24.88).

128. WM 21 (5.13.88).

129. WM 13 (5.27.88), 2, 3 (6.10.88).

130. *Hansard* col. 91 (reply by J.C.G. Botha, Minister of Home Affairs, to P.G. Soal, PFP) (2.24.88).

131. *Hansard* cols. 10786–89 (5.20.88).

132. WM 3 (6.10.88); *Hansard* col. 1973 (reply by A.J. Vlok, Minister of Law and Order, to J. van Eck, Ind) (6.28.88).

133. WM 1 (6.17.88).

134. WM 1 (6.24.88), 1 (7.222.88), 3 (7.29.88); St (7.19, 21- 23.88); EP (7.27.88); BD (7.28.88); CT 7.29.88).

135. WM 5 (7.22.88), 2 (8.26.88).

136. PAB No. 93/88.

137. NW (7.30.88).

138. PAB No. 96/88; WM 3 (7.29.88), 16 (8.5.88); STi (7.31.88).

139. St 2 (10.13.88), 5 (10.14.88), 15 (10.21.88), 10 (10.26.88); PN 18 (10.13.88); BD 1 (10.13.88), 3 (10.27.88); CT 2 (10.13.88), 6 (10.14.88); C 9 (10.14.88); So 8 (10.14.88); DFA 11 (10.14.88), 6 (10.27.88); EPH 6 (10.14.88); CP 2 (10.16.88); NN 3 (10.13.88); NW 8 (10.25.88).

140. NW 5 (10.20.88); St 2 (10.21.88); BD 3 (10.21.88); CT 2 (10.22.88); C (10.22.88).

141. CT 7 (10.24.88); St 3 (10.28.88); NN 3 (10.27.88).

142. CT 7 (10.28.88), (10.29.88); So 6 (10.31.88).

143. St 3 (10.31.88).

144. He issued a first warning to *Free Azania* the same day. St 15 (11.2.88); WM 1 (12.2.88).

145. CT 6 (11.2.88); St 1, 12 (11.2.88); PN 12 (11.2.88); EPH 8 (11.2.88); DD 16 (11.3.88); So 8 (11.3.88).

146. STri (11.6.88); SSt (11.6.88).

147. St (11.7.88).

148. SSt 2 (11.20.88); PN 3, 8 (11.21.88); CT 7 (11.21.88), 2 (11.22.88), 3 (11.23.88); So 3 (11.21.88); C 10 (11.22.88); St 6 (11.22.88), 3 (11.24.88), 1 (11.25.88), 16 (12.5.88); WM 8 (12.2.88), 4 (1.27.89), 2 (6.23.89), 7 (3.2.90).

149. WM 4 (1.13.89), 11 (2.24.89), 5 (3.3.89); NYT A15 (1.12.89).

150. *Hansard* cols. 289-92 (2.9.89).

151. *Hansard* cols. 2922-76 (D.J. Dalling, PFP; J.C.G. Botha, Minister of Home Affairs; C.J. van R. Botha, F.J. van Deventer, J.T. Delport, NP; P.G. Soal, PFP) (3.16.89).

152. *Hansard* col. 5894 (J.C.G. Botha, Minister of Home Affairs) (4.19.89).

153. WM 8 (6.30.89).

154. St (8.17.89); WM 5 (8.18.89), 3 (9.1.89), 4 (9.22.89), 7 (10.13.89), 3 (11.24.89), 3 (12.8.89).

155. Association of Democratic Journalists (1989).

156. WM 9 (9.15.89).

157. CT 5 (6.14.88); C 11 (6.15.88); St 4 (6.15.88), 3 (6.16.88), 3 (6.29.88), 11 (7.1.88).

158. NN (6.30.88) (7.7, 13.88).

159. WM 13 (12.9.88).

160. Catholic Bishops' Publishing Co. v State President and another 1990 (1) SA 849 (A).

161. Staatspresident v United Democratic Front 1988 (4) SA 830 (A) (decided after the *New Nation* had filed its heads of argument).

162. Nkondo v Minister of Law and Order 1986 (2) SA 756 (A).

163. WM 3 (11.10.89), 1 (11.17.89)3 (11.24.89).

164. WM 6 (2.2.89).

165. NN 1 (1.4.90); SSt 8 (2.4.90).

166. NN 12 (2.16.90); WM 7 (3.2.90).

167. Including "The Shadowed Mind," "Natal: South Africa's Killing Fields," and "The Sun Will Rise" (about the Sharpeville Six). WM 7 (3.16.90), 3 (3.23.90)6, 21 (4.5.90), 3 (9.7.90); St (4.4.90); *ACAG Update* 4 (4.90).

168. *Hansard* col. 9087 (E. Louw, Minister of Home Affairs) (5.14.90).

169. WM 3 (9.7.90).

170. C 13 (3.8.90), 17 (6.13.90), 26 (1.31.91); NM 3 (6.13.90); A 19 (6.14.90); So 8 (1.31.91).

171. *ACAG Update* 4 (2.90), 1 (7.90), 3 (8.90), 4 (9-10.90).

172. Transvaal Attorney General Klaus von Lieres lost a R35,000 claim against *Vrye Weekblad* for alleging that he had conducted "a petty vendetta" against the paper and engaged

in "selective prosecution." WM 5 (10.5.90), 5 (2.21.92). Law and Order Minister Leon Mellet accepted R15,000 to settle a R200,000 claim against the paper. *ACAG Update* 5 (April 1991).

173. WLD Nos. 24659 and 24969/89; WM 7 (11.16.90), 10 (11.23.90), 5 (11.30.90), 3 (12.8.90), 5 (1.18.91), 6 (1.25.91), 6 (4.5.91), 7 (4.12.91), 5 (2.21.92), 3 (8.28.93), 2 (12.3.93); NYT 12 (1.19.91).

174. WM 3 (4.5.91), 3 (6.14.91), 11 (7.19.91). The book was Mzala (1988).
Inkatha had used this strategy until the Supreme Court held that an artificial person could not be defamed. WM 5 (12.5.86), 3 (5.22.87).

175. WM 3 (3.3.91); *ACAG Update* 3 (3.91).

176. WM 2 (3.22.91).

177. WM 5 (4.5.91).

178. WM 11 (9.11.92), 2 (10.23.92). Government had prosecuted its predecessor, the *Rand Daily Mail*, for the same offense twenty-seven years earlier. See H. Suzman (1993: 190–92).

179. FW 27 (6.20.91).

180. WM 3 (4.30.91); St 8 (5.9.91); FW 19 (8.1.91). On *The New African* see Ntshakala & Emdon (1991).

181. Louw (1991: 209).

182. WM 8 (1.21.94).

183. WM 4 (7.31.92).

184. BD 11 (7.28.92); WM 5 (2.5.93). Efforts to buy the Sowetan and merge it with the *Sunday Nation* failed. WM 8 (1.21.94).

185. Rees & Day (1980); Heard (1990: 139-44); H. Suzman (1993: 190- 92); WM 7 (10.30.92), 1 (11.6.92).

186. WM 6 (9.24.93).

187. WM 18-19 (4.30.93); see generally Mazwai et al. (1991).

188. For an account of the PAB by its chairman during this period, see van Rooyen (1991).

Chapter 9: THE ALEXANDRA TREASON TRIAL

1. Jochelson (1988a: 15–16); Sarakinsky (1984: i, 1–2); Harvey (n.d.); Tourikis (1981).

2. Harvey (n.d.).

3. Jackson (n.d.); Lodge (1983: 13–14). The last event was depicted in the movie about Ruth First, "A World Apart."

4. Harvey (n.d.).

5. Jackson (n.d.); Sarakinsky (1984: 6, 17–21, 24, 26–27); Jochelson (1988a: 17); H. Suzman (1993: 88); Lodge (1983: ch.7).

6. Jochelson (1988a: 17, 21, 26); Jackson (n.d.); Sarakinsky (1984: 49–50, 54–55).

7. Jochelson (1988a: 22, 29, 83–84); Jackson (n.d.); Sarakinsky (1984: 54, 61).

8. Carter (1991b: 200); Jochelson (1988a: 83–85, 90, 100); Jackson (n.d.). Jochelson has since published two briefer accounts of Alexandra politics during the 1980s (1988b; 1990).

9. Sarakinsky (1984: 71–74); Jochelson (1988a: 94); SSt (2.9.86).

10. Jochelson (1988a: 96–99, 101–02, 108–09); Sarakinsky (1984: 75); Harvey (n.d.); Augustyn & Marais (n.d.: 1–2).

11. Jochelson (1988a: 111–14); Manoim (n.d.).

12. RDM (2.25.85); So (3.21.85), (4.17.85); Jochelson (1988a: 118– 19); Manoim (n.d.).

13. Jochelson (1988a: 130–36); Manoim (n.d.).

14. Jochelson (1988a: 115, 120); Manoim (n.d.).

15. St (1.3.86), (1.8.86), (2.17.86), (2.18.86), (2.19.86), (4.4.86), 4.18.86); So (1.13.86), (2.17.86), 1 (2.18.86), (4.17.86); C (1.13.86), (2.17.86), 1 (2.18.86), (2.20.86), (4.17.86); SSt (2.16.86); CP (2.16.86); STi 10 (2.16.86); BD (2.17.86), 1 (2.18.86); Manoim (n.d.); Carter (1991a: 118–20, 136); Jochelson (1988a: 137–38); Mufson (1990: 126–29, 319).

16. St 1 (2.18.86), 1 (2.19.86), 3 (2.20.86), (2.21.86), (2.25.86), (2.27.86); BD (2.19.86), (2.21.86); C (2.19.86), (2.20.86), (2.23.86), (2.26.86); So (2 (2.19.86), (2.20.86), (2.21.86); WM 3 (3.7.86); STi (2.23.86); G (2.25.86); O (2.23.86); Labour Monitoring Group (1986).

17. So (2.18.86); St (2.19.86).

18. C (2.19.86).

19. SABC (2.18.86), (2.19.86); Carter (1991a: 116); STri (3.2.86).

20. So (2.21.86); C (2.21.86); St 1 (2.22.86); SSt (2.23.86); Jochelson (1988a: 139–41); Legal Education Centre (1986: 4–6).

21. St (2.24.86), (2.28.86); WM (2.28.86); CP (3.2.86); So (2.25.86), 3.3.86).

22. C (3.3.86), (3.5.86), (3.6.86); WM (2.28.86); St (3.5.86), (3.6.86), (3.12.86); So (3.5.86), (3.6.86), (3.7.86), (3.10.86); BD (3.5.86), 1 (3.6.86); STi (3.9.86); SSt (3.16.86); CP (3.16.86), (3.23.86); Manoim (n.d.); Legal Education Centre (1986: 6–7).

23. So (3.10.86), (3.17.86), (3.18.86), (4.1.86); St (3.12.86), (3.13.86), (3.19.86), (3.27.86), (4.4.86); SSt (3.16.86); CP (4.6.86).

24. St (3.27.86), (4.16.86), (4.22.86), (4.23.86), (4.24.86); So (4.1.86), (4.16.86), (4.17.86), (4.23.86); C (4.17.86); CP (4.20.86); BD (4.22.86), (4.23.86); *Speak Alexandra* 1 (5.15.86).

25. So (4.14.86); Manoim (n.d.); Carter (1991: 130, 136); Lodge et al. (1991): 336). Sisulu was detained for this for more than two years.

26. St (3.18.86), (4.22.86); CP (4.20.86); So (4.21.86); BD (4.22.86); C (4.22.86); Jochelson (1988: 149–50).

27. *Hansard* cols. 4551–53, 7958–60 (D.J. Dalling, PFP) (4.30.86, 5.11.86); WM (5.2.86).

28. C 1 (4.23.86), 1 (4.24.86), (4.25.86), 1 (4.26.86); St (4.23.86), (4.24.86), (4.26.86), (4.29.86); WM (4.25.86); BD (4.23.86), 1, 3 (4.24.86), 3 (4.25.86); So (4.24.86), (4.29.86); CP 1 (4.27.86); SSt 1 (4.27.86); STi (4.27.86); STr (4.27.86); G (4.24.86); *Speak Alexandra* (5.15.86); Jochelson (1988a: 151–52); Legal Education Centre (1986: 9–10).

29. So (4.25.86); St (4.25.86); STi (4.27.86).

30. CP (4.27.86); So (4.28.86), (4.29.86); C (4.29.86); BD (4.29.86); St (4.29.86); WM (5.2.86); Manoim (n.d.).

31. C (4.25.86), 1 (4.26.86), (4.30.86); SSt (4.27.86); BD (4.30.86); St (4.30.86); So 12 (4.30.86); STi (5.5.86).

32. SSt (5.4.86), (6.8.86); C (5.1.86); BD (5.1.86).

33. So (5.5.86), (5.9.86); St 3 (5.7.86), 2 (5.10.86), (5.16.86); BD ((5.9.86); CP (5.11.86); WM (5.9.86); CT 2 (5.10.86); C 3 (5.10.86); Manoim (n.d.).

34. CP (5.11.86); STi 1 (5.11.86); SSt (5.11.86); St (5.12.86), (5.13.86); C (5.12.86), (5.13.86); CT (5.12.86); BD (5.12.86), (5.13.86).

35. BD 6 (5.12.86).

36. PN 10 (5.12.86); FM 54, 57 (5.16.86).

37. St (5.14.86), (5.15.86), (5.16.86), (5.19.86); SSt (5.18.86); C (5.14.86), 1 (5.15.86), (5.16.86), 2 (5.17.86), (5.19.86); BD (5.15.86); STi (5.18.86); CP (5.18.86), (5.25.86); WM 8 (5.23.86).

38. So (5.20.86), (5.26.86), (5.28.86), (6.10.86); St (5.22.86), 7 (5.24.86), (5.30.86), (6.12.86); SSt (11.16.86); Manoim (n.d.); Jochelson (1988a: 153–54).

39. CP (6.8.86); C (6.11.88); BD (6.11.88).

40. CP 1 (6.29.86); C (6.13.86); WM 8, 11 (7.19.86), 14 (7.25.86); NYT (6.29.86); Jochelson (1988a: 186); Manoim (n.d.).

41. So (8.1.86), (9.21.86), (12.29.86); St (8.1.86), (12.1.86), (3.16.86); CP (8.3.86), (11.16.86); WM (7.31.87); BD (10.22.87); Jochelson (1988a: 188, 199, 201, 215–16, 218); Manoim (n.d.); Mashabela (1988: 12, 20, 23).

42. Unless otherwise noted, information about this trial is from Meer (1989).

43. WM 3 (8.16.85), 5 (10.25.85).

44. WM 3 (12.6.85), 2 (12.13.85); So (2.4.86).

45. WM 8 (2.7.86), 9 (3.6.86), 3 (3.21.86), (3.27.86), 3 (4.11.86), 3 (6.6.86), 5 (6.27.86).

46. WM 2 (1.24.86), 5 (2.14.86), 3 (10.31.86), 1 (11.28.86), 2 (1.23.87), 1 (3.13.87), 1 (3.20.87), 1, 5, 18 (4.3.87), 10 (7.3.87), 7 (8.7.87), 4 (9.18.87), 5 (11.13.87); R. Moss (1990); Wescott (n.d.); D. Davis (1990a).

47. WM 2 (2.27.87).

48. All of his statements are from an August 1990 interview.

49. Affidavit of Det. Sgt. Trevor Allen Scot, Security Branch Investigation Team, Sandton (3.26.87).

50. C 4 (2.14.87).

51. Moses Mayekiso and others v Attorney General, WLD Case No. 4969/87.

52. G (5.6.87); T (5.26.87), (10.28.87); WM 10 (10.23.87); *News on Sunday* (9.13.87); *The Age* (9.14.87).

53. NYT (11.26.87); WM (11.20.87); St (11.19.87); BD (11.19.87).

54. WM (4 (10.31.86), 3 (11.7.86), (11.20.87); STr (5.1.88); G (10.19.87); I (10.19.87); letter from Dr. Michael Lobban, Department of Law, University of Durham (3.23.92).

55. WM 10 (10.23.87); CP 4 (2.21.88).

56. WM 18 (12.6.91), 25 (2.21.92).

57. WM 4 (10.31.86), 3 (11.7.86).

58. He also allowed Mayekiso's parents, who had travelled from Transkei, to visit him in the cells during the trial. WM 25 (2.21.92).

59. St (10.22.87), (11.18.87); BD (11.4.87), (11.9.87); So (11.18.87).

60. 1.30.88.

61. St 2 (4.21.88); see also the *Weekly Mail* and *The Cape Times*.

62. R v Endemann, 1915 TPD 142; R v Leibbrandt, 1944 AD 282.

63. S v Mayekiso and others 1988 (4) SA 738 (W); WM 5 (5.27.88); CT 9 (6.7.88).

64. C (8.2.88), (8.3.88); BD (8.2.88), (8.3.88).

65. State Exhibit HHH.

66. St 2 (9.8.88); So 4 (9.12.88), 2 (10.26.88); NN 7, 9 (9.15.88); BD 3 (9.16.88).

67. Interview with defense attorney Norman Manoim (July 1991).

68. 4.5.86.

69. I am grateful to Michael Lobban for this insight.

70. C 8 (12.13.88); NW 1 (12.15.88); St 10 (12.20.88); CP 5 (12.18.88).

71. C (2.2.89), (2.4.89); BD (2.2.89), 2 (2.7.89); CT 2 (2.2.89).

72. So (2.19.89); C (2.10.89); BD (2.10.89); CP (2.12.89); STr (2.19.89); WM (2.17.89).

73. S v Zwane and others 1989 (3) SA 253 (W).

74. S v Baleka and others 1988 (4) SA 688 (T).

75. WM 1, 3 (12.9.88), 1, 12 (12.15.88), 5 (1.26.89).

76. So 3 (4.4.89); BD (4.4.89); St (4.4.89); NN 2 (4.5.89).

77. So (4.10.89), 6 (4.26.89).

78. WMl 8 (4.7.89).

79. St 1 (4.25.89), (4.29.89); C (4.25.89).

80. St 1 (4.25.89), 4 (4.29.89).

81. NN (4.27.89); see also CP 9 (4.30.89).

82. St 10 (4.26.89); SSt 12 (4.30.89).

83. NW 14 (4.27.89).

84. FM 48 (4.28.89); St (5.5.89).

85. PN 20 (4.25.89); So 6 (4.26.89).

86. NW 14 (4.27.89); CT 10 (4.26.89); So 6 (4.26.89).

87. NYT A3 (4.25.89); WP A10 (4.25.89); STr (4.20.89).

88. NN (4.27.89).

89. CT 3 (4.26.89); St 1 (4.25.89); So 6 (4.26.89); *South* (4.28.89).

90. WM 13 (4.28.89).

91. BD (5.5.89); SSt (4.30.89); NN (5.5.89).

92. SSt 2 (4.30.89); NN (5.5.89); WM (6.2.89).

93. WM 13 (5.26.89); 14(2) SALB 36 (6.89); ACAG 8 (12.89); Alexandra Joint Negotiating Forum (1991); interview with Norman Manoim and Amanda Armstrong (July 1990).

94. NYT A4 (12.16.89); LAT A3 (12.16.89).

95. DM 4 (7.9.90).

96. So 3 (11.15.90); STi 22 (11.11.90); EP 10 (11.20.90).

97. WM 2 (3.15.91), 8 (3.22.91), 1 (3.28.91), 6 (5.3.91), 6 (5.17.91), 5 (3.12.93).

98. WM 4 (7.17.87), 3 (4.8.88).

99. S v. Ruben Mcetywa, Regional Court, STD, Case No. 41/1851/90 (7.11.90). See also S v Albert Tekululi and Absolom Sibisisi, Regional Court, STD, Case No. 41/2631/90 (10.22.90); interview with attorneys Mpueleng Pooe and Levi Modise, Bell, Dewar & Hall (July 1991).

100. WM 8 (6.14.91).

101. CALS and Nadel (1991). Interviews with Stephen Goldblatt, Bram du Plessis and Levi Modise and visit to Alexandra (July 1991).

102. WM 12 (4.30.92), 12 (10.29.93).

103. Although treason was charged in the Yengeni case in the Western Cape, the Masina case in the Northern Transvaal (Delmas 2) and the Broederstrom 3, the state withdrew that count before conviction. Manoim (1989).

104. Manoim (1989).

105. Van Dijkhorst appeared to find UDF leaders guilty on this ground. R. Moss (1990: 148–49).

106. Gilbey (1993: 145 et passim).

107. See Burman (1989); Burman & Schärf (1990); Schärf (1989; 1990); Schärf & Ngcokoto (1990); Seekings (1989; 1992); Hund & Kotu-Rammopo (1983); Hund (1988); G. van Niekerk (1988); Grant & Schwikkard (1991); Lodge et al. (1991). On violence in South African society, see McKendrick & Hoffman (1990). Street committees were even more common, see PLANACT (1990).

108. Quoted from WP (10.15.87) by Price (1991: 255).

109. *Hansard* cols. 7912–14 (L. Wessels, NP) (6.11.86). He was appointed Deputy Minister of Law and Order on March 31, 1988.

110. NYT B8 (3.14.88), quoted in Price (1991: 255).

111. I am grateful to Michael Lobban for reminding me of this revealing gaffe.

112. *Sechaba* (March 1984); National Executive Committee, "ANC Call to the Nation: The Future Is Within Our Grasp!" (Lusaka, April 25, 1985); Alex Mashinini, "Dual Power and the Creation of People's Committees," *Sechaba* 25 (April 1986); Carter (1991a: 117).

113. So did songs, see Kivnick (1990).

114. Meer (1989: 27–28).

115. SSt 12 (4.30.89).

Chapter 10: BAKWENA BA MAGOPA

1. Platzky & Walker (1985); see also Desmond (1971); Lodge (1983: ch. 4); SACBC & SACC (1984); SAIRR (1983; 1984; 1985); Platzky (1985; 1986; 1987); E. Unterhalter (1987); Cole (1987); Lawyers Committee for Human Rights (1987); Cowling (1990); Robertson (1990); Murray & O'Regan (1990); Dolny & Klug (1992); Christopher (1994).

2. *Hansard* col. 2534 (9.1.81).

3. *Hansard* col. 844 (2.11.83).

4. Unless otherwise noted, all information and quotations come from papers filed in the application for an interdict against the removal.

5. Deeds of Transfer (1922; 1931); Godfrey Archibald Godley for Department of Native Affairs (10.4.22); So (10.3.83); TRAC (1986a); Haysom (1986c).

6. Undated memorandum probably submitted to the January 1982 Commission of Inquiry.

7. Haysom (1986c).

8. In response to a Parliamentary question by Helen Suzman, Koornhof revealed that D. Rautenbach, "who has a Diploma Iuris," concluded that the allegations were unfounded. *Hansard* cols. 13–14 (2.1.84).

9. Memorandum (10.4.83); Haysom (1986c).

10. Undated but probably March; it may have been from migrant laborers on the Reef.

11. Anonymous notes of a field trip (10.4.83).

12. Haysom (1986c).

13. CP (9.18.83).

14. St (9.23.83).

15. SE 15 (9.25.83).

16. So (9.30.83).

17. SE (10.2.83).

18. So 4–5, 7 (10.2.83).

19. So (10.11.83).

20. 9 *Learn and Teach* (1983).

21. St (11.17.83); RDM (11.18.83).

22. St (11.19.83).

23. St (11.21.83), 2 (11.22.83).

24. Haysom (1986c).

25. Shadrack More v Minister of Co–operation and Development and J de Villiers, TPD Case No. 20215/83.

26. St (11.23.83).

27. Steven Sihewula v Mr Kotze and Minister of Bantu Administration and Development, SECLD (Solomon, AJ, 11.22.77). For a discussion of the underlying legislation, see Marcus (1990b).

28. RDM (11.23.83); So (11.23.83); CP 8 (11.28.83); Black Sash (1983a).

29. NYT §1 p.6 (11.27.83).

30. WP §1 p.1 (11.27.83).

31. WP A10 (11.28.83).

32. Unfortunately, the account of Magopa in her autobiography is cursory and erroneous. H. Suzman (1993: 202–03).

33. CP (11.27.83).

34. SACC Press Conference, "The Mogopa Removals" (11.30.83).

35. NYT (11.30.83); CP 8 (12.4.83); *Seipone* 1 (12.3.83).

36. St (12.1.83); STr 4 (12.4.83).

37. NYT (11.30.83).

38. NS (12.2.83); SE (12.4.83).

39. Black Sash (1983a: 3).

40. NYT (12.3.83); WP (12.3.83); St (12.3.83). The first two articles, by Allister Sparks, were reprinted in *South African Outlook* (2.84).

41. St (12.1.83); CP (12.4.83); RDM (12.5.83).

42. Black Sash, Press Statement on SABC/Radio Setswana Coverage of Mogopa.

43. STr 4 (12.4.83).

44. St 1 (12.56.83); RDM (12.7.83); Black Sash, Daily Summary on Magopa (12.6.83); Black Sash (1983b).

45. Black Sash (1983b).

46. RDM (12.10.83).

47. STi (12.11.83).

48. PN (12.12.83).

49. Haysom (1986c: 15).

50. RDM (12.15.83).

51. Black Sash, Memo (2.20.84); TRAC (1986a: 5).

52. NYT A6 (1.13.84). The Pacific News Service also distributed the November NPR broadcast story. *Bacon's* (1.22.84).

53. *Hansard* cols. 130–31 (H. Suzman, PFP) (1.31.84).

54. *Hansard* cols. 273, 280–83 (C.W. Eglin, PFP; R.F. Botha, Minister of Foreign Affairs) (2.2.84); RDM (2.3.84).

55. St (2.9.84).

56. T (2.11.84).

57. Gill de Vlieg, "The St. Valentine's Day Removal at Magope" (2.16.84).

58. WP A38 (2.16.84); Spink (1991: 107–11). Government stonewalled repeated Parliamentary questions about compensation, claiming the matter was sub judice. *Hansard* col. 356 (reply by Minister of Co-operation and Development to G.B.D. McIntosh, PFP) (3.4.85), col. 1228 (Reply by Deputy Minister of Development and Land Affairs to Helen Suzman, PFP) (4.23.85), cols. 160, 1228 (replies by Minister of Co-operation and Development to H. Suzman, PFP) (2.25.86, 4.23.86).

59. RDM (2.16.84); STr (2.19.84); WP A38 (2.16.84); TRAC (1986a: 506); Black Sash, Memorandum (2.20.84).

60. RDM (2.18.84).

61. T (2.15, 16.84).

62. STr (2.19.84).

63. CP (2.19.84).

64. *Hansard* cols. 1195–1206 (H. Suzman, PFP; B.H. Wilkens, Deputy Minister of Development and Land Affairs) (2.16.84).

65. St (2.21.84); RDM (2.21.84).

66. RDM 8 (2.24.84); Black Sash, Memorandum (2.20.84).

67. The report was by Profs. J.Q. Heyns and P.B. van der Walt and Dr. P. Rousouw, acting "in a personal capacity." *DRC News* (3–5.84); RDM (3.3.84)). Contrast the contemporaneous "Mogopa Uprooted," 36(3) *Wits Student* 11–13 (3.16.84).

68. St (5.12.84).

69. WP A1, A14 (5.5.84). The editorial was reproduced in the *Guardian Weekly* 10 (5.13.84).

70. CP (5.27.84).

71. SAIRR (1984: 441).

72. St 2 (8.14.84).

73. St 1 (2.2.85).

74. NW 12 (2.15.85); SAIRR (1985: 328).

75. §9 of the Laws on Co–operation and Development Amendment Bill, No. 89–85(GA).

76. *Hansard* col. 7435 (G. van N. Viljoen, Minister of Co–operation, Development and Education) (6.12.85).

77. St (5.22.85).

78. CT 4 (5.21.85).

79. FM 53 (5.24.85).

80. *Hansard* col. 7415 (H. Suzman, PFP) (6.12.85).

81. CT 6 (6.11.85); FM 65 (6.21.85).

82. WM 11 (6.21.85).

83. NYT A12 (8.30.85).

84. Giliomee (n.d.).

85. CP 6 (8.25.85); WM 4 (8.23.85), 7 (8.30.85); see White (1988); Claassens (1990).

86. More v Minister of Co–operation and Development and another 1986 (1) SA 102 (A) (Trengove, J, with Rabie, CJ, and Kotze, Botha and Grosskopf, JJ).

87. Id. 113.

88. Id. 114.

89. Id. 115–16.

90. PN 3 (9.20.85).

91. So 4 (9.24.85).

92. WM 5 (10.4.85).

93. WM 9 (10.11.85).

94. WM 5 (11.8.85), 5 (11.15.85), 9 (9.26.86).

95. WM 3, 5 (11.22.85).

96. WM 2 (2.7.86), 5 (3.14.86), 13 (9.19.86).

97. WM 5 (3.14.86, (3 (7.25.86).

98. WM 5 (10.24.86), 1 (11.21.86), 1 (11.28.86).

99. See generally his account of representing the Magopa, Haysom (1990c).

100. TRAC (1988a: 7–8); WM 5 (2.20.87).

101. TRAC (1988a: 8); 13 *TRAC Newsletter* (8.87); St 1 (7.30.87).

102. *Hansard* col. 2582 (P.G. Soal, PFP) (7.29.87).

103. *Hansard* col. 2653 (G. van N. Viljoen, Minister of Education and Development Aid) (7.29.87).

104. St 1, 11 (7.30.87), (8.12.87); NN 19 (7.30.87); ND (8.9.87).

105. TRAC (1988a: 10).

106. NN 14 (8.5.87); CT 2 (7.30.87); FM 60 (8.14.87).

107. NN 2 (8.26.87); Jaffee (1987).

108. Press statement (8.4.87); BD (8.5.87); CT 4 (8.5.87); WM 5 (7.31.87); St 1 (7.30.87); So 6 (8.6.87).

109. WM 5 (7.31.87); St 11 (7.30.87), 7 (8.24.87), (8.26.87); ND 6 (8.9.87); BD (8.3.87); TRAC (1988a: 10).

110. STi 2, 13 (9.6.87).

111. BD 4 (9.8.87).

112. CT 4 (9.8.87).

113. So 7 (9.9.87).

114. CT 10 (9.9.87).

115. A 16 (9.10.87).

116. *Sash* 35 (12.31.87).

117. St (9.14.87); Aninka Claassens, Memorandum (1.12.88).

118. "The Agricultural Base of the Community: Reasons for Being Situated in the Maize Triangle"; Mogopa Land Proposals (10.5.87).

119. St (10.5.87).

120. NN 2 (2.18.88).

121. St 3A (2.15.88).

122. So 7 (2.17.88).

123. The minutes appear to have been prepared by government retrospectively on February 10, 1989 to substantiate its version (emphasis in the original).

124. Annexures M2 and M3 to the application for ejectment (translated from Afrikaans).

125. Minister of Agriculture and Water Supply and Minister of Education and Development Aid v Daniel Molefe, Matthew Mpshe, Peter Chief More and Jacob More, TPD Case No. 2077/89.

126. NN 4 (2.16.89).

127. WM 10 (2.17.89).

128. BD 2 (2.15.89); see also St (2.13.89).

129. Assistant Director, Division of Financial Aid, Department of Agriculture and Water Supply. I am grateful to Cherie van Onselen for translating the applicant affidavits and judgments from Afrikaans.

130. C 8 (2.25.89); cf. PN 5 (2.27.89).

131. C 9 (4.26.89).

132. So 2 (4.27.89).

133. CP 2 (4.30.89).

134. BD 2 (4.28.89), 2 (5.2.89).

135. WP (5.1.89); reprinted in So 6 (5.10.89).

136. C 8 (5.30.89).

137. BD 2 (5.3.89).

138. STi 10 (5.7.89).

139. STi 18 (5.7.89).

140. WM 6 (4.14.89), 11 (5.12.89), 17 (5.26.89), 6 (2.15.91).

141. WM 3 (1.13.89).

142. WM 14 (6.26.87), 3 (9.11.87), 6 (11.17.89); 1 *Land Update* (5.90).

143. WM 7 (12.8.89), 5 (12.15.89).

144. WM 2 (12.15.89).

145. BD 2 (5.11.89); WM 1 (5.12.89); STr 25 (5.14.89); see also WP (5.3.89).

146. NN 2 (8.17.90).

147. Appellate Division No. 573/89.

148. WP A16 (8.27.90); NYT §1 p.4 (9.2.90); DM 2 (8.27.90); WM 3 (8.31.90).

149. C 4 (9.25.90).

150. WM 10 (1.18.91), 20 (3.25.91).

151. WM 12, 29 (2.8.91).

152. White Paper on Land Reform A2.11(f); WM 1 (3.15.91).

153. WM 6 (7.5.91), 10 (9.11.92).

154. WM 4 (7.24.92).

155. WM 17 (8.21.92).

156. WM 3 (11.27.92).

157. WM 2 (12.18.92).

158. Minister of Agriculture and Agricultural Development, Petronella Jacomina Hall, Albertus van Zyl, Gottlieb Johannes Niemand, Jacobus Nicolaas van Antwerp, Hendry Victor Louis Olver, Gert Petrus Jacobus Coetzer, and Andries Terreblanche v Levi Segopolo and 86 others, TPD Case No. 8380/91.

159. Olifile Levy Segopolo and the Community of Goedgevonden v Eugene Ney Terre Blanche and the Afrikaner Weerstandsbeweging, TPD Case No. 9969/91.

160. BD (3.14.91).

161. *Farmer's Weekly* 7 (4.26.91).

162. C (4.20.91).

163. C (5.9.91) (quoting a *Financial Times* interview).

164. Minister of Agriculture and Agricultural Development and others v Levy Segopolo and others 1992 (3) SA 967 (T).

165. WM 15 (5.24.91), 7 (6.7.91), 7 (1.10.92).

166. WM 6 (10.29.93).

Chapter 11: MOUTSE AND KWANDEBELE

1. GN 2106, GG 5771 (11.16.56); Proc. 174, GG 142 (12.29.61).

2. GN 1887, GG 2909 (10.30.70).

3. GN R1274 (8.10.62).

4. Proc. R225, GG 3666 (9.29.72).

5. For the history of the Ndebele, see Delius (1989).

6. McCaul (1987: 4).

7. GN 2143, GG 2217 (11.22.68).

8. Proc. 135, GG 4337 (7.19.74); McCaul (1987: 5).

9. McCaul (1987: 57).

10. Proc. R871 (5.20.77); GN R2021, GG 5766 (10.7.77).

11. Procs. R204–05, GG 6661 (9.14.79).

12. McCaul (1987: 6).

13. McCaul (1987: 59).

14. RDM 11 (11.29.83); SE 11 (7.24.83).

15. Proc. R60, GG 7499 (3.20.81).

16. McCaul (1987: 6–9, 57).

17. Government of the Republic of South Africa and another v Government of KwaZulu and another 1983 (1) SA 164 (A).

18. RDM 11 (11.29.82).

19. McCaul (1987: 58).

20. *Hansard* col. 10734 (P.G.J. Koornhof, Minister of Co–operation and Development) (6.30.83).

21. RDM 4 (2.22.83); SE 11 (7.24.83).

22. §6, Laws on Co–operation and Development Amendment Act 102 of 1983.

23. *Hansard* col. 10831 (H. Suzman, PFP; P.G.J. Koornhof, Minister of Co–operation and Development) (8.8.83).

24. *Hansard* cols. 11041–51 (N.J.J. Olivier, PFP; P.G.J. Koornhof, Minister of Co–operation and Development) (8.10.83); RDM (8.4.83), 1 (8.10.83).

25. TRAC (1988b: 116).

26. §12, Laws on Co–operation and Development Amendment Act 83 of 1984 (amending §37B, National States Constitution Act of 1971); *Hansard* cols. 470, 1295 (replies by G. van N. Viljoen, Minister of Co–operation and Development to P.G. Soal, PFP) (3.11.85, 4.26.85); McCaul (1987: 60–61); SAIRR (1984: 504).

27. *Hansard* cols. 10–11 (P.G.J. Koornhof, Minister of Co–operation and Development) (Standing Committees, 5.2.84).

28. McCaul (1987: 6).

29. McCaul (1987: 9–10); CT 7 (8.13.86). In 1986 Heunis claimed that 46.5 percent of eligible voters in KwaNdebele participated. *Hansard* cols. 2326–27 (reply to P.G. Soal, PFP) (6.19.86). But only men were eligible, and most of them were at work outside KwaNdebele.

30. So 7 (2.13.85), 3 (2.26.85), 1 (3.12.85), 1 (4.17.85); FM (3.15.85); WM 3 (6.21.85), 2 (11.15.85); SM 2 (2.17.85), 4 (4.28.85); PN 8 (2.25.85); *Hansard* cols. 977, 1511 (replies by G van N. Viljoen, Minister of Co–operation and Development, to P.G. Soal and H. Suzman, PFP) (4.8.86, 5.15.85); McCaul (1987: 62–65); TRAC (1988b: 118–19); Haysom (1986a: 68–70); LRC (1989: vol. 2); SAIRR (1985: 284, 308–09).

31. *Hansard* cols. 977, 2131–34 (replies by J.C. Heunis, Minister of Constitutional Development and Planning, to P.G. Soal, PFP) (4.8.86, 6.4.86).

32. McCaul (1987: 61, 64). The PFP made only a pro forma objection. *Hansard* cols. 7396–97 (R.A.F. Swart, PFP) (6.12.85).

33. WM 5 (11.22.85), 6 (12.13.85); So (11.20.85); St (11.19.85); BD 3 (11.20.85); DN (8 (11.20.85); CP 2 (12.8.85); SSt 4 (12.8.85); Haysom (1986a: 73); McCaul (1987: 61, 66–67); TRAC (1986a: 2); SAIRR (1985: 284–86, 306–07).

34. BD 2 (12.6.85); CT 11 (12.6.85), 11 (12.9.85); So 5 (12.9.85); FM 21 (12.20.85).

35. CT 12 (12.10.85).

36. So 6 (12.20.85).

37. A 14 (12.23.85).

38. EPH 2 (12.17.85); NYT A4 (12.18.85); CT 2 (12.19.85); So 4 (12.19.85); *Hansard* cols. 153–56 (reply by A.J. Vlok, Deputy Minister of Defence and Law and Order, to P.G. Soal, PFP) (2.25.86); Haysom (1986a: 73–74); TRAC (1986a: 2); McCaul (1987: 67).

39. Procs. R227, R228, GG 10053 (12.31.85, 1.1.86); WM 12 (1.10.86); PN 3 (1.2.86), 2 (1.4.86); CT 1 (1.3.86), 1 (1.4.86); NM 3 (1.6.86); So 4 (1.14.86); C 2 (1.3.86), 4 (1.4.86); TRAC (1986a: 2), (1988b: 121); McCaul (1987: 68–69); Haysom (1986a: 76–77);

40. So 1, 8 (1.3.86); BD 1 (1.3.86); CT 1 (1.4.86), 2 (1.6.86); FM 36 (1.10.86); T (1.3.86); C 2 (1.4.86); McCaul (1987: 69); TRAC (1986a: 3).

41. St 8 (1.20.86).

42. CT 6 (1.7.86); see also 6 (1.6.86).

43. EPH 4 (1.7.86).

44. A 8 (1.6.86).

45. EP 8 (1.6.86).

46. NM 6 (1.20.86).

47. PN 8 (1.4.86).

48. CT 1 (1.6.86); CP 4 (1.12.86); WM 6 (1.24.86); McCaul (1987: 68–69).

49. WM 5 (2.28.86), 8 (6.30.86); St (3.20.86); So (3.20.86); McCaul (1987: 78–79); Ritchken (1989: 427).

50. T (1.2.86).

51. NYT 1 (1.2.86).

52. WP (1.4.86), (1.7.86).

53. St 16 (3.3.86).

54. WP (1.7.86); CT (1.6.86); CP (1.12.86); C 8 (1.8.86), 5 (1.10.86); PN 5 (1.10.86); So 2 (1.10.86); McCaul (1987: 69–70).

55. So 1 (1.13.86).

56. PN 7 (1.17.86); C 3 (1.17.86); FM 57 (1.24.86), 60 (1.31.86); NN 3 (1.16.86); CT 2 (1.17.86); McCaul (1987: 73).

57. So 4 (1.28.86); Haysom (1986a: 66); McCaul (1987: 77–78).

58. CT 11 (2.5.86), 2, 10 (2.6.86), 8 (2.7.86); BD (2.5.86); A 12 (2.7.86); WM 5 (2.28.86); McCaul (1987: 81).

59. *Hansard* cols. 226–27, 234–35 (H. Suzman, PFP) (2.5.86), cols. 623–24 (reply by G. van N. Viljoen, Minister of Education and Development Aid, to H. Suzman, PFP) (3.18.86); FM 57 (1.24.86); So 1 (2.7.86), 6 (2.10.86), 4 (2.11.86), 7 (2.17.86), 1 (4.9.86), 4 (4.14.86); A 4 (2.7.86); CT 4 (2.6.86), 2 (2.8.86); C 10 (2.8.86); PN 3 (2.5.86), 3 (2.10.86); TRAC (1986a: 5–6); McCaul (1987: 72, 74–76).

60. *Hansard* cols. 106–11 (replies by B.H. Wilkens, Deputy Minister of Development and Land Affairs, to P.G. Soal and H. Suzman, PFP) (2.18.86).

61. PN 2, 12 (2.14.86); DD 3 (2.14.86); CT 2 (2.15.86); McCaul (1987: 73).

62. A 1 (2.17.86); PN 7 (2.18.86), 20 (2.20.86); FM 57 (2.28.86); C 8 (2.18.86); NW 2 (2.18.86); CT 2 (2.18.86).

63. St 14 (2.18.86); DN 8 (2.18.86); PN 14 (2.18.86), 10 (3.10.86), 12 (3.11.86); CT 10 (2.20.86).

64. *Hansard* col. 1448 (J.W. Greeff, Speaker) (3.4.86); St 4 (3.5.86); C 13 (3.5.86); WM 2 (3.7.86); CT 4 (2.19.86). The action had been filed on February 28.

65. C 11 (3.7.86); CT 6 (3.6.86); *Eye Witness* (3.7.86); FM 69 (3.14.86); NN 3 (3.25.86); Commonwealth Group (1986: 60); Dugard et al. (n.d.: 10).

66. *Hansard* cols. 3738–40 (4.18.86).

67. *Hansard* cols. 2100–01 (reply by J.C. Heunis to P.G. Soal, PFP) (6.3.86); C 12 (4.5.86), 4 (4.19.86), 3 (5.8.86); McCaul (1987: 72, 81); see generally SAIRR (1986: 681–92).

68. PN 11 (4.8.86); St (5.14.86); So (5.7.86); WM 5 (5.23.86); TRAC (1988b: 123–26); McCaul (1987: 79–80, 86); Ritchken (1989: 428); LRC (1989: 32).

69. WM 1 (5.16.86); So 5 (5.16.86); McCaul (1987: 81–82).

70. STi 2 (5.18.86); CP 5 (5.18.86).

71. So 1, 4 (5.15.86), 4 (5.16.86); CT 1 (5.15.86); C 2 (5.15.86); WM 1 (5.16.86); G (5.15.86); NYT (5.15.86); A 10 (5.16.86); STi 2 (5.11.86); EP 8 (5.12.86); TRAC (1988b: 126–27); McCaul (1987: 82–93).

72. C 4 (5.16.86), 13 (5.20.86); So 11 (5.20.86); FM 48 (5.23.86); McCaul (1987: 85–86).

73. CT 2 (5.27.86), 6 (6.30.86); SSt 2 (7.20.86); WM 2 (6.6.86), 5 (7.4.86), 1 (7.18.86); So 2 (7.17.86); CP 11 (6.8.86), 2 (6.29.86); McCaul (1987: 87–91); TRAC (1988b: 129).

74. SSt 2 (7.27.86); STr 3 (7.27.86); WM 3 (7.25.86); PN 1 (7.24.86), 1 (7.25.86), 15 (7.29.86); C 5 (7.25.86); BD 1 (7.30.86); Finnegan (1988); McCaul (1987: 91–92, 94).

75. WP A1 (8.3.86).

76. SSt 1 (8.3.86); STr 6 (8.3.86); WM 1 (8.1.86), 2 (9.12.86); So 4 (8.7.86); McCaul (1987: 94–95).

77. PN 6 (8.11.86) (quoting the *Guardian*); A 1 (8.4.86), 12 (8.5.86); FM 52 (8.8.86); So 4 (8.1.86); STi 20 (8.3.86); WA 3 (8.2.86); DN 6 (8.5.86); see also NYT (7.30.86).

78. G (8.4.86); WP A1 (8.3.86); NW 2 (8.12.86); CT 7 (8.13.86); So 3 (8.4.86); WM 1 (8.1.86); C 5 (8.2.86); CP 1 (8.3.86); STi 19 (8.10.86); McCaul (1987: 86).

79. WM 3 (8.8.86); STi 19 (8.10.86); NN 6 (8.13.86); McCaul (1987: 97).

80. WM 14 (8.15.86); CP 5 (8.17.86); NN 3 (8.13.86); *Sash* 24 (8.31.86); McCaul (1987: 97–98).

81. C 1 (8.13.86); PN 3 (8.14.86); DN 4 (8.16.86); So 9 (8.15.86).

82. CT 6 (8.14.86); So 4 (8.14.86); NW 8 (8.14.86); A 8 (8.15.86); NN 6 (8.13.86); SSt 16 (8.17.86); CP 2 (8.17.86); see also PN (8.13.86); DN 10 (8.13.86).

83. GN 9, Umthetho Ogadangisiwe (Official Gazette) (8.12.86); these were reissued with slight modifications by GN 4 (3.27.87), GN 3 (6.12.87), GN 7 (7.8.87), and GN 24 (12.28.87). So 2 (8.14.86), 9 (8.15.86); A 1 (8.14.86); NN 1 (8.13.86); PN 3, 7 (8.14.86); WM (11.21.86); McCaul (1987: 99–100).

84. C 16 (9.9.86); A 8 (9.10.87); FM 53 (9.12.86); McCaul (1987: 99–100)

85. WM 3 (10.9.86), 3 (10.17.86), 5 (11.14.86), 6 (5.8.87); McCaul (1987: 100–01).

86. PN 13 (11.17.86), 15 (11.18.86); WM 13 (11.21.86), 5 (11.28.86), 1 (5.22.87); FM 57 (11.21.86); STr 7 (11.23.86).

87. TPD Case No. 3409/86.

88. PN 5 (5.29.86).

89. Mathebe v Government of the Republic of South Africa and Others, TPD Case No. 9171/86.

90. Interviews (August 1990, July 1991).

91. St (11.26.86), 4 (11.27.86); WM 5 (11.28.86).

92. PN 5 (12.3.86); St 3 (12.3.86); WM 2 (12.5.86). I am grateful to Cherie van Onselen for translating the unreported Afrikaans judgment; I have reworked the language slightly.

93. BD 3 (12.4.86), 3 (12.5.86); CP 4 (12.7.86); So 7 (12.8.86); McCaul (1987: 103).

94. Mahlangu v Mahlangu and another 1989 (2) SA 132 (T); WM 2 (1.30.87), 3 (3.30.87), 2 (4.24.87); CP 1 (2.22.87), 1 (3.22.87); STr 25 (3.1.87). LRC attorneys were arrested three times, prohibited from entering the homeland, and forbidden to interview detainees. LRT (1988: 27–28).

95. C 14 (5.6.87), 21 (5.7.87); PN 5 (5.6.87), 22 (5.7.87); So 4 (5.7.87); WM 6 (5.8.87); WP (5.7.87); McCaul (1987: 104). South Africa expected to spend R5m on the stadium, R2.9m

on the Supreme Court, and R1.46m on a broadcasting center. *Hansard* cols. 1247–48 (reply by G. van N. Viljoen, Minister of Education and Development Aid to P.G. Soal, PFP) (4.21.86).

96. C 13 (5.8.87), 2 (5.9.87), 11 (5.11.87); BD 8 (5.7.87); PN 13 (5.22.87); WM 2 (5.15.87); McCaul (1987: 104).

97. Affidavits in support of the interdict application, Siphila Dlamini and others v KwaNdebele Minister of Justice and others, TPD Case No. 9298/87 (filed May 19); SSt 1 (5.24.87); G 9 (5.12.87); CP 1 (5.17.87); NN 1, 19 (5.21.87), 1 (5.28.87); PN 13 (5.22.87), 2 (5.29.87); BD 15 (5.27.87); C 3, 16 (5.28.87); CT 11 (5.28.87); McCaul (1987: 104); Finnegan (1988: 215–34).

98. C 5 (5.29.87); CT 3 (5.29.87); So 9 (5.29.87); NN 1 (5.28.87); WM 4 (6.5.87).

99. *Hansard* col. 51 (reply by J.C. Heunis, Minister of Constitutional Development and Planning, to P.G. Soal, PFP) (6.2.87).

100. *Hansard* cols. 23–24, 229–30 (P.W. Botha, State President; H. Suzman, PFP) (5.19, 21.87), col. 1127 (reply by J.C. Heunis, Minister of Constitutional Development and Planning, to P.G. Soal, PFP) (10.6.87); C 4 (6.3.87), 9 (6.10.87), 11 (6.16.87), 12 (6.17.87); PN 3 (6.10.87); CT 13 (6.10.87), 12 (6.17.87), 6 (6.20.87); So 2 (6.11.87); FM 28 (6.12.87); WM 11 (6.12.87); SSt 21 (6.14.87); A 26 (6.24.87).

101. Cornelius Mahlangu v KwaNdebele Commissioner of Police, TPD Case No. 16943/87; William Magolego v Mbhokotho and others, TPD Case No. 9121/87; Nomsa Mdaka v Lt C J Jones and others, TPD Case No. 11866/87; Thomas Ngwenya v Sibanyoni and others, TPD Case No. 11296/87; WM 6 (6.26.87), 2 (7.10.87), 3 (7.17.87); NN 1 (7.9.87); STi 19 (7.19.87).

102. BD 2 (7.20.87); WM 5 (7.31.87), 5 (8.7.87), 4 (8.14.87); CP 4 (11.8.87), 9 (12.6.87).

103. *Hansard* cols. 2574–87, 2653–55 (P.G. Soal, PFP; G. van N. Viljoen, Minister of Education and Development Aid) (7.29.87); PN 5 (7.30.87); C 4 (8.12.87); NN 2 (8.13.87); So 2 (9.9.87); G (9.22.87); GN 15, Umthetho Ogadangisiwe (9.14.87).

104. *Hansard* cols. 5736–37, 5811–12 (P.G. Soal, PFP; G. van N. Viljoen, Minister of Education and Development Aid) (9.11.87).

105. C 12 (9.23.87); FM 61 (9.25.87); BD 9 (9.26.87); St 9 (9.26.87); So 1 (9.24.87), (9.30.87).

106. C 15 (9.8.87); BD 5 (9.8.87); Government of Lebowa v Government of the Republic of South Africa and Another 1988 (1) SA 344 (A) (Grosskopf, J, with Rabie, CJ, and Joubert, Hefer and Vivier, JJ).

107. C 13 (9.30.87); CT 5 (9.30.87); So 7 (9.30.87).

108. Wm 3 (10.2.87); CP 2 (10.11.87).

109. Gibson Thlokwe Mathebe and others v KwaNdebele Commissioner of Police and another, TPD Case No. 14181/87.

110. WM 10 (3.4.88).

111. *Hansard* cols. 839–71 (M.J.D. van Wyk, C.J. Darby–Lewis, CP; P.G. Soal, PFP; G. van N. Viljoen, Minister of Education and Development Aid) (2.15.88). NP backbenchers and the PFP had opposed the incorporation two years earlier, *Hansard* cols. 5188, 11657–82 (M.H. Veldman, NP; H. Suzman, PFP) (5.7.86, 9.5.86).

112. *Hansard* cols. 360–62, 961–86 (J.A. Rabie, P.A.S. Mopp, UDP; G. van N. Viljoen, Minister of Education and Development Aid) (2.9, 15,88). Debate in the House of Delegates was perfunctory, *Hansard* cols. 1363–77 (2.17.88). C 10 (12.18.87), 4 (2.16.88); BD 4 (2.16.88); PN 2 (12.19.87); WM 7 (4.8.88), 8 (11.20.92, 16 (11.27.92).

113. Chief Gibson Tlokwe Mathebe v KwaNdebele Minister of Law & Order and another, TPD Case No. 3593/88.

114. Chief Gibson Tlokwe Mathebe v KwaNdebele Minister of Law and Order and another, TPD Case No. 3594/88.

115. Interview with John Dugard (July 1991); STi 2 (3.6.88); CT 3 (3.7.88); C 13 (3.8.88); BD 3 (3.8.88); NN 5 (3.17.88); Written Representations (1988: 43).

116. Mathebe v Regering van die Republiek van Suid–Afrika en andere 1988 (3) SA 667 (A) (Grosskopf, J., with Viljoen, Hefer, Vivier, and Boshoff, JJ); C 11 (3.30.88); BD 3 (3.30.88); FM 42 (4.8.88).

117. WM 2 (3.31.88); PN 2 (4.12.88); STi 12 (4.10.88); CP 5 (4.10.88); So 6 (4.5.88).

118. WM 4 (4.29.88); STi 2 (5.1.88); A 6 (5.4.88), 11 (5.20.88); PN 6, 16 (5.24.88), 14 (5.26.88); BD 12 (4.28.88); So 12 (4.5.88), 6 (4.28.88); interview with John Dugard (July 1991).

119. *Hansard* cols. 9298, 12935–36 (D. Lockey, LP) (5.9.88, 6.2.88).

120. *Hansard* col. 9569 (S. Pachai, PPSA, Deputy Minister of Environment Affairs) (5.10.88).

121. *Hansard* col. 9578 (G. van N. Viljoen, Minister of Education and Development Aid) (5.10.88).

122. *Hansard* col. 12316 (M. Rajab, PFP) (6.1.88).

123. *Hansard* cols. 12383–86 (W.C. Malan, NDM) (6.2.88).

124. *Hansard* cols. 12405, 12586–89 (H. Suzman, PFP; J.C. Heunis, Minister of Constitutional Development and Planning) (6.2–3.88).

125. *Hansard* col. 12955 (J.C. Heunis, Minister of Constitutional Development and Planning) (6.6.88).

126. Proc. R104, GG 11360 (6.24.88); *Hansard* col. 1964 (reply by J.C. Heunis, Minister of Constitutional Development and Planning, to H. Suzman, PFP) (6.28.88); A 10 (6.10.88); FT 54 (6.10.88); NN 3 (9.15.88); Written Representations (1988).

127. December 2, 1987, *Hansard* col. 737 (reply by J.C. Heunis, Minister of Constitutional Development and Planning, to H. Suzman, PFP) (3.25.88). For the history of Botshabelo, see Colin Murray (1992).

128. *Hansard* col. 5792 (G. van N. Viljoen, Minister of Education and Development Aid) (9.11.87).

129. Proc. R169 (12.2.87); *Hansard* cols. 418, 669 (replies by J.C.G. Botha, Minister of Home Affairs, and G. van N. Viljoen, Minister of Education and Development Aid to P.C. Cronjé, PFP) (2.23.87, 8.25.87); C 19 (12.3.87); So (12.7.87); G (12.11.87); WM 7 (12.4.87), 3 (1.22.88); NCAR (n.d.).

130. *Hansard* cols. 833, 9044–45 (N.J.J. Oliver, P.G. Soal, PFP) (5.4–5.88); col. 737 (reply by J.C. Heunis, Minister of Constitutional Development and Planning, to H. Suzman, PFP) (3.25.88).

131. *Hansard* cols. 9299–300 (G.L. Leeuw, LP) (5.9.88).

132. *Hansard* col. 9306 (G. van N. Viljoen, Minister of Education and Development Aid) (5.9.88).

133. Lefuo v Staatspresident en 'n ander 1989 (3) SA 924 (O) (Malherbe, J, with Hattingh and Findlay, JJ); Plaskett (1990b).

134. WM 4 (9.2.88); CP 10 (10.15.88).

135. *Hansard* cols. 6830–31 (G. van N. Viljoen, Minister of Education and Development Aid) (4.29.89).

136. Bill 76–89(GA). *Hansard* cols. 4898, 9486, 9887–9928, 10625–30, 10658–61, 10671 (4.6, 5.12, 22, 26.89); WM 5 (4.21.89).

137. Staatspresident en 'n Ander v Lefuo 1990 (2) SA 679 (A).

138. WM 15 (4.28.89).

139. C 23 (1.26.89), 11 (12.8.90).

140. Paulina Machika en vier ander v Die Staatspresident en 16 ander, TPD Case No. 17864/87; WM 7 (10.30.87); L 7 (11.8.87).

141. Nomsa Mdaka v W O Magangwa and others, TPD Case No. 17726/87.

142. Affidavits in Paledi Mathebe and another v Minister of Law and Order and others, TPD Case No. ?/87; WM 4 (11.6.87).

143. TPD Case No. 20066/87; WM 3 (12.24.87), 5 (1.15.88).

144. Peter Thabo Ncube v Minister of Law and Order and others, TPD Case No. 20813/87; David Mabosa Mahlangu v KwaNdebele Commissioner of Poliice and another, TPD Case No. 2598/88; WM 2 (1.15.88), 1 (2.19.88); NN 1 (2.18.88).

145. *Hansard* col. 8644 (P.W. Botha, State President) (5.3.88).

146. C 12 (4.9.88); PN 2 (4.9.88), 1 (5.19.88); DN 3 (4.14.88); CT 9 (4.15.88); NW 4 (4.16.88); So 10 (4.21.88); *Hansard* col. 1358 (reply by J.C. Heunis, Minister of Constitutional Development and Planning, to W.J.D. van Wyk, CP) (5.10.88), cols. 12629–30 (P.G. Soal, PFP) (6.3.88).

147. Interview with Geoffrey Budlender (July 1991); BD 3 (4.29.88); PN 4 (4.29.88); So 1 (4.29.88); SSt 2 (5.1.88).

148. Machika en andere v Staatspresident en andere 1989 (4) SA 19 (T). I am grateful to Cherie van Onselen for translating the Afrikaans judgment; I have slightly modified her wording.

149. CT 5 (5.21.88), 4 (5.25.88), 4 (5.26.88); C 9 (5.21.88), 12 (5.26.88); CP 1 (5.22.88), 11 (5.29.88); So 4 (5.27.88); STr 7 (5.22.88); FM 47 (5.27.88); WM 11 (6.3.88).

150. *Hansard* cols. 15125–46 (C.W. Eglin, PFP; J.W. Maree, NP) (6.29.88).

151. *Hansard* cols. 15164–84) (J.C. Heunis, Minister of Constitutional Development and Planning; L.T. Landers, LP, Deputy Minister of Population Development; T. Abrahams, LP) (6.29.88).

152. *Hansard* cols. 15216–28 (6.29.88).

153. PN (6.24.88); C 8 (6.28.88), 8 (6.30.88), 10 (8.11.88), 10 (8.24.88), 8 (9.8.88); BD 5 (8.24.88); A 8 (6.28.88), 10 (6.29.88), 4 (8.11.88), 6 (8.24.88); *Hansard* cols. 15233, 15407–30, 16327–33 (8.19, 23.88, 9.2, 7.88).

154. A 2 (9.16.88); SSt 6 (9.18.88).

155. Umthetho Ogadandigisiwe No. 131 (11.4.88).

156. PN 14 (11.15.88).

157. So 3 (12.7.88), 3 (1.12.89), 1 (2.8.89); PN 12 (12.8.88), 5 (12.9.88); WM 6 (12.15.88); FM 25 (12.23.88), 48 (2.17.89); NN 2 (12.22.88); St 4 (1.12.89), 4 (1.14.89).

158. TPD Cases No. 331/87, 2780/87, 6631/87, 8298/87, 9121/87, 9205/87, 11866/87, 12813/87, 14607/87, 16943/87, 17726/87, 20066/87, 20134/87, 20239/87, 20813/87, 400/88, 2598/88, 4679/88, 16369/88, 16943/88, 507/89, 934/89. St 19 (9.28.89), 2 (9.29.89), 2 (10.12.89), 2 (10.19.89), 2 (11.1.89), 3 (11.3.89), 2 (11.8.89), 3 (11.28.89), 3 (2.21.90), 3 (4.3.90), 3 (4.20.90); WM 3 (12.1.89), 3 (9.21.90); LRC (1989).

159. St 2 (11.6.89).

160. St 3 (5.4.90); BD 4 (5.4.90).

161. GN 549, GG 8825 (7.20.83).

162. *Hansard* cols. 11337–45, 11392–412, 11657–82 (9.1,–2, 5.86) (R.A.F. Swart, PFP; H.J. Tempel, NP; F. Hartzenberg, CP).

163. *Hansard* cols. 4142–60 (P.G.Soal, PFP; J.H.W. Mentz, NP; G. van N. Viljoen, Minister of Education and Development Aid) (8.19.87).

164. On the appointment of chiefs, see D. Unterhalter (1990).

165. Proc. R220, GG 11644 (12.30.88); Proc. 15, Bophuthatswana GG 264 (12.30.88); Pupsey Ntsanyana Sebogodi v State President and another, TPD Case No. 19332/88; for background on Bophuthatswana, see Butler et al. (1977).

166. All facts extraneous to the trial are taken from memoranda by attorneys Clive Plasket (Cheadle Thompson & Haysom, 5.89), James Sutherland and Greg Nott (Bell Dewar & Hall, 5.89), Clive Plasket and Brendan Barry to Deputy Minister of Foreign Affairs (6.91), Clive Plasket to Cosatu (1991), J. Wills and Tefo Raditapole (1.10.91), and WM 5 (3.31.89), 3 (8.4.89), 5 (8.11.89).

167. WM 5 (3.31.89), 5 (7.14.89), 3 (8.4.89), 5 (8.11.89).

168. *Hansard* cols. 6792–94, 6799, 6840–41 (P.G. Soal, PFP; L.C. Abrahams, LP; G. van N. Viljoen, Minister of Education and Development Aid) (4.26.89).

169. Nkgokoloane Dadelik Majafa v State President and others, TPD Case No. 13145/89.

170. Black Sash (1990: 30).

171. WM 1 (7.6.89), 5 (7.14.89), 3, 7 (7.27.89); Black Sash (1990: 30); National Land Committee (1990a).

172. *Hansard* cols. 9142–43, 9280–310 (C.J. van der Merwe, Minister of Development Aid; J. Douw, LP) (5.15–16.90).

173. Hughes (1971).

174. For an account of such practices in the Ciskei, see Haysom (1983).

175. Among the many fruitless lawsuits seeking to halt state violence, see Jacob Mnyakeni v KwaNdebele Minister of Law and Order and others, TPD Case No. 19407/86; Siphila Dlamini and others v KwaNdebele Minister of Justice and others, TPD Case No. 8298/87; Thomas Ngwenya v Sibanyoni and others, TPD Case No. 11296/87; Mary Tshabalala v KwaNdebele Minister of Justice, Law and Order, TPD Case No. 14607/87; Paledi Mathebe and another v Minister of Law and Order and others, TPD Case No ?/87; Ramotlogedi Johannes Makitla v State President and others, TPD Case No. 408/88; Frans Nkopodi Phatlane v State President and others, TPD Case No. 5729/88; David Maboa Mahlangu v KwaNdebele Commissioner of Police and another, TPD Case No. 2598/88.

176. *Hansard* cols. 243–44 (J.H. Hoon, CP) 2.5.86).

Chapter 12: DISESTABLISHING OUKASIE

1. GN 775 (5.11.28); GN 999 (6.15.28). Unless otherwise noted, all information about Oukasie is from Bekker et al. (1988); for other accounts of these events, see Morris (1986; 1989; 1990).

2. Axelrod et al. (1986: 1–2).

3. *Brits Pos* 1 (4.10.70) (translated from Afrikaans).

4. WM 5 (5.9.86).

5. TRAC (1986b: 2).

6. FM (2.28.86); Currin et al. (1991: 20); Bekker et al. (1988: 13); *Hansard* col. 822 (reply by J.C. Heunis, Minister of Constitutional Development and Planning, to P.G. Soal, PFP) (9.9.87).

7. TRAC (1986b: 4); SSt (4.23.86).

8. St (5.30.86), 3A (2.6.90); BD (2.27.86); C (5.29.86); CP (7.1.86); WM 5 (3.14.86); TRAC (1986b: 5); Bekker et al. (1988: 14).

9. BD (2.28.86); St (2.28.86), (3.12.86); FM (2.28.86); *Hansard* cols. 233–35 (reply by J.C. Heunis, Minister of Constitutional Development and Planning, to R.A.F. Swart, PFP) (2.27.86).

10. St 7 (3.27.86); TRAC (1986b: 4); Axelrod et al. (1986).

11. Unless otherwise noted, all information is taken from the founding affidavit.

12. BD (4.10.86); St 4.11.86).

13. M J Mahlaela v M B de Beer 1986 (4) SA 732 (T).

14. So (4.24.86); St (4.24.86), 1 (4.25.86).

15. St (5.19.86); BD (5.14.86); CP (6.1.86). *The Sunday Star* 19 (10.26.86) reported incorrectly that Mahlaela still had no house.

16. CT (5.22.86).

17. WM (5.30.86), 4 (10.24.86); C (5.29.86); St (5.30.86), (6.6.86); CP (6.1.86); TRAC (1986b: 5).

18. Quoted in Axelrod et al. (1986: 4–5).

19. Axelrod et al. (1986); Morris (1986: 47); BD 5 (12.3.86).

20. GN 2177 (10.17.86).

21. During the 1986 debate on repeal a PFP MP said: "The amendment of section 5 of the Black Administration Act as well as the repeal of the Blacks (Urban Areas) Act...means that the legal machinery for the forced removal of Blacks is now being done away with." *Hansard* col. 7671 (N.J.J. Olivier, PFP) (6.9.86).

22. C (10.17.86); BD (10.17.86); St (10.17.86), (11.26.86); SSt 19 (10.26.86); FM 31 (10.31.86).

23. STi 19 (10.26.86); CP 5 (11.11.86).

24. NYT A3 (10.18.86); St (10.18.86), (10.24.86); So (10.20.86), 14 (10.23.86), 4, 12 (10.27.86); CT 2 (10.20.86); C (10.20.86), 13 (10.23.86); PN 1 (10.21.86); STi 19 (10.26.86); SSt 19 (10.26.86); BD 7 (10.28.86); FM 62 (10.24.86); NN 2 (10.23.86).

25. FM 62 (10.24.86); SSt 19 (10.26.86); PN 17 (10.28.86), 10 (11.11.86); St (10.20.86); EPH 12 (10.30.86); STi (10.26.86); So 4 (10.23.86), 4 (10.28.86), 15 (10.31.86); WM (10.24.86).

26. C 11 (10.29.86), 12 (10.30.86); So 15 (10.31.86); CP 8 (11.2.86); FM 31 (10.31.86), 48 (11.7.86).

27. NYT (10.17.86), A15 (10.20.86), (11.3.86), (11.23.86). The last also described removals from Langa, Lawaaikamp, Duncan Village, and Red Location.

28. WP (10.17.86); CSM 1 (11.19.86).

29. SSt 19 (10.10.86); FM (11.7.86); C 2 (11.15.86).

30. PN 9 (11.4.86), 5 (11.5.86), 17 (11.11.86); FM 48 (11.7.86); So 3 (11.7.86); CP 2 (11.9.86).

31. St (11.17.86), (11.19.86), (11.26.86); So 7 (11.19.86), 3 (11.25.86); NN (11.20.86); PN 3 (11.21.86), (11.27.86).

32. So (12.3.86); BD 3 (12.3.86); St (12.3.86), (12.4.86); C (12.3.86).

33. BD 4 (12.29.86).

34. PN 7 (12.17.86). The other probably was *The Citizen* (1.1.87).

35. T (1.19.87).

36. BD (1.16.87), 7 (4.14.87); St (1.16.87), (2.24.87); So 4 (1.20.87), (4.10.87); PN 3 (1.21.87), 17 (1.22.87); NN 3 (4.9.87).

37. *Hansard* cols. 216, 303 (reply by J.C. Heunis, Minister of Constitutional Development and Planning, to E.K. Moorcroft, PFP) (2.23.87); St (3.5.87); FM 47 (3.20.87).

38. NN (3.12.87); So 3 (3.19.87); St 12 (3.10.87), 5 (3.12.87); BD 6 (3.9.87); CT 13 (5.11.87); Bekker et al. (1988: 4).

39. *Hansard* cols. 872, 1088, 1360 (replies by P.J. Badenhorst, Deputy Minister of Development Planning and C.J. van der Merwe, Deputy Minister of Constitutional Planning, to C.J. Derby–Lewis and A. Gerber, CP) (9.9.87, 9.15.87, 10.6.87); C 4 (9.16.87), (10.7.87).

40. FM 54 (10.30.87); So 4 (10.19.87); St (11.3.87).

41. BD 1 (1.12.88).

42. *San Jose Mercury News* §B (1.20.88); *San Francisco Chronicle* (1.20.88); *In These Times* (1.21.88); St (1.21.88); So 5 (1.22.88); PN 9 (1.25.88).

43. H. Suzman (1993: 203–04); *Hansard* col. 271 (2.9.88).

44. St 5 (2.24.88), (2.29.88); NN 8 (3.3.88); FM 67–68 (3.25.88); Co–op News 12 (3.9.88) (Berkeley).

45. St (3.27.88), 10 (3.30.88), 3 (3.31.88), 6 (4.4.88); CT 4 (3.29.88); WM 2 (3.31.88), 7 (4.8.88); So 7 (3.30.88); WSJ (3.30.88); PN 10 (3.31.88); *Hansard* cols. 600, 731 (reply by J.C. Heunis, Minister of Constitutional Development and Planning, to A. Gerber and C.J. Derby–Lewis, CP) (3.22, 25.88).

46. *Hansard* cols. 5897–5902, 5959–86 (G. van N. Viljoen, Minister of Education and Development Aid; A. Gerber, CP) (4.14–15.88)

47. GN 25–26, GG 1–13 (4.26.88).

48. St 1 (4.27.88), 11 (4.28.88); BD (4.27.88), 2 (4.28.88); CT 7 (4.29.88); So 5–6 (4.29.88); STi 2 (5.1.88); SSt 13 (5.8.88); PN 12 (4.29.88).

49. So 18 (5.25.88); St 3 (5.30.88), 3 (6.2.88); C 2 (5.30.88); STr 7 (5.29.88); *Hansard* col. 1372 (reply by J.C. Heunis, Minister of Constitutional Development and Planning, to S.S. van der Merwe, PFP) (5.10.88), cols. 11261–64, 12405–06 (H. Suzman, PFP; J.C. Heunis, Minister of Constitutional Development and Planning) (5.23.88, 6.2.88).

50. Mufson (1990: 291–93).

51. Currin et al. (1991: 11, 13–15); Morris (1990: 58, 61–63). Police never identified the attackers. There is a striking parallel to the 1983 police killing of Saul Mkhize, who led resistance to the removal of Driefontein. See White (1988: 722).

52. Bekker et al. (1988); Barron et al. (1988).

53. *Hansard* col. 2274 (reply by J.C. Heunis, Minister of Constitutional Development and Planning, to K.M. Andrew, PFP) (9.28.88).

54. CP 4 (11.6.88).

55. Joseph Makama and others v Administrator of the Transvaal, TPD Case No. 19317/88; St 4 (1.4.89); CT 6 (1.7.89); CP 2 (1.15.89).

56. CP 15 (1.22.89); So 9 (4.13.89).

57. *Hansard* cols. 324, 490 (replies by J.C. Heunis, Minister of Constitutional Development and Planning, to J.J. Walsh, PFP and A. Gerber, CP) (3.13, 21.89).

58. NN 4 (7.28.89); PN 5 (8.3.89), 3 (8.4.89); C 4 (8.3.89), 12 (8.4.89).

59. Hleka v Johannesburg City Council 1949 (1) SA 842 (A).

60. So 5 (8.9.89); PN 3, 9 (8.9.89); BD 2 (8.10.89); SSt 13 (8.13.89).

61. St 2, 8, 9 (8.9.89); PN 8 (8.9.89); BD 2 (8.9.89).

62. STi (8.13.89).

63. So 7 (8.14.89), 6 (8.15.89); St 3 (8.14.89); Morris (1990: 51).

64. CP 5 (10.1.89); St 2 (12.15.89), 3 (1.12.90), 10 (4.13.91); So 2 (1.29.90), 5 (6.12.90), 2 (7.26.90), 9 (4.11.91); C 10 (5.23.90), 13 (6.21.90), 4 (4.11.91); PN 2 (4.11.91); NN 18 (6.7.90), 3 (4.12.91); Currin et al. (1991: 11).

65. C 4 (1.26.91); St 5 (1.28.91); So 4 (1.28.91).

66. NN 5 (2.1.91); PN 2 (4.13.91); CP 11 (5.19.91); Ngale & Budlender (1991); Bouwer Viljoen Inc. (1991).

67. BD 13 (2.28.92); St 3 (3.2.92); NN 9 (3.13.92); So 3 (11.20.92); FW 24 (12.3.92).

68. This sense of belonging, which is found in working class and ethnic neighborhoods in the West, emerges most vividly in fiction and autobiography, e.g., Mphahlele (1967; 1971); Mattera (1987); Rive (1986); Mathabane (1986).

69. See Black Sash (1988b); G. Budlender (1988b); Roos (1988; 1989); C. Lewis (1989); O'Regan (1989; 1990); Keightley (1990); Swilling et al. (1991); Crankshaw (1993).

Chapter 13: THE ROLES OF LAW

1 See Lodge et al. (1991: 289-314).

2 Exemplified in such titles as "Time Longer Than Rope" (Roux, 1964); "Endgame in South Africa?" (Cohen, 1986); "Can South Africa Survive? Five Minutes to Midnight" (Brewer,

1989b); "South Africa: No Turning Back" (Johnson, 1988); and "The Mirror at Midnight: A South African Journal" (Hochschild, 1990).

3 Gilbey (1993: ch. 14).

4 On the difficulty of testing theories of legitimation, see Hyde (1983); for attempts to apply such theories to South Africa, see Ashforth (1990); D. Davis (1990c); Friedrichs (1990; 1992).

5 Berman (1950).

6 Mandela (1964).

7 WM (2.3.89).

8 Diar (1990: chaps. 4, 17).

REFERENCES

Abbreviations

CALS: Centre for Applied Legal Studies
CIIR: Catholic Institute for International Relations
HRC: Human Rights Commission
HSRC: Human Sciences Research Council
ICJ: International Commission of Jurists
LRC: Legal Resources Centre
LRT: Legal Resources Trust
NCAR: National Committee Against Removals
NLC: National Land Committee
SAIRR: South African Institute of Race Relations
SAJHR: South African Journal on Human Rights
SALB: South African Labour Bulletin
SALJ: South African Law Journal
SAR: South African Review
SPROCAS: Study Project of Christianity in Apartheid Society
THRHR: Tydskrif vir Hedendaagse Romeinse–Hollandse Reg
TRAC: Transvaal Rural Action Committee

Abel, Richard L. 1985a. "Law Without Politics: Legal Aid under Advanced Capitalism," 32 UCLA Law Review 474.

_____. 1985b. "Lawyers and the Power to Change," 7(1) Law & Policy (special issue).

Acta Juridica. 1979. "The First International Conference on Human Rights in South Africa," [1979] Acta Juridica.

African National Congress. 1989. "Constitutional Guidelines for a Democratic South Africa," 5 SAJHR 129.

_____. 1991. "A Discussion Document on the Structure of a Constitution for a Democratic South Africa," 7 SAJHR 233.

Akerson, David J. 1989. "An Inquest–Law Inquest," 5 SAJHR 209.

Albertyn, Cathi. 1986. "Forced Removals and the Law: The Magopa Case," 2 SAJHR 91.

_____. 1991. A Critical Analysis of Political Trials in South Africa, 1948–88. Ph.D. dissertation, law, University of Cambridge.

Albertyn, Cathi and Dennis Davis. 1990. "The censure of 'communism' and the political trial in South Africa," in Sumner.

Alexandra Joint Negotiating Forum. 1991. The Alexandra Accord. Johannesburg: Storyteller Communications.

Allen, Francis A. 1974. The Crime of Politics: Political Dimensions of Criminal Justice. Cambridge, Mass.: Harvard University Press.

Amnesty International. 1986. Imprisonment under the Pass Laws. New York: Amnesty International.

_____. 1987. Argentina: The Military Juntas and Human Rights. Report of the Trial of the Former Junta Members, 1985. London: Amnesty International Publications.

_____. 1992. South Africa, State of Fear: Security force complicity in torture and political killings, 1990–1992. London: Amnesty International.

Anon. 1972. The State v. The Dean of Johannesburg. Johannesburg: SAIRR (prepared by a member of the legal profession).

Antonio, R.J. 1972. "The Processual Dimension of Degradation Ceremonies: The Chicago Conspiracy Trial: Success or Failure?" 23 British Journal of Sociology 287.

Arendt, Hannah. 1977. Eichmann in Jerusalem. New York: Penguin.

Armstrong, Amanda. 1987. "'Hear No Evil, See No Evil, Speak No Evil': Media Restrictions and the State of Emergency," 4 SAR 199.

_____. 1989. "Media Restrictions and the State of Emergency," in Haysom & Plaskett.

Arnold, Thurman. 1935. The Symbols of Government. New Haven: Yale University Press.

_____. 1937. The Folklore of Capitalism. New Haven: Yale University Press.

Aron, Nan. 1989. Liberty and Justice for All: Public Interest Law in the 1980s and Beyond. Boulder, Colo.: Westview Press.

Ashforth, Adam. 1990. The Politics of Official Discourse in Twentieth–Century South Africa. Oxford: Clarendon Press.

Association of Democratic Journalists. 1989. Standing on the Truth. Johannesburg: ADJ.

Atchison, John. 1988. Numbering the Dead: Political Violence in the Pietermaritzburg Region. Pietermaritzburg: Centre for Adult Education, University of Natal.

Attenborough, Richard. 1987. Richard Attenborough's Cry Freedom: A Pictorial Record. New York: Knopf.

Auerbach, Jerold S. 1976. Unequal Justice: Lawyers and Social Change in Modern America. New York: Oxford University Press.

Augustyn, Tess and Sandra Marais. n.d. Preliminary Report on a Socio–Economic Survey Done in Alexandra. Pretoria: UNISA (University of South Africa), Department of Sociology.

Axelrod, M., P. Axelrod, G. Faller, N. Legge, A. Morris, G. Mendelowitz, L. Mostert and L. Platzky. 1986. Upgrading the Brits Old Location: Feasibility Report. Brits: Brits Action Committee and Brits branches of MAWU and NAAWU.

Balbus, Isaac. D. 1973. The Dialectics of Legal Repression: Black Rebels before the American Criminal Courts. New York: Russell Sage.

Bam, Fikile, 1984. "A New Trend towards Legal Reform in South Africa (The Hoexter Commission's Report)" (unpublished).

_____. 1985. Poverty Law in South Africa: Perspectives from the Second Carnegie Enquiry into Poverty and Development in Southern Africa (unpublished).

Bannan, John F. and Rosemary S. Bannan. 1974. Law, Morality and Vietnam: The Peace Militants and the Courts. Bloomington: Indiana University Press.

Barberton Commission. 1984. Report of the Committee of Inquiry into the Events at the Barberton Maximum Security Prison (Town) on 20 and 30 September 1983 and Related Matters. Pretoria: Government Printer.

Barkan, Steven E. 1977. "Political Trials and the *Pro Se* Defendant in the Adversary System," 24 Social Problems 324.

_____. 1985. Protesters on Trial: Criminal Justice in the Southern Civil Rights and Vietnam Antiwar Movements. New Brunswick, N.J.: Rutgers University Press.

Barnes, Julian. 1993. The Porcupine. New York: Vintage.

Barron, Peter, Eric Buch, Paulo Ferinho and John Gear. 1988. Medical Survey of Community Health in Oukasie. Johannesburg: Community Agency for Social Enquiry.

Baskin, Jeremy. 1991. Striking Back: A History of Cosatu. London: Verso.

Baskir, Lawrence M. and William A. Strauss. 1978. Chance and Circumstance: The Draft, the War, and the Vietnam Generation. New York: Vintage.

Basson, Dion. 1987. "Judicial Activism in a State of Emergency: An Examination of Recent Decisions of the South African Courts," 3 SAJHR 28.

Baxter, Lawrence G. 1984. Administrative Law. Cape Town: Juta.

_____. 1985a. "Section 29 of the Internal Security Act and the Rule of Law," 1985 Reality 5.

_____. 1985b. "Legal Education and Public Policy," 1 Natal University Law and Society Review 15.

_____. 1985c. "Doctors on Trial: Steve Biko, Medical Ethics and the Courts," 1 SAJHR 137.

Becker, Theodore L., ed. 1971. Political Trials. New York: Bobbs–Merrill.

Beinart, B. 1962. "The Rule of Law," [1962] Acta Juridica 99.

Bekker, Simon, Alan Morris, Mark Orkin, Marshall Buys, Geoff Budlender and Anthea Jeffery. 1988. Socio–Economic Sample Survey of Oukasie. Johannesburg: Community Agency for Social Enquiry.

Belknap, Michael R. 1978. Cold War Political Justice: The Smith Act, the CIA, and American Civil Liberties. New York: Greenwood Press.

_____. 1981. American Political Trials. New York: Greenwood Press.

Bell, A.D. and R.D.A. Mackie, eds. 1985. Detention and Security Legislation in South Africa. Durban: Centre for Adult Education, University of Natal.

Bell, Derrick. 1987. And We Are Not Saved. New York: Basic Books.

Bell, Geoff et al. 1977. The Battle of Grunwick.

Bendix, Sonia. 1989. Industrial Relations in South Africa. Johannesburg: Juta.

_____. 1992. Industrial Relations in South Africa (2nd ed.). Johannesburg: Juta.

Benjamin, Paul. 1987. "Trade Unions and the Industrial Court," 4 SAR 253.

_____. 1989. "Re–establishing Managerial Power? Changing Patterns in Labour Law," 5 SAR 275.

Benjamin, Paul, Reagan Jacobus and Chris Albertyn, eds. 1989. Strikes, Lock–outs and Arbitration in South African Labour Law: Proceedings of the Labour Law Conference 1988. Johannesburg: Juta.

Bennett, T.W., D.J. Devine, D.B. Hutchinson, I. Leeman and D. van Zyl Smit. 1988. Law under Stress: South African Law in the 1980s. Cape Town: Juta.

Bennhold, Martin. 1989. "Lawyers in Exile," 17 International Journal of the Sociology of Law 63.

Bennun, M.E. 1993. "Boipatong and After: Reflections on the Politics of Violence in South Africa," 21 International Journal of the Sociology of Law 49.

Berat, Lynn. n.d. Legal Aid and the Indigent Accused in South Africa: A Proposal for Reform (unpublished).

_____. 1989. "Doctors, Detainees and Torture: Medical Ethics v. the Law in South Africa," 25 Stanford Journal of International Law 499.

_____. 1991. "The South African Judiciary and the Protection of Human Rights: A Strategy for a New South Africa," 5 Temple International and Comparative Law Journal 181.

Berman, Harold J. 1950. Justice in Russia: an interpretation of Soviet law. Cambridge, Mass.: Harvard University Press.

Bernstein, H. 1972. South Africa: The Terrorism of Torture. London: Christian Action Publications.

Bernstein, Helen. 1989. The World That Was Ours: The Story of the Rivonia Trial. London: SAWriters.

Bernstein, Hilda. 1978. No 46—Steve Biko. London: International Defence and Aid Fund.

Bernstein, Richard. 1992. "French Collaborators: The New Debate," 39(12) New York Review of Books 37.

Bindman, Geoffrey, ed. 1988. South Africa: Human Rights and the Rule of Law. London: Pinter.

Bisharat, George Emile. 1989. Palestinian Lawyers and Israeli Rule: Law and Disorder in the West Bank. Austin: University of Texas Press.

Bjornland, Eric C. 1990. "The Devil's Work? Judicial Review under a Bill of Rights in South Africa and Namibia," 26 Stanford Journal of International Law 391.

Blaauw, Loammi C. 1989. "Alternatives to Military Service," 5 SAJHR 240.

Black, Michael. 1992. "Alan Paton and the Rule of Law," 91 African Affairs 53.

Black Sash. 1983a. Circular No. 18 (December 1). Johannesburg: Black Sash.

_____. 1983b. Diary of Events at Mogopa since 18th November 1983 (December 14). Johannesburg: Black Sash.

_____. 1986. Working Notes for Advice Offices (unpublished).

_____. 1988a. "Greenflies": Municipal Police in the East Cape. Johannesburg: Black Sash.

_____. 1988b. Of Squattters, Slums, Group Areas, and Homelessness. Johannesburg: Black Sash.

_____. 1990. Grasping the Prickly Pear: The Bophuthatswana Story. Johannesburg: Black Sash.

Blair, Jon. 1978. The Biko Inquest. London: Rex Collins.

Blom–Cooper, L.J. 1959. "The South African Treason Trial: R v. Adams and others," 8 International and Comparative Law Quarterly 59.

Boetie, Dugmore. 1989. Familiarity Is the Kingdom of the Lost. New York: Four Walls Eight Windows.

Bonner, David. 1985. Emergency Powers in Peacetime. London: Sweet & Maxwell.

Bonnin, Debbie and Ari Sitas. 1988. "Lessons from the Sarmcol Strike," in Cobbett & Cohen.

Boulle, J.J. 1985. "The Inscrutable Face of the Ministerial Sphinx," 102 SALJ 264.

_____. 1987. "Constitutional Law in South Africa, 1976–1986," [1987] Acta Juridica 55.

Bouwer Viljoen Inc. 1991. Application to Independent Development Trust for Capital Subsidy Scheme Funding for Upgrading and Extension of Oukasie (unpublished).

Boyle, Kevin, Tom Hadden and Paddy Hillyard. 1975. Law and State: The Case of Northern Ireland. London: Martin Robertson.

_____. 1980. Ten Years On in Northern Ireland. London: Cobden Trust.

Branch, Taylor. 1988. Parting the Waters: America in the King Years, 1954–1963. New York: Simon and Schuster.

Brassey, M.S.M., H. Cheadle, E. Cameron and M.P. Olivier. 1987. The New Labour Law: Strikes, Dismissals and the Unfair Labour Practice in South African Law. Cape Town: Juta.

Brewer, John D. 1987. After Soweto: An Unfinished Journey. New York: Oxford University Press.

_____. 1989a. "Internal Black Protest," in Brewer (1989b).

_____, ed. 1989b. Can South Africa Survive? Five Minutes to Midnight. London: Macmillan.

Breytenbach, Breyten. 1984. The True Confessions of an Albino Terrorist. London: Faber and Faber.

Brittain, Victoria and Abdul S. Minty, eds. 1988. Children of Resistance. Statements from the Harare Conference on Children, Repression and the Law in Apartheid South Africa. London: Kliptown Books.

Brogden, M.E. 1989. "The Origins of the South African Police—Institutional versus Structural Approaches." [1989] Acta Juridica 1.

Brogden, Mike and Clifford Shearing. 1993. Policing for a New South Africa. New York: Routledge.

Bronner, Ethan. 1989. Battle for Justice: How the Bork Nomination Shook America. New York: W.W. Norton.

Brookes, E. and J.B. Macauley. 1958. Civil Liberty in South Africa. Cape Town: Oxford University Press.

Bruinders, Timothy. 1988. "The Unrepresented Accused in the Lower Courts: S v Radebe; S v Mbonani 1988 (1) SA 191 (T)," 4 SAJHR 239.

Budlender, Debbie. 1989. Assessing US Corporate Disinvestment: The CASE Report for the Equal Opportunity Foundation. Braamfontein: Community Agency for Social Enquiry.

Budlender, Geoff. 1984. "Lawyers and Poverty: Beyond `Access to Justice.'" Second Carnegie Inquiry into Poverty and Development in Southern Africa (Conference Paper No. 91) (unpublished).

_____. 1985. "Incorporation and Exclusion: Recent Developments in Labour Law and Influx Control," 1 SAJHR 3.

_____. 1986. "Influx Control in the Western Cape: From Pass Laws to Passports," 11(8) SALB 34 (Sept/Oct).

_____. 1988a." Law and Lawlessness in South Africa," 4 SAJHR 139.

_____. 1988b. "South African Legal Approaches to Squatting," 242 De Rebus 160.

_____. 1988c. "On Practising Law," in Corder.

_____. 1988d. Defining and Focussing the Casework of the LRC (unpublished).

_____. 1989. "On Citizenship and Residence Rights: Taking Words Seriously," 5 SAJHR 37.

_____. 1990. "Urban Land Issues in the 1980s: The View from Weiler's Farm," in Murray & O'Regan.

_____. n.d. Lawyers, Conflict and Social Justice (unpublished).

Bumiller, Kristin. 1988. The Civil Rights Society: The Social Construction of Victims. Baltimore, Md.: Johns Hopkins University Press.

Burchell, Jonathan. 1988. "Contempt of Court by the Media: Another Opportunity to Extend Press Freedom is Lost: S v Harber 1988 (3) SA 396 (A)," 4 SAJHR 375.

Burdzik, Jean and Dawid van Wyk. 1987. "Apartheid Legislation 1976–1986," [1987] Acta Juridica 119.

Burman, Sandra. 1989. "The Role of Street Committees: Continuing South Africa's Practice of Alternative Justice," in Hugh Corder, ed. Democracy and The Judiciary. Cape Town: IDASA.

Burman, Sandra and Wilfried Schärf. 1990. "Creating People's Justice: Street Committees and People's Courts in a South African City," 24 Law & Society Review 693.

Butcher, Goler Teal. 1986. "Legal Consequences for States of the Illegality of Apartheid," 8 Human Rights Quarterly 404.

Butler, Jeffrey, Richard Elphick and David Welsh, eds. 1987. Democratic Liberalism in South Africa: Its History and Prospect. Cape Town: David Philip.

Butler, Jeffrey, Robert I. Rotberg and John Adams. 1977. The Black Homelands of South Africa: The Political and Economic Development of Bophuthatswana and KwaZulu. Berkeley: University of California Press.

Caiger, Andrew. 1991. "Context and the Judicial Function in South Africa." Paper presented to the annual conference of the Socio–Legal Studies Association, Leicester (April).

Cameron, Edwin. 1982. "Legal Chauvinism, Executive–mindedness and Justice—L C Steyn's Impact on South African Law," 99 SALJ 38.

_____. 1987. "Nude Monarchy: The Case of South Africa's Judges," 3 SAJHR 338.

_____. 1988. "Civil Disobedience and Passive Resistance," in Corder.

Cameron, Edwin, Halton Cheadle and Clive Thompson. 1988. The New Labour Relations Act: The Law after the 1988 Amemdments. Cape Town: Juta.

Cameron, Edwin, H. Rudolph and Dirk van Zyl Smit. 1980. "Judicial Appointments, Public Confidence and the Court Structure: Proposals for a New Approach," [1980] De Rebus 430.

Cammack, Diana. 1989. "South Africa's War of Destablilisation," 5 SAR 191.

Canan, Penelope and George W. Pring. 1988. "Studying Strategic Lawsuits against Public Participation: Mixing Quantitative and Qualitative Approaches," 22 Law & Society Review 385.

Carlson, Joel. 1973. No Neutral Ground. New York: Thomas Y. Crowell.

Carnegie Quarterly. 1981. "Pursuing Justice in an Unjust Society: The Centre for Applied Legal Studies in South Africa," 29(1&2) Carnegie Quarterly.

Carroll, Lewis (Charles Dodgson). 1946. Alice in Wonderland and Through the Looking Glass. New York: Grosset & Dunlop.

Carter, Charles. 1991a. "Community and Conflict: The Alexandra Rebellion of 1986," 18 Journal of Southern African Studies 115.

_____. 1991b. "'We are the Progressives': Alexandra Youth Congress Activists and the Freedom Charter, 1983–85," 17 Journal of Southern African Studies 197.

_____. 1991c. Comrades and Community: Politics and the Construction of Hegemony in Alexandra Township, South Africa, 1984–87. D.Phil. dissertation, Oxford.

Casper, Jonathan D. 1972. Lawyers Before the Warren Court: Civil Liberties and Civil Rights, 1957–1966. Urbana: University of Illinois Press.

Catholic Institute for International Relations. 1982. Torture in South Africa. London: CIIR.

_____. 1988. Now Everyone Is Afraid: The Changing Face of Policing in South Africa. London: CIIR.

_____. 1989. Out of Step: War Resistance in South Africa. London: CIIR.

Centre for Applied Legal Studies and National Association of Democratic Lawyers. 1991. Community Dispute Resolution Resource Committee. Johannesburg: CALS.

Chaskalson, Arthur. 1985a. "Legal Control of the Administrative Process," 102 SALJ 419.

_____. 1985b. "Responsibility for Practical Legal Training," [1985] De Rebus 116 (March).

_____. 1989. "The Past Ten Years: A Balance Sheet and Some Indicators for the Future," 5 SAJHR 293.

_____. n.d.a. "The Role of a Legal Resources Centre" (unpublished).

_____. n.d.b. "Is There a Place for Legal Advice Bureaux and Law Clinics?" (unpublished).

Chaskalson, Arthur and Sheena Duncan. 1984. Influx Control: The Pass Laws. Paper presented to the Second Carnegie Inquiry into Poverty and Development in Southern Africa, Cape Town (April 13–19) (unpublished).

Cheh, Mary M. 1986. "Systems and Slogans: The American Clear and Present Danger Doctrine and South African Publications Control," 2 SAJHR 29.

Chestnut, J.L., Jr. and Julia Cass. 1990. Black in Selma: The Uncommon Life of J.L. Chestnut, Jr. New York: Anchor Books.

Christenson, Ron. 1986. Political Trials: Gordian Knots in the Law. New Brunswick, N.J.: Transaction Books.

Christopher, A.J. 1994. The Atlas of Apartheid. New York: Routledge, Chapman & Hall.

Claassens, Aninka. 1990. "Rural Land Struggles in the Transvaal in the 1980s," in Murray & O'Regan.

Clark, J. 1985. "The Juridification of Industrial Relations: A Review Article," 14 Industrial Law Journal 69.

Coaker, J.F. 1972. "The Image of the Law in the Minds of White South Africans," in Randall.

Cobbett, William and Robin Cohen, eds. 1988. Popular Struggles in South Africa. London: James Currey.

Cock, Jacklyn. 1992. Colonels and Cadres: War and Gender in South Africa. Cape Town: Oxford University Press.

Cock, Jacklyn and Laurie Nathan, eds. 1989. War and Society: The Militarisation of South Africa. Cape Town: David Philip.

Coetsee, Kobie. 1988. "Response to Mr Edwin Cameron," 4 SAJHR 94.

Cohen, Robin. 1986. Endgame in South Africa? The Changing Structures & Ideology of Apartheid. London: James Currey and Paris: UNESCO Press.

Cohen, Stanley. 1972. Folk Devils and Moral Panics: The Creation of the Mods and Rockers. London: Macgibbon & Kee.

Cole, Josette. 1987. Crossroads: The Politics of Reform and Repression, 1976–1986. Johannesburg: Ravan.

Coleman, Max and David Webster. 1986. "Repression and Detentions in South Africa," 3 SAR 111.

Columbia Human Rights Law Review. 1989. "Human Rights in the Post–Apartheid South African Constitution," 21 Columbia Human Rights Law Review 1–251.

Commonwealth Group of Eminent Persons. 1986. Mission to South Africa: The Commonwealth Report. Harmondsworth: Penguin.

Conlon, Gerry. 1990. Proved Innocent: The Story of Gerry Conlon of the Guildford Four. Harmondsworth: Penguin.

Cooper, George. 1979/80. "Public Interest Law—South African Style," 11 Columbia Human Rights Law Review 105.

Cooper, Jeremy and Rajeev Dhavan, eds. 1986. Public Interest Law. Oxford: Basil Blackwell.

Corbett, M.M. 1981. "Judicial Review and the Problems of Southern Africa," 12 Loyola University [of Chicago] Law Journal 175.

Corder, Hugh. 1984. Judges at Work: The Role and Attitudes of the South African Appellate Judiciary, 1910–1950. Cape Town: Juta.

_____. 1987a. "The Judicial Eye: Change and the Courts," in D.J. van Vuuren, ed. Change in South Africa (Power Sharing). Durban: Butterworth.

_____. 1987b. "The Supreme Court: Arena of Struggle," in Wilmot G. James, ed. The State of Apartheid. Boulder, Colo.: L. Rienner.

_____, ed. 1988. Essays on Law and Social Practice in South Africa. Cape Town: Juta.

_____. 1989a. "Crowbars and Cobwebs: Executive Authority and the Law in South Africa," 5 SAJHR 1.

_____. 1989b. "The Judicial Branch of Government: An Historical Overview," in D.P. Visser, ed. Essays in Legal History. Cape Town: Juta.

Coulter, Jim, Susan Miller and Martin Walker. 1984. State of Siege: Miners' Strike 1984. Politics and Policing in the Coal Fields. London: Canary Press.

Cover, Robert M. 1975. Justice Accused: Antislavery and the Judicial Process. New Haven: Yale University Press.

Cowen, Dennis V. 1961. The Foundations of Freedom. Cape Town: Oxford University Press.

Cowling, M.G. 1987. "Judges and the Protection of Human Rights in South Africa: Articulating the Inarticulate Premiss," 3 SAJHR 177.

_____. 1990. "Forced Removals in KwaZulu: From Bad to Worse," 6 SAJHR 303.

Crankshaw, Owen. 1993. "Squatting, Apartheid, and Urbanisation on the Southern Witwatersrand," 92 African Affairs 31.

Crapanzano, Vincent. 1986. Waiting: The Whites of South Africa. New York: Vintage.

Crenshaw, Kimberlé. 1988. "Race, Reform and Retrenchment: Transformation and Legitimation in Antidiscrimination Law," 101 Harvard Law Review 1331.

Currin, Brian, David Bam and Mpho Molefe. 1991. Commission of Inquiry into the Cause of Violence in Oukasie Township, Brits. Pretoria: Lawyers for Human Rights.

Dangor, Achmat. 1990. The Z Town Trilogy. Johannesburg: Ravan Press.

Davenport, T.R.H. 1961. "Civil Rights in South Africa, 1910–1960," [1960] Acta Juridica 11.

_____. 1987a. "Unrest, Reform and the Challenges to Law, 1976–1986," [1987] Acta Juridica 1.

_____. 1987b. South Africa: A Modern History (3rd ed.). Johannesburg: Macmillan.

Davidson, Eugene. 1966. The Trial of the Germans. New York: Collier Books.

Davidson, Joshua. 1985. "Note: The History of Judicial Oversight of Legislative and Executive Action in South Africa," 8 Harvard Journal of Law and Public Policy 687.

Davies, Robert. 1987. "South African Regional Policy Post–Nkomati: May 1985–December 1986," 4 SAR 341.

_____. 1989. "South African Regional Policy Before and After Cuito Cuanavale," 5 SAR 166.

Davis, Dennis M. 1980a. "Human Rights—A Re-examination," 97 SALJ 94.

_____. 1980b. "Human Rights—A Rebutter," 97 SALJ 616.

_____. 1982. "The Rule of Law and the Radical Debate," [1981] Acta Juridica 65.

_____. 1985a. "Political Trials in South Africa," in Davis & Slabbert.

_____. 1985b. "Positivism and the Judicial Function," 102 SALJ 103.

_____. 1987a. "The Chief Justice and the Total Onslaught," 3 SAJHR 231.

_____. 1987b. "Competing Conceptions: Pro–executive or Pro–democratic—Judges Choose," 3 SAJHR 96.

_____. 1987c. "Post–apartheid South Africa—What Future for a Legal System?" [1987] Acta Juridica 220.

_____. 1988. "Legality and Struggle: Towards a Non–instrumentalist View of Law," in Corder.

_____. 1990a. "Violence and the Law: the Use of the Censure in Political Trials in South Africa," in Manganyi & du Toit.

_____. 1990b. "The judges' crucible: ideology of law and ideology of struggle," in Mark Swilling, ed. Views on the South African State. Pretoria: HSRC.

_____. 1990c. "The Delmas Trial and the Danger of Political Trials for the Legitimacy of a Legal System," 6 SAJHR 79.

Davis, Dennis and Hugh Corder. 1988. "A Long March: Administrative Law in the Appellate Division," 4 SAJHR 281.

Davis, Dennis and Mana Slabbert, eds. 1985. Crime and Power in South Africa: Critical studies in criminology. Cape Town: David Philip.

Davis, Stephen M. 1987. Apartheid's Rebels: Inside South Africa's Hidden War. New Haven: Yale University Press.

Dean, W.H.B. 1976a. The Riots and the Constitution: an address to the Civil Rights League. Cape Town: CRL.

_____. 1976b. "The Role of Law in the Elimination of Racial Discrimination," [1976] Acta Juridica 157.

_____. 1983. "Reason and Prejudice: The Courts and Licensing Bodies in the Transvaal," in E. Kahn, ed. Fiat Justitia: Essays in Memory of O.D. Schreiner. Cape Town: Juta.

_____. 1984. "The Legal Regime Governing Urban Africans in South Africa—An Administrative–Law Perspective," [1984] Acta Juridica 105.

_____. 1986. "Our Administrative Law: A Dismal Science?" 2 SAJHR 164.

Dean, W.H.B. and Dirk van Zyl Smit, eds. 1983. Constituitonal Change in South Africa—The Next Five Years. Cape Town: Juta.

de Antonio, Emile. 1964. Point of Order! New York: Norton.

Delius, Peter. 1989. "The Ndzundza Ndebele," in Philip Bonner, Isabel Hofmeyr, Deborah James and Tom Lodge, eds. Holding Their Ground: Class, Locality and Culture in 19th and 20th Century South Africa. Johannesburg: Witwatersrand University Press and Ravan Press (History Workshop 4).

Dendy, Mervyn. 1987. "Ministerial Liability for the Focus of the Force: Curbing the Over–Zealous Policeman," 3 SAJHR 82.

_____. 1989. "When the Force Frolics: A South African History of State Liability for Delicts of the Police," [1989] Acta Juridica 20.

Denman, Earl. 1985. The Fiercest Fight: A documented account of the struggle against Apartheid in South Africa. Worthing: Churchman Publishing.

Desmond, Cosmas. 1971. The Discarded People: An Account of African Resettlement in South Africa. Braamfontein: Christian Institute of South Africa.

de Tocqueville, Alexis. 1958. Democracy in America (2 vols.) (Phillips Bradley ed.). New York: Vintage Books.

de Villiers, B., D.J. van Vuuren and M. Wiechers, eds. 1992. Human Rights: Documents That Paved the Way. Pretoria: HSRC.

Diar, Prakash. 1990. The Sharpeville Six. Toronto: McClelland & Stewart.

Didcott, J.M. 1989. "Salvaging the Law" (The Second Ernie Wentzel Memorial Lecture). Johannesburg: CALS.

Dikobe, Modikwe. 1973. The Marabi Dance. Oxford: Heinemann.

Dlamini, C.R.M. 1988. "The Influence of Race on the Administration of Justice in South Africa," 4 SAJHR 37.

Dlamini, Moses. n.d. Hell–Hole Robben Island. Trenton, N.J.: Africa World Press.

Dlodlo, Andreas. 1987. "The Influence of Government Policy on Sentences in Magistrates' Courts." LL.M. dissertation, University of Natal.

Dolny, Helena and Heinz Klug. 1992. "Land Reform: Legal Support and Economic Regulation," 6 SAR 322.

Dorfman, Ariel. 1991. "Death and the Maiden," 20(6) Index on Censorship 5 (June).

Dorsen, Norman and Leon Friedman. 1973. Disorder in the Courts. New York: Pantheon.

Dreyer, Peter. 1980. Martyrs and Fanatics: South Africa and Human Destiny. London: Secker & Warburg.

Driver, E.J. 1969. Elegy for a Revolutionary. London: Faber and Faber.

Dromey, Jack and Graham Taylor. 1978. Grunwick: The Workers' Story. London: Lawrence and Wishart.

Dugard, John. 1970. "The Courts and Section 6 of the Terrorism Act," 87 SALJ 289.

_____. 1971. "The Judicial Process, Positivism and Civil Liberty," 88 SALJ 181.

_____. 1972a. "South African Lawyers and the Liberal Heritage of the Law," in Randall.

_____. 1972b. "Judges, Academics and Unjust Laws: The Van Niekerk Contempt Case," 89 SALJ 271.

_____. 1973. "A Review of South African Legal Education," in Legal Aid in South Africa.

_____. 1974. "The Political Trial: Some Special Considerations," 91 SALJ 59.

_____. 1978. Human Rights and the South African Legal Order. Princeton, N.J.: Princeton University Press.

_____. 1982a. "A Triumph for Executive Power: An Examination of the Rabie Report and the Internal Security Act 74 of 1982," 99 SALJ 589.

_____, ed. 1982b. Report on the Rabie Report: An Examination of Security Legislation in South Africa. Johannesburg: CALS (Occasional Paper No. 3).

_____. 1984. "Should Judges Resign?—a Reply to Professor Wacks," 101 SALJ 286.

_____. 1985. "Training Needs in Sentencing in South Africa," 1 SAJHR 93.

_____. 1987a. "*Omar*: Support for Wacks's Ideas on the Judicial Process," 3 SAJHR 295.

_____. 1987b. "Human Rights and the Rule of Law I," in Butler et al.

_____. 1987c. "The Quest for Liberal Democracy in South Africa," [1987] Acta Juridica 237.

_____. 1987d. "The Jurisprudential Foundations of the Apartheid Legal Order," 18 Philosophical Forum 115.

_____. 1989. "Human Rights, Humanitarian Law and the South African Conflict," 2 Harvard Human Rights Yearbook 101.

_____. 1992. "Human Rights, Apartheid and Lawyers: Are there any lessons for lawyers from common law countries?" 15 University of New South Wales Law Journal 439.

Dugard, John, Nicholas Haysom and Gilbert Marcus. 1992. The Last Years of Apartheid: Civil Liberties in South Africa. New York: Ford Foundation and Foreign Policy Association.

Dugard, John, Nicholas Haysom and Dolly Mokgatle. n.d. Why the Incorporation of Moutse into KwaNdebele Should Be Rejected (unpublished).

du Plessis, Menan. 1983. A State of Fear. Cape Town: David Philip.

_____. 1989. Longlive! Cape Town: David Philip.

du Toit, Andre. 1977. The Politics of Civil Rights in South Africa. Cape Town: Civil Rights League.

_____. 1988. "Understanding Rights Discourses and Ideological Conflicts in South Africa," in Corder.

du Toit, Dirk C. 1986. "Cowboys and Crooks: Judges and Legislative Intention," 2 Tydskrif vir Regwetenskap.

Dworkin, Ronald. 1977. Taking Rights Seriously. Cambridge, Mass.: Havard University Press.

_____. 1985. A Matter of Principle. Cambridge, Mass.: Harvard University Press.

_____. 1986. Law's Empire. Cambridge, Mass.: Belknap Press.

Dyzenhaus, David. 1982. "L C Steyn in Perspective," 99 SALJ 380.

_____. 1983a. "Judging the Judges and Ourselves," 100 SALJ 496.

_____. 1983b. "Positivism and Validity," 100 SALJ 454.

_____. 1984. "Judging the Judges and Ourselves II," 101 SALJ 553.

_____. 1985. "Judges, Equity and Truth," 102 SALJ 295.

_____. 1986. "Bail, Security and Rights," 2 SAJHR 85.

_____. 1991. Hard Cases in Wicked Legal Systems: South African Law in the Perspective of Legal Philosophy. Oxford: Clarendon Press.

Edelman, Murray. 1964. The Symbolic Uses of Politics. Urbana: University of Illinois Press.

_____. 1971. Politics as Symbolic Action. Chicago: Markham.

_____. 1977. Political Language: Words that Succeed and Policies that Fail. New York: Academic Press.

_____. 1988. Constructing the Political Spectacle. Chicago: University of Chicago Press.

Ellmann, Stephen. 1990. "Lawyers against the Emergency," 6 SAJHR 228.

_____. 1992. In a Time of Trouble: Law and Liberty in South Africa's State of Emergency. Oxford: Clarendon Press.

Eprile, Tony. 1989. Temporary Sojourner and other stories. New York: Simon & Schuster.

Epstein, Jason. 1970. The Great Conspiracy Trial. New York: Vintage Books.

Essa, Saira and Charles Pillai. 1987. Steve Biko: The Inquest. Johannesburg: Thorald's Africana Books.

Essop, Ahmed. 1984. The Emperor. Johannesburg: Ravan Press.

Falk, Richard A. 1968. "Observer's Report on The State v. Tuhadeleni and others," in ICJ, Erosion of the Rule of Law in South Africa. Geneva: ICJ.

Fanon, Frantz. 1982. Black Skin, White Masks. New York: Grove Press.

Farmelo, Laura B. 1984. Narrative Report to Ford Foundation: Individual Grant for Comparative Study of South African and American Race Relations Law and the Potential for Fostering Social Change Through the Legal Process in South Africa. New York: Ford Foundation.

Farrell, Michael. 1986. Emergency Legislation: The Apparatus of Repression. Derry: Field Day Theater Co. (Pamphlet No. 11).

Feit, E. 1971. Urban Revolt in South Africa, 1960–64. Evanston, Ill.: Northwestern University Press.

Fernandez, L.D. 1984. A Comparison betwen the Legal Aid Systems of South Africa and West Germany in Theory and Practice. Ph.D. dissertation, University of the Witwatersrand.

_____. 1985. "The Law, Lawyers and the Courts in Nazi Germany," 1 SAJHR 124.

ffrench–Beytagh, G.A. 1973. Encountering Darkness. London: Collins.

Fine, Alan. 1987. "Trends and Developments in Organised Labour," 4 SAR 219.

Fine, Bob with Dennis Davis. 1990. Beyond Apartheid: Labour and Liberation in South Africa. Johannesburg: Ravan.

Fine, Bob and Robert Millar, eds. 1985. Policing the Miners' Strike. London: Lawrence & Wishart.

Fine Derrick. 1989. "Kitskonstabels: A Case Study in Black on Black Violence," [1989] Acta Juridica 44.

Fine, Derrick and Desirée Hansson. 1990. "Community responses to police abuse of power: Coping with the kitskonstabels," in Hansson & van Zyl Smit.

Fine, Robert, F. de Clerq and D. Innes. 1981. "Trade Unions and the State: the question of legality," 7 SALB 39.

Finkielkraut, Alain. 1992. Remembering in Vain: The Klaus Barbie Trial and Crimes Against Humanity. New York: Columbia University Press.

Finnegan, William. 1986. Crossing the Line: A Year in the Land of Apartheid. New York: Harper & Row.

_____. 1988. Dateline Soweto: Travels with Black South African Reporters. New York: Harper & Row.

Finnemore, Martheanne and Roux van der Merwe. 1986. Introduction to Industrial Relations in South Africa. Johannesburg: Lexicon.

First, Ruth. 1965. 117 Days: An Account of Confinement and Interrogation under the South African Ninety–Day Detention Law. Harmondsworth: Penguin.

Forbath, William. 1989. Law and the Shaping of the American Labor Movement. Cambridge, Mass.: Harvard University Press.

Forder, Jay. 1990. "Conscription," in Robertson et al.

Forman, Lionel and E.S. Sachs. 1957. The South African Treason Trial. London: John Calder.

Forsyth, C.F. 1980a. "Human Rights and Ideology: A First Examination," 97 SALJ 103.

_____. 1980b. "Human Rights and Ideology: Litis Contestatio," 97 SALJ 623.

_____. 1985. In Danger for their Talents. Cape Town: Juta.

_____. 1988. "The Sleep of Reason: Security Cases before the Appellate Division," 105 SALJ 679.

_____. 1991. "Interpreting a Bill of Rights: The future task of a reformed judiciary?" 7 SAJHR 1.

Forsyth, C.F. and J. Schiller. 1981. "The Judicial Process, Positivism, and Civil Liberty II," 98 SALJ 218.

_____, eds. 1985. Human Rights: The Cape Town Conference. Cape Town: Juta.

Foster, Don and Clifford Luyt. 1986. "The Blue Man's Burden: Policing the Police in South Africa," 2 SAJHR 297.

Foster, Don and Diane Sandler. 1985. A Study of Detention and Torture in South Africa: Preliminary Report. Cape Town: Institute of Criminology, University of Cape Town.

Foster, Don and Donald Skinner. 1990. "Detention and Violence: Beyond Victimology," in Manganyi & du Toit.

Foster, Don, with Dennis Davis and Diane Sandler. 1987. Detention & Torture in South Africa: Psychological, legal & historical studies. Cape Town: David Philip.

Fraenkel, E. 1969. The Dual State. New York: Octagon.

Franey, Ros. 1983. Poor Law: The mass arrest of homeless claimants in Oxford. London: Campaign for Single Homeless People et al.

Freeman, Alan. 1978. "Legitimizing Racial Discrimination Through Antidiscrimination Law: A Critical Review of Supreme Court Doctrine," 62 Minnesota Law Review 1049.

Friedman, Leon, ed. 1965. Southern Justice. New York: Pantheon.

_____. 1970. "Political Power and Legal Legitimacy: A Short History of Political Trials," 30 Antioch Review 157.

Friedman, Maggie and David Webster. 1989. Suppressing Apartheid's Opponents: Repression and the state of emergency: June 1987–March 1989.

Friedman, Steven. 1987. Building Tomorrow Today: African Workers in Trade Unions, 1970–1984. Johannesburg: Ravan.

Friedrichs, David O. 1990. "Law in South Africa and the Legitimacy Crisis," 14 International Journal of Comparative Law and Applied Criminal Justice 189.

_____, ed. 1992. "Law and the South African Legitimacy Crisis," 16 Legal Studies Forum 127–205.

Fudge, Judy and Harry Glasbeek. 1992. "The Politics of Rights: A Politics with Little Class," 1 Social and Legal Studies 45.

Fugard, Sheila. 1984. A Revolutionary Woman. London: Virago Press.

Fuller, Lon. 1958. "Fidelity to Law," 71 Harvard Law Review 630.

Gardiner, Gerald. 1957. "The South African Treason Trial," 48 Journal of the International Commission of Jurists 43.

Garfinkel, Harold. 1956. "Conditions of Successful Degradation Ceremonies," 61 American Journal of Sociology 420.

Gauntlett, J.J. 1989. "Proceeding against the Police," [1989] Acta Juridica 8.

Gaventa, John. 1980. Power and Powerlessness: Quiescence and Rebellion in an Appalachian Valley. Oxford: Clarendon Press.

Gaylin, Willard. 1970. In the Service of Their Country: War Resisters in Prison.

Geary, Roger. 1985. Policing Industrial Disputes: 1893 to 1985. Cambridge: Cambridge University Press.

Geldenhuys, Odette. 1985. Directory of Advice Centres in the Western Cape. Cape Town: UCT Centre for Intergroup Studies.

Gerhart, Gail. 1978. Black Power in South Africa: Berkeley: University of California Press.

Gifford, Tony. 1984. Supergrasses: The Use of Accomplice Evidence in Northern Ireland. London: Cobden Trust.

Gilbey, Emma. 1993. The Lady: The Life and Times of Winnie Mandela. London: Jonathan Cape.

Giliomee, Hermann. n.d. Land Reform and the SA Government (unpublished).

Giliomee, Hermann and Lawrence Schlemmer, eds. 1985. Up Against the Fences: Poverty, passes and privilege in South Africa. New York: St. Martin's Press.

Ginn, John L. 1992. Sugamo Prison, Tokyo. An account of the trial and sentencing of Japanese war criminals in 1948, by a U.S. participant. Jefferson, N.C.: McFarland & Co.

Goldberg, Arthur J. 1985. "The Status of Apartheid under International Law," 13 Hastings Constitutional Law Quarterly 1.

Goldstone, Richard. 1990. Report of the Commission of Enquiry into the Incidents at Sebokeng, Boipatong, Lekoa, Sharpeville and Evaton on 26 March 1990. Pretoria: Government Printer.

_____. 1992. Report of the Commission of Inquiry regarding the Prevention of Public Violence and Intimidation (Second Interim Report, May 27).

Goodman, Geoffrey. 1985. The Miners' Strike. London: Pluto Press.

Gosiger, Mary C. 1986. "Strategies for Divestment from United States Companies and Financial Institutions Doing Business with or in South Africa," 8 Human Rights Quarterly 517.

Gould, William. 1981. "Black Unions in South Africa: Labour Law Reform and Apartheid," 17 Stanford Journal of International Law 99.

Grant, B. and P.J. Schwikkard. 1991. "People's Courts?" 7 SAJHR 304.

Great Britain, House of Commons, Foreign Affairs Committee. 1991. Report on South Africa. London: HMSO.

Green, M.A. 1987. "What Role Can Judges Play in Mitigating Apartheid? A Study of the Urban African Legal Regime," [1987] Wisconsin Law Review 325.

Green, Penny. 1990. The Enemy Without: Policing and class consciousness in the miners' strike. Milton Keynes: Open University Press.

Green, Pippa. 1986a. "A Place to Work: Sarmcol Workers Co–ops," 11(4) SALB (Feb–Mar).

_____. 1986b. "Review: Sarmcol Workers' Play," 11(5) SALB 121 (Apr–May).

Greenberg, Jack et al. 1986. "The Role of Law and Lawyers in South Africa," in Nancy Wight, ed. Law and Current World Issues. New York: Oceana.

Grodin, Joseph R. 1989. In Pursuit of Justice. Berkeley: University of California Press.

Grogan, John. 1986. "News Control by Decree," 103 SALJ 118.

_____. 1988a. "Judicial Control of Emergency Detention: A Glimmer of Hope," 4 SAJHR 225.

_____. 1988b. The Media Emergency Regulations, 1988: A Guide for Journalists. Grahamstown: Department of Journalism and Media Studies, Rhodes University (Occasional Paper No. 2).

Gross, P.H. 1979. "South Africa," in Frederick H. Zemans, ed. Perspectives on Legal Aid: An International Survey. Westport, Conn.: Greenwood Press.

Grundy, Kenneth W. 1983. The Rise of the South African Security Establishment. Cape Town: South African Institute of International Affairs.

_____. 1988. The Militarization of South African Politics. Oxford: Oxford University Press.

Gusfield, Joseph R. 1963. Symbolic Crusade: Status Politics and the American Temperance Movement. Urbana, Ill.: University of Illinois Press.

_____. 1981. The Culture of Public Problems: Drinking–Driving and the Symbolic Order. Chicago: University of Chicago Press.

Hachten, William A. and C. Anthony Giffard. 1984. Total Onslaught: The South African Press Under Attack. Madison: University of Wisconsin Press and Braamfontein: Macmillan.

Hahlo, H.R. and E. Kahn. 1960. South Africa: The Development of its Laws and Constitution. Cape Town: Juta.

_____. 1968. The South African Legal System and its Background. Cape Town: Juta

Hahlo, H.R. and I.A. Maisels. 1966. "The Rule of Law in South Africa," 52 Virginia Law Review 1.

_____. 1971. "Scandalizing Justice: The Van Niekerk Story," 21 University of Toronto Law Journal 378.

Hain, Peter. 1984. Political Trials in Britain. London: Allen Lane.

Hakman, Nathan. 1972. "Political Trials in the Legal Order: A Political Scientist's Perspective," 21 Journal of Public Law 73.

Halberstam, David. 1980. "The Fire Next Time," 245(5) Atlantic Monthly 81 (May).

Hall, Stuart. 1980. Drifting into a Law and Order Society. London: Cobden Trust.

Hall, Stuart, Chas Critcher, Tony Jefferson, John Clarke and Brian Roberts. 1978. Policing the Crisis: Mugging, the State, and Law and Order. London: Macmillan.

Halliday, Terence C. 1987. Beyond Monopoly: Lawyers, State Crises, and Professional Empowerment. Chicago: University of Chicago Press.

Handler, Joel F. 1978. Social Movements and the Legal System: A Theory of Law Reform and Social Change. New York: Academic Press.

Hanlon, Joseph. 1986. Beggar Your Neighbours: apartheid power in Southern Africa. London: CIIR and Bloomington, Ind.: James Currey.

Hansson, D.S. 1989. "Trigger–happy? An Evaluation of Fatal Police Shootings in the Greater Cape Town Area, from 1984 to 1986," [1989] Acta Juridica 118.

Hansson, Desirée and Dirk van Zyl Smit, eds. 1990. Towards justice? Crime and state control in South Africa. Cape Town: Oxford University Press.

Hariman, Robert, ed. 1990. Popular Trials: Rhetoric, Mass Media, and the Law. Tuscaloosa: University of Alabama Press.

Harms, L.T.C. 1990. Report of the Commission of Inquiry into Certain Alleged Murders. Pretoria: Government Printer.

Harring, Sidney L. 1983. Policing a Class Society: The Experience of American Cities, 1876–1915. New Brunswick, N.J.: Rutgers University Press.

Harris, Bede. 1987. "'Religious Convictions' and Conscientious Objection," 3 SAJHR 240.

Harrison, David. 1981. The White Tribe of Africa: South Africa in Perspective. Berkeley: University of California Press.

Hart, H.L.A. 1958. "Positivism and the Separation of Law and Morals," 71 Harvard Law Review 593.

Harvey, Richard. n.d. A Chronology of Recorded Events in Alexandra, 1905–1985 (unpublished).

Hay, Douglas, 1975. "Property, Authority and the Criminal Law," in Hay et al.

Hay, Douglas, Peter Linebaugh, John G. Rule, E.P. Thompson, and Cal Winslow. 1975. Albion's Fatal Tree: Crime and Society in Eighteenth–Century England. New York: Pantheon.

Hayden, Tom. 1970. Trial. New York: Holt, Rinehart & Winston.

Haysom, Nicholas. 1983. Ruling with the Whip: A report on the violation of human rights in the Ciskei. Johannesburg: CALS (Occasional Paper No. 3).

_____. 1984. "The Industrial Court: Institutionalising Conflict," 2 SAR 278.

_____. 1986a. Mabangalala: The Rise of Right–Wing Vigilantes in South Africa. Johannesburg: CALS (Occasional Paper No. 10).

_____. 1986b. "The Langa Shootings and the Kannemeyer Commission of Enquiry," 3 SAR 278 [reprinted in 8 Human Rights Quarterly 494 (1986)].

_____. 1986c. Plight of the Magopa People. Letter to Hon Dr. G van N Viljoen (December 2).

_____. 1987a. "License to Kill Part I: The South African Police and the Use of Deadly Force," 3 SAJHR 3.

_____. 1987b. "License to Kill Part II: A Comparative Survey of the Law in the United Kingdom, United States of America, and South Africa," 3 SAJHR 202.

_____. 1988. Vigilantes and the Militarisation of South Africa (unpublished).

_____. 1989a. "Public Safety and the South African Courts," 2 Harvard Human Rights Yearbook 111.

_____. 1989b. "Policing the Police: A Comparative Survey of Police Control Mechanisms in the United States, South Africa and the United Kingdom," [1989] Acta Juridica 139.

_____. 1990a. "Vigilantism and the policing of African townships: Manufacturing violent stability," in Hansson & van Zyl Smit.

_____. 1990b. "Policing," in Robertson et al.

_____. 1990c. "Rural Land Struggles: Practising Law Democratically," in Murray & O'Regan.

_____. 1992. "The Total Strategy: The South African Security Forces and the Suppression of Civil Liberties," in Dugard et al.

Haysom, Nicholas and Steven Kahanovitz. 1987. "Courts and the State of Emergency," 4 SAR 187.

Haysom, Nicholas and Laura Mangan, eds. 1987. Emergency Law. Johannesburg: CALS.

Haysom, Nicholas and Gilbert Marcus. 1985. "'Undesirability' and Criminal Liability under the Publications Act 42 of 1974," 1 SAJHR 31.

Haysom, Nicholas and Clive Plasket. 1988. "The War Against Law: Judicial Activism and the Appellate Division," 4 SAJHR 303.

_____, eds. 1989. Developments in Emergency Law. Johannesburg: CALS.

Helliker, Kirk, Andre Roux and Roland White. 1987. "'Asithengi': Recent Consumer Boycotts," 4 SAR 33.

Hellman, Ellen, ed. 1949. Handbook on Race Relations in South Africa. Cape Town: SAIRR.

Heard, Anthony Hazlitt. 1990. The Cape of Storms: A Personal History of the Crisis in South Africa. Fayetteville: University of Arkansas Press.

Herbstein, Denis. 1991. "How Canon Collins and friends smuggled £100,000,000 to South Africa and were never found out," Observer 49 (May 5).

Herd, Norman. 1976. The Bent Pine (The Trial of Chief Langalibalele). Johannesburg: Ravan Press.

Hiemstra, Victor. 1990. Report of the Commission of Inquiry into Alleged Irregularities in the Security Department of the City Council of Johannesburg. Pretoria: Government Printer.

Higginbotham, Jr., A. Leon. 1990. "Racism in American and South African Courts: Similarities and Differences," 65 New York University Law Review 479.

_____. 1992. "An Open Letter to Justice Clarence Thomas From a Federal Judicial Colleague," 140 University of Pennsylvania Law Review 1005.

Hillyard, Paddy. 1993. Suspect Community: People's Experience of the Prevention of Terrorism Acts in Britain. London: Pluto Press.

Hindson, Doug. 1980. "The New Black Labour Regulation: limited reform, intensified control," 6(1) SALB 45 (July).

_____. 1987a. Pass Controls and the Urban Proletariat in South Africa. Johannesburg: Ravan Press.

_____. 1987b. "Orderly Urbanisation and Influx Control: from Territorial Apartheid to Regional Spatial Ordering in South Africa," in Richard Tomlinson and Mark Addleson, eds. Regional Restructuring Under Apartheid: Urban and Regional Politics in Contemporary South Africa. Johannesburg: Ravan Press.

Hindson, Doug and Marian Lacey. 1983. "Influx Control and Labour Allocation: Policy and Practice since the Riekert Commission," 1 SAR 97.

Hlatshwayo. M. 1987. "To you comrades P Sibiya, S Ngubane, F Mnikathi, A Nkabande," 12(2) SALB 2 (Jan–Feb).

Hochschild, Adam. 1990. The Mirror at Midnight: A South African Journey. New York: Viking.

Hoexter Commission. 1983. Report of the Commission of Inquiry into the Structure and Functioning of the Courts (RP 78/1983). Pretoria: Govt Printer.

Hoexter, Cora. 1986. "Judicial Policy in South Africa," 103 SALJ 436.

Hogan, Gerard and Clive Walker. 1989. Political violence and the law in Ireland. Manchester: Manchester University Press.

Hooper, Charles. 1989. Brief Authority. Cape Town: David Philip (first published 1960).

Hope, Christoper. 1988. White Boy Running. New York: Doubleday.

Horowitz, Donald L. 1991. A Democratic South Africa? Constitutional Engineering in a Divided Society. Berkeley: University of California Press.

Horrell, Muriel. 1971. Action, Reaction and Counter–action: A Brief Review of Non–White Political Movements in South Africa (2d ed.). Johannesburg: SAIRR.

_____. 1978. Laws Affecting Race Relations in South Africa (to the end of 1976). Johannesburg: SAIRR.

_____. 1982. Race Relations as Regulated by Law in South Africa, 1948–1979. Johannesburg: SAIRR.

Hughes, Everett C. 1971. The Sociological Eye (2 vols.). Chicago: Aldine–Atherton.

Human Rights Commission. 1989. Freedom of the Press. Braamfontein: HRC (Fact Paper FP4).

_____. 1990. Children and Repression, 1987–1989. Braamfontein: HRC.

Human Rights Quarterly. 1988. "South Africa's Children: A Symposium on Children in Detention," 10(1) Human Rights Quarterly (February).

Hund, John. 1988. "Formal Justice and Township Justice," in John Hund, ed. Law and Justice in South Africa. Johannesburg: Institute for Public Interest Law and Research.

Hund, John and Malebo Kotu–Rammopo. 1983. "Justice in a South African Township: The Sociology of Makgotla," 16 Comparative and International Law Journal in Southern Africa 179.

Hurst, J. Willard. 1945. "Treason in the United States," 58 Harvard Law Review 226–72, 395–444, 806–57.

Hutchinson, Allan and Patrick Monahan. 1987. The Rule of Law: Ideal or Ideology. Toronto: Carswell.

Huyse, Luc and Steven Dhondt. 1993. La répression des collaborateurs, 1942–1952: un passé toujours présent. Brussels: CRISP.

Hyde, Alan. S. 1983. "The Concept of Legitimation in the Sociology of Law," [1983] Wisconsin Law Review 379.

Ietswaart, Heleen F.P. 1987. "The Allende Regime and the Chilean Judiciary," in Yash Ghai, Robin Luckham and Francis Snyder, eds. The Political Economy of Law: A Third World Reader. Delhi: Oxford University Press.

Indicator South Africa. 1988. Political Conflict in South Africa: Data Trends, 1984–1988. Durban: Indicator Project South Africa.

Ingraham, Barton. 1979. Political Crime in Europe: A Comparative Study of France, Germany and England. Berkeley: University of California Press.

International Commission of Jurists. 1960. South Africa and the Rule of Law. Geneva: ICJ.

_____. 1962. South African Incident: The Ganyile Case. Geneva: ICJ.

_____. 1968. Erosion of the Rule of Law in South Africa. Geneva: ICJ.

_____, ed. 1975. The Trial of Beyers Naude: Christian Witness and the Rule of Law. London: Search Press.

_____. 1978. Detention of Children in South Africa. Geneva: ICJ.

_____. 1992. Agenda for Peace: An Independent Survey of the Violence in South Africa. Geneva: ICJ.

International Defence and Aid Fund for Southern Africa. 1990. Review of 1989: Repression and Resistance in South Africa and Namibia. London: IDAF Publications Ltd.

Jackson, Bernard with Tony Wardle. n.d. The Battle for Orgreave. Brighton: Vanson Wardle Productions.

Jackson, Gordon S. 1993. Breaking Story: The South African Press. Boulder: Westview Press.

Jackson, John D. 1980. Justice in South Africa. Harmondsworth: Penguin.

Jackson. n.d. Chronology of the Events and History of Alexandra (unpublished).

Jaffee, Georgina. 1984. "The Retrenchment Process," 2 SAR 125.

_____. 1987. "The Magopa people: another dream smashed," 49 Work in Progress 19 (September).

Jaffee, Georgina and Karen Jochelson. 1986. "The Fight to Save Jobs: Union Initiatives on Retrenchment and Unemployment," 3 SAR 51.

Jagwanth, Saras. 1992. "Policing of the Conflict in the Greater Pietermaritzburg Area—A Perception Study," 8 SAJHR 536.

Jamieson, A. 1989. The Heart Attacked: Terrorism and conflict in the Italian State. London: Marion Boyars.

Jaster, Robert Scott and Shirley Kew Jaster. 1993. South Africa's Other Whites: Voices for Change. New York: St. Martin's Press.

Jochelson, Karen Jane. 1988a. Urban Crisis: State Reform and Popular Reaction. A Case Study of Alexandra. B.A. honours dissertation, University of the Witwatersrand.

_____. 1988b. "People's power and state reform in Alexandra," 56/57 Work in Progress 11 (Nov–Dec).

_____. 1990. "Reform, Repression and Resistance in South Africa: a case study of Alexandra Township, 1979–1989," 16 Journal of Southern African Studies 1.

Johns, Sheridan and R. Hunt Davis, Jr., eds. 1991. Mandela, Tambo, and the African National Congress: The Struggle Against Apartheid, 1948–1990. A Documentary Survey. New York: Oxford University Press.

Johnson, Shaun, ed. 1988. South Africa: No Turning Back. London: Macmillan.

_____. 1991. "Resistance in Print I: Grassroots and Alternative Publishing, 1980–84," in Tomaselli & Louw (1991a).

Jones, Chris and Tony Novak. 1985. "Welfare Against the Workers: Benefits as a Political Weapon," in Huw Beynon, ed. Digging Deeper: Issues in the Miners' Strike. London: Verso.

Joseph, Helen. 1966. Tomorrow's Sun: A Smuggled Journal from South Africa. New York: John Day.

_____. 1986. Side by Side. London: Zed Books.

Joubert, Elsa. 1980. Poppie. Johannesburg: Jonathan Ball.

Journal of Southern African Studies. 1992. "Political Violence in Southern Africa," 18(3) JSAS (September).

Kadish, Mortimer R. and Sanford H. Kadish. 1973. Discretion to Disobey: A Study of Lawful Departures from Legal Ethics. Stanford, Ca.: Stanford University Press.

Kahn, Ellison. 1949. "The Pass Laws," in Hellman.

_____. 1961. "Crime and Punishment, 1910–1960," [1960] Acta Juridica 191.

_____. 1966. "When the Lion Feeds and the Censor Pounces: A Disquisition on the Banning of Immoral Publications in South Africa," 83 SALJ 278.

_____. 1970. "The Death Penalty in South Africa," 39 THRHR.

Kane–Berman, John. 1978. Soweto: Black Revolt—White Reaction. Johannesburg: Ravan.

_____. 1993. Political Violence in South Africa. Johannesburg: SAIRR.

Kannemeyer, Donald. 1985. Report of the Commission Appointed to Inquire into the Incident which occurred on 21 March 1985 at Uitenhage (RP74/1985). Pretoria: Government Printer.

Kaplan, Karel. 1990. Report on the Murder of the General Secretary. Columbus: Ohio State University Press.

Karis, Thomas. 1961. "The South African Treason Trial," 76 Political Science Quarterly 217.

_____. 1965. The Treason Trial in South Africa: A Guide to the Microfilm Record of the Trial. Stanford, Ca.: Hoover Institution.

Karis, Thomas and Gwendolyn M. Carter, eds. 1972–77. From Protest to Challenge: A Documentary History of African Politics in South Africa, 1882–1964 (4 vols.). Stanford, Ca.: Hoover Institution.

Kaufmann, Sam. 1991. "Human Rights in South Africa: A Continuing Struggle," 22(2) Ford Foundation Letter 6.

Keightley, Raylene. 1990. "The Trespass Act," in Murray & O'Regan.

_____. 1992. "International Human Rights Norms in a New South Africa," 8 SAJHR 171.

Keneally, Thomas. 1983. Schindler's List. Harmondsworth: Penguin.

Kenney, Henry. 1992. Power, Pride and Prejudice: The Years of Afrikaner Nationalist Rule in South Africa. Johannesburg: Jonathan Ball.

Kentridge, Felicia. 1982. Report on Recent Trends in the Organisation of Legal Services in South Africa (unpublished).

Kentridge, Matthew. 1990. An Unofficial War: Inside the conflict of Pietermaritzburg. Cape Town: David Philip.

Kentridge, Sydney. 1980. "The Pathology of a Legal System: Criminal Justice in South Africa," 128 University of Pennsylvania Law Review 603.

_____. 1981. "The Theories and Realities of the Protection of Human Rights under South African Law," 56 Tulane Law Review 227.

_____. 1982. "Telling the Truth about Law," 99 SALJ 648.

_____. 1987. Law and Lawyers in a Changing Society (First Ernie Wentzel Memoral Lecture). Johannesburg: CALS.

Keren, Michael. 1993. "Law, Security and Politics: an Israeli Case Study," 21 International Journal of the Sociology of Law 105.

Kessler, Mark. 1987. Legal Services for the Poor. Westport, Conn.: Greenwood Press.

Kettle, Martin and Lucy Hodges. 1982. Uprising! The police, the people and the riots in Britain's cities. London: Pan.

Kinoy, Arthur. 1989. Rights on Trial: The Odyssey of a People's Lawyer. Cambridge, Mass.: Harvard University Press.

Kirby, Michael. 1989. "Effective Review of Administrative Acts: The Hallmark of a Free and Fair Society," 5 SAJHR 321.

Kirchheimer, Otto. 1961. Political Justice: The Use of Legal Procedure for Political Ends. Princeton, N.J.: Princeton University Press.

Kivnick, Helen Q. 1990. Where Is the Way: Song and Struggle in South Africa. New York: Penguin Books.

Klíma, Ivan. 1993. Judge on Trial. New York: Knopf.

Klug, Heinz. 1988. "The South African Judicial Order and the Future: A Comparative Analysis of the South African Judicial System and Judicial Transitions in Zimbabwe, Mozambique, and Nicaragua," 12 Hastings International and Comparative Law Review 173.

Kluger, Richard. 1975. Simple Justice: The History of Brown v. Board of Education and Black America's Struggle for Equality. New York: Vintage.

Kruss, Glenda. 1987. "The 1986 State of Emergency in the Western Cape," 4 SAR 173.

Kuper, Leo. 1956. Passive Resistance in South Africa. London: Jonathan Cape.

Labedz, Leopold and Max Hayward, eds. 1967. On Trial: The Case of Sinyavsky (Tertz) and Daniel (Arzak). London: Collins and Harvill.

Labour Law Unit, University of Cape Town. 1988. Conference on Laws against Trade Unions and Political Organizations. Cape Town: UCT Labour Law Unit.

Labour Monitoring Group (Johannesburg). 1986. "Mayekiso Stoppage," 11(5) SALB 11 (Apr–May).

Labour Monitoring Group (Natal). 1985. "Monitoring the Sarmcol Struggle," 11(2) SALB 88 (Oct.–Dec.).

Landis, Elizabeth. 1961. "South African Apartheid Legislation," 71 Yale Law Journal 1–52, 437–500.

Laurence, Patrick. 1990. Death Squads: Apartheid's Secret Weapon. Harmondsworth: Penguin.

Lawyers' Committee for Civil Rights Under Law. 1983. Deaths in Detention and South Africa's Security Laws. Washington, D.C.: LCCRUL.

Lawyers Committee for Human Rights. 1986a. The War Against Children: South Africa's Youngest Victims. New York: LCHR.

_____. 1986b. Mamelodi: South Africa's Response to Peaceful Protest. New York: LCHR.

_____. 1986c. Deaths in Custody: Seven Recent Cases in South Africa. New York: LCHR.

_____. 1987. Crisis in Crossroads. New York: LCHR.

Lawyers for Human Rights. 1991. Phola Park, Community under Siege. Pretoria: LHR.

Lee, H.P. 1990. "A Fragile Bastion under Siege—The 1988 Convulsion in the Malaysian Judiciary," 17 Melbourne University Law Review 386.

Lee, Robin and Lawrence Schlemmer, eds. 1991. Transition to Democracy: Policy Perspectives. Cape Town: Oxford University Press.

Legal Aid in South Africa. 1974. Proceedings of a Conference held in the Faculty of Law, University of Natal, Durban, from 2nd–6th July, 1973. Durban: Faculty of Law, University of Natal.

Legal Education Centre, Black Lawyers Association. 1986. Dark City: Report on Unrest in Alexandra. Johannesburg: BLA.

Legal Resources Centre. 1989. Written Representations to the Commission of Enquiry into the 1986 Unrest and Alleged Mismanagement in KwaNdebele (May 22) (unpublished).

Legal Resources Trust. 1981–90. Annual Reports. Johannesburg: LRT.

Lelyveld, Joseph. 1985. Move Your Shadow: South Africa Black and White. New York: Times Books.

Lemon, Anthony. 1987. Apartheid in Transition. Boulder, Colo.: Westview Press.

Leon, R.N. 1986. "A Bill of Rights for South Africa: Address," 2 SAJHR 60.

Levin, Jay. 1986. "Torture Without Violence: Clinical and Ethical Issues for Mental Health Workers in the Treatment of Detainees," 2 SAJHR 177.

Levine, Adeline Gordon. 1982. Love Canal: Science, Politics, and People. Lexington, Mass.: Lexington Books.

Lewin, Hugh. 1981. Bandiet: Seven years in a South African prison. London: Heinemann.

Lewin, Julius. 1959. "Power, Law and Race Relations in South Africa," 30 Political Quarterly 389.

_____. 1963. Politics and Law in South Africa. London: Merlin Press.

Lewis, Carole. 1989. "The Prevention of Illegal Squatting Act: The Promotion of Homelessness?" 5 SAJHR 233.

Lewis, Robin. 1980. Real Trouble: A Study of Aspects of the Southall Trials. London: Runnymede Trust.

Lippman, Matthew. 1993. "They Shoot Lawyers, Don't They?: Law in the Third Reich and the Global Threat to the Independence of the Judiciary," 23 California Western International Law Journal 257.

Lipton, Merle. 1985. Capitalism and Apartheid: South Africa, 1910–84. Cape Town: David Philip.

Lobban, Michael. 1990. "Black Consciousness on Trial: The BPC/SASO Trial, 1974–1976." Johannesburg: African Studies Centre, University of the Witwatersrand (Seminar Paper 276).

_____. n.d. White Man's Justice: South African Political Trials in the Black Consciousness Era. Oxford: Oxford University Press (forthcoming).

Lodge, Tom. 1983. Black Politics in South Africa since 1945. London: Longmans.

_____. 1989. "The United Democratic Front: Leadership and Ideology," in Brewer (1989b).

Lodge, Tom, Bill Nasson, Steven Mufson, Khehla Shubane and Nokwanda Sithole. 1991. All, Here, and Now: Black Politics in South Africa in the 1980s. New York: Ford Foundation and Foreign Policy Association.

Lonsdale, John, ed. 1988. South Africa in Question. London: James Currey.

López, Gerald P. 1992. Rebellious Lawyering: One Chicano's Vision of Progressive Law Practice. Boulder, Colo.: Westview Press.

Louw, P. Eric. 1991. "Resistance in Print II: Developments in the Cape, 1985–1989: *Saamstaan, Grassroots*, and *South*," in Tomaselli & Louw (1991a).

Louw, P. Eric and Keyan Tomaselli. 1991a. "The Struggle for Legitimacy: State Pressures on the Media, 1950–1991," in Tomaselli & Louw (1991a).

_____. 1991b. "Impact of the 1990 Reforms on the 'Alternative Media,'" in Tomaselli & Louw (1991a).

Lowenstein, Karl. 1948. "Reconstruction of the Administration of Justice in American Occupied Germany," 61 Harvard Law Review 419.

Luckham, Robin. 1981. "Imperialism, Law and Structural Dependence: The Ghana Legal Profession," in C.J. Dias, R. Luckham, D.O. Lynch, and J.C.N. Paul, eds. Lawyers in the Third World: Comparative and Developmental Perspectives. Uppsala: Scandinavian Institute of African Studies and New York: International Center for Law in Development.

Lukas, J. Anthony. 1970. The Barnyard Epithet and Other Obscenities: Notes on the Chicago Conspiracy Trial. New York: Harper & Row.

MacCormick, Neil. 1978. Legal Reasoning and Legal Theory. Oxford: Oxford University Press.

_____. 1981. H.L.A. Hart. London: Edward Arnold.

_____. 1982. Legal Right and Social Democracy. Oxford: Oxford University Press.

_____. 1985. "A Moralistic Case for A–Moralistic Law?" 20 Valparaiso University Law Review 1.

_____. 1986. "The Interest of the State and the Rule of Law," in P. Wallington and R.M. Merkin, eds. Essays in Memory of Professor F.H. Lawson. London: Butterworths.

Macdonald, John, Christian Ahlund and Jeremy Sarkin. 1990. Signposts to Peace: An Independent Survey of the Violence in Natal, South Africa. Geneva: ICJ.

Mahomed, Ismail. 1989. "Disciplining Administrative Power—Some South African Prospects, Impediments and Needs," 5 SAJHR 345.

Majodina, Thole. 1986. "A Short Background to the Shooting Incident in Langa Township, Uitenhage," 8 Human Rights Quarterly 488.

Major, Reginald. 1973. Justice in the Round: The Trial of Angela Davis. New York: Third Press.

Malan, Rian. 1990. My Traitor's Heart: A South African Exile Returns to Face His Country, His Tribe, and His Conscience. New York: Atlantic Monthly Press.

Mandela, Nelson. 1960. "Courtroom Testimony," in Johns & Davis.

_____. 1964. "I Am Prepared to Die," in Johns & Davis.

Manganyi, N. Chabani and André du Toit, eds. 1990. Political Violence and the Struggle in South Africa. London: Macmillan.

Manoim, Norman. 1989. Changing Nature of Treason Trials in South Africa (unpublished).

_____. n.d. Chronology of Events in Alexandra in 1985. (unpublished).

Marcus, Gilbert. 1985a. The Freedom Charter: A Blueprint for a Democratic South Africa. Johannesburg: CALS (Occasional Paper No. 9).

_____. 1985b. "Respect for the Courts: Myth and Reality," 1 SAJHR 236.

_____. 1985c. "The Abdication of Responsibility: The Role of Doctors in the Uitenhage Unrest," 1 SAJHR 151.

_____. 1985d. "The Wider Reaches of Censorship," 1 SAJHR 69.

_____. 1988a. "Fine Distinctions, Scientific Censorship and the Courts," 4 SAJHR 82.

_____. 1988b. "Reasonable Censorship?" in Corder.

_____. 1989. "Fanning Revolution, Unrest and Violence: A Case Study of Censorship under the Emergency," 2 Harvard Human Rights Yearbook 125.

_____. 1990a. "Censorship under the emergency," in Robertson et al.

_____. 1990b. "Section 5 of the Black Administration Act: The Case of the Bakwena ba Mogopa," in Murray & O'Regan.

_____. n.d. An Examination of the Restrictions Imposed on the Press and Other Publications which appear in practice to affect members of the black group more severely [sic] than other groups. Pretoria: HSRC.

Maré, Gerhard. 1992. Brothers Born of Warrior Blood: Politics and Ethnicity in South Africa. Johannesburg: Ravan.

Maré, Gerhard and Georgina Hamilton. 1987. An Appetite for Power: Buthelezi's Inkatha and South Africa. Johannesburg: Ravan.

Maree, Johann, ed. 1987. The Independent Trade Unions, 1974–1984: Ten Years of the South African Labour Bulletin. Johannesburg: Ravan.

Martin, David and Phyllis Johnson, eds. 1986. Destructive Engagement: Southern Africa at War. Harare: Zimbabwe Publishing House.

Martin, Meredith. 1988. In the Name of Apartheid: South Africa in the Postwar Period. New York: Harper & Row.

Marx, Anthony W. 1992. Lessons of Struggle: South African Internal Opposition, 1960–1990. New York: Oxford University Press.

Mashabela, Harry. 1988. Townships of the PWV. Johannesburg: SAIRR.

_____. 1989. Fragile Figures? — The 1988 PWV Township Elections. Johannesburg: SAIRR.

_____. 1990. Mekhukhu: Urban African Cities of the Future. Johannesburg: SAIRR.

Mathabane, Mark. 1986. KafMathews, A.S. 1964. "A Bridle for the Unruly Horse," 81 SALJ 312.

_____. 1965. "An Unfortunate Rebuff," 82 SALJ 454.

_____. 1971. Law, Order and Liberty in South Africa: Cape Town: Juta.

_____. 1978. The Darker Reaches of Government. Cape Town: Juta.

_____. 1985a. "The Rule of Law—a reassessment," in E. Kahn, ed. Fiat Justitia, Essays in memory of O D Schreiner. Cape Town: Juta.

_____. 1985b. "The South African Judiciary and the Security System," 1 SAJHR 199.

_____. 1986. Freedom, State Security and the Rule of Law. Cape Town: Juta.

_____. 1987. "Human Rights and the Rule of Law II," in Butler et al.

Mathews, A.S. and R.C. Albino. 1966. "The Permanence of the Temporary: An Examination of the 90– and 180–Day Detention Laws," 83 SALJ 25.

Mathews, M.L. 1982/83. "Subjective Discretion Clauses and the Jurisdiction of the Court—An Analytical Approach," 1982/83 Natal University Law Review 51.

Mathews, M.L., Philip B. Heymann, and A.S. Mathews, eds. 1993. Policing the Conflict in South Africa. Gainesville: University Press of Florida.

Mattera, Don. 1987. Sophiatown: Coming of Age in South Africa. London: Zed Press.

Maylam, Paul. 1990. "The Rise and Decline of Urban Apartheid in South Africa," 89 African Affairs 57.

Mazwai, Thami, Arthur Konigkramer, Connie Molusi, Kaizer Nyatsumba, Dawn Lindberg, Lionel Abrahams, Nomavenda Mathiane, Joe Thloloe and John Kane–Berman. 1991. Mau–Mauing the Media: New Censorship for the New South Africa. Braamfontein: SAIRR.

Mbeki, Govan. 1991. Learning from Robben Island. Cape Town: David Philip.

McCaul, Coleen. 1987. Satellite in Revolt. KwaNdebele: An Economic and Political Profile. Johannesburg: SAIRR.

McConnell, W.H. 1974. "Political Trials East and West," [1974] Saskatchewan Law Review 131.

McKee, Grant and Ros Franey. 1988. Time Bomb: Irish Bombers, English Justice and the Guildford Four. London: Bloomsbury.

McKendrick, Brian and Wilma Hoffmann, eds. 1990. People and Violence in South Africa. Cape Town: Oxford University Press.

McQuoid–Mason, David J. 1982. An Outline of Legal Aid in South Africa. Durban: Butterworths.

_____. 1984. "Problems Associated with Legal Representation of Africans in the Urban Areas of South Africa," [1984] Acta Juridica 181.

_____, ed. 1985. Legal Aid and Law Clinics in South Africa. Durban: University of Natal.

_____. 1986a. "Detainees and the Duties of District Surgeons," 2 SAJHR 49.

_____. 1986b. "The Organisation, Administration and Funding of Legal Aid Clinics in South Africa," 1(2) Natal University Law and Society Review 189.

_____. 1988. "The Responsibility of Doctors during the State of Emergency," [1988] Acta Juridica 65.

Medical Association of South Africa. 1983. Report on Medical Care of Prisoners and Detainees. Supplement to South African Medical Journal (May 21).

Meer, Fatima, ed. 1985. Unrest in Natal: August 1985.... Durban: Institute for Black Research.

_____. 1989. Treason Trial—1985. Durban: Madiba Publishers.

_____. n.d. Robert McBride and Greta Apelgren: The Magoos Bombing: A Sociological Report for the Defence. Johannesburg: Skotaville.

Memmi, Albert. 1968. Dominated Man. New York: Orion Press.

_____. 1984. Dependence. Boston: Beacon Press.

_____. 1990. The Colonizer and the Colonized. London: Earthscan.

Mermelstein, D., ed. 1987. The Anti–Apartheid Reader: The Struggle Against White Racist Rule in South Africa. New York: Grove Press.

Merrett, Christopher. 1990. "In a State of Emregency: Libraries and Government Control in South Africa," 60 Library Q. 1.

Merrit, N. 1988. Detentions and the Crisis in the Pietermaritzburg Area, 1987–1988. Pietermaritzburg: Centre for Adult Education, University of Natal.

Mgogi, Wallace. 1992. "The Work of the Legal Resources Centre in South Africa in the Area of Human Rights Promotion and Protection," 36 Journal of African Law 1.

Mihalik, Janos. 1980. Gevangenisstraf: Noodsaklikheid vir Alternatiewe Straawe. Ph.D. dissertation, law, University of South Africa.

_____. 1989. "Restrictions on Prison Reporting: Protection of the Truth or a Licence for Distortion?" 5 SAJHR 406.

Millner, M.A. 1961. "Apartheid and the South African Courts," 14 Current Legal Problems 280.

Milton, J.R.L. 1970. "A Cloistered Virtue," 87 SALJ 424.

Mitchell, Richard H. 1992. Janus–Faced Justice: Political Criminals in Imperial Japan. Honolulu: University of Hawaii Press.

Mitford, Jessica. 1969. The Trial of Dr. Spock. New York: Knopf.

Mkhondo, Rich. 1993. Reporting South Africa. London: James Currey.

Mokgatle, D.D. 1987. "The Exclusion of Blacks from the South African Judicial System," 3 SAJHR 44.

Monama, Ramarumo. 1983. Is This Justice? A Study of the Johannesburg Commissioners' ('Pass') Courts. Johannesburg: CALS (Occasional Paper No. 4).

Moodie, T. Dunbar. 1975. The Rise of Afrikanerdom: Power, Apartheid, and the Afrikaner Civil Religion. Berkeley: University of California Press.

Moodley, Inthiran. 1990. "Mass dismissals," in Robertson et al.

Morris, Alan. 1986. Forced removals continue: old Brits location under threat," 11(8) SALB 46 (Sept–Oct).

_____. 1989. "The South African State and the Oukasie Removal," 8 Transformation 24.

_____. 1990. "The Complexities of Sustained Urban Struggle: The Case of Oukasie," 2(2) South African Sociological Review 49.

Moseki, Mojalefa. 1988. "Black journalists under apartheid," 7/88 Index on Censorship 22.

Moss, Glenn. 1979. Political Trials. South Africa: 1976–1979. Johannesburg: University of the Witwatersrand, Development Studies Group (Information Publication 2).

Moss, Rose. 1990. Shouting at the Crocodile: Popo Molefe, Patrick Lekota, and the Freeing of South Africa. Boston: Beacon Press.

Mphahlele, Ezekiel. 1967. In Corner B. Nairobi: East African Publishing House.

_____. 1971. Down Second Avenue. Garden City, N.Y.: Doubleday.

Müller, Ingo. 1991. Hitler's Justice: The Courts of the Third Reich. Cambridge, Mass.: Harvard University Press.

Mufson, Steven. 1990. Fighting Years: Black Resistance and the Struggle for a New South Africa. Boston: Beacon Press.

Mullin, Chris. 1990. Error of Judgement: The Truth about the Birmingham Bombings. Swords, Ireland: Poolbeg.

Mulloy, Eanna. 1986. Emergency Legislation: Dynasties of Coercion. Derry: Field Day Theater Co. (Pamphlet No. 10).

Munnik Commission. 1987. Report of the Commission of Inquiry into Certain Advertisements. Pretoria: Government Printer.

Mureinik, Etienne. 1985a. "Fundamental Rights and Delegated Legislation," 1 SAJHR 111.

_____. 1985b. "Discretion and Commitment: The Stock Exchange Case," 102 SALJ 434.

_____. 1985c. "Liversidge in Decay," 102 SALJ 77.

_____. 1986. "Administrative Law in South Africa," 103 SALJ 615.

_____. 1987. "Security and Integrity," [1987] Acta Juridica 197.

Murray, Christina and Laura Mangan. 1987. "Hangings in Southern Africa: The Last Ten Years," 3 SAJHR 387.

Murray, Christina and Julia Sloth–Nielsen. 1988. "Hangings in Southern Africa: The Last Ten Years," 4 SAJHR 391.

_____. 1989. "Hangings in South Africa: The Last Ten Years," 5 SAJHR 490.

Murray, Christina, Julia Sloth–Nielsen and Colin Tredoux. 1990a. "Correspondence," 6 SAJHR 102.

_____. 1990b. "The Death Penalty in the Cape Provincial Division: 1986–1988," 5 SAJHR 154.

Murray, Christina and Catherine O'Regan, eds. 1990. No Place to Rest: Forced Removals and the Law in South Africa. Cape Town: Oxford University Press and UCT Labour Law Unit.

Murray, Colin. 1992. Black Mountain: Land, Class and Power in the Eastern Orange Free State, 1880s–1980s. Edinburgh: Edinburgh University Press for International African Institute.

Murray, Martin. 1987. South Africa: Time of Agony, Time of Destiny. The Upsurge of Popular Protest. London: Verso.

Mzala. 1988. Gatsha Buthelezi: Chief with a double agenda. London: Zed Books.

Naidoo, I. 1982. Island in Chains. Harmondsworth: Penguin.

Nathan, Laurie. 1987. "Resistance to Militarisation: Three Years of the End Conscription Campaign," 4 SAR 104.

National Committee Against Removals. n.d. Botshabelo: Incorporation Now, Independence Next? Cape Town: NCAR.

National Council for Civil Liberties. 1980a. Southall, 23 April 1979: The Report of the Unofficial Committee of Enquiry. London: NCCL.

_____. 1980b. The Death of Blair Peach: Supplementary Report of the Unofficial Committee of Enquiry. London: NCCL.

_____. 1984. Civil Liberties and the Miners' Dispute: First Report of the Independent Inquiry. London: NCCL.

_____. 1986a. Stonehenge: A report into the civil liberties implications of the events relating to the convoys of summer 1985 and 1986. London: NCCL.

_____. 1986b. No Way in Wapping: The effect of the policing of the News International dispute on Wapping Residents. London: NCCL.

National Land Committee. 1990a. Land Update. Johannesburg: NLC.

_____. 1990b. The Bantustans in Crisis. Johannesburg: NLC.

Neumann, Franz. 1972. Behemoth: The Structure and Practice of National Socialism, 1933–1944. New York: Octagon Books.

New York Review of Books. 1970. Trials of the Resistance. New York: NYRB.

Ngale, Phineas and G.M. Budlender. 1991. Oukasie Development Trust—Upgrading and Extension of Oukasie, Brits (unpublished).

Nicholson, Chris. 1986. "Nothing Really Gets Better: Reflections on the Twenty–Five Years Between Sharpeville and Uitenhage," 8 Human Rights Quarterly 511.

Niehaus, Carl. 1994. Fighting For Hope. Cape Town: Human & Rousseau.

Nienaber, G.M. 1983. "Discretions, Ouster Clauses and the Internal Security Act," 46 THRHR 211.

North, James. 1986. Freedom Rising. New York: New American Library.

Norton, M.L. 1982/83. "The Political Trial in South Africa: The Quest for Legitimacy," 1982/83(3) Natal University Law Review 97.

Ntshakala, Siza and Clive Emdon. 1991. "The New African: Hopes, Struggles and Problems," in Tomaselli & Louw (1991a).

Ogilvie Thompson, N. 1972. "Speech on the Centenary Celebration of the Northern Cape Division," 89 SALJ 30.

Okojie, Paul. 1991 "Black People and the Miscarriage of Justice: A Review of the Campaign to Free the Tottenham Three," 16(3) Sage Race Relations Abstracts 21 (August).

Olgiati, Vittorio. 1989. "The Law 'In Motion' and the Role of Lawyers during the Fascist Dictatorship in Italy." Presented to the ISA Research Committee on Sociology of Law, Caracas (July 3–8).

Olson, Peter. 1991. "The US Human Rights Program in South Africa, 1986–89," 13 Human Rights Quarterly 24.

O'Regan, Catherine. 1989. "No More Forced Removals? An Historical Analysis of the Prevention of Illegal Squatting Act," 5 SAJHR 361.

_____. 1990. "The Prevention of Illegal Squatting Act," in Murray & O'Regan.

Ormond, R. 1985. The Apartheid Handbook. Harmondsworth: Penguin.

Orr, Wendy. 1988. "Call to the International Community," in Brittain & Minty.

Orwell, George. 1949. 1984. Harmondsworth: Penguin.

Osiel, Mark. 1984. "The Dilemmas of Latin American Liberalism: The Case of Raimundo Faoro," 21 Luso–Brazilian Review.

_____. 1986. "The Making of Human Rights Policy in Argentina," 18 Journal of Latin American Studies 135.

Ottaway, David. 1993. Chained Together: Mandela, de Klerk, and the Struggle to Remake South Africa. New York: Times Books.

Ottaway, Marina. 1993. South Africa: The Struggle for a New Order. Washington, D.C.: Brookings Institution.

Parry, Sarah. 1981. Outcasts From Justice—the consequences of banning orders under the Internal Security Act. Johannesburg: CALS (Occasional Paper No. 2).

Parsons Commission. 1992. Report of the Commission of Enquiry into the 1986 Unrest and Alleged Mismanagement in KwaNdebele. Pretoria: Government Printer.

Paton, A.S. 1987. Save the Beloved Country. Melville: Hans Strydom.

Pattee, George. 1953. The Case of Cardinal Aloysius Stepinac. Milwaukee: Bruce Publishers.

Pauw, Jacques. 1991. In the Heart of the Whore: The Story of South Africa's Death Squads. Halfway House: Southern Book Publishers.

Peterson, Horace C. and Gilbert C. Fite. 1957. Opponents of War, 1917–18. Madison: University of Wisconsin Press.

Pheto, M. 1983. And Night Fell: Memoirs of a Political Prisoner in South Africa. London: Allison and Busby.

Pitts, Joe W. (Chip), III. 1986. "Note: Public Interest Law in South Africa," 22 Stanford Journal of International Law 153.

Piven, Frances Fox and Richard A. Cloward. 1977. Poor People's Movements: Why They Succeed, How They Fail. New York: Pantheon.

PLANACT. 1990. The Soweto Rent Boycott: A Report by PLANACT. Johannesburg: Planact.

Plasket, Clive. 1986a. "The Eastern Cape Bench, Civil Liberties and the 1985/1986 State of Emergency," 2 SAJHR 142.

_____. 1986b. "Anton Piller Orders and Police Stations," 2 SAJHR 67.

_____. 1989. "Sub–Contracting the Dirty Work," [1989] Acta Juridica 165.

_____, ed. 1990a. Policing and the Law. Cape Town: Juta.

_____. 1990b. "Homeland Incorporation: The New Forced Removals," in Murray & O'Regan.

_____. 1992. "The Final Word on Anton Piller Orders Against the Police," 8 SAJHR 569.

Plasket, Clive and P.L. Firman. 1984. "Subordinate Legislation and Unreasonableness: The Application of Cruse v Johnson ([1898] 2 QB 91) by the South African Courts," 47 THRHR 416.

Platzky, Laurine. 1985. "Relocation in South Africa: A Review," 1 SAJHR 270.

_____. 1986. "Reprieves and Repression: Relocation in South Africa," 3 SAR 381.

_____. 1987. "Restructuring and Apartheid: Relocation during the State of Emergency," 4 SAR 451.

Platzky, Laurine and Cherryl Walker. 1985. The Surplus People: Forced Removals in South Africa. Johannesburg: Ravan Press.

Posel, Deborah. 1990. "Symbolizing Violence: State and Media Discourse in Television Coverage of Township Protest, 1985–7," in Manganyi & du Toit.

_____. 1991. The Making of Apartheid, 1948–61: Conflict and Compromise. Oxford: Clarendon Press.

Price, Robert M. 1991. The Apartheid State in Crisis: Political Transformation in South Africa, 1975–1990. New York: Oxford University Press.

Prior, Andrew. 1989. "The South African Police and the Counter–Revolution of 1985–1987," [1989] Acta Juridica 189.

Rabie Commission. 1981. Report of the Commission of Inquiry into Security Legislation (RP90/1981). Cape Town: Government Printer.

Radford, E.J. and W. Leeb. 1986. "An Investigation into the Effects of Job Loss on the African Township of Mpophomeni." Pietermaritzburg: University of Natal, Department of Psychology.

Ramgobin, Mewa. 1986. Waiting to Live. New York: Vintage.

Randall, Peter, ed. 1972. Law, Justice & Society. Johannesburg: SPROCAS.

Rauh, Joseph L., Jr. 1993. "Nomination and Confirmation of Supreme Court Justices: Some Personal Observations," 45 Maine Law Review 7.

Rayner, Mary. 1986. "Law, Politics, and Treason in South Africa," 8 Human Rights Quarterly 471.

_____. 1987. Turning a Blind Eye? Medical Accountability and the Prevention of Torture in South Africa. Washington, D.C.: Committee on Scientific Freedom and Responsibility, American Association for the Advancement of Science.

_____. 1990. "From Biko to Wendy Orr: the Problem of Medical Accountability in Contexts of Political Violence and Torture," in Manganyi & du Toit.

Raz, Joseph. 1979. The Authority of Law. Cambridge: Cambridge University Press.

Ream, Davidson. 1970. "The Right to Counsel in South Africa," 18 UCLA Law Review 335.

Rees, Mervyn and Chris Day. 1980. Muldergate: The Story of the Info Scandal. Johannesburg: Macmillan.

Reifner, Udo. 1982. "Individualistic and Collective Legalization: The Theory and Practice of Legal Advice for Workers in Prefascist Germany," in Richard L. Abel, ed. The Politics of Informal Justice, vol. 2: Comparative Studies. New York: Academic Press.

_____. 1986. "The Bar in the Third Reich: Anti–Semitism and the Decline of Liberal Advocacy," 32 McGill Law Journal 96.

Republic of South Africa. 1991. White Paper on Land Reform. Pretoria: Government Printer.

Rhadamanthus. 1970. "Contempt of Court? The Trial of B. van D. van Niekerk," [1970] Acta Juridica 77.

Rickard, Carmel. 1990. "Natal conflict and strategies for peace," in Robertson et al.

Riekert Commission. 1979. Republic of South Africa, Report of the Commission of Inquiry into Legislation Affecting the Utilization of Manpower (RP 32/1979). Pretoria: Government Printer.

Riekert, Julian G. 1982. "Police Assaults and the Admissibility of 'Voluntary' Confessions," 99 SALJ 175.

_____. 1985a. "The Silent Scream: Detention without Trial, Solitary Confinement and Evidence in South African 'Security Law' Trials," 1 SAJHR 235.

_____. 1985b. "The DDD Syndrome: Solitary Confinement and a South African Security Law Trial," in Bell & Mackie.

Ritchken, Edwin. 1989. "Introduction," 5 SAR 391.

Rive, Richard. 1986. 'Buckingham Palace,' District Six. New York: Ballantine Books.

Robertson, Janet. 1971. Liberalism in South Africa, 1948–1963. Oxford: Clarendon Press.

Robertson, Michael. 1987. "'Orderly Urbanization': The New Influx Control," in Rycroft et al.

_____. 1989. "The Participation of Judges in the Present Legal System: Should Judges Resign?" in Hugh Corder, ed. Democracy and the Judiciary. Cape Town: Idasa.

_____. 1990. "Dividing the Land: An Introduction to Apartheid Land Law," in Murray & O'Regan.

_____, ed. 1991. Human Rights for South Africans. Cape Town: Oxford University Press.

Robertson, Michael, Chris Albertyn and Megan Seneque, eds. 1990. South African Human Rights and Labour Law Yearbook. Cape Town: Oxford University Press and Durban: Centre for Socio–Legal Studies.

Rockman, Gregory and Eugene Abrahams. 1989. Rockman: One man's crusade against apartheid police. Melville: Senior Publications.

Roebuck, Julian C. and Stanley C. Weaber. 1978. Political Crime in the United States: Analyzing Crime by and against Government. New York: Praeger.

Roos, Johan. 1987. "Labour Law in South Africa, 1976–1986: The Birth of Legal Discipline," [1987] Acta Juridica 94.

_____. 1988. "On Illegal Squatters and Spoliation Orders," 4 SAJHR 167.

_____. 1989. "On Illegal Squatters and Spoliation Orders II," 5 SAJHR 395.

Rose, David. 1992. A Climate of Fear: The Murder of PC Blakelock and the Case of the Tottenham Three. London: Bloomsbury Publ.

Rosenberg, Gerald N. 1991. The Hollow Hope: Can Courts Bring About Social Change? Chicago: University of Chicago Press.

Rostron, Bryan. 1991. Till Babylon Falls. London: Coronet Books.

Roux, Edward. 1964. Time Longer Than Rope: A history of the black man's struggle for freedom in South Africa. Madison: University of Wisconsin Press.

Rudolph, H.G. 1979. "Man's Inhumanity to Man Makes Countless Thousands Mourn! Do Prisoners Have Rights?" 96 SALJ 640.

_____. 1980. "Racial Insensitivity and the Appellate Division," 4 SACC 66.

_____. 1984. Security, Terrorism and Torture: Detainees' Rights in South Africa and Israel—A Comparative Study. Cape Town: Juta.

Rycroft, A.J., L.J. Boulle, M.K. Robertson and P.R. Spiller, eds. 1987. Race and the Law in South Africa. Cape Town: Juta & Co.

Sabin, Arthur J. 1993. Red Scare in Court: New York versus the International Workers Order. Philadelphia: University of Pennsylvania Press.

Sachs, Albie. 1973. Justice in South Africa. Berkeley: University of California Press.

_____. 1975. "The Instruments of Domination in South Africa," in Thompson & Butler.

_____. 1985. "Towards the Reconstruction of South Africa," 12 Journal of Southern African Studies 49.

_____. 1990a. The Jail Diary of Albie Sachs. Cape Town: David Philip.

_____. 1990b. "Towards a Bill of Rights in a Democratic South Africa," 6 SAJHR 1.

_____. 1991. Human Rights in a New South Africa. Cape Town: Oxford University Press.

_____. 1993. Advancing Human Rights in South Africa. Cape Town: Oxford University Press.

Saltman, Michael and Henry Rosenfeld. 1990. "Rule of law versus political interest," 14 Contemporary Crises 1.

Sampson, Anthony. 1956. Drum: A Venture into the new Africa. London: Collins.

_____. 1958. The Treason Cage: The Opposition on Trial in South Africa. London: Heinemann.

Sanders, A.J.G.M. 1986. "A Bill of Rights for South Africa?" 1 South African Public Law 1.

Sarakinsky, M. 1984. From 'freehold township' to 'model township'—a political history of Alexandra: 1905–1083. B.A. honours dissertation, Development Studies, University of the Witwatersrand.

Saul, John and Stephen Gelb. 1981. The Crisis in South Africa: Class Defence, Class Revolution. New York: Monthly Review Press.

Savage, Michael. 1984. Pass Laws and the Disorganization and Reorganization of the African Population in South Africa. Rondebosch: South Africa Labour and Development Research Unit, School of Economics, University of Cape Town.

Scarry, Elaine. 1985. The Body in Pain: The Making and Unmaking of the World. New York: Oxford University Press.

Schärf, Wilfried. 1989. "The Role of People's Courts in Transitions," in Hugh Corder, ed. Democracy and the Judiciary. Cape Town: Institute for Democratic Alternatives in South Africa.

_____. 1990. People's Courts: The Sociology of Township Justice. Cape Town: University of Cape Town, Institute of Criminology.

_____. n.d. Police Abuse of Power and Victim Assistance during Apartheid's Emergency (unpublished).

Schärf, Wilfried and Baba Ngcoto. 1990. "Images of Punishment in the People's Courts of Cape Town 1985–7: from Prefigurative Justice to Populist Violence," in Manganyi and du Toit.

Schafer, Stephen. 1974. The Political Criminal. New York: Free Press.

Scheingold, Stuart A. 1974. The Politics of Rights: Lawyers, Public Policy, and Political Change. New Haven: Yale University Press.

Schlemmer, Lawrence and Valerie Moller. 1985. "Constraint, stress and reaction: the responses of migrant contract workers to their situation," in Giliomee & Schlemmer.

Schneider, Martin. 1987. "The Last Word," 6(5) Leadership in South Africa 21.

Schneir, Walter and Miriam Schneir. 1965. Invitation to an Inquest: A New Look at the Rosenberg–Sobell Case. New York: Doubleday.

Schoombee, Hannes and Dennis Davis. 1986. "Abolishing Influx Control—Fundamental or Cosmetic Change?" 2 SAJHR 208.

Schrag, Philip G. 1972. Counsel for the Deceived: Case Studies in Consumer Fraud. New York: Pantheon.

Schreiner, O.D. 1967. The Contribution of English Law to South African Law; and The Rule of Law in South Africa. London: Stevens & Sons.

Schrire, Robert. 1991. Adapt or Die: The End of White Politics in South Africa. New York: Ford Foundation and Foreign Policy Association.

Schultz, John. 1993. The Chicago Conspiracy Trial (rev. ed.). New York: Da Capo Press.

Scott, Craig and Patrick Macklem. 1992. "Constitutional Ropes of Sand or Justiciable Guarantees? Social Rights in a New South African Constitution," 141 University of Pennsylvania Law Review 1.

Scraton, Phil, ed. 1987. Law, Order and the Authoritarian State. Milton Keynes: Open University Press.

Scraton, Phil and Phil Thomas, eds. 1985. "The State v The People: Lessons from the Coal Dispute," 12(3) Journal of Law and Society (Winter).

Seegers, Annette. 1988. "Extending the Security Network to the Local Level," in Chris Heymans and Gerhard Totemeyer, eds. Government by the People. Cape Town: Juta.

Seekings, Jeremy. 1989. "People's Courts and Popular Politics," 5 SAR 119.

_____. 1992. "The Revival of 'People's Courts': Informal Justice in Transitional South Africa," 6 SAR 186.

Seidman, Gay. 1993. Manufacturing Militance: Workers' Movements in Brazil and South Africa, 1970–1985. Berkeley: University of California Press.

Selvan. R.L. 1986. "The District Surgeon's Dilemma," 5 SAJHR 219.

Shamir, Ronen. 1992. "The Bar Association Hasn't Got the Guts to Speak: The Untold Story of the American Bar Association's Committee on the New Deal." Chicago: American Bar Foundation (Working Paper 92–02).

Sharpeville Commission. 1960. Report of the Commission of Inquiry into Sharpeville, 21 March 1960 in terms of GN 169 GGE 6404 of 1 April 1960. Pretoria: Government Printer.

Sher, Mark. 1985. "From *dompas* to disc: the legal control of migrant labour," in Davis & Slabbert.

Silver, Louise. 1979. "The Statistics of Censorship," 96 SALJ 120.

_____. 1983. "Trends in Publication Control: A Statistical Analysis," 100 SALJ 520.

_____. 1984. A Guide to Political Censorship in South Africa. Johannesburg: CALS (Occasional Paper No. 6).

Simkins, Charles. 1983. Four Essays on the Past, Present and Future Distribution of the Black Population of South Africa. Cape Town: South Africa Labour and Development Research Unit.

_____. 1986. Reconstructing South African Liberalism. Johannesburg: SAIRR.

Simon, Paul. 1992. Advice and Consent: Clarence Thomas, Robert Bork and the Intriguing History of the Supreme Court's Nomination Battles. Bethesda, Md.: National Press Books.

Simpson, A.W.B. 1988. "Rhetoric, Reality, and Regulation 18B," [1988] Denning Law Journal 123.

Skolnick, Jerome H. 1966. Justice Without Trial: Law Enforcement in a Democratic Society. New York: John Wiley.

_____. 1969. The Politics of Protest. New York: Ballantine Books.

Slabbert, Mana. 1981. South Africa's Legal System: Justice for All? Prospects and Problems. Cape Town: UCT Institute of Criminology.

Smith, Bradley F. 1977. Reading Judgment at Nuremberg. New York: Basic Books.

Snow, Peter G. 1975. "Judges and Generals: The Role of the Argentine Supreme Court during Periods of Military Government," 24 Jahrbuch des Öffentlichen Rechts der Gegenwart 609.

Snyman, Johannes Hendrik. 1970. South Africa and the Rule of Law: Testimony of a Supreme Court Judge. London: South Africa Society.

Soggot, David. 1986. Namibia: The Violent Heritage. New York: St. Martin's Press.

Soper, Philip. 1977. "Legal Theory and the Obligation of a Judge: The Hart/Dworkin Dispute," 75 Michigan Law Review 511.

_____. 1984. A Theory of Law. Cambridge, Mass.: Harvard University Press.

South Africa, Department of Foreign Affairs. 1968. South Africa and the Rule of Law. Pretoria: Government Printer.

South African Catholic Bishops' Conference and South African Council of Churches. 1984. Relocations: The Churches' Report on Forced Removals. Johannesburg: SACBC and SACC.

South African Institute of Race Relations. 1978–1986. Annual Survey of Race Relations in South Africa. Braamfontein: SAIRR.

South African Journal on Human Rights. 1987. "Focus on Omar," 3 SAJHR 295–337.

_____. 1992. "Focus on Rudman," 8 SAJHR 90–125.

South African Labour Bulletin. 1985a. "Interview: Sarmcol BTR Strike," 10(8) SALB (July–Aug).

_____. 1985b. "Document: The BTR Sarmcol Strike—June 1985," 10(8) SALB 33 (July–Aug).

_____. 1985c. "BTR: The International Factor," 11(1) SALB 2 (Sept).

_____. 1986. "Solidarity Stoppage at Dunlop," 11(5) SALB 13 (Apr–May).

South African Law Journal. 1980. "The Didcott Memorandum and Other Submissions to the Hoexter Commission," 97 SALJ 651.

_____. 1989. "The Relaunch of the Society for the Abolition of the Death Penalty in South Africa," 106 SALJ 39.

Sparks, Allister. 1990. The Mind of South Africa. New York: Alfred A. Knopf.

Sperling, Gerald B. and James E. McKenzie, eds. 1990. Getting the Real Story: Censorship and Propaganda in South Africa. Calgary: Detselig Enterprises.

Spiller, P.R. 1982–85. "History of the Natal University Law Faculty," [1982/83] Natal University Law Review 1, [1984] Natal University Law Review 7, 1 Natal University Law and Society Review 1.

Spink, Kathryn. 1991. Black Sash: The Beginning of a Bridge in South Africa. London: Methuen.

Stadler, Alf. 1987. The Political Economy of Modern South Africa. Cape Town: David Philip.

Stalker, John. 1988. Stalker: Ireland, 'Shoot to Kill' and the 'Affair.' Harmondsworth: Penguin.

Stern, Gerald. M. 1977. The Buffalo Creek Disaster. New York: Vintage.

Stewart, Gavin. 1987. "'Perfecting the free flow of information': media control in South Africa, 12 June to 18 November, 1986," 1/87 Index on Censorship 29.

Steyn, L.C. 1967. "Regsbank en Regsfakulteit," 30 THRHR 101.

Steytler, N.C. 1988. The Undefended Accused. Johannesburg: Juta.

_____. 1989. "Policing 'Unrest': The Restoring of Authority," [1989] Acta Juridica 234.

_____, ed. 1990a. Policing Political Opponents. Cape Town: Oxford University Press.

_____. 1990b. "Policing political opponents: Death squads and cop culture," in Hansson & van Zyl Smit.

Straker, Gill, with Fatima Meer, Rise Becker and Madiyoyo Nkwale. 1992. Faces in the Revolution: The Psychological Effects of Violence on Township Youth in South Africa. Cape Town: David Philip and Columbus: Ohio University Press.

Stuart, K. 1986. The Newspaperman's Guide to the Law (4th ed.). Durban: Butterworth.

Strydom, Lauritz. 1965. Rivonia Unmasked! Johannesburg: Voortrekkerspers.

Sumner, Colin. 1983. "Rethinking deviance: Towards a sociology of censures," 5 Research in Law, Deviance and Social Control 187.

_____, ed. 1990. Censure, Politics and Criminal Justice. Milton Keynes: Open University Press.

Sutcliffe, Michael, Alison Todes and Norah Walker. 1990. "Managing the Cities: An Examination of State Urbanization Policies since 1986," in Murray & O'Regan.

Sutcliffe, Michael and Paul Welling. 1988: "Inkatha versus the Rest: Black Opposition to Inkatha in Durban's African Townships," 87 African Affairs 325.

Suttner, Raymond. 1984a. "Political Trials and the Legal Process," 2 SAR 63 [reprinted in 24 Crime and Social Justice 61 (1985)].

_____. 1984b. The Freedom Charter—The People's Charter in the Nineteen–Eighties. (26th T B Davie Memorial Lecture, UCT).

_____. 1986. "The Judiciary: Its Ideological Role in South Africa," 14 International Journal of the Sociology of Law 47.

Suttner, Raymond and Jeremy Cronin. 1986. 30 Years of the Freedom Charter. Johannesburg: Ravan.

Suzman, Arthur. 1968. "South Africa and the Rule of Law," 85 SALJ 261.

_____. 1973. Law and Order and the Rule of Law in South Africa. Johannesburg: SAIRR (Topical Talk No. 30).

Suzman, Helen. 1993. In No Uncertain Terms: A South African Memoir. New York: Knopf.

Swilling, M., R. Humphries and K. Shubane, eds. 1991. Apartheid City in Transition. Cape Town: Oxford University Press.

Swindle, Howard. 1993. Deliberate Indifference: A Story of Murder and Racial Injustice. New York: Viking.

Taylor, Peter. 1987. Stalker: The Search for the Truth. London: Faber and Faber.

Taylor, Telford. 1993. The Anatomy of the Nuremberg Trials: A Personal Memoir. New York: Knopf.

Teubner, G.C.M., ed. 1988. Autopoietic Law, a New Approach to Law and Society. Berlin: De Gruyter.

_____. 1990. State, Law, Economy as Autopoietic Systems: Regulation and Autonomy in a New Perspective. Berlin: De Gruyter.

Thomashausen, Andre E.A.M. 1984. "Human Rights in South Africa: The Case of Bophuthatswana," 101 SALJ 467.

Thompson, Clive. 1988. "Trade Unions using the Law," in Corder. Thompson, E.P. 1975. Whigs and Hunters: The Origins of the Black Act. New York: Pantheon.

Thompson, E.P. 1975. Whigs and Hunters: The Origin of The Black Act. New York: Pantheon.

Thompson, Leonard. 1985. The Political Mythology of Apartheid. New Haven: Yale University Press.

Thompson, Leonard and Jeffrey Butler, eds. 1975. Change in Contemporary South Africa. Berkeley: University of California Press.

Thornton, Peter. 1987. The Civil Liberties of the Zircon Affair. London: NCCL.

Thornton, Robert. 1990. "The Shooting at Uitenhage, 1985: The Context and Interpretation of Violence," in Manganyi & du Toit.

Tomaselli, Keyan and P. Eric Louw, eds. 1991a. The Alternative Press in South Africa. Bellville: Anthropos and London: James Currey.

_____. 1991b. "The South African Progressive Press Under Emergency, 1986–1989," in Tomaselli & Louw (1991a).

Tomlinson, Richard. 1988. "South Africa's Urban Policy: A New Form of Influx Control," 23 Urban Affairs Quarterly 487.

Tourikis, P.N. 1981. The "Political Economy" of Alexandra Township: 1905–1958. B.A. honours dissertation, Industrial Sociology, University of the Witwatersrand.

Transvaal Rural Action Committee. 1986a. Newsletter No. 10 (April). Johannesburg: TRAC.

_____. 1986b. Newsletter No. 11 (July). Johannesburg: TRAC.

_____. 1988a. Mogopa: And Now We Have No Land. Johannesburg: TRAC.

_____. 1988b. "Kwandebele—The Struggle Against 'Independence,'" in Cobbett & Cohen.

Trapido, Stanley. 1970. "Liberalism in the Cape in the 19th and 20th Centuries," in Institute of Commonwealth Studies, Collected Seminar Papers (vol. 4). London: ICS.

_____. 1980. "The 'Friends of the Natives': Merchants, Peasants and the Political and Ideological Structure of Liberalism at the Cape, 1854–1910," in Shula Marks and A. Atmore, eds., Economy and Society in Pre–Industrial South Africa. London: Longmans.

Trichardt, A.P. and H.C. Trichardt. 1986. "Civil Disobedience," [1986] De Rebus 216 (May).

Tun Salleh Abas with K. Das. 1989. May Day for Justice. Kuala Lumpur: Magnus Books.

Turk, Austin T. 1972. "The Limits of Coercive Legalism in Conflict Regulation: South Africa," in Ernest Q. Campbell, ed. Racial Tensions and National Identity. Nashville: Vanderbilt University Press.

_____. 1981. "The Meaning of Criminality in South Africa," 9 International Journal of the Sociology of Law 123.

_____. 1982. Political Criminality: The Defiance and Defense of Authority. Newbury Park, Ca.: Sage Publications.

Turnbull, Malcolm. 1988. The Spy Catcher Trial. London: Heinemann.

Tushnet, Mark. 1987. The NAACP's Legal Strategy against Segregated Education, 1925–1950. Chapel Hill: University of North Carolina Press.

Tushnet, Mark and Katya Lezin. 1991. "What Really Happened in Brown v. Board of Education?" 91 Columbia Law Review 1867.

Tyson, Harvey, ed. 1987. Conflict and the Press: Proceedings of the Star's Centennial Conference on the Role of the Press in a Divided Society. Johannesburg: Argus.

Unicef. 1987. The Impact of Apartheid, Warfare, and Destabilization on Children in Southern and South Africa. Paris: Unicef.

_____. 1989. The Impact of Apartheid, Warfare, and Destabilization on Children in Southern and South Africa (2nd ed.). Paris: Unicef.

United Nations. 1973. Maltreatment and Torture of Prisoners in South Africa. New York: UN.

United States Congress, House Committee on International Relations, Subcommittee on Africa. 1977. Resolutions to investigate Steven Biko's death and to condemn the Government of South Africa for massive violations of civil liberties of the people of South Africa. 95th Congress, 1st Session, H.Res. 809, H.Conc. Res. 398 (October 26).

United States, Department of State. 1989. "South Africa," in Country Reports on Human Rights Practices for 1988. Washington, D.C.: USGPO.

Unterhalter, David. 1986. "Legal Professional Privilege: A Rule of Evidence or a Procedural Right?" 2 SAJHR 312.

_____. 1990. "Legitimate Expectation and the Law of Chiefs," in Murray & O'Regan.

Unterhalter, Elaine. 1987. Forced Removal: The Division, Segregation and Control of the People of South Africa. London: International Defence and Aid Fund for Southern Africa.

Upham, Frank K. 1987. Law and Social Change in Postwar Japan. Cambridge, Mass.: Harvard University Press.

Useem, Michael. 1973. Conscription, Protest and Social Conflict. New York: Wiley.

van Blerk, A. 1982 "The Irony of Labels," 99 SALJ 365.

_____. 1988. Judge and Be Judged. Cape Town: Juta.

van den Wyngaert, Christine. 1986. "Criminal Justice in South Africa: A European Perspective. An Observer's Report on *S v Passtoors*," 2 SAJHR 278.

van der Horst, Sheila T. and Jane Reid, eds. 1981. Race Discrimination in South Africa: A Review. Cape Town: David Philip.

van der Merwe, Hendrik W. 1989. Pursuing Justice and Peace in South Africa. New York: Routledge.

van der Spuy, E. 1989. "Literature on the Police in South Africa: An Historical Perspective," [1989] Acta Juridica 262.

van der Vyver, Johan David. 1976. Seven Lectures on Human Rights. Cape Town: Juta.

_____. 1980. "The Section 114 Controversy—and Governmental Anarchy," 97 SALJ 363.

_____. 1982. "Parliamentary Sovereignty, Fundamental Freedoms and a Bill of Rights," 99 SALJ 557.

_____. 1986. "Judicial Review under the New Constitution," 103 SALJ 236.

_____. 1988a. "State Sponsored Terror Violence," 4 SAJHR 55.

_____. 1988b. "The State President and Indemnity under the Defence Act," 4 SAJHR 153.

van der Westhuizen, Johann and Henning Viljoen. 1988. A Bill of Rights for South Africa. Johannesburg: Butterworth.

van Manen, Willem C. n.d. The Passtoors Trial: a report to the International Commission of Jurists and the Nederlands Juristen Comite voor Mensenrechten on a treason trial in South Africa, April–May 1986.

van Niekerk, Barend. 1969. "…Hanged by the Neck until You Are Dead," 86 SALJ 457.

_____. 1975. "The Role and Function of the Radical Lawyer in South Africa," 1 Natal University Law Review 147.

_____. 1978. "The Uncloistering of Virtue," 95 SALJ 362.

_____. 1979. "Mentioning the Unmentionable: Race as a Factor in Sentencing," 3 SACC 151.

_____. 1981. "Judicial Visits to Prisons: The End of a Myth," 98 SALJ 416.

van Niekerk, G.J. 1988. "People's courts and people's justice in South Africa," 21(2) De Jure 292.

van Rooyen, Kobus. 1991. "Publications Appeal Board: Court or Inquisition?" 7 SAJHR 342.

van Zyl Smit, Dirk. 1984. "Public Policy and the Punishment of Crime in a Divided Society: An Historical Perspective on the South African Penal System," 21/22 Crime and Social Justice 146.

_____. 1987. "Normal Prisons in an 'Abnormal' Society?: A Comparative Perspective," 3 SAJHR 147.

_____. 1988a. "South African Prisons and International Law," 4 SAJHR 21.

_____. 1988b. "Indigence and the Right to Counsel: *S v Khanyile* 1988 (3) SA 795 (N)," 4 SAJHR 363.

Venter, F. 1973. "The Withering of the Rule of Law," 8 Speculum Juris 69.

Vogler, Richard. 1991. Reading the Riot Act: The magistracy, the police and the army in civil disorder. Milton Keynes: Open University Press.

Vose, Clement E. 1959. Caucasians Only: The Supreme Court, the NAACP, and the Restrictive Covenant Case. Berkeley: University of California Press.

Wacks, Raymond. 1984a. "Judges and Injustice," 101 SALJ 266.

_____. 1984b. "Judging Judges: A Brief Rejoinder to Professor Dugard," 101 SALJ 295.

Webster, David. 1987. "Repression and the State of Emergency," 4 SAR 141.

Webster, Eddie. 1985. Cast in a Racial Mould: Labour Process and Trade Unionism in the Foundries. Johannesburg: Ravan.

Weinstein, Jack B. 1992. "A Trial Judge's Second Impression of the Federal Sentencing Guidelines," 66 Southern California Law Review 357.

Weisberg, Richard. 1984. The Failure of the Word: The Protagonist as Lawyer in Modern Fiction. New Haven: Yale University Press.

_____. 1991. "Legal Rhetoric Under Stress: The Example of Vichy," 12 Cardozo Law Review 1371.

Weisbrod, Burton A., Joel F. Handler and Neil K. Komesar. 1978. Public Interest Law: An Economic and Institutional Analysis. Berkeley: University of California Press.

Wells, Julia C. 1994. We Now Demand!: The History of Women's Resistance to Pass Laws in South Africa. Johannesburg: Witwatersrand University Press.

Wellstone, Paul D. 1978. How the Rural Poor Got Power: Narratives of a Grass–Roots Organizer. Amherst: University of Massachusetts Press.

Weschler, Lawrence. 1993. "An Afrikaner Dante," New Yorker 78 (November 8).

Wescott, Shauna. n.d. Trial of the 13. Johannesburg: Black Sash.

West, Martin. 1983. "From Pass Courts to Deportation: Changing Patterns of Influx Control in Cape Town," 82 African Affairs 476.

White, Lucie E. 1988. "To Learn and Teach: Lessons from Driefontein on Lawyering and Power," [1988] Wisconsin Law Review 699.

Wicomb, Zoë. 1987. You Can't Get Lost in Cape Town. New York: Pantheon.

Wiehahn Commission. 1979. Report of the Commission of Inquiry into Labour Legislation (RP47/1979). Pretoria: Government Printer.

Woffinden, Bob. 1987. Miscarriages of Justice. London: Hodder & Stoughton.

Wolpe, Harold. 1980. "Towards an Analysis of the South African State," 8 IJSL 399.

_____. 1988. Race, Class and the Apartheid State. London: James Currey.

Woods, Donald. 1978. Biko. London: Paddington Press.

_____. 1987. Filming with Attenborough: The Making of Cry Freedom. New York: Holt.

Work in Progress. 1987. "Sarmcol forces rethink on industrial court," 50–51 Work in Progress (Oct–Nov).

Written Representations to the Committee of Inquiry into the Constitutional and Political Future of Moutse (September 14, 1988).

INDEX

Abiola, Chief M. K. O., 303
Adversaries, construction of, 524-26
Advisory Commission on Land Allocation
    (ACLA), 419-20, 423
African National Congress (ANC): Alexandra
    treason trials and, 333, 334, 341, 347, 356,
    365, 368, 372; on censorship, 266, 301; on
    conscription and conscientious objection,
    119; Freedom Charter, 13; Inkatha violence
    and, 200, 202, 208; legalization of, 17;
    New Nation and, 274, 275, 277, 278, 279-
    80; outlawing of, 2, 12, 15; pass laws and,
    24; police torture and killing of members,
    252
Afrikaner Resistance Movement (AWB), 420,
    421-22, 423
Agence France Presse, 260
Albertyn, C. J., 133, 190
Alexandra (township): brief history of, 311-
    15; treason trials, 329-83; uprising in
    January-June 1986, 315-26
Alexandra Action Committee (AAC), 5, 321,
    322-26, 376, 377
Alexandra Civic Association (ACA), 317, 319
Alexandra Crisis Committee, 321
Alexandra Liaison Committee (ALC), 313, 314
Alexandra Residents Association (ARA), 314
Alexandra Town Council, 315, 318
Alexandra Women's Organization (AWO),
    314
Alexandra Youth Congress (AYCO), 314, 319
Allen, Brian, 142, 143
Al-Qalam, 296-97
Andrew, Ken, 54, 90
Andrews, Johannes, 399, 423
Anglican Church, 71, 83, 110, 122
Apartheid: Alexandra as pawn in, 312; cen-
    sorship and, 304-305; forced removals and,
    385, 405, 410, 425, 426, 427; ideology of
    and law, 541-45; incorporation of black
    communities into homelands and, 436,
    486; judiciary as ally against, 524; lessons

of South Africa, 547-49; Nazism and, 99-
    100, 122; police violence and, 257; role of
    law in struggle against, 1-3, 535-42; SARM-
    COL-MAWU dispute and, 167-72; sexual
    discrimination and, 492-93. *See also* Pass
    laws
Argus newspapers, 263
Armstrong, Amanda, 374
Association of Democratic Journalists, 293,
    299
Association of Law Societies, 19-20
Attenborough, Richard, 232, 294-95
Auden, W. H., 1
Authoritarianism, legality and resistance to, 3
Awetha, Abdul, 202
Awetha, Dumisani, 194
Azanian People's Organisation, 233-34, 251

Bahurutshe Ba Ga Moilwa, 484
Bahurutshe Ba Sebogodi, 480
Bakwena Ba Magopa. *See* Magopa
Ball, Chris, 263
Ballack, Capt. Frantz, 248
Bantoane. *See* Moutse
Bantu Affairs Administration Board, 24
Bapela, Obed, 319, 324, 325, 329-69, 375,
    377, 382
Batzofin, Saul, 106, 107
Beea, Mike, 314, 316-17, 319, 320, 325, 329,
    358, 368, 380
Beeton, Lt., 218
Benzien, Jeff, 245
Berg, Maj. R. F., 221
Berman, Harold, 533
Berman, Justice H. L., 417
Bernard, Sgt. Ferdinand, 250
Bester, Charles, 91, 106, 111-12
Bezuidenhout, C. J., 40, 226-27
Bieder, Owen, 362, 370
Biko, Steve, 4, 211-14, 219, 231-32, 233, 248,
    253, 255, 257
Bindman, Geoffrey, 13

Black, use of term, 1
Blackburn, Molly, 211, 217, 226, 227, 239
Black Lawyers Association, 21
Black Sash: on censorship, 269, 279, 289; on conscription and conscientious objection, 70, 90, 107; on disestablishment of Oukasie, 505; on forced removal of Magopa, 393, 397, 398, 402, 403, 404, 406, 408, 410, 412, 432; on incorporation of black communities into homelands, 443, 445, 446, 462; on *Komani* case, 27, 29-30, 31, 34, 35-36; on *Rikhoto* case, 54; pass laws and political activism of, 61, 64; on police brutality, 211, 221
Bodley, Mrs. D. N., 32-33
Boerestaat Party, 115
Boesak, Dr. Allan, 104, 315, 316-17, 395, 428
Bolo, Mkhululi, 303
Bophuthatswana: forced removal of Magopa to, 405-23; incorporation of Braklaagte into, 480-84, 488-90; incorporation of Leeuwfontein into, 484-86, 488-90
Botha, Det. Sgt. Calla, 250
Botha, Chris, 412
Botha, Lt. Gerrit, 178
Botha, Maj. Louis, 201
Botha, Pik, 260, 296
Botha, P. W., 16, 18, 214, 261-62, 439-40, 442, 451, 463
Botha, Stoffel, 262, 265, 266-69, 270, 271, 272, 290-91, 292, 293, 294, 297-98, 304, 305, 306-307, 308, 377
Botshabelo (township), 470-72, 491
Bowman, Gilfillan and Blacklock (law firm), 388
Boya, Tom, 505, 506
Bozolli, Belinda, 361, 475
Bradley, Sgt. W. W. G., 230
Braklaagte (ethnic group), 480-84, 488-90, 494
Brand, John, 155, 158-59, 167, 168, 177, 192, 204
Brassey, Martin, 132, 140-41, 147, 155, 157, 168, 171
Bredenkamp, Louis, 113-14
Bredenkamp, Mag. P. H., 93, 94, 103, 106-107
Breytenbach, Breyten, 16, 378
Breytenbach, Wynand, 115
British Broadcasting Corporation (BBC), 293
British Tyre & Rubber (BTR), 127, 150, 152, 156, 160. *See also* SARMCOL
Brits (city of), 495-517
Brits Action Committee (BAC), 495, 501, 503, 504, 506, 507, 509, 511, 515, 516, 521
Broome, Justice, 197

Browde, Jules, 284, 287-89, 400, 415
Browde, Selma, 312
Brown, Gavin, 144, 147, 149
Brown, Leonard, 497, 511, 515
Brown, Marge, 408
Bruce, B. David, 91, 92-105, 109, 116, 117, 118, 119, 120, 121, 122
Bruce, Ursula, 99, 122
Buchner, Jac, 201
Buddhism, 77
Budlender, Geoffrey, 25-43, 56, 63, 412, 413, 498-99, 501, 503, 506, 509, 510-12, 515
Buechner, Brig. Jacques, 198
Bundy, Colin, 361
Burger, Lt. Col. Staal, 250
Burger, Steve, 324, 325
Business Day, 289, 290
Buthelezi, Chief, 165, 169, 194, 195, 196, 199, 201, 202, 207, 208, 209, 264, 302, 454
Buthelezi, Manas, 315, 316-17
Buti, Sam, 313, 314, 315, 316, 318, 380
Buys, Marshall, 497, 504, 507, 510, 511

Cachalia, Azhar, 199
Cairns, Father Ronald, 361
Calata, Fort, 213-14
Cameron, Edwin, 79, 87, 88, 94-95, 113, 122
Campaign for an Open Media, 301
The Cape Times, 260, 263, 279, 289, 292
Cape Town Development Board (CTDB), 504
Catholic Institute for International Relations, 284
Cele, Mzikayifani, 181
Celliers, Koos, 395
Censorship, government: after 1989, 301-303; legal and political impact of, 303-309; *New Nation* and, 5, 272-90, 300; repression under emergency of 1985-87, 259-72; repression under emergency of 1988-89, 290-300
Centre for Applied Legal Studies, 20
Chalmers, Edward, 227
Chaskalson, Arthur, 25, 46, 328, 513-14
Chauke, Khazamola Sanuel, 43
Cheadle, Halton, 195, 234-36, 241
Cheadle, Thompson, and Haysom (law firm), 20
Cherry, Janet, 72
Chikane, Rev. Frank, 251, 277
Chikane, Moss, 364
Chonco, Goodenough Bhekinkosi, 178, 180, 190, 206
Chueu, Maredi, 435, 438, 442, 445, 450-51
Church of the Province of South Africa (CPSA), 281

Churches. *See* Anglican Church; Church of the Province of South Africa; South African Catholic Bishops Conference; South African Council of Churches; Southern Cape Council of Churches

The Citizen, 271, 303, 305

City of London Anti-Apartheid Movement, 331

City Press, 303

Claasens, Aninka, 411, 412

Class, structure of post-apartheid society, 522

Coertze, State Attorney, 421, 424-25

Coetsee, Justice H. J., 17, 104-105, 111

Coetsee, Kobie, 68, 116

Coetzee, Capt. Dirk, 249, 250

Coetzee, Michael, 218

Coetzee, Neil, 214, 215, 216, 217, 219-22, 223, 225, 226

Coetzee, P., 177, 178-93

Coetzee, P. J., 263

Colonialism, 547

Combrink, Justice, 199, 202

Communication, and language in legal proceedings, 206, 349, 380, 537

Community Dispute Resolution Resource Committee, 372-73

Congress of South African Trade Unions (COSATU), 16, 174-209, 325, 501

Congress of Traditional Leaders of South Africa (Contralesa), 201-202, 465, 493

Conscientious objection. *See* Conscription

Conscription, resistance to, 4: analysis of political impact of, 117-24; Appellate Division decisions, 107-109; *Bruce* case, 92-105; collective opposition in 1980-87, 68-77; collective opposition in 1988-89, 105-107; collective opposition in 1990-92, 113-16; individual defiance in 1980-88, 77-78; individual defiance in 1989-92, 109-13; Toms case, 78-92

Conservative Party (CP): on censorship, 298; on conscription and conscientious objection, 70; on incorporation of black communities into homelands, 466-67, 479, 491; on influx control, 60, 62; on police brutality, 212, 213. *See also CP Patriot*

Consumer boycotts, 214, 255, 312, 319, 332, 366

Corbett, Chief Justice, 108, 123, 300

Cosatu News, 264

Council of Unions of South Africa (COSATU), 55, 264, 276

Cover, Robert, 9

CP Patriot, 302

Criminal law, government manipulation of, 532. *See also* Police

Criminal Procedure Act, 108

Cronjé, Pierre, 198

Croucamp, Andre, 112

Cruywagen, Willem, 511

Cry Freedom (film), 294-95, 308

Curlewis, Justice, 285, 286-89, 307, 308, 309

Daily Dispatch, 289, 303

Dalling, David, 244, 298, 299, 321

Dandala, Rev. Hamilton, 217-18

Daniels, Dr., 218

Daniels, Justice H., 263

Dawjee, Mahomed Faizal, 297

de Beer, M. B., 495, 499, 500, 512, 513

de Beer, Mag. E., 251

de Beer, Sam, 447

de Cock, Mag. E. L., 251

de Jager, Chris, 104

de Klerk, Maj. Charl, 114

de Klerk, F. W., 14, 17, 200, 249, 250, 252, 301, 308

de Klerk, Justice, 467

de Kock, Maj. Eugene, 250

Delmas treason trials, 364-65, 378, 379, 382

Delport, Dr. J. T., 292, 472

der Heyde, Peter auf, 114

de Tocqueville, Alexander, 11-12

de Villiers, Chris, 114, 115, 116

de Villiers, I. W. B., 460-61, 477

de Villiers, Mag., 392, 422, 426

de Villiers, Nicholas, 461

de Vlieg, Gill, 402

de Vries, Dr. Isaak, 271, 326-27

de Vries, Koos, 271

Dewe, Jack, 303

de Witt, C. C., 154

Dhlomo, Oscar, 176, 180, 193, 198, 264

Didcott, Justice John, 72, 123, 164-65, 200

Die Stem (journal), 272, 282, 305

Die Volkstem, 282

Dirading, Michael Isaac, 315, 325

Ditshwantso tsa Rona, 313-14

Dladla, Philip, 143, 165

Dlamini, Robert, 193

Dompas, 23-24

Drury, Alan, 367

Dugard, John, 88-89, 438, 443, 451, 460, 468, 473

Duma, Bufana, 249

Duma, Richard, 192

Duncan, Sheena, 27, 30, 31, 34, 41, 43, 47, 58, 59, 397, 403, 445

du Plessis, I. P., 227, 230, 255

du Plessis, Lt. Lourens, 252

du Preez, Gert, 55

du Preez, Max, 296

Dutch Reformed Church, 68, 405, 428
Duze, Themba, 214, 215

Eastern Province Herald, 260-61, 263, 303
Eastern Transvaal Development Board, 42
East Rand Development Board, 440
Ecumenical Lay Centre, 154
Education, as legal and political strategy,
    531-33. *See also* National Education Crisis
    Committee (NECC)
Edwards, Lt. Karl, 217
Eglin, Colin, 401
Ekangala Action Committee, 440-41
Eksteen, Justice J. P. G., 236, 238
Eloff, Justice C. F., 436, 477-78
Els, Lt. Deon, 233
Emergency camps, disestablishment of
    Oukasie and, 509–510, 512–513, 514, 518
Employers, repeal of influx control laws and,
    62-63. *See also* SARMCOL; Unions, black
    trade
End Conscription Campaign (ECC), 71-77, 83,
    105-107, 113-16, 118
Engagement, modes of, 527-29
Engelbrecht, Andries, 270-71, 305
Erasmus, Minister of Justice F. C., 18
Erwin, Alec, 196
Essack, Moulana, 78
Ethnicity, incorporation of black communities
    into homelands, 436-95
Evans, Gavin, 113, 118
Evening Post, 303
Executive branch, relationship between law
    and politics, 8

Faku, Sgt. A. T., 218, 219-21, 239, 242, 256
Family, influx control and, 62. *See also*
    Lodger's permits; Pass laws
Fani, Paul, 229
Fatharly, Peter, 156
Fazzie, Henry, 215
Federation of South African Trade Unions
    (FOSATU), 55, 128, 130, 151, 346
Feminism, South African, 492
Ferreira, Fred, 53-54
Findlay, Justice, 471
First, Ruth, 249
Flattery, Sgt. John, 93, 94-95, 117, 118
Flemmert, Lt. Dawid, 222, 223
Flemmert, Gregory, 299-300
Floris, Leon William, 250
Forced removals: incorporation of black
    communities into homelands compared to,
    487; legal and political analysis of, 424-34;
    of Magopa people, 386-423. *See also*

Homelands; Incorporation; Resettlement
    policy
Foreign Correspondents' Association, 296
Fourie, Col. F. J., 232
Foxcroft, Justice J. G., 90
Fraser, Ian, 275
Free Azania, 264
Freeth, Rev. John, 88
Friedman & Friedman (law firm), 177, 179

Gabela, Jerome, 246
Galanakis, George, 303
Galela, Champion, 213
Gandhi, 15, 20
Gastrow, Peter, 199, 213, 472
Gay and lesbian rights movement, 87-88,
    120-21
Gcabashe, Bheki, 199
Gcani, Tembile, 224
Gcina, Ivy, 225-26, 243
Gender. *See* Women's suffrage
General Council of Trade Unions of Japan,
    331
George Mahlangu, Majozi, 459, 463, 464, 479,
    480, 494-95
George, Vusumzi, 215, 217, 222-23, 243
Gerber, Andrew, 508, 510
Giddons, Michael, 332-33
Giles, G. S., 133, 136, 142-43, 149, 154-55,
    159
Gluckman, Dr. Jonathan, 252
Godolozi, Qoqawuli, 213
Goldstein, Justice, 422-23, 426, 428, 430, 432
Goldstone, Judge Richard, 34, 63, 249
Goniwe, Matthew, 213-14, 242, 251-52
Gordon, Justice G., 294, 308
Government. *See* Law; Police; Politics;
    Violence, state
Graff, Michael, 112, 121
Grant, John, 316, 319, 349-50
Grassroots, 290, 292, 297, 303
Grobler, Dr. Jan, 498, 499, 503, 505
Grootboom, Umbulelo, 293
Grosskopf, Justice, 363, 379, 382, 436
Gumede, Archie, 193-94, 199
Gunter, J., 59
Gwala, Harry, 125, 301, 371

Hadebe, Reggie, 202
Hammarsdale Youth Congress (HYC), 193
Hammond-Tooke, W. D., 474
Hani, Chris, 249
Harber, Anton, 290, 295-96, 302, 306
Harms, Judge Louis, 250-51
Hartman, David, 77
Hashe, Sipho, 213

Haysom, Nicholas, 391, 392, 400-401, 402, 406, 409, 411, 413, 414, 415, 418, 423, 426, 427, 433, 447
Heard, Anthony, 260
Heita, Andreas, 248
Hendrickse, Allan, 106
Henning, Mattheus, 177
Hesp, A. R., 126-27
Heunis, Chris, 260, 281, 440, 442, 443, 445, 449-50, 457, 458, 462, 463, 468, 470, 476, 478, 481, 498, 501, 502, 504, 505, 507, 508, 510, 512, 518
Hills, Brig. Johannes, 233, 235
Hilton-Barber, Brett, 303
Hlengwa, Clement, 252
Hlongwane, Billy, 319
Hoffman, Mag. D., 245-46
Hoffman, Mag. F., 245
Hofmeyr, Reinald, 48
Holocaust, 99
Holomisa, Bantu, 252
Homelands: forced removal of Magopa to, 5-6, 386-423; involuntary incorporation of black communities into, 436-95; legal and political analysis of resettlement policy, 424-34
Horack, John, 262
Hough, Danie, 518-19
Howick Rubber Workers Union, 125
Human, A. C., 343-46, 356-57, 379, 381, 414-15
Hurley, Denis, 81

Ideology: apartheid and law, 543-47; of individualism, 168
Ihubane, R. J., 479
Ilanga, 264, 303
Incorporation, of black communities into homelands, 436-95
Independence, of homelands. See Homelands
Individualism, ideology of, 168
Industrial Court, arbitration of SARMCOL-MAWU dispute, 154-67
Influx control. See Pass laws
Inkatha, 4: violence in Alexandra, 372; violence against MAWU, 151, 165, 169
Inter-American Press Association, 290
International Commission of Jurists, 13
International Congress of Free Trade Unions, 331
International Defence and Aid Fund, 21
International Metalworkers' Federation, 325
International Press Institute, 289
Ironside, Rod, 55
Islam, conscription and conscientious objection, 77

Jack, Mkhuseli, 226-28, 243, 255, 293
Jackson, Derek, 264
Jaffer, Mansoor, 292
Jam, Sgt. Phumzile, 215, 226, 239
Jamile, Samuel, 192, 196, 197
Jehovah's Witnesses, 73, 112-13, 121
Jenkins, Prof. Trefor, 238
Johannesburg Democratic Action Committee, 324
Jones, Justice, 242
Joseph, Humphrey, 264
Joubert, Chief Justice Christiaan P., 418
Joubert, Dr. W. A., 328
Judaism, conscription and conscientious objection, 77, 95, 99-100
Judges: as ally against apartheid, 524; relationship between law and politics, 8
Jury nullification, 8

Kabinde, Esther, 36
Kannemeyer, Justice, 212, 244
Karodia, Ashraf, 233
Kentridge, Felicia, 25, 34
Kentridge, Sydney, 76, 77
Kgatitsoe, Elisha, 406-407, 428
Kgatitsoe, Lazarus, 392
Kgatitsoe, Lucas, 410, 411, 428
Kgatitsoe, Matthew, 402
Khumalo, Joseph, 192, 196
Khumalo, M. Z., 165, 192, 193, 201, 208
Khumalo, Mpiyake, 49
Khumalo, Sam, 497
Khumalo, Sithembiso, 194
Khuzwayo, Zazi, 192
Kikine, Sam, 55
Kimble, Carrie, 420
King, Rev. Edward, 89
Klaaste, Aggrey, 391
Klerk, Hennie, 56
Knoetze, John, 31, 35, 39, 41, 42-43, 49, 55, 59
Knudsen, J. M., 31
Komani case, 24-43, 58, 61-65
Komani, Veli Willie, 24
Kompe, Lydia, 517, 520
Kondile, Sizwe, 249
Koornhof, Dr. Piet, 27, 28, 48-49, 53, 54, 55, 57, 58-59, 63, 120, 385, 395, 398, 402-403, 433, 437, 439
Kose, Peter, 441
Kriegler, Justice Johann, 250, 302
Kriel, Ashley, 245
Krugel, W. F., 328
Kruger, Paul, 296
Kruger, Scholtz, 56

Krynauw, Dr. Japie, 233, 238
Kuhn, Andries, 461
Kumleben, Justice, 109
Kumm, Sgt., 227
Kunene, Meshack, 371
Kunutu, Placid, 447
Kuny, Denis, 467
KwaNdebele, incorporation of Moutse into, 5-6, 436-95

Labour Party: on censorship, 291; on incorporation of black communities into homelands, 468, 478, 486
Lang, Dr. Ivor, 231, 232, 233, 235, 238, 254, 255, 257
Langbridge, Stephen, 467
Language, communication in legal proceedings, 206, 349, 380, 538
Laubscher, Maj. D. L. E., 228-29
Law: censorship, 303-309; conscription and conscientious objection, 117-24; disestablishment of Oukasie, 519-24; forced removal of Magopa, 424-34; framework for approaching relationship of to politics, 7-21; ideology of apartheid and, 543-47; incorporation of black communities into homelands, 486-95; Inkatha violence, 203-209; lessons of South Africa, 547-49; pass laws, 61-65; police and state violence, 243-52, 253-57; role of in struggle against apartheid, 1-3, 532-40; SARMCOL-MAWU dispute, 167-72; specificity of case study approach, 545-47; strategies of private parties in struggle against apartheid, 524-33; treason trials, 373-83
Lawyers, South Arican legal system, 17-21
Lawyers for Human Rights, 21
Learn and Teach (journal), 272, 294
Lebowa, incorporation of Moutse into KwaNdebele, 436-95
Leeuwfontein (township), 484-86, 488-90, 494
Legal formalism, 490
Legal Resources Centre (LRC): disestablishment of Oukasie, 503, 506, 511, 512; forced removal of Magopa, 388; founding of, 20-21; *Komani* case, 24-43; incoporation of black communities into homelands, 461; pass laws and political activism, 61-65; *Rikhoto* case, 43-60
Legal system, description of South African, 17-21
Legislatures: conscription laws and judicial authority, 123; relationship between law and politics, 8
Legitimation, concept of, 530-31

le Grange, Louis, 261
Lekota, Patrick, 327, 364
Lemmer, J. J., 292
Lepa, Jemima, 392
Lerm, Brig. Hertzog, 457-58, 463
le Roux, Frank, 57
Lesbians and Gays Against Oppression Committee, 87
Levy, Andrew, 145, 150, 162-64, 166, 169, 170
Levy, Justice Harold, 248
Lewis, David, 55
Liebenberg, Dr. Nikolaas, 78-79
Linda, Mbulelo, 293
Lockey, Desmond, 450, 455
Lodger's permits, 24-43
Loewe, Mike, 293
Lombard, Juan, 233
London, Dr. Leslie, 77
London World Television News, 260
Lotz, G. J., 221
Louw Dr., 218
Louw, Eugene, 115, 116, 301
Louw, Rev. Fremont, 395
Louw, Lionel, 316-17
Louw, Steven, 105
Louwrens, Col. James, 197
Lubowski, Anton, 250
Luthi, Templeton, 222, 225
Lyster, Richard, 177

Mabaso, Mxegeni Joseph, 175, 177, 178, 180, 181, 183, 184, 189, 190, 191, 192, 203, 204, 207
Mabena, Jonas, 480
Mabhogo, David, 436-37
Mabiletsa, Emily, 504
Machika, Paulina, 473-74
Madibikane, Shadrack, 403
Madlala, Sipho, 202
Maduna, Vusi, 193
Mafole, Ntwe, 195
Magamela, M. E., 241
Magerman, Arthur, 314
Magolego, R. F., 460
Magopa, forced removal of to homeland, 5, 386-434
Mahlaela, Moshe Jan, 498–99, 500, 501, 511
Mahlangu, Chief Andries, 437, 462, 463, 464, 474, 478
Mahlangu, Prince Cornelius, 453, 455, 458, 461, 462, 463-64, 475, 491
Mahlangu, F. K., 441, 455, 457, 458, 462, 463, 487
Mahlangu, George, 459, 463, 464, 479, 480, 494-95

Mahlangu, Prince James, 452, 456, 458, 461, 462, 463, 464, 478
Mahlangu, K. S., 464
Mahlangu, Chief Makhosana Klaas, 446
Mahlangu, Matthew, 504
Mahlangu, Paradise, 456
Mahlangu, Simon, 436
Mahlangu, Solly, 437, 456, 462, 464, 474, 478
Mahli, Tommy, 346-47, 374
Majafa, Nkgokoloane Dadelik, 483, 485
Majebe, Pakamile, 81
Majola, Moses, 180, 181-82, 183-84, 185-88, 189-90, 206, 207
Makama, Joseph, 512-13
Makau, Patrick, 249
Makhanya, Rev. Morote, 518
Makhatini, John, 127
Makubire, Harry, 313
Makutu, Beauty, 40
Malan, Maj., 444
Malan, Magnus, 68, 72, 105-106, 107, 113, 251
Malan, N., 33
Malcomess, John, 227
Malebane-Metsing, Rocky, 519
Malgas, Ernest, 224-25
Malindi, Amos, 364
Mallet, Brig. Leon, 299-300
Mamabolo, Levy, 502
Mamogale, Chief Lerothodi, 390, 423
Mandela, Nelson: censorship of, 294; on End Conscription Campaign, 116; law career of, 20; prosecution and jailing of, 2, 15; release of, 17
Mandela, Winnie, 16, 87, 318, 374-75
Maneli, Bubele, 239
Mangcotywa, Leslie, 215-16, 228-29, 243
Mangope, Lucas, 424, 482, 484-85, 487
Manoim, Irwin, 290
Manoim, Norman, 374
Manthata, Thomas, 364
Manuel, Col. John, 249
Maphala, Albert, 318
Maphumulo, Chief, 201
Mapoch, King, 455-56, 458, 464, 476
Mapuma, Eric, 214
Marais, Etienne, 105
Marais, Jaap, 456
Marais, P. J., 78, 85-88, 89
Marais, Piet, 419, 423
Marcus, Gilbert, 234
Marule, Simon, 245
Marx, Brig. Christo, 246-47
Marx, Frans, 49, 55
Marx, Col., 204
Maseka, Theresa, 319

Mashatile, Paul, 314, 324
Mashiane, Mafiri Maria, 33-34
Mashigo, Refilwe, 361
Mashile, Paul, 318
Mashiqana, Siyolo, 222
Mason, Cedric, 331-32, 381
Mass Funeral Coordinating Committee (Alexandra), 317-18
Mathebe, Gibson, 473
Mathebe, Godfrey, 444, 447, 468, 473
Mathebe, Chief L. C., 439, 441-42, 443-44, 447, 450-51, 460, 466, 467, 468
Matlala, Nano, 464
Matoto, Lulamile, 238-39
Matsepe-Casaburri, Dr. Ivy, 303
Mavuso, J. S. A., 512-13, 514
MAWU. See Metal and Allied Workers Union
Mayekiso, Kola, 335, 347, 349, 367
Mayekiso, Moses, 314, 316, 320-21, 322, 323, 329-69, 374, 377-78, 380, 381
Mayekiso, Mzwanele, 324, 325, 329-69
Mbanjwa, D., 137
Mbeki, Govan, 280, 281
Mbeki, Thabo, 199
McCall, Justice, 155-56, 157, 159-60, 163
McCarthy, Mag. A. S., 249
Mchunu, M. M., 175, 181, 183, 184, 190, 191, 204
Mchunu, Thulani, 190
Mchunu, Vela, 190, 192-93, 196, 201, 207, 208
Mdakane, Richard, 324, 325, 329-69
Mdakane, Zephaniah, 320, 340, 379
Media: on Alexandra treason trials, 330-31, 334, 369-70; on "black-on-black" violence, 173-74; on black trade unions, 162; on disestablishment of Oukasie, 505; on forced removal of Magopa, 393-95, 396-97, 398, 401, 403, 416, 432-34; on incorporation of black communities into homelands, 443, 444, 445-46, 446-47, 453, 454-55, 457, 463, 465; on police torture in East Cape, 236-38, 242; publicity as legal and political strategy, 535. See also Censorship
Media Workers Association of South Africa, 289, 293
Medical Association of South Africa (MASA), 231-32
Mellet, Brig., 293
Mene, Stanford, 242
Mentoor, Edward, 224
Metal and Allied Workers Union (MAWU): Alexandra treason trials and, 374; labor dispute with SARMCOL, 4, 125-72; Oukasie township and resettlement policy, 500. See also Mpophomeni

Methodist Synod, 71
Meyer, Defence Minister, 114, 115
Meyer, R. P., 471
Mhlawuli, Fidelo, 213-14
Mhlongo, William Silika, 33
Military. *See* Conscription; South African
   Defense Force
Milne, Justice, 326-27, 379
Milne, Natal Judge President, 18
Minaar, Dirk Jacobus, 414, 415, 421
Mitchell, Capt. Brian, 246, 247
Mkhize, Angelica, 194, 198
Mkhize, Sipho, 192
Mkonto, Sparrow, 213-14
Mmapaletsebe, Evelyn Manana, 29
Mncube, Andreas, 180, 181-82, 183, 184, 189,
   206
Mncwabe, Jerome, 194
Mngadi, Sthembiso, 193
Mnikathi, Nomuza Flomena, 175, 181, 186
Mnikathi, Phillip, 192
Moatshe, Rev. P., 515-16
Modernity, tradition and, 542-43. *See also*
   Women's suffrage
Modimoeng, David, 504
Modimoeng, Joyce, 503
Moerane, Marino, 327
Mohamed, Ashraf, 233-34
Mohamed, Ismail, 18, 327
Mohatshe, Jacob, 497
Mohlala, Frank, 55
Moilwa, Chief Moswana David, 484, 485, 486
Moitse, Naude, 321, 324
Moitse, Ntema Johanna, 33
Mokaba, Peter, 493
Mokoena, Bishop Isaac, 290
Mokua, Bertha, 505
Molala, Nkosi, 457
Molefe, Daniel, 415, 417
Molefe, Popo, 327, 364, 381
Molepo, Rev. Thomas, 317
Molepo, Wilson, 317
Moloatsi, Jacob, 390-91
Molokoane, Abel, 504, 516
Mompati, Ruth, 87
Mönnig, Heinrich, 75
Morale, Mapule, 342
More, Henry, 411, 428
More, Isaac, 389, 390, 402
More, Jacob, 386-88, 389, 399, 402, 404, 405,
   424
More, Philip, 393, 397
More, Shadrack, 387, 391, 392, 401-402
More, Simon, 386
Morobe, Murphy, 446, 462
Morrison, Dr. George de Villiers, 34, 58, 426

Mostert, Brig. Floris, 250
Moswane, Thayini Lettie, 40
Mothers Against War, 107
Motlana, Dr. Nthato, 100-102, 121, 403
Motor Assemblers and Components Workers
   Union (MACWUSA), 214-15
Moutse, incorporation of into KwaNdebele,
   5-6, 436-95
Mpetha, Oscar, 124
Mphokeli, Sgt., 229, 239
Mpofu, Pozisa Patricia, 29
Mpophomeni (township), Inkatha violence
   in, 4, 174-209
Mpshe, Andrew, 389
Msibi, Sam, 303
Msizane, Godfrey, 324
Mtetwa, C. J., 165, 201
Mthembu, Jerry, 315, 379
Mthembu, Johannes, 194-95
Mthembu, Mandla, 198
Mthembu, Sarah, 319, 338, 351, 359, 361
Mthimkulu, Simon, 252
Mtshali, Jacob, 314
Mtsweni, Klaas, 456, 459
Munnik, Judge President ?, 263
Mvelase, N. M., 178
Mvelase, V. V., 176, 180, 194, 196, 208
Mxenge, Griffiths, 249
Mxenge, Victoria, 202, 214, 251
Myburgh, Justice, 475, 489
Myburgh, Mag. J. P., 245
Myeni, Musa, 200
Mzolo, Romanus, 175, 190

Naidoo, Jay, 370
Naidoo, Krish, 20
Nair, Billy, 243-44
The Namibian, 302
Nampala, Nikodemus, 248
Nani, W. O., 228
Natal Student Congress, 275
Natal Witness, 299
National Association of Democratic Lawyers,
   21
National Automobile and Allied Workers
   Union (NAAWU), 214, 500
National Committee Against Removals, 412,
   443
National Education Crisis Committee (NECC),
   275
Nationalism, black, 367-68
National Party: on censorship, 266, 298, 307;
   disenfranchisement of blacks by, 12; on
   incorporation of black communities into
   homelands, 489; on influx control, 60;

police brutality and, 213; translation of racist ideology into law by, 14-15
National Press Union, 261, 262
National Union of Mineworkers, 370
National Union of South African Students, 69
Naudé, Beyers, 16, 315, 316-17
Nazism, apartheid and, 99-100, 122
Ncane, Mlungisi, 233
Ndebele. *See* KwaNdebele
Ndiyane, Rodwell, 215, 216, 221-22, 225, 226
Ndlovu, Bogart, 199
Ndlovu, Moses, 127
Ndlovu, Phikelela, 202
Ndlovu, Velaphi, 176, 194, 195, 196
Ndou, Samson, 320
Ndzondelelo Secondary School, 229
Ndzundza Tribal Authority (NTA), 462
Nederduitse Gereformeerde Kerk (NGK), 405, 428
Neer, Dennis, 214-15, 219-21, 228, 243
Neethling, Gen. Lothar, 249-50, 302
Nel, D. J. L., 260, 261
Nel, Col. J. T., 79, 80
Nel, Louis, 397-99, 433, 440, 503
Nel, Lt. Winnifred, 236
Nesi, Const. V. M., 230-31, 233
The New African, 299, 303
New Era, 297
New Nation: banning of issues of, 264, 271; censorship of, 5, 259, 292, 299, 300, 301-303, 304, 305, 307-308, 309; closing of, 272-90; establishment of, 261-62
New Republic Party (NRP): on conscription and conscientious objection, 70; on police brutality, 213
Newslink, 303
Newspaper Marketing Bureau, 303
Newsweek, 260, 261
Ngcezula, Fezile, 230
Ngcina, Peter, 229
Ngcobo, Const. Roy, 247
Ngcobo, Sipho, 322
Ngcobo, Thulani, 194, 195
Ngubane, Simon, 175, 181, 186
Ngubeni, Emanuel, 320
Ngwenya, S'kumbuso, 202
Nicholson, Mrs. J., 27-28
Niemand, A. J., 49
Nieuwoudt, Gerrit, 228-29
Nieuwoudt, Maj. Gideon, 242
Nieuwoudt, Lt. J. G., 215, 222
Nieuwoudt, Magistrate S. M., 178-93, 204-205, 209
Nkabinde, Alpheus Mziwakhe, 177-78
Nkayi, Phila, 303
Nkomo, Mzakelwa Alpheus, 178

Nkondo, Curtis, 323
Nkosi, Celiwe Rita, 42
Nkosi, Philemon and Martha, 50
Noemdoe, Louis, 264
Nofemela, Butana Almond, 249-50
Ntombela, David, 184, 194, 197-98, 199, 201, 202, 205, 207, 208
Ntuli, Piet, 437, 438, 453, 454
Ntuli, Victor, 193
Nujoma, Sam, 271
Nupen, Charles, 45, 49-52, 64
Nyoka, Caiphus, 245
Nyuka, Patrick, 293
Nzama, Sibongeseni, 192
Nzimande, Raphael, 165

Odendaal, Brig. Gert, 236
O'Donovan, Justice J. B., 46, 47
Oliphant, Reggie, 293
Olivier, Mag. B. J., 250
Olivier, Prof. J. A., 229
Olivier, Nic, 52, 54-55, 406
Omar, Dullah, 78, 251
Omar, Imam Rashid, 77
Oosthuizen, M. J., 154
Organisation of Lesbian and Gay Activists, 88
Orr, Kathleen, 234
Orr, Dr. Wendy, 4-5, 218-19, 221, 223, 224-25, 229, 230, 231, 232, 233, 234-36, 237-38, 242, 243, 253, 255-57
Orsmond, Bishop Reginald, 273
Oukasie (township), disestablishment of, 6, 497-524
Oukasie Civic Association, 518, 519
Oukasie Development Trust, 519
Out of Step (ECC magazine), 290

Pachai, Somaroo, 450
Padi, Richard, 315
Pan African Congress (PAC): outlawing of, 2, 12, 15; pass laws and, 24
Pass laws, 3-4: *dompas* and disenfranchisement of blacks, 23-24; *Komani* case, 24-43, 60-65; *Rikhoto* case, 43-65
Passtoors, Heleen, 13
Paton, Alan, 3, 238
Paulsen, Col., 227-28
Peter, Welile, 233
Phalatse, Harvey, 318
Phatudi, Cedric, 437, 438, 439, 440, 442, 448, 449
Pienaar, Chief Magistrate J. J., 18
Piroshaw, Camay, 55
Pluddemann, Peter, 75
Police, 4-5: Alexandra uprising of 1986, 315-16, 321-22, 340; forced removal of

Magopa, 403, 421-22; incorporations of black communities into homelands, 440, 443, 444, 445, 453, 457-58, 463, 467, 476, 483, 484-85; involvement in Inkatha violence, 175-76, 177, 178, 192, 193, 194, 196, 198, 200-201, 202, 203-204, 207; legal responses to violence of, 243-52; Oukasie and resettlement policy, 499, 503, 511; Port Elizabeth in 1985-86 emergency, 214-43, 253-57; reputation for brutality, 211-14; SARMCOL security department and, 125-26, 127, 150, 165, 168; tension between law and politics, 9. See also Violence, state

Police, Prisons, and Defence Acts, 304, 306

Political trials, clash between law and politics, 10-11. See also Treason trials

Politics: censorship, 303-309; conscription and conscientious objection, 117-24; disestablishment of Oukasie, 519-24; forced removal of Magopa, 424-34; framework for approaching relationship of law to, 7-21; incorporation of black communities into homelands, 486-95; Inkatha violence, 203-209; pass laws, 61-65; police and state violence, 253-57; SARMCOL-MAWU labor dispute, 167-72; treason trials, 373-83

Pooe, Alex, 399-400

Pooe, Ephraim, 417

Pooe, Ezekiel, 404-405, 428

Port Elizabeth, 1985-86 emergency and police violence, 214-43

Port Elizabeth Advice Centre, 215

Port Elizabeth Black Consumers Boycott Committee (PEBCO), 213, 227

Port Elizabeth News Agency, 293

Port Elizabeth Youth Congress (PEYCO), 215, 226

Post & Telecommunication Workers Association, 276

Pretorius, Louis, 390

Prince, Lt. Patricia, 225, 231, 236

Prinsloo, Lt., 228

Proactivity, as legal and political strategy, 529-30

Progressive Federal Party (PFP): on censorship, 260, 261, 266, 291, 298, 299; on conscription and conscientious objection, 68, 69-70; on disestablishment of Oukasie, 512, 514; on forced removal of Magopa, 404, 409; on involuntary incorporation of black communities into homelands, 439, 440, 454, 459, 464-65, 466, 469, 478, 479; on police brutality, 212, 213, 244, 245; on Rikhoto case, 59, 60

Quakers, 68

QwaQwa (homelands), 470-72, 491

Rabie, Chief Justice, 13, 18

Racism, judiciary and institutional, 524. See also Apartheid; Ethnicity

Radebe, Andries, 419-20

Rala, Alex, 216-17, 222, 228-29

Ramakobye, Sello, 497, 502

Rametse, Darkie, 318

Ramodike, M. N., 477

Rampou, George, 402

Rand Daily Mail, 302

Rantho, Joanna, 515

Rathbone, Gary, 112, 119

Rathebe, Enoch, 389

Rathebe, Timothy, 402

Ravan Press, 264

Raw, W. V., 69

Reactivity, as legal or political strategy, 528-30

Reddy, Sgt. Perumal, 190

Release Mandela Campaign, 263

Religion. See Anglican Church; Buddhism; Church of the Province of South Africa; Dutch Reformed Church; Islam; Judaism; South African Catholic Bishops Conference; South African Council of Churches; Southern Cape Council of Churches

Rensburg, Ihron, 218, 243

Rent boycotts, 358, 366

Resettlement policy, disestablishment of black townships, 495-517. See also Forced removals; Incorporation

Residence rights, 43-60. See also Pass laws

Resistance, strategies of in Oukasie, 521

Rikhoto case, 43-65

Rikhoto, Mehlolo Tom, 44

Robb, Noël, 24-25, 27, 28

Robbins, Ron, 151

Rockman, Lt. Gregory, 249, 300

Rontsch, Wally, 114

Rooinasie, Rashid, 77

Roux, Justice, 463-64, 491

Roux, P. E., 126, 131, 134, 144, 148, 154-62, 168, 171-72

Rumpff, Chief Justice, 26

Rumpff, F. L. H., 469, 472

Rural Foundation, 412

Russell, Patrick, 88

Russell, Archbishop Philip, 395

Russell, Capt. Stanley, 79

Saamstaan (Stand Together), 264, 290, 293

Saan newspapers, 263

Sabelo, Winnington, 202
Sachs, Albie, 14, 15
St. Oliver's Catholic Mission, 461
Sampson, Reginald John, 125-54, 168-70
Sandenbergh, Maj. Cecil, 232, 235
Sanford, Pauline, 175
Sangster, Colin, 112-13
SARMCOL. *See* South African Rubber
   Manufacturing Company Ltd.
SARMCOL Workers Cooperative (SAWCO),
   153
SASPU National, 264
Satchwell, Kathleen, 93, 99, 106
Saturday Star, 303
Sauls, Frederick, 234
Sauls, Helen and Moira, 234
Saunders, Dudley, 303
Saunders, Juliette, 260-61
Saunders, Dr. Stuart, 219
Save Alexandra Party (SAP), 313, 314
Save the Press Campaign, 293, 295
Scheepers, Capt. J. C., 227
Scheepers, Maj., 403
Schmidt, Benno, 362-63, 367
Schnetler, Brig. E. S., 224, 229, 240
Scholts, Magistrate J. J., 177-78, 180, 203
Scholtz, J. J., 45-46, 49-52, 64
Schok, Justice P., 24
Schoon, Marius, 249
Schoon, Brig. W. F. S., 250
Schreiner, Justice, 46-47
Schreiner, William Geoffrey, 127-54, 168-70,
   347
Scott, D. G., 44
Sebogodi, John, 482
Sebogodi, Pupsey, 482
Segopolo, Levy, 420-21
Selebi, Jackie, 104
Selikowitz, Justice, 76-77
Senego, Beauty, 28
Separate Amenities Act, 15
Seria, Rashid, 272, 293, 306
Severance pay, 130-31, 132, 157
Shabalala, Nhlanhla, 190
Shabalala, Thokozile, 196-97
Shabalala, Thomas Mandla, 197, 199
Shaku, M. L., 447
Shango, Phillip, 246
Sharpeville Six, 13, 280, 468
Shezi, Bheka, 251
Shifidi, Immanuel, 248
Shifite, Oswald, 89
Sibiya, Khulu, 104
Sibiya, Micca Mnikwa, 175, 179, 181, 186,
   189, 190, 203, 205, 208-209

Sibiya, Phineas, 143, 153, 155, 175, 181, 186,
   189
Silango, Vusi, 320, 321
Simkins, Charles, 58
Sister Community Project, U.S.-South Africa,
   509
Sisulu, Albertina, 281
Sisulu, Walter, 371
Sisulu, Zwelakhe, 261, 268, 279, 285, 300,
   301, 319, 373
Sithebe, Stephen, 165, 200, 201
Sithole, Clayton Sizwe, 248
Sithole, Stephen, 358-59, 379
Skosana, Simon, 435, 436, 437, 438, 439, 441,
   444-45, 447, 448, 452, 454, 455, 456, 457,
   458, 459, 474-75, 477, 486
Slovo, Joe, 87, 296
Smalberger, Justice J. W., 108, 213
Smith, Danie, 392-93
Smith, Derek, 303
Smith, Percy, 218, 225
Soal, Peter, 411-12, 464, 472, 515
Social movements, relationship between law
   and politics, 8
Soga, Rev. de Villiers, 217-18, 243
Soggot, David, 334-63
Sogoni, Mbulelo, 229
Sokhela, Vincent, 198
Solomon, Justice, 242
Sotho. *See* Moutse
South, 271, 282, 290, 292, 299, 300, 303, 306,
   308
South Africa: centrality of law in, 11-14;
   legal system of, 17-21; lessons from expe-
   rience of, 549-51; politics of law in, 14-17.
   See also Apartheid; Law; Politics
South African Allied Workers Union
   (SAAWU), 47, 276, 326-27
South African Broadcasting Company
   (SABC), 57, 259
South African Catholic Bishops' Conference,
   71, 261-62, 269, 273, 302, 508
South African Christian Leadership Assembly
   (SACLA), 82-83, 85
South African Communist Party (SACP), 2,
   12, 277-78, 280
South African Congress of Trade Unions
   (SACTU), 125
South African Council of Churches (SACC),
   68, 289, 395, 409
South African Defence and Aid Fund, 20
South African Defense Force (SADF), military
   capacity and role of, 2. *See also*
   Conscription; Police
South African Institute of Race Relations, 462

South African Media Council, Code of Conduct, 269, 270
South African Medical Association, 212, 231-32, 316
South African Police (SAP). *See* Police
South African Press Association, 259
South African Rubber Manufacturing Company Ltd. (SARMCOL), labor dispute with MAWU, 4, 125-72. *See also* Mpophomeni
South African Society of Journalists, 289, 293
Southern Cape Council of Churches, 247
Sowetan, 272-73, 289, 293, 299, 305, 306
Soweto rebellion (1976), 24, 313
Sparg, Marion, 331
Sparks, Allister, 393-94, 416
Spoelstra, Justice T. T., 435, 461, 476, 480, 487
Stadler, Maj. Gen. Herman, 249-50
Stadler, Brig. H. D., 333, 363
Stafford, Justice E., 495, 499, 500, 520, 522
Stals, Leizel, 30-31
Stander, Mag. M. P. H., 244
The Star, 268-69, 273, 289, 299, 302
Steel and Engineering Industries Federation of South Africa, 329-30
Steele, Richard, 71
Steenhuizen, Armand, 29
Steenkamp, Mayor Japie, 498, 519
Stegmann, Justice, 73
Stewart, David, 261
Steyn, Jan, 48
Steyn, L. C., 18
Steyn, Lt. Pieter, 225
Storey, Rev. Alan, 114
Strachan, T. E., 151
Strike, of MAWU against SARMCOL, 138-54. *See also* Unions
Strydom, Justice J. J., 18-19, 20, 214, 215, 219-21, 222, 226, 330
The Sunday Star, 279, 303
Sunday Times, 292
Sunday Tribune, 292
Surplus People's Project, 385
Sutherland, James, 467
Suttner, Raymond, 14
Sutton, Richard, 48
Suzman, Helen, 3, 19: on Alexandra township, 321; on conscription and conscientious objection, 91, 104; on disestablishment of Oukasie, 507, 508, 510, 522-23; on forced removal of Magopa, 394, 401, 403, 404, 406, 427; on incorporation of black communities into homelands, 439, 446, 449, 451, 455, 456, 463, 469; on *Komani* decision, 34, 38; on pass laws, 60;

on police brutality, 212, 213; on *Rikhoto* decision, 47, 49, 52, 54, 55, 57, 58, 59
Swanepoel, Frans, 391
Swart, J. D. M., 287-89
Swart, Ray, 406
Swing, William Lacy, 422

Tambo, Oliver, 20, 73, 277, 278, 379
Tamboer, James Michael, 214, 215, 218, 222, 223
Taylor, Lt., 228
Tempel, Hendrik, 409
Temple, Matthew, 113
Terblanche, Capt. Deon, 247
Terre'Blanche, Eugene, 420, 421, 423
Terrorism Act, 15
Theron, Mag. J., 452
Thloloe, Joe, 292-93
Thompson, Desmond, 75
Thompson, E. P., 3, 9
Thompson, Ogilvie, 18
Thupudi, Setshego Maria, 40
Thusago, Calvin, 303
Thusi, Morris Sipho, 177, 181, 182-83, 186, 188, 189, 190, 206
Thusong Youth Centre, 324
Toms, Dr. Ivan, 71, 76, 78-92, 109, 117, 118, 119, 121, 122
Toms, Millicent, 107
Torr, Douglas, 109-11, 120, 121, 122
Toubman, Lt. Georgina, 233
Townships, disestablishment of black, 495–517. *See also* Forced removals; Incorporation
Tradition, modernity and, 544-45. *See also* Tribalism; Women's suffrage
Transvaal Law Society, 19, 20
Transvaal Rural Action Committee (TRAC), 409, 410, 418, 443, 468, 503, 507, 508, 515
Treason trials, 5: Alexandra trials, 329-83; Delmas trials, 364-65, 378, 379, 382; of UDF members, 326-28
Tredoux, Attie, 271
Trengrove, Wim, 177, 179-93, 197, 203, 204, 207, 209
Treurnich, Capt. H. D., 234
Tribalism, 173-74. *See also* Ethnicity
Trust Feeds massacre (December 1988), 246-47
Tsenoli, Lechesa, 200
Tshabalala, Paul, 329-69, 375, 380
Tshabalala, Vincent, 314
Tshawane, Rev. Joseph, 277
Tshikalange, David, 250
Tshungu, Justus, 294
Tswana (ethnic group), 485-86

Tswekae, Mercy Seoposengwe, 41
Tucker, Benjamin, 231-32
Tugwana, Gabu, 261-62, 272, 278, 281-82, 301, 302
Tungata Sgt. Butler, 217, 222-23, 240, 242, 256
Tungata, M. A., 214, 216, 219-21
Tutu, Bishop Desmond, 78, 88, 91, 251, 290, 316-17, 389, 395, 396, 428

Umafrika, 303
Umkhonto we Sizwe (ANC military wing), 2, 12
Unions, black trade: Alexandra treason trials and, 374; labor dispute between SARM-COL and MAWU, 4, 125-72; Oukasie and resettlement policy, 502; police violence against, 214-15
United Auto Workers (UAW), 331, 367
United Christian Action network, 290
United Democratic Front (UDF): censorship regulations and, 263; creation of, 16; disappearance of activists, 213-14; on incorporation of black communities into homelands, 455, 456; Inkatha violence in Mpophomeni and, 174-209; treason trials of members, 5, 326-28
United International Pictures, 294
United Nations: Convention on the Political Rights of Women, 475; special committee against apartheid, 289
United States Embassy: on censorship, 269-70; on forced removal of Magopa, 396, 422; on incorporation of black communities into homelands, 447, 453. See also U.S.-South Africa Sister Community Project
United Workers of South Africa (UWUSA), 156, 175, 201, 208
Upbeat, 272
Urban Councils Association, 521
Urban Foundation, 55-56, 59
U.S.-South Africa Sister Community Project, 509
Usembenzi, 273

Vaal Civic Association, 259
Valente, Riccardo, 361
van der Hoven, Hermanus, 248
van der Merwe, C. J., 486
van der Merwe, Mag. J., 106
van der Merwe, Stoffel, 266-67, 290, 292, 295, 305
van der Merwe, Justice W. J., 416-17, 483
van der Walt, Dr., 219, 221, 227
van der Walt, Hennie, 496
van der Walt, Louisa, 93-94, 96-98, 100-102

van der Walt, Justice Piet J., 311, 331-69, 376, 380, 381-83
van der Westhuizen, Gen. Christoffel, 251
van der Westhuizen, Lt. Gen. Ronnie, 247
van Dijkhorst, Justice Kees, 261, 327-28, 364-65, 382, 495, 513-15, 517, 522
van Dyk, Judge Hendrik, 382, 393, 402, 459-61
van Eck, Jan, 78, 291-92
van Heerden, P. A., 43, 52
van Niekerk, Barend, 14
van Niekerk, Justice, 284
van Pittius, Gey, 326-27
van Staden, Dr., 218
van Tonder, Robert, 115, 273
van Wet, Hennie, 198
van Wyck, Freddie, 216, 221, 225
van Wyck, L., 31
van Zyl, Abraham, 251
van Zyl, C. S., 127, 138, 144, 168, 169
Verhoef, Mag. Hein, 109-11, 112, 114, 121
Veriava, Dr. Yusuf, 238
Vermaak, Solly, 395, 426
Verster, Joe, 252
Vesi, Paulus, 202
Viljoen, Abraham, 455
Viljoen, Dr. Gerrit, 406, 408-409, 410-11, 412, 413, 414, 424, 426, 435, 440, 442, 449, 464, 466-67, 468-69, 470, 479, 481-82, 483, 487
Viljoen, M., 385, 391
Vincent, Mike, 303
Violence, "black-on-black": background of, 173-74; government fomentation of, 424; Inkatha murders in Mpophomeni, 174-209
Violence, state: forced removals as, 385; legal responses to, 243-52; Port Elizabeth in 1985-86 Emergency, 214-43, 253-57. See also Police
Vlok, (Law and Order Minister) Adriaan, 71, 106, 199, 246, 248, 263, 293, 317, 377
von Willich, W. S., 179, 183, 184, 186, 191, 203, 204
Vorster, B. J., 68
Vorster, C., 110
Vorster, Mag. F. M., 251
Vosloo, Ton, 262-63
Voting rights, of women in homelands, 473-80, 492-93
Vrye Weekblad, 296, 301, 302, 303

Wages, labor disputes and, 135, 150
Walt, Ethel, 393, 402, 443
War Resisters International, 105
Watermeyer, Dr. G. S., 238
Wattrus, Capt., 246
Weaver, Tony, 263

Webster, David, 14, 250
Weekend Star, 303
Weekly Mail, 261, 263, 272, 282, 290, 292, 295, 296, 299, 301, 302, 303, 306
Weir, Ian, 137
Welsh, R. S., 477
Wentzel, Greyling, 437
Wentzel, K. N., 177
Wentzel, Louis, 224
Western Cape Administration Board (WCAB), 31
West German Catholic Services, 276
West Rand Administration Board (WRAB), 28-31, 35-36, 43, 313
Wiehahn Commission, 16
Wild, Francois Gerhadus Johannes, 416
Wilkens, Ben, 403, 406, 408, 424, 450, 453, 467, 481
Wilkinson, Philip, 77-78, 119
Williamson, Justice, 246
Wilson, Justice Andrew, 200, 247
Winkler, Harald, 71
Winter, Col Eric, 252
Women's suffrage, in homelands, 473-80, 492-93
Woods, Donald, 232, 295
Woods, Gavin, 165, 201

Working conditions, labor disputes and, 135
Work in Progress, 272, 282
A World Apart (film), 295
Worrall, Dr. Dennis, 212

Xhego, Michael, 217, 221-22, 224, 228-29, 243

Yapi, Virginia, 31
Yawitch, Joanne, 460
Young South Africans for a Christian Civilisation, 301-302
Yutar, Percy, 20

Zietsman, Judge, 252
Zion Christian Church, 61
Zondi, Lawrence, 126
Zondi, Musa, 195-96
Zondi, Philip, 196
Zulu. *See* Inkatha; KwaNdebele
Zuma, C. S., 194
Zuma, David, 178
Zuma, M., 175
Zuma, Shiyaboni, 180, 181-82, 184-85, 186, 188, 189, 195, 205, 206, 207, 208
Zwane, Tex, 319